Belly
Dance
Step by Step

Belly
Dance
Step by Step

LAURA COOPER

Gaia Books Limited

A GAIA ORIGINAL
Books from Gaia celebrate the vision of Gaia, the self-sustaining living Earth, and seek to help its readers live in greater personal and planetary harmony.

Editor	Jinny Johnson
Designer	Sara Mathews
Photography	Sarah Skinner
Production	Jim Pope
Direction	Joss Pearson, Patrick Nugent

® This is a Registered Trade Mark of Gaia Books Limited

First published in the United Kingdom in 2004 by
Gaia Books Limited, 66 Charlotte Street, London W1T 4QE

ISBN 1-85675-174-0
A catalogue record of this book is available from the British Library

Printed in Singapore by Imago

10 9 8 7 6 5 4 3 2 1

CAUTION
Belly dance is generally a safe form of exercise for healthy women. If, however, you have back problems or you are in any doubt about your medical condition, check with your doctor before starting belly dance. Most women can also continue belly dancing while pregnant but, again, check with your doctor to make sure.

Contents

INTRODUCTION 6
The origins and history of belly dancing

CHAPTER 1 GETTING STARTED 12
Where to dance, what to wear and selecting music

CHAPTER 2 PREPARATION 18
Learning the proper posture and how to stretch
and warm up your body before dancing

CHAPTER 3 BASIC ELEMENTS 26
The basic steps for building a belly dance routine,
from hip drops to dervish turns

CHAPTER 4 ADDING MYSTERY 70
Bringing beauty and subtlety to your dance with a veil

CHAPTER 5 DRAWING ON POWER 98
Mastering the art of sword work in your dance

CHAPTER 6 WINGS 108
Adding spectacular drama to your steps by the use of wings

CHAPTER 7 VARIETY: THE SPICE OF LIFE 116
Introducing different props, such as candles, canes and zills

CHAPTER 8 THE ORIENTAL FANTASY 126
Performance: perfecting your art by dancing for others

RESOURCES 139
INDEX 141

Introduction

"This above all; to thine own self be true."
WILLIAM SHAKESPEARE

By picking up this book you've confessed, at least to yourself, that at heart you are a romantic. I admitted the very same thing to myself years ago and like any romantic I am forever living in my imagination, in love with mystery, captivated by beauty, intoxicated with music, enraptured by emotion and obsessed with adventure. At the age of seven, I gazed upon the artefacts of King Tutankhamen's tomb on exhibit at the Smithsonian Museum. As I peered into the clear case that held the pharaoh's golden mask, I became hypnotized by its dazzling intricacy and subtle whispers of the past. From then on I was fascinated by ancient history – the grandeur of lost empires, the mysteries of the old world and the magic of the past.

I started belly dancing as a way to indulge my imagination while connecting with one of the lost eras that interested me most: the height of the Middle Eastern empire around the 1600s. That was a time in which tremendous strides were made in fields such as philosophy, medicine, art and poetry. Belly dancing seemed a delightful way to bring my interest in the ancient world into my very modern life. With its sensuous, feminine history, this art form was irresistible to me. I threw myself into its history and practice, and I hope, through this book, to share my enthusiasm with you.

The name belly dance is most likely derived from the French phrase *dance du ventre* or "dance of the stomach". Most modern dancers embrace this as an historical accuracy while others view it as a pejorative term created by tourists who made forays into the Middle East in the early 19th century. Belly dancing can also be referred to as "oriental dance", a title which covers both Middle Eastern and Near Eastern dance styles. Another name is *raks sharqui*, Arabic for "dance of the east". Although this term is primarily used to describe Egyptian cabaret style, it now has broader usage in America.

Dancing is a living, breathing element of human existence. Like all living things, it grows and changes with the world around it. Although it may not seem like it now, the roots of belly dancing are firmly entrenched in religious rituals focusing on goddess worship and/or fertility. Many ancient artefacts showing softly rounded women with large hips and breasts support anthropological theories promulgating the high status of women in archaic divinity structure because of their ability to give birth. The early pagan communities often worshipped a matriarchal deity and extolled the magic and fascination of the ability of women to create life. There is considerable historical evidence linking the ritualistic fertility dances of these cultures, which were symbolic re-creations of giving birth, to modern belly dancing. The sharp hip movements, deliberate muscular contractions and spasms, as well as sinewy undulations, demonstrate strong connections to the body's responses during labour and delivery.

But how did these rituals metamorphose into a form of mainstream public entertainment? The facts on this are limited and sketchy, but many people agree it was gypsy tribes who first drew dancing out into the street and developed it into theatre. The gypsies originally hailed from India and spoke in a Hindi-based language called Romany. Some time around the 5th century AD as a result of local oppression, need for work and sometimes banishment, the Romany gypsies began to migrate to other parts of the known world. Scholars suggest that many first travelled west into Afghanistan and Persia. From there, some migrated north to Turkey and on to Europe while others went south, following the coastline until they reached Egypt and other parts of North Africa. One of the ways that gypsies supported themselves during their nomadic journeys was by providing entertainment for the people of the communities in which they stopped.

The Romany left a cultural influence on many areas where they settled and the spell of their dance style remains strong in Central Asia, where Islamic communities have thrived for centuries. It is especially concentrated in Turkey and Egypt. The sophisticated religious belief structure of Islam had tremendous influence on all forms of entertainment and celebratory practice, dancing included. As a result of cultural segregation between the sexes, Muslim women were permitted only to be entertained by and celebrate with other women in closed quarters.

Belly dancing developed in different ways in each country the gypsies migrated through. In Turkey, after Fatih Sultan Mehmet II conquered Constantinople in 1453, the gypsies settled in the newly titled city of Istanbul. When entertainment was requested for the women, they were amused by female-only dancers and musicians called *chengis*. There are two theories for the origin of this name – the harp-like instrument called the *chang* or the Turkish word for gypsy, *chingene*. Working in organized groups, comprising the business leader, dancers and musicians, referred to as a *kol*, the *chengis* danced at bath houses, harems and other communal locations for women. They built an artistic style that is the root of many of the movements in belly dancing today. The complex hip work, shimmies and varied facial expressions, as well as veil dancing and finger cymbal playing, can be linked back to the gypsy *chengis,* who remained highly regarded and extremely popular until the end of the 19th century.

The strength of the dance form gradually failed when the power of the Ottoman Empire began to wane. Considerable economic collapse, social

upheavals and modernizations ate away at the foundation of the *chengis* dancing troupes until what remained was a shadow of its former brilliance. In Turkey today, *chengis* dancing has become belly dancing and is primarily a tourist attraction, rather than secular entertainment.

As the gypsies continued their migration south into Egypt, the dancers were liberated for a time regarding their audiences. Performances were no longer exclusive to women. Gypsies also danced for the public at celebrations, wedding processions and in front of coffee houses and market places where the flow of people and money was greatest. Referred to as the *ghawazee*, their repertoire was a mix of music and dancing, including their own unique torso movements, native dances and improvised performances with veils, sticks, swords and candles. Some theorize that it was this public practice of dancing that generated the idea of adding coins to the performers' costume. As the gypsies danced, people who stopped to observe them would toss coins to their feet as tips. Without safe places to store their earnings, dancers sewed the money onto their clothes for safekeeping or used the coins to purchase jewellery which could always be worn.

Generally, public dancing was tolerated by the authorities because they earned a substantial revenue by taxing performers' profits. However, religious complaints and opinion finally outweighed the financial benefits, and public *ghawazee* dancing was outlawed in the city of Cairo in 1834.

Punishments for breaking the edict were severe, including physical abuse for a first offence and years of hard labour for repeated offences, generally ending in banishment. At some point between 1849 and 1856, however, the ban was lifted and dancing was allowed to return to Cairo, although the sanction against dancing in public remained. The dance moved inside to a music-hall type environment and Egyptian cabaret-style dancing was born. At the turn of the century, it was given the name of belly dancing.

Belly dancing's expansion into Europe and America came from the ever-increasing flow of tourists into the Middle East. Dance troupes were contracted by foreigners and taken to exhibition forums in London, Paris and Chicago to perform their unique music and dancing. Their art was praised for its unique excitement – and condemned as lewd and scandalous because of its dramatic physical demonstrations. Belly dancing's popularity, even under this intense public scrutiny, remained undeniable and grew tenfold at the 1893 Chicago World's Fair with the publicity surrounding a belly dancer named Little Egypt. Reputedly of Syrian descent, Little Egypt sparked a wave of controversy. Her pelvic- and torso-focused dancing was imitated by so many to such an exaggerated extent that she began to protest against the impostors for distorting her performance into sheer vulgarity. This is one of the earliest examples of belly dancing being twisted into overt public sexuality from its more subtle origins.

Mme MATA HARI
«Danse Indienne»

BOYER

The fantasized and often distorted version of belly dancing grew at a rapid pace, becoming a popular subject in books, art and Hollywood movies. Its image dominated by the burlesque temptress style fed to us by a sex-hungry entertainment industry, belly dancing was not something that appealed to most of the female population. But in recent years more and more women have discovered the true elements of this incredibly feminine and self-affirming art form. By combining the best of the ancient and the modern, contemporary belly dancers have been able to rejuvenate the dance from the taints of yesterday to the visual delight of today, appealing to people of all ages and backgrounds.

It is with dedicated love for and appreciation of belly dancing that I write this book. I hope that it brings you on a journey through history as well as acting as an inspiring passage to your inner spirit – and a way to express it to yourself and the world.

1 Getting started

Learning to belly dance has almost unlimited benefits and you will feel improvements in both your physical and mental wellbeing soon after you start. On a spiritual level, belly dancing promotes a positive body image. Today's fashion is for an almost emaciated thinness which borders on the unhealthy and can have negative physiological effects. Low body weight can affect mood, increase stress on the heart, disrupt the sleep cycle and deregulate normal gland functioning. It may also be linked to erratic menstrual cycles. Just think – a woman's desire to be supermodel-thin might damage one of the quintessential aspects of being female! Few women are born with the build and metabolism to achieve the current popular body image, leaving a very hard and disappointing road for others, who strive to measure up but cannot because of their natural shape.

Belly dancing is a wonderful way to counteract these negative body images and celebrate the more natural, curvaceous feminine form in all its shapes and sizes. In the ancient world, when belly dancing came into being, thinness was a sign of poverty, sickness and starvation. For a woman of those times, having a soft layer surrounding her bones showed that she was well fed and healthy, possessed financial means and was endowed with security and happiness. Remember that when you look at your body in the mirror!

Most people are more open to learning when they feel relaxed and comfortable and this is certainly true for belly dancing. One of the best things about belly dancing is that you can really let yourself go, physically and mentally. The easiest way to facilitate this release is to take a few moments to create a good space where you can dance.

CREATING A POSITIVE DANCE ENVIRONMENT

If you are at home, find somewhere that allows about 2m (6ft) of space all round your central point. The measurements don't have to be exact, but you need enough room to move with as little restriction as possible. You should also have a large mirror in front of you in which you can see yourself from about 60cm (2ft) above your head down to your toes.

Privacy is important, particularly when you first start. Dancing in the daylight which streams through your windows during the day is a delight, but this does expose you to the curious eyes of passers-by. However, if you drape lengths of sheer fabric in a variety of colours over your window you will have the benefits of natural light, tinted into different hues, while protecting your dance retreat from the gaze of others. You can buy extremely inexpensive polyester chiffon in any colour which takes your fancy from your local fabric shop.

This simple technique can be used in the evening as well. When dancing after sunset, low, soft lighting is preferable to the hard glare of fluorescents. If you do not have a dimmer switch, cover your lights with lengths of dark-hued sheer fabrics.

Day or night, scented candles are a delightful addition to your setting. Use a variety of candles on candlesticks and in bowls and glasses to add a soothing and mysterious atmosphere to your dance space. Some dancers prefer to use the heady scent of burned patchouli or sandalwood incense to create a spiritual dance space. Incense sticks or cones are perfect. Just make sure you have the right burner so you avoid burns or fire. Others like to anoint their pulse points with earthy musky oils so that when they start to move, their body heat causes the fragrance to be released.

The aim when creating positive space at home is to build a spiritually warm atmosphere, which brings you emotional contentment and security. However, if you prefer to practice in a professional studio, look for one that has windows with full shade coverage and a floor made of varnished hard wood which is smooth to the touch. The surroundings should be clean and without obstacles.

WHAT TO WEAR

Next, think about proper dress for dancing. There is a wonderful variety of clothing for belly dancing beyond the costumes you see on professionals wearing. Whatever you wear to dance in, try to find something that matches the following requirements.

• Choose something that does not restrict your movement in any way. Freedom of body expression is essential to good belly dancing. Beginners often feel most comfortable in a sports bra top. These special tops are made for exercises that are more demanding than beginning belly dance and are ideal for supporting your breasts, while allowing freedom for your arms and shoulders and leaving your midriff visible. Other options are shelf bra tank tops or cotton yoga shirts folded up above your midriff.

• Be brave and allow for a top that fully exposes your midsection. No matter how big or small, you don't have to be shy – allow your belly and hips to show. No holding back now! For your legs, a pair of lightweight running or yoga tights rolled over at the waist down to your hip bones is a great inexpensive choice.

• Find something light and feminine such as a gypsy-style shawl or silk scarves to drape round your hips.

Once you get into belly dancing you might like to invest in practice clothing to make you look the part. There are plenty of wonderful belly dance clothes to choose from which will make you feel like you just stepped out of an Oriental painting. Try costume-type bra tops, vest tops, cholis and tie-arounds for your upper body. Underneath, flowing harem pants and billowy gypsy skirts give unlimited range of movement and feeling.

Coin belts come in every colour and design you can think of and are worth every penny for the fun they add to your dancing. When purchasing, give the coin belt a good shake to see how loud the coins ring. The louder, the better! This exciting jingling adds incredible spirit and authenticity to the dance and can spark your imagination like nothing else.

RELAX YOUR MIND AND BODY

To bring yourself into the right frame of mind and lift your spirits, start with some breathing exercises to relax your mind and body and release tension.

• Stand or sit comfortably and close your eyes.
• Relax your abdominal muscles and inhale deeply for five heartbeats. Let your stomach extend fully so you draw in as much air as possible.
• When five beats are up, hold the air in your lungs for two beats and then release your breath completely for another six beats. You should feel your shoulders and neck muscles relaxing.
• Repeat this exercise at least four times. If you are feeling particularly tense, repeat the breathing technique until you feel calm and peaceful.

Imagination is a powerful tool that will also help you get into the right frame of mind. There is inspiration everywhere and it is always helpful to conjure up a romantic image that helps drain away daily stress. While you are practising your breathing, let your imagination take you somewhere magical. My favourite phrase in belly dancing is "anything is possible".

Maybe your mind will take you to a simple flower garden with cool grass under your feet, or to a white sandy beach with the ocean lapping the shore. My personal favourite is to imagine myself in a desert oasis in the early evening, with a cool and gentle breeze flowing over me. Wherever you wish to go at that moment is fine.

SELECTING MUSIC

The music of the Middle East has incredible soul and touches upon all aspects of human emotion. Whatever you are feeling, from joy and sadness to ecstasy and surprise, you can find music to match your mood. The most common instruments in Middle Eastern music are the *oud*, the *nay*, the *kunoon* and the *dumbek*. To the dancer, however, the most important of these instruments is the *dumbek*, or drum. It establishes the tempo of the music and by following the rhythm of the drum, you can establish the proper pace for dancing.

The single best tool a dancer has to keep her dancing in time with her music is what she learned in primary school – counting from one to eight! As you practice the techniques in this book, count out loud to the beats in the music. When your timing skills improve, you can start counting in your head instead of out loud. This is a simple technique, but unfortunately, many dancers, once they feel they have mastered counting, give up on it. This nearly always leads to sloppy technique. The strongest dancers keep counting no matter what level of expertise they reach.

In the early stages of dancing, the easiest way to find the beat is by marching to it. Simply step from left to right, tapping each foot when you hear the sound of the *dumbek* drum. There are some inspiring popular rhythms in traditional music which are helpful for a beginning belly dancer to get to know.

The traditional eight-count beat is the simplest and is basically eight uniform beats sounded one after another:
(one two three four five six seven eight)
Doom doom doom doom doom doom doom doom
●   ●   ●   ●   ●   ●   ●   ●

Another popular rhythm is the *chiftitelli*. It is so closely associated with the Middle East that even people who aren't interested in Arabic music will recognize it:
(one twothree fourfive six seven eight)
Doom doomdoom doomdoom dom dom dom
●   ●●   ●●   ●   ●   ●

The *moqsoom*, mostly used for creative hip work, is very simple:
(onetwo pause three pause onetwo pause three)
Domdom dom domdom dom
●●   ●   ●●   ●

A very advanced rhythm that has its origins in Turkey and Greece is the complex nine/eight rhythm. The nine/eight is an amazing musical annotation that is very rapid and energetic:
(one two three four five six SEVEN eight nine)
Doom doom doom doom doom doom DOOMdom doom

●　　●　　●　　●　　●　　●　　●●　　●

SUGGESTED ALBUMS FOR BELLY DANCING

When you first start belly dancing, the music and artists will be unfamiliar to you. Beginners risk spending lots of money on music only to find that its unsuitable for dancing. To avoid this, I've chosen some musicians and albums with excellent music for the beginner.

TURKISH: OMAR FARUK TEKBILEK
Gypsy Fire
Crescent Moon
Dance into Eternity
Firedance

ETHNIC COMPILATIONS: GEORGE ABDO
Best of Bellydance from Egypt, Lebanon, Arabia and Turkey

EGYPTIAN: HOSSAM RAMSEY
Source of Fire
Rhythms of the Nile
Secrets of the Eye

MODERN/POP BELLY DANCE MUSIC
Natasha Atlas: *Halim*
Alabina: *The Voice of Alabina*
Amr Diab: *The Best of Amr Diab*

NEW AGE BELLY DANCE MUSIC
Jehan Kamal: *Serpent Rising*
Azam Ali: *Portals of Grace*
Vas: *In the Garden of Souls*

2 Preparation

With any form of instruction I believe that it is vital for a student to learn each element of the new skill correctly the first time it's taught. First impressions stick with you. When something is learned properly the first time, it's remembered that way for life. Each type of dance has its own foundation of techniques which beginners must understand and master before they can move on, and belly dancing is no exception. The four most important skills for the beginner to learn are primary dance counting, weight distribution, muscle isolation and correct body posture (p.20).

DANCE COUNTING

Every dancer must follow the technique of counting, especially in the beginning. Belly dance music has a wide range of complex rhythms, but the best one for learning is a simple eight-count beat – the drum or underlying rhythm repeats every eight beats. With that in mind, for the dance steps to operate in time with the music, a count of eight is used to monitor and manage every step at all times. Each step and each move are given a count or set of counts that will total eight beats.

WEIGHT DISTRIBUTION

Each step we take – walking, running, dancing or even skipping – is accompanied by shifts in body weight. When you are dancing, understanding your body weight and where it is held will bring an improvement in grace and balance. As we stand still, our weight is evenly distributed, with 50 percent on each side. If the right knee is bent, our weight naturally shifts to the left side to offset the lack of balance on the right. If the left leg is lifted up off the ground, then 100 percent of the weight is supported by the right leg.

   To help understand this concept, place your right foot in front of your left and sway your upper body back and forth in a rocking motion. Feel how your body shifts the weight backward and forward to maintain balance. In the foundation position (p.20), note that when you lean back, 70 percent of your weight will be on your back leg while 30 percent is on your front leg.

MUSCLE ISOLATION

Isolation is the term dancers use to describe the act of intentionally moving only one part of the body at a time, while keeping the other parts still and relaxed. In other words, you isolate the muscles that you want to use and freeze those you're not using. Isolation helps develop your muscles properly during practice for stronger and more distinct movements.

PROPER POSTURE: THE FOUNDATION

Stand with your feet 30cm (12in) apart and parallel, knees unlocked. Straighten your spine until there is not even the slightest slouch in your upper body. Gently push your shoulders back and lift your chin to a comfortable level, about 1cm (½in) higher than normal. Flex your abdominal muscles until your stomach is slightly lifted and you feel tension in your lower abdomen. You body should appear calm but proud.

UPPER BODY

Having your arms in the proper position makes the difference between looking graceful and looking awkward. With your arms bent slightly at the elbow, raise them at your sides until your hands are about chest level. Bend your wrists, just slightly raising your hands.

LOWER BODY

Bend your knees just a little so that they are soft, then slide your left foot 15cm (6in) forward. Rise up onto the ball of your left foot, arching your heel sharply upward. Take a moment to note your weight distribution. At first, many people stand in this posture with 50 percent of their weight on each foot. In this position, 70 percent of the body weight should be on the back leg, and 30 percent on the front. If you are standing with a 50/50 distribution, lean back slightly and your weight will naturally shift onto the back leg. Don't lean all the way back – just enough to transfer more than half your weight to your back leg.

HAND POSITIONS

There are two basic hand positions – both are easy
to achieve, yet look elegant. These positions help you
learn how to hold your hands beautifully, without
distracting from what the rest of your body is doing.

BASIC 1: THE BASIC HAND
Keeping your wrist arched, straighten your
right hand until it is sharp and tense. Hold
for a few moments, then slightly relax so
there is a softness in the joints. Slightly raise
your little finger and forefinger while
dropping your middle finger and thumb.

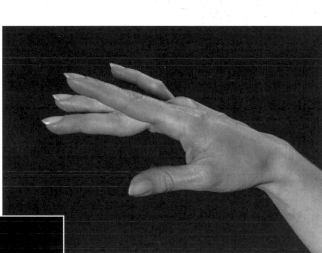

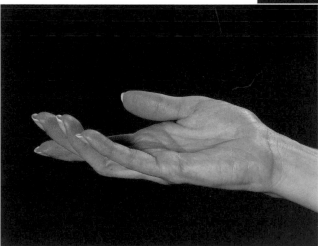

BASIC 2: THE OFFERING HAND
Hold out your hand with the palm and forearm
facing upward. Starting with the little finger,
allow your fingers to curl up very slightly while
keeping your forefinger almost perfectly straight.

STRETCH AND WARM UP

Before any physical activity, it is important to stretch and warm up your body to prevent injury as well as soreness. It's also easier to achieve the natural movements of belly dancing after some gentle stretches. Practice these stretches daily and your flexibility – and your dancing – will improve.

NECK STRETCH

Begin by slowly rolling your head right round in a circle. Roll four times to the left and four to the right.

1 Keeping your left arm and shoulder relaxed, take your right hand and reach it over your crown. Rest your fingertips over your left ear and breathe in. When you breathe out, gently pull your head down and to the right. Make sure you don't lift your left shoulder. Take two breaths, feeling your neck muscles uncoil, and release.

2 Repeat this exercise on the other side, resting your left hand on your right ear and gently pulling your head to the left. Repeat twice more on each side.

HIP-RELEASING STRETCH

Stand with your feet shoulder-width apart and raise your arms out to your sides. Keeping your feet flat on the ground, bend your knees and gently push your hips as far as you can to the right. Try almost to sit without falling over, as though you're balancing the littlest part of your cheek on a stool while still supporting yourself with your legs! Hold this position for ten seconds and breathe. You will feel your hip joints starting to pull and release.

Return to the center and stretch to your left side, again holding for ten seconds.

Repeat twice more. Speed up by shifting all the way out to the left and right in one fluid movement, gently bouncing once or twice on each side.

BACK-RELEASING STRETCH

The hip and torso movements in belly dancing use the muscles that encircle your pelvis and run down your lower back. Stretching these muscles before you practice will help you develop flexibility and strength, and improve the quality of your dancing.

1 Stand with your feet parallel and raise both arms straight up above your head. Keep your shoulders pressed down.

2 Slowly bend forward with a flat back (don't curl down), hinging at the waist and gently bending your knees until your torso is parallel with the floor.

3 Drop your hands down in front of you and touch the floor. If you cannot touch the floor, gently bend your knees and simply reach as far as is comfortable for you. Take a deep breath and relax. When you are supported by your hands, flex and release your knees a few times on each side in a walking motion.

4 Bend both knees together until you can grasp your ankles. Gently pull down with your arms while attempting to straighten your legs. Hold for a count of 30 seconds. You should feel a nice stretch across your back and hips as your muscles gradually let go their tension. Release and roll up. Repeat once more.

HAMSTRING STRETCH

This stretch will help to loosen tight hamstrings and calf muscles. Don't force your muscles. If you cannot reach your ankles, just gently stretch as far as you can. You know your body best, and it's the only one you have, so be careful with it!

1 Take a wide step to your left so that your feet are about 1.2m (4ft) apart. Stretch out your arms, reaching from your shoulders as though you're trying to touch the walls. Feel your shoulder blades begin to release. Slowly bend forward with a flat back (don't curl down), hinging at the waist while gently bending your knees until your torso is horizontal with the floor.

2 Rotate your body to the right and reach down with both hands to grasp your right ankle. Take a deep breath in. As you breathe out, pull gently on your ankle, bringing your lower body down for 20 seconds and allowing your calf and hamstring muscles to release. Rise up and repeat the stretch on the other side.

3 When you've stretched both sides, return to the center. Drop directly down, reaching as far as you can toward both your ankles. Grasp them firmly. Breathe in and as you breathe out, gently pull on your ankles and allow your hip muscles to release. Repeat all the stretches.

WRIST-RELEASING STRETCH

Graceful hands are important in belly dancing,
so keep your wrists supple with this stretch.

1 With palms together, hold
your hands at chest level.

2 Press your palms together
and lower your arms until your
hands are at abdomen level.
Make sure you keep your lower
palms touching. Hold for a
count of five. Repeat twice.

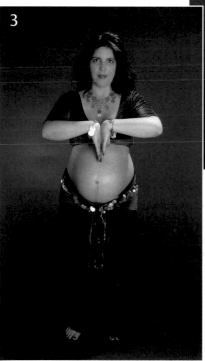

3 Switch your hands so
that your palms are facing
outward and your fingers
are pointing down. Press
your hands together.

4 Gently drop your elbows
down to lift your wrists
slightly until you feel a stretch
in your forearms. Hold for a
count of five. Repeat twice.

3 Basic elements

When you were a child you had to learn to walk before you could run. Before walking, you had to learn to stand, and before standing came crawling. The truth is, belly dancing is no different! Dedicating time and patience to the measured and steady progression of your abilities is the best way to learn the basic movements on the following pages. These steps make up the primary vocabulary of beginner belly dance and it is vital to master them before leaping into more complex motions.

When finding your way through the instructions, try not to skim over movements that come easily to you. Rather, practice them and focus on understanding why your body responds so well to those particular physical patterns. This knowledge will help if you reach a stumbling block with another movement. Should this happen, don't get frustrated – be patient and allow yourself time to think through the step, grasping each component, then putting the movement together.

As you grow more comfortable with the steps, I urge you to experiment and improvise. Try alternating between fast and slow as you practice, noting how the contrast changes the steps. Vary the level of energy you put into the movements, performing some with sharp, muscular jerks and others with soft and gentle fluidity. You'll be amazed at the difference these easy changes will make in all your basic (and later more complex) practice movements.

Turning and spinning (pp.65–69) are especially delightful to experiment with, but a bit more tricky. Have you ever seen a professional dancer turn and turn and never appear to get dizzy? That is because of the technique called "spotting". To spot, look straight ahead and focus on a single point in front of you. Turn round as far as you can without removing your eyes from that point. When you can't turn any further, quickly spin your head round with the turn to look over the other shoulder. Locate the original point you focused on until your body catches up. Repeat this five times quickly. Now spin five times without spotting. Feel the difference? No matter how fast/slow or sharp/smooth your movements, spotting will spare you many swimming heads and stumbles.

Simple as these steps may seem, when put together in artful combinations, they can be used to build stunning dances and routines. While adding more and more steps to your dance vocabulary, really allow yourself to play around by "layering" them. That means taking the separate techniques and layering one on top of the other to develop a string of movements that add up to a dance. Layering is truly where the fun begins – by applying it, your skills will develop from the simplicity of a planned series of steps to joyfully intricate, spontaneous dancing.

HIP DROPS

This is the ideal step for learning how to move and isolate your hips and a very important movement in belly dancing.

1 First double check that your body is in a strong foundation position with proper weight distribution (p.20).

2 Lift your left hip slowly by contracting the muscles that run down the left side of your abdomen. As you lift your hip, don't lift the rest of you! Keep your head in an even position by allowing your left knee to bend a little and your right to straighten slightly, while pulling your hip up.

3 When your hip is as high as it can go, hold it there for two counts, then drop it sharply by releasing the contraction and actively using your leg and pelvic strength to force the hip down lower than its original position in foundation. Hold it there for another two counts, accentuating the down motion. Raise the hip slowly, again counting one, two in your head, and sharply drop it while counting three, four. Repeat on your right side.

HIP LIFTS

This a simple variation of the hip drop. During the hip drop, the down/dropping motion is accentuated. In a lift, it is the opposite – the upward motion is accentuated.

1 Starting in foundation position (p.20) and using the same count speed as the hip drop, sharply lift your hip with a jerk.

2 Hold for two counts and slowly release your hip back down to foundation level.

PRACTICE

Perform ten hip lifts on the right and ten on the left. Speed up so that it only takes one count to lift your hip and one count to drop it for another ten lifts.

PRACTICING THE HIP LIFT AND HIP DROP TOGETHER

Using two counts, practice 20 hip drops on the left and 20 on the right. Then repeat, but using only one count per hip drop. Switch to high and low hip drops for 20 on each side. Finally, transition into hip lifts by completing a hip drop, holding it for one beat, then moving quickly into a hip lift. Remember, for hip lifts and drops to look as they should, always accentuate the drop or lift with a brisk, sharp movement and keep the opposing release soft.

HIP SNAPS AND HIP THRUSTS

These moves may look simple, but to master them you must be able to control your hip muscles while relaxing your knees, to allow your hips more range.

LEFT AND RIGHT HIP SNAP

1 As you stand in foundation (p.20), bend your supporting leg 7.5cm (3in) more than usual. Increasing the bend on the supporting leg gives your hips more room to move. In one fast movement, bend your right leg down, straighten your left leg slightly and sharply snap your left hip out to the left.

2 Then quickly bend your left leg down, straighten your right and sharply snap your right hip out to the right. Alternate left and right in short sharp movements until you've done ten snaps on each side. Each snap should equal one count.

FRONT AND BACK

3 Now, just as fast as with the left and right snap, softly bend your knees and snap your pelvis a little to the front by tightening your abdomen muscles sharply. A small fast snap is enough – any more can look vulgar.

PRACTICE

Snap your hips sharply to the left and right for eight counts, then front and back for eight counts. Now try a belly dance technique called the "box" – this means sharply performing a dance step in four different directions: front, side, back and side. The hip snap box is based on four counts. Begin by snapping your hips to the left, then back, over to the right and finally to the front. Repeat four more times, then finish with two sets of side hip snaps.

4 Then snap to the back by arching your spine and pushing your pelvis back. Repeat the front and back snaps ten times in each direction. Keep the movements distinct and tight, counting one for each snap.

HIP THRUST

1 Start in the foundation position (p.20), keeping your hips straight and knees softly bent. With your right foot, step about 60cm (2ft) to the right. Lift your heel, arching your foot, and place 70 percent of your weight on your supporting left leg.

2 Isolating the rest of your body, thrust your right hip sharply up and out for one count. Slowly bring your hip back in, also for one count.

Pull your right leg back and step out with your left foot. Lift your left heel and thrust your hip out to the left for one count. Again, bring the hip back in for a single count.

Unlike the hip drops and lifts, the thrust is meant to be danced to two counts – one out, one in. You could speed it up to one count, but the music must be very fast for the step to look right.

HIP THRUST RETURN

A small adjustment to the hip thrust can add another dimension to the step. Starting again on the right side, instead of sharply thrusting your hips out, push them out gently and quickly snap them back into place. This accents the movement in instead of the movement out.

PRACTICE

Perform ten hip thrusts on your right side and ten on your left. Follow with alternate right and left hip thrusts.

ADDING DETAIL

On the thrust, switch your hands into the offering position (p.21), then roll them back into basic (p.21) on the return.

JOINING THE HIP THRUST AND RETURN

Dance ten hip thrusts to each side, if possible without pausing in between. Follow with hip return thrusts on each side. Now, why not try accenting both the out and in movement?

HIP ROLLS

Although the hip roll movement draws attention to the hips, it is your footwork and leg strength that make it possible. The reverse hip roll is a more subtle movement – our anatomy prevents it being as broad and dramatic as the regular roll.

HIP ROLL

1 For the first count, step out to the right so that your feet are shoulder-width apart and flat on the ground. Sit out as far as you can to the right and bend your knees slightly. Your weight should be 70 percent on your right leg, 30 percent on your left.

2 For the second count, arch your right foot as high as you can while tightly contracting the muscles that run down the right side of your torso. This will dramatically lift your hip. Make sure that you don't bob up and down by keeping your head and body at the same height as when you started the arch and contraction. Allowing your knees to bend and flex naturally with the hip roll helps you to keep level.

3 For the third count, roll your hips from the right to the left in one smooth movement. Push your hips as far as you can to the left, while shifting your weight to the left leg. Once you have rolled to the left, release your contracted muscles and drop your arched foot flat on the ground while sitting out. This final position is the perfect starting point for the left hip roll – repeat from step 1, but with your left hip.

PRACTICE

Practice and speed control will help you smooth out your hip rolls. Speed up the movements to two counts only and eliminate any pauses between steps. Try not to let your foot fall sharply to the floor, but place it down softly in a light release. After ten more two-count sets, speed up to only one count per roll. After ten of these, you should see the hip roll forming as you get used to the technique. At first it helps to repeat the following in your head while performing the rolls: right up, push, down, left up, push, down.

REVERSE HIP ROLL

1 Begin by moving into the beginning stance of a right hip roll, but don't push your hips so far. Remember to soften your knees and keep your height consistent.

2 Tightly contract the muscles on your left side and sharply arch your left foot. Unlike the hip roll in which you keep your hips thrust out while contracting, in the reverse hip roll you must keep your hip pulled in as close as possible to your center point during the lift and contraction.

3 While your hip is in the lifted position, push it gently out to the left. Release the contracted muscles and drop your arched foot. Again, allow your knees to bend and flex naturally with the movement so that you remain level. The mantra for the reverse hip roll is as follows: left up, push left, drop, right up, push right, drop.

PRACTICE

Slowly repeat the reverse hip roll five times on each side. As with the regular hip roll, speed up to one count per roll and smooth it out.

To practice the hip roll and reverse hip roll together, first dance ten hip rolls, alternating left and right. Pause for one count and then move quickly into ten reverse hip rolls, alternating left and right.

VARIATION

During hip rolls and reverse hip rolls, try bending your knees deeply and dancing a few low rolls, gradually straightening your legs until you return to your normal height.

LARGE HIP CIRCLES

As with the hip rolls, the best way to learn the large hip circle is to break it down into four separate steps totalling eight counts, then bring the steps together.

PREPARATION

Stand in basic foundation (p.20), with your feet shoulder-width apart. As in the hip-releasing stretch (p.22), push your hips as far as you can to the right, keeping your feet flat on the floor, for two counts. Then push your hips to the left for two counts. Alternate between left and right for eight counts, then return to center.

Next, bend your knees about 7.5cm (3in) and contract your lower abdominal muscles. This will raise your pelvis and support your spine as you lean back slightly. Make sure that your lower back doesn't arch. Hold for two counts, then tilt your body forward until you have reversed your position.

1 Begin by sitting out to the right as far as is comfortable for two counts.

2 Slowly round your hips forward, leaning back with your pelvis tucked under and your spine straight for two counts.

3 Next, push your hips out to the left as far as is comfortable for two counts.

4 Follow with a forward lean, again with a straight back, for two counts.

PRACTICE

Repeat the sequence four times until you feel confident with the steps. To tie the movements together and build a wide, graceful hip circle, don't hold each step but flow from one to another, connecting them without any pauses.

ADDING ELEGANT ARM MOVEMENTS

The addition of elegant arm movements will add visual
interest and complexity to your hip circles.

1 For the first four counts as you round
the circle to the right, switch your
hands to the offering position (p.21).

2, 3 Slowly bring your arms
together at chest level, softly
crossing them close to your
body as your hips round from
right to forward, back and left.

4 As your hips round back to the
right, return your arms slowly to the
basic position (p.21) with palms
down. Just gorgeous!

PRACTICE

Perform four large hip circles
with elegant arm movements
to the right, followed by
another four to the left.
Experiment with changing the
speed of the entire movement,
alternating between left and
right hip circles at fast and
slow speeds.

HIP TWISTS

A fun, energetic movement, the hip twist can be danced on the spot or used as the hip twist walk, a travel step.

2 Twist your left hip sharply forward and round to the right while turning your foot in the same direction. Softly twist your hip back to the starting position while gently lifting your foot off the floor in a small kick. Put your foot back down in the same place you kicked off from and dance another hip twist. Repeat eight times, then switch to the right hip.

FORWARD HIP TWIST
1 Stand in basic foundation (p.20). On the first count, gently step forward on your left foot, planting it firmly on the ground in front of you.

BACK HIP TWIST
3 Begin by performing a forward hip twist, but do not forcefully thrust your hip forward. Just softly extend it with a gentle push.

4 Snap your hip back sharply, using the momentum to kick your foot lightly off the floor before setting it down again. Repeat eight times on the left side. Then switch, repeating the movement eight times on your right side.

PRACTICE

Dance the forward hip twist using one count for each step. Twist on the left for eight counts (four twists), then speed up until only one beat is required for a full twist. Repeat on the right side. Follow with a full set of back hip twists on both sides with the same tempo as above.

HIP TWIST WALK

I Perform a full left hip twist, accentuating the forward motion.

2 Twist your hip back energetically, softly kicking your foot up off the floor.

3 Instead of placing your left foot back down for another hip twist, use it to take a large step, about 30cm (12in), forward, turning your toes moderately out to the left.

4 Immediately step forward with your right foot, moving quickly into a right hip twist. As your right foot lifts off the ground, take a large step forward. Now quickly step forward with your left foot, repeating the entire segment from the beginning. Continue alternating left and right. This easy travel step will take you right across the floor if you let it!

VARIATION

Feel free to dance as many hip twists as you like between each walk step.

THE BODY INTENSE SHIMMY

The body intense shimmy demonstrates belly dancing's roots in fertility and the ritualistic act of giving birth better than any other movement. It's also the most widely recognized step and unique to belly dance.

1 Contrary to popular belief, the shimmy emanates from the knees, not the hips! Select some music with a rapid tempo and stand in foundation (p.20). Modify your foundation pose by placing your feet side by side and flat on the ground. Relax your knees, bending them slightly so that they are loose and supple.

Take a few long breaths. Many of us have a tendency to hold our breath and contract our muscles when doing something strenuous, such as shimmying, but that is the fastest way to run out of energy. As you learn to shimmy, breathing evenly and deeply will help you keep going longer and prevent your knees from locking.

2 Bend your right knee and notice that your left hip lifts slightly. Do not lock your left knee and try your best to keep it soft. Return your right knee to its starting position, also without straightening or locking it.

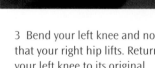

3 Bend your left knee and notice that your right hip lifts. Return your left knee to its original position.

4 Now slowly bend your knees, alternating left and right. As each knee rises and drops so will the opposite hip. This is the cornerstone of the shimmy. Remember not to straighten your legs so much that your knees lock. Keep them soft.

Gradually speed up your knee bends until you feel you can go no faster. There you are – that is a fully fledged shimmy!

5 After about a minute or so of shimmying, you may start to feel a burn in your thigh muscles – that means you are doing the movement properly. After two minutes of shimmying, you may start to sweat and that's even better. Shimmying takes incredible energy, so sweating is another sign that you are moving the correct way. Once the shimmy motor is running, you can relax and your body will almost shimmy by itself.

SHAKE THAT BELT
A coin belt is a wonderful prop when learning to shimmy. The spirited sound not only serves as an inspiration but also indicates the speed of your shimmy.

BELLY ROLL

Don't be disheartened if you aren't able to perform this movement straight away. It takes time to develop the muscle control necessary to roll your entire abdomen. Keep trying and you will get there.

PREPARATION

Place your hands on your belly, one above the other. Fully relax your stomach – let it hang as though it has no muscles at all. Take a deep breath in and then breathe out, feeling the muscles under your hands working. The lower abdomen is generally engaged before the upper abdomen. Repeat three more times until you are in tune with your breathing.

Relax your stomach again and, rather than waiting for a breath, contract ONLY your lower abdominal muscles. Relax. Then contract ONLY your upper ab muscles. Now that you have an idea of the different muscles, try a belly roll.

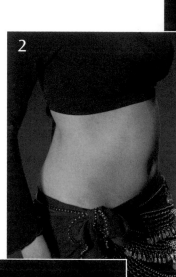

1 Relax your belly entirely and contract your lower abdominal muscles.

2 Gradually release the lower abs and simultaneously begin to contract the upper ones.

3 As your upper abs clench and pull in close to your body, fully relax your lower abs.

4 Finally, flex your lower abs while relaxing the upper muscles, then begin the series again. If you can do this four or five times successfully you will find yourself performing a bona fide belly roll as you contract and release your abdominal muscles.

VARIATION

Once you can do the normal belly roll, try it in reverse! Instead of starting by contracting the lower abdominal muscles, contract the upper ones, then move on to the lower. As you contract the lower set, release the upper abdominals so that the roll appears to reverse direction and wave down rather than up.

SENSUOUS UNDULATION

Another staple in belly dance, the undulation is both unusual and sensual without being overtly suggestive. Pulling the undulation sequence together takes patience and practice. It is especially important that you look in a mirror as you try this technique so that you can see your entire body working and make sure you're moving correctly.

PREPARATION STEPS FOR UNDULATION

Instead of facing front in the foundation stance, turn your body until you are at a 45-degree angle to the mirror. Thrust your chest forward as far as you can for two counts, arching your upper spine and pushing your shoulders back (see chest thrust p.44). Then roll your shoulders forward and compress your upper body into a deep slouch for two counts. Repeat both the thrust and the slouch four more times.

Now, using parts of the hip circle (p.34), tuck your pelvis up by contracting your abdominal muscles and lean back with bent knees for two counts. Lift up from your chest while straightening your knees moderately and lean forward, hinging at the waist, also for two counts. Repeat four times.

PUTTING THE MOVEMENT TOGETHER

In order to develop the necessary clean, snakelike movements, you now need to connect the four two-count steps detailed above into an eight-count undulation. Remember, taking it slowly and speeding up gradually is the best way to develop muscle control and learn this technique correctly.

1 Begin with the arch. Firmly push your chest as far forward as you can, keeping your shoulders pressed back.

2 Keeping the arch strong, allow your lower back to release and push your hips back. Extend and lengthen your body up toward the ceiling, leading with your chest.

3 Start to lean back. Support your lower spine by tucking your pelvis slightly up and in.

4 With knees softly bent, continue to lean back as far as you can go without any strain to your spine or abdominal muscles.

5 Curl in your chest and roll your upper body forward until your entire body is almost crouched into a reverse C shape.

To finish the undulation, strongly arch your chest out and push your hips back again. Continue with the forward momentum and lead with your chest until you rise up and slide into the beginning position. Keep repeating the undulation with as few pauses as possible. It will be choppy in the beginning, but as your body grows accustomed to the movements, it will smooth out.

PRACTICE

Dance four undulations with your body facing 45 degrees to the right, then four more with your body entirely in profile. Switch to the left profile and dance four undulations, then turn 45 degrees to the left and dance four more. As you grow accustomed to moving your body in this way, try to avoid the tendency to speed up. An undulation is meant to be slow and soothing like ocean waves, not wiggly like a worm. Only when you are sure that you've mastered the movement should you consider adding speed as a variation.

VARIATION: HIGH/LOW UNDULATIONS

Standing in foundation (p.20), step forward on your right foot in a rocking motion. Then rock back on your left foot. Practice this gentle sway for 16 counts, two counts forward and two counts back. When the next forward rock begins, arch your chest forward and begin the undulation. As you rock back, finish the undulation with the lower part of your body.

Try adding a dip to the undulation by bending your knees on one full undulating rock back and forth, then standing on your toes for a second full rock back and forth. Alternate between high and low undulations while rocking on your feet for a count of 16.

CHEST THRUSTS AND CHEST CIRCLES

CHEST THRUST SIDE TO SIDE
1 Keeping your shoulders relaxed and your
hips directly over your legs, isolate your chest
and thrust it out to the right as far as you can.
Imagine that your legs and hips are frozen
solid and there is a rope around your
shoulders pulling you directly to the right.

2 Return to the center and push to the left. The
visual effect should be that the upper and lower
halves of your body are on two separate planes
and are moving independently of one another.
   If it looks as if you are not really moving, but
simply bending your chest to the left and right in
almost a slump on each side, try counteracting this
by slightly lifting the shoulder on the side in which
you are thrusting. In other words, if you are pushing
your chest to the right, lightly lift your right
shoulder. When you are pushing to the left, gently
lift your left shoulder. This will square out the upper
part of your body, making the movement distinct.

PRACTICE
Perform ten chest thrusts, alternating
to the left and right, for two counts
each. Then speed up to one count on
each side. Try playing with the timing
by holding a left thrust for two counts,
then alternating right and left for one
count and vice versa.

CHEST THRUST FRONT AND BACK
1 Chest thrusts can be danced front to back as well as side to side. Imagine that instead of pulling you right and left, the rope is now pulling you forward and back. Thrust your chest forward as far as you can, pulling your shoulders back and arching your upper spine.

2 Then roll your shoulders forward and curve your back so that it appears as if you are slouching, with your chest caving in.

CHEST CIRCLES
Perform a "box" (p.30) of chest thrusts with your upper body. Each move should be two counts. Thrust forward, return to center. Push to the right, return to center. Thrust back, return to center. Push to the left, return to center. Next, repeat the box, but without returning to center after each movement. Repeat five times, then smooth the sequence out. Remove any pauses in between steps and slowly rotate your chest to each point using one count. A chest circle will take a total of four counts to achieve.

CHEST THRUST PRACTICE
Alternate between pushing forward and back ten times for two counts each. Try experimenting with timing as you did with the side to side thrusts.

CHEST CIRCLE PRACTICE
Perform a chest circle for four more four-count rotations, then speed up to two-count rotations in each direction.

BEAUTIFUL BACKBENDS

This step should be learned gradually. Only increase the arch when your back is fully supported by strong, well-developed abdominal and lower back muscles.

1 Stand with your feet shoulder-width apart and your hands in basic one (p.21). On your dominant side, step directly back with the corresponding foot. Step far enough to bring the toes of your back foot in line with the heel of your front foot. Unlock your knees and allow them to bend softly.

Contract your abdominals and tuck your pelvis slightly forward. Keeping your abdominal muscles tight will support and straighten your lower back. It is very important not to allow your lower spine to collapse onto itself so keep those abs rock solid!

WARNING

If you have, or have had, any spinal or neck pain or injury, do not perform this movement under any circumstances. Even if you are without pain or injury, try this step only with the aid of another person, who can catch you if you start to fall over backwards.

2 Tilt your head back slightly and, keeping your shoulders pressed down, slowly bend back about 7.5cm (3in). Allow your knees to bend naturally with the movement. Pause and check your body to make sure your lower back isn't arching yet. If this is easy for you, go back another 7.5cm (3in). Check your body again. If you are feeling strain in your neck or spine, slowly come up again. This means that your muscles are not developed enough to go farther and you must only drop this far until they are strong enough to do more.

3 If you still feel comfortable, drop back another 7.5cm (3in) and raise the arm opposite your supporting leg.

4 Continue to dip back slowly by 7.5cm (3in) increments until the first sign of strain, then come back up 7.5cm (3in). This point is your maximum range until your muscles are stronger.

If your neck and upper back feel very strong, gently tilt your head back and look at the ceiling. Hold for a few moments. Slowly come back up, leading with your chest.

PRACTICE

As you fall gently into your backbend, note at which point you start to develop tension in your neck and spine and come back up. Fall back again, this time holding the backbend at the very point before you feel the strain for five seconds. Repeat five times. Break for a minute or two, then repeat. If you practice every day, your backbend should become deeper and more secure as your muscles gain strength.

ADDING ELEGANT ARM MOVEMENTS

Making the backbend beautiful is easier than the backbend itself. Raise your arms in front of you and simply strike a pretty pose with your hands. Use basic hands or offering hands (p.21) to make this technique look more elegant and less gymnastic. Adding forward snake arms (p.54) is another wonderful way to enhance the movement without drawing attention away from the bend itself.

COBRA NECK SLITHER

Begin by repeating the neck stretches (p.22) before attempting the cobra neck slither. The unusual head movements in belly dance are unlike anything in Western dance styles.

PREPARATION

Inhale deeply and relax your shoulders. Place your fingertips on your neck, directly below the angle of your jawbone. Gently circle your fingers until you find the muscle underneath. This is the muscle you need to engage to perform the cobra. Gently slide your neck to the right. As you do, feel the muscle on the left side of your neck moving. Repeat in the other direction, feeling the muscles on the right side work. This movement is more of a push than a pull, so it is important not to overextend your neck. Even just a small movement in each direction is enough to make an impact. As your neck becomes more flexible from doing neck stretches and the slither, your range will improve.

1 Raise your arms up above your head so they are parallel to your ears. Firmly press your shoulders down and back, un-crowding your neck. Place your palms together and lower them until your elbows are bent at a 45-degree angle. This lovely face frame is a perfect complement to the cobra.

2, 3 Now, as you practiced, simply slither your head left, then right. Make sure you don't tilt your head in the direction you are moving to compensate for limited neck flexibility. It's best to perform the movement correctly, no matter how small. To add a further oriental touch, smile a little and move your eyes back and forth in the direction of your slither.

VARIATION

Instead of standing still and placing your palms together with straight wrists, twist your wrists and cross them, meeting the palms in the middle (right). Step dramatically forward, slithering as you go.

POSES

Here are some examples of beautiful hand and arm poses you can use in your dance. Posing during a dance routine is an excellent way for the dancer to have a short break, while allowing observers to take in visual details that might otherwise be missed.

OFFERING

ARABY PUSH

EGYPTIAN GODDESS

FINALE POSTURE: RA'S CROWN

SHOULDER SHAKE

Use your shoulders to express a wide range of feelings and concepts in belly dancing. Just as you can say "I don't know" by shrugging your shoulders, you can also express flirtation, playfulness – even pride – by shoulder movements as you dance.

1 Stand in foundation with basic arms (p.20). Look at the position of your hands and imagine that each one is resting on a wall so that it cannot move. Relax your shoulders completely and raise them about 1cm (½in) or so.

2 Push your right shoulder forward without moving your arm or hand – remember, there is a wall there. Repeat eight times, making sure you keep your arm still. Perform another set, but now sharpen the movement by putting the accent on the push. Switch to your left shoulder and repeat for eight counts on the left side. Again, repeat and sharpen the movement for eight counts. Alternate your shoulders left and right sharply, so as one shoulder is pushed out, the other is pulled in.

VARIATION
For a playful, 1930s-style belly dance step, dip your body slowly to the left, center, then right, while practicing the shoulder shake. This is a classic belly dance movement which, when combined with the shoulder shake, takes you right back to the sultan's palace!

PRACTICE
Alternate pushing each shoulder forward for two counts, totalling 16 beats. Speed up to one count per push and soften the movement so it becomes a gentle shake, rather than sharp accents. Don't overdo the shake – the focus is meant to be on your shoulders, not other parts of you!

HAND MOVEMENTS

These movements are often the last skills to be mastered by a new belly dancer. The need for grace and subtlety means that hands must be used conservatively, so as not to draw attention away from other parts of the body. You may find that these beautiful positions carry over into your everyday life – in the way you hold a teacup, use your hands as you speak, or even in the way you rest your hands at a computer keyboard.

CIRCLING HANDS

Practice this simple technique of circling hands from basic one (p.21) to basic two, or offering hand (p.21), every day until it becomes second nature. It will make a wonderful difference in your dancing and can be used in just about any of the dance steps.

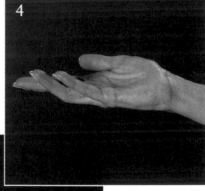

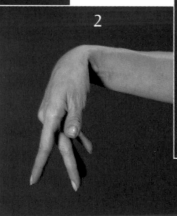

1 Start with your right hand in basic one position.

2 Drop your wrist and stiffen your fingers while sweeping your hand counterclockwise in a full half circle.

3 Continue to rotate your wrist until your forearm and palm are facing up.

4 Release your stiffened fingers into basic two, or the offering hand position.

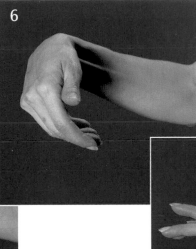

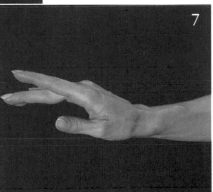

5 Straighten your wrist and, gently curling your fingers, softly fold your hand at the base knuckles.

6 Rotate your wrist clockwise while sweeping your hand down and around until the palm and forearm are facing down.

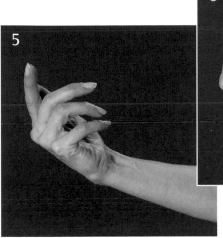

7 Then, smoothly drop your wrist while lifting your hand, returning your fingers to basic one.

SPANISH HANDS

When the Arabs inhabited Spain, the cultures had an interesting impact on each other. You can see the cross-cultural influence in this Spanish hands technique. A powerful modification on circling hands, it adds further elegance to those simple movements.

1 Start by holding one hand, bent at the wrist in basic one position (p.21), over your head, with fingers pointing at the ceiling. The other hand should also be in basic one, but held at waist level, fingers pointing down. Starting with the index fingers on the upper and lower hands, fold over each finger at the base knuckles one at a time, while rotating your wrists around in a circle (see basic to offering hand switch, opposite).

2 As you turn your wrist, straighten your fingers and arch them back until they have returned to a relaxed basic position.

SNAKE ARMS

Sensuous and almost eerie, snake arms are meant to entice and hypnotize. Start by learning the single snake arms, then move on to the alternating version.

SINGLE SNAKE ARMS

1 Stand with your feet flat on the floor and arms at your sides, palms facing inward. Lift your right arm, keeping it slightly bent at the elbow as if holding a large rolled-up towel under your arm. Roll your shoulder forward so that your elbow is pointing toward the ceiling.

2 Raise your arm, leading with your elbow until it is just above shoulder height, or as high as you can manage. Beginning with your wrist, lift your hand gradually.

3 As your hand continues to lift, rotate your elbow to point down. Softly bend your fingers and turn your palm out, while gradually lowering your arm until it is at your side. Repeat the step eight times, then start again with your left arm.

DON'T WORRY!

The muscles used to perform these techniques are rarely used in daily life. Don't be surprised if you find that after practicing this movement your arms and hands are shaky. This is a natural result of tired muscles and will pass in a few hours.

ALTERNATING SNAKE ARMS

1 Begin with your right arm, slowly lifting it until you rotate your elbow and change the direction of your hand. At the moment when you begin to drop your right arm, start the step on the left side of your body by raising your left arm.

2 As your left elbow reaches shoulder level and rotates to turn down, your right arm should be once again beginning its ascent. Each arm should be working slowly in the opposite direction to the other. This technique takes lots of coordination so be patient and take it slowly.

PRACTICE

Begin by snaking both arms at the same time for four counts as you raise them, and four counts as you lower them. Then lift only the left for four counts, followed by the right for four counts. Move back into snaking both arms together. Finally, as the arms come back down, lift only the left. As you begin to lower it, immediately bring up the right to start alternating snake arms. Speed up the alternating snake arms to two counts per movement. Repeat six times.

DANCING WITH SNAKE ARMS

When you feel you have mastered snake arms, try bringing them into your dance practice. You can do just about anything with strong snake arms. Try stepping forward on your right foot into a deep lunge, while your arms are snaking to your sides. When you have reached the deepest part of your lunge, hold it and slowly bring your snaking arms forward so that your hands are crossing in front of you. Snake in this position for a few moments, then slowly move your arms back to your sides and slightly behind you. Step back from your lunge, stop snaking and slowly bring your arms to the front in prayer position.

LEGS AND FEET: BASIC STANCES

There are two basic methods of standing in belly dance, and the steps on the following pages should be practiced using both methods. You can either dance with your feet flat on the ground or high on the ball, also called releve.

FLAT FOOT
The flat foot position is just what it sounds like. Stand with your entire foot flat on the floor and your body weight equally distributed.

RELEVE
In the releve, or arched foot position, stand high on the ball of the foot with your heels off the ground as if you were stretching up to reach something. All your weight is supported by the ball of the foot and the joints of your first two toes. Very different from the "on points" position in ballet when the dancer stands on the tips of her toes, releve offers more security and stability.

PRACTICE
To practice the releve position, stand with your feet flat and parallel. Raise your heels off the ground until your feet are fully arched and hold for five seconds. Relax and repeat three times more.

Rise up on your heels again and hold the position for two minutes or as long as you can manage. You might find your calves tire after only 30 seconds, so stop when you need to. Your ankles may feel very weak, but this is normal at first so don't worry unless you're in any pain – if you are, stop. The muscles are simply weak and need to be developed. Keep practicing and your calves and ankles will quickly become stronger.

Although many dancers like to wear fashionable high-heeled shoes, I feel these are out of place in most forms of belly dancing. Dancing in releve (right) adds the same height and elegance as high heels and is more in keeping with belly dancing's historic natural roots.

THE BASIC WALK

Simple and classy, the basic walk is the fastest and most graceful way to make an entrance. When walking normally, your heel touches the ground before the rest of your foot. In a belly dance walk it is the opposite – you place your toes on the ground first.

1 Stand with your arms at your sides and your feet parallel to one another, 15cm (6in) apart. Lift your right foot 10cm (4in) off the ground and glide it forward.

2 Place your toes on the floor first, followed by your heel.

3 Repeat with your left foot, touching toes down first as before. Continue, alternating left and right. Lift your chin slightly and walk as smoothly as you can, without too much head bobbing, around your space.

ADDING ARMS

There are no particular arm movements associated with this walk. You can simply keep your arms in basic or do something much more complex, such as alternating snake arms (p.55). Experiment and do what works for you.

PHARONIC WALK

If you're in the mood for drama when entering the dance space, try the pharonic walk. An interpretation of postures depicted in Ancient Egyptian hieroglyphics, it conveys a sense of grandeur – of a queen or goddess entering the room.

1 Stand with your right side at a 45-degree angle to the front and your head held up. Raise your arms above your head. Cross your hands at the wrists so your palms meet in prayer position.

2 Pointing your toes, lift your left knee until your foot is almost level with your right knee.

3 Slowly and deliberately extend and straighten your leg and place your foot flat on the floor, toes first.

4 Repeat, stepping and lifting your right leg.

PRACTICE

Walk slowly and deliberately, taking time and care with each step, until you reach the center of the dance space.

THE INDIE CROSS STEP

This walk has its origins in ethnic artistic expression –
there are many statues of Indian gods and goddesses
portrayed as moving in a cross step. Because there are two
full steps to each movement, the Indie cross step can be
danced with two or four counts. We'll begin with four.

1 Lift your right leg, bending at the
knee and toes pointed, to the side so
that it is directly under your right
arm. Swing your leg over the left and
step to the far left across your body
for two counts.

2 Transfer your weight onto the
right leg by leaning slightly forward
for another two counts.

3 Next, lift your left leg to the side and
swing it over the right for two counts.

4 Step far right until you can lean
and transfer your weight to the
left foot for the final two counts.

ADDING ARMS

As you step with your right foot,
slowly make a left snake arm
(p.54) until your weight is
completely forward. When stepping
to the left, slowly make a right
snake arm until your weight is
completely forward.

PRACTICE

Removing any pauses in the
sequence, cross step forward to
the front of the room. Turn and
step around your space, making
one full circle.

GHAWAZEE SLIDE STEP

Based on three movements and four counts, this is a playful, fast-moving ghawazee (or gypsy) step, which can be used as a travelling step and/or hip step.

1 Lift your right leg and step forward about 60cm (2ft).

2 Shift your body weight onto your right foot. Steps 1 and 2 should total only one count.

3 Slide your left foot forward until it is about 10cm (4in) behind your right heel for count two.

4 Finally, for count three, transfer your weight onto your back foot, then step forward again with your right foot. Pause for the fourth count.

Beginning another four counts, step forward with your left foot, passing the right. Glide your right foot 7.5–10cm (3–4in) forward to your left, and then step forward again with your left foot. Repeat the entire movement from step 1.

PRACTICE

The way to learn this step is practice. Keep repeating with alternating feet, slowly gaining in speed until you look as if you're skipping. Experiment with large and small steps.

DEBKE

A traditional folk dance step, the eight-step full debke traces its roots back to the desert tribes, who used it as part of their cultural celebrations.

1 Using one count for each step, begin by crossing your left foot in front of your right, stepping almost parallel to your current stance.

2 Then with your right foot, step directly sideways to the right.

4 Step one more time to the right with your right foot. Touch the floor lightly with the tip of your toe. This sequence should take four counts.

3 With your left foot, now cross behind your right, stepping parallel.

5 Cross your right foot over your left, stepping almost parallel.

6 With your left foot, step directly sideways to the left.

7 With your right foot, step behind your left.

8 With your left foot, step again to the left, touching the floor lightly with the tip of your toe. This sequence should take up the final four counts. Start again at step 1.

ADDING ARMS

For a fun experiment, raise your arms, bending at the elbows until your hands are parallel to your head. Bend your wrists until your palms are flat and facing the ceiling. When stepping to the left, look in that direction and, keeping your arms stiff, raise your right arm about 7.5cm (3in) higher than your left.

When you step to the right, return your right arm to its original level and raise the left while looking right.

PRACTICE

Perform the full debke right and left and then try it forward in each direction on the diagonal right and left. Try holding your arms in a variety of positions – be as creative as you want.

KASHLIMAR

Also a traditional folk step, the kashlimar can be performed in one place or used to travel across your dance space. Each step in the sequence is equal to one count.

1 Step forward with your right foot. As you transfer your weight forward, lift your left foot slightly off the floor.

2 Now reverse direction and step down with your left foot. Rock back your weight and lift your right foot slightly off the ground. Continue shifting your center of gravity back and step about 60cm (2ft) behind your left foot with your right.

3 When all your weight is on your right leg, lift your left foot slightly. Place it down and rock forward. Transfer your weight to your left leg.

4 Step forward with your right foot until it is back in its original position (see step 1).

PRACTICE
Gently keep the kashlimar step going for eight full repetitions. Then try changing direction by stepping 45 degrees to the right side for four full steps. Step forward and back again for another four, then 45 degrees to the left for four counts.

ADDING ARMS
Easy, relaxed arm movements are best for this gentle travel step. When stepping forward, gently swing your arms to the front, leading with your wrists. When stepping back, gently swing your arms behind you, again leading with your wrists.

FRONT CROSS STEP TURN

1 Again working with four counts, dip down and forward slightly, while stepping 15–30cm (6–12in) across your right foot with your left. Rise high onto the ball of your right foot. Begin an ascending snake arm (p.54) on the right, leading with your elbow toward the ceiling and keeping your left arm in basic.

2 Pivot on both feet until you are facing the back of the room with your right arm high above your head, still leading with your elbow.

4 Begin a descending right snake arm and an ascending left, at the same time pivoting on your feet until you are once more facing front. Most of your weight should be on your left leg. Follow through and finish your arm movements on the left and right.

3 Lower your right arm and lift your left, continuing to lead with your elbows back to basic. With your left foot, quickly step across your right, pivoting until you are once more facing the front of your dance space.

PRACTICE

Repeat back and forth four times on each side or until you feel secure. If you begin losing your balance, don't worry – you're just getting dizzy. Take a break and try again later.

THREE-POINT TURN

This turn is danced with two or four counts, even though it is three steps. Unlike the cross step turn (p.65), which is on the spot, this turn moves you a few feet in each direction. Start slowly. Try four-counts, then speed up to two.

1 Begin count one by stepping out 60–90cm (2–3ft) to the right with your right leg.

2 Cross your left leg in front of your right, passing it by about 60cm (2ft) for a second count.

3 As you place your left foot down, pivot on your feet until you are facing the back of your dance space.

4 Sweep your right leg behind your left, passing it by about 60cm (2ft). As you place your right leg down, simultaneously pivot on your feet until you are facing the front of the room again for count three. Pause for the fourth count, then try a three-point to the left.

PRACTICE
Repeat in the opposite direction, now stepping left, right, left. Try the turns with some spotting (p.27) so you don't get too dizzy.

ADDING ARMS
Add arm movements by bringing your arms together at chest level as you pivot to the back of the room, and separating them when you return to face front.

THREE-POINT DROP

I love this step. It reminds me of dramatic dance scenes in Hollywood movies of the 1940s, when temple priestesses are shown dancing seductively for their goddess, unaware that they are being spied upon by scoundrels or thieves.

1 Start by following the steps for a basic three-point turn to the right. On the last step, as you place your right foot down, transfer 70 percent of your body weight onto it.

2 Bend your knee and slide your left foot away from you so that you are in a full lunge supported by your right leg. Drop your head gently but fully forward. Sweep your left arm down in front until your palm is on the floor. Simultaneously swing your right arm high up behind you. This slide and drop replaces the fourth beat pause in the original turn.

3 Then taking a full four counts, flip your head up and peer straight ahead, while slowly beginning to rise from the lunge.

4 To come up, gradually lower your right arm. At the same time, drag your left foot in to meet your right while straightening your right knee, until you are back to your starting position. Repeat this in the other direction, lunging onto the left foot and sliding back with the right. Your right arm should be forward, with your hand touching the ground, while your left is raised straight up behind your body. Rise up slowly as before, gradually dropping your left arm and sliding your right foot in.

PRACTICE

Repeat six times, alternating turn by turn, left and right.

ACCENTUATING THE FACE

The quick flip of the head in this step is a perfect chance to convey different feelings and expressions. Experiment, just for fun. As you lift your head dramatically from the drop, try looking very serious for one lift, then joyful for the next. Maybe you can put a gleam of mischief in your eye or even a look of shock or dismay.

DERVISH TURN

The whirling dervishes are ceremonial Sufis who split off from traditional Islam sometime in the 13th century. Part of their practice is spinning gracefully in circles, with one palm facing the sky and the other facing the earth. Many people associate the whirling dervish with frantic speed, but the real dervishes start slowly, then build up pace as they whirl. The same is true for this turn. Be prepared to get a little dizzy because you cannot spot (p.27) with this turn!

WARNING
People suffering from neck pain or any spinal condition should not perform the head accents included in this step.

1 Stand with your feet parallel and flat on the ground. Tilt your head slightly to one side and raise your arms to your sides so they are parallel with your shoulders. To start, both hands should be in basic (p.21). Begin spinning slowly and evenly, using small steps. After two rotations, switch your right hand from basic to offering (p.21) and speed up a little.

2 After one more rotation, begin to roll your head around your shoulders as you spin.

3 If you have long hair and your neck muscles are strong and flexible enough, flip your hair around as your head is circling on your shoulders.

4 Pick up speed until you are whirling very quickly for three or four more rotations. Continue to whip your head and hair around.

5 When you are ready to finish the turn, stop rolling your head and slowly come to a halt. As you do so, return your right hand to basic and lower your arms to chest level.

6 Carefully flip your head, tossing your hair back over your shoulders for a terrific finale.

4 Adding mystery

Belly dancers portrayed in films or paintings usually have a veil. Sometimes covering the face or body, sometimes held in the hands, the diaphanous veil seems to defy gravity as it floats about the dancer – a wonderful image that never fails to captivate the observer.

STYLES AND TYPES OF VEIL

Most veils are rectangular, but half-circles and triangles are not uncommon. Veils are generally made from magic silk, silk chiffon or polyester chiffon, but almost any fabric can be used provided it is light and beautiful. Veils can be very simple or decorated with complex sequin and bead designs.

CHOOSING THE VEIL THAT'S RIGHT FOR YOU

Try to choose a veil that looks good with whatever you like to dance in but is not exactly the same colour. It should be significantly lighter or darker so that it contrasts with your clothes or costume and doesn't get lost. Deep shades like burgundy or royal purple are wonderful if you're feeling moody and serious, while delicate pastels and springtime shades are perfect for joyful and spirited dancing.

Next, decide what length of veil will work best for you. Too short a veil restricts the movements you can do with it and interrupts its gentle floating. Too long a veil will drag on the ground, and if you step on it, the smooth fabric will make your feet slide out from under you so fast that you won't know what happened until you're flat on the floor! One handy guide I use for my students and myself is to measure the length of your arms, fingertip to fingertip. Then add on another 90cm (3ft) so that the veil will drape from each fingertip by 45cm (18in). Don't worry if you can't find a veil with the exact measurements; a difference of 5–7.5cm (2–3in) is fine.

The next question is, how much float should the veil have? Which veil you choose depends on how you'd like to use it. Is it purely ornamental or is it an extension of your feelings and body? In Egyptian belly dancing, which is primarily cabaret style, the dancers generally enter with a veil, spend a few minutes or so dancing with it, then discard it to continue their routine. When a dancer plans on using a veil like this, a highly ornate veil is a good choice and it can be made of heavier, highly decorated fabric. Since the dancer isn't really using the veil much, the increased weight won't disturb her routine.

However, I'd like to encourage you to use the veil more fully, so you may want to choose something light and airy for your first veil. If you're purchasing a veil, throw the fabric high into the air and without letting it go, allow it to float down. The veil that takes the longest to sink is the right one!

THE BEAUTY OF THE VEIL

I consider the veil to be an integral part of the dance, adding incredible beauty and feeling. Don't be surprised if you fall in love with veil work and become afflicted with "veilitis". This is a condition that only affects belly dancers, compelling them to buy veils in all their favourite colours until their wardrobes are exploding in rainbows. There is no known cure except lack of storage space!

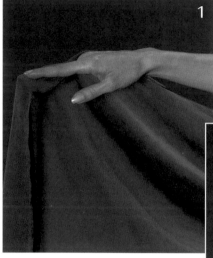

HOW TO HOLD A VEIL

1 Grasp the veil draped behind you, with an even amount of fabric cascading from your hands on each side. Hold your right hand in basic one position (p.21) and drape the veil over your last three fingers, while threading it between your index and middle finger.

2 Experiment with different hand positions to help get a feel for dancing with the veil.

MAKING A VEIL

Making your own veil is easy and gives a wonderful personal touch to your costume. Take your measurements (p.71), pop into your local fabric supplier and ask to see some silk or polyester chiffon. Select the colour you like, unroll a length or two and wave it about to see how light it is and how well it floats. Don't be shy! The fabric that is the lightest is the best choice. Ask for the fabric to be cut, rather than torn, which can cause pulls in the body of the fabric and fray the edges.

To seam your veil, fold each edge over by 5mm (¼in) and press with a warm iron. Fold over another 5mm (¼in) and press again so that you have fully rolled hems. With a needle and thread or sewing machine, stitch along the middle of the hems to secure them. Press the entire veil once more and you are ready to start dancing.

BODY GLIMPSING

Body glimpsing is a way of using the veil to reveal parts of the body briefly, then hide them again, giving the impression of letting someone in on a secret. This technique can be used to focus on any one part of your body at a time.

1 Cascade the veil round you by quickly crossing your arms in front of your chest, enclosing your body.

2 Quickly unfurl the veil and leading with your elbows and wrists, raise both arms above your head. Perform a quick high and low undulation.

3 Rapidly close the veil across your chest again and turn your body to the right.

4 Open the veil, leading with your elbows and wrists, but this time lower your right arm and raise your left. Dance six hip drops on the right side. Close the veil and turn to face the left. Open your veil as in step 2, but with your left arm up and right arm low. Dance one hip thrust, forward and back, then wrap yourself in the veil again.

WAYS OF WEARING YOUR VEIL

In a full routine, the veil dance is not usually performed until the second or third piece of music. Instead of having to interrupt her dance to fetch the veil, a belly dancer carries her veil draped around her body until she needs it – a practice called "wrapping". Wraps should be simple and allow for unrestricted movement as well as easy unwrapping. As you learn to wrap your veil, let it drape in loose folds like a flowing waterfall of fabric. Make sure no part of the veil is hanging on the floor where it could cause you to slip and fall.

THE BASIC WRAP

1 With the veil behind you, take the left side and tuck a part of it into your right shoulder strap or sleeve.

2 Take the right side and tuck part of that into your left shoulder strap or sleeve. The veil will be wrapped loosely round your waist and crossed over your chest, with the excess fabric hanging from your shoulders.

THE TOGA

1 Hold the veil in front of you. With your right hand, tuck the veil inside your costume at your right hip. Make sure nothing is dragging on the floor on that side.

2 With your left hand, wrap the veil behind you and pass it to your right hand. Bring the veil under your right arm and tuck the remaining length of fabric into your left shoulder strap.

THE GODDESS

1 Hold the veil in front of you and with your right hand, tuck it inside your costume at your right hip.

2 As you did with the toga, take the veil in your left hand and wrap it behind you, passing the fabric into your right hand.

3 Instead of bringing the veil under your right arm, bring it up and over your shoulder. Allow it to drape down in front. Take a small bit of the veil where it rests on the top of your shoulder and tuck it into the top of your sleeve or shoulder strap. With your left hand, grasp the excess veil, which is hanging down in front, at least 30cm (12in) up from the bottom of the veil.

4 Tuck the veil that you are holding in your left hand into the front of your costume on the left side, by your belly. With your right hand, do the same with the excess veil on your right side. The veil will billow out from your waist and hang in gentle waves.

THE SEDUCTION OF UNVEILING

Unveiling is one of the most sensuous elements of belly dancing. But it needs to be performed with great care and elegance if it is to convey sensuality rather than overt sexuality. Classic dancers and appreciative viewers prefer the gentle delicacy of a caress across the cheek rather than an jarring slap across the face, so to speak.

UNVEILING IN A SPIN

A pleasingly subtle method of unveiling is to unwrap while spinning. This technique takes time and skill to master but is well worth it. There are only two rules to follow when learning this technique: first, never look at your veil or your hands; second, only one hand at a time should be used to untuck your veil. The technique is shown here with the toga wrap, but any of the styles shown on pp.74–75 can be unwrapped in a spin.

1 Begin by reminding yourself of the last point where your veil is tucked in. Start slowly spinning with small steps, as if you were dancing a dervish turn.

2 Languidly grab the veil at the last tuck point and gently, without looking, pull the veil straight out from the tuck.

3 Little by little, continue unwrapping by pulling the veil from each point while spinning.

4, 5 Depending on how you tucked the veil, you may need to switch it to the other hand, toss it over your shoulder or even swirl it round your head.

6 When the veil is at its last tuck point, keep spinning and grab it with your free hand. Gently pull it free.

7 Remain spinning and manipulating the veil until there is the same amount of veil on each side. Slowly come to a halt and pose until you gather your dizzy wits from all that turning!

UNVEILING IN STEPS

If you find the unveiling spin (pp.76–77) a bit overwhelming, try unveiling in steps. The technique is not just to pull out the tucks one at a time while standing in place, but to unveil step by step in between some elegant dance movements.

PART ONE: CREATING A SAIL
1 The technique is shown here using the toga wrap but is possible with any of the veil wrap styles on pages 74–75. With your back facing the front of your dance space, begin hip rolling (p.32) left and right. With your right hand, grasp the first tuck point at your shoulder.

2 Slowly pull the veil free from the first tuck point.

3 Begin unwrapping your body by bringing the veil across your chest to the right. When the veil is directly in front of you, take hold of it in your left hand and adjust it until you have one side in each hand. Raise the veil above your head and lean diagonally to the right while spinning to the left. The veil will catch the air and billow out behind you like a tall sail.

4 Dance two rotations, then switch directions by leaning to the left and spinning to the right. After another two rotations, come to a gentle halt facing front and hold the veil up at an even level behind you.

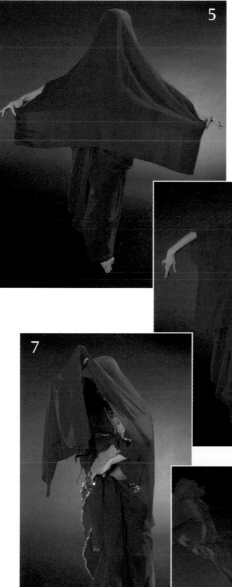

PART TWO: CREATING A TENT

5 With both arms, drape the veil over your head, pulling it gently so that it reaches down to your waist. Since your waist and face can't be seen, this is the chance to peek at where the last tuck point is – but don't move your head.

6 Perform some elegant snake arms (p.54) or perhaps a shimmy (p.38) and a few reverse hip rolls (p.33) until you're sure of the position of the last tuck point.

7 Turn your back to the front of the room again and with your left hand grab the veil at your waist. Reach your right arm over your face to take hold of the veil from its left side. (Although the dancer here is shown facing the front to demonstrate what is happening, this step should always be performed with your back to the audience so no one can see how you magically unveil.)

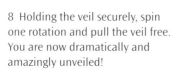

8 Holding the veil securely, spin one rotation and pull the veil free. You are now dramatically and amazingly unveiled!

UNDERSTANDING LIFT AND CASCADE

These simple veil movements will help you learn how to control your veil so that it flows like a gentle breeze and appears soft as a cloud. Once you understand the nature of lift and cascade, anything is possible.

Unless otherwise indicated, always begin veil steps in basic foundation (p.20), holding the veil behind you.

PREPARATION

Holding the veil firmly in each hand, quickly but gently raise your arms, lifting the veil. Drop them slowly, allowing the veil to gather air and cascade down as it falls. Experiment with the speed of lifting and dropping, while observing how the veil falls and where it catches the most air in relation to how fast you move your arms. The technique is to drop your arms fast enough not to interrupt the fall of the veil, while making sure that they are moving slowly enough not to drag down the material.

LIFT AND CASCADE

1 Leading with your wrists, quickly raise your arms and lift the veil. Just as you reach up as far as you can, flick your wrists to extend your hands upward with a snap. This will kick the veil up another foot or so, giving it more height.

2 With this added height, the veil will take longer to cascade down your body. Again leading with your wrists, gently and without pulling, guide the veil down behind you.

CASCADING BACK AND FORTH

1 Stand with your palms facing up. As you did with the lift and cascade, sweep your arms up above your head. But instead of letting them drop behind you, arc your arms forward, so that they pass over your head to the front of your body, with the veil trailing behind.

2 Allow your arms to drop at a pace that permits the veil to cascade gently down to the ground. Reverse the sweep without drag or interruption by passing your arms back over your head so that the veil can cascade down behind you again.

PRACTICE

Begin by lifting the veil four times behind you. Follow with another four lifts, including wrist flicks to see how high you can get the veil to go. Then repeat front and back cascades six times and finish with four consecutive left and right cascades.

CASCADING LEFT AND RIGHT

Standing with the fabric behind you, drop your arms to your sides and extend them backward. Swing them together left and right. As you reach the final swing to the right, raise your right arm and perform a single lift and cascade. Your left arm should remain behind you.

When the cascade is complete, begin swinging your arms again, but this time allow the final swing to lead into a lift and cascade on your left side. As a last step, cut out the in-between swings and just perform left and right cascades one after the other.

MAKING THE VEIL DANCE

Beautiful veil work often comes from your own inspiration, rather than in formalized steps. These next few movements focus on providing you with a core of veil steps, while allowing you the freedom to experiment with the veil as an extension of your body.

VEIL SWITCH

1 One of the most elegant movements, this is also one of the simplest. The step moves the veil gracefully around the body without looking jerky or awkward. The step requires eight counts. Begin in the veil foundation position.

2 Raise your right arm and circle it around behind you, moving it clockwise and over your head for two counts.

3 When your right arm begins to reach the front of your body, bend your left elbow, bringing your hand closer to your abdomen. Continue to move your right arm past your left until it sweeps fully to the front for one count.

4 Hold both arms out again until they are back in their original position, with the exception that the veil is now in front of you. This is also one count.

5 With your left arm, bring the veil across the front of your body to the right. As your left arm passes your right arm, lead your right hand through the gap in the veil to pass to the left for one count.

6 Continue moving your left arm over and round your head until the veil is behind you for one count.

7 Return your left arm to its original position and slowly raise both arms above your head to finish. Let this section of the step comprise the final two counts.

PRACTICE
Repeat the right veil switch, then the left veil switch, four times each. Return to a right veil switch and perform one for eight counts, then four, then two. Repeat on the left.

SPINNING THROUGH THE DOOR

Take a few moments to review the cross step turn (p.65), both left and right, before learning this step.

1 Raise your left arm and lower your right, holding the veil securely in both hands. Keeping your left arm high, sweep your right arm under and inside your left, while beginning a left cross step turn for two counts.

2 Begin to pivot on both feet and arch your back gently. As you spin round to face the back of your dancing space, your left arm should remain aloft as the right arm begins to arc in a wide circular upward swing. This also takes two counts.

3 Continuing the turn without breaking the momentum for another two counts, sweep your left arm down and behind you, also in a wide circular arc. Quickly follow your left arm with your right while completing the pivot around to face front.

4 For the final two counts, as your left arm begins to swing back up to waist level during the completion of the turn, sweep your right arm out and down, also to waist level, until both arms are level. Repeat in the other direction.

PRACTICE

Start in a beautiful pose of your choosing and slowly switch the veil from left to right. Repeat twice, then change direction for another two switches. Finish with spinning through the door, once to the left and once to the right.

KISSING THE AUDIENCE

This is one step in which the dancer completely controls the veil's movements. The veil can be notoriously erratic and you never quite know if it's going to cooperate with you or not. But you can rely on this step to do what it is supposed to do if you perform the movements correctly.

1 Standing in a low foundation with the veil behind you, lean slightly forward. Leading with the upper sides of your arms and wrists, lift your arms up and forward, and cross them moderately in front.

2 Immediately flip the veil high up in front of you and out to your sides in a dramatic, V-shaped sweep.

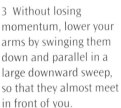

3 Without losing momentum, lower your arms by swinging them down and parallel in a large downward sweep, so that they almost meet in front of you.

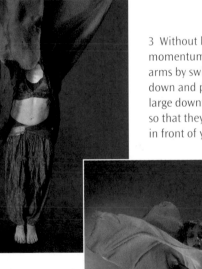

PRACTICE

Repeat and experiment with speed to see what works best with your particular veil. This move should be done quickly and smoothly, but not so fast as to make the veil whippish. Because it is so beautiful, the kiss can be performed to each side as a whole set. So, a kiss front, turn to the left and kiss, then back and kiss, and lastly to the right and kiss. Smooches all around!

4 Follow through and complete the step by continuing the downward swing to thigh level. Finally swing your arms up and out to your sides, returning to the foundation position.

CREATING WINGS AND OFFERING VEIL

CREATING WINGS

1 Cascade the veil to the front and, with your arms extended diagonally away from your body, hold the veil draped over each thumb.

2 Flip the veil up and toward you, while sweeping your hands underneath until it comes to rest on top of your arms. Release it and repeat the flip three more times.

3 As you complete the last flip, gently extend your arms further out to your sides until the veil is taut. Hold the taut area against your neck while raising your arms high at the sides. Release. Now, in one quick, fluid movement, flip the veil, extend your arms and hit your neck with the taut veil edge. The veil will naturally collect itself at your neck as you raise your arms high at your sides. Release by tossing the veil down and gently forward in front of you.

OFFERING VEIL

Although the offering veil is a separate step, it is also a nice way to close the creating wings veil. From the last wings position, bend your knees and lean forward. Gradually lower your arms and the veil will naturally slide down your chest and come to rest on your forearms. Begin slow, forward snake arms until the veil moves to rest across your wrists. Grasp the veil with your thumbs and sweep your arms underneath, flipping the veil forward and down. Cascade the veil back to rest behind you and return to foundation.

ANDROMEDA VEIL

When Andromeda's mother boasted that her daughter was more beautiful than the sea nymphs, they exacted revenge by pressuring Poseidon to release a sea monster to ravage the people of the land. The only way to stop the rampage was to sacrifice Andromeda to the creature. Chained to a rock by the sea and whipped by the ocean and wind, she bravely awaited her fate but was saved by Perseus. This veil movement is named for her.

PREPARATION

From the offering veil position, raise your arms high in the air, but without holding the veil in both hands. Allow the veil to fall over your shoulders. Lower your arms to your sides and bow slightly.

1 Lean softly to the left and look at your left arm. Swing it outside and round the veil until the fabric is wrapped twice round your wrist, resembling a cuff. Hold your left arm steady and gracefully lean to the right. Swing your right arm round the veil until it also has a veil cuff.

2 Raise both arms, now bound by veil chains, and sway back and forth, as though chained to a rock like Andromeda.

3 To release, lower your arms slowly while bending your knees and leaning forward. Slowly, using small circular movements, unwrap the veil from your arms. Lean further forward until gravity pulls the veil down to rest on your forearms and across your chest. Sweep your hands underneath and grasp the long side of the veil, flipping it over and straightening up. Cascade the veil back to rest behind you and return to foundation.

SANDSTORM VEIL

Complicated but visually stunning, the sandstorm is well worth learning. It is meant to be performed on the side of the body, to the left or right. As you master the movement, look in the mirror and you'll see the veil creating an amazing vortex like the eye of a sandstorm.

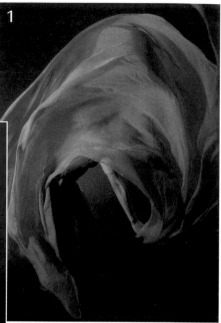

1 Cascade the veil forward and turn your body to face the left. Place your left hand on your right hip and with your right arm, flip the veil forward in a wide arc.

2 With a flat back, lean forward until both edges of the veil are resting on the floor in front of you.

3 Take your right arm and flip the veil back the same way you flipped it forward, in a high wide arc.

4 As your right arm passes your face, flip your left arm back, also sweeping in a high wide arc.

5 Continue moving your right arm in a full circle around the side of your body while following it with your left.

6 When your left arm is directly above your head, move to rest your hand on the back left side of your head.

7 Finish the right arm sweep by allowing it to pass once more over your head and down behind you. Flip the veil over your forearm. At this point your right arm will have completed one and a half circles.

FINISHING TOUCHES
Here are two ways of completing the step. One is to reverse the storm until the veil is back in the start position. The other is called "sailing through the storm".

REVERSING THE STORM
Begin with your left arm. Sweep it in the opposite direction (forward and around) until the veil is no longer wrapped round it. Now simply sweep the veil forward in the same way it was swept back, following with your right arm until you are back in the starting position.

SAILING THROUGH THE STORM
Instead of flipping forward to release, hold the veil firmly in your left hand, which is resting on your head, and grasp the other end gently with your right thumb. Lift your right arm high into the air and begin spinning to the right, creating a large sail billowing behind you. To release, gradually slow to a halt and with both hands flip the veil forward to the ground, leaning with it. Cascade the veil back and return to veil foundation.

PRACTICE
Perform three complete sets of sandstorm veil, then try it on the other side. For a final step, move into sailing through the storm right after each sandstorm.

USING THE VEIL AS AN ACCENT

As well as being an extension of the body of the dancer, the veil can also act as a subtle accent to the movements, adding interest and drama to relatively simple steps.

PRINCESS VEIL FRONT FACE FRAME
1 Cascade the veil in front of you and turn your hands until your palms are facing the ceiling.

2 Raise your arms up and bend them at the elbows. Rotate your hands out and round to the back so they meet at the top of your head, fingertips touching.

BACK FACE FRAME
Holding the veil behind you, raise your arms. Bending at the elbows, lean slightly back and touch your hands together over your head in the prayer position (right).

DANCING WITH THE FACE FRAME
When the veil frames your face to the front, most of your body is covered. The cobra neck slither (p.48) works perfectly because it is an interesting move in itself and loses nothing but gains everything by being framed. With the back face frame, the entire body is exposed. The cobra neck slither is again an excellent choice, as are hip drops (p.28) and hip rolls (p.32).

STEPPING OVER THE CURTAIN

1 Begin with a slow front cascade. With as much drama as you can muster, drop your body gently toward the front as the cascade rolls forward.

2 Guide the veil down and in, so that it hits your ankles and gathers there. Come up and dramatically flip your hair out of your face with an arched back.

3 Slowly straighten your spine and rise up a little. Carefully and sensuously step over the veil with your left foot. Place your foot firmly on the floor and shift all your weight onto it. Pause for a count.

4 Complete the step by following with your right foot so the veil is completely behind you.

When using this technique, less is more. Only do this accent once in a dance, otherwise it can look as if you're skipping rope. It can be followed by other movements, such as body glimpsing (p.73), lift and cascade (p.80) or veil switch (p.82).

THE BUTTERFLY

The butterfly is tricky and takes some coordination, so be patient. Thinking carefully about how your arms move will help you to perform the step correctly.

1 Cascade the veil to the front.

2 Sweep your left arm under the veil, bringing it up to chest level.

3 The middle of the veil will now have a twist in the center and the left side will rest over your left shoulder.

4 Begin turning to the right and stop quickly when you come around to the front after the second rotation.

5 Gently dip low by bending your knees. At the same time, sweep your right arm down, forward and up, while sweeping your left arm down, back and up.

6 The veil will still have a twist in the middle, but it will now rest over your right shoulder. Begin turning again, this time toward the left. After the second rotation, stop again in the center. Dip low and swing your right arm down and back while sweeping your left arm down, forward, then up. The veil will now be resting back on your left shoulder. Start spinning again and switch after the second rotation. Release by unflipping the veil from whichever arm it is resting on in your final turn.

PRACTICE
It's best to follow this complex, fast-moving step with something simple and slow. Perform three full butterflies. After the release (step 6), perform a half veil switch (p.82) or a cascade (p.80) to position the veil behind you.

THE ENVELOPE

Deeply mysterious and sensuous, the envelope walks
the fine line between suggestion and seduction because
of its method of final unveiling. Temper this by adding
a sense of playfulness and character to the earlier steps.

1 The envelope should always start mid-spin. This
distracts the audience and prevents them from
predicting what will happen next. Start spinning
in whichever direction you feel most comfortable
and raise your arms to shoulder level.

2 As you turn, bring your arms
and hands together until they
meet in the center. Grab both
ends of the veil in your right
hand, releasing the left. Push
gently against the veil with your
left hand to pull it taut.

3 Lift the veil over your head until you are
completely surrounded by the material. It may
catch on your hair on the way up, but don't let
that interrupt you. Your hair will eventually fall
inside and rest back where is supposed to.

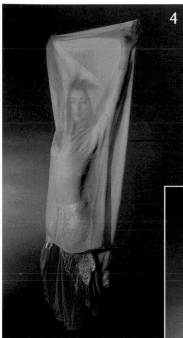

4 Gradually stop spinning and begin some of your favourite dance movements. You can face to the front or diagonally, depending on the movement you choose. For example, hip rolls (p.32), chest circles (p.45) and shimmies (p.38) should be performed facing front. Hip drops (p.28) and undulations (p.42) should be done on the diagonal for maximum effect.

5 While dancing some hip-focused movements, spread the opening of the veil at the top by separating your thumb and forefinger. Look up and lower the veil down over your head until it is in front of your eyes.

Bring the veil forward so that you can see out of it. Here's a chance to use facial expressions to convey emotions. A fun idea to try is to peer out of the veil meaningfully, looking left to right as if you're searching for someone. Get someone's attention and give a playful wink.

6 Wrap your arms behind your head, placing your hands almost on top of your crown, creating a mask effect with the veil. Very deep and low hip rolls work well for this part of the envelope. Finish this mischief by spinning again, just two rotations, and lifting the veil back up above you.

FINISHING THE ENVELOPE

7 Finishing the envelope and releasing the veil is a delight because the exit is as beautiful as the entrance. With the veil above your head, allow your left hand to peek out at the top and begin snaking it down.

8 Slowly lower your right arm while extending the snaking motion down your left. As your right arm continues its descent, allow your head to come out and follow it with your chest. When your upper body begins to be exposed, movements such as chest circles (p.45) or undulations (p.42) are a great way to slide out of the envelope.

9 When your entire body down to your hips is out of the envelope, finish in one fluid motion. Turn round to the back, grab the left side of the veil with your free (left) hand so you have one end in each hand.

10 Turn to face front. With a flourish, separate the veil ends for a full body view until your arms are raised high behind you. Slowly lower them back down to the veil foundation position.

SPINNING BARREL TURN

All the turns and spinning techniques taught earlier can be accented with veil work. The three-point (p.66), dervish (p.68) and cross step (p.65) turns are fast enough to gather air and lift the veil so it surrounds you like a gossamer mist. Using the veil's versatility, add this turn to your repertoire.

1 Begin by spinning slowly to the right, making small steps. As your body begins its second turn, drop your right arm in a circular sweep downward and raise your left arm in a circular sweep upward.

2 Without breaking the momentum, sweep your right arm up and your left arm down as your body continues turning to face the back of your dance space.

4 Keep spinning and circling your arms while gaining in speed. The veil will flow round you, creating an almost uninterrupted halo of fabric, similar to a rolling barrel.

3 As you spin forward, continue the downward sweep of the left arm across your lower body, while circling your right arm high over the crown of your head.

5 Drawing on power

Sword dancing embodies the warrior goddess in every woman. It empowers a dancer and allows her to extend her vision to include incredible images of power, freedom, risk, danger and mystery. As you learn to dance with a sword, always take your time and go slowly. The sword dance is so stunning, compelling and magical that there is never any need to rush it. Move carefully and deliberately, instilling feeling and heart into each step, and the routine will do the rest!

Beginners should start with a very dull practice sword and handle it with great care to avoid injury. Most practice swords are made of lightweight compressed aluminum or layered tin, with a thin simple handle and covered scabbard. The blade itself is gently curved and usually two sided, meaning that there is a cutting edge running across the bottom as well as the first few inches of the top. A practice sword will have only one point at the tip, with the blade and the point filed very dull to minimize injury if an accident or slip should occur.

Professional swords are extremely beautiful and sophisticated but can cause injury if mishandled. I advise my students not to pick up a professional sword until they have mastered the dance with a practice one. A rule of thumb is when you are completely comfortable with your practice sword and can get through the entire sword lesson four times back to back without losing the sword even once, you can consider taking the leap to the professional sword.

The most common professional sword is the scimitar. Forged out of heavy steel and weighing about 2kg (4½lb), the scimitar's blade is usually about 1m (3ft 3in) long. It has a single curved cutting edge and boasts a very ornate handle that counterbalances the weight of the blade.

HOLDING THE SWORD

Remember that even a dull sword is still a weapon and should be held like one, with respect and delicacy. Always hold the handle of the sword with your dominant hand – the hand you write with. Grasp the sword in front of you with the blade facing the ceiling, gripping the handle firmly with your entire fist. Open your other hand into the offering position and rest the blade of the sword delicately on your first two fingers. Don't ever grab and hold the blade with a full hand or fist. From this position, lift the blade up in front of you and take a close look at it. If there is a sharp edge on the top and the bottom, then it is a double-edged sword. In that case, lightly slide your fingers toward the handle until they are past the second blade. If there is no second blade, then wherever your hand most feels comfortable is perfect.

PLACING THE SWORD ON YOUR HEAD

The practice sword must be extremely blunt. Swords do fall off, especially at first, so it is essential to practice your disaster recovery techniques before you start learning to sword dance.

PREPARATION

In order to learn without fear, you must love your sword. Hold the sword in your hands. Run your fingers across the blade and grasp it tightly in both hands to learn where it can be caught so it doesn't injure you. Toss it up and down gently and catch it with both hands. Once you are comfortable with your sword, you will know how to prevent disasters or repair them with dignity.

PLACING THE SWORD

1 Hold the sword out in front of you at a level just below your hips. Grasping the handle with one hand and supporting the blade with two fingers of the other hand, begin making large undulations.

2, 3, 4 As you undulate, slowly begin to turn around and gradually raise the sword until it is high above your head. This can be done at a moderate pace with a half turn, or in a slow, powerful style with one full turn or more.

TIP

If your hair is very fine or smooth and the sword keeps slipping off your head, a good dose of extra-hold hairspray will give your hair enough texture to grasp the sword.

5 When your back is facing front, begin hip rolling with wide, deep movements. Without bobbing, gradually lower the sword onto your head. Remove your supporting fingers and balance the sword with the hand holding the handle. If the sword feels shaky, adjust it with your dominant hand.

6 Gradually stop hip rolling. Lift your left foot up and over your right, placing the ball of your foot firmly on the floor next to your right foot.

7 Pivot on your feet slowly so as not to knock the sword off-balance and turn around to face front again.

PRACTICE

Try snake arms (p.54), hip drops (p.28) , hip thrusts (p.31), hip rolls (p.32), basic walking (p.58) and undulations (p.42), all with the sword in place.

The key to good sword work is to make sure your head doesn't bob up and down – if it does, the sword will slide off. Look in the mirror and find a point behind you that you can use as a mark. It should be exactly at the middle of the blade. This small spot is your "bob" mark. By focusing on this spot, you'll be able to see if you are bobbing and correct yourself. To prevent bobbing, bend your knees a little more than usual to increase the movement range.

ADJUSTING THE SWORD

If you feel the sword starting to slip, reach up with your dominant hand, grasp the handle and gently readjust the sword's position. If the sword dips unevenly to the left, slide it to the right and vice versa.

TAKE CARE

Always be aware of safety. If the sword has slipped beyond a point where it can be adjusted or caught, then hop out of the way and let it drop. It will make a clang, but no harm will be done. Your dainty little toes are much more important than a piece of metal.

FLOOR WORK
Boasting a Hollywood level of drama and sensuality, floor work with the sword demands considerable skill and grace on the part of the dancer. Start by learning the body movements without the sword. When you've memorized them thoroughly, add the sword.

PREPARATION: DESCENDING TO THE FLOOR
With the sword on your head, place 80 percent of your weight on your left leg. Slide your right leg forward, around and behind you in a large wide circle. Slide your left leg forward into a deep lunge until your right knee touches the floor. Transfer 80 percent of your body weight onto your right knee by leaning back until you are in a full kneel. Slide your left foot forward until your leg is completely extended. Then sweep your left leg around to the back and drag it forward until it is parallel with your right leg and you are kneeling on both knees. This step does take a lot of strength; if you cannot do it yet, just kneel down on both knees, one leg at a time. Keep practicing as best you can without hurting yourself and you will succeed when your muscles are stronger.

IN THE LAMP
1 While on your knees, hold your hands in front of you in prayer position. Begin to circle your hips around to the right. On the third circle, as your hip reaches the left side, push it out and down until you are almost sitting on your heels far over to the left. Place your arms in the genie position, with your left arm low and right arm high. Pause for a moment.

2 Resume the hip circle while lifting up and returning to center as your hips move to the right.

3 After two more hip circles, when your hip reaches the right side, push it out and down until you are almost sitting on your heels far to the right. This time, reverse the genie arm position, so your right hand is low and the left hand is high. Pause for a moment and lift up, returning to center while resuming your hip circle. Without breaking the hip circle, repeat the movement three more times on each side.

LAZY CROSS KICK

1 Begin by kneeling with your knees slightly apart and your arms in foundation with basic hands. Sit down on your heels, using the soles of your feet as a cushion for your bottom.

2 Reach your left arm behind you and lean diagonally back in that direction until your palm is flat on the floor. Bend your elbow, transferring your weight to your arm and away from your right leg.

PRACTICE

Despite its name, this step isn't so lazy. Don't be surprised if you have trouble keeping your leg up at first. Just keep at it and you will improve.

3 When free from pressure, extend your right leg straight out and lift it 10cm (4in) off the floor. With your free arm, reach over across your chest.

4 In one very slow continuous motion, swing your right leg across the floor all the way to your left side without dropping it, while swinging your right arm to the left side in a gentle gliding motion. Return your leg back to the left in the same way, simultaneously returning the arm to the right. Repeat the leg/arm cross twice more before coming out of the movement.

THE RESURRECTION

I always encourage my students to use creative visualization to add an extra layer of emotion to their developing skills. In order to perform this movement properly, think about the image you are trying to convey – the idea that a mummy, stiff and dead, is being resurrected and slowly coming alive. Another great visualization is to think of a caterpillar building a stiff cocoon round itself, then emerging as a beautiful butterfly. Remember to carry out this movement as slowly as you possibly can to promote the concept of metamorphosis.

1 After descending to the floor, slowly sit back to the right of your heels. One by one, carefully swing your legs out in front of you and to the right, so that your left side is facing front. Keeping your spine very straight, hinge at the waist and lean forward, reaching for your feet. Cross your arms at the wrists and begin slow, sultry snake arms.

2 Curl your spine and begin to lean back, snaking your arms and hands up over your body. As your hands pass over each part of you (feet, calves, thighs, hips and so on), lock that part stiff. The idea is that you are mummifying yourself for eternity.

WARNING
You need to be very strong to perform this movement, so if you feel any strain in your lower spine or neck as you lean back, stop and don't go any further.

3 Keep snaking and leaning back until your shoulder blades rest on the floor. Keep your chin tucked firmly into your chest and your head elevated. Snake your arms out to the sides.

4 Slowly place your hands on the floor and swing them out to the sides until they are diagonally extended from each shoulder. Hold for a moment.

5 Leading with your chest, push into the floor with your arms using all your strength. Flex your abdominal muscles and lift up off the floor until you are back in a sitting position. The mummy has been resurrected!

REMOVING THE SWORD

Even though, at this point, the essential elements of the sword routine are over, the removal of the sword should be as ceremonial as the placing of it on your head.

A SIMPLE METHOD

1 Leading with your elbow and then your wrist, raise your dominant arm up. When it is at shoulder level, extend your arm and turn it until your palm is facing up. Again leading with the wrist, bend your elbow and grasp the handle of the sword.

2 Carefully lift the sword straight off your head. Reach your free hand up to the blade so it rests gently on your fingertips. Without bending your elbows, lower the sword in front of you, following its descent with your eyes.

3 Stop lowering the sword when your arms are just above waist level, then move into a lovely pose of your choosing.

A FANCY OPTION

In this finale step, you remove the sword while spinning. Begin to turn and, using the method described in step 1, raise your dominant arm up and grasp the sword handle. Continue spinning and lift the sword straight up. Lower it in front of you, supporting the blade with two fingers of your other hand until it is at face level. Stop spinning and continue lowering the sword until your arms are at waist level. Move into a beautiful pose to finish the set.

TRIPLE CIRCLE

At the climax of this movement, three parts of you will be circling: your arms, your body and your hips! The triple circle can be used before the sword is placed on your head or after it has been removed.

1 Holding the sword at chest level, hip roll (p.32) in wide circles, left and right. Make your circles as big and bold as you can.

2 Begin to draw a circle around your body with the sword by slowly raising it up while hip rolling, then bringing it over your head.

3 Maintaining the hip rolls, continue the circular path by bringing the sword down the other side of your body, then dipping it low in front to set up another rotation. Once you've grasped the hip roll and sword circle concept, you're ready for the next step – adding the third circle!

4 With small, delicate steps, slowly begin a spin. It is important to use the raising and lowering of your feet during the hip rolls to your advantage by working your steps in time with the rise and fall. When your foot pulls up for the hip roll, just as it reaches the top of the ball, lift it a small amount and take a step in the direction you want to spin. Lower the full foot to the ground. As you lift your other foot for the hip circle to the other side, repeat the step, again lowering the full foot to the ground afterwards. Continue this stepping in the direction you want to spin and you will find yourself in a full triple circle: one with your hips, one with your sword and one with your body.

6 Wings

Drama, beauty and an incredible delight for the eyes are just a few of the words that spring to mind when describing wings. To dance with wings is to feel like a queen before all of humanity, a rose amid brambles, or streaming silk on rough burlap. Although wings are a modern addition to the world of belly dance, they manage to conjure up images of the great pharaohs, terrible gods and temperamental goddesses of Ancient Egypt.

There are two types of wings currently used by belly dancers. The style you choose will depend to some extent on the concept you'd like to convey. In one type, the wings wrap around the upper arm over the bicep and tricep muscles and conjure a look reminiscent of the glorious hieroglyphs of herons and bird deities on the walls of the great temple of Karnak. The second type attaches around the neck like a gilded collar. The material left flowing behind looks like the monarch's cape displayed in so many etchings of the wealthy in Ancient Egypt.

Traditionally, wings were made of thick, but lightweight, gold or silver lamé. Now they are also available in a dazzling rainbow of colours, textures and fibres, ranging from the boldest of satins to subtle pastel chiffons. Each wing is constructed from a large semicircle of material with a complex pleated design pressed into it. The pleats allow for very small creases where the band attaches to the body and gradually grow larger toward the edges of the material. A long pocket is sewn into the upper edge of the wing for a wooden dowel to be inserted. The dowel not only allows you to grasp the wing and keep it stable but also acts as an extension of your arm, creating extraordinary reach. When the wings are extended, the length and symmetrical folds of the fabric create an illusion of feathers catching the wind while in movement.

The dramatic scale and appearance of wings makes them a wonderful accompaniment to your dancing but also restricts their use. It's almost impossible to practice wing techniques at home because you need somewhere with a high ceiling and a great deal of empty space. Most dancers rent studio space for wing practice. Actual performances with wings are rare because only a full stage or a large restaurant with plenty of space can accommodate them.

Regardless of these obstacles, wings are an integral component of your dance practice so do your best to learn them. Whichever design or material you choose, wherever you find to dance, one of the most delightful aspects about dancing with wings is that almost everything you manage to do with them is shatteringly gorgeous – an eye-popping, jaw-dropping, heart-pounding spectacle!

GETTING FAMILIAR WITH WINGS

The best way to begin learning wings is just to play with them. Imagine you are a little girl again and someone has given you a pair of wings. You would probably run round the house trying to fly. Well, do just that now – play with your wings, swing them, circle them, flap them. Let your imagination soar for a few minutes as you experiment. This activity will help you grow accustomed to the feel and dynamics of dancing with wings.

HOW TO HOLD WINGS

Stand in the basic foundation pose (p.20), but with your arms at your sides. With the wings hanging loose, manoeuvre the fabric until it is behind the dowels. With the dowels in the front of the wings, grab each one firmly, with knuckles facing out. You are ready to begin total wing enchantment!

EXPERIMENTATION

Turn in circles, watching your wings billow out. Swing your arms back and forth, marvelling at the dancing fabric. By experimenting, you can develop fun movements and poses that are all your own. But do write down any interesting steps you discover before you forget them.

POSES

The wings are so spectacular that simple poses can be a primary part of any wing piece. Adding poses in between steps is a perfect way to accent the exciting, flowing beauty of the wings.

THE HATHOR

THE OSIRIS

THE ISIS

THE HORUS

HALO TURN

1 Begin by spinning slowly, using small steps, around to the left. As your body begins to turn, drop your left arm in a circular sweep downward and raise your right arm in a circular sweep upward. Continue to sweep your arms around until you are facing the back of your dance space and both your arms are up in the air circling toward the right.

2 As you spin forward, begin sweeping your right arm in an arc downward, crossing in front of your body, followed by your left. Keep spinning your body and circling your arms while gaining in speed. The wings will whip round you, creating an amazing full body halo.

COCOON

1 Raise your arms up and out at your sides, keeping your elbows locked. Stop when your arms are parallel to the floor. Keeping your wrists perfectly straight, bend your elbows until the wings are very close to your body, like a cocoon.

2 Begin spinning with small steps. The wings will catch the air and the flowing material will cover you demurely, front and back, while allowing the briefest glimpses of your face. To finish with a flourish, bring both arms down to each side with energy and speed. Then sweep the wings forward, out to the side and up, holding them high for drama!

WING SWISH

1 Grasping the dowels from the outside, raise your right arm high, extending it diagonally from the shoulder. Cross your left arm delicately across your lower body.

2 Quickly wave your right arm in a wide semi-circular movement down and across your body to the left.

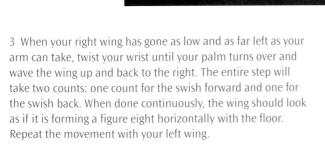

3 When your right wing has gone as low and as far left as your arm can take, twist your wrist until your palm turns over and wave the wing up and back to the right. The entire step will take two counts: one count for the swish forward and one for the swish back. When done continuously, the wing should look as if it is forming a figure eight horizontally with the floor. Repeat the movement with your left wing.

PRACTICE

Swish the wings one at a time, starting on the right for four full steps. Then switch to the left and swish four times. Then bring both arms together and perform two full simultaneous swishes.

THE PROUD/MOURNFUL HERON

1 Start in a right leg foundation (p.20). Hold the wings up high on each side of your body. With your left foot, take a large step, 1.2m (4ft) or so, forward. Keep your spine straight and stretch your arms out and behind you.

2 Simultaneously bend your left knee as much as you can, keeping your right leg almost straight, until you are very close to the ground in a deep forward lunge. Keeping your arms straight, curl your body forward while swinging the wings gently up, then forward and down in a large beautiful arc.

3 As the wings descend, curve your body forward as far as you can, dipping your head down to face the ground and rolling your shoulders in. The very tips of the wings should almost touch the floor.

TIP
If your legs are not very strong, you should only lunge a little until your body builds the strength it needs to sink all the way down. If you have any back pain, injury or weakness, don't do the backbend.

4 Suddenly straighten your back and, at the same time, swing the wings up to shoulder level. Crest the wings outward at a gentle descending angle.

5 Keeping the fluidity of the movement, tilt your head and body backward and finally sweep the wings into a high wide arc behind you. Step back and repeat on the right side, starting with your right foot.

ADDING EMOTION

This versatile wing step can be used in both playful and solemn dances. All the dancer has to do is to make some small alterations in her expression to change the feeling of the dance.

To make this step playful, hop into the lunge and quickly rise up from the forward sweep with a jolt of energy, happy eyes and a wide joyful grin.

To create a mournful mood, dance the entire step with thoughtful deliberation. Relax your face muscles so there isn't the slightest hint of tension. While sliding into the lunge, peer down so that you are looking at the floor until the wings begin to come up and back. When the wings are just about at the final proud heron stage, throw your head back and switch your gaze from the ground to the ceiling. Repeat this in the other direction.

7 Variety: the spice of life

As well as the sword, veil and wings, there are a number of other props you can use to create interest and drama in your dance.

CANDLES

These are very popular props. Most candle dancers work with a large silver tray, bearing candles in all shapes and sizes, which they balance on their head. Dancing with a tray of fire on your head is at once terrifying and awesome – a technique certainly worth learning! As with the sword, candles can be dangerous if not handled correctly, so take care. And for safety's sake, I recommend that you keep a fire extinguisher in your dance space with you, especially while learning. Take your time when selecting your tray and if you want to start out with something fancy, go ahead. It needn't be brand new. In fact, some of the most beautiful and charming trays I have seen have been old, bought at second-hand shops or antique markets.

CANE

Dancing with a cane may have its roots in a masculine battle dance, or *tahtiyb,* from the Upper Egypt farmland regions. In a simulated fighting style, the men danced with long hardwood sticks, using powerful, aggressive movements. The mock skirmish consisted of much waving and striking of the sticks as well as energetic hops and leaps. Over time, a feminine adaptation emerged with a more lighthearted and playful style, substituting a delicate hooked cane for the stick. When choosing a cane, look for one that is long enough to lean on, narrow enough for your hand to grasp, and light enough for you to lift without effort.

FINGER CYMBALS

I like the Turkish name for these – *zills* – but they are known as *sil sil* in Arabic, *salasih* in Farsi and *zagat* in Egyptian. Musical instruments for fingers date back to 200 BC, when dancers in celebrations would clack together two wooden or ivory sticks in each hand. As cultures progressed, so did the quality of instrumentation. Some evidence suggests that it was the Greeks who first began playing a metal form of finger instrument, but nobody is sure. The only firm fact about finger cymbals is that learning to play them is HARD, but worth every ounce of effort.

Zills are a musical instrument, so it's important to select them for their sound, not beauty. Listen to them chime a few times before you buy and check they make a clear bell-like ring (not a clack) that resonates for at least three seconds after the strike. Generally the longer the sound resonates, the better the zills.

CANDLES

Dancing with a tray of candles requires the same care and concentration as dancing with a sword, and sword techniques (pp.98–107) can be used with candles. However, unlike the sword, you must hold the tray of candles firmly with both hands at all times – never with just fingers or one hand – to be sure you don't drop it and get burned.

As a beginner, don't light the candles until you are absolutely in control of the tray and feel no fear or insecurity about your skills. As for sword, the rule of thumb is when you can get through the entire candle lesson four times back to back without losing the tray even once, you can consider taking the leap to lighting the candles. When you do light them, don't immediately launch into a full routine. The fire on your head may make you nervous at first, so practice the movements, one at a time, very slowly until you feel comfortable. As your confidence grows, you can begin to put movements together to build a routine.

PLACING THE CANDLES

In order to balance the tray, it is vital to position the candles evenly. When choosing candles there are two options. You might like to choose one candle that has a large base measuring 5–7cm (2–3in) and is 10–15cm (4–6in) tall, with 15 or so more slender pillar candles of varying heights to place around it. Or you may prefer to use 20 pillars of different heights, carefully placed with the highest in the center and the shortest around the edges of the tray as shown here.

Fix the candles to the tray with candle adhesive or sticky tack. Do NOT light the candles.

NEONIC DROPS

This advanced step is named after the first dancer I ever saw perform it, while balancing a tray of 30 candles on her head. When she danced this step, the drop was so sudden and unexpected that it almost seemed as if she had tripped. The audience literally gasped in admiration. Such a step requires great skill and lots of practice but is well worth working for.

1 From foundation (p.20), step forward with your left foot, transferring 70 percent of your weight onto it. Without bouncing up first (as many people do) and knocking the tray off balance, immediately drop into deep lunge.

2 Slowly come back up in a reverse, well-controlled undulation. Beginning at the hips, curve in your waist and stomach.

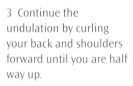

3 Continue the undulation by curling your back and shoulders forward until you are half way up.

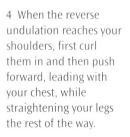

4 When the reverse undulation reaches your shoulders, first curl them in and then push forward, leading with your chest, while straightening your legs the rest of the way.

TIP

If you have trouble keeping a tray on your head, stick a thin piece of grip foam to the underside. Grip foam is the material used to make rubber cloths to help open jars or non-skid pads for under the rug. Use the smallest amount possible to secure the tray to your head so it is as inconspicuous as possible.

PRACTICE

Step forward with your right foot and repeat the drop and reverse undulation. Practice this step around your dance space.

KNEE WALK

Whenever I see this step, I always think of youthful temple daughters worshipping their goddess during a ritual by bowing down on their knees in respect and adoration. In more practical terms, the knee walk is a great way to take you across the floor without interrupting a floor routine.

TIP
While learning this step, wear knee pads to avoid bruising or injury. When practicing or performing the knee walk, wear harem pants in slippery fabric or some other leg covering. The fabric will protect your skin from chafing and burns from the floor when you slide.

1 Begin by resting firmly on your knees with your arms in basic at a 45-degree angle.

2 Slide your left knee forward and diagonally to the left, forcing your body into a deep lunge. Simultaneously begin a left snake arm (p.54), reaching out in the same direction as your knee.

3 Drag your right knee forward to meet your left. As your right leg slides forward, complete the left snake arm and begin a right snake arm. Raise your body back up to its original height.

4 Slide your right knee forward and diagonally to the right. This will once again force your body into a deep lunge. Complete the right snake arm and begin another on the left as you drag your left knee to the right, returning to the starting position.

BACKBEND UNDULATION

1 Start in the same position as for the knee walk, but turn your body to profile. Spread your knees apart a full 1.2m (4ft) while touching your toes together behind you. This triangular leg support spreads your body weight to help maintain balance. Begin snaking both arms forward.

2 Keeping your chin parallel with the floor, lean back as far as you can without strain, supporting yourself with your thigh muscles. Keep snaking your arms in front of you – they are a convenient counterbalance to the force of gravity pulling you backward.

3. Hunch your shoulders slightly and curl your upper body forward – don't just pop straight up – pulling in your abdominal muscles while almost sitting fully on your feet.

4 When your upper body is directly over your knees, lift up off your feet, roll your shoulders back and push your chest forward. Arch your back and come up from the sitting position by leading forward and upward with your chest. Return to the starting position and repeat!

WARNING
As with all backbends, perform this movement slowly and with extreme care to avoid injuring your back.

CANE STEPS

LEAPING SKIP STEP

1 Hold the base of the cane with your right hand and the crook with your left. Stand in right foot foundation with the cane at chest level in front of you. Turn slightly to the left until the right side of your body is somewhat forward. With a small hop, jump forward and as you land, bend your knees to lower your body into a dip. Try not to lean forward as you dip, just lower your center of gravity. Lift the cane up above your head.

2 Follow the dip with a fast energetic leap straight up into a left foot releve (p.56). At the same time, bend your right knee, raise your leg with a hip lift and straighten your arms to hold the cane high above your head.

As you descend, lower your arms back to chest level and pivot to the right until the left side of your body is slightly facing front. Repeat the movement on the other side.

HIP PUSH STEP

1 Start in the same position as for the leaping skip step, but hold only the bottom of the cane in your right hand. Rest the crook on your right shoulder.

Softly extend the first finger of your left hand while curling over the others. Rest the side of your forefinger against the left side of your forehead in a delicate salute.

2 Lifting your right leg and bending at the knee, hip snap (p.30) to the back. On the release of the snap, place your right foot forward, about 30cm (12in) past your left, and hip snap forward on your right side. Repeat four times, then switch to the other side for another four.

SWINGING THE CANE: PREPARATION

Grasp the cane firmly, 5cm (2in) from the bottom, with your dominant hand. Your fingers should be firmly wrapped round the entire stalk. Swing the cane round twice in a clockwise direction, without relaxing your grip. Reverse and swing counterclockwise. Notice that your wrist has trouble spinning gracefully with the cane and torques uncomfortably left and right. The following steps demonstrate how to twirl a cane smoothly without strain on your wrist.

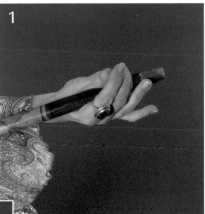

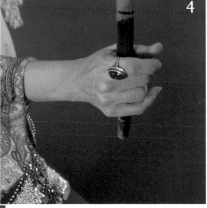

SWINGING THE CANE

1 Grasp the cane firmly. Release all fingers except your forefinger and thumb and keep a firm grip with those.

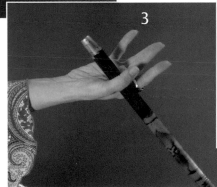

2 Begin to swing the cane in a counterclockwise direction, still holding only with your thumb and forefinger. Allow the cane to swing down in a wide arc while resting on your other fingers.

4 When the momentum of the cane brings it to a point when it is vertical to the floor, gently close all your fingers around it until until you have it back in a firm grip.

3 As the cane begins to swing up, the end will lift off the fingers it's resting on. Extend those fingers, preparing for the final step.

PRACTICE

Spin the cane slowly and carefully, making one spin at a time and pausing before the next, until you feel comfortable. Then start spinning the cane more rapidly, removing the pauses so that one spin flows seamlessly into the next. For a final experiment, spin the cane once on your right side. Then, keeping it in the same hand, cross your arm over your chest to the opposite side and swing the cane once on the left side. Repeat.

ZILLS

Often viewed as just another prop to the dance, many dancers forget that zills, or finger cymbals, are a musical instrument and require practice to master. Poorly played zills can, and will, undermine even the greatest of dancers. But I urge you to not be afraid! Embrace the zills, practice and the payback will be tremendous.

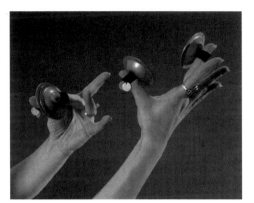

WEARING THE ZILLS

You need two sets of zills for proper instrumentation. A zill should be attached to your thumb and middle finger by elastic running through the hole at the top of the zill. One technique is to run a loop of elastic through the hole, measure it to your finger and tie a knot on the inside of the zill. Another is to use small safety pins to hold the elastic in place. The zills should fit tightly but not be so tight that the tips of your fingers turn blue. If necessary, loosen the elastic. Like different notes, zill chimes vary in strength and style.

BASIC RING

1 Position the zills on the thumb and middle finger of each hand.

2 Quickly strike your left thumb and middle finger together, pulling the zills apart right after the impact. Immediately separating the zills allows the chime to reverberate and linger.

3 Repeat with your right hand.

PRACTICE

Ring the zills in each hand slowly, one after another, allowing the chime to linger. Speed up gradually, striking left then right until you have a steady rapid pace. Stop. Begin again, but ring the zills softly at first, building in volume by adding pressure to each strike.

WIND CHIME

Hold your zills apart in each hand, palm up, with your left hand in front of your right. Move your left hand directly toward you, and your right hand directly away from you so that the edges of the left zills strike the edges of the right zills as they pass each other, moving in opposite directions. This will create a magical wind-chiming effect, which seems almost fairylike. Repeat the set to practice and perfect your technique.

SAMPLE RHYTHMS

Practice to a slow drumbeat from your favourite music.
For 8 drumbeats, single strike your right zill only once on each beat. Repeat on the left.
For the next 8 beats, quickly double strike (R,L) on each beat.
Finally, for another 8 beats, quickly triple strike (R,L,R) on each beat.

Traditional gallop 8 counts, one set of strikes per drumbeat:
Triple strike, triple strike, triple strike… (RLR, RLR, RLR).

Rolling gallop 13 very fast alternating single strikes for every 8 counts:
Single strike R, single strike L, single strike R… (R,L,R,L,R,L,R,L,R,L,R,L,R).

Beladi 9/8 count beat using single and triple strikes:
This is a tough one to teach in a book, so forgive this silly technique, but it works!
Strike R, Strike R, Holy Cow (R,L,R), Strike R, Holy Cow (R,L,R), Strike R, Strike L.
In other words: (R, L, R-L-R, R, R-L-R, R,L).

Chiftitelli 8-count accent rhythm with pauses:
Triple strike, triple strike, triple strike, single, single, single
(R-L-R, R-L-R, R-L-R, pause, R, R, R). Or:
Single strike, double strike, double strike, pause, single, single single
(R, RL, RL, pause, R, R, R).

USING ZILLS IN THE DANCE

A dancer can't just play zills – she has to play them and dance to their music. Stand in place and begin to play a steady single strike beat. March on the spot to it. Increase to double and then triple strike beat while continuing to march. After 16 triple strikes, begin to march forward and around your dance space while triple striking. Not as easy as it sounds.

As you get better at marching to the triple beat, try different steps such as the ghawazee step (p.61) and hip twist (p.36). When you have successfully combined those steps with zill playing – this takes some time, so don't lose hope – move on to playing other rhythms with the zills.

Practice will make perfect. If you're really struggling, don't get frustrated and give up. Keep playing and it will all come together.

8 The Oriental fantasy

Thomas Alva Edison said, "Genius is one percent inspiration, 99 percent perspiration". Belly dancing is no different. With the solid foundation of steps taught in the previous chapters, there is no limit to how much dancing you can do. The best way to improve your dancing is to practice, practice, practice! Each time you rehearse your dance steps, your body will grow more familiar with the movements and they will get easier and easier. One of the most enjoyable ways to practice, rather than just repeating each step over and over, is to build a dance routine. The routine brings all the steps together and blends them into one flowing dance.

Before I was a professional dancer, I spent many happy hours alone in my living room, dancing my heart out to the routines I developed. After a year or so, I began to feel a compelling desire to share my dancing with other people. Being an incurable romantic, I wanted to give them a chance to escape from their everyday lives into the magic of an Oriental dream. I wanted to take them with me to the places I went in my mind while I was dancing. Perhaps by now you might be feeling the same thing.

If you're thinking about performing for other people, you're probably feeling a strange mix of emotions – excitement, curiosity, suspense and hope, mingled with nervousness, insecurity and fear. Some people refer to the latter as stage fright. Revel in all the positive emotions and let them inspire you! As for the negative emotions, there are some really easy techniques to help you manage them.

OVERCOMING YOUR FEARS

Many beginners worry about what people will think when they see them dance for the first time. An easy remedy for stage fright is to invite only people you know and trust to your early performances. Family and close friends are excellent support for the fledgling dancer. If you're planning to dance in a public place for the first time you might worry about what strangers will think about you and your dancing. Well, there are two types of people in the world as it relates to belly dancing – those who know how to belly dance and those who don't. For those who don't, anything you do is going to be marvellous because they don't know any better. And those who do belly dance remember how it felt to be new and will be compassionate.

Another common phobia is the fear of forgetting the steps of the dance. There is only one cure for that – practice! If you keep rehearsing a routine, your body and mind will reach a point where the movements become second nature. The thought processes of which step comes after which will melt away as your body takes over and gets you moving.

BUILDING A ROUTINE

Many teachers propose different formulas for dancing which include some components and exclude others, based on their personal vision of belly dancing. It seems, however, that the most creative and talented dancers do not allow themselves to be limited by convention. They incorporate all their scope and talent, adding a touch of their own personality to the routine. With that in mind, I suggest a six-segment routine which touches on all your new skills as a dancer as a great place to begin.

ENTRANCE (1–2 minutes)
The entrance, as you move into your dancing space, is as much a part of the dance as anything else. It's generally best to use graceful arm movements and dramatized walks and save everything else for the body of the routine. Enter slowly and moodily, using the pharonic walk (p.59), or leap into position with joy, using the ghawazee step (p.61).

DANCING OR ZILL SET (2–4 minutes)
As the entrance concludes, the first full dance piece is perfect for energetic dancing, with or without the chiming of zills to get you, and any audience, revved up. Zills add vigour and life to a speedy opening number.

VEIL (4–5 minutes)
Nobody likes to see the same dance over and over. Changing the mood by moving into veil work, light and ethereal as an evening summer breeze, will add some depth and variety.

PROPS (CANDLES 6–8 minutes, CANE 4–5 minutes, SWORD 6–8 minutes, WINGS 4–5 minutes)
Generally considered the climax of the routine, the pace of this segment really depends on what you'd like to dance with. Sword and candle work is thoughtful and slow, while the folklike nature of the cane will speed things up again. Dancing with wings can be either fast or moderate, depending on the music and the image the dancer wants to convey.

FIFTH SET (2–3 minutes)
This piece is usually the moment where dancers perform what is called a drum solo. In many Middle Eastern musical compositions, there are segments when the drum beats without the accompaniment of other instruments. The rhythm becomes more lively and the dancer reflects this by changing the smoothness of her routine to sharp, passionate hip movements in time with the beat changes. The solo can also include shimmies (p.38) and anything else in the dancer's vocabulary that accents the drum set.

FINALE (2–3 minutes)
This is a farewell dance which is combined with elegant gestures of personal achievement. Common to the finale are bright smiles, winks and plenty of graceful bowing. It is also a demonstration of gratitude – to yourself and your soul for completing the routine as well as to the audience, if there is one, for watching with kindness and interest.

DANCE ROUTINES

The dance instructions on the next few pages are designed to help you practice much of what you have learned, not only to improve your skills, but also to provide you with a taste of what a routine should encompass. The dances are not subscribed any time counts so you can experiment with the speed and pauses as you wish. It's generally best for beginners to take more counts rather than less to complete a step.

Select your pieces of music: one for your entrance, one for a fast dance and another for a medium tempo veil routine. Find a long, slow composition that works well for your prop routine and a speedy number for your finale.

GETTING READY
Put on your veil in a style that appeals to you (pp.74–75). If you plan on dancing with zills, place them on your fingers. Select your prop and place it on the floor toward the front of your dance space – close enough to be accessible, but far enough away so you don't trip over it.

ENTRANCE
For a dramatic entrance, start your slow entrance music and get ready to become queen of the Nile! Stand outside the dance space and slowly begin a pharonic walk with prayer hands over your head. Pause and head slither left and right. When you reach the center of your space, incorporate other slow movements such as snake arms, hip rolls and undulations. Repeat your entrance until the music is finished, using the basic walk or indie cross step, along with a variety of head and arm combinations.

FAST DANCE WITH OR WITHOUT ZILLS

When the fast music picks up, wait until you hear the fourth solid beat before starting to dance. If playing zills, begin playing with first dance step. Then:

- 8 hip drops left
- 8 hip drops right
- 2 hip thrusts each, front, side and back on the left
- 2 hip thrusts each, front, side and back on the right
- 4 high/low hip drops left
- 4 high/low hip drops right
- Hop
- Shimmy!

- 4 kashlimar steps on the spot
- 1 box of hip snaps
- 3-point turn left
- Shoulder shake
- 3-point turn and drop right

Gradually rise up, taking at least 4 counts
- 4 alternating hip rolls
- 4 hip lifts right
- 4 hip lifts left
- 2 undulations
- Hop
- Shimmy!

- Pivot to back
- 3 ghawazee steps back, pivot
- 3 ghawazee steps front
- 2 large hip circles
- 4 small chest circles
- 4 alternating left and right reverse hip rolls
- 2 hip twists left
- 2 hip twists right
- Hop
- Shimmy!

Repeat for practice until your music piece is complete. ▶

MEDIUM TEMPO VEIL

For the first 20 seconds of the veil music:

- 8 slow undulations, high and low, 2 each front, back, left, right
- Slow alternating snake arms front and back

FOR THE REST OF THE MUSIC

- Unveil in steps (advance to spin when the steps are mastered)
- 1 slow veil switch left
- 2 fast veil switches right
- Cascade forward; allow veil to drop slowly
- Soft shoulder shake
- Flip into wings
- Release forward
- Cascade back
- 4 alternating left and right cascades
- Cascade forward
- Walkover
- 3 slow barrel turns left
- 3 simple turns on the spot, veil held high
- 1 body glimpse right with 2 hip drops
- 1 body glimpse left with 2 hip drops
- 1 body glimpse front with 2 undulations
- Basic walk in a wide circle with shoulder shake
- Return to center
- 3 alternating hip rolls while lowering arms to sides
- Shimmy and raise arms up slowly to center
- Spin into envelope
- 4 alternating hip rolls
- 1 box hip snaps
- Lower veil in front of eyes and peek out; wink!
- Wrap veil round head
- Shimmy and raise veil back up
- Slowly snake out of envelope
- Spin
- 2 sandstorm veils
- 1 sandstorm veil with sailing through storm
- Stop spinning abruptly and drop arms quickly to release sail
- 1 veil switch right
- 2 fast veil switches left
- Left spin through the door
- Cascade back
- 1 body glimpse front with full hip circle
- 1 body glimpse left with undulation
- 1 body glimpse right with undulation
- Wrap your arms round your chest in a hug, sway left and right leading with your shoulder

Repeat for practice until music piece is complete. ▶

VERY SLOW PROP ROUTINE

(Use with sword or candles – practice sword or unlit candles only)
Enter holding prop firmly in front of you. Take it slowly!

- 3 circle turns all the way around
- Hip roll in place and raise prop above your head
- 3-point turn left
- Pause
- Cobra neck slither
- 3-point turn right
- Chest circle
- Pause
- Shimmy and lower prop to waist level
- 4 alternating hip rolls
- 8 walking hip twist steps in a circle
- 4 hip drops while raising prop above head
- Half 3-point turn so your back is facing front
- Carefully place prop on head
- Very slowly complete turn
- Descend to floor
- Knee crawl
- Resurrection
- Cross kick
- Backbend undulations
- Raise to kneeling position
- Shimmy and ascend
    Repeat for practice until music piece is complete.

FAST FINALE

Quickly but gracefully discard your prop.
If playing zills, turn your back to the front, alternate hip rolls
and return them to your fingers. Turn round and begin to play

- Ghawazee step in wide circle around dance space
- 3 alternating hip twist walks front
- Large bow
- Pivot to right
- 3 alternating hip twists right
- Shoulder shake
- Pivot to left
- 3 alternating hip twists left
- Shimmy
- Pivot to back
- 3 alternating hip twists back
- Look over shoulder to front, shoulder shake
- 3-point turn forward with drop
- Gradually come up; wink
- Large bow left
- Large bow right
- Shoulder shake, dipping left and right
- Spin
- Bow one more time and exit gracefully.

COSTUME

Costumes play a vital role in great belly dancing. They can be handmade or bought and should reflect a dancer's personal taste. There are costumes to suit all shapes and sizes. They come in every colour and in a wide range of fabrics, such as velvet, silk, chiffon and lightweight cottons. If a dancer can imagine it, it can be made! Here are a few costume types.

CABARET TURKISH/EGYPTIAN

These two styles are very similar. An intricately beaded and tasselled bra and belt set is draped over up to three loose skirts and/or harem pants, and worn with matching gloves, wrist cuffs, armbands and headband.

EGYPTIAN MERMAID COSTUME

Almost exactly the same as the Egyptian cabaret, the mermaid costume is distinguished by a form-fitting stretchy skirt, which smoothes over the hips and flares out at the bottom in six to eight long panels.

TRIBAL COSTUME

Lush, original adornments give tribal costumes their unique gypsy look. The top is often two pieces – a bra or choli top with a vest that closes at the solar plexus. The gored skirt is made of generous lengths of fabric so it catches the air and circles out wildly while the dancer is moving. Rich sewn-on details include coins, small bells, mirrors, cowry shells and fat dancing tassels. Some dancers also wear a decorated turban made of different scraps of brightly coloured fabrics wrapped round the head and tied at the back.

BELADI DRESS

Perfect for folk and cane dancing, the beladi dress is a classy full-length dress with long or short sleeves. A fringed, beaded or coined sash is often tied round the waist for accent.

OTHER ESSENTIAL ACCESSORIES

Bracelets, necklaces, rings, earrings, armbands, anklets and a beaded headband – if the costume doesn't come with one.

OPTIONAL ACCESSORIES

Belly or toe rings.

MAKE-UP

As integral as the costume is a well made-up face. There are two main schools of thought when it comes to make-up. The first approach is simply to glamorize your current style by selecting bolder and brighter shades of cosmetics and applying them more thickly so that they show up under strong lights. Or you can play up the Oriental fantasy by applying more dramatic make-up, including heavily kohled and extended eyes, strongly arched brows and blushed cheeks. Body glitter and adhesive jewels are nice additional touches.

To bring out the best in every face, a dancer's make-up kit must include certain items: oil-free liquid foundation in one shade lighter than her skin colour and matching oil-free loose powder, stick and liquid eyeliner, several different shades of blusher and eye shadow, lipsticks, an eyebrow pencil that is the same shade as the darkest part of your hair, and black mascara. Waterproof cosmetics are best as they won't run when you sweat. Handy make-up accessories are eyelash curlers, cotton swabs, absorbent beauty sponges, brushes in different sizes and make-up remover for mistakes.

DANCER ETIQUETTE

At the beating heart of the dance lie its most powerful elements – mystery, fantasy and sensuality. Belly dancing is the passage to unlocking these and many other beautiful and pure emotions from within you in a unique and exclusively feminine way. Unfortunately, belly dancing suffers from an oppressive stigma, which affects its image and worldwide acceptance. To the enduring disappointment of the dancing community, many people who are unfamiliar with the history and practice of this particular style of dancing often confuse it with burlesque, striptease and other types of flesh-focused entertainment.

A combination of factors lies at the root of this debasement. Due to early European and American opposition by religious authorities and the Hollywood portrayal of belly dancers as temptresses, belly dancing became cheapened in the eyes of many as a corrupt and immoral thrill with a negative impact on society. That couldn't be further from the truth.

All forms of perfection have their cheap imitations and belly dancing is no exception. Misconduct by imposters in belly dancing costumes, as well as inappropriate portrayal of the art by the media, have diluted our legitimacy. But as long as there are still true belly dancers out there, the art of the belly dance is redeemable. The dancer herself must re-educate the viewing public and participants and show them what belly dancing really is – and what it is not.

ALWAYS BE A LADY

As a professional dancer and instructor, the single most important point that I try to impress upon my students is that first and foremost, a dancer is ALWAYS a lady. To do justice to belly dancing, her conduct must be unimpeachable under all circumstances . She must behave with elegance and dignity, and have impeccable manners. When she dances, she must be dignified, not dirty; sensuous, not sexual; and beautiful, not bawdy. There are a few etiquette techniques which if consistently followed will not only build a dancer's reputation as a legitimate artist but will also help stand as a reminder that we are not part of the sex trade world.

First, never dance for a male-only audience, such as at bachelor parties. Dancing under those circumstances creates an immediate link to the sex-for-sale concept.

Second, never allow tip money to be tucked into any part of your costume. Dancer or not, your physical being is sacred, and must not be handled by strangers in such a fashion. If you are in a public place, an appropriate alternative is to allow generous donators to sprinkle paper money down upon you in a benevolent shower. After this it is perfectly acceptable and

encouraged to demonstrate your gratitude with a small curtsy or graceful bow to your admirers.

Third, never stoop or kneel to gather your tips from the floor. Make a gentle request to your employer, or an employee of the establishment, to pick them up for you. If an employee collects money for you, it is courteous to give him or her a little tip in return.

Fourth, know your art inside and out from an historical perspective. Most people know nothing about belly dancing, other than what they see in the media, which is hungry for shock and scandal. Often a dancer will be faced with questions such as "Wasn't this really just a dance for harem girls to perform in front of the sultan?" or "How can you consider this to be family entertainment when your body is so exposed?" In these circumstances it is up to the dancer to remedy the misconceptions through education. Take any opportunity to explain what true belly dancing is. Know your history and be prepared to explain the facts to the curious and interested. It's a wonderful feeling when you see someone come to understand the integrity buried beneath the pop culture myth.

As you grow in the dance, keep close to your heart the awareness that the movements touch on all stages of our lifespan from birth to adolescence through to old age and passing on. Wherever you are in your own life and however you are feeling, you can pour your emotions and experience into your dancing and share them with the world. Emotions of joy, sadness and even anger can all be part of your dance.

When I stumbled into my first belly dance class I never suspected how it would enhance my life in so many positive and incredible ways. I hope with all my heart that belly dancing brings the same passion and joy to your life as it has to mine.

Resources

SUGGESTED READING
Historical
Al-Rawi, Rosina-Fawzia B., trans. by Arav, Monique, *Grandmother's Secrets: The Ancient Rituals and Healing Power of Belly Dancing*, Interlink Pub. Group, 2000

Buonaventura, Wendy and Farrah, Ibrahim, *Serpent of the Nile: Women and Dance in the Arab World*, Interlink Pub. Group, 1998

Carlton, Donna, *Looking for Little Egypt*, International Dance Discover Books, 1995

Nieuwkerk, Karin van, *"A Trade like Any Other": Female Singers and Dancers in Egypt*, Univ. of Texas Press, 1995

Richards, Tazz (editor), and Djoumahna, Kajira (introduction), *The Belly Dance Book: Rediscovering the Oldest Dance*, Backbeat Press, 2000

Stewart, Iris J., *Sacred Woman, Sacred Dance: Awakening Spirituality Through Movement & Ritual*, Inner Traditions Intl. Ltd., 2000

Thornton, Lynne, *Women As Portrayed in Orientalist Painting*, Art Books Intl. Ltd., 1996

Costuming
Brown, Barry and Brown, Dawn Devine, *Costuming from the Hip*, Ibexa Press, 1997

Brown, Barry and Brown, Dawn Devine, *From Turban to Toe Ring*, Ibexa Press, 2000

Brown, Barry and Brown, Dawn Devine, *Bedlah, Baubles, and Beads*, Ibexa Press, 2001

Personal Care
Buonaventura, Wendy and Eady, Isobel (Illustrator), *Beauty and the East: A Book of Oriental Body Care*, Interlink Pub. Group, 2000

MAGAZINES
Bennu
Associated Artists of Middle Eastern Dance Inc.
A non-profit organization
72 Park Terrace West, Suite E48
New York, NY 10034-1351

Habibi
PO Box 42018
Eugene, OR 97404

Zaghareet!
P.O. Box 1809
Elizabeth City, NC 27906

SHOPPING ABROAD
Egypt
Mr Mahmoud Abd El Ghaffar
"Al-Wikalah"
75 Gawfar El Qayid St
Al-Musky
Al-Azhar
Cairo, Egypt
Tel: 20 2 589 7443
Fax: 20 2 390 0357

Turkey
Madame Bella
"Boutique Bella"
Fulya Cad. Erse Han No. 3-5 D.16
Mecidiyeköy, Istanbul
Turkey
Tel: 90 212 272 2029,
Fax: 90 212 288-3699

COSTUMES
Costumes online USA
Ready-made designs
www.topkapidesigns.com (Turkish)
www.home.earthlink.net (Turkish)
www.egyptworld.com (Egyptian)
www.pyramidimports.com (Egyptian)

Nourhan Sharif Dancewear
http://www.nourhansharif.com

Alia Michelle Designs
http://aliamdesigns.com/

Custom-made designs
http://www.aliamdesigns.com/
www.domba.com

Costumes online UK
www.whirling-dervish.co.uk
www.khalganikostumes.com
www.theshimmyshop.co.uk
www.faridadance.com

CLASSES
Try looking at the links listed below or get in
touch with your local leisure center or dance
school for classes

Information online USA
www.bellydanceny.com

Information online UK
www.mosaicdance.org
www.footwork.org/ghazala/main.htm
http://www.shira.net/dir-uk.htm (directory of
instructors)
Council for dance education and training
http://www.cdet.org.uk/index2.htm

BELLY DANCERS
www.dancingmoonlight.com (author's website)
www.geocities.com/mimibellydance
www.enchantressofbioluminosity.com/
www.rajadance.com
www.bellydancersonline.com
http://www.bellydancer.info/
www.vers.com/kanari
www.mysticbellydancer.com

MUSIC
Omar Faruk Tekbilek (Turkish)
Faruk has 10 fabulous CDs. His soulful voice
and compositions never fail to inspire.
My personal favourites are
Dance into Eternity
Cresent Moon
Alif
www.omarfaruktekbilek.com

Hossam Ramzy (Egyptian)
Hossam is world famous for his music. His
perfect percussion rhythms are wonderful to
learn from. My personal favourites are:
Secrets of the Eye
Source of Fire
Rhythms of the Nile

Jehan Kemal (fusion)
Not only an utterly stunning dancer, Jehan has
a mysterious and spiritual voice that is the very
epitome of femininity in the dance.
My personal favourites are:
The Goddess Dance series
Sacred Waters
Heartbeat
www.jehanarts.com

Index

A

accessories 135
Andromeda veil 87
Araby push 50
arms
  movements 35, 47, 58
    debke 63
    indie cross step 60
    kashlimar 64
    snake arms 54-55
    three-point turn 66
  poses 20, 50

B

back face frame 90
back hip twist 36
back-releasing stretch 23
backbends 46, 47, 121
basic hand 21
basic walk 58, 101
beladi 125, 135
belly dancing
  history 7-11, 38
  learning 13, 27
belly roll 40
belts, coin 15, 38
body glimpsing 73, 91
body intense shimmy 38-39
"box" 30, 45
breathing exercises 15
butterfly 92-93

C

cabaret 11, 134
Cairo 10-11
candles 10, 14, 117-121, 129, 133
  backbend undulation 121
  knee walk 120
  neonic drops 119
cane 122-123, 129
  hip push step 122

leaping skip step 122
  swinging 123
cascade 80, 91, 93
chengis 8, 10
chest circles 44, 45, 95
chest thrusts 44-45
chiftitelli 16, 125
circling hands 52-53
cobra neck slither 48
cocoon 112
coins 10, 15, 38
costume 14-15, 134-135
counting 16, 19
creating wings 86
cross step turn 97

D

dance counting 16, 19
dance environment 13-14
dance routines 127, 130-133
debke 62-63
dervish turn 68-69, 97
dress 14-15, 134-135

E

Egypt 8, 10-11
Egyptian goddess 50
Egyptian mermaid costume 134
emotion 115, 127
entrances 128, 130
envelope 94-96

F

face frames 90
feet, stances 56
fertility dances 8, 38
finales 129, 133
finger cymbals see zills
flat foot position 56
floor work 102-105
folk steps

debke 62-63
  kashlimar 64
forward hip twist 36
foundation position 19, 20
front cross step turn 65
front face frame 90

G

ghawazee 10
ghawazee slide step 61
goddess worship 7
gypsies 8, 10

H

halo turn 112
hamstring stretch 24
hands
  movements 52-53
  positions 21, 31, 47, 50
Hathor pose 111
hips
  circles 34, 35
  drops 28, 29, 95, 101
  lifts 29
  movements 23
  push step 122
  rolls 32, 33, 79, 95, 101
  snaps 30
  steps 61
  stretches 22
  thrusts 30, 31, 101
  twists 36, 37
Horus pose 111

I

in the lamp 102
indie cross step 60
instruments 16, 117, 124
Isis pose 111
Istanbul 8

K

kashlimar 64
kissing the audience 85
knee walk 120
kol 8

L

layering 27
lazy cross kick 103
leaping skip step 122
legs, stances 56
lift 91
lift and cascade 80
Little Egypt (belly dancer) 11

M

make-up 135
moqsoom 16
muscle isolation 19
music 8, 10, 16-17, 117, 124

N

neck stretches 22, 48
neonic drops 119

O

offering hand 21
offering pose 50
offering veil 86
Osiris pose 111

P

pharonic walk 59
placing the sword 100-101
poses 20, 50, 111
princess veil front face frame 90
proud/mournful heron 114-115

R

Ra's crown 50
releve 56
resurrection 104-105
reverse hip roll 32-33
rhythms 16, 125
rolling gallop 125
Romany 8
routines 128-133

S

sailing through the storm 89
sandstorm veil 88
sensuous undulation 42-43
shimmies 38-39, 79, 95
shoes 56
shoulder shake 51
slithers 48
snake arms 47, 54-55, 60, 101
    alternating 55
    front cross step turn 65
    single 54
    unveiling 79
Spanish hands 53
spinning barrel turn 97
spinning through the door 84
spotting 27, 66
stances, basic 56
stepping over the curtain 91
stretches 22-25
Sufis 68
swinging the cane 123
swords 99-107, 129
    floor work 102
    in the lamp 102
    lazy cross kick 103
    resurrection 104-105
    triple circle 107

T

tahtiyb 117
three-point drop 67
three-point turn 66, 97
toga wrap, unveiling 78
traditional gallop 125
travelling steps
    ghawazee slide step 61
    kashlimar 64
trays 117, 119
tribal costume 134
triple circle 107
Turkey 8
turns
    cross step 97
    dervish 68-69, 97
    front cross step 65
    halo 112
    spinning barrel 97
    three point 66

U V

undulations 42-43, 73, 95, 101, 121
veils 71-97, 128, 130, 132
    Andromeda 87
    back face frame 90
    basic wrap 74
    body glimpsing 73
    butterfly 92-93
    cascade 80-81
    creating wings 86
    envelope 94-95
    front face frame 90
    goddess 75
    kissing the audience 85
    offering veil 86
    sailing through the storm 89
    sandstorm 88
    spinning barrel turn 97

spinning through the door 84
stepping over the curtain 91
switch 82-83, 91, 93
toga 74
unveiling
   in a spin 76-77
   in steps 78-79

W

walks 36-37, 58-59, 101, 120
warm up 22
weight distribution 19, 20
windchime 125
wings 109-115, 129
   cocoon 112
   halo turn 112
   poses 111
   proud/mournful heron 114-115
   swish 113
wrist-releasing stretch 25

Z

zills 117, 124-125, 128, 131
   basic ring 124
   in the dance 125
   windchime 125

AUTHOR'S ACKNOWLEDGMENTS

My endless love and gratitude first and foremost to my husband, whose unwavering support and dedication I cannot not live without.

Deep and warm appreciation to my cakes at Gaia Books, Sara and Jinny, who held my hand through this whole project even though they are on the other side of the Atlantic.

Many loving thanks to my family, immediate and extended, who always believe I can do anything. And tender gratefulness to my dear Kindred Spirits, especially The Neon, whose companionship are ever my safe havens.

PUBLISHER'S ACKNOWLEDGMENTS

Gaia Books would like to thank the following for their help in the making of this book: Naia, Mimi, Andrea Anwar, Raja, Leyla, Kanari, Fahdida, Elisabeth, Aquila and Heidi, who modelled and danced for the step by step photographs; Heidi Steinberg and Joey McGill for make-up; Nourhan Sharif Dancewear and Alia Michelle Designs for costumes; Claire Hayward and Ann Marie Philip for design assistance; Joel Porter for technical support; Elizabeth Wiggans for compiling the index; Michael Beacom and Jeff Solomon at Sterling.

Photographic credits: All photographs are by Sarah Skinner except for those on pages 9, 10 and 11 from the Mary Evans Picture Library. Sarah Skinner would like to give special thanks to Kevin Fox, Ursula Jones and Jack Skinner.

Contents

Acknowledgements   xiii

About the authors   xiii

The history of *Voluntary but not Amateur*   xiv

Foreword   xv

Chapter 1:

Before you start – legal structures and charitable status   1

Legal structures   1

    Unincorporated associations   2

    Charitable trusts   3

    Limited companies   4

    Community interest companies   5

    Charitable incorporated organisations   6

    Industrial and provident societies   7

    Changing the structure   8

    Local authority influence   11

Charitable status   11

    What is a charity?   11

    Excepted charities   12

    Exempt charities   12

    Charitable purposes   12

    Public benefit   14

    Dual registration   14

    Advantages   15

    Restrictions   16

Minimising the risk of personal liability   20

    Liability of committee members   20

Chapter 2:

Setting up and running an organisation   22

Setting up the organisation   22

    Drafting and agreeing the constitution   22

    Models   34

    Adopting the constitution   34

    Registering as a charity   36

    The committee   37

    Documentation   40

    Setting up registers   40

    Noting important dates   42

Contents

Running the organisation 43
  Meetings 43
  Changes in organisational membership 44
  Changes in committee membership 45
  Moving the administrative office 46
  Annual accounts, annual reports and annual returns 46
  Changes to the constitution 47
  Dealing with crises 48

Equality and diversity policy 49
  Legal obligations 49
  The policy 49

Checklist: The first committee meeting 53

Checklist: Annual general meetings 55

Checklist: Electing committee members 56

Checklist: Committee members' roles and responsibilities 57

Chapter 3:

Employees' and workers' rights 61

The definitions 61
  Employees and workers 61
  Volunteers 61
  Agency staff 62
  Seconded staff 62
  Self-employed people 62
  Trainees 63

Employment rights: a summary 63
  Workers' rights 63
  Additional rights for employees 64

Contracts of employment and written statements 66
  Contents of the contract 66
  Statement of employment particulars 66

Deciding on terms and conditions 68
  Pay 68
  Working time, holidays and time off 69

Discrimination 71
  Context 71
  Who is protected 72
  The scope of equality legislation 74
  Strengthening enforcement 79
  Other equality legislation 79
  Fixed-term employees 81
  Part-time workers 82

Contents

Equal opportunities in employment: good practice   83
  Monitoring effectiveness   83

Family legislation   84
  Maternity   84
  Paternity   86
  Adoption   87
  Parental leave   88
  Dependants' leave   89
  Flexible working arrangements   90
  Dignity at work   93

Disciplinary and grievance policy and procedures   95
  Defining the scope of the policy   95
  Developing procedures   95
  Grievance procedures   96
  Representation   97

Unions   97
  Workers' rights   97
  Union recognition   97
  Union agreements   98
  The rights of recognised trade unions   98
  Union officials   99
  Time off for union learning representatives   99
  Employee representatives   99
  Consultation with employees   99
  The Information and Consultation of Employees Regulations 2004   100

Taking on other organisations' staff   100
  Information   101
  Consultation   101
  An economic, technical or organisational justification   101
  Pensions   101

Public interest disclosure – 'whistle-blowing'   102

Redundancy   102
  Notifying those involved   103
  Selection for redundancy   105
  Offers of alternative work   105
  Time off to look for work   106
  Redundancy pay   106
  Good practice   106
  Claiming money owed   107

Providing references   107

Employment tribunals   108

Contents

Chapter 4:
Recruiting and paying people

Recruiting and paying people 109

Making an appointment 109
  The legal requirements 109
  Reviewing posts 109
  Selection panels 109
  The recruitment process 110
  Probationary periods 116
  Taking on freelance and self-employed workers and consultants 116
  Taking on volunteers 118
  Restrictions on employing people 120

Paying people 124
  Payslips 124
  Deductions 124
  Employees leaving 126
  At the end of the tax year 127
  Filing accounts 127
  Temporary and casual staff 127
  Students 127
  Volunteers 128
  Employers' childcare contributions 128
  Maternity, paternity and adoption pay and benefits 128
  Outsourcing payroll services 129

Sick pay and leave 130
  Statutory sick pay 130
  Sickness/ill health policies and procedures 132

Pensions 134
  State pensions 134
  Additional provision 134
  Occupational pension schemes 135
  Stakeholder pensions 136
  Personal pension plans 137
  Group personal pensions 137
  Recent and forthcoming changes 137
  Further information 138

Keeping records 138

Monitoring emails and internet access 138
  Developing an internet/email policy 139

Reorganisation 142
  Unfair dismissal 142
  Procedures for reorganisation 143

Chapter 5:

Health and safety

Health and safety   144

Legislation   144
  Regulations   144
  Enforcement   144
  Responsibilities of committee members and staff   145

General duties under the HSW Act   145
  Duties to employees   145
  Home-based workers   145
  Duties to non-employees   145
  Duties to users of premises   146
  Duties of employees   146

Other general requirements of the HSW Act   146
  Health and safety policy statement   146
  Health and safety poster   147
  Safety representatives   147
  Consultation with employees who are not represented
  by a recognised trade union   147
  Safety committees   148

Regulations under the HSW Act   148
  The management of health and safety at work   148
  Workplace health, safety and welfare   153
  Personal protective equipment   155
  Work equipment   156
  Manual handling   157
  Managing asbestos   158
  Display screen equipment   158
  Fire safety   160

Other health and safety laws and regulations   162
  Smoking   162
  Electrical apparatus   163
  Hazardous substances   163
  First aid   164
  Occupational road risk   164
  Working hours   165
  Noise   165
  Corporate manslaughter   165
  Duties relating to premises   166
  Public health laws   166
  Accidents and diseases   167
  Health and safety policies   167
  Stress   168

Checklist: Health and safety policy   169

Work-related stressors   172

Contents

Chapter 6:
Premises and environmental concerns

Premises and environmental concerns 173

Unincorporated organisations 173

Incorporated organisations 173

Types of property interests 173
Mortgages for freehold and long leasehold properties 173
Leasing premises 174
Holding a licence 175

Finding premises 175
Access for disabled people 176

Deciding about premises 178
Points to check in a lease or licence 178
Is the lease or licence right for you? 181

Signing deeds, including leases and mortgage agreements 181
Unincorporated association and trusts 181
Incorporated organisations 182

Sharing premises 182
Those belonging to another organisation 182
Those belonging to your organisation 183
Co-locating 183
Hiring out parts of premises 184

Planning and building regulations 185
Development 185
Use of buildings and land 185
The appearance of a building 186
Listed property and buildings in conservation areas 186
Tree preservation orders 186
New buildings 186
Obtaining planning permission 186
Building regulations 187

Paying rates 187
Mandatory rate relief 188
Discretionary rate relief 188
Empty rate relief 188

Disposing of premises 188
Requirements of Section 36 of the Charities Act 1993 188
Documentation 189

Equipment leases 190
Types of agreement 190
Hire purchase 190

The green office 191
Legislation 191
Voluntary sector environmental organisations 194
Environmental policy and practice 194

Model deed of appointment 200
Background 200
Agreement 200

Chapter 7:

Insurance 202

General rules 202
The extent of the duty 202
Who should be covered? 202
Incorporated organisations 202
Unincorporated organisations 203
Material facts 203
Exclusions 203
Amount of cover 203
Completing the proposal 204
Liability 204
Making a claim 204

Types of insurance 204
Compulsory insurance 204
Insurance that may be required 205
Discretionary insurance 208

Risk management 210

Further information 210

Chapter 8:

Financial management 211

Legal requirements – accounts 211
Charities 211
Accounting records 212
Annual accounts 213
Audit or examination of accounts 216
Trustees' annual reports 218
Public access to accounts 220

Legal requirements – PAYE 221

Legal requirements – value added tax 221

Contents

Legal requirements – income tax and corporation tax   223
   Charities   223
   Non-charitable organisations   224

Gift Aid   224

Duties of the committee – financial procedures and responsibilities   224
   Specific duties of the treasurer   225
   Financial systems and procedures   226

Budgets and cash flow   228
   The budget process   228

Bank accounts   230

Record keeping   231
   Checking the records   232
   Bank statements and bank reconciliation   232

Charities' reserves   233

Working with auditors or independent examiners   233
   Responsibilities of the auditor or examiner   233
   Appointing an auditor or examiner   235

Chapter 9:

Services and activities   237

Equal opportunities in service delivery   237
   Legal requirements   237
   Working for public authorities   240
   Good practice   240

Contracting to provide services   244
   Types of funding agreements   244
   The contracting process   245
   Should an organisation take on a service?   245
   Liability   248
   Main headings of a contract   248

Handling data and information   249
   Data protection   249
   Electronic marketing   251
   Freedom of information   252
   Copyright   252
   Defamation   253

Activities   254
   Meetings   254
   Processions   255
   Protest and private land   255
   Further information   256
   Loudspeakers   256

Street parties	257
Selling, preparing and storing food	257
Licensing premises	257

Campaigning and political activity | **259**
Trustees' duties	259
Permitted activities	259
Campaigning methods	260
Elections	260
Use of premises	260
Legislation	260
Further information	261

Fundraising | **261**
Regulation	261
Fundraising statements	261
Right to a refund	262
Trading	262
Exempt fundraising events	262
Gift Aid	262
Payroll giving	263
Gifts of shares and securities	263
Collections	263
Sponsored activities	265
Lotteries, raffles and bingo	265
Minibuses and coaches	268

Confidentiality and information sharing | **269**
| Confidentiality policies | 271 |

Human Rights Act | **272**
| Organisations with public functions | 272 |

Chapter 10:

Closing down

	273

Glossary of terms used | 273

Is closure necessary? | **275**
| Cash flow forecast | 275 |
| Balance sheet | 275 |

Planning for survival | **276**
Reducing staff costs	276
Reducing costs of premises	277
Reducing other costs	277
Increasing income	278
Mergers	279
The rescue plan	280

Contents

Winding up   281
   Solvent organisations   281
   Insolvent organisations   283
   Liability for debts   286
   Notification of closure   286
   Record retention   287

Glossary   289

Contacts   291

Index   297

Acknowledgements

The Directory of Social Change acknowledges the huge part that London Voluntary Service Council has played in the history of *Voluntary but not Amateur* and we are very pleased to have the opportunity to publish the eighth edition.

DSC would like to thank Bates Wells & Braithwaite for supplying their legal expertise. In particular: Principal Legal Editor, Sarah Bull; and Legal Editors: Rosamund McCarthy, Malcolm Robson, Alice Faure Walker, Bill Lewis, Siobhan McGoay, and Ben Maitland.

The authors would like to thank the following individuals and organisations for their invaluable input.

Shemle Begum (Liberty) – meetings, processions and protests; **Charity Commission** – trustee indemnity insurance, campaigning, charitable collections; **Chris Chilton** (Pensions Trust) – pensions, **Chris Church** – green office; **Jacky Crowley** (Health @ Work) – health and safety; **Amanda Eastwood** (Community Transport Association) – minibuses and coaches; **Victoria Howse** (Ethical Property Foundation) – premises; **Bill Hyde** (Community Transport Association) – minibuses and coaches; **Alan Lawrie** – service contracts; **Ursula Murray** – equal opportunities and diversity; **Ken Pennykid** (Keegan & Pennykid) – insurance; **Satinder Pujii** (Directory of Social Change) – paying people, **Margaret Sharkey** (London Hazards Centre) – health and safety; **Jill Thornton** (Directory of Social Change) – paying people; **Paul Ticher** – data protection and confidentiality; **Frank Ward** (Community Matters) – licensing and gambling.

About the authors

Ruth Hayes

Ruth is an independent social researcher with particular interests in employment, housing, health, crime and community safety, and in voluntary sector developments. She works across all sectors including central and local government, the private sector, academic institutions, the voluntary sector and charitable trusts.

Jacki Reason

Jacki Reason is a freelance editor and writer with 30 years' experience of the voluntary sector. She is former head of London Voluntary Service Council's Information and Publications Department, writes carers' information packs for local authorities and currently edits *London Age*, for Age Concern London and *Community*, for Community Matters. She has sat on a number of boards of voluntary organisations and is project manager of *Portraits for Posterity*, recording the portraits and stories of Holocaust survivors.

The history of *Voluntary but not Amateur*

As the '8th edition' on the front cover suggests, *Voluntary but not Amateur* (VBNA) has a long history. A glimpse through early editions provides for fascinating reading. The most striking feature is the rapid escalation in VBNA's size. The first edition, published in 1985 in pillar box red, was a mere 68 pages, with text printed in 12 point and with cartoons throughout following the fate of the Crumbly Mansions Community Association as it grappled with the law. Over time the cartoons disappeared and the print size decreased to make way for more text. By the time of the fifth edition in 1998 the book had grown to such a size as to demand an index. The current edition is more than four times the size of the first VBNA.

VBNA's widening girth reflects an expansion in the law. Early editions, for example, covered health and safety legislation on one page, whereas the subject now demands a dedicated chapter; maternity rights were dealt with in a column and paternity rights in a couple of sentences as a matter of good practice. Alongside new legislation came a clutter of acronyms such as SORPS, TUPE, CRB, PUWER and WEEE that now need explaining. The voluntary sector itself played a role in bringing about changes in the law. For example, its activities can no longer be summarised under the 'four heads of charity' described in previous editions, but now require thirteen, and the growth in the social enterprise movement saw the creation of community interest companies.

VBNA also provides advice and information on good practice, again giving an insight into the concerns of the time. Early editions had whole chapters on using computers (including the ambiguous headings: 'Manipulating figures' and 'Choosing a dealer'). They also had a chapter on fundraising – remember the Manpower Services Commission and the Urban Programme? These have been replaced with sections on 21st-century concerns such as contracting to provide services, use of e-mail and internet policies, the green office and developing family-friendly working practices.

VBNA has always been a production with a cast of thousands: on page xiv are listed the many people who have helped us to put together the present edition. But special thanks must go to the London Voluntary Service Council, which dreamt up the idea of VBNA back in the 1980s (when we were both working in the Council's Research and Information Department) and published the first seven editions, before graciously handing the publication over to the Directory for Social Change in 2007. Ultimately, though, VBNA is a tribute to every one of those heroic staff and committee members who over the past 20 years have learned to manage the fast-growing complexity of voluntary sector law and good practice.

Foreword

In the 24 years since the first edition of *Voluntary but not Amateur* was published, both the voluntary sector and wider society have seen extraordinary changes that were unimaginable in 1985. Coincidentally, we were in the midst of recession then and today find ourselves in another, which may well turn out to be even worse. Charities and voluntary organisations will be needed more than ever, but will face a tough climate for fundraising. Also media coverage will undoubtedly be harder to come by as other issues take the front pages.

Faced with the dual problems of escalating demand for services and increasingly stretched income, the sector needs resilience, effective governance and a first-principles approach. One of the strengths of *Voluntary but not Amateur* is that it summarises the processes people need to master when involved in running a voluntary organisation. It captures both best practice scenarios and legal requirements in one comprehensive volume, helping voluntary organisations understand everything from organisation management to employment law, campaigning and fundraising. It provides a back-to-basics resource for those running voluntary and charitable organisations, as well as a comprehensive update of recent legislation.

In 2009, the sector needs to work even more effectively than before, and so it has to be as clear about its role and as focused on its direction as possible. It must ensure its resources go where they will make the most impact, not on unnecessary duplication or ineffective recruitment practices.

We need a robust and well-equipped voluntary sector that will survive the tests ahead. Planning for these is a real challenge in itself, especially for smaller organisations. *Voluntary but not Amateur* is an excellent place for them to start.

I am delighted to welcome this new edition, and hope it will be used even more widely than its predecessors.

Baroness Neuberger DBE

Chapter 1

Before you start – legal structures and charitable status

This chapter examines the advantages and disadvantages of each legal structure open to a voluntary organisation. It then describes which organisations are eligible for charitable status and outlines the restrictions of such status. Reference is made to a number of Charity Commission publications (usually indicated by a CC or RR reference) which, unless otherwise indicated, are available from www.charity-commission.gov.uk or 0845 3000 218 (textphone 0845 3000 219).

Legal structures

The legal structures for a voluntary organisation are:

Unincorporated	Incorporated
Unincorporated association	Charitable incorporated organisation (expected to be available during 2009)
Charitable trust	Company limited by guarantee
	Company limited by shares
	Community interest company
	Industrial and provident society

Any organisation, whatever its size, needs a set of **governing rules** defining what it is set up to achieve and including its internal rules and procedures (outlined in chapter 2). The governing rules are set out in the **governing document**. The precise form of this depends on the legal structure adopted.

Legal structure	Governing document
Unincorporated association	Constitution or rules
Charitable trust	Trust deed, deed of trust or declaration of trust
Charitable incorporated organisation	Constitution
Company limited by guarantee	Memorandum and articles of association
Company limited by shares*	Memorandum and articles of association
Community interest company	Memorandum and articles of association
Industrial and provident society	Rules

A not for profit company may be limited by shares, although this is rare. It is extremely unusual for a company limited by shares to have charitable status.

Throughout the book, we will be using the term 'constitution' to cover all forms of governing document. Constitutions are described in detail in chapter 2.

Most voluntary organisations will be run by a management committee, which can be known by a number of titles, including the following:
- committee
- executive committee
- management committee
- council of management
- board of trustees (most commonly used by charities)
- board of directors (most commonly used by companies).

Unincorporated associations

An unincorporated association is not required by law to seek approval of any kind before setting up, nor does it have to register with any regulatory body unless it is legally charitable (see *Charitable status*, page 11). However, it may still have to register with some bodies before starting to operate: for example, HM Revenue & Customs (HMRC), the local environmental health department, the Commission for Social Care Inspection or Ofsted. An unincorporated association with a small income, which does not intend to employ staff, enter into contracts or acquire property, may need only a set of basic rules. These should state the association's aims, the powers it has to achieve them and its management procedures.

Advantages

An unincorporated association is essentially a membership organisation and can draw up its own democratic constitution setting out the rules by which it will be run. It is quick and cheap to set up: unless you are applying for charitable status no other agency need be involved and there are no fees to pay, unless you take legal advice about the constitution. It is also simple and cheap to run: you do not have to submit accounts (unless the organisation is a charity, or accounts are required by a funder). It can generally be wound up more easily than companies, charitable incorporated organisations (CIOs) or industrial and provident societies (IPSs), provided the constitution allows for this (see chapter 10).

Unincorporated associations can register as charities and gain all the advantages of charity status listed later in this chapter. They must generally register if their objects are charitable and their annual income is over £5,000.

Disadvantages

An unincorporated association has no separate legal existence, and remains for most purposes a collection of individuals. As a result, in most cases:

- it cannot acquire property in its own name; property must be held by individuals or an incorporated body acting on its behalf
- legal proceedings cannot be taken by the association in its own name, but must be taken by individuals representing it
- its activities may be restricted as funders may prefer to donate larger sums to organisations with a more formal structure
- it may find it difficult to borrow money. Many banks and other financial institutions will insist on incorporation before providing loan finance
- individual members of the management committee can be held personally responsible for the association's obligations and debts (see *Liability of committee members*, page 20).

As a charitable unincorporated association develops, its trustees may apply to the Charity Commission to become an **incorporated body of trustees**. If the Commission accepts the application, this overcomes the first two disadvantages listed above, as the charity property is then held in the name of the association and the trustees can enter into contracts or take proceedings in the name of the incorporated body. See *Incorporation of charity trustees* (CC43) for further details. Applications must be made on the form in the application pack *How to apply to the Charity Commission for a Certificate of Incorporation* (CHY 1093), available from www.charity-commission.gov.uk.

Note that becoming an incorporated body of trustees is *not* the same as the unincorporated association converting to an incorporated organisation (known as 'incorporation': see *Changing from unincorporated to incorporated*, page 8). In particular, only incorporation will protect committee members against being personally responsible, in most situations, for the association's liabilities and debts. If liability of management committee members is a concern, you should seriously consider forming an incorporated organisation (see *Minimising the risk of personal liability*, page 20).

The constitution

The Charity Commission and other organisations have devised model constitutions. Alternatively, you could adapt one being used by a similar organisation; see *Models*, page 34.

Charitable trusts

An organisation that has no need for members, is unlikely to employ many staff and wants a simple structure to allow a small number of people to manage money or property for a charitable purpose could consider setting up a trust. However, only those organisations with charitable aims may use this structure and if they meet the requirements for charity registration detailed on pages 11–14 they must register with the Charity Commission.

There are three parties involved in a trust:
- the first, and future, donors of money or property
- the trustees (the Charity Commission usually requires three), who become the nominal owners of the trust property
- the beneficiaries (the people who will benefit from the trust).

As with all voluntary organisations, the trustees must ensure that the property or money is used for the purposes set out in the trust deed (a trust's constitution); as with all charities, the trustees should not generally benefit personally from trust property.

Advantages

Trusts can be set up quickly and cheaply, although you may need legal advice to make sure that the trust is valid. Apart from asking the Charity Commission to approve the trust deed and, in rare cases, paying stamp duty to HMRC, you do not need to involve any other regulatory body (although it may be necessary to register with some bodies once operating). Small trusts are also cheap to administer. If the trust deed has provision for changes, amendments can be made fairly easily but, as with any charity, the Charity Commission may need to approve any alterations to the aims and objectives clauses. Regulation by the Charity Commission gives a trust credibility.

Trustees can acquire and manage property on behalf of the trust, and the trust deed can give trustees powers to raise and borrow money to fulfil the trust's aims.

Disadvantages

Organisations set up as charitable trusts that meet the requirements for charity registration (see page 11) must register as charities and therefore be subject to all the restrictions on registered charities set out later in this chapter.

Trusts are essentially undemocratic. Unlike other legal structures, there is generally no membership structure, although the trust deed can allow for members and elected trustees. Trustees are generally the only people with legal powers to make decisions relating to the trust.

As with unincorporated associations, trusts have no separate legal existence. Property cannot be held in the name of the trust, legal proceedings cannot be taken in its name, and there is a risk that the trustees will be held personally responsible for the trust's obligations and debts (see *Liability of committee members*, page 20). Trustees can apply to the Charity Commission to be incorporated (see page 8), which enables them to hold property, enter into contracts and take court action in the name of the trust. But even if the trustee body becomes incorporated in this way trustees can be personally liable for the trust's debts. In order to avoid this, the trust may want to consider converting into an incorporated body (see *Changing from unincorporated to incorporated*, page 8).

The constitution

The constitution of a charitable trust is called a **trust deed**, **deed of trust** or **declaration of trust**. There are several models available, including *Charitable trusts: model trust deed* (GD2) (from www.charity-commission.gov.uk/registration) and the Charity Law Association's *Trust deed for a charitable trust* (approved by the Charity Commission) available, for a charge, from admin@charitylawassociation.org.uk.

Limited companies

There are two types of limited company. In a company limited by shares members (shareholders) invest money in the hope of gaining a profit; this type of company is generally found in the commercial sector, although some social enterprises may take this legal form.

The second kind is a **company limited by guarantee**. This is appropriate for organisations that aim to pursue some social or political cause. There are no shareholders and any profits are generally reinvested in the company (profits cannot be distributed to the members if the company has charitable status). All members must guarantee to pay a nominal sum (usually £1, and almost always less than £10) if the company is wound up.

A limited company must have a two tier structure: that is, having both members and directors (board or committee members), but these can be the same people.

A limited company with charitable aims must register with the Charity Commission if it meets the requirements listed on pages 11–14.

Advantages

A company is an **incorporated organisation**. This means that it has a distinct legal identity separate from that of its members, and therefore:

- can buy, own and sell property in its own name
- may take or defend legal proceedings in its own name
- can protect individual members of the organisation and, in most circumstances, members of the management committee from personal liability.

The liability of individual members (people with a right to vote at general meetings of the members) and **board members** (also known as **committee members** or **directors**) is

different. As the extent of individual members' personal liability is limited to the amount they agree to guarantee, they are therefore almost totally protected against personal liability in an incorporated organisation.

Under company law the board of directors is responsible for running the company; the directors generally have no personal liability unless they:

- act fraudulently
- are fined for breach of a statutory duty or a criminal offence
- act in breach of trust or duty, or
- continue running the company when they know, or ought to know, that it is or will inevitably become insolvent.

Committee members' liability is discussed further under *Minimising the risk of personal liability*, on page 20. Insolvency is described in chapter 10.

Companies must have a membership, which usually has the power to elect, and always has the power to remove, committee members. The structure works equally well for any size of organisation.

Because a company is incorporated and therefore has a separate legal identity, owning and transferring property is relatively simple. Even when the committee or membership changes, ownership of the property remains in the name of the company, so there is no need for any formal process to transfer ownership.

Although most companies have to use the word 'Limited' as part of their name, the majority of voluntary organisations are exempt from this requirement (see *Name,* in chapter 2).

It may be easier for a company to borrow money, for the lender knows that the organisation, rather than a changing group of individuals, is responsible for repayment. However, banks may still ask for personal guarantees from individual committee members who will then be liable to repay the loan if the company defaults.

Once the memorandum and articles of association (the company's constitution) are agreed, company registration (with the Registrar of Companies) takes eight to ten working days provided there are no complications. The registration fee is small (£20 in 2008/09).

Disadvantages

Companies' activities are regulated by the **Companies Acts 1985 to 2006** and are usually subject to more controls and bureaucracy than other legal structures.

Annual returns and accounts must be submitted to the Registrar of Companies (for which there is a charge: £30 or £15 online in 2008/09). The company must keep registers of members and directors, which must be available for public inspection (see *Setting up registers,* in chapter 2).

Companies have to notify the Registrar of Companies whenever a committee member leaves or a new one is appointed, or a committee member's personal details change. They must also notify the Registrar if they enter into any legal charge (for example, if they borrow money from a bank and the bank has a mortgage over the company's property).

The constitution

The constitution of a limited company consists of two parts:*

■ the **memorandum of association**, which contains the company's aims, the powers it has to pursue them, and the extent of members' liability

■ the **articles of association**, which describe the company's rules, including its procedures for electing the committee members (company directors) and keeping accounts.

*From 1 October 2009, under the **Companies Act 2006**, the memorandum of association of all new companies will mention only the subscribers (that is, the initial members). All other provisions previously set out in the memorandum will be included in the articles of association, so companies will have a single constitutional document. Existing companies will not need to change their constitutions.*

Community interest companies (CICs)

CICs, established by the **Companies (Audit, Investigations and Community Enterprise) Act 2004**, are limited liability companies designed for social enterprises (non-charitable, not for profit organisations pursuing community benefit). A CIC can be a private company limited by guarantee or by shares, or a public limited company. They are regulated by the Regulator of Community Interest Companies.

A CIC is registered as a company in the usual way, but also needs to satisfy a 'community interest test': that is, to show that its activities are being carried out in the interests of the community or wider public and that access to its benefits will not be confined to an unduly restricted group. CICs cannot distribute assets to their members – this is known as an 'asset lock'.

A CIC limited by shares has the option of issuing shares that pay a dividend to investors. The dividend payable will be capped in order to protect the asset lock.

An organisation that is legally charitable (see page 11) cannot register as a CIC, although it can establish CICs as subsidiaries.

Advantages

A CIC is a corporate body and therefore has the same advantages as any other company.

CICs are specifically identified with social enterprise and, for some organisations, may be a more suitable structure than having charitable status.

Unlike charities, CICs can usually pay their board of directors.

Disadvantages

Since a CIC cannot be legally charitable it will not have the benefits of charitable status. CICs are regulated by the CIC Regulator as well as Companies House.

The constitution

A CIC's constitution has the same format as that of a limited company (see page 4), but its memorandum must contain a statement that the company is a community interest company, and the memorandum and articles must comply with the detailed requirements of the CIC regulations.

For further details see www.cicregulator.gov.uk.

Charitable incorporated organisations (CIOs)

The charitable incorporated organisation (CIO) was introduced in the **Charities Act 2006**. Designed specifically for charities, the CIO has the advantages of a corporate structure, but without the complexities of company law. As with limited companies, CIOs will have a two tier structure, with both directors/trustees and members, but again, these can be the same people.

> At the time of writing draft CIO regulations and model constitutions were out for consultation. Where appropriate we have included brief details. The final legislation will be published as the **Charitable Incorporated (General) Regulations**, probably in late 2009.

Advantages

A CIO is an **incorporated organisation**, and therefore has the same advantages of being a legal entity and of having limited liability as a company (see page 4). However, CIOs will enjoy a number of further advantages over a charitable company, including:

- only one regulator (the Charity Commission)
- less onerous accounting regulations
- a single annual return and simpler filing requirements

- simpler requirements relating to the reporting of constitutional and governance changes
- lower costs
- more straightforward arrangements for mergers
- simpler constitutional forms
- greater constitutional flexibility
- an enforcement regime that does not penalise the charity for the misconduct of its directors
- a clear set of duties for charity trustees and members that reflect its charitable nature.

CIOs are charities, and so have all the advantages of charitable status described on page 15.

Disadvantages

CIOs will also have all the restrictions of charitable status described on page 16 and, in some cases, may face more restrictions than other registered charities.

They will be more complicated to set up and run than an unincorporated association, and will have a number of additional requirements, including:

- keeping registers (see *Setting up registers*, in chapter 2)
- submitting accounts and annual returns to the Charity Commission, regardless of income (see *Annual accounts, annual reports and annual returns*, in chapter 2)
- a less flexible form of constitution.

The legal structure is new, and therefore untried. In particular, it will not be possible to rely on company law to answer difficult questions about how to run a CIO.

The constitution

Model constitutions will be available from the Charity Commission. The draft regulations propose two model forms: for an 'association' type of charity (where the members are distinct from the people who run the charity) and for a 'foundation' type of charity (where the charity trustees will be the only members).

For further information about CIOs see www.charitycommission.gov.uk or www.cabinetoffice.gov.uk/third_sector.

Industrial and provident societies (IPSs)

To qualify for registration under the **Industrial and Provident Societies Act 1965** a society must generally have at least three members, carry on an industry, business or trade and be either a cooperative society or a community benefit society.

There is no statutory definition of a **cooperative society**, but the Financial Services Authority (FSA), which regulates IPSs, uses the following criteria:

- members should have a common economic, social or cultural need or interest (a 'community of interest')
- business must be conducted for the members' mutual benefit
- control of the society must lie with all members, be exercised by them equally and should not be based, for example, on how much each member has put into the society
- officers of the society should generally be elected by the members, who may also vote to remove them from office
- where part of the business capital is the common property of the cooperative, members should receive only limited compensation (if any) on any share or loan capital which they subscribe. Interest on share and loan capital must not be at a rate higher than is necessary to obtain and retain enough capital to run the business
- if the rules allow profits to be distributed to members, this must be according to the extent to which they have participated in the business of the society
- there should normally be open membership.

An organisation for the **benefit of the community** (a community benefit society) must usually:

- be run for the benefit of the community, not the members of the society

- have rules forbidding the distribution of its assets among members
- allow all members an equal say in controlling its affairs
- restrict the interest rate paid on its share or loan capital
- have 'special reasons' for registering as an IPS rather than as a company (that is, some concrete advantage or benefit that would be lost or unobtainable if the organisation were a company).

Examples of acceptable special reasons include:

- wanting to operate on the basis of 'one member, one vote'
- practical business reasons (which should be explained)
- being part of a group structure of societies sharing common accounting and/or IT systems.

For further details see the Notes to the FSA's *Mutual societies application form*, available from the small firms section of www.fsa.gov.uk.

Advantages

IPSs are incorporated organisations, which means that they can hold property and take legal action in their own name. Most importantly, committee members are protected from personal liability under contracts and can generally be personally liable only if they act fraudulently or in breach of trust, or continue to run the organisation when they ought to know that it has no reasonable chance of avoiding insolvent liquidation (see chapter 10).

IPSs use a set of rules to register with the FSA. Most societies applying for registration do so through one of the organisations (sponsoring bodies) that has agreed model rules with the FSA and which can support new IPSs through the process. Using model rules limits the chance of mistakes, may reduce the fee payable and can shorten the time taken to register.

Under the **Cooperatives and Community Benefit Societies Act 2003** a community benefit society can implement an asset lock to ensure that assets are only used for community benefit.

Disadvantages

If the organisation does not use model rules, registration can be a lengthy, expensive process (£950 in 2008/09). If a sponsoring body's model rules are used, the fee is reduced (to between £40 and £950, depending on the number of changes made to the model) although the sponsor may charge an additional fee. Registration using model rules should be dealt with in a matter of weeks, but may take longer.

Annual returns and accounts must be submitted to the FSA. Registers of members and officers must be kept and be available for certain members of the public (see *Setting up registers*, in chapter 2). An IPS has to pay the FSA an annual fee (in 2008/09 between £55 and £415) depending on its total assets.

At the time of writing an IPS cannot register with the Charity Commission, even if it is charitable, and therefore will not receive a registered charity number. Some regard this as an advantage as it means less regulation, but some funders can award grants only to registered charities. It is expected that, from October 2009, charitable IPSs that meet the requirements for charity registration (see page 11) will need to register with the Charity Commission, unless they are registered social landlords.

A charitable IPS should submit its constitution to HMRC for recognition as charitable, otherwise it will not be able to claim the tax advantages of charitable status (see page 15) and may have to pay corporation tax. A charitable IPS is eligible for rate relief in the same way as other charities (see page 15).

Provided their rules do not specify an earlier date, IPSs have seven months to submit their annual return after the end of a financial year. This period is shorter than that required for companies.

Further information about IPSs is available from the FSA (see www.fsa.gov.uk/pages/doing/small_firms/msr/societies/index.shtml).

Changing the structure

It is possible to move from one form of legal structure to another as an organisation develops and its needs change. For example, it may start with a steering group and no constitution, merely a set of agreed objectives, and move on to develop a more formal constitution.

Changing from unincorporated to incorporated

In time, your organisation may want to own property, take on staff or enter into long-term contracts and thus consider becoming a company limited by guarantee or a CIO. This is perfectly possible. A new organisation (the company/CIO) will need to be established, the assets and liabilities of the original organisation will be transferred to the company/CIO, and the original organisation is likely to be wound up.

Under **Section 74** of the **Charities Act 1993** (as amended by the **Charities Act 2006**) trustees of an unincorporated charity can transfer the charity's assets to a CIO by resolution, passed by a majority of at least two-thirds of the trustees voting. They must also be satisfied that the transfer to the CIO will further the purposes for which the assets are held and that the objects of the CIO are substantially similar to those of the transferring charity.

The following points need to be considered when making such a change.

Date of transfer: If possible arrange the timing of the transfer on the last date of, or half-way through, the original organisation's financial year so that both organisations have either a full or a six-month period of accounts.

Bank accounts: The company/CIO may need to open new bank accounts, although banks sometimes allow the old account number to be retained. The new committee may therefore have to pass resolutions appointing new cheque signatories.

Officers: Company/CIO officers will need to be elected, following procedures laid down in the governing document.

Contracts of employment: Employees will be affected by the TUPE regulations (see chapter 4). Their contracts of employment will transfer from the original organisation to the new company/CIO. The original organisation must inform the employees prior to the transfer about what is proposed, providing the information specified in chapter 4.

Pensions: If the organisation is a member of a defined benefit multi-employer pension scheme (see *Pensions*, in chapter 4) the transfer will almost certainly trigger obligations under the **Pensions Act 2004** and the Pensions Regulator will need to be informed. This is a complicated area and you should take advice from the Pensions Regulator (www.thepensionsregulator.gov.uk) and, if appropriate, the Charity Commission. For further information see *Defined benefit pension schemes – questions and answers* (from www.charity-commission.gov.uk/ supportingcharities) and *Multi-employer withdrawal arrangements* (from www.thepensionsregulator.gov.uk).

Premises: If the original organisation leases premises, the landlord will need to agree to transfer the lease to the new organisation. If the trustees hold property for the unincorporated organisation, ownership will need to be transferred to the incorporated organisation. In both circumstances it is essential to take legal advice. The rules on disposal of premises are discussed in more detail in chapter 6.

Equipment: On the date of transfer, all equipment owned by the original organisation must be transferred to the company/CIO. One way of dealing with this is for an officer representing the original organisation and a committee member or officer from the company/CIO to sign a single sheet of paper confirming the transfer of all equipment. Check whether a transfer of ownership invalidates any guarantees on the equipment. If so, it may be appropriate to leave them in the name of the committee members of the original organisation until the guarantee has expired, although note that this should be properly documented and may affect other aspects of the transfer, such as the accounts. Where equipment is not owned outright, but is held under a leasing or hire purchase arrangement, check the terms of the arrangement with the leasing or hire company. The company will almost certainly need to be consulted or at least told about the new arrangements.

Insurance: The company/CIO will need new insurance policies. In some situations it may be appropriate for the old insurance policies to be maintained: for example, where property remains with the old organisation for some reason, or where claims under the old policy are a possibility, such as in the case of childcare organisations (where it is possible that someone who was in the care of the organisation when a child will make a claim for abuse when he/she is older). Additional types of insurance may be needed (for further details see chapter 7).

Funding: Funding agreements will have to be transferred to the company/CIO, with the funders' permission. Many funders would want to give their consent before any conversion process is started; you should always seek confirmation that a grant made to the original organisation will continue after the conversion.

Membership: When a new company is set up, the only members will be those people who signed the memorandum and articles of association (constitution). It is likely that when a CIO is set up, the names of the first members must be included in the constitution. One of the first tasks of the new committee will be to ensure that all members from the original organisation are admitted into membership, following the procedures laid down in the articles of association.

Co-options: The first committee members of a limited company (directors) or CIO (trustees) are the people who put themselves forward as the first directors/trustees on the application to Companies House/the Charity Commission for registration (see *Adopting the constitution*, in chapter 2) as part of the process of setting up the company/CIO. Any additional committee members should be elected, appointed or coopted under the provisions in the articles of association/CIO constitution.

Letterheads: The new organisation will need a new letterhead (see *Documentation*, in chapter 2).

Charity number: If the company is registered as a charity it will have to apply for a new charity registration number (see *Registering as a charity*, in chapter 2). As the CIO will be a new legal entity it will have a new registered charity number.

Notifying other agencies: You should let other agencies and organisations with whom you deal, including banks, funders and suppliers, know of the change of legal status.

It is sensible to take legal advice on the transfer. A lawyer can ensure that the assets and liabilities are properly transferred to the company/CIO; there are mechanisms in charity legislation that can help reduce the amount of paperwork required. The trustees of the old organisation may wish for some form of indemnity from the new company/CIO in relation to their liabilities: this is best dealt with formally with legal help.

Action on the transfer date

The following transfers should take place:
- money in bank or building society accounts
- responsibility for outstanding cheques and liabilities
- employees' contracts
- equipment and premises (unless they are to be left in the names of the original committee members).

The original organisation will continue to exist until the final accounts have been prepared and audited (if required, see chapter 8), and submitted to a general meeting if required, and the winding up procedures in the constitution have been followed.

The final meeting

After the transfer date a general meeting of the original organisation may be held to discuss:
- agreement of the audited accounts for the final period up to the date of transfer
- a resolution to wind up the organisation.

Note that in some situations it may not be appropriate to wind up the old organisation: for example, if substantial legacies to the old organisation are expected. The rules on this are complicated and specialist advice may be needed.

Converting a charitable company, an industrial and provident society or a community interest company to a charitable incorporated organisation

This is a relatively straightforward procedure.

The company/IPS/CIC must pass either a special resolution or a unanimous written resolution of the members to convert. It must then send the Charity Commission a copy of:
- the resolution to convert to a CIO
- the proposed constitution
- the resolution adopting the proposed constitution
- plus any other documents prescribed by regulations or requested by the Commission.

The Commission will notify the appropriate registrar.

Where a charitable company converts to a CIO, if the liability of each member is £10 or less, the guarantee is extinguished. If the guarantee is greater than £10, the new constitution must provide for the members to contribute to the assets of the CIO if it is wound up.

If the Charity Commission grants the application, it will:
- enter the CIO in the register of charities

- send the appropriate registrar the resolutions of the converting company/IPS/CIC and the entry in the register relating to the CIO.

Converting an industrial and provident society to a company

An IPS that wishes to convert into a company (either limited by guarantee or a CIC) must pass a special resolution. Under the **Industrial and Provident Societies Act 1965**, the resolution can serve as the memorandum of a company. If the IPS wishes to convert to a CIC the memorandum and articles must comply with CIC legislation.

The **Industrial and Provident Societies Act 2002** sets out the following voting requirements for a special resolution:

- not less than 50% of the qualifying members must vote on the resolution, and
- not less than 75% of those who vote must vote in favour.

The IPS must hold a second meeting to confirm the special resolution not less than 14 days and not more than one month after the first meeting. The resolution to confirm must be passed by the majority of those qualifying members who vote.

For further details see www.fsa.gov.uk/pages/doing/small_firms/msr/societies.

Local authority influence

Companies and IPSs with 20% or more local authority representation on the committee may be subject to additional regulations. These are very complex and you should take legal advice.

Charitable status

Charities in England and Wales are governed by the **Charities Acts 1992, 1993** and **2006**. The Charities Act 2006 received Royal Assent in November 2006 and is being brought into force over several years. The 2006 Act makes many amendments to the **Charities Acts 1992** and **1993** and needs to be read closely with them. At the time of writing the government

had committed to producing a consolidated Act in the 2008/09 parliamentary session.

The government must conduct a review of the Act before November 2011, including its effect on public confidence in charities and the willingness of individuals to volunteer.

A plain English guide to the Act and an implementation plan is available from www.cabinetoffice.gov.uk/third_sector/law_and_regulation.aspx.

> **Note:** The Charities Act 2006 is only applicable in England and Wales. Scottish charities are governed by the **Charities and Trustee Investment (Scotland) Act 2005** and regulated by the Office of the Scottish Charity Regulator (OSCR) (www.oscr.org.uk); Northern Irish charities are governed by the **Charities Act (Northern Ireland) 2008** and regulated by the Charity Commission for Northern Ireland (CCNI). This section therefore only applies to charities in England and Wales (but see *Dual registration*, page 14).

This section describes which organisations in England and Wales have charitable status and which have to register with the Charity Commission under the Charities Acts; it then examines the advantages of being a charity and the restrictions of charitable status.

What is a charity?

To be charitable an organisation must:
- be not for profit
- have exclusively charitable purposes (see page 12)
- operate for the public benefit (see page 14).

A charitable organisation whose gross annual income exceeds £5,000 and is not legally excepted or exempt from registration (see page 12) must register with the Charity Commission, whatever its legal status. At the time of writing if charities under the threshold want to register they need to convince the Commission there are exceptional circumstances that justify registration (see *Registering as a charity* (CC21)). Although the Charities Act 2006 does contain provisions allowing charities under the income threshold to register voluntarily if they wish to, these provisions are unlikely to come into force before late 2009.

Excepted charities

Some charities, including some churches, Scouts and Girl Guides and some armed forces charities, have historically been excepted from registering. Under the 2006 Act such charities whose income is over £100,000 will have to register. At the time of writing these provisions were due to come into force in January 2009, and such charities were likely to be able to register voluntarily from October 2008. In time all currently excepted charities may have to register, although this will not come into force before the Act is reviewed in 2011.

Exempt charities

Some charities are exempt from registering under the **Charities Act 1993** because they are considered to be adequately supervised by, or accountable to, some other public body, such as the FSA or the Housing Corporation. These include charitable IPSs (see page 7), some universities and museums. They are, however, subject to the legal rules generally applicable to charities and some of the provisions of the Charities Acts.

The Charities Act 2006 changes the exempt charity regime in two respects, although these changes are not due to come into force until late 2009. Some charities (or groups of charities) will lose their exempt status, on the grounds that no suitable supervisory body can be identified for them. Charitable IPSs, for example, will lose their exempt status unless they are also registered social landlords. These charities will, at least initially, only need to register with the Charity Commission if their income is over £100,000; as with excepted charities this threshold may come down over time. Some charities and groups of charities

will remain exempt, but the Charity Commission will have wider powers to intervene in their activities.

Charitable purposes

To be a charity an organisation must have exclusively charitable purposes (its objects or aims, which are usually stated in its constitution) and be established for the public benefit (see page 14).

The **Charities Act 2006** introduced 13 charitable purposes. These replaced the previous four heads of charity (relief of poverty, advancement of education, promotion of religion, and other purposes beneficial to the community in a way recognised as charitable). The new purposes are:

1. The prevention or relief of poverty
2. The advancement of education
3. The advancement of religion
4. The advancement of health or the saving of lives
5. The advancement of citizenship or community development
6. The advancement of the arts, culture, heritage or science
7. The advancement of amateur sport
8. The advancement of human rights, conflict resolution or reconciliation or the promotion of religious or racial harmony or equality or diversity
9. The advancement of environmental protection or improvement
10. The relief of those in need by reason of youth, age, ill health, disability, financial hardship or other disadvantage
11. The advancement of animal welfare
12. The promotion of the efficiency of the armed forces of the Crown, or of the efficiency of the police, fire and rescue services or ambulance services
13. Other purposes recognised as charitable and any new charitable purposes which are similar to another charitable purpose.

Examples

Below are examples of the types of charities and charitable purposes that fall within categories 1–11 and 13. For further details and more examples see *Commentary on the descriptions of charitable purposes in the Charities Act 2006*, available at www.charity-commission.gov.uk/spr/corcom1.asp.

1. The prevention or relief of poverty

- Making grants or loans to individuals or organisations that assist particular groups of poor people
- Providing legal, debt management or financial advice.

2. The advancement of education

- Parent teacher associations, playgroups and physical and out-of-school education
- Providing apprenticeships and vocational training opportunities (see *RR3: Charities for the relief of unemployment*)
- Museums (see *RR10: Museums and art galleries*).

3. The advancement of religion

- Advancing a particular religion or supporting religious societies and institutions
- Providing and maintaining places of worship, churchyards and other religious burial places.

4. The advancement of health or the saving of lives

- Providing (conventional and/or complementary, alternative or holistic) medical treatment, care and healing
- Hospital Leagues of Friends or hospital radio
- Medical research
- Promoting healthy living
- Assisting the victims of natural disasters or war
- Providing life saving or self defence classes.

5. The advancement of citizenship or community development

- Promoting civic responsibility, good citizenship and volunteering
- Promoting urban and rural regeneration (see *RR2: Promotion of urban and rural regeneration*)

- Promoting the voluntary sector, the efficiency and effectiveness of charities and the effective use of charitable resources
- The promotion of community capacity building (see *RR5: The promotion of community capacity building*)
- Charities concerned with social investment.

6. The advancement of the arts, culture, heritage or science

- Art galleries and arts festivals (see *RR10: Museums and art galleries*) and local arts societies
- Promoting crafts and craftsmanship
- The preservation of historical traditions, ancient sites, buildings or monuments.

7. The advancement of amateur sport

- Amateur sports clubs
- Multisports centres
- Promoting a particular amateur sport or game.

8. The advancement of human rights, conflict resolution or reconciliation or the promotion of religious or racial harmony or equality and diversity (see *RR12: The promotion of human rights*)

- Promoting human rights, at home or abroad
- Promoting restorative justice and other forms of conflict resolution or reconciliation
- Mediation
- Promoting good relations between persons of different racial groups and equality and diversity
- Enabling people of one faith to understand the religious beliefs of others.

9. The advancement of environmental protection or improvement (see *RR9: Preservation and conservation*)

- The conservation of flora, fauna or the environment generally
- Promoting sustainable development and biodiversity, recycling and sustainable waste management
- Researching the use of renewable energy sources.

10. The relief of those in need, by reason of youth, age, ill health, disability, financial hardship or other disadvantage

- The care, upbringing or establishment in life of children or young people
- Relief of the effects of old age or disability
- Providing housing.

11. The advancement of animal welfare

- Promoting kindness and preventing or suppressing cruelty to animals and animal sanctuaries
- Caring for and rehoming abandoned, mistreated or lost animals.

12. Other purposes currently recognised as charitable and any new charitable purposes which are similar to another charitable purpose (also see *RR1a: Recognising new charitable purposes*)

- Providing facilities for recreation and other leisure time occupation in the interests of social welfare (see *RR4: The Recreational Charities Act 1958*)
- Disaster funds
- Gifts for the benefit of a particular locality
- Promoting mental or moral improvement or the moral or spiritual welfare or improvement of the community
- Promoting the sound administration and development of the law
- Rehabilitating ex-offenders and crime prevention.

Public benefit

As well as being established for one or more of the above purposes, to be charitable an organisation must show that its purposes are for the **public benefit**. The Charities Act 2006 does not define public benefit, but requires the Charity Commission to issue guidance promoting awareness and understanding of the meaning of the term.

Principles

The Charity Commission's general guidance *Charities and public benefit* states that an organisation must show that it meets two key

principles, and that within each principle there are factors that must be considered in all cases:

- **Principle 1**: There must be an identifiable benefit or benefits:
  1a: it must be clear what the benefits are
  1b: the benefits must be related to the aims
  1c: benefits must be balanced against any detriment or harm.
- **Principle 2**: Benefit must be to the public, or a section of the public:
  2a: the beneficiaries must be appropriate to the aims
  2b: where benefit is to a section of the public, the opportunity to benefit must not be unreasonably restricted by geographical or other restrictions, or by ability to pay any fees charged
  2c: people in poverty must not be excluded from the opportunity to benefit
  2d: any private benefits must be incidental.

The law also requires a statement of how the charity has delivered public benefit to be included in the trustees' annual report.

At the time of writing the Commission had published some and was working on other specific guidance for six subsectors: educational charities, religious charities, charities charging fees, charities for the relief of poverty, charities promoting social inclusion and non-religious belief charities, and was consulting on public benefit and the advancement of moral or ethical belief systems.

For further information, and a copy of the guidance, see www.charity-commission.gov.uk/publicbenefit/.

Dual registration

A charity established in England and Wales that carries out certain activities in Scotland or Northern Ireland will need to apply for registration with OSCR/CCNI (**dual registration**). For further details see *Dual registration,* in chapter 2.

Advantages

Tax relief

The main advantages of charitable status relate to taxation. Charities have the following tax advantages:

- **income and corporation tax**: charities do not generally pay income or corporation tax on their profits. Profits earned from trading activities by charities are potentially taxable but can be exempt from tax in some situations, including where:
  - the trade is part of the charity's main function or the work is mainly carried out by the beneficiaries, or
  - the profits fall within the annual turnover limit described on page 16, or
  - the income was generated by a fundraising event which fell within a specific exemption.

In all these cases the profits from the trade must be used solely for the purposes of the charity

- **stamp duty land tax**: charities are exempt from stamp duty land tax on land acquisitions. To claim exemption complete the relevant section of form **SDLT1** (available from 0845 302 1472). For further details see www.hmrc.gov.uk/so or telephone the stamp taxes helpline: 0845 603 0135
- **capital gains tax**: charities do not pay capital gains tax as long as any gain is used for charitable purposes
- **value added tax** (VAT): most trading by charities is subject to normal VAT rules, even if the profits from the trading are exempt from other forms of tax. Charities can, however, take advantage of some special VAT exemptions, including the sale of donated goods, certain supplies to disabled people and certain charity fundraising events. For further details see *Legal requirements – value added tax*, in chapter 8
- **donations**: under Gift Aid (see chapter 9) charities can recover tax on donations from individuals, and companies can reclaim the tax on charitable donations, making charity giving more attractive. A raft of other tax breaks on charitable donations by individuals can also help. For example, outright gifts of shares to charity are not subject to a stamp duty charge and there is no capital gains tax on gifts to charity, and usually no inheritance tax. There are also special reliefs for some gifts of shares and securities.

Rate relief

A charity is entitled to an 80% reduction on the non-domestic rate on any building it uses wholly or mainly for charitable purposes (**mandatory relief**). The local authority has the discretion to waive the remaining 20% (**discretionary relief**). For further details see *Paying rates*, in chapter 6.

Fundraising

Some funders, particularly trusts, have a policy of grant aiding only registered charities. Having charitable status and, in particular, a charity number (which registered charities are automatically given) also provides credibility when raising money from the public.

Advice

Charity Commission Direct (0845 300 218; textphone 0845 3000 219) offers free advice on all aspects of charity law. The Commission's website www.charity-commission.gov.uk includes a wide range of publications and a Knowledge Base, with answers to frequently asked questions.

Small charities

The Charity Commission takes a 'light touch' approach to charities whose annual income is under £20,000, and publishes a number of information sheets specifically for small charities. For further details see www.charity-commission.gov.uk/supportingcharities/sculist.asp.

Restrictions

Campaigning

Charities must not have directly political aims, and are therefore restricted in the nature and extent of their campaigning work. The law does, however, allow some political activity by charities as long as it is directly relevant to their work and does not involve party politics. The Charity Commission's revised guidance *Campaigning and political activities by charities* (CC9), published in March 2008, clarifies the distinction between **non-political campaigning** (raising awareness of issues, mobilising support and ensuring the law is observed) and **political campaigning** (trying to change the law or to change policies of local, national or international governments).

Campaigning is covered in greater detail in chapter 9.

Election meetings

Under the **Representation of the People Act 1983** certain charities may be required to allow election candidates to use their premises free of charge. For further details see *Charities and elections*, available at www.charity-commission.gov.uk/supportingcharities/elect.asp.

Trading

There are some restrictions on a charity's trading activities. The charity must be sure that it has power under its constitution and under charity law to carry out the trading activity. Profits from such activity will be subject to tax unless a special exemption applies.

Activities that are generally permitted by charity law, and are tax free, are:

- selling its services as part of its charitable work (**primary purpose trading**) – for example, by providing educational or community care services, or a charity which is a theatre charging people to see productions
- trading if the trading is ancillary to the charity's primary purpose (**ancillary trading**) – for example, selling food and drink in a theatre restaurant or bar to members of the audience
- selling goods produced by its beneficiaries – for example, items made in a sheltered workshop
- selling donated goods, land, buildings and investments
- running a lottery, provided it complies with all requirements for small or society lotteries (see *Lotteries, raffles and bingo*, in chapter 9)
- organising fundraising events (see *Fundraising*, in chapter 9), although the Charity Commission may be concerned if they pose a significant financial risk to the charity.

A charity may want to run a trading activity connected to its main activities. For example, a shop run by a charitable art gallery or museum may sell a range of goods. Some may be directly related to the gallery or museum – for example, works of art or educational books – but other goods such as mugs or sweatshirts may be sold solely to raise funds. In the latter case, the trading activity is known as **non-primary purpose trading**. A charity may want to run trading activities that are not directly linked to its main activities: this is also non-primary purpose trading. Such trading is only exempt from tax if:

- the total turnover from all trading and other incidental fundraising activities does not exceed the annual turnover limit (see below), **or**
- where the total turnover exceeds the annual turnover limit, there was a reasonable expectation that it would not do so, **and**
- in either case the profits are used for the purposes of the charity.

Annual turnover limit

The annual turnover limit is:

- £5,000, or
- if greater than £5,000, 25% of the charity's total incoming resources, up to a maximum of £50,000. For example, if the charity's total gross income is £160,000, all the turnover from its non-charitable trading will be taxable if it exceeds £40,000 (that is, 25% of £160,000).

Total incoming resources	Maximum permitted turnover
Under £20,000	£5,000
£20,001–£200,000	25%
Above £200,000	£50,000

The charity will need appropriate power in its constitution to carry out non-primary purpose trading. The Charity Commission's advice at the time of writing was that a charity should not carry out such trading if it posed a significant risk to the charity's assets.

If the proposed trading is not permitted by the constitution, is not recommended by the Charity Commission or would attract tax it is advisable to consider setting up a trading company (see below). Note, however, that there are many complications in running a trading subsidiary company alongside a charity, and it is easy to end up with the charity subsidising a non-charitable body, which is in breach of charity law. The exemptions outlined in this section allow a charity to undertake a measure of non-charitable trading without setting up a trading subsidiary.

Charities that are trading by entering into contracts with public bodies to provide services should refer to *Charities and public service delivery – an introduction and overview* (CC37), and see *Contracting to provide services,* in chapter 9.

Using a separate trading company

If a charity wants to trade over and above permitted and tax-free activities, it can set up a separate trading subsidiary. There are several advantages. First, using a trading company means that the trading can be structured tax efficiently. Second, using a trading company can protect the charity from the risks involved in trading. For example, if the trading is carried out by the charity directly and the turnover from the trade is insufficient to meet the costs of carrying on the trade, the difference has to be financed from the charity's assets. If the trading is carried on by a separate trading company, this will usually

bear any losses; if there is a shortfall the trading company may face insolvency but the charity's assets should be protected, provided the trading company has been properly run.

The charity or its trustees will control the subsidiary, which will pay its profits to the parent charity. The most common way of doing this is by regular Gift Aid donation to the charity (see chapter 9); this is also tax efficient. The subsidiary may also need to make interest and capital payments on loans from the parent charity: the latter are not tax deductible.

The parent charity must meet the following requirements:

- its constitution must not include any restrictions on purchasing shares in a private company
- there must be some clear benefits to the charity in having the trading company – a reasonable expectation of profits and income based on proper assessments of risk and income
- the two organisations must have totally separate accounts and, if the same staff work for both, it must be possible to distinguish what they do for each organisation. It must also be possible to distinguish the separate costs of, for example, any shared premises, equipment and stationery
- the charity must not subsidise the trading company; costs for shared staff, premises, equipment etc. must be properly apportioned and the charity must charge the trading company for all resources used by the company (note that there may be VAT implications in these recharges)
- the charity must think carefully before investing funds in the trading subsidiary. The investment can usually be by way of loan or shares and in either case the charity will need constitutional power to make the investment and will need to comply with its duties regarding investing (see *Investments* on page 227). At the very least the trustees should consider business plans, cash flow forecasts, profit projections and other available information in order to satisfy

themselves as to the financial viability of the trading subsidiary. The investment in the trading venture should not be speculative. Any loan should usually be on commercial terms, including a proper rate of interest and repayment terms, and should be secured. Improper investment in a trading subsidiary can affect the charity's tax breaks.

There may be some disadvantages in setting up a trading company, including:

- the possibility of losing rate relief if premises are partly used for non-charitable purposes
- the additional costs and staff time of establishing and operating a trading company
- the additional time involved in running two separate organisations with two separate committees
- the potential conflict of interest between trustees or directors of the two bodies (the Charity Commission recommends that at least one director of each body is independent of the other)
- restrictions on investment in the trading company
- any profit made by the trading company is subject to corporation tax. Generally, most of the profits will be donated to the charity and attract tax relief through Gift Aid (see *Gift aid*, page 224) but any profits retained, including money the trading company uses to invest in its development, are taxable
- arrangements may be needed between the two bodies for the use of land
- the difficulty of apportioning costs between the charity and the trading company
- the potential VAT implications for the charity when it recharges the non-charity for staff time, use of premises, use of equipment, etc.

For further information about all aspects of charity trading, including trading subsidiaries, see *Trustees, trading and business activities* (CC35), from www.charity-commission.gov.uk and *Charities – trading and business activities*, from www.hmrc.gov.uk/charities.

Users on the committee

Many voluntary organisations see user participation as a vital way of ensuring services are relevant and accessible. However, a charity that is considering having its service users on the management committee must take care to ensure there is no conflict of interest.

The Charity Commission advises that user committee members should be excluded from taking any part in decisions directly affecting their interests or those of anyone closely connected to them. For example, in a charity helping people in financial need, a user committee member may need to be excluded from decisions where grants are allocated.

There is no legal bar to all the committee members being users, but as a guide the Charity Commission suggests that users make up no more than a third of the committee.

For further information see *Users on board* (CC24).

Payments to committee members

There are restrictions on the charity paying its committee members (trustees) for anything over and above reasonable out of pocket expenses. Payment to trustees, even for doing specific pieces of work for the charity or renting premises to the charity, is only allowed if it is provided for in the constitution, authorised by the Charity Commission or covered by a new legal provision introduced by the **Charities Act 2006**.

Under this new provision charity trustees, or those connected to them (such as spouses, civil partners, relatives or businesses), may receive remuneration (payment in cash or kind) for providing services to the charity or goods supplied in connection with those services as long as:

- the terms are set out in a written agreement
- the amount is reasonable
- the trustees (exercising reasonable care and skill) are satisfied that the arrangement is in the best interests of the charity (this usually

means that it will save the charity money or provide a better service)

- the number of trustees benefiting form a minority of the charity's trustees
- the constitution does not prohibit the relevant person from receiving payment
- a trustee who stands to benefit takes no part in any decision about the agreement.

This power might be used, for example, to pay a trustee for a piece of research, computer consultancy or graphic design, the use of a trustee's firm for a building job or using a trustee's premises. The power does not cover:

- paying a trustee for carrying out normal trustee duties
- employing a trustee or anyone connected with a trustee on a full or part time contract.

If your constitution prohibits this type of payment, it will have to be amended to make such a payment. However, in many cases you will not need to obtain Charity Commission approval for such a change. Even if there is express prohibition in the constitution, a charity can pay up to £1,000 each year to trustees without reference to the Charity Commission, as long it is happy that the payments are in the best interests of the charity.

Any payments to committee members, whether as an employee or not (see below), may be subject to tax. In some circumstances they may be subject to the rules about the national minimum wage (see *Minimum wage*, in chapter 3), and may affect the committee member's entitlement to state benefits.

Note: A trustee cannot act as auditor to their charity.

For further information see *Trustee expenses and payments* (CC11).

Employees on the committee

If a charity wishes any of its employees to be committee members, the constitution must specifically allow for this. A clause to this effect will need to be negotiated with the Charity Commission. Such clauses are not common, particularly for smaller charities. Even if the

constitution contains the appropriate clause, an employee should only be appointed as a committee member if:

- it is in the interests of the good administration of the charity, and
- the employee is excluded from meetings where terms of employment are discussed.

The number of employee places will generally be restricted, and they must be in the minority.

Even though these restrictions mean that most employees cannot play any formal role in making the most important management decisions, they can still be involved through consultation. Unless prohibited by the organisation's constitution, it is always possible to invite employees to attend and speak (but not vote) at trustee meetings.

Liability for breach of trust

A charity's committee members can be personally liable if any losses result where they have acted in breach of trust. This is discussed further under *Minimising the risk of personal liability*, on page 20.

Publicity and administrative requirements

All charities must make their annual accounts available to any member of the public on request, but can make a reasonable charge. In practice, accounts filed with the Charity Commission, can be obtained from the Commission's website or by contacting the Commission. Charities whose annual income exceeds £10,000* and all CIOs must submit an annual return, their annual accounts and a trustees' annual report to the Charity Commission (see *Annual accounts, annual report and annual returns*, in chapter 2, and *Trustees' annual* reports, in chapter 8). Charities that are not CIOs whose income is below this threshold are asked to complete an annual update, and must inform the Commission of any changes to the details held on the register of charities.

At the time of writing, the Office of the Third Sector had agreed to increase this threshold to £25,000, probably relating to accounting periods starting from 1 April 2009.

Minimising the risk of personal liability

All voluntary organisations will want to protect members and committee members from personal liability for losses. In most organisations there is minimal risk, but where risks do occur organisations should choose the most appropriate legal structure.

Liability of committee members

It is important to understand the following ways in which committee members can become personally liable:

- for breach of trust if the organisation is a charity
- for negligence to service users, staff, or anyone else
- for breach of statutory duties in carrying out the organisation's activities
- under contracts entered into by the organisation.

Where there is no management committee the liability rules below may apply to the organisation's members.

Breach of trust

Committee members of a charity who have acted in breach of trust may be personally required to repay the charity for any losses incurred, whatever the legal structure. This can include where committee members have:

- acted fraudulently (for example, stealing money from the charity)
- gained personal benefit from their role – for example, receiving payment or other benefits not allowed under its constitution and not authorised by the statutory power (see *Payments to committee members*, page 18) or by the Charity Commission
- allowed the charity to carry out an activity not permitted under its constitution or under charity law if this causes loss to the charity. For example, if the charity engaged in political campaigning which was not allowed, committee members might have to

repay to the charity the cost of any publicity material produced
- acted outside the charity's objects, beneficiary group or area of benefit
- been seriously negligent and this has resulted in losses to the charity (for example, by allowing it to engage in some risky venture without taking proper steps to protect its position).

Provided trustees act sensibly and seek advice when necessary from, for example, valuers, solicitors, accountants or the Charity Commission, there should be no reason for them to act in breach of trust. It is particularly important for organisations that operate on the fringe of acceptable charity activity (for example, campaigning), to get advice if they have any doubt about whether the activities are permitted under charity law.

Even if a committee member has acted in breach of trust, the court or the Charity Commission has power to relieve them of personal liability if it is satisfied that they acted reasonably and honestly.

It may also be possible for the charity to obtain trustee indemnity insurance against personal liability for an act taken in breach of trust by an honest mistake (see chapter 7).

Negligence

If an organisation is incorporated, the organisation itself rather than individual committee members would usually be liable for negligence if it is sued for loss, damage or injury arising as a result of an organisation's action or inaction (for example, giving incorrect legal advice). In practice, organisational and personal liability can be avoided in many cases by taking out adequate insurance (public liability and/or professional indemnity insurance), and the committee should take responsibility for arranging this (see chapter 7). If the organisation has employees, it must take out employer's liability insurance.

In unincorporated organisations individual committee members would be liable for negligence. They should have a right of reimbursement out of the organisation's funds, but may be out of pocket themselves if the organisation runs out of funds and there is a shortfall. If the organisation did not have enough resources to meet the claim, it might be forced into insolvency, but if the committee members had acted properly they should be protected from personal liability (see *Insolvent organisations*, in chapter 10).

Breach of statutory duties

Committee members have a number of statutory duties: for example, in relation to employees, health and safety and company law. Failure to perform many of these duties, such as those under the Health and Safety at Work Act or related regulations (see chapter 5) and the submission of company accounts and reports on time (see chapter 8), is an offence that may be punishable by fines or, in some cases, imprisonment.

You can reduce the risk of such offences occurring by ensuring you have access to people – whether committee members, staff, volunteers or professional advisers – who are aware of the full range of obligations, and by having proper procedures and monitoring in place.

Contracts

Voluntary organisations can enter into a number of contracts including:

- employment contracts
- contracts with consultants or freelance workers
- leases on premises
- other leases – for example, for equipment or cars
- contracts to provide services
- opening an account – for example, with a stationery supplier.

Many contracts, especially those relating to leasing premises, vehicles or equipment, contain clauses requiring payment over a number of years. Unless there is provision to terminate the contract or assign (transfer) it, an organisation will continue to be liable to make the payments until the lease has ended.

In an incorporated organisation, the organisation itself will be liable to make the payments even if its funding has ceased. If it cannot meet its obligations, it is wound up and any assets are distributed among the people to whom it owes money (see chapter 10).

For unincorporated organisations there is no such escape, so taking on contracts and leases increases the risk of personal liability for the committee members of such organisations.

An unincorporated organisation must enter into a lease or contract of any kind through:

- named individuals or the whole committee, who will be responsible for making payments under the terms of any contract or lease
- appointing holding trustees or a custodian trustee (for leases or investments) (see *Holding trustees*, in chapter 2); if there are holding trustees this is best done using a trust deed which states that they are entitled to an indemnity from the main body or its committee members
- applying to the Charity Commission, if a charity, to become an incorporated body of trustees (see page 36).

Personal liability can be limited to some extent by:

- ensuring the contract can be terminated on at least reasonable notice if funding runs out
- stating in the contract that it is being entered into by a person in the capacity of a trustee on behalf of the organisation and that the trustee is not to be personally liable for any breach of contract.

Chapter 2

Setting up and running an organisation

This chapter covers the process for getting an organisation up and running once you have decided whether to be charitable and which structure to use.

Throughout the chapter we use 'constitution' to refer to all forms of governing document (see *Legal structures,* in chapter 1, for further details).

Unless otherwise indicated, Charity Commission publications mentioned (usually indicated by a CC reference) are available from www.charity-commission.gov.uk or Charity Commission Direct (0845 3000 218; textphone 0845 3000 219).

Setting up the organisation

Drafting and agreeing the constitution

A constitution sets out the rules for governing an organisation. Some rules are determined by your legal structure and whether you wish to be legally charitable; others will depend on how you want to manage your affairs. A constitution will:

- ensure your organisation's aims are clear and agreed by your members
- provide mechanisms for making decisions and resolving disputes
- ensure accountability
- give you credibility with banks and funders
- allow your organisation to enter into contracts
- clarify liability and lines of responsibility
- allow your organisation, if legally charitable, to register as a charity and gain the benefits of charitable status
- enable holding or custodian trustees to be formally appointed and, if necessary, hold property on trust for an organisation (see chapter 6)

- if you wish, allow you to register your organisation as a company, charitable incorporated organisation (CIO) or an industrial and provident society (IPS)
- help your organisation to affiliate to the local council for voluntary service or other second tier (umbrella) organisation.

Broadly, a constitution has the following sections:

- name of the organisation
- objects and beneficiaries (and area of benefit, if defined)
- powers
- membership
- members' meetings
- the management committee, officers and committee meetings
- keeping accounts
- altering the constitution
- dissolution.

Name

A constitution should start with the name of the organisation. You may wish to include a simple power to change the name.

There are some restrictions on the names a voluntary organisation can use; these vary according to the legal form and whether it is registered as a charity.

A company cannot use a name that is the same as another company's and can also be ordered to change its name if it is too like that of another company. Under new rules introduced in October 2008, a company can also be ordered to change its name if it is the same as or similar to a name which another person is already using (even if that other person is not a company). The person concerned would need to raise a successful objection with the Company Names Adjudicator (see www.ipo.gov.uk/cna). Certain 'sensitive' words cannot be included in a company's name – for example, 'charity', 'foundation' or 'trust' – or can only be used where particular conditions are satisfied (for example, 'charity' can only be used if the company provides a letter of non-objection from the Charity Commission). For further information see *Company names* (GBF2), available from www.companies-house.gov.uk.

An IPS cannot have a name the Financial Services Authority (FSA) considers to be undesirable. This would include cases where the name is similar to that of an existing society, company or charity, or where it would be offensive.

The Charity Commission can require a charity to change its name if it is the same as or too like the name of an existing charity, and in certain other situations, such as where the name is misleading or offensive. The Commission can refuse to register the name of a CIO in similar circumstances.

You can check online whether a proposed name is already in use by contacting Companies House (www.companies-house.gov.uk), the Community Interest Company Regulator (www.cicregulator.gov.uk), the FSA (www.mutuals.fsa.gov.uk) or the Charity Commission (www.charity-commission.gov.uk).

Organisations must also check whether there is a trade mark registration identical with or similar to their company name; if so they risk facing legal action for trade mark infringement – you can check the trade mark register at www.ipo.gov.uk. Even if there is no trade mark registration, it is wise to avoid a name already in use, because there is a risk of having a claim of 'passing off' brought against the organisation; a shared name could also be confusing to potential users.

A company limited by guarantee does not have to use the word 'limited' or the Welsh equivalent 'cyfngedig' at the end of its name if:

- its objects are the promotion of commerce, art, science, education, religion, charity or any profession or anything incidental or conducive to those objects, and

- its memorandum and articles (constitution):
  - require its profits or other income to be used to promote its objects
  - prohibit the payment of dividends to members, and
  - on winding up, require the assets to be transferred to another body with similar objects, or to one whose objects are the promotion of charity.

If a company wants to use this exemption, its solicitor, a director or the company secretary (see page 37) must complete form **30(5)(a)** – a statutory declaration that the company complies with the above requirements. From October 2009 charitable companies will be able to exclude 'limited' or 'cyfngedig' from their name without making a formal declaration.

A CIC's name must end with 'community interest company' or 'CIC', or the Welsh equivalent, 'cwmni buddiant cymunedol' or 'cbc'. An IPS must end its name with 'limited' or 'cyfngedig'. It is possible to apply to the FSA for exemption where the society's objects are wholly charitable or benevolent.

Objects, beneficiaries and area of benefit

The objects define the organisation's main purposes (why it exists and what it hopes to achieve).

Describe **objects** broadly. For example, if you want to run a youth club it is better to describe your objects as promoting services for young people, so that you can take on new activities without changing your constitution.

To register as a charity, all objects in the constitution must be recognised by the Charity Commission as being charitable (see *Charitable purposes*, in chapter 1) and for the public benefit (see *Public benefit*, in chapter 1). Once registered, charitable companies cannot change any of their objects without the Commission's consent. Consent would also usually be required for changes to the objects of an unincorporated charity. The Charity Commission publishes example charitable objects for a range of charitable purposes, available from www.charity-commission.gov.uk/registration.

The clause will give an indication of the charity's **beneficiaries**: that is, the people the organisation serves. In many cases the beneficiaries will be the public at large: for example, everyone may potentially benefit from the work of an environmental organisation. In other cases, the benefits will be focused on a particular group (for example, those living in a certain area) and the constitution can make this clear. Note that for charities, the public benefit of the organisation's work must be made clear, so restrictions on the class of beneficiaries must generally be reasonable and appropriate (see *Public benefit*, in chapter 1).

A range of legislation forbids discrimination in the provision of services on the grounds of sex, marital status, racial group, disability, religion or belief and sexual orientation, but there are circumstances where it is possible to provide exclusive services. For further information see *Equal opportunities in service delivery*, in chapter 9.

> The **Equality Bill 2008**, which at the time of writing was due to be debated in the 2008/09 parliamentary session, proposes to ban age discrimination in the provision of goods, services and facilities.

The objects may also describe the **area of benefit**: the geographic area served – for example, a county, district or parish. When describing your area of benefit, remember that your organisation may grow, so adding 'and the surrounding area' will give some flexibility. It is possible for the area of benefit to be worldwide.

Powers

This clause explains what your organisation is allowed to do to achieve its objectives. It is advisable to include a broad range of powers to allow for growth. These could include: the

power to fundraise, employ and pay staff, recruit volunteers, buy or lease premises and equipment, enter into contracts, work in partnership with other organisations, borrow or raise money, and take out insurance. It is also useful to include the power to delegate decision making. (Under provisions introduced in the **Charities Act 2006**, charities no longer need explicit constitutional power to take out and pay for trustee indemnity insurance.)

Membership

All voluntary organisations, apart from some charitable trusts, will have a membership structure. In legal terms a member is an individual or an organisation who agrees to abide by the terms of the constitution in return for rights given under that constitution: for example, the right to vote at general meetings.

> **CIOs:** A CIO must have one or more members. The draft regulations propose two forms of CIO (foundation and association – see *Models*, page 34). In a foundation CIO the only members are the trustees.

The constitution should include details of:
- who is eligible for membership
- categories of membership where relevant
- how membership is approved and recorded
- membership subscriptions and how they are decided
- members' meetings
- conditions of membership
- members' rights
- the circumstances in which membership ends.

The extent to which these matters are outlined in the constitution will vary. For example, some organisations may include details of the membership categories; in others the committee members will decide the categories, which allows for flexibility as circumstances change.

Note that although most legal forms require a membership structure, organisations may not always want a large membership. Some charities, in particular, choose to restrict their membership to the members of the committee from time to time. This structure is not uncommon for charitable companies. In such cases committee members wear two hats: sometimes their trustee 'hat', and sometimes their members' 'hat' – for example, where constitutional changes need members' approval. If this format is used, it is helpful to provide in the constitution that the only members will be the committee members, rather than having to remember to change the members, following the appropriate procedures, each time the committee members change.

Eligibility: This will depend on the organisation's aims and objectives, key activities and catchment area. Charities that wish to have an open democratic membership might make full membership – that is, with voting rights – open to any individual aged 18 years or over, or any corporate body or unincorporated association interested in furthering the charitable objects. It is important that a charity's members understand that they must exercise their membership rights only in the interests of the charity, and not for any private interest.

Organisations with a defined area of benefit should clarify whether membership is open to people who work in the area as well as those who live there.

Membership categories: There can be two types of membership – voting and non-voting. Voting members must be dealt with in the constitution. It is possible to have more than one category of voting member: the constitution can either set out categories or provide that the committee will establish different categories.

Non-voting members do not have to be referred to in the constitution, although they can be. Although such members can play an important role in supporting the organisation they are not technically 'members' and do not have rights such as being able to attend and vote at the annual general meeting.

Group membership

Organisations as well as individuals can often become members. If an incorporated organisation is a member of another body (if allowed for in its constitution), it will generally exercise its membership rights by appointing a representative (or representatives) to act on its behalf. Unless your constitution states otherwise, organisational members and their representatives will have the same rights and obligations as individual members.

Technically, an unincorporated association cannot be a member of another organisation because it has no separate legal existence, and must appoint a nominee to join on its behalf. The nominee then becomes a member, whose name must appear in the membership register (see *Setting up registers*, page 40). However, many organisations ignore this and will allow an unincorporated association to join in the same way as an incorporated organisation and to appoint a representative to act on its behalf.

CIOs: The draft model constitutions have been prepared on the basis that an unincorporated association could not become a member of a CIO, but as explained in the previous paragraph an individual member could represent an unincorporated body. The draft CIO regulations also propose that if an association CIO (see note on page 28) wishes to have corporate members, the constitution must deal with how they will be represented at members' meetings.

New members

The constitution should describe procedures for applying for membership and approving new members. Many organisations have an application form containing a signed declaration of support for the organisation and an agreement to abide by its rules and values. Some ask for a copy of organisational members' constitutions and annual reports for proof of their eligibility.

Resignation

The procedures for resigning from membership should be described and should include a requirement for resignations to be made in writing.

Terminating membership

This clause could state that individuals would cease to be members upon death, if they resigned, were no longer eligible – for example, because they stopped working or living in the area – or did not pay their subscription.

There should also be a rule setting out grounds for expulsion: for example, by bringing the organisation into general disrepute. The decision making procedures need to be described. One method is for the management committee to propose an expulsion, an appeals committee to review the case, and the final decision to be taken by ordinary members in a general meeting. Whatever method is chosen, there must be a balance between members' rights and the ability of an organisation to protect its reputation. The member concerned should be given an opportunity to state their case, accompanied by an advocate if necessary. The reasons for expulsion should be recorded. If an organisation is thinking of expelling a member, it is advisable to seek legal advice, to ensure that the procedure is conducted properly.

When an individual or organisation ceases to be a member for any reason the list of members must be updated.

Subscriptions

Many organisations have subscriptions or membership fees. Some organisations charge a nominal amount, to cover the administrative costs involved in running a membership organisation; others see subscriptions as a useful way of generating income. It is common to have different membership rates: for example, unwaged people may have free or subsidised membership.

Some constitutions state how the level of subscription is set, how often the amount is reviewed, when fees are to be paid (usually either annually or quarterly), and any arrangements for reduced payments for people joining throughout the year. These matters are generally decided either at the annual general meeting (AGM) or by the management committee.

Another option is to include a clause giving the management committee, or a members' general meeting, the power to decide the rules relating to membership and subscriptions. This allows more flexibility, because the rules can be changed without having to amend the constitution.

However, procedures for dealing with lapsed subscriptions and termination of membership should be included in the constitution.

If a membership subscription is not purely a donation, it may need to be treated as a trading activity for tax purposes (for details see chapter 8). This can be a complex area, so it may be sensible to speak to your accountant.

Conditions of membership

Members of a company limited by guarantee agree to pay a fixed amount (usually £1 or £5) if the company is wound up. IPS members agree to buy a share from the society (usually for £1).

There are no specific requirements for members of unincorporated associations. Some have 'open membership', where the constitution states that anyone fulfilling certain criteria (for example, living on a specific estate or in a particular town) is automatically a member.

Members' rights

In some cases, the rights of members are automatically implied by law. Any non-automatic rights must be included in the constitution. These could include rights to:

- put resolutions to the AGM
- have copies of non-confidential committee meeting minutes

- attend committee meetings as observers
- stand for election to the committee
- nominate candidates to stand in committee elections.

Meetings

There are several types of meetings.

Members' meetings

These are usually called 'general meetings' but may also be described as 'open meetings' and are for all members of the organisation. In small organisations, all the decisions can be made directly by members taking part in general meetings, but this is not always practical. Most organisations elect a management committee to handle the day-to-day running of the organisation (see *The committee, officers and committee meetings*, page 28). Companies must give a minimum of 14 days' notice for members' meetings; the constitution may require a longer period.

> **CIOs:** The draft regulations do not include a minimum notice period for general meetings, but the draft model constitutions provide for a 14 day minimum notice period.

Annual members' meetings: Many organisations, particularly those with large memberships, regard it as good practice to have one formal meeting of all members each year – an **annual general meeting (AGM)**. This is typically the meeting where you deal with the formal business of your organisation, such as:

- approving the minutes of the previous AGM and dealing with matters arising
- receiving the annual report
- receiving the accounts
- electing the committee and officers for the next year
- approving any changes to the constitution
- considering any resolutions put forward
- appointing auditors or independent examiner.

In some cases an AGM is a legal requirement, or may be required by funders. For further details see page 44.

Your constitution could list the contents of the agenda for the AGM. It should state the manner and period of notice, the quorum needed, and the minute-taking and voting procedures. If you want members to be able to submit motions, the constitution should explain where and by when they have to be sent, and how other members will be notified.

The constitution can also allow for other general meetings. There could be a clause allowing for a certain number of general meetings to be held, say three a year. You may also want to permit a specified proportion of members (perhaps one third or a half) to write to the secretary requesting a general meeting. Company law gives a specified proportion of the members rights to demand a general meeting, even if this is not specifically stated in the constitution. As with the AGM, the constitution should specify the manner and notice period, the quorum needed, and voting and minute-taking procedures.

Failing to give notice of members' meetings

It is useful to add a clause stating that accidental failure to give a member notice of a meeting does not invalidate that meeting.

Dispensing with members' meetings

Many constitutions allow for a resolution to be passed in writing, provided a copy of the resolution is signed by all voting members (that is by 100% of those who are entitled to attend and vote at general meetings). Under the **Companies Act 2006** written resolutions can be passed by the members even if this is not specifically stated in the constitution: for ordinary resolutions, approval is required from a simple majority of members entitled to vote; for special resolutions (see page 28), approval is required from a minimum of 75% of members entitled to vote.

Voting procedures

Issues that might be covered in this clause include:

- who may vote at each meeting
- the proportion of votes necessary to agree a motion/resolution – a simple majority or, say, two-thirds
- whether the same voting procedure is used for resolutions and for committee member elections
- whether a motion has to be agreed by a specified proportion of those eligible to vote, or of those actually present
- whether the chair has a normal vote, a casting vote, or both
- whether the members can appoint a proxy – a person entitled to vote on behalf of someone who cannot attend a meeting. If so, there should be a rule requiring written proof of the appointment of a proxy to be sent to your organisation before the meeting so that its validity can be checked
- how a poll can be demanded: a poll involves checking votes against a membership list rather than voting simply on a show of hands. Many constitutions allow members to ask for a secret ballot if they wish.

Note that company law is quite prescriptive about the voting procedures to be used at members' meetings, and not all company law requirements can be overridden in the constitution. Companies should therefore make sure their constitutions dovetail properly with company law. For example, company law prescribes the proportion of votes required for resolutions: there are two types of resolution, an **ordinary resolution**, which requires a simple majority, and a **special resolution**, which requires a 75% majority. Some matters require approval by special resolution: for example, changes to the company's constitution. Company law also provides that members must be able to appoint a proxy. The chair cannot have a casting vote at company members' meetings unless this was allowed for in the company's constitution before 1 October 2007.

CIOs: The draft regulations propose that the following must be included in the constitution:

- the procedure to be followed if members are to be given the power to use proxy or postal votes
- if CIO members have the right to request a poll, details of how the poll is demanded and conducted.

Quorum

A clause should specify the minimum number of voting members needed to take decisions. The number required should not be set too high as this may cause difficulties in arranging meetings that enough people can attend. The procedures for an inquorate meeting (that is, with too few voting members present) should be described. One option is to adjourn the meeting until the same time the following week, at which juncture it would be deemed to be quorate regardless of how many people attended (also see *Management committee meetings*, page 32)

The management committee, officers and committee meetings

Management committee membership

Committees' powers vary, but their key role is to manage an organisation's affairs. The constitution should include clauses on:

- how many people should serve on the committee
- how long someone remains in office: in some organisations the whole committee retires at each AGM but can stand for re-election; other organisations prefer to elect committee members for a two or three year term, or to have a proportion (say, a third) retiring each year on a rolling programme
- who is eligible for committee membership, specifically whether committee members must also be members of the organisation and whether certain people are ineligible.

Note: Committee members of unincorporated charities must be aged 18 or over. IPS members and company directors (committee members) must be aged 16 or over. The

Charity Commission recommends that organisations should carefully consider the number of trustees aged under 18 who are appointed, taking into account the scale, complexity of activities and governance of the organisation, and the range of skills and experience required on the committee. It also advises you to alert parents/guardians of the duties and responsibilities involved before inviting someone aged under 18 to become the director of a charitable company. You should also check whether the company's insurance covers for breach of duty by a director aged under 18.

> **CIOs:** The draft CIO regulations propose a minimum age of 16 for appointment as a trustee.

The following people cannot be committee members of charities:

- those who have been convicted of any offence involving deception or dishonesty, unless the conviction is spent under the Rehabilitation of Offenders Act 1974 (see *Ex-offenders*, in chapter 3)
- undischarged bankrupts* and people who have made formal agreements with creditors under the Insolvency Act 1986
- anyone who has previously been removed from trusteeship of a charity by the court or the Charity Commission
- anyone disqualified from being a company director.*

It is an offence to act as a charity trustee while disqualified unless the Charity Commission has given a waiver under **Section 72(4)** of the **Charities Act 1993**.

These rules also apply to non-charitable companies.

A committee member found to be in one of the above categories should cease to act.

Note: Most organisations working with children or providing care services to vulnerable adults must carry out Criminal Records Bureau checks for their committee members. If an organisation is registering as a charity, the Charity Commission will ask for a declaration that the checks have been made for the current trustees (see *Criminal record checks*, in chapter 4).

Selecting the committee

The constitution should explain how the first management committee will be chosen and how members are to be appointed in successive years.

Election: The most usual way of becoming a committee member is through election by the membership at the AGM or by postal or electronic ballot. Branch organisations may have a two stage process whereby people are elected locally and their names are put to the AGM at which the management committee is chosen.

An organisation wishing to elect its committee at the AGM should explain in the constitution the procedures for:

- nominations – these could be required in advance, for example at least 14 days before the AGM, or nominations could be made at the AGM itself
- informing members about candidates, where relevant – for example, through written notification at least one week before the AGM
- voting – whether by post, electronically or at the meeting, and if at the meeting, whether by secret ballot or by a show of hands. Also, whether different categories of members have different voting rights.

Consider the implications of holding elections through a postal or electronic ballot: the process could take up to two months. If you prefer this approach, the constitution should explain:

- how the ballot is organised
- the procedures and timescales for nominations
- how members are informed about candidates
- the number of votes for each category of member.

Some constitutions do not set out the details of election procedures. Instead, they allow the committee to make rules (which may be called 'standing orders' or 'bylaws') on how elections must be held.

Appointment: You may also wish to allow committee members to be appointed by other organisations: for example, those using your organisation's services. Such members would not have to stand for election unless the constitution states they have to be approved by a general meeting or by the committee.

Co-option: Some constitutions include rules to allow the committee to co-opt additional committee members in order to:

- fill a committee vacancy (sometimes called a 'casual vacancy'); see *Filling vacancies*, below
- introduce specific skills or different perspectives onto the committee – for example, those of service users.

In most cases the management committee chooses co-opted members. Their status may differ from that of full members.

Filling vacancies

The constitution should also describe the procedures for filling committee vacancies if, for example, a member resigns between elections. The options for replacing an elected committee member are generally either a co-option or the holding of another election.

Subcommittees

It is useful to have a clause in the constitution allowing the management committee to appoint subcommittees to deal with specific topics: for example, staff, finance or services delivered. You may wish to allow subcommittees to include people who are not members of the main management committee. Whenever the management committee of a charity delegates to a subcommittee it should be clear about what is being delegated and how the subcommittee will report back on what it is doing. All delegation should be kept under review. It is advisable for the constitution to state that subcommittees must report on their activities to the full management committee.

Note that under charity law committees cannot delegate decision-making to subcommittees, or anyone else, unless they have specific power to do so, so it is useful to include a power to delegate (see *Powers*, page 24).

Holding trustees

An unincorporated association's constitution should allow the appointment of 'holding trustees' or a custodian trustee to make it easier to own or lease property. Since an unincorporated association has no separate legal existence, a lease will usually be granted to named individuals or an incorporated body. As it would be impracticable to have the whole committee named as trustees, the organisation is given the power to appoint a few people or an incorporated body to represent it. Holding trustees can be, but do not have to be, members of the committee.

Holding trustees entering into any form of contract (including an equipment or premises lease) will continue their responsibilities until that lease expires, even if they cease to be committee members or no longer have any involvement with the organisation. If any of these arrangements are likely to be long term, or to involve financial risk, you should consider becoming incorporated (see *Minimising the risk of personal liability*, in chapter 1). This will then enable you to enter into the lease or own the property, without having to appoint holding trustees or a custodian trustee. For further details see chapter 6.

Officers

The constitution will often state the officers needed and who is eligible, and describe how they are to be appointed.

IPSs must have a secretary. Under the **Companies Act 2006** private companies (which includes most voluntary sector companies) no longer need appoint a company secretary. In charities, a paid employee can be the secretary but cannot generally be a member of the committee (see *Employees on the committee*, in chapter 1).

Most organisations appoint a chair. Some may also appoint a committee secretary and treasurer. Some have other officers such as a vice chair and membership secretary. For details about officers' duties see *Checklist: Committee members' roles and responsibilities*, page 57, and *Duties of the treasurer*, in chapter 8.

The constitution should set out the procedures for electing officers. The main options are election by the membership at the AGM or election by the management committee. There may also be clauses specifying how long officers can stay in post and the procedure for filling vacancies.

Sometimes, the constitution allows the committee to decide how much power is delegated to individual officers. In this case the committee could make its own rules (**standing orders**) which set out the powers that have been delegated to subcommittees and officers.

The constitution may also state:

- who is responsible for keeping minutes and preparing and distributing agendas
- that the treasurer is responsible for keeping accounts.

In companies and IPSs the company secretary (if there is one)/secretary has responsibilities laid down by law (see the checklist *Main duties of a company secretary*, page 59). It may be necessary to distinguish in the constitution between the company secretary/secretary and an honorary secretary (for example, a membership or committee secretary).

Terminating the period of office

This clause describes ways in which people can cease to be committee members and officers: for example, when their term of office expires, for non-attendance without good reason (in this case the minimum number of meetings should be defined), or on grounds of misconduct (again the grounds should be

defined). State whether their membership is automatically terminated, or if the committee takes that decision. Also state that if an appointing organisation withdraws its appointee (see *Appointment*, page 30), that person automatically ceases to be a committee member.

Members of a company can remove a committee member by passing a resolution by a simple majority at a general meeting, provided appropriate procedures have been followed.

If a committee member can be dismissed for non-attendance, ensure that:

- regular checks are kept on attendance
- any member nearing the limit is warned
- the committee is informed if someone's limit is reached.

If a committee member can be dismissed on grounds of misconduct, ensure that:

- any proposed resolution conforms with the constitution and that proper notice has been given
- the committee member is informed of the meeting at which the removal is to be considered and is given written details of any allegations
- enough time is allocated at the meeting for the matter to be properly considered and for the committee member to have an opportunity to speak
- the vote on any resolution is counted and recorded in the minutes
- reasons for removal are recorded.

To ensure fairness it may be worth setting up an external appeal system using independent people to consider the case. It is sensible to consult your legal advisers if you wish to remove a committee member.

Powers to suspend

The constitution could include powers to suspend officers or committee members or, at the very least, to require them to leave the committee meeting. To avoid such a power being misused, consider including a provision enabling the officer or committee member to appeal to a general meeting.

Management committee meetings

The constitution or standing orders should state:

- how often the committee should meet. This could be set as a minimum. The Charity Commission would expect the committee members of even the smallest charity to meet at least twice a year
- who is responsible for calling meetings. This is usually the secretary, but it is sensible to give one or two other committee members the power to arrange a meeting if the secretary fails to do so
- the length of notice that must be given. Often this is seven days, but a clause could state that a meeting can be called at shorter notice if a specified number of committee members agree
- that the notice of a meeting must include the venue, date and time, together with the agenda
- the voting procedures. Generally each committee member has one vote, although committee members should not vote on any matter in which their interests conflict with those of the organisation (see *Conflicts of interest*, below). The chair may have a casting vote
- the quorum, and the procedures for an inquorate meeting. The constitution could give an inquorate committee power to meet to co-opt new committee members, or to call a general meeting at which new committee members can be elected.

There could also be a clause saying that certain items cannot be discussed unless members have been given advance notice. If this is the case, include provision for overriding this clause in an emergency.

Written resolutions: A clause could give the committee the power to make decisions without actually meeting, by means of all the members signing a written resolution.

Virtual meetings: The constitution may provide for committee meetings to be held by telephone or video conference, for example, provided all participating can communicate simultaneously with the other participants.

Conflicts of interest: Both charity law and company law require management committee members to avoid situations where there might be a conflict between their personal interests and those of the organisation. This can apply to situations of personal financial interest, and also to circumstances where there might be a conflict of loyalties, such as where an individual is trustee of two charities, one of which is applying to the other for funding.

Whatever the legal form of the organisation, its constitution should include details of procedures to be followed in the event of a conflict. Committee members should declare any potentially conflicting interests when they join the committee and on an ongoing basis: it is useful to keep a register of interests. Committee members should also be asked at the beginning of committee meetings whether they have any new interests. The constitution should generally provide that conflicted committee members must withdraw from any discussions on a matter in which they have an interest (unless invited to take part), withdraw during the vote, have no vote on the matter and not be counted in the quorum for that part of the meeting.

Charity and company constitutions may need to contain specific wording to take account of charity and company law requirements.

See also *Payments to committee members*, in chapter 1.

Minutes: There should be a clause stating that committee meeting minutes must be kept in a proper minute book. The task is generally the responsibility of the secretary. This is a requirement of company law, and is good practice in all cases.

Observers at committee meetings: Some constitutions specify who can attend meetings as observers; alternatively the decision could be left to the discretion of the management committee.

Keeping accounts

All voluntary organisations are advised to keep accounts, and most are legally required to do so. For further information see chapter 8.

The constitution should contain a general statement that all funds raised will be used to further the organisation's aims and objectives. There should be clauses relating to the keeping of up-to-date financial records and the role of the treasurer (if there is one) in making financial reports to the rest of the committee. Other clauses can:

- cover procedures for determining the financial year (there may be legal restrictions on what this can be)
- specify that the management committee can decide the rules relating to signatories on bank accounts
- state that the accounts must be audited or examined in accordance with legal requirements (see chapter 8).

The auditors are generally formally elected at the AGM, although company and IPS law allow for the 'deemed' (assumed) reappointment of auditors from year to year provided certain conditions are met. Auditors have the right to see financial records, the minutes of meetings and bank statements, and may also have the right to be notified of any general meeting.

Under company law the members of a company are able to dismiss auditors, and all organisations should consider including this power. Anyone auditing the accounts of a charity, company or IPS is required by law to be independent of the organisation. Other organisations should specify those who may not act as auditors, including committee members, trustees, employees and their relatives.

Altering the constitution

Generally amendments to the rules of an unincorporated organisation are made at the AGM or a special meeting called for this purpose. The clause should state:

- the amount of notice required to hold the meeting
- how members will be notified of proposed changes
- the majority required for alterations to be carried (usually two thirds or three quarters of those voting or those eligible to vote)
- where relevant, that the Charity Commission must give prior approval for changes in the objects clause and certain other clauses relating to the use of the charity's money or property. The Commission is likely to insist that the constitution contains a clause requiring its written consent before such changes are made.

Guidance on the wording of these clauses can be found in *Choosing and preparing a governing document* (CC22).

The **Companies Act 1985** describes the process for altering a company's constitution (there is no need for this to be specified in the constitution); if the company is also a registered charity some alterations need the Charity Commission's consent. A CIC will need approval from the CIC Regulator for any changes to its objects.

Dissolution

The dissolution or termination clause describes the procedures for winding up an organisation. In unincorporated organisations the power to decide such a move usually rests with members of the organisation at a general meeting. There should be a clause stating the amount of notice the committee must give to the members (usually at least 21 days) and the proportion of membership required to agree dissolution.

The procedures for winding up a company or IPS depend on whether the organisation is solvent or insolvent, and are governed by the **Insolvency Act 1986** (even if the organisation is solvent).

> **CIOs:** The draft regulations propose that the provisions of the Insolvency Act 1986 will also apply to CIOs. The full rules will be in the Charitable Incorporated Organisations (Insolvency and Dissolution) Regulations, which will probably be published in 2009.

The dissolution clause will specify what happens to any assets remaining after the debts have been paid. In general any remaining assets will have to be transferred to an organisation with similar objectives. There is usually a provision forbidding the distribution of assets or property, directly or indirectly, among members; in the case of a charity this restriction **must** apply.

A CIO's constitution must state whether members are liable to contribute to its assets if it is wound up and, if so, up to what amount.

The clause may also state that the committee is responsible for winding up the affairs of the organisation and notifying the relevant agencies.

Models

Model constitutions are available. The Charity Commission has models for organisations wishing to register as charities, either as an unincorporated association (**GD3**) or as a company limited by guarantee (**GD1**). It has also produced a *Model declaration of trust* (**GD2**) for organisations wishing to become charitable trusts. All are available from www.charity-commission.gov.uk. The Commission will advise any charitable organisation on developing a constitution. The Charity Law Association has also produced models for charitable companies, charitable trusts and charitable associations, approved by the Charity Commission, available (for a charge) from admin@charitylawassociation.org.uk. Some large national charities have agreed standard constitutions with the Charity Commission for their branches or affiliates or for specific types of organisation. They are listed on the Charity Commission's website at www.charity-commission.gov.uk/registration.

> **CIOs:** At the time of writing two draft model constitutions for CIOs were proposed: for an association type of charity (where the members are distinct from the people who run the charity) and for a foundation type of charity (where the charity trustees will be the only members). The models will be available from www.charity-commission.gov.uk. Note that CIO constitutions must be in the same form as the models, or as near to that form as circumstances allow.

Models for CICs are available from www.cicregulator.gov.uk. IPSs planning to use a set of model rules can get advice from the sponsoring organisation (see *Industrial and provident societies – advantages*, in chapter 1). The FSA can provide forms and guidance notes on how to register a new IPS as well as general advice on registration.

Inevitably, model constitutions are general and will probably need adapting to meet your specific needs. It is advisable to seek legal advice or advice from a voluntary sector support organisation such as a council for voluntary service when drawing up a constitution.

Adopting the constitution

Unincorporated associations

Once the constitution has been agreed between yourselves (and, if applicable, your solicitor and/or funders) the next step is for those involved formally to adopt the constitution, either by holding a meeting or by the first members signing the document.

Companies limited by guarantee

Under company law it is possible for a private limited company (which includes most voluntary sector companies) to have only one director. However, it is nearly always advisable for voluntary sector companies to have more than one. Under the **Companies Act 2006** private companies no longer need to appoint a company secretary, although they may do so voluntarily (and must do so if required by the articles of association).

To adopt a constitution (the memorandum and articles of association), you must follow these procedures:

- At least one person must sign both the memorandum and the articles of association as the 'subscriber(s)' – that is, the founder member(s) – of the company, in front of a witness, who must also sign.
- The first director(s) must complete and sign form **10**, which also gives details of the company secretary, if there is one, and the company's registered office. If there are more than two directors photocopy page 2 of the form or use form 10 continuation sheets. The subscribers or their agent, who could be the solicitor filing the application on their behalf, must also sign.
- At least one director, the company secretary (if there is one) or the solicitor handling the registration must sign a form **12**, a statutory declaration confirming compliance with company law – this must be done after the other documents have been signed and dated.
- A voluntary sector company using a name which does not include the word 'limited' must complete form **30(5)(a)**.*

All the above must be submitted to the New Companies Department at Companies House, together with two bound and signed copies of the memorandum and articles of association and payment of £20 (in 2008/09), payable to 'The Registrar of Companies'. If the company is being formed electronically different procedures apply: physical signatures are not required. The fee is reduced to £15 for online registration (although the organisation helping to form the company electronically will generally also charge its own fee).

Forms 12 and 30(5)(a) must be witnessed by a commissioner for oaths, notary public, justice of the peace or solicitor, once the memorandum and articles have been completed and signed.

All forms mentioned can be downloaded from www.companieshouse.gov.uk or ordered from 0303 1234 500; minicom 02920 381245.

Provided the correct documentation is submitted and the name is acceptable, the Registrar of Companies will register the company, give it a registered number and send a Certificate of Incorporation to the contact address given on the forms or to the registered office.

Note: the procedures for company formation, particularly the names of the forms required, will change from October 2009. At the time of writing, the details were not known.

Community interest companies

CICs follow the same process as other companies, but must also complete form **CIC 36**, signed by its first directors, which includes a declaration that the company, when formed, will not be an excluded company (that is, politically motivated) and that it will carry out its activities for the benefit of the community, or a section of the community (known as a **community interest statement**). CICs have to pay an additional fee of £15, which Companies House collects on behalf of the CIC Regulator.

Form CIC 36 (and the other company formation forms) and model memoranda and articles of association can be downloaded from www.cicregulator.gov.uk.

Industrial and provident societies

If you are not using model rules, it is advisable to check with the FSA about your proposed rules. Once the rules are agreed in principle and, for a charitable IPS, accepted by HMRC, submit the application using a **Mutual Societies Application Form,** available from the FSA, with the registration fee (which will depend on whether you are using model, adapted or new rules) and two bound and signed copies of the rules.

Charitable trusts

Charitable trusts must carry out the following procedures:

- The first trustees must 'execute' the trust deed: that is, sign it in front of an independent witness (who must also sign against each signature, and give his or her address).
- The trust should check whether the deed must be stamped by HMRC.

Stamp duty

If the deed declares trust over:

- stocks and shares, it should be sent to HMRC's Edinburgh Stamp Office, in case it attracts stamp duty
- an interest in land, it does not require stamping (there is a separate procedure for Stamp Duty Land Tax)
- cash, it will not require stamping.

For further information contact the Stamp Duty Helpline (0845 603 0135).

Charitable incorporated organisations*

Registration will be by application to the Charity Commission using a model constitution. Once the constitution is agreed, you will need to send it to the Commission, together with any other documentation the Commission requires, which is likely to include a registration application form and other documents listed in the form.

The draft CIO guidance states that Charity Commission Direct will either acknowledge the application or ask you for any missing information. Once it has received all the documents, it will send the application to the Registration Unit. The Unit aims to provide an initial response within 15 working days and to decide on an application for registration in an average of 40 days.

Once the Commission has accepted a CIO's application, it will enter the CIO on the Register of Charities and send a copy of the entry to the CIO's principal office; the CIO will become an incorporated body by virtue of that registration.

*At the time of writing the CIO structure was not expected to be available until late 2009. For further information see www.charity-commission.gov.uk.

Registering as a charity

For organisations other than CIOs (including charitable trusts), once the constitution has been formally adopted or the company has been formally incorporated, you need to send the following to Charity Commission Direct:

- the completed application form (**CC5a**) and declaration form (**CC5c**), signed by all the trustees (available from the Commission as part of its registration pack)
- a copy of your constitution
- if a company, a copy of the certificate of incorporation (unless you are unable to register with Companies House until the Charity Commission has consented to the use of the word 'charity' or 'charitable' in the company name)
- evidence that the organisation's gross annual income is over £5,000, which can be a letter pledging funding.

Note: there is no fee for charity registration.

Charity Commission Direct may ask you for missing information. Once it has received all the documents, it will send the application to the Registration Unit. Registration takes an average of eight to twelve weeks.

Once the Commission is satisfied with the constitution, the charity is entered on the Register of Charities and you will be notified of:

- the registration number
- the details recorded on the Register of Charities
- the requirements after registration.

Dual registration

A charity established in England and Wales that carries out certain activities in Scotland, including occupying land or premises in Scotland and carrying out activities in any office, shop or similar premises, will need to apply for registration with the Office of the

Scottish Charity Regulator (OSCR) (**dual registration**). This may mean the charity will need to alter its constitution. The Charity Commission has agreed standard wording with OSCR to enable such charities to register. For further information see www.charity-commission.gov.uk/supportingcharities/oscrguide2.asp. Charities registered with OSCR will need to comply with the rules for Scottish registered charities, which differ in some respects from the Charity Commission's requirements: see www.oscr.org.uk. English and Welsh charities operating in Northern Ireland will also need to register with the Charity Commission for Northern Ireland, which is due to be established in late 2009, but at the time of writing the registration regime in Northern Ireland promises to be more less onerous than registration with OSCR.

The committee

First members and appointing the committee

Unincorporated associations

The first members of an unincorporated association will usually be those people who attended the meeting to agree the constitution and/or signed the constitution. The procedure for admitting new members will have to be used before anyone else can join and is given the right to vote (see *Changes in organisational membership*, page 44).

If a meeting is used to set up the group and agree its constitution, those attending generally elect the first committee members and officers. If the group is set up by signing a constitution it will need to follow the procedures in the constitution for electing a committee and officers, probably by holding a general meeting.

Companies and industrial and provident societies

The initial members are those who signed the memorandum and articles of association (companies) or rules (IPSs). A company must name its first committee members and company secretary (if it has one) in its application for

incorporation (form 10). It may need to follow the procedures in the articles of association to increase the committee membership by cooptions or elections and to appoint other officers. An IPS will have a secretary named in its application for registration and will have to elect a committee in accordance with its rules. A company's directors and members can be the same people.

Charitable incorporated organisations

The initial members (at least one) will be those who are named as such in the constitution. They will typically be those who apply to the Charity Commission for the CIO to be constituted.

A CIO's constitution must state how committee members are appointed and who can stand. A CIO's committee members and members can be the same people.

Trusts

Trusts do not usually have a membership. The first trustees (committee members) are generally named in the trust deed, or in the trustees' declaration CC5c (see *Registering as a charity*, page 36).

Committee members' and officers' roles

Potential committee members and officers should be clear about their roles and responsibilities, which should be agreed at the first committee meeting. It is useful to draw up 'role descriptions' for all committee members: the checklist on pages 57–60 should help (for details of the treasurer's role see *Duties of the treasurer*, in chapter 8). Company directors and charity trustees have particular duties imposed on them by law.

For the rest of this chapter we will use the following terminology:
- **committee:** the body that runs the organisation
- **committee members:** the members of the committee
- **secretary:** the company secretary of a company, the secretary of an IPS and the secretary of any other organisation.

The first committee meeting

The procedures to be followed before, during and after the first committee meeting are outlined in the checklist *The first committee meeting* (page 53).

The agenda should include the following items.

Co-options to the committee

Check whether the constitution gives powers to co-opt others onto the committee and, if so, decide whether to exercise these powers. If an election at a general meeting is the only method of expanding committee membership, it may be necessary to hold such a meeting soon.

Election of officers

The usual options for electing officers (if they have not already been appointed as part of the setting-up process) are:

- by the committee at its first meeting
- by the committee pending an AGM, or
- by members at an AGM.

If the constitution does not allow the committee to appoint officers you will have to wait until the first AGM.

Membership

You may want to expand membership as soon as possible. The constitution should describe the necessary procedures. In some cases only the committee can agree new members, but some constitutions allow the responsibility to be delegated to a subcommittee, individual officers or staff.

Address for administrative purposes

All charities must notify the Charity Commission of their contact address and of any changes to that address. Companies must notify the Registrar of Companies and IPSs must notify the FSA of their first registered office, and of any changes to that address.

The registered address must generally be printed on all correspondence and many other documents.

Companies and IPSs must have their full registered name clearly displayed outside the premises (or in the case of companies, somewhere it can reasonably be seen by a visitor).

Bank accounts

Your constitution may describe the requirements for cheque signatories. Before the first meeting, obtain the necessary bank forms (**bank mandates**); most banks have different forms for different legal structures. The bank will require the committee to pass and minute a standard resolution which includes the decision to appoint cheque signatories. The signatories must sign the necessary paperwork; the person chairing the meeting, and possibly the secretary, will need to sign to confirm the appointment of the signatories.

Registered charities should inform the bank of their charitable status because charities with an annual income above £10,000 and all CIOs, regardless of income, must include their charitable status on their cheques.

Under the **Cooperatives and Community Benefit Societies Act 2003** charitable IPSs whose names do not include 'charity', 'charitable' or the Welsh equivalents must include a statement that they are charitable on their cheques. Under the **Charities Act 2006**, CIOs whose names do not include 'charitable incorporated organisation' or 'CIO' or the Welsh equivalent must include a statement that they are a CIO on their cheques.

In order to avoid fraud and money laundering, banks now have stringent requirements for setting up bank accounts and will request personal information about cheque signatories. They will also need to confirm the identity of the organisation itself (through its constitution, and charity and/or company registration if applicable) and the identities of the main office holders.

Insurance

Chapter 7 describes the insurances that organisations must consider and those that are optional but advisable. It is a good idea to have insurance proposals completed and ready to send off before, or as soon as, the organisation is set up. If this is not possible, insurance must certainly be organised before taking on any responsibilities such as managing premises or recruiting workers or volunteers.

Premises

Organisations planning to take on premises should consider the requirements set out in chapter 6 relating to leasing or owning premises.

Developing organisational policies

There are a number of policies that an organisation should develop, either as a legal requirement or as good practice. These include:

- **Health and safety**: Organisations with employees are legally required to have a health and safety policy and carry out a risk assessment, and these must be in writing if there are five or more employees. It is good practice to have these in writing even if there are no employees, or fewer than five. See chapter 5 for further details.
- **Disciplinary and grievance**: All employers must have disciplinary and grievance procedures. See chapter 3 for further details.
- **Dignity at work**: It is good practice to develop policies that address bullying and harassment at work, see chapter 3.
- **Equal opportunities and diversity**: It is good practice to develop an equal opportunities and diversity policy as soon as possible. This should be followed when making any decisions about services, membership, staff and volunteer recruitment, and committee membership. Equal opportunities and diversity are discussed at the end of this chapter and in chapters 3 and 9.
- **Rules on handling money and petty cash**: see chapter 8.
- **Data protection**: A data protection policy is important, to ensure the organisation complies with the law (see chapter 9).

- **Confidentiality**: It is good practice to have a policy on confidentiality (see chapter 9).
- **Email and internet use**: Although there is no obligation for organisations to develop an email/internet policy for their staff, it is advisable to do so, to avoid risk from inappropriate use (see chapter 4).
- **Environmental**: It is also good practice to develop a policy that ensures the organisation has environmentally friendly policies and procedures. This is discussed further in chapter 6.

The financial year

The constitution may stipulate a financial year; if not, the committee has discretion to do so. Many organisations link their financial year to that of their major funder(s). Companies House must be informed of any change to a company's accounting reference date on form **225** before the end of the period allowed for sending in the accounts. (The form number is due to change in 2009; see www.companieshouse.gov.uk for up-to-date information.)

Auditors/independent examiners

For many voluntary groups it is a statutory requirement to have their accounts audited or independently examined (see chapter 8). Some funders may also require audited accounts. Clarify the requirements before the first committee meeting.

If an auditor is required, make the appointment as soon as possible and certainly before the end of the first financial year.

Delegating powers

Check the constitution to see whether decision making can be delegated. Larger organisations may wish to establish standing orders to delegate powers to a number of subcommittees. Smaller organisations could delegate responsibility to officers or individual committee members. It is particularly important that charity committee members should only delegate decision making where they have constitutional or statutory power to do so. The committee members must be clear about the terms of the delegated authority and the delegation should be kept under review.

Annual general meetings

The constitution may require an AGM to be held before the end of the first financial year, and if so, the first committee meeting may want to consider its timing. It could be combined with a launch and, if required, the election of committee members.

For further details on AGM requirements see page 44.

Appointing staff

In organisations appointing staff the committee should agree:

- an equal opportunities and diversity policy, which includes recruitment, shortlisting and interview procedures
- job particulars
- terms and conditions of employment, and in particular any entitlements which are greater than the statutory minimum (for example, sickness pay, maternity, paternity and adoption leave and pay, parental leave entitlement, annual leave entitlement and redundancy pay)
- disciplinary and grievance procedures.

They must also ensure that a written health and safety policy is in place if five or more people are to be employed. Staff recruitment is covered in chapter 4.

Setting up minute-taking systems

Set up a system for keeping minutes of committee meetings and general meetings. Companies must keep minutes in a form that prevents tampering or forgery (for example, a book or numbered loose leaf pages initialled by the chair); it is good practice for all organisations to do so.

Documentation

A company's full name, registered number, registered office address and place of registration must be shown on all business letters and order forms. If 'limited' is not part of

the company's name its status as a limited company must be included.

Registered charities whose income exceeded £10,000 in the previous financial year must give their status ('Registered charity') on their letterhead, fundraising material and financial stationery such as order forms and invoices. It is useful to include the registration number ('Registered charity number ...'). CIOs must include their name on similar documents, and those whose name does not include 'charitable incorporated organisation' or 'CIO' or the Welsh equivalent must also include a statement that they are a CIO.

Charitable IPSs whose names do not include 'charity', 'charitable' or the Welsh equivalents must declare their charitable status on correspondence and certain other documents.

Companies are not legally obliged to list directors' names on their stationery. However, if they do so they must include the names of **all** directors and must amend the stationery whenever directors change.

All VAT-registered organisations must include their VAT registration number on letterheads and financial documents.

Electronic communications

External emails and other electronic communications sent outside the organisation and websites should include the same information as printed materials. Emails sent within an organisation do not need to contain this information. Under the **Companies Act 2006** companies' emails amounting to business letters or invoices, as well as companies' websites, must include their registered name, number, address, place of registration and, if it is not clear from the name, limited company status.

Setting up registers

Companies and IPSs must keep certain registers (lists), with separate pages for members, committee members and secretaries (if any). Registers can be contained in a simple bound book or kept using some other means, including on a computer, provided they are secure and, where relevant, can be printed out.

Unincorporated associations do not have to keep such registers but it is good practice to do so.

Register of members

Companies and IPSs must have a register of members, and for individual members must include their:

- name and address
- date of joining
- date of resignation or removal (company members' names must stay on the register for at least ten years after this date).

For organisations that are members, the register should list their names and can also include (but does not have to) the name of their representatives. Unincorporated organisations cannot generally be members of a company or IPS, so their representatives become the members, and the names of the organisations they represent can also be included in the register (see *Group membership*, page 25).

The register, or a duplicate, is usually held at the registered office. Companies can, in some circumstances, keep the register elsewhere and if they do, must notify Companies House on form **353** where it is kept. (This can be done online; see www.companieshouse.gov.uk for further details.) The register must be available for public inspection in the case of a company, and more limited inspection in the case of an IPS. If not kept in a bound book it must be in a form that prevents it being falsified.

An IPS's register of members must state the number of shares owned by each member.

Registers of officers and committee members

IPSs must also keep a register of officers' names and addresses, showing when they were appointed.

Companies must have a register of directors (committee members) and a register of company secretaries, if appointed. A company secretary who is also a member of the committee must be entered in both registers.

The register of company directors must contain the following information:

- date of appointment or election
- date of ceasing to be a director
- full name
- any previous name used in the past 20 years or since the director was aged 18 (apart from any change of name on marriage). (From October 2009 the age limit will be reduced to 16, and the requirement will be for names used formerly for business purposes, which could include a name changed on marriage.)
- home address, including post code*
- date of birth
- nationality
- business occupation
- every company the person concerned is, or has been, a director of at any time in the previous five years. If there are no such companies, the register should say so. (This requirement will no longer apply after October 2009.)

The register of company secretaries need include only their name, home address,* former name(s), date of appointment as secretary and date of ceasing to be secretary.

*Under the **Companies (Particulars of Usual Residential Address) (Confidentiality Orders) Regulations 2002** company directors and secretaries can apply to the Secretary of State for permission to keep their private address confidential. This facility is only available to those who can demonstrate actual or potential serious risk of violence or intimidation. For further information telephone Companies House on 0303 1234 500. From 1 October 2009, under the **Companies Act 2006**, the directors' and secretaries' register can include a service address rather than a residential address; this can be the company's registered office. The company must still keep* *a register of directors' residential addresses, but this will not be open to public inspection.*

Similarly, after 1 October 2009, although directors' residential and service addresses will need to be filed with Companies House, only the service addresses will be made public.

CIOs: The draft regulations propose that an association* CIO will need to maintain separate registers of members and trustees and that a foundation* CIO (that is, where the trustees are the only members) will need to keep a single register, with the following information:

Register of members
- Members' names and correspondence address
- Date of joining
- Date of leaving.

Register of trustees – individuals
- Name, former name and correspondence address
- Normal place of residence (that is, country, state or part of the UK)
- Nationality
- Business occupation
- Date of birth.

Register of trustees – body corporate or firm
- Corporate or firm name
- Registered or principal office
- Certain particulars relevant to the form of incorporation.

Where a CIO has a single member this must be stated in the relevant register.

The register(s) must be kept available for inspection either at the CIO's principal office or some other convenient place.

The CIO's members (or trustees in a foundation CIO) and members of the public have the right to inspect the register(s).

*See Models, page 34

Register of charges

This is necessary if a company enters into any charges: for example, taking out a loan that requires security or collateral.

CIOs: The draft regulations propose a requirement for CIOs to keep a register of charges.

Completing the necessary forms

Registration authorities will send most of the forms that have to be completed. But companies will need to get their own supply of forms 288a, 288b and 288c, which must be sent to Companies House whenever a director (committee member) or company secretary is appointed or elected or ceases to hold the position, or there is any change in the details relating to directors or the company secretary. These forms are available free from www.companieshouse.gov.uk or by telephoning 0303 1234 500; minicom 02920 381245. They can be submitted online; see www.companieshouse.gov.uk for further details.

Noting important dates

The secretary and treasurer need to ensure that dates and periods of notice – for example, that needed to notify members of an AGM – stated in the constitution or required by law, and deadlines for submitting charity and/or company forms, are complied with (see *Checklist: Main duties of a company secretary*, page 59).

Auditing accounts

Some organisations need to have their accounts audited or independently examined before their AGM (see *Auditing or examining accounts*, in chapter 8).

Committee elections

In many organisations the management committee is elected at the AGM. Proxies, postal and electronic methods of election can generally only be used if allowed by the constitution.* If elections are carried out using these methods check the timetable laid out in the constitution.

*Under the **Companies Act 2006** company members have the right to appoint a proxy to attend and vote on their behalf at a meeting, even if the company's constitution prohibits proxy voting. The Act also makes some provision for electronic communication.*

Filing accounts

CIOs, other charities whose income is £10,000* or over, companies and IPSs must file their annual accounts, audited if required, with the relevant registrar or registrars. CICs have to file a **community interest report** along with their accounts. The secretary and treasurer need to note the date by which these accounts must be filed. For companies, late submission incurs an automatic fine.

* At the time of writing, the Office of the Third Sector had agreed to increase this threshold to £25,000. This is likely to apply to accounting periods starting from 1 April 2009, but as the changes require secondary legislation, you should check with your accountant or the Charity Commission whether they have come into force.

Running the organisation

Meetings

Notice of meetings

The constitution should set out the notice required for general meetings. This is usually either 14 or 21 days. Some constitutions also specify notice for committee meetings, and the method of giving notice. If the constitution does not specify notice for meetings the committee should adopt standing orders setting out its requirements.

Companies must give at least 14 days' notice of general meetings. Notice of company general meetings must include a statement of the right to appoint proxies and, if a special resolution (see *Voting procedures*, page 28) is proposed, the notice must include the text of

the resolution and the fact that it is proposed as a special resolution.

> **CIOs:** The model association constitution provides for a minimum notice period of 14 days for a general meeting.

Communicating electronically

The **Companies Act 2006** widened companies' powers to use email and their websites to communicate with members. Depending on the type of communication, this requires amendments to the constitution, members' express consent and in some cases both:

- to communicate all documents to a member via email requires individual agreement from the member
- to communicate all documents via the company's website requires either actual consent from the member or **deemed** (assumed) **consent**. Reliance on the deemed consent rules requires either an amendment to the constitution *or* a members' resolution. The company can then ask members for permission to communicate via the website: if they do not reply they can be assumed to have given their consent.

For further details see *ICSA guidance on electronic communication with shareholders 2007*, available from www.icsa.gov.uk.

> **CIOs:** The rules for CIOs are likely to be similar, but the draft regulations propose that if a CIO wants to communicate some or all documents electronically this must be stated in its constitution. The draft model association constitution (see *Models*, page 34) includes wording allowing for electronic communication.

Preparing for the meeting

Some constitutions describe the content of agendas and the rules governing meetings. The following matters need to be clear before any meeting:

- whether the chair has a casting vote in the case of a tie (under the Companies Act 2006 companies cannot give the chair a casting vote at members' meetings unless this was included in the constitution before 1 October 2007)
- who is taking minutes
- whether a subcommittee has the delegated powers to make the required decisions.

Auditors of companies and IPSs must receive notice of all general meetings and are entitled to speak on matters concerning the audit, accounts and other financial matters.

Virtual or electronic meetings

Organisations may wish to conduct meetings by electronic means, whereby participants can both see and hear each other: for example, by using video conferencing or internet video facilities. This could be useful if you need to make an emergency decision, and it may make it easier for some disabled committee members to participate (although it could exclude visually or hearing impaired members). The Charity Commission's view is that a meeting held electronically, where all those present can see and hear each other, is allowed unless there is an express prohibition in the constitution. A meeting held by teleconference, at which all present can hear each other but not see each other, is only permitted if the constitution allows it.

It is not uncommon for trustee meetings to be held in this way, although for charities the Charity Commission recommends that at least one face-to-face meeting be held each year. An organisation would be well advised to think carefully before holding a virtual members' meeting, and to take appropriate advice.

Some constitutions permit resolutions to be passed without holding meetings: for example, by each member or committee member signing a copy of the resolution.

Under the **Companies Act 2006** members' written resolutions no longer require unanimous approval. Ordinary resolutions require approval from a simple majority of members eligible to vote and special resolutions require approval from 75% of members eligible to vote.

If the technology is available and the constitution allows it, written resolutions may be approved by email. The Companies Act 2006 includes provision for written resolutions to be approved by email provided certain conditions are met.

For further details on running meetings see *Charities and meetings* (CC48) and chapter 5 of *Just about managing?*

Annual general meetings

Your constitution may specify some of the content of the AGM (see *Annual members' meetings*, page 27).

Because trusts do not have a membership, there is generally no constitutional requirement to hold an AGM.

Under the **Companies Act 2006** private companies (which include most voluntary sector companies) do not need to hold an AGM unless this is a constitutional requirement. However, funders may expect organisations to hold one, and it is a useful way of communicating with members. Companies must give a minimum of 14 days' notice of an AGM, although the constitution can require a longer period.

> **CIOs:** The draft model constitution for an association CIO (see *Models*, page 34) provides for the first AGM to be held within 18 months of registration, and for subsequent AGMs to be held at intervals of not more than 15 months.

Changes in organisational membership

New members

The constitution should describe the procedures for admitting new members – both individual and, where relevant, organisational (see *Group membership*, page 25). In some cases the committee must make the decision; if so, new membership should be an item on every agenda. If permitted by the constitution it may be possible to delegate the decision to a subcommittee, officers or staff. If so, the committee should pass a resolution to this effect, which should be recorded in the minute book.

In IPSs, members usually pay £1 for their share and receive a share certificate. Other organisations may charge a membership subscription, if permitted in the constitution.

All organisations should have a method of recording acceptance of membership: for example, an application form that includes the statement 'I wish to become a member of ... and agree to abide by its constitution', together with the member's signature. All new members should be given appropriate written material: for example, a copy of the constitution, annual report and equal opportunities and diversity policy.

Your equal opportunities and diversity policy should ensure that any decision to refuse membership is justified and that reasons are recorded.

Terminating membership

Terminating membership is covered on page 26.

Recording changes

Companies, CIOs and IPSs must enter details of membership changes in the register of members (see page 41). Other organisations should keep a record to ensure that all members are invited to the AGM and other general meetings and are given any other privileges of membership.

Changes in committee membership

Procedures for electing or appointing committee members, terminating committee membership and filling vacancies are described in *The committee, officers and committee meetings*, page 28.

Information for new committee members

All new committee members should be given the information they need to carry out their responsibilities: for example, a copy of the constitution, induction pack, role description, annual report and accounts, minutes and papers for the last two or three committee meetings (and the next meeting, if available), and the organisation's main policies (see *Developing organisational policies*, page 39).

Changes in officers

Procedures for changing officers will be set out in the constitution.

Always ensure that the appointment of officers is clearly noted in the minutes of the general or committee meeting at which the appointment took place.

Recording changes

Companies, CIOs and IPSs must update the relevant register (directors and company secretaries – if used – for companies; trustees for CIOs; officers for an IPS) when there is a change (see *Setting up registers*, page 40).

Companies must inform Companies House within 14 days of any changes in committee membership or in committee members' details using form **288a** (new committee members and changes in company secretary), **288b** (resignations) or **288c** (changes in personal details). This can be done online; for further details see www.companieshouse.gov.uk.

Where officers' names appear on an organisation's stationery, ensure that this is amended as necessary. Note that if the name of one company director appears on the stationery, then *all* directors must be included.

The law and good practice on organisational and committee membership are covered in greater detail in chapter 2 of *The voluntary sector legal handbook*.

Moving the administrative office

An organisation changing its administrative office should carry out the following procedure:

■ check whether the constitution includes specific rules about changes of office

■ ensure that the decision is made by a meeting and recorded in the minutes

■ ensure that other organisations have the new address including, in particular, the bank, insurers, funders and the Charity Commission (if relevant)

■ if the change also means that a company's registered office changes, include the new address on stationery and some other documents (see *Documentation*, page 40)

■ if you are a company, submit form **287** to Companies House within 14 days (see www.companieshouse.gov.uk for details of how to submit this online)

■ if you are an IPS, inform the FSA

■ if you are a company or an IPS, ensure that the full registered name is at or outside the new registered office (see *Address for administrative purposes*, page 38).

Annual accounts, annual reports and annual returns

Accounts and reports

Chapter 8 covers the law and good practice on bookkeeping and producing accounts. It also explains when accounts need to be audited or independently examined. This section looks at the role of the committee in managing the annual accounts and audit and producing annual reports.

Accounts of companies and IPSs must be approved and signed by the committee. Under company law, private companies (which include most voluntary organisations) no longer need to present approved accounts to members, although this may be a constitutional requirement and is good practice. In any case, all company members must receive a copy of the accounts (this can be done electronically, with members'

approval; see *Communicating electronically*, page 43). An IPS must send an annual return, which includes financial information, to all its members (see *Annual returns*, page 47).

A company or IPS will therefore need to carry out the following procedure:

■ the organisation's staff and/or treasurer prepare initial accounts

■ the committee and/or staff prepare a report that expands on the accounts, explains the organisation's work during the year and contains information required under company, IPS and/or charity law (the trustees' annual report; see *Trustees' annual reports*, in chapter 8). CICs must also prepare an annual community interest report to show that the organisation is still satisfying the community interest test, and submit it to the CIC Regulator

■ the audit/independent examination, if required, is completed and the auditor/ independent examiner is satisfied that they can give the necessary certificate

■ the auditor/independent examiner presents a draft set of accounts and the report on the accounts to the committee

■ the committee approves the draft and authorises the necessary signatures to the accounts and report as required by company, IPS and/or charity law

■ those authorised sign a copy of the accounts and report

■ signed copies of a company's accounts and report are sent to members with a copy of the auditor's/independent examiner's certificate.

The process will be similar for other types of organisation, but the constitution may require final approval of the accounts to be given by the AGM. In this case the committee would approve the draft and circulate it to members beforehand.

An organisation's first auditor will have been appointed by the committee or at a general meeting or AGM. Companies no longer need to reappoint auditors annually if the members have appointed them, unless required by their constitution or by the members.

In unincorporated charities that require an audit (see chapter 8), the committee should appoint the auditor unless the constitution specifies that this is to be done at a general meeting.

Submitting the accounts and report

Companies must send their annual accounts and report to Companies House within nine months of the end of their financial year (for accounting years starting after 6 April 2008; ten months for accounting years before this date).

IPSs must submit their annual return to the FSA within seven months of the end of the financial year.

Registered charities whose gross income exceeds £10,000* and all CIOs must send their annual accounts and report to the Charity Commission within ten months of the end of the financial year. Smaller charities only need to send them to the Charity Commission on request.

At the time of writing, the Office of the Third Sector had agreed to increase this threshold to £25,000. This is likely to apply to accounting periods starting from 1 April 2009, but as the changes require secondary legislation, you should check with your accountant or the Charity Commission whether they have come into force.

Annual returns

Registered charities whose annual gross income exceeds £10,000 (see note above), all CIOs, IPSs and companies must submit annual returns to the relevant regulatory bodies. Charitable companies must submit separate annual returns to both the Registrar of Companies and the Charity Commission. CICs must also submit a community interest report to the CIC Regulator.

Charities whose income is below the £10,000 threshold (see note above) and which are not CIOs are asked to complete an annual update form and must inform the Charity Commission

of any changes to the details held on the Register of Charities.

The Charity Commission will send the annual return form for completion. Companies House and FSA annual return forms can be downloaded from their respective websites (www.companieshouse.gov.uk; www.fsa.gov.uk). It is then simply a case of following the instructions on the form and submitting it by the deadline. Companies must pay a fee (£30 in 2008/09, or £15 if submitted online).

Changes to the constitution

Many constitutions include procedures for amending clauses. This will often involve a meeting, with a specified amount of notice to be given of any resolution, and a specified majority to vote in favour of an amendment before it can be passed.

Most registered charities must receive the Charity Commission's written consent before considering any amendment to their objects. As soon as any amendment has been passed, you must send a copy of the resolution making the change to the Charity Commission. If there are major changes the Commission will also need a copy of the revised constitution. Unincorporated charities no longer need the Commission's approval for changes to administrative powers and procedures.

Amending a CIO's constitution requires a resolution to be passed by a 75% majority of those voting at a general meeting (including proxy and postal votes, if permitted), or unanimously if passed otherwise than at a general meeting. Certain amendments, including changes to the CIO's objects, require the Charity Commission's approval. Changes do not take effect until they are registered with the Commission.

CIOs: The draft regulations propose giving a CIO the option to restrict the power to amend its constitution – for example, by requiring a higher majority of the vote to pass amendments.

Amending a company's constitution requires 75% of voting members to pass a special resolution. Unless required by the constitution, this need not involve holding a meeting. If the company is a charity, changes to the objects clause, the clauses dealing with the distribution of property on winding up, and the trustee benefits clauses can only be made with prior Charity Commission consent. A copy of the revised constitution must be submitted to the Registrar of Companies within 15 days, with a signed copy of the special resolution which made the change showing the date on which it was passed. If the change required prior consent from the Charity Commission, a copy of the consent must also be submitted to Companies House. Charitable companies must also send the Charity Commission a copy of the revised constitution.

An IPS must register the amendment with the FSA. A special meeting may be needed to amend the constitution.

You may need to inform the bank of any amendment to the constitution; check the original bank mandate for details.

Funders may also need to be informed of any changes; some require that they be informed or even that they should give their consent before any change can be made. Failure to comply with such requirements could put grants at risk.

An organisation changing its name must ensure that the new name is immediately used on all stationery, external emails, websites, cheques and other financial documents and publications. Companies and IPSs must also change the name on their registered office. You will also need to go through the process outlined under *Name*, on page 22, and notify regulatory bodies of your change of name.

Dealing with crises

Emergency decisions

Constitutions may include provision for making decisions outside the normal cycle of committee meeting. The main methods are:

- allowing a committee meeting to be held at short notice at the chair's discretion
- allowing a decision to be made by circulating a copy of a proposed resolution to each committee member and obtaining their signatures
- delegating decision making to a subcommittee or officers
- making a decision by telephone or email.

Note that if the method used is not authorised by the constitution, the decision should be ratified at the next meeting. If this is the case, the method should only be used if the organisation is absolutely certain that the decision will be ratified.

No quorum

Without a quorum (which should be specified in the constitution), a meeting cannot make a decision.

If there are not enough committee members to make a quorum, or the committee membership falls below the minimum specified in the constitution, the committee can usually meet only to call a general meeting or, if permitted under the constitution, co-opt or appoint new members to the committee.

Some constitutions include procedures for dealing with inquorate general meetings: for example, adjourning the meeting to a later date and deeming the reconvened meeting as being quorate however many people turn up, thus enabling decisions to be made.

Misconduct by officers or committee members

If the organisation is not a company the constitution must include specific powers to remove a committee member or officer. Otherwise, a general meeting must be called to amend the constitution so that the committee or the general meeting is given the power to remove the person concerned. However, this approach is likely to cause considerable friction within the organisation and damage its reputation externally.

Under company law, the members can dismiss a director at a general meeting, provided appropriate procedures are observed. There may also be constitutional powers to remove a director.

The accused person must, in all cases, be given an opportunity to present their case at the meeting at which the removal is discussed, and under company law has the right to ask the company to circulate written representations.

In all cases, if the constitution gives the committee the right to appoint signatories, the committee has the authority to stop anyone guilty of misusing funds from signing cheques. The committee also has the power to require the person concerned to return any property belonging to the organisation immediately, and can take legal action to recover this property if required.

Equality and diversity policy

This section starts by outlining the legal context and then examines the components of an equality and diversity policy.

Legal obligations

A wide range of legislation prohibits discrimination, harassment and victimisation of employees and (generally) service users on the grounds of race, colour, nationality, gender (including transgender people), disability, age, sexual orientation and religion or belief.* Part time and fixed term workers are also protected and must be treated no less favourably than other workers.

An organisation will be liable if an employee discriminates against a colleague or user, and may be responsible for paying compensation or damages to the victim, unless it can show it

has taken reasonable practical steps to prevent discrimination by, for example, having and implementing appropriate policies and training. There is also a duty to protect workers from sexual harassment by service users.

The Equality Bill 2008 will contain powers to outlaw unjustifiable age discrimination by those providing goods, facilities and services and carrying out public functions. The government is considering whether to include powers to extend the current protection for workers who are harassed by a client because of their sex to protection from such harassment on all other grounds. (At the time of writing the Bill was due to be debated in the 2008/09 parliamentary session.)

Employment legislation is explained within *Discrimination* in chapter 3, and in chapter 4; chapter 9 describes the law and good practice in relation to service delivery.

The policy

Although it is not required by law, organisations should develop a policy to state their position on equality and diversity, which should be accompanied by procedures for implementation and monitoring. Such a policy will help you:

- comply with the law
- show staff, volunteers and users that you are committed to fairness
- improve employment practices and services
- ensure that all those involved in the organisation understand their rights and responsibilities as regards equality and diversity, and the procedures for dealing with any breach of the policy
- attract, develop and retain high quality staff, volunteers and committee members
- obtain grants and service contracts; most public agencies now require a policy as a condition of grant aid or contracts.

It is important to understand the concepts involved in developing a policy. Briefly, equal opportunities or equality means eliminating discrimination by giving groups of people the same rights when accessing, for example, employment, pay and conditions, training and services. These rights are enshrined in legislation outlined in chapters 3 and 9.

With diversity comes an appreciation that individuals from different backgrounds can make a positive contribution through their varied experiences and ideas.

Developing the policy

Avoid simply adopting another organisation's policy. The process of policy development provides important learning opportunities:

- examining your processes, practices and services will help you develop tailor-made activities to bring about change
- gathering information will help you to measure your success in implementing the policy
- involving staff and their representatives, volunteers, the committee and, where relevant, users will ensure that everyone's skills and experiences are included as well as increasing their commitment.

There is no standard format for a policy but you should think about including the following components:

- a declaration of intent
- the scope of the policy
- overall aims
- objectives and action plan
- implementation procedures
- monitoring and review processes
- reference to supporting policies.

Declaration of intent

This is a public statement that you are committed to promoting equality and diversity and will take steps to challenge unfair discrimination and harassment. The statement could also acknowledge that you value the unique contribution each person brings to your organisation through their experience, knowledge and skills.

The statement is usually included in publications, on websites and other written material, and incorporated into job advertisements.

Scope of the policy

This will define whom you wish to target. As well as meeting the legal requirements to include race, colour, nationality, gender (including transgender people), disability, age, sexual orientation and religion or belief, you may wish to include other categories – such as social class – or target other groups such as carers.

This section can also define who within the organisation is covered by the policy: for example, all paid staff, volunteers, trainees and self-employed people as well as members and affiliated organisations.

Overall aims

These could include:

- achieving equality and diversity as an employer, service provider and purchaser of services/goods and in relations with other organisations
- all staff and volunteers achieving their full potential in an environment promoting dignity and mutual respect
- treating all staff fairly and equally in relation to pay and other benefits, recruitment, promotion, transfer, training, dismissal and redundancy.

Objectives and action plan

For example:

- all staff, committee members and, where relevant, volunteers and trainees, to receive training on equality and diversity. Anyone involved in recruitment or promotion decisions to be trained in non-discriminatory recruitment and selection techniques
- all workers to have access to support. For example, if certain workers, such as women, black or minority ethnic workers, lesbian or gay workers, disabled workers or those of different faiths want to set up a support group, this will be encouraged
- the composition of the organisation's committee and membership to reflect the community served

- employment at all levels of the organisation to reflect the community served, likewise the volunteer profile
- premises and equipment to be accessible to staff, volunteers, the committee and users
- measures of positive action to be taken where appropriate
- policies, procedures and services to be regularly reviewed to ensure they remain relevant
- equality and diversity to be advocated (for example, by requiring all members to have, or be developing, their own policy)
- an equality and diversity dimension to be introduced into all areas of work, recruitment and service provision, and into service procurement
- services to be developed through consultation with users and potential users, information on services to be widely available, and systems to be developed to assess service delivery and consumer satisfaction.

The objectives should include clear and measurable targets with a realistic timetable, and state who has overall responsibility for the policy and for each action.

Implementation procedures

Final responsibility for implementing the policy lies with the committee as a whole, but day-to-day management is usually delegated to a named committee member and a senior member of staff, whose duties will include:

- ensuring the policy is communicated so that everyone – including staff, members, committee members, officers, volunteers, self-employed workers, trainees and users – knows the standards of conduct expected and what to do if discrimination occurs
- identifying staff and committee members' equality and diversity training needs including, for example, recruitment practices and changes in legislation
- involving staff representatives at all stages
- monitoring the policy
- ensuring that other policies and procedures are regularly reviewed

- handling harassment, bullying and discrimination complaints
- reporting to the committee and membership on progress in implementing the policy.

You must ensure that those responsible are given enough time to perform these duties effectively and possess the appropriate authority, including:

- the ability to report directly to the committee
- powers to launch an investigation into a complaint of discrimination, bullying or harassment (which should be carried out by more than one person)
- powers to examine written materials (but bear in mind confidentiality issues)
- a budget to carry out this work.

Monitoring and review

Equality and diversity policies should be continually monitored, to measure their effectiveness and to highlight areas that need to be revised. It is good practice to develop a monitoring policy to manage data collection. The policy should be specific to the needs of your organisation and outline:

- the rationale for monitoring
- who is responsible for monitoring
- data to be collected and analysed
- how the data will be used.

The policy should state that any breach of confidentiality in respect of monitoring data will be a disciplinary offence.

Monitoring involves collecting statistical information, and should cover the composition of your:

- job applicants (advertising, applications, shortlisting and selection)
- the workforce (including promotion, training and use of disciplinary and grievance procedures)
- volunteers
- membership
- the committee, subcommittees and working groups
- service users.

See chapters 3 and 9 for information about monitoring employees and service users, and *Data protection*, in chapter 9, for the legal requirements on handling data.

Reference to supporting policies

Equality and diversity policies generally refer to supporting policies and procedures. These could include:

- staff recruitment (see chapter 4)
- staff training and support
- conditions of service, including pay and benefits and redundancy (see chapters 3 and 4)
- grievance and disciplinary policy and procedures (see chapter 3)
- dignity at work policy (see chapter 3)
- employment of disabled people and physical access (see chapter 3)
- working arrangements; for example, carers' policy or work–life balance policy (see chapter 3).

Checklist:

The first committee meeting

Before the meeting

- [ ] set up the necessary registers
- [ ] set up a system for keeping minutes of committee meetings and general meetings
- [ ] organise safe storage for:
  - the original of the constitution
  - copies of documents submitted to regulatory bodies
  - registers
  - minute books, including meeting papers
  - financial records
  - signed copies of annual accounts and reports
  - legal documents such as leases, employment contracts and insurance policies
- [ ] check the constitution for procedures to elect officers and committee members, and for rules on cheque signatories
- [ ] draft role descriptions for officers and committee members
- [ ] obtain bank mandate forms and identify the documentation required by the bank
- [ ] consider what insurances are necessary and obtain quotes and proposal forms
- [ ] where relevant, obtain the information the committee needs to make decisions about entering into licences or leases for premises
- [ ] where relevant, invite organisations entitled to appoint or nominate committee members to put forward appointees or nominees
- [ ] check the constitution for:
  - the committee's powers to co-opt additional members
  - rules on admitting new members
  - rules about delegation to subcommittees, officers or staff
- [ ] check funders' requirements regarding year end
- [ ] check constitutional, legal and funders' requirements regarding the audit/inspection of accounts
- [ ] draft stationery, ensuring that it complies with legal requirements.

At the meeting

Ensure that decisions are formally made and minuted about:

- [ ] cheque signatories
- [ ] insurance policies
- [ ] delegating authority for completing and signing insurance proposal forms
- [ ] staff recruitment

☐ taking on premises

☐ delegating responsibility to subcommittees and/or officers (where relevant)

☐ developing the organisation's policies and procedures

☐ registration with regulators – for example, HMRC or the Information Commissioner.

After the meeting

☐ update the necessary registers

☐ order stationery

☐ obtain the necessary signatures on the bank mandate and any additional information the bank requires from signatories (if not done at the meeting)

☐ enter into the minute book the requirements for the bank resolutions and sign the bank mandate to confirm that this has been done

☐ return forms to the bank to set up account(s)

☐ obtain and file the necessary insurance policies, ensuring copies of proposal forms are made and kept

☐ ensure that everyone involved with the organisation is made aware of their responsibilities, including the organisation's policies

☐ if a company, complete and send the following forms to Companies House, as appropriate: **288a** new committee members; **288b** committee resignations; **288c** changes in committee members' personal details; **225** any change in the accounting reference date; **353** if the register of members is to be kept somewhere other than at the registered office

☐ keep a record of all decisions to delegate authority.

Checklist:

Annual general meetings

Note that private companies (which include most voluntary organisations) no longer need to hold an AGM unless their constitution requires it, although some may choose to do so.

Before the meeting

☐ check the timescale within which the AGM must be held (see page 44), ensure that correct notice is given of the AGM and that notices are sent in accordance with the constitution

☐ where relevant, follow the necessary procedures in relation to the auditing/ examination of accounts (see *The auditing or examining process*, in chapter 8)

☐ check the constitution for any agenda requirements

☐ check the rules on elections and prepare the necessary material

☐ ensure the auditor/examiner is informed of the meeting

☐ if a company, ensure that there is a sufficient supply of form **288a** to be completed at the AGM by new committee members.

At the meeting

☐ ensure that resolutions are passed and, if required under the constitution, that the accounts and the committee's report are received and/or approved

☐ ensure that elections are held

☐ ensure that minutes are kept.

After the meeting

☐ ensure that a company's new committee members complete and sign form **288a,** and that form **288b** is completed for committee members who are no longer serving, then send the forms to Companies House

☐ submit financial documents to the appropriate regulatory bodies (see *Submitting the accounts and report*, page 47) and ensure that copies are available for inspection by all members in line with the constitution and, in the case of a company or an IPS, at the registered office

☐ update the appropriate registers

☐ ensure that the minutes are written up

☐ carry out induction procedures for new committee members (existing committee members may also find this useful).

Checklist:

Electing committee members

Some constitutions detail the election procedures. If there are no requirements, the committee should agree the format (see *Selecting the committee*, page 29).

Before the meeting

Check:

☐ the categories of elected committee members

☐ who can vote for which categories

☐ nomination procedures, including timescales.

Circulate (as appropriate):

☐ requests for nominations, with instructions

☐ information about nominees, if this is being sent out before the meeting

☐ proxy, electronic or postal ballot papers, if allowed under the constitution. Under the **Companies Act 2006** company members have the right to appoint a proxy to attend and vote on their behalf at a meeting, even if the company's constitution prohibits proxy voting.

Prepare (as appropriate):

☐ ballot papers

☐ a list of those entitled to vote for each category of member

☐ the agenda structured in such a way that vote counting can take place without interrupting the flow of the meeting.

At the meeting

Ensure (as appropriate) that:

☐ ballot papers are given to those entitled to vote, with an explanation of the voting procedure (including who can vote for which categories of member)

☐ people not running for election are available to count votes

☐ results are announced, and recorded in the minutes

☐ the necessary information relating to new members is completed for the register of committee members, and that companies complete form **288a** (appointments) and form **288b** (resignations).

Checklist:

Committee members' roles and responsibilities

Duties of all committee members

Committee members have overall responsibility for the organisation's strategic direction, and for ensuring that it meets its legal duties, remains solvent and well run, and delivers the outcomes for which it was set up.

The main duties and tasks are outlined below. For further details see *Good governance. A code for the voluntary and community sector*, available from www.ncvo-vol.org.uk/ publications.

Legal duties

- [ ] ensuring that the organisation meets its objectives, complies with the rules set out in its constitution and acts legally in all its activities (taking advice when necessary)

- [ ] providing proper accounts of the organisation's activities to its members, funders and regulatory bodies (as appropriate)

- [ ] ensuring that the organisation's resources and assets are well managed and used to pursue its objects

- [ ] keeping up to date with the organisation's activities

- [ ] keeping abreast of, and complying with, legislation that may affect the organisation's work and direction

- [ ] ensuring that the organisation has effective health and safety policies and procedures and that they are effectively monitored

- [ ] ensuring that the necessary insurance policies are taken out and periodically reviewed

- [ ] ensuring that the organisation meets all its contractual and other obligations

- [ ] regularly attending committee meetings and working jointly with other members.

Managerial tasks

- [ ] setting policy and short, medium and long-term objectives

- [ ] identifying, discussing and agreeing new areas of work

- [ ] ensuring that there are systems for regularly monitoring and evaluating the organisation's work

- [ ] being a good employer

- [ ] supervising and supporting senior staff and ensuring that other employees and volunteers are properly supervised and supported

- [ ] ensuring that the organisation's policies and procedures are implemented and monitored

- [ ] promoting the organisation.

Main duties of the chair

The tasks of a chair can be divided into four key areas, some of which could be delegated to a vice chair.

Planning and running the organisation's meetings

These include the AGM, any other members' meetings and committee meetings.

Planning meetings includes:

☐ ensuring that the organisation holds the meetings required by its constitution

☐ helping to plan agendas, checking the minutes of previous meetings and ensuring that these and any background papers are distributed beforehand

☐ being briefed about each agenda item

☐ ensuring that outstanding matters are followed up.

Running meetings involves:

☐ ensuring that the meeting is quorate

☐ obtaining agreement to, and then signing, the minutes of the previous meeting

☐ making sure that all agenda items are discussed

☐ ensuring that all participants who wish to do so have the opportunity to make a contribution, or in large meetings deciding who speaks

☐ fairly summarising issues and options before a decision is taken

☐ making sure that voting procedures are complied with

☐ clarifying decisions.

Dealing with matters relating to the membership, other officers and users

This involves:

☐ ensuring that members' rights as stated in the constitution are met

☐ helping to deal with disciplinary action against members and other officers

☐ helping to deal with disputes between members, users and the organisation.

Supervising senior staff

The chair is often responsible for supervising and supporting the work of the senior member of staff, although this may be done by another committee member.

Helping with the management of the organisation

This involves:

☐ making decisions and taking action between committee meetings (taking **chair's action**) if permitted by the constitution or authorised by the committee

☐ helping to deal with any staff problems

☐   assisting with staff recruitment.

Other duties

The chair often acts as a spokesperson, which could include:

☐   representing the organisation at external events

☐   liaising with the press on behalf of the organisation (this could be delegated to a press officer)

☐   taking an active role in fundraising campaigns.

Main duties of a company secretary

Unless stated in the constitution, private companies (which include most voluntary organisations) no longer need a company secretary. However, the duties outlined below must still be carried out. If the constitution allows, some may be delegated to paid staff, volunteers, a solicitor or others. A member of staff (or anyone else with the necessary knowledge) can be the company secretary.

Note: In this section we refer to 'directors', which are a company's committee members.

The company secretary will normally undertake the following:

☐   maintaining and updating the registers (see page 40)

☐   ensuring the company files statutory information promptly, including accounts, annual returns (form **363**); change of directors, secretaries and their details (forms **288a/b/c**); change of registered office (form **287**); and change of accounting reference date (form **225**)

☐   providing members, directors and auditors (where required) with notice of meetings

☐   providing members and auditors with proposed written resolutions

☐   sending copies of resolutions to Companies House

☐   supplying a copy of the accounts to members and others entitled to receive notice of general meetings

☐   keeping, or arranging for the keeping, of copies of all members' resolutions passed otherwise than at general meetings, and of minutes of all meetings

☐   ensuring that people entitled to do so can inspect company records

☐   the custody and use of the company seal (if used). If the company has a seal, it is good practice to keep a sealing register (a list of documents on which the company seal has been used).

For further details see *Directors and secretaries* (GBA1), available from the 'guidance booklets' section of www.companies-house.gov.uk.

Main duties of a committee secretary

Many organisations, both incorporated and unincorporated, have an elected committee secretary. If there is no secretary, the relevant tasks can be undertaken by committee members or staff.

Companies

In a company the elected secretary might help the company secretary (if there is one) prepare for and administer meetings and assist with other administration (see above).

Unincorporated associations

In unincorporated associations, the secretary often takes on responsibilities similar to those of the company secretary (see above), specifically in relation to meetings, maintaining lists of members' and committee members' names and addresses, and ensuring annual reports and accounts are submitted to the relevant agencies.

Preparing for meetings

This involves:

- [ ] sending notices of all meetings to members, within the time required by the constitution or by law

- [ ] making arrangements for meetings

- [ ] in consultation with the chair, preparing the agenda and distributing it with any background papers

- [ ] checking that members have carried out tasks agreed at the previous meeting.

Helping in meetings

This involves:

- [ ] making sure that the minutes of the previous meeting are agreed, and signed by the chair

- [ ] taking and producing minutes of the meetings: recording the names of those attending and apologies, major decisions, any votes taken and agreed further action.

Other administration

This could involve:

- [ ] dealing with incoming correspondence and keeping records of outgoing correspondence

- [ ] keeping records of membership subscriptions

- [ ] ensuring members are provided with the organisation's constitution, annual report and policies.

Chapter 3

Employees' and workers' rights

Employing people brings new responsibilities, and before taking these on you must be aware of your legal obligations and your employees' rights. First, it is important to understand that different types of people providing work have different rights. These are explained below.

The definitions

The following definitions are used throughout this chapter and in chapter 4.

Employees and workers

The precise definition of 'employee' and 'worker' differs slightly across employment legislation, but in general the following descriptions apply:

- **employee**: someone who works under the terms of a contract of employment, including many of those working on short-term contracts, whether written, agreed orally or implied by the nature of the relationship. Employees enjoy all of the employment rights described below
- **worker**: someone who agrees to do the work themselves (that is, they cannot subcontract the work), whether under a contract of employment or any other contract, and where your organisation is not simply a client or customer of their business. So someone who has their own business (for example, a person who runs a catering business providing sandwiches at your AGM) will not count as a worker. However, someone being paid to make sandwiches for the AGM when they do not run a catering business would be a worker. 'Workers' can include agency workers, casuals and some freelances, but generally excludes someone who is genuinely running their own business as a self-employed person (see *Self-employed people*, page 62). Workers have some, but not all, employment rights.

All employees are workers, but not all workers are employees.

Further information about many of the employees' and workers' rights described in this chapter is available on the Department for Business, Enterprise and Regulatory Reform's (BERR) website www.berr.gov.uk.

Volunteers

There are several definitions of volunteering, but most centre around the carrying out of unpaid work for the benefit of others. As long as volunteers receive only reimbursement for genuine and documented out of pocket expenses, and only the training necessary for their work, they are unlikely to be employees or workers.

But those who work within what can be described as a 'contractual' relationship may become entitled to employment or workers' rights and could, for example, qualify for the national minimum wage (See *Minimum wage*, page 68). The following could define a contractual relationship:

- payment for anything other than expenses
- training or perks which are not necessary for the person's work
- if volunteers have little control over the rules governing their work – for example, the hours they are expected to work
- if the organisation is obliged to provide work and the volunteer is obliged to do that work – that is, 'mutuality of obligation'.

For further details on the legal status of volunteers see *Volunteers and the law*, published by Volunteering England, available from www.volunteering.org.uk or the Volunteering England Infoline (0800 028 3304).

Organisations have a duty of care towards their volunteers, and must meet their responsibilities under the **Health and Safety at Work Act 1974** (see chapter 5). Volunteers should be insured under either employers' or public liability cover, and their actions covered by public liability insurance and/or professional indemnity insurance (see chapter 7).

Although volunteers are not covered by the same discrimination legislation as employees and workers, your equal opportunities and diversity policy (see chapter 2) should cover volunteer recruitment and management and include procedures for dealing with complaints of discrimination, harassment or bullying. Points to consider when recruiting volunteers are discussed under *Taking on volunteers*, in chapter 4.

Agency staff

Agency staff are placed to work for an organisation for a limited period. There is usually a contract between the agency and the organisation, as well as one between the agency and the individual. In these situations, the organisation is unlikely to be the employer.

Under legislation to implement the **EU Agency Workers Directive** in the UK, which is expected to come into effect in 2009, agency workers who have been in a job for 12 weeks will be entitled to equal treatment. This has been defined to mean at least the basic working and employment conditions (for example, pay and holidays) that would apply if the worker had been recruited directly by the employer to do the same job. It will not cover occupational social security schemes (for example, sickness benefit and pension schemes).

Agency workers are protected against discrimination through equality legislation (see *Discrimination*, page 71). They also have the right to receive the national minimum wage (see *Minimum wage,* page 68), enjoy the same rights as employees under the Working Time Regulations (see page 69) and part-timers' rights (see page 82), and have the right to join a union.

Seconded staff

Seconded staff are employed by one organisation and loaned to another for a limited period. There should be a written agreement between the seconding employer, the host organisation and the secondee,

clarifying the terms of the secondment, in particular whether the seconding organisation remains the employer.

It is unlawful for the host organisation to discriminate against secondees under equality legislation (see *Discrimination*, page 71), and the host organisation owes them a responsibility under the Health and Safety at Work Act 1974 (see chapter 5).

Self-employed people

People are generally defined as self-employed if they run their own business and bear the responsibility for the success or failure of that business. To qualify for self-employed status, people have to meet a number of criteria relating to their working practices, including: the ability to choose the work taken and where and when to do that work; providing their own work equipment; the agreement of a fixed price for the job, regardless of how long it takes; and having a number of clients at the same time. Self-employed people are registered as such with HM Revenue & Customs (HMRC), and pay their own tax and national insurance. They are responsible for their own public liability insurance (and professional indemnity insurance if they provide a professional service, see chapter 7). They are not entitled to employment rights or to workers' rights (except rights in relation to whistle-blowing; see *Public interest disclosure*, page 102).

For suggestions about the content of a self-employed person's contract see *Taking on freelance and self-employed workers and consultants*, in chapter 4.

If you treat people as self-employed when they should be treated as employees, HMRC PAYE and National Insurance Contributions Offices can demand tax and national insurance payments even if these have not been deducted from the fees paid to the individual. There may also be penalties for and interest due on late payment. It is also possible that someone on a self-employed contract may subsequently claim that they are an employee and be entitled to employment rights such as paid holidays and unfair dismissal. It is therefore advisable to check with your PAYE office before assuming someone is self-employed.

If you are employing consultants supplied through another organisation such as a company, that organisation is responsible for paying their tax and national insurance. Unlike self-employed people, workers supplied by another organisation are protected under equality legislation against discrimination by the host organisation (see *Discrimination*, page 71).

Trainees

Whether trainees have employees' rights depends on the circumstances. Those placed by colleges, and who are not paid by the host organisation, are not usually classified as employees or workers and therefore have no rights associated with employment. Those placed for longer periods or who are paid may acquire employment or workers' rights. Always clarify whether trainees are to be treated as employees. In all cases the host organisation has responsibilities to trainees under the Health and Safety at Work Act 1974 (see chapter 5).

There are special responsibilities owed to trainees aged under 18 in health and safety legislation, to compensate for their lack of experience or lower awareness of risks (see *The management of health and safety at work*, in chapter 5).

Trainees who are not employees will not be covered by employers' liability insurance if they are injured owing to the employer's negligence or failure to comply with health and safety law. It is therefore essential to ensure that your public liability insurance covers any trainees working for your organisation (see chapter 7).

Below we outline employment rights for workers (which includes employees) and additional rights for employees only.

Employment rights: a summary

All employees (see page 61) have rights during employment: those given by statute (**statutory rights**) and those acquired through their contract of employment (**contractual rights**). Some rights apply to all employees as soon as they start work; others depend upon length of service and continuity of employment. Continuity of employment, or continuous service, means how long a person has worked for the same employer, even if the job has changed. In some cases work with a previous employer also counts towards continuity.

Workers' rights

When someone applies for a job

Everyone has the right not to be discriminated against because of their race, sex, age, disability (unless this is objectively justified; see page 78), sexuality, gender reassignment status, religion or belief or trade union membership.

As soon as someone starts work

All workers, from their first day at work, have a number of rights.

Pay
- an itemised pay statement showing how much they earn and any deductions (see *Paying people*, in chapter 4)
- the national minimum wage, and not to be dismissed because they qualify for the national minimum wage or because they have sought to enforce their right to do so (see *Minimum wage*, page 68)
- protection from unauthorised deductions made from wages (see *Paying people*, in chapter 4).

Annual leave and working hours

(see *Working Time Regulations*, page 69).

- twenty-four, or from 1 April 2009, 28 days' paid annual leave if working full time or pro rota if part time
- rest breaks and maximum working hours per week and, if night workers, access to health checks.

Protection from discrimination

(see *Discrimination*, page 71)

- equal pay and conditions for work of equal value
- not to be discriminated against on grounds of race, including colour, nationality or ethnic or national origins
- not to be discriminated against on grounds of sex, pregnancy, marital status or past, current or future actions in relation to gender reassignment
- not to be discriminated against on grounds of disability
- not to be discriminated against on grounds of age
- not to be discriminated against on grounds of sexual orientation, including orientation towards someone of the same sex (lesbian/gay), opposite sex (heterosexual) or both sexes (bisexual)
- not to be discriminated against on grounds of religion or belief
- not to be discriminated against on grounds of part-time working or fixed-term status (unless objectively justifiable)
- not to be discriminated against on the grounds of refusing to opt out of a 48-hour week.

Trade union activity

(see *Unions*, page 97)

- in organisations employing 21 or more people, to have a union recognised by the employer if desired by the majority of the workforce
- union membership (in almost all cases) and to take part in union activities
- not to belong to a union
- not to be victimised or unfairly dismissed on grounds of union membership or activities

- not to be discriminated against at work or when applying for a job through an employer keeping a record of trade union members
- reasonable paid time off to carry out duties and undergo relevant training as an official of a recognised union or as an employee representative
- reasonable time off to perform duties as a union learning representative
- reasonable time off (which need not be paid) for activities of a recognised union.

Protection from dismissal and victimisation

- not to be dismissed or victimised on grounds of race, sex, sexuality, age, religion or belief or disability (see *Discrimination*, page 71)
- not to be dismissed in breach of their contract
- not to suffer a detriment or be dismissed after 'blowing the whistle' on illegal or dangerous activities carried out by their employer (see *Public interest disclosure*, page 102).

Other rights

- to be accompanied by a colleague or trade union official during disciplinary or grievance hearings (see *Disciplinary and grievance policy and procedures*, page 95)
- to compensation if they become ill or injured during the course of employment as a result of the employer's negligence (see *Legislation*, in chapter 5).

Additional rights for employees

As soon as someone starts work

Time off (apart from union activity)

- reasonable time off with pay to perform functions as a safety representative (in organisations with five or more staff) (see *Safety representatives,* in chapter 5)
- reasonable time off (which need not be paid) for public activities (see *Time off for public duties*, page 71)

■ if aged 16 or 17, for those who have yet to gain a certain educational or training standard, to reasonable paid time off to study or train for a qualification to help them achieve that standard. Certain employees aged 18 have the right to complete training already begun (**Employment Rights Act 1996** amended by the **Teaching and Higher Education Act 1996**) (see *Time off for study or training – young people*, page 71).

Protection from dismissal and victimisation

■ not to be dismissed during the first 12 weeks of lawfully organised industrial action (**Employment Relations Act 1999**)

■ not to be dismissed for activities relating to being a representative for consultation about redundancy or business transfer (see *Redundancy*, page 102)

■ not to be dismissed for participating in the election of an employee representative (see *Redundancy*, page 102)

■ not to be victimised or dismissed on grounds of activities as a safety representative, for making a complaint about a health and safety matter or for taking steps to protect themselves or leaving a place where they reasonably believe they are in danger (see *Safety representatives*, in chapter 5)

■ not to be victimised or dismissed because they have asserted a statutory right (that is, they have required the employer to comply with statutory obligations) (**Employment Rights Act 1996**).

Family responsibilities

■ to reasonable unpaid time off to deal with unexpected or sudden emergencies relating to dependants. A 'dependant' would include a partner, parent, child and others who live with the employee who reasonably rely on the employee for assistance (see *Dependants' leave*, page 89)

■ female employees are also entitled to:
 – paid time off for antenatal care (see *Maternity*, page 84)
 – 52 weeks' maternity leave (see *Maternity*, page 84)
 – the right to return to the same job on the same pay and conditions after maternity leave (see *Maternity*, page 84)
 – the right not to be unfairly dismissed for any reason connected with their pregnancy (see *Maternity*, page 84)
 – the right to a written statement of the reasons for dismissal if they are dismissed at any time while they are pregnant or on statutory maternity leave (see *Right not to be dismissed*, page 85).

Other rights

■ to work in a healthy, safe environment (see *General duties under the HSW Act*, in chapter 5)

■ to statutory sick pay after they have been off sick for four days in a row and are earning more than the national insurance lower earnings limit (LEL). There are some exceptions; see *Sick pay and leave*, in chapter 4.

After one calendar month

■ one week's minimum notice of dismissal (**Employment Rights Act 1996**)

■ pay during medical suspension (**Health and Safety at Work Act 1974**)

■ wages if laid off (**Employment Rights Act 1996**)

■ a statement of terms of employment particulars (see page 66). The employer has two months in which to issue a statement (**Employment Rights Act 1996**).

After 26 weeks

■ thirty-nine weeks' statutory higher rate maternity pay (see *Maternity, paternity and adoption pay*, in chapter 4) if earning more than the national insurance LEL

■ the option of one week's or two consecutive weeks' paternity leave and, if earning more than the LEL, statutory paternity pay (see *Paternity*, page 86, and

Maternity, paternity and adoption pay, in chapter 4)

- forty-two weeks' adoption leave and, if earning more than the LEL, statutory adoption pay (see *Adoption*, page 87, and *Maternity, paternity and adoption pay*, in chapter 4). The right to a written statement of the reasons for dismissal if dismissed at any time during adoption leave (see *Right not to be dismissed*, page 85)
- parents of children aged under 16 (or 18 if disabled) and carers of an adult relative can make a written request for more flexible working arrangements (see *Flexible ways of working*, page 92).

After one year

- not to be dismissed for an unfair reason or through an unfair procedure (note that for some unfair dismissals there is no qualifying period) (**Employment Rights Act 1996**) or for a reason connected to a transfer under **Transfer of Undertakings (Protection of Employment) Regulations 2006 (TUPE)**
- to be given written reasons for dismissal within 14 days of a request (**Employment Rights Act 1996**)
- to take up to 13 weeks' unpaid parental leave to care for each child during their first five years or, in the case of a disabled child, up to 18 weeks' leave until the child's 18th birthday. Similar rights exist for adopted children. (See *Parental leave*, page 88.)

After two years

- to redundancy payment, if earning more than the national insurance LEL
- to reasonable time off work to look for work or training if under notice of redundancy (see *Redundancy*, page 102).

After employment ends

- to protection against discrimination once the employment had ended. Such discrimination could include failure to provide a reference and not dealing with a grievance post-termination (see *Post-employment discrimination*, page 75).

Contracts of employment and written statements

A contract of employment exists the moment someone accepts the offer of a job (even if orally), and is binding on both sides, as long as the offer or acceptance does not depend on some condition such as satisfactory references or a medical check. If such conditions are made, the contract comes into effect as soon as they are satisfied or the day the person starts work (even if the conditions have not yet been satisfied).

Contents of the contract

Contracts consist of **express terms** and **implied terms**. Express terms are those specifically stated in, for example, the letter of appointment, the terms and conditions of employment, and any union agreement with that employer. Implied terms are those not actually stated. These include the employer's duty to pay wages, comply with statutory requirements, provide a safe work environment and treat the employee with respect. For the employee, implied terms include being ready and willing to work, obey reasonable instructions and be honest.

A contract does not have to be in writing. Any ongoing arrangement in which someone receives money or other reward in return for work is likely to be a contract, even if there is nothing in writing.

Statement of employment particulars

Under the Employment Rights Act 1996 all employees are entitled to a statement of employment particulars if their job lasts for at least one month, and must receive the statement within two months of their start date. The information can be provided in a separate written statement, a contract of employment or a letter of appointment.

Employees must give their consent to any change to the statement and must receive written notice of the change within one month of its taking effect.

Essential

The written statement must cover:

- names of employer and employee, and address of the employer
- the date(s) the current employment, and any previous employment counting as continuous employment, began
- job title or brief description of the job
- scale or rate of pay, method of calculating pay and any entitlement to increases such as annual increments
- interval of payments (weekly or monthly)
- hours of work (including any terms and conditions relating to normal working hours and overtime)
- the place(s) of work, whether an employee is or could be required or permitted to work at other places
- holiday entitlement (including entitlement to public holidays)
- where the employment is temporary, the period for which it is expected to continue, or if a fixed-term contract, the date on which it is to end
- any collective agreements that directly affect the terms and conditions of employment and, if the employer is not a party to them, by whom they were made
- details of terms relating to any employment abroad for more than one month.

The following must also be provided within two months of starting work, either within the statement itself or in a separate document given to employees either directly or via, for example, the staff handbook (in this latter case the statement of particulars must specify where the information is available):

- terms and conditions relating to sick leave and sick pay
- details of, and terms relating to, pensions and pension scheme(s), including whether the employment is covered by a pensions contracting out certificate. If there is no pension scheme this should be stated

- details of dismissal, disciplinary and grievance rules and procedures. The following details must be written into the statement:
  - the name or job title of the person to whom the employee can apply in order to solve a grievance and how to make the application
  - the person to whom the employee can apply if dissatisfied with any disciplinary decision or decision to dismiss them
- the amount of notice the employer and employee must give; either the statutory legal minimum or the amount established in a collective agreement or other agreed amount (as long as it is more than the statutory minimum).

For an example of a written statement of employment particulars meeting the requirements of the legislation see Acas's publication *Self help guide: producing a written statement*, available at www.acas.org.uk. Also see the BERR publication *Written statement of employment particulars: guidance*, available at www.berr.gov.uk/employment/employment-legislation/employment-guidance.

Optional

Employers do not have to include the following in the statement of particulars but may consider it good practice to do so:

- reimbursement arrangements for travel and subsistence
- time off for religious holidays (see *Religious holidays*, page 71)
- a provision for extended leave – for example, to allow workers to visit relatives abroad (but remember that there is a risk of indirect race discrimination on the basis of national origin if people from the UK without relatives abroad are denied comparable opportunities for leave)
- childcare: a voluntary organisation may not have the funds to run a crèche, but it could consider contributing towards childminding costs (see *Employer's childcare contributions*, in chapter 4)
- probationary periods: if confirmation of employment is subject to a probationary

period (see *Probationary periods*, in chapter 4), this should be stated in the contract. During a probationary period the length of notice required from/by either side is normally reduced, and the disciplinary procedure may be simplified

■ a statement that employees must comply with the organisation's policies, such as equal opportunities, health and safety, data protection, confidentiality and child protection (if applicable).

If the following are more generous than statutory entitlements, these too should be included:

■ maternity, paternity and adoption leave and pay arrangements (see pages 84 to 88)

■ arrangements for leave to look after dependants and compassionate leave (see page 88)

■ arrangements for flexible working (see page 90)

■ time off for public duties and union activities (see pages 71 and 97)

■ redundancy pay (see *Redundancy*, page 102).

Deciding on terms and conditions

The following sections set out employees' minimum statutory rights. You may provide more generous terms and conditions, and suggestions to this effect are given under some sections. However, before doing so consider the financial implications – particularly in relation to sick pay, maternity, paternity and adoption pay and redundancy pay. You need to strike a balance between enabling the organisation to function effectively with adequate resources and providing generous terms and conditions to employees.

You must also consider the long-term implications. Your organisation may be able to afford generous terms and conditions now, but might not be able to in the future. It may be difficult to reduce contractual terms without making your organisation vulnerable to

legal claims. These are not easy matters to resolve and it is sensible to get independent advice.

Pay

All workers are entitled to an itemised pay statement showing how much they earn and any deductions, and are protected from unauthorised deductions made from their wages (see *Paying people*, in chapter 4).

Minimum wage

The **National Minimum Wage Act 1998** sets a minimum hourly rate for the basic pay of almost all workers. In October 2008 the minimum hourly rates were:

■ the adult rate of £5.73 for workers aged 22 years and over

■ the development rate of £4.77 for those aged between 18 and 21

■ the youth rate of £3.53 for 16–17 year olds.

If a worker lives in accommodation provided by an employer, an amount can be deducted from wages that takes that worker below the minimum wage. In 2008 the sum that can be offset for accommodation is £4.46 per day (£31.22 per week).

The minimum rates apply to most workers, including pieceworkers, homeworkers, sessional staff, agency workers, part-time staff and casual workers and freelance workers who fall within the definition of worker (see *The definitions*, page 61). The main exceptions include:

■ people who are 'genuinely self-employed' (see *Self-employed people*, page 62)

■ apprentices under the age of 19 and those who are 19 or over and in the first 12 months of their apprenticeship

■ a volunteer worker in a hostel with charitable status who receives free accommodation and food as well as expenses for any work-related travel, but who does not receive monetary payments

■ some trainees on government or European training programmes

- residential members of charitable religious communities
- volunteers, if the only money they receive is for actual expenses, and they receive no benefits other than training necessary for their voluntary work, and/or reasonable (non-monetary) subsistence or accommodation
- volunteers who receive money for subsistence if they are placed by one voluntary organisation in another one.

However, some people who consider themselves 'volunteers' could be entitled to a minimum wage if given additional non-job related training, or any payment apart from genuine reimbursement for expenses, or other benefits, as these arrangements could amount to a contract. For example, BERR has announced that reimbursement for care costs is a benefit, and will entitle volunteers who receive it to the minimum wage. For further details on the position of volunteers and the minimum wage see *Volunteers and the law*, from www.volunteering.org.uk.

Keeping records

Employers must keep adequate records to show that the minimum wage is being paid, and workers must be given access to their records within 14 days of a written request.

If there is a dispute, the employer must prove that the national minimum wage has been paid. Records must be kept for three years (and in a form which enables the information kept about a worker in respect of a pay reference period to be produced in a single document), but BERR advice is to keep them for at least six years, as workers can take out a claim for up to this period.

For information and advice on the national minimum wage telephone 0845 6000 678. For free copies of the BERR publication *A detailed guide to the national minimum wage* ring 0845 6000 678 or visit www.berr.gov.uk.

Working time, holidays and time off

Working Time Regulations 1998

Workers aged over 18 are entitled to:

- a 48-hour limit on their working week, in most cases averaged over 17 weeks. Most workers can make a written and signed agreement to work more hours, and can cancel this agreement at any time by giving between one week and three months' notice
- from 1 April 2009, 5.6 weeks' or 28 days' annual paid leave, which can include public holidays (see *Holidays*, page 70). Workers can no longer exchange any part of this entitlement for pay
- a 20-minute in-work rest break if they work more than six hours
- rest breaks of 11 consecutive hours over each 24-hour period
- a day off each week, or two days off each fortnight.

Working time hours include paid overtime, job-related training, time spent travelling during the course of work and working lunches. Not included are hours spent travelling to and from work, lunch breaks, evening classes or day release courses.

Part-time workers must receive the same entitlements (with paid holiday on a pro rata basis). Mobile workers in some sectors (for example, transport) and some other types of worker currently remain outside the scope of the regulations.

Night workers

A night worker is defined as someone who works at least three hours between 11 pm and 6 am. Night workers can work no more than eight hours in any 24-hour period, averaged over 17 weeks and cannot opt out of this limit. They have the right to a free health assessment before they start working nights and on a regular basis afterwards to ensure they are suitable for night work.

Young workers

Workers aged 16 and 17 years must not work more than eight hours a day or 40 hours a week. Unlike the situation for adult workers, these hours cannot be averaged out and there is no opt-out available. Young workers generally cannot work at night (but there are some exceptions). They also have the following rights:

- a 30-minute rest period in every 4.5 hours worked
- a 12-hour rest period between each working day
- two days off each week.

Keeping records

Employers must keep records to show that workers are taking their daily, weekly and annual entitlements to time off, and are not working more than the maximum allowed hours. They do not have to record the working hours of anyone who has opted out of the 48-hour week, but employers must still keep a record of their names. They should keep a record of the names of the night workers, when a health assessment was offered, if it was accepted and the result of any assessment. Records must be kept for two years.

Enforcement of the regulations is split between two bodies. The entitlements (for example, rest periods and breaks and paid annual leave) are enforced through employment tribunals. The working time limits are enforced by the Health and Safety Executive and by local authorities.

Holidays

Under the **Working Time Regulations 1998** all workers, including those on fixed-term contracts, are entitled to 4.8 weeks' or 24 days' paid annual leave. From April 2009 this will be increased to 5.6 weeks (or 28 days) including bank holidays. Part-time workers have a pro rota entitlement.

Note that, if existing employees' contracts allow statutory leave plus bank holidays (or if this has become custom and practice), employers who do not want to give bank holidays on top of the increased statutory leave will need to agree a variation (change) to the contract, either with each individual employee, or through a union.

Workers must give their employers notice before taking a holiday. The notice must be twice as long as the period of leave requested: for example, four weeks' notice for a two-week holiday. The employer can refuse permission by giving counter notice at least as long as the leave requested, in this example two weeks.

Most employers specify the leave year in the contract, which is normally the same as the organisation's financial year. If there is no such agreement then the leave year starts on the date the worker took up post (if they started after 1 October 1998) or on 1 October (if they started work before then).

If a worker resigns before taking all their holiday allowance for the proportion of the leave year worked they must be paid their outstanding entitlement. If someone has taken more than their entitlement when they leave, the employer can make a pay deduction to compensate for the overpaid days only if this is allowed for in the contract of employment.

Unless their contracts say otherwise, employees continue to accrue contractual holiday entitlements while off sick. Statutory holiday leave will also accrue.

Employees on maternity leave, adoption leave and paternity leave accrue their entitlement to statutory and contractual leave. However, statutory annual leave cannot be taken at the same time as maternity leave. Before an employee goes on maternity or adoption leave they may wish to consider taking any outstanding leave and perhaps delaying the start of their leave. Alternatively, it may be possible to take annual leave in the period between the expiration of maternity or adoption leave and the expiration of the leave year.

Religious holidays

You should develop a policy to guide employees on how any requests for leave for religious festivals will be handled. The policy must not favour one religion or belief over others, or the holding of a religion or belief over non-belief, and must confirm your willingness to accommodate such requests. For further details see the Acas publication *Holidays and holiday pay*, available from www.acas.org.uk.

Time off for public duties

Under the **Employment Rights Act 1996** employees are entitled to time off (which need not be paid) for certain public duties. These include acting as a:

- magistrate
- local authority councillor

or a member of:

- a police authority
- a statutory tribunal
- a relevant health body
- the managing or governing body of an educational establishment
- the governing body of a further or higher education corporation
- the Environment Agency
- a board of prison visitors.

The amount of time off must be 'reasonable' for the duties involved and for the employee's needs. For further information see BERR leaflet *Time off for public duties*, available from www.berr.gov.uk.

At the time of writing the government was consulting on modernising the list of activities that entitle people to time off; see www.communities.gov.uk/publications/communities/timeoffconsultation.

Time off for study or training – young people

Employees aged 16 or 17 who have not achieved a certain standard in their education or training have the right to reasonable time off with pay to study or train for a relevant qualification which will help them obtain that standard. Certain employees aged 18 have the right to complete study or training already started. This can be in the workplace, at college, with another employer or a training provider, or elsewhere. There is no qualifying period. For further details see *Time off for study or training*, available from www.connexions-direct.

Time off for training – adults

At the time of writing the government was consulting on a new right to ensure that employers consider seriously employees' requests for unpaid time off for training. It is expected that the right would mirror the right to flexible working (see page 90) and would apply to all employees with at least 26 weeks' service.

Discrimination

Context

The European Union has established a common framework to tackle unfair discrimination in the fields of employment, self-employment and occupational and vocational training on six grounds: sex, race, sexual orientation, religion or belief, age and disability. The framework comprises three directives: the Race Directive 2000, the Employment Directive 2000 and the Equal Treatment Directive 1975 (amended 2002). To comply with these directives the government has:

- amended earlier race and sex discrimination legislation through the **Race Relations Act 1976 (Amendment) Regulations 2000** and the **Sex Discrimination Act 1975 (Amendment) Regulations 2003 and 2008**
- introduced new legislation to ban discrimination on the grounds of religion and sexuality, the **Employment Equality (Religion or Belief) Regulations 2003** and the **Employment Equality (Sexual Orientation) Regulations 2003**

- introduced the **Disability Discrimination Act 1995 (Amendment) Regulations 2003**
- introduced the **Employment Equality (Age) Regulations 2006** and **Amendment Regulations 2008**.

Who is protected

The Race Relations Act and Regulations make it illegal to discriminate against anyone because of their race, colour, ethnic origin, nationality or national origin. Ethnic origin is not defined in the legislation. However, discrimination cases have clarified the position of certain groups of people. For example, Jews, Romany gypsies and Sikhs were found to be ethnic groups, whereas Travellers were not. Scottish and English people are racial groups.

The **Sex Discrimination Act 1975 and Regulations** make it illegal to discriminate against anyone because of their sex or marital status. The **Pregnant Workers Directive 1992** provides special protection for pregnant women and outlaws less favourable treatment on the grounds of pregnancy or maternity. The **Sex Discrimination (Gender Reassignment) Regulations 1999** cover discrimination in employment and vocational training on the grounds of gender reassignment (often known as transsexuality). The regulations make it illegal to discriminate against anyone who plans to undergo, is undergoing or who has undergone gender reassignment. There is no obligation on a transsexual person to disclose their status as a condition of employment. If they choose to disclose, this cannot in itself be a reason for not offering employment, and non-disclosure or subsequent disclosure cannot be grounds for dismissal.

The **Equality Bill 2008** proposes a clarification of the definition of gender reassignment to recognise that not all transsexual people undergo medical supervision. At the time of writing the Bill was due to be debated in the 2008/09 parliamentary session.

The Disability Discrimination Act 1995 (DDA) governs disability discrimination. The Act has been amended by the **Disability Discrimination Act 1995 (Amendment) Regulations 2003**.

Under the Act someone is considered to have a disability if they have:

- a physical, sensory or mental impairment which has a substantial and long-term (has lasted or could last over 12 months) adverse effect on their ability to carry out normal day-to-day activities. 'Normal day-to-day activities' include: mobility; manual dexterity; physical coordination; continence; ability to lift, carry or move everyday objects; speech, hearing or eyesight; ability to communicate; memory or ability to concentrate or understand; and perception of risk of physical danger
- a progressive illness, such as multiple sclerosis, which has any adverse effect on their ability to carry out normal day-to-day activities
- a severe disfigurement, such as a burns injury, even if it has no adverse effect on day-to-day activities.

Included in the illnesses and disabilities so far accepted as falling within the definition of the Act are Aids/HIV, back pain, long-term depression, diabetes, schizophrenia, dyslexia, epilepsy and ME.

Under the **Disability Discrimination (Blind and Partially Sighted Persons) Regulations 2003** anyone registered with the local authority as blind or partially sighted, or certified as blind or partially sighted by an ophthalmologist, is defined as disabled for the purposes of the DDA. They do not have to show that the condition has a substantial adverse effect on their day-to-day activities. The DDA also includes people with cancer or HIV from the point of diagnosis.

People who have had a disability within the meaning of the Act are protected even if they no longer have that disability. For example, it would be discrimination to refuse to interview or recruit someone if they revealed they had had a disability in the past.

> The **Equality Bill 2008** will simplify the definitions of disability discrimination and the different justification tests allowing disability discrimination. It will also repeal the list of capacities which forms part of the definition of whether a person is disabled. At the time of writing the Bill was due to be debated in the 2008/09 parliamentary session.

The Employment Equality (Religion or Belief) Regulations 2003, amended by the **Equality Act 2006,** outlaw discrimination in employment and vocational training on the grounds of any religion, religious belief or philosophical belief. Religion or belief is not explicitly defined, but would include: collective worship, a clear belief system, a profound belief affecting the way of life or view of the world. The regulations cover beliefs such as Paganism and Humanism and those with religious or similar beliefs. The Act has implications for hours of work, annual leave dates, dress/appearance and facilities for religious observance.

The Employment Equality (Sexual Orientation) Regulations 2003 outlaw discrimination in employment and vocational training on the grounds of sexuality towards people of the same sex (lesbians and gay men), the opposite sex (heterosexuals) and the same and opposite sex (bisexuals). They cover discrimination on grounds of perceived as well as actual sexuality (that is, assuming – correctly or incorrectly – that someone is lesbian, gay, heterosexual or bisexual). There is an exemption if the job involves working for an 'organised religion', which allows the employer to apply a genuine occupational requirement (see page 78) to comply with the doctrines of the religion or to avoid conflicting with the religious convictions of its followers. This exception has been narrowly interpreted by the courts but would apply to jobs for members of the clergy and other staff working for the religion. Under the **Civil Partnerships**

Act 2004 employers must provide civil partners with the same benefits as those provided to married employees: for example, survivor pensions, flexible working, statutory paternity pay, paternity and adoption leave, or health insurance. There is no duty to provide benefits to unmarried couples, but if you give benefits to opposite sex unmarried partners, they must be offered to same sex partners.

The Employment Equality (Age) Regulations 2006 prohibit discrimination against employees on grounds of age (covering recruitment, terms and conditions, promotions, dismissals and training). People aged under 18 and over 65 can now claim unfair dismissal, statutory redundancy payments and statutory sick pay as the age limits for these have been removed. The Regulations have also introduced a retirement procedure which employers must follow: employees have the right to request staying on past the employer's retirement date (see *Retirement*, page 77). An employer can justify age discrimination only if they can prove that it is a proportionate way of achieving a legitimate aim. Examples could include the need to ensure health and safety of employees or the need for an employee to be in the post for a reasonable time before retirement.

An employer can discriminate on the grounds of age without having to justify doing so:

- where there are benefits linked to length of service. If, for example, employees 'earn' additional holiday entitlements after a certain length of service, these can continue, even though this may indirectly discriminate against younger people as they are less likely to have been with an employer long enough to qualify. However, the length of service required must be less than five years; if more than five years the employer must show there is a genuine business reason
- to meet other legislative requirements such as payment of different rates under the national minimum wage (see page 68).

All equality legislation applies to contract and agency workers and job applicants as well as employees and workers. Specifically, in terms of employment, discrimination is forbidden in:

- recruitment and selection
- terms and conditions of work
- promotion
- training and development
- pay and fringe benefits
- discipline and grievance
- redundancy
- retirement ages
- occupational pensions.

Discrimination can also occur after employment: for example, by not providing a reference (see *Post-employment discrimination*, page 75).

The scope of equality legislation

Direct discrimination

Underpinning all the legislation is the concept of unlawful direct discrimination and treating someone less favourably because of their gender, race, disability, sexual orientation, religion or age.

Indirect discrimination

This occurs when there is unjustified 'provision, criterion or practice' (for example, selection criteria, policies, benefits, employment rules or any other practices) that, although they may be applied to everyone, have the effect of putting certain people at a disadvantage. The motive can be intentional or unintentional.

Unlike direct discrimination, indirect discrimination is not unlawful if it can be justified by an employer, who must show that there is a legitimate aim (for example, a real business need) and that the practice is proportionate to that aim (that is, necessary and with no alternative means available).

Discrimination by association

Discrimination by association is where an individual is discriminated against through their association with another person. For example, a worker may be harassed by colleagues because his or her friends are bisexual. The harassment is on the basis of the friends' sexuality and not that of the individual. The Race Relations Act 1976, the Employment Equality (Religion or Belief) Regulations 2003 and the Employment Equality (Sexual Orientation) Regulations 2003 protect workers who are discriminated against on the basis of the race, religion or belief, or sexual orientation of an associated person. At the time of writing the government was consulting upon providing protection in other areas for discrimination by association as part of the Equality Bill 2008.

Victimisation

This means treating people less favourably because they have made a complaint under anti-discrimination legislation or supported someone else in making a complaint.

Harassment

The **Race Relations Act 1976 (Amendment) Regulations 2003** state that harassment on the grounds of race, ethnic or national origin is unlawful. Harassment occurs when someone's actions or words, based on race or ethnic or national origin, are unwelcome and violate another person's dignity or create an environment that is intimidating, hostile, degrading, humiliating or offensive. Similar definitions exist in the **Employment Equality (Religion or Belief) Regulations 2003** and **Employment Equality (Sexual Orientation) Regulations 2003** and the **Disability Discrimination Act 1995 (Amendment) Regulations 2003.**

The **Equal Treatment Amendment Directive 2002** provides the first statutory definition of harassment in this context ('unwanted conduct related to the sex of a person') and sexual harassment (when 'any form of unwanted verbal, non-verbal or physical conduct of a sexual nature occurs'). The **Sex**

Discrimination Act 1975 (Amendment) Regulations 2008 broadened the definition of harassment so that a claim of harassment can be made by anyone, regardless of their sex and regardless of whether they were the intended target of the harassment. So a witness to the harassment (for example, someone who feels offended, intimidated or degraded by having to watch offensive behaviour towards a colleague, or listen to sexually offensive jokes) can make a claim even if they were not the intended target (**third party harassment**).

Employers must also take reasonably practicable steps to protect workers from sexual or sex harassment by third parties, where such harassment is known to have occurred on at least two previous occasions, even if it had not been committed by the same person. This duty includes protecting workers from harassment by service users.

> The government, through the **Equality Bill 2008**, is considering whether to extend the protection for workers who are harassed by a client because of their sex, to protection from such harassment on all other grounds. At the time of writing the Bill was due to be debated in the 2008/09 parliamentary session.

Post-employment discrimination

It is unlawful to discriminate against or harass someone on the basis of their race, sex, age, disability, religion or belief or sexuality after the termination of their employment, providing the actions are closely connected to the employment relationship.

Examples of post-employment discrimination would include: failure to provide a reference; providing a bad reference on the grounds that a person had claimed or threatened to claim discrimination while they were employed; not pursuing a grievance made during the course of employment after the person has left.

Additional rights of disabled people

The **DDA** introduces specific definitions of discrimination in relation to disabled workers:

- **direct discrimination.** 'A person directly discriminates against a disabled person if, on the grounds of the disabled person's disability, he treats the disabled person less favourably than he treats or would treat a person not having that particular disability whose relevant circumstances, including his abilities, are the same as, or not materially different from, those of the disabled person'
- **less favourable treatment.** Treating a disabled person less favourably for a reason relating to their disability
- **failing to make reasonable adjustments in relation to a disabled person.** This means an employer must make adjustments to the physical working environment (for example, doorways, toilets, office furniture) and/or the employer's criteria or practices (for example, selection and interview procedures, the terms and conditions of service) to avoid a disabled worker, or potential worker, being put at a disadvantage.

Reasonable changes could include:

- making adjustments to premises
- allocating some of a disabled person's tasks to someone else
- altering working hours (for example, a person taking medication with side effects that are worse in the morning may start work later in the day)
- assigning a different place of work: for example, the ability to work at home during rehabilitation periods
- allowing absence from work for rehabilitation, assessment or treatment
- providing additional training
- acquiring or modifying equipment (for example, installing speech browser software)
- modifying instructions or reference manuals (for example, providing oral instruction)
- modifying testing or assessment procedures (for example, giving people more time to complete tests)

- providing a reader or interpreter
- providing additional supervision (for example, a support worker).

Always consult a disabled person about any reasonable adjustments they might need to enable them to do the job.

The law lists a number of factors that would determine 'reasonable':
- how effective the adjustment is in preventing the disadvantage
- how practicable it is for the employer to make the change
- the cost of the adjustment
- the resources available and the ability to raise finance.

The Act covers agency staff as well as those employed directly by the organisation. However, unless such staff are working for an organisation on a long-term basis, it is unlikely that it would be reasonable to expect the organisation to make extensive adjustments.

Good practice

The Act prohibits discrimination against disabled people, and organisations are required to make special arrangements for their benefit. For example, an employer could provide special training, specially adapted equipment or special conditions of service. One source of funding to help with adjustments for an existing or prospective employee is Access to Work (see below).

Examine your premises and equipment to make sure they are suitable for disabled workers. Some factors to consider are listed below. Seek advice either from the specific employee or worker for whom the adaptations are being made, or through a disability access audit. For further information see *Access for disabled people*, in chapter 6.

The *Code of practice for employment and occupation*, available from www.equalityhumanrights.com, describes the duties of employers in preventing discrimination against disabled people in work or seeking work. The Department for Work and

Pensions' *Employ ability* scheme provides advice to employers on all aspects of working with disabled people; see www.dwp.gov.uk/employability.

The local authority may be prepared to help with adaptations, particularly to WCs, if the organisation agrees to make them available for public use.

Employment schemes for disabled people

Access to Work (AtW)

The Department for Work and Pensions runs this scheme to help both employed and unemployed disabled people. The amount of help available depends on the employment status of the worker concerned and the support needed. All the approved costs are paid for workers who are unemployed and starting a new job, are self-employed, or have been in the job for less than six weeks. Regardless of employment status, the scheme will also pay up to all the approved costs of help with support workers, fares to work and communicator support at interview.

For people working for an employer who have been in the job for six weeks or more, AtW pays a proportion of the costs of support. The employer will have to pay the first £300 of the approved cost and then 20% of the total up to £10,000.

All help provided is for a maximum period of three years, after which the support will be reviewed.

Job Introduction Scheme

This scheme allows employers to give a disabled person a 'taster' of a job if they think they have the required skills and experience but are concerned about the practical implications of recruiting them. Employers receive a grant to employ a disabled person on a full or part-time basis usually for six weeks. The disabled person receives the 'rate for the job' during this time.

For further details about Access to Work, the Job Introduction Scheme and other matters concerning employing and retaining disabled employees contact the Disability Employment Adviser at the local Jobcentre Plus office.

The Disability Symbol

This is the recognition, indicated by a circular symbol (usually green) with two ticks, that is given by Jobcentre Plus to employers who have agreed to take action to meet five commitments regarding the employment, retention, training and career development of disabled employees. These five commitments are:

■ to interview all disabled applicants who meet the minimum criteria for a job vacancy and consider them on their abilities
■ to ensure there is an opportunity to discuss with disabled employees, at any time but at least annually, what can be done to develop and use their abilities
■ to make every effort to ensure any employee who becomes disabled can stay in work
■ to ensure that all employees develop sufficient disability awareness to make these commitments work
■ to review the five commitments annually, plan ways to improve on them and let employees and Jobcentre Plus know about progress and future plans.

Additional rights of older people: retirement

The **Employment Equality (Age) Regulations 2006** introduced a national default retirement age of 65 (to be reviewed in 2011). Employers may retire employees or set retirement ages at or above 65, but compulsory retirement below 65 is unlawful unless it can be objectively justified (which will be only in very rare circumstances).

Definitions

■ **pension age:** the age at which someone can receive their pension
■ **retirement age:** either the statutory default of 65 or the normal retirement age

■ **normal retirement age:** the age at which employers require employees in the same kind of position to retire. A normal retirement age below 65 must be objectively justified
■ **intended retirement date (IRD):** can be either the retirement age or the normal retirement age.

Employees have the right to ask to continue working beyond their retirement date and employers must consider such requests, using the following procedure:

■ Between six and twelve months before the IRD, you should notify the employee in writing of their IRD and of their right to ask to work beyond that date.
■ An employee who wants to make such a request must inform their employer, in writing, between three and six months before their IRD of their desire to continue working indefinitely, for a stated period or until a certain date.
■ The employer can either:
  – agree to the request and amend the contract of employment to reflect the new date and any changes to working practices, or
  – arrange to meet the employee within a reasonable period to hear their case. The employee can bring a companion to that meeting, who must be either a colleague or a union representative. The companion may address the meeting but cannot answer questions on the employee's behalf.
■ After the meeting the employer may decide to accept the proposal, to suggest an alternative date and/or working pattern or to refuse the proposal. The employee must be notified in writing within a reasonable timescale.
■ The employee may seek an appeal meeting if:
  – their request is refused outright, or
  – the extension is for a shorter period than requested
■ The decision from that meeting must be made in writing and dated.

For further details see the Acas publication *Guidance on age and the workplace: a guide for employers* available from www.acas.org.uk.

Liability for discrimination

Employers are liable for any act of discrimination or harassment in the workplace unless they can show they have taken steps to prevent it. This is known as **vicarious liability**. The perpetrators may also be ordered to pay compensation. It is good practice for employers to protect their workers from discrimination or harassment by third parties, such as service users, as well as by colleagues.

Burden of proof

Once an individual can show that there has been potential discrimination, the employer has to defend the case and show that the reason for different treatment is justifiable and not discriminatory.

Genuine occupational requirement

In some circumstances it is possible to discriminate in favour of a person of a particular race (including ethnic or national origin), sex, age, sexual orientation, disability status, religion or belief where there is a genuine occupational requirement (GOR). GORs apply in relation to recruitment, promotion, transfer, training and dismissal.

Examples would include:

- to provide personal welfare services to people of a particular race where someone of the same race will provide the services most effectively
- in single sex accommodation where the employee has to live in and there is only sleeping or sanitary provision for one sex
- where there is a need to present a 'public face', or a role model.

Guidelines

Use the following guidelines when seeking to apply a GOR:

- Remember that a GOR applies to a particular job, and not to the organisation as a whole. Each post to which a GOR may apply must be considered separately in terms of the duties of the job and its context.
- GORs should be identified at the beginning of the recruitment, training or promotion process, before the vacancy is advertised. Advertisements sent to potential applicants should clearly show that the GOR applies, and this point should be repeated throughout the selection process.
- When claiming a GOR you must be able to demonstrate the tasks for which an exemption is to be claimed. A GOR cannot be justified in relation to specific tasks if there are already enough employees who can perform these tasks.
- Where the organisation has a religious ethos, a GOR exemption can be claimed only if the nature of the role and the context within which it is carried out has sufficient profile or impact within the organisation to affect its overall ethos.
- A GOR can only be claimed where it is necessary for the relevant duties to be carried out by someone of a particular sexuality, or religion or faith, not just because it is preferable.
- A GOR must be reassessed each time a post becomes vacant.
- The GOR cannot be used to establish a balance or quota of employees of a particular religion or faith, or sexuality.

Before implementing a GOR, seek legal advice or consult the EHRC or Equality Direct (see *Sources of advice*, page 79).

Positive action

Positive action describes the measures that can be taken to improve representation of groups that are in the minority within a workforce to counteract the effects of past discrimination and help abolish stereotyping.

The Discrimination Acts and Regulations allow employers to set targets to monitor the number of people from under-represented groups and support and train such people. An employer must show either:

- that in the past 12 months there were none, or a very small number, of that group employed in that type of work, or
- (in the case of gender) that the training is needed because the potential trainees have not been in full-time employment due to domestic or family responsibilities.

Employers are also allowed, when recruiting, to encourage members of a particular group to apply for certain kinds of work, as long as the group doing that particular kind of work was under-represented in the preceding 12 months.

The **Equality Bill 2008** proposes an extension of positive action so that employers can take into account, when choosing between two equally qualified candidates, under-representation of disadvantaged groups: for example, women and people from minority ethnic communities. At the time of writing the Bill was due to be debated in the 2008/09 parliamentary session.

Sources of advice

The **Equality and Human Rights Commission (EHRC)** (www.equalityhumanrights.com) has replaced the Commission for Racial Equality, Equal Opportunities Commission and Disability Rights Commission. It provides advice to individuals and employers, and supports some individuals in making complaints about discrimination, usually in test cases. EHRC has a law-enforcing role and has the power to carry out formal investigations, issue non-discrimination notices and, where necessary, seek an injunction to prevent discrimination from continuing. It is responsible for a series of Codes of Practice which contain practical guidance on eliminating discrimination and promoting equality of opportunity. Although there is no legal requirement to comply with these Codes, an employment tribunal will take non-compliance into account when determining a case of unlawful discrimination.

Equality Direct is a telephone helpline (0845 600 3444) and website service (www.equalitydirect.org.uk) managed by Acas that provides advice on equality legislation and good practice. Acas has also produced a series of guidance notes on equality in the workplace, available from www.acas.org.uk or 08457 47 47 47 (textphone users ring 08456 06 16 00).

Strengthening enforcement

The **Equality Bill 2008** proposes allowing tribunals to make wider recommendations in discrimination cases, which will go beyond benefiting the individual taking the case to provide benefits for the rest of the workforce. The government will explore further how to allow discrimination claims to be brought on combined multiple grounds, such as where someone is discriminated against because she is a black woman, and will consider introducing representative actions in discrimination law, to allow trade unions, the EHRC and other bodies to take cases to court on behalf of a group of people who have been discriminated against. At the time of writing the Bill was due to be debated in the 2008/09 parliamentary session.

Other equality legislation

Equal pay

The **Equal Pay Act 1970** makes it unlawful for employers to discriminate between men and women in terms of their contracts of employment, where they are doing the same work or work of equal value. It covers all contractual benefits, not just pay (including holiday entitlement, pension, childcare benefits, sickness benefits and car allowances).

The Act covers both direct and indirect discrimination:

- **direct discrimination** occurs where one sex is paid less than the other for comparable work because of their sex
- **indirect discrimination** is where the pay system may appear fair between men and women but in practice one sex is at a disadvantage.

Equal work can be defined as:

- **like work**, work which is the same or broadly similar
- work rated as **equivalent** through a job evaluation scheme
- work which is of **equal value**. This is based on the demands of the job, and may include factors such as effort, skill and decision making.

The **Employment Act 2002** introduced an equal pay questionnaire to make it easier for employees to request information from their employer when deciding whether to bring an employment tribunal case. Employers do not have to complete the questionnaire, but failure to reply (or evasive replies) may be taken into account if a tribunal has to decide whether the Equal Pay Act is being infringed. The questionnaire is available from www.equalities.gov.uk.

As there are data protection concerns about the questionnaire, employers are advised to obtain the consent of third party employees (those who may be used as comparators) before disclosing information about their pay. Get legal advice before seeking such consent or disclosing information.

The former Equal Opportunities Commission published the *Code of practice on equal pay*. Failure to comply with it is not a breach of the law, but the Code can be taken into account whenever a court or tribunal has to decide whether the Equal Pay Act is being infringed. Copies are available via the EHRC website www.equalityhumanrights.com.

The **Equality Bill 2008** proposes a ban on secrecy clauses which prevent people discussing their own pay, and a requirement for the government to gather and publish evidence on the effectiveness of equal pay audits in closing the gender pay gap. At the time of writing the Bill was due to be debated in the 2008/09 parliamentary session.

Pensions

The **Pensions Act 1995** prohibits direct and indirect discrimination in access to occupational pension schemes, or in the way employees are treated under the scheme rules.

Ex-offenders

The **Rehabilitation of Offenders Act 1974 (ROA)** gives people the right not to reveal certain convictions after specified periods, which vary according to the sentence and the age of the person when convicted. Such convictions are said to be **spent**. For example, for people aged 18 or over when convicted, a period of imprisonment of between six and 30 months becomes spent after ten years. Sentences longer than 30 months are never spent.

Positions which involve access to children, vulnerable adults or money are generally exempt from the non-disclosure provisions. In these circumstances, applicants must disclose spent convictions provided they are told that the posts are exempt under ROA. Application forms for such jobs should ask about criminal convictions and state that the post is exempt under ROA (see *Application forms*, in chapter 4). For further information about these provisions see the Home Office leaflet *Wiping the slate clean* (available from www.homeoffice.gov.uk). For many (but not all) exempt positions there is a statutory duty on the employer to carry out a criminal records check (see chapter 4). Even where there is no duty to carry out a check, it may be required by funders.

For further information about employing ex-offenders see *Employing people with criminal records*, available from www.cipd.co.uk.

Equality schemes

Public authorities have a duty to tackle discrimination and promote equality in relation to race, gender and disability either individually or under the umbrella of a **single equality scheme**. The three equality duties are similar in spirit; for each, a public authority must:

- promote equality of opportunity
- promote good relations with target groups and the rest of society
- promote positive attitudes
- eliminate harassment and unlawful discrimination.

Most authorities have also introduced the **equality standard** as a voluntary best value performance indicator, which requires them to mainstream age, disability, gender, race, religion or belief and sexual orientation into council policy and practice.

Voluntary organisations working in partnership with or providing services on behalf of a public authority (either through grant aid or contracts) may need to comply.

Details of each of the duties are available on www.equalityhumanrights.com.

The **Equality Bill 2008** proposes a new equality duty on public bodies, which will bring together the three existing duties and extend to gender reassignment, age, sexual orientation and religion or belief. Public bodies will be required to report on gender pay, minority ethnic employment and disability employment. At the time of writing the Bill was due to be debated in the 2008/09 parliamentary session.

Fixed-term employees

The **Fixed-term Employees (Prevention of Less Favourable Treatment) Regulations 2002** prevent employees on fixed-term contracts being treated less favourably than comparable employees on permanent contracts, unless there are genuine business reasons. The regulations apply to people on contracts that last for a specific period, until a specific task has been completed, or until a specified event takes place or does not take place. It would include, for example, seasonal staff employed for a specific period, as well as employees covering for maternity leave. The regulations do not apply to agency workers.

This means that fixed-term employees have the right to:

- the same pay and conditions, including for example holiday and sick pay
- the same or an equivalent benefits package (for example, season ticket loans)
- access to occupational pension schemes, or salary equivalent to the employer pension contribution, or a contribution to a stakeholder or private pension scheme (see *Pensions*, in chapter 4)
- the same training and promotion opportunities and ability to apply for permanent jobs with an organisation.

However, fixed-term employees do not have the right to the same pay, conditions and benefits if their overall terms and conditions are just as good or better than those for permanent employees. For example, an employer can choose to give better pay instead of pension rights.

A fixed-term employee may write to their employer asking for a written statement explaining the reasons for any less favourable treatment. An employer must respond within 21 days. Less favourable treatment can be justified in one of two ways. The employer must show:

- there are genuine business reasons, or
- that, in terms of pay and benefits, the fixed-term employee's package as a whole is at least equal to that of permanent colleagues.

Other rights

When a fixed-term contract comes to the end of its term and is not renewed, employees have a number of rights including:

- protection from unfair dismissal (after one year's service)
- a written statement of reasons for dismissal
- statutory redundancy pay if they have at least two years' continuous service and their contract is ending because of redundancy.

The use of successive fixed-term contracts is limited to four years unless a longer period can be justified for genuine business reasons. Employers and employees may increase or decrease this period or agree a different way to limit the use of successive fixed-term contracts via collective or workforce agreements. A renewal of the fixed-term contract after four years' continuous service will be treated as a permanent contract (unless the use of a fixed-term contract can be justified), and an employee has the right to ask their employer for a written statement confirming that their contract is permanent. The employer must respond within 21 days.

There is no legal requirement to include a notice clause in a fixed-term contract, but it may be advisable to have one, as it allows you to end the contract if it becomes genuinely necessary (for example, if funding for a piece of work unexpectedly comes to an end). Without such a notice period, the employee may be able to claim damages to cover their losses for the outstanding period of the contract.

Part-time workers

The **Part-time Workers (Prevention of Less Favourable Treatment) Regulations 2000** give part-time workers the same contractual rights (that is, those laid down in the terms and conditions of employment) as comparable full-time workers. Unlike fixed-term rights, which apply only to employees, part-time rights apply to all workers (see *The definitions*, page 61), including employees and most other people working under a contract. Under the regulations 'full-time' is defined as the number of hours considered by the employer to be full-time for that type of work, and 'part-time' is anything which is not full-time. Workers do not have to work a minimum number of hours to qualify for employment rights.

Specifically, the rights apply to:

- rates of pay (unless this can be justified on objective grounds – for example, where a performance-related pay scheme is in place and the full-time worker and the part-time worker are shown to have different levels of performance)
- overtime pay. Part-timers do not have an automatic right to overtime payments once they work beyond their normal hours. However, once they have worked up to the normal hours of a full-timer over the same period, they are entitled to the same hourly rate of overtime
- benefits such as season ticket loans on a pro rata basis, unless an exception can be objectively justified
- annual leave on a pro rata basis
- sick pay and maternity pay on a pro rata basis unless different treatment can be justified on objective grounds
- contractual maternity, paternity, parental, adoption and dependants' leave on a pro rata basis
- access to any career break schemes, unless this can be objectively justified
- access to training and career development, including promotion. Wherever possible, training must be organised at times that suit most workers, including part-timers
- access to occupational pension schemes, unless different treatment is justified on objective grounds
- treatment when selected for promotion and redundancy.

A part-timer who believes they are being treated less favourably than a full-timer can ask their employer for a written statement of reasons. The employer must respond within 21 days.

Equal opportunities in employment: good practice

Organisations should develop an equal opportunities and diversity policy to ensure that no worker or job applicant, volunteer or trainee suffers direct or indirect discrimination, harassment or victimisation, and that:

- both paid and unpaid posts are advertised so as to encourage applications from a wide variety of communities
- applicants for both paid and unpaid work are treated fairly
- the training needs of specific groups of people are recognised
- disabled people's needs are met through adaptations to premises, policies and procedures and through the purchase of specific equipment
- there are procedures to monitor and review the policy.

Monitoring effectiveness

It is essential to establish systems to monitor the effectiveness of an equal opportunities policy. Begin by analysing the composition of your workforce to identify posts or departments where people likely to suffer discrimination are over-represented (in poorly paid jobs) or under-represented (in more senior posts). The policy should state how often this analysis needs to be carried out, and require systems to record the composition of those people:

- applying for and being shortlisted for a post
- appointed to a post
- seeking career training and development
- seeking promotion and being promoted
- seeking redress under the grievance procedure and those against whom the procedure is used
- against whom disciplinary action is taken
- being dismissed
- made redundant.

You should also record how people learn about vacant posts, so that advertising procedures can be monitored. It is also important to monitor the composition of volunteers, trainees and self-employed workers.

Monitoring should be based on a system of records covering race, gender, age and disability. You may wish to discuss with workers and their representatives whether to monitor other characteristics, such as religion, sexuality, marital status and caring responsibilities. However, remember that some people may not have the confidence to be open about being lesbian, gay, bisexual or transsexual, which could lead to under-reporting. It may be better to concentrate on introducing robust strategies to combat discrimination rather than collecting monitoring data in the first instance.

Age

You can either ask someone their age, or decide to group options into categories such as 17 or under, 18 to 24, 25 to 34 and so on.

Gender

As well as male and female, some organisations ask people whether they are transgender male or transgender female.

Race

Most organisations use the same questions and categories as the 2001 census. These are:

'What is your ethnic group? Chose ONE section from A to E, and then tick the appropriate box to indicate your cultural background.

A White. Tick box options of: British; Irish; Any other White background (please write in).

B Mixed. Tick box options of: White and Black Caribbean; White and Black African; White and Asian; Any other Mixed background (please write in).

C Asian or Asian British. Tick box options of: Indian; Pakistani; Bangladeshi; Any other Asian background (please write in).

D Black or Black British. Tick box options of: Caribbean; African; Any other Black background (please write in).

E Chinese or other ethnic group. Tick box options of: Chinese; Any other (please write in).'

Disability

Many organisations use the census question: 'Do you consider yourself to have any longstanding illness, health problem or disability that affects your daily activities or the work that you do?' If the answer is yes, some then ask people to describe their disability by ticking all the options that apply to: hearing, visual, speech, mobility, physical, unseen disability (for example, diabetes), learning, mental health, severe disfigurement, other.

Sexual orientation

If you wish to ask this question use the following categories – but again, stress that participation is voluntary: Heterosexual, lesbian, gay, bisexual, transsexual, prefer not to say (but see *Monitoring effectiveness*, page 83).

Religion

The categories used in the census were: None, Christian, Buddhist, Hindu, Jewish, Muslim, Sikh, any other religion. You should consider adding: Prefer not to say.

Data protection

All information collected will be defined as 'sensitive' under the Data Protection Act (see chapter 9). People should be told why monitoring is necessary and that participation is voluntary. The names of those being monitored must remain confidential, and information should be stored in a statistical form only, otherwise an employer can collect it only with explicit consent from the individual. The Information Commissioner's *Employment practices code*, available from www.ico.gov.uk, includes a chapter on record keeping for equal opportunities purposes.

Setting standards and dealing with complaints

The equal opportunities policy should ensure that volunteers, trainees and self-employed people are aware of the standards of behaviour required when dealing with anyone connected with the organisation. Volunteers and trainees guilty of discriminatory behaviour should face disciplinary action. Contracts with self-employed people should give you the right to terminate their services in the event of proven inappropriate behaviour.

Trainees and volunteers should have access to a grievance procedure if they consider they are being discriminated against, harassed or treated unfairly.

Family legislation

This section describes the rights of employees who become parents either through giving birth or adoption. It then discusses the rights of parents and other carers to take paid and unpaid leave and make a request for flexible working arrangements. Maternity, paternity and adoption pay are explained in chapter 4.

Maternity

A pregnant employee has the following rights, set out in the **Employment Rights Act 1996**, the **Employment Relations Act 1999**, the **Maternity and Parental Leave Regulations 1999**, the **Employment Act 2002**, the **Work and Families Act 2006** and the **Sex Discrimination Act 1975 (Amendment) Regulations 2008**:

- paid time off for antenatal care
- maternity leave of 52 weeks
- maternity pay benefits, usually statutory maternity pay or maternity allowance
- not to be dismissed or treated unfairly because of her pregnancy or the fact that she has taken maternity leave
- to return to work after the baby is born.

Employers also have certain obligations to ensure the health and safety of pregnant employees (see chapter 5).

Paid time off for antenatal care

All pregnant employees, regardless of length of service, can take paid time off for antenatal care, including relaxation and parentcraft classes, as long as these are advised by their doctor, midwife or health visitor. The employer can ask to see an appointment card or medical certificate, once the pregnancy has been confirmed.

Maternity leave and pay

Length of maternity leave

All pregnant women, regardless of length of service and number of hours worked, have a right to 52 weeks' maternity leave. They can also extend maternity leave by up to four weeks by taking that year's quota of parental leave (see page 88).

Starting maternity leave

By no later than the end of the 15th week before the **expected week of childbirth (EWC)** the woman must tell her employer that she is pregnant, give the date of the EWC and the start date of her maternity leave (although she can change this date by giving 28 days' notice). You can ask for written notice of the start date of maternity leave and can request a copy of form **MAT B1** stating the EWC.

Within 28 days of receiving the woman's notification you must confirm with her in writing the date her leave will end, and you should assume that this will be after 52 weeks.

A pregnant employee may start her maternity leave any time after the beginning of the 11th week before the EWC. A week begins on a Sunday for this purpose. The maternity leave period will start automatically if the baby is born before the date given, or if the woman is absent from work because of the pregnancy in the four weeks before the EWC.

Terms and conditions

A woman is entitled to her normal terms and conditions of employment throughout the 52-week maternity leave, except those relating to normal wages or pay. She continues to be employed and therefore her leave counts towards her period of continuous employment. Annual holiday entitlements also accrue; these will be either those specified in her contract of employment or, from 1 April 2009, the equivalent of 28 days' paid leave under the Working Time Regulations 1998 (whichever is the higher, see *Holidays*, page 70). Under the **Social Security Act 1989** she will be entitled to her usual pension contributions. A woman returning to work after maternity leave must also benefit from any general improvements to the rate of pay (or other terms and conditions) introduced for her grade while she has been away.

Right to health and safety

Employers must take account of health and safety risks to new and expectant mothers when assessing risks in work activity. If the risk cannot be avoided, you must take steps to remove the risk or offer suitable alternative work (with no less favourable terms and conditions); if no suitable alternative work is available, you must suspend the new or expectant mother on full pay for as long as is necessary to protect her health and safety or that of her baby. The health and safety rights of pregnant and breastfeeding mothers are described in chapter 5.

Right not to be dismissed

A woman, regardless of length of service, cannot be dismissed or treated unfairly because of her pregnancy, or for any reasons connected with her pregnancy or childbirth.

A woman who is dismissed while she is pregnant or on maternity leave must be given written reasons for her dismissal. If she is made redundant during her maternity leave she must be offered a suitable alternative vacancy, where available; she does not have to apply or be interviewed for the vacancy but should be offered it in priority over her colleagues. If there is no alternative vacancy your normal redundancy procedure applies.

Keeping in touch days

During maternity leave you may make reasonable contact with an employee, and must keep her informed of promotion opportunities and information about her job that she would normally have access to if at work.

Both parties may wish to enter into a more formal contact arrangement through **keeping in touch** days. Under the scheme employees are allowed up to ten days' paid work without forgoing their SMP or MA payments. The work must be the type of work she normally performs under her employment contract, but may include training or any other activity to help her keep in touch with the workplace. Work for any part of one day (for example, attending a morning meeting) counts as a full day. Neither the employer nor employee is obliged to enter into the arrangement.

Returning to work

Under health and safety regulations women cannot work within two weeks of giving birth (or four weeks if the work is in a factory). This is known as **compulsory maternity leave**.

Women intending to return to work at the end of maternity leave do not have to provide employers with further notification unless they want to return beforehand, in which case they must provide eight weeks' notice. This notice does not have to be in writing.

All women returning from maternity leave have the right to go back to the same job on the same terms and conditions.

Women who wish to change their working pattern on return from maternity leave (or at any time before the child's 16th birthday, or 18th birthday if the child is disabled) have the right to request a flexible working pattern (see *Flexible working arrangements*, page 90).

If an employee cannot return to work at the end of leave because she is ill, this should be treated as sickness absence, and if she does not want to return she must give the notice period stated in her contract.

Improving on the statutory requirements

Employers may want to offer more generous terms than the statutory requirements. This need not incur extra expense: for example, the letter writing process could be simplified and the time limits increased. If funds are available (and are likely to remain available into the future) the employer may offer contractual maternity pay at a higher rate than statutory maternity pay, but note that contractual maternity pay cannot be recovered from HMRC.

Any improvements agreed should be included in the written terms and conditions. For further information see the BERR publication *Pregnancy at work – what you need to know as an employer*, available from www.berr.gov.uk/publications.

Paternity

Paternity leave

The **Employment Act 2002** introduced rights of paternity leave and pay for employees. To qualify for paternity leave, the parent must:

- expect to have responsibility for the child's upbringing
- be the biological father of the child, or the mother's husband or partner or civil partner
- have worked continuously for the organisation for 26 weeks ending with the 15th week before the baby is due (EWC).

Employees can choose to take either one week or two consecutive weeks' paternity leave, which can start from:

- the day the baby is born
- a specified number of days or weeks after the baby is born
- a specific date after the first day of the week of the EWC.

Leave can start on any day of the week (but not before the baby is born), but must be taken within 56 days of the baby being born or, if the baby is born before the week it was due, within 56 days of the first day of that week.

Parents must inform their employers, in writing or on the self-certificate form **SC3**, of their intention to take paternity leave by the end of the 15th week before EWC. They must state:

■ the week the baby is due
■ whether they wish to take one or two weeks' leave
■ when they want their leave to start.

They can alter the date on which they want leave to start but must give their employer 28 days' notice.

Employees are entitled to their normal terms and conditions of employment during paternity leave, except those relating to normal pay (unless otherwise stated in their contract). They are entitled to return to the same job, and are protected from unfair treatment or dismissal for taking or seeking to take leave.

For further information see the BERR publication *Working fathers. Rights to leave and pay: guide for employers and employees,* available from www.berr.gov.uk.

> Under the **Work and Families Act 2006**, the government announced plans to introduce a separate right to **additional paternity leave and pay** (APL&P) before the end of the 2008/09 Parliament. The scheme will be in addition to current paternity leave and pay. It will provide certain employees (generally fathers) with an opportunity to take up to 26 weeks' leave to care for their child during the first year of its life. Some of this leave could be paid, if certain conditions are met, notably if the mother returns to work. The government also intends to introduce keeping in touch days (see page 86) for fathers who take up additional paternity leave when introduced.

Adoption

Rights to leave and pay for adoptive parents were introduced in the **Employment Act 2002**.

Adoption leave

Paid adoption leave is available to employees who are adopting a child on their own, or for one member of a couple who are adopting together. The couple can decide who will take the paid leave. The other member of the couple, or the partner of the adopter, may be able to take paid paternity leave.

To be eligible the parent must:
■ be newly matched with a child for adoption by an adoption agency, and
■ have worked continuously for their employer for 26 weeks before the beginning of the week in which they were notified of the match.

The parent taking adoption leave is entitled to 52 weeks' adoption leave. Provided the other parent has the necessary 26 weeks' continuous employment, they are entitled to one or two consecutive weeks' paternity leave with paternity pay (see *Paternity*, page 86).

Parents can choose to start their leave from:
■ the date of the child's placement, or
■ a fixed date, which can be up to 14 days before the expected date of placement.

If the placement breaks down during adoption leave, an employee on adoption leave (but not paternity leave) can remain on leave for up to eight weeks after the end of the placement.

Adopters must inform their employer of their intention to take leave within seven days of being notified that they have been matched with a child for adoption. They must tell their employer:

■ when they expect the child to be placed with them
■ when they want their leave to start; they can alter this date as long as they give 28 days' notice

- the date when they expect any statutory adoption pay to start – at least 28 days in advance.

Within eight weeks the employer must write to the adopter setting out the date on which they expect them to return to work, assuming that the 52-week entitlement is being taken. Employers can ask for evidence from the adoption agency to prove their entitlement to leave.

Right not to be dismissed

Adopters cannot be dismissed or treated unfairly because of their adoption. An employee who is dismissed during adoption leave is entitled to a written statement of the reasons regardless of their length of service and regardless of whether they have requested a statement.

Employees are entitled to their normal terms and conditions of employment throughout their 52-week adoption leave or two weeks' statutory paternity leave (adoption), except those relating to normal pay (unless otherwise stated in their employment contact).

As with women on maternity leave, there is an option, if both parties agree, for adopters to take up to ten keeping in touch days during their adoption leave period (see *Keeping in touch days*, page 86).

Adopters intending to return to work at the end of their full adoption leave do not have to give any further notice to their employers. Those wanting to return beforehand must give eight weeks' advance notice.

For further information see the BERR publication *Adoption leave and pay*, available on www.berr.gov.uk.

Parental leave

The **Employment Relations Act 1999** and **Maternity and Parental Leave (Amendment) Regulations 2002** govern the right of parents (including birth mothers and fathers, adoptive parents and other legal guardians) who are employees to take unpaid leave for a limited period to look after children aged under five or under 18 if disabled.

Qualifying periods and leave entitlements

To be eligible parents must have completed one year's service with their employer. Parents can start taking leave when the child is born or placed for adoption or as soon as they have completed one year's service, whichever is later.

The main elements of parental leave are:
- 13 weeks' parental leave for each child until their fifth birthday
- if the child is adopted, 13 weeks' leave up to five years following the placement, or until their 18th birthday if that is sooner
- parents of disabled children can take 18 weeks' parental leave for each disabled child born or adopted
- both parents can take up to 13 weeks' unpaid parental leave per child.

The parent remains employed while on leave with terms such as contractual notice and redundancy terms still applying. In addition:
- where leave is for four weeks or less the parent has the right to return to the same job. For longer periods the parent is entitled to return to the same job or, if not practicable, to a similar job with the same or better status, terms and conditions
- when parental leave follows maternity leave, the parent is entitled to return to the same job if reasonably practicable, or a similar job with similar or better conditions.

Mothers can take parental leave immediately after maternity leave, provided any notice requirements set in the workplace or fallback scheme (see below) and other conditions, such as the qualifying period, are met.

The fallback scheme

The statutory fallback scheme on how leave is taken and required notice periods applies unless an employer has improved arrangements through a workforce or collective agreement, or in individual contracts. Under the scheme:

- parents can take leave in blocks of one week or more, up to a maximum of four weeks a year per child. Parents of a disabled child can take leave in single days or longer periods as they wish
- parents must give 21 days' notice of leave with start and end dates (this does not have to be in writing)
- the employer can postpone the leave for up to six months if there are genuine business reasons. The employer must:
  - discuss an alternative date with the parent, with the same amount of leave as requested
  - give written notice of the postponement, with reasons, within seven days of receipt of the parent's advance notice, and confirm new dates
- the employer cannot postpone leave if it is asked for immediately after a child is born or is adopted.

Workforce agreement

Wherever possible develop your own agreements on parental leave through individual, workforce or collective agreements. Individual agreements should be incorporated into an employee's contract of employment; workforce or collective agreements automatically become part of their contracts.

A workforce agreement can improve upon, but cannot offer less than, the fallback scheme provisions: for example, employers could allow all parents to take leave in one-day blocks. It could also improve on the minimum regulations by:

- extending entitlement to those with informal childcare responsibility such as grandparents
- setting a shorter qualifying period than one year. This may particularly help parents who are returning to the labour market
- allowing leave for parents of older children
- increasing the total length of leave to more than 13 weeks (18 weeks for parents of disabled children) or disregarding leave taken in a previous job

- ensuring that at least part of the leave is paid.

To be valid, a workforce agreement must:

- be in writing
- be shown to all employees to whom it will apply, together with a guide explaining what it means
- be signed when it comes into effect, either by employee representatives or, in organisations with 20 or fewer employees, by most of the workforce or other appropriate representatives.

There is no statutory duty to keep records of parental leave taken, but because when a parent changes jobs their new employer could ask about the amount of leave taken, it is advisable to keep such records.

For further information see the BERR publication *Parental leave: a guide for employers and employees*, available on www.berr.gov.uk.

Dependants' leave

Under the **Employment Relations Act 1999** all employees, regardless of length of service, have the right to take reasonable unpaid time off work to deal with an emergency involving a dependant, and not to be dismissed or victimised for doing so.

A dependant is defined as the partner (including a same sex partner), child or parent of the employee, or someone who lives with them as part of their family, such as a relative or friend. It does not include tenants or boarders living in the home.

In cases of illness or injury, or where care arrangements break down, a dependant may also be someone who reasonably relies on the employee for assistance. This may be where the employee is the primary carer or the only person who can help in an emergency.

An unexpected or sudden emergency could include when a dependant:

- is ill and needs an employee's help
- is involved in an accident or assaulted

- needs an employee to arrange their longer term care
- needs an employee to deal with an unexpected disruption or breakdown in care, such as a childminder failing to turn up
- goes into labour
- dies and the employee needs to make funeral arrangements or attend a funeral.

There is no set limit to the time off that can be taken; it is a question of what is reasonable. In most cases, the amount of leave will be one or two days, but this will depend on individual circumstances. Employees should tell their employers as soon as possible about their absence, the reason for it and how long they expect to be away from work.

This right is intended to cover unforeseen situations. If people know in advance that they will need time off, they should be able to arrange to use their annual leave entitlement or apply for any contractual entitlement to compassionate or other types of leave.

Dependants' leave does not include a right to pay, but many employers consider it good practice to give a contractual right to reasonable paid time off or to give a manager the authority to agree paid time off on a discretionary basis.

For further information see the BERR publication *Time off for dependants: A guide for employers and employees* available on www.berr.gov.uk.

Flexible working arrangements

Under the **Employment Act 2002** and **Work and Families Act 2006** employers must seriously consider requests from employees who are parents or carers of an adult relative to adopt flexible working patterns. Employees are protected from suffering unfair treatment or dismissal for making an application under the right.

Any request accepted will represent a permanent change to the employee's contractual terms and conditions unless otherwise agreed. The employee has no right to revert to the previous working pattern unless this has been agreed between the parties. It is of course possible to offer a trial period before any changes are permanently introduced.

Making the request

To be eligible parents must:

- have parental responsibility for a child under six (the government has proposed increasing this to 16 from April 2009) or a disabled child under 18. This includes biological parents, legal guardians, adoptive and foster parents and their partners, including same sex partners, as long as they have parental responsibility for the child. The parent may make a request up until the last appropriate birthday of the child (currently sixth or 18th, but from April 2009, 16th or 18th).

Carers must:

- be or expect to be caring for a spouse, partner, civil partner or relative, or
- live at the same address as the adult in need of care.

Both parents and carers must:

- have worked for the employer continuously for 26 weeks at the date the application is made
- not have made another application to work flexibly during the previous 12 months (only one application can be made each year).

Examples of the working patterns that employees can apply for include a change in the number of hours worked, a change in times when required to work, or a change in the place of work (including a request to work from home, whether for all or part of the week). For further details of flexible working options see *Flexible ways of working*, page 92.

The onus is on the employee to make an application in writing or on form **FW (A)** (from www.berr.gov.uk/employment/

workandfamilies/flexible-working/flexforms/
index.html) well in advance of when the
changes would take effect (there is no set time
limit, but the guidance suggests at least 14
weeks). The application must be dated and
must:

- state that the application is being made
  under the statutory right to request a
  flexible working pattern
- describe the relationship to the child or
  adult being cared for and confirm the
  employee's child rearing or caring
  responsibility
- set out the flexible working pattern applied
  for and the date that the proposed changes
  would start
- describe any effects that the employee
  thinks the proposed changes would have
  on the organisation and explain how these
  might be dealt with
- state whether a previous application has
  been made to the employer, and if so when.

Considering an application

Employers must consider all applications and
decide whether they can accommodate the
new working pattern. It is good practice to
acknowledge receipt of the request. The
employer must:

- within 28 days, either agree to the proposed
  changes in writing or arrange to meet the
  employee concerned to consider the
  application
- allow the employee, if they wish, to bring a
  companion from the organisation
- within 14 days of the meeting, inform the
  employee of the decision by stating in a
  written and dated letter that:
  - the request is accepted, and that a start
    date, description of the new job and
    conditions such as a trial period are
    established, or
  - a compromise agreed at the meeting is
    confirmed, or
  - the request is rejected. In this case the
    clear business reasons for the rejection
    (see next paragraph), together with
    notification of the appeals process,
    should be included. Form **FW(C)** (from

www.berr.gov.uk/employment/
workandfamilies/flexible-working/
flexforms/index.html) (application
rejection) can be used to reject a request.

The business reasons for refusing an
application must be one of the following:

- burden of additional costs
- detrimental effect on the ability to meet
  demand
- inability to reorganise work among existing
  staff
- inability to recruit additional staff
- detrimental impact on quality
- detrimental impact on performance
- a lack of suitable work available when the
  employee proposes to work
- planned structural changes.

Appealing against the decision

An employee must lodge a written appeal
within 14 days of the date of the rejection letter.
The employer has 14 days to arrange a
meeting after receiving notice of an appeal. The
employee can bring a companion, who must be
a worker employed by the organisation, to the
appeal. The employer must inform the
employee of the outcome in writing within 14
days. The written outcome of the appeal acts
as the employer's final decision and is
effectively the end of the formal procedure.

At the time of writing the government was
consulting on how to make dealing with
flexible working requests easier for employers;
see *Consultation on implementing the
recommendations of Imelda Walsh's
independent review,* available from
www.berr.gov.uk.

Good practice

To improve upon the legal minimum,
employers could develop a work–life balance
policy which:

- states that the organisation is committed to
  a work–life balance and believes that there
  are benefits to both the organisation and its
  employees

- makes flexible working options open to everyone, female and male, not only for caring responsibilities, but for out-of-work learning, volunteering, travelling, religious commitments, and at all stages of a career, including people approaching retirement
- describes the procedures for requesting alternative working practices
- describes the appeals procedure
- describes alternative ways of working available within the organisation
- offers a trial period before an employee makes a commitment to new working practices.

Other legislation

Other legislation may influence how employers deal with requests for flexible working. For example, a woman's request to work part time after returning from maternity leave may count as indirect discrimination under the **Sex Discrimination Act**. The **Part-time Workers (Prevention of Less Favourable Treatment) Regulations** come into force when a request is granted for a reduction in hours. Employers must also check that any health and safety requirements have been satisfied, particularly if the employee is to work from home (see chapter 5).

For further information see the BERR publication *Flexible working: the right to request and duty to consider: guidance for employers and employees*, available from www.berr.gov.uk, or the *Voluntary sector work–life development pack*, available free for voluntary groups from www.working.families.org.uk or 020 7253 7243.

Flexible ways of working

Flexitime

Many organisations operate a system of flexitime to give people the freedom to work the hours that suit them. The key elements of a flexitime scheme are:

- **band width**: the hours over which the system operates – that is, the earliest starting and latest finishing times. A limit is usually placed on the number of hours that can be worked in one day – often nine (the maximum under the Working Time Regulations is 13, or eight for a worker aged under 18)
- **core hours**: the periods when all employees must be present, other than for authorised absence (for example, 10am–12pm and 2pm–4pm)
- **flexible times**: the periods during which starting and finishing times may be varied, subject to the demands of the job. The hours worked during these periods are credited to the employee's total working hours
- **lunchtime**: in general a break of between half an hour and two hours (all employees must take at least half an hour), usually between the core hours
- **accounting period**: the period in which employees must complete their contractual hours – often four weeks. For example, a full-time worker contracted to work a 35-hour week will need to work 4 x 35 (140) hours during a four-week accounting period.

Flexitime is of particular benefit to employees with caring responsibilities, disabled employees and those wishing to study or pursue outside interests.

Job sharing

Job sharing is where two people share one full-time job. Each sharer does a proportion (often half) of the work and receives that proportion of the pay, contractual and statutory holidays and other benefits. Job sharing does not require any organisational restructuring or changes in establishment levels.

Working at home

Some people may wish to divide their working time between home and the office. Before this happens employers must carry out a risk assessment of the activities undertaken by staff working from home. See *Home-based workers*, in chapter 5.

School-hours working/term-time working

These are both specific types of part-time working. School-hours working involves someone working only during school hours. Term-time working allows an employee to take unpaid leave during the school holidays.

Compressed hours

This allows people to work their total number of agreed hours over a shorter period: for example, employees might work their full weekly hours over four rather than five days. It is essential to ensure that they do not exceed the number of hours/days permitted under the **Working Time Regulations** (see page 69).

V-time (voluntary reduction in hours)

V-time allows people to trade pay for time off. Staff are given the option of reducing full-time working hours for an agreed period, usually a year, with the right to return to full-time work afterwards. Time off can be negotiated as a reduction in the working week, or as a block of time during the year. They are paid only for the hours they actually work.

Career breaks

Career breaks, or sabbaticals, are extended periods of leave, normally unpaid. Employers usually specify a minimum number of years' service for which someone must have worked before they are eligible for a career break.

Advantages

There are benefits to flexible working. For individuals, the opportunity to work flexibly can improve their ability to balance home and work responsibilities. Employers gain by being able to retain skilled staff, which in turn reduces recruitment and training costs. This is particularly relevant for the voluntary sector, which is often unable to compete in the labour market in terms of salaries and other financial benefits.

Some drawbacks

Introducing flexible working patterns has implications for management practices, especially in relation to monitoring and supervision. The additional management time and costs can be substantial, particularly in small organisations: supervising four part-timers will require far more input than supervising two full-timers. Communication can be more complex, especially if it is not possible to hold staff meetings at a time when everyone can attend. If one job sharer leaves it can be difficult to find an appropriate match. If someone reduces their hours, there may not be a corresponding reduction in workload and/or expectation, and the person can end up being expected, or feeling obliged, to do a full-time job on part-time pay.

For further information on flexible working patterns see the Acas guide *Flexible working and work–life balance* or contact Working Families (www.workingfamilies.org.uk).

Dignity at work

Employers have legal responsibilities to prevent bullying and harassment at work. First, they have a duty of care for all their workers. If the mutual trust and confidence between the employer and workers is broken (for example, through bullying at work), then an employee can resign and claim constructive dismissal on the grounds of breach of contract. Allowing sustained bullying or harassment to take place could also contravene the **Health and Safety at Work Act 1974**. Under this Act, employers must take reasonable care to protect the health of their workforce from excessive and sustained levels of stress arising from the way in which work is organised, and the way people deal with each other at work (see chapter 5). Employers who fail to tackle harassment and bullying in the workplace may be liable under the discrimination acts (see *Discrimination*, page 71). The **Criminal Justice and Public Order Act 1994** created a criminal offence of 'intentional harassment', whether in the workplace or elsewhere; harassment may also be a criminal offence under the **Protection from Harassment Act 1997**.

Both the employer and perpetrator(s) may be liable for any damages arising from types of harassment in the workplace (see *Discrimination*, page 71).

The definition of harassment used by Acas is: 'unwanted conduct affecting the dignity of men and women in the workplace. It may be related to age, sex, race, disability, religion or belief, nationality or any personal characteristic of the individual, and may be persistent or an isolated incident. The key is that the actions or comments are viewed as demeaning and unacceptable to the recipient'.

Bullying may be characterised as: 'offensive, intimidating, malicious or insulting behaviour, an abuse or misuse of power through means intended to undermine, humiliate, denigrate or injure the recipient'.

Bullying and harassment are not always face-to-face activities. They may be carried out through written communications, email and the telephone. Not only are such activities unacceptable on moral grounds, but they can severely harm an organisation through, for example, poor performance, absenteeism, high employee turnover and a damaged reputation with users.

It is good practice to develop a dignity at work policy that includes measures to prevent bullying and harassment and to deal with complaints. As far as possible involve everyone in the organisation in its development, including paid staff, volunteers, the union, management committee and users.

Policy checklist

Here are some suggestions about the content of a dignity at work policy:

- a statement of commitment from senior management
- an acknowledgement that bullying and harassment are or may be problems for the organisation
- a clear statement that bullying and harassment will not be tolerated and that failure to comply with the policy is a disciplinary offence

- examples of unacceptable behaviour. Although it is easy to agree on what constitutes extreme forms of bullying and harassment, it is the more subtle actions that are most difficult to define as unacceptable. Acas and the TUC provide the following suggestions:
  - spreading malicious rumours or insults (especially on the grounds of age, race, sex, sexuality, disability or religion or belief)
  - ridiculing or demeaning someone
  - picking on them
  - setting them up to fail
  - unfair treatment
  - shouting at someone
  - exclusion or victimisation
  - overbearing supervision or other misuses of power or position
  - unwelcome comments, actions or advances of a sexual nature
  - making unfounded threats or comments about job security
  - deliberately undermining a competent worker by overloading and constant criticism
  - intentionally blocking promotion or training opportunities
- the scope of the policy. Make it clear that bullying and harassment of users, volunteers, trainees, self-employed workers and members of the management committee as well as paid staff will not be tolerated
- the measures that will be taken to prevent bullying and harassment
- the responsibilities of supervisors and managers
- describe the investigation procedures (including timescales for action)
- describe the grievance and disciplinary procedures (including timescales for action) or refer to those procedures
- allow people to complain to someone of their own sex, race, age group and, where relevant, experience of a disability
- allow people to be represented throughout the process by a union official, an employee representative or a friend

- ensure that an independent person will deal with any complaint
- guarantee confidentiality and protection against victimisation or retaliation
- ensure that the policy is communicated across the organisation
- ensure that those who are responsible for dealing with complaints are properly trained
- if possible ensure that an adviser or counsellor is available to support those suffering harassment or bullying
- allow for regular reviews to monitor the effectiveness of the procedures.

For further details see the Acas publication *Bullying and harassment at work: guidance for employers* (available from www.acas.org.uk) and the TUC leaflet *Bullied at work? Don't suffer in silence* (available from www.tuc.org.uk or the TUC Know Your Rights Hotline on 0870 600 4882).

Disciplinary and grievance policy and procedures

New arrangements for disciplinary and grievance procedures have been introduced under the **Employment Act 2008** and will take effect from 6 April 2009. Until then employers must comply with the minimum steps set out in the statutory dismissal procedure contained in *Disciplinary, dismissal and grievance procedures: guidance for employers*, available from www.berr.gov.uk.

An **Acas code of practice on discipline and grievance** will replace statutory procedures. Although compliance with the Code is not a legal requirement, failure to do so may be taken into account by an employment tribunal, if an employee takes out a claim for unfair dismissal. The final version of the code: *ACAS code of practice 1 – disciplinary and grievance procedures* is available from www.acas.org.uk.

Defining the scope of the policy

Organisations should develop a policy on how to deal with unacceptable behaviour. This should start with a definition of such behaviour. As well as including obvious offences such as harassment, bullying and petty theft, the list could cover matters such as timekeeping, misuse of telephones and email, misuse of office stationery and postage, carelessness in respect of health and safety, performance and behaviour, and unauthorised absence.

As regards performance, the policy should use the same procedures to address incompetence or neglect of work duties ('capability') as to address the inability to carry out tasks because of illness or disability ('incapacity'), although you may wish to distinguish between performance and behaviour issues in the language you adopt.

Gross misconduct

The policy should specify the type of behaviour that will be treated as gross misconduct and might result in dismissal without notice. Examples could include:

- theft or fraud
- physical violence
- bullying or harassment
- bringing the organisation into serious disrepute
- drunkenness or drug abuse
- serious infringement of health and safety rules
- serious negligence which causes or might cause unacceptable loss, damage or injury
- sending abusive or offensive emails
- downloading pornographic, racist, sexist or other unacceptable material from the internet.

Developing procedures

When drawing up a disciplinary procedure, follow the Acas *Code of practice*, available from www.acas.org.uk. The code says that, wherever possible, you should first attempt to resolve the problem informally. If informal approaches fail, then more formal procedures should be adopted, which are:

- set down in writing, specific and clear about those to whom they apply
- agreed wherever applicable with unions or employee representatives
- are clearly understood by employees and managers.

Acas lists the key elements of a formal process:

- Issues should be dealt with promptly; meetings and decisions should not be unduly delayed.
- Employers should act consistently and ensure that like cases are treated alike.
- The problems should be properly investigated to establish the facts of the case.
- Any disciplinary meeting should, as far as possible, be conducted by a manager who was not involved in the matter that gave rise to the dispute, but if there is a performance problem the immediate manager should be involved.
- An employee should be informed of the basis of the problem and have an opportunity to put their case before any decisions are made.
- An employee has the right to be accompanied at any disciplinary or grievance meeting.
- An employee should be allowed to appeal against any formal decision made.

It is good practice to keep written records during disciplinary cases and a written record should be kept of the outcome.

If the offence is proven, in most cases the employer imposes a disciplinary penalty. This is usually a verbal or written warning, depending on the seriousness of the matter and the warnings prescribed under the disciplinary procedure. Any warning should describe the nature of the problem, the improvement required, the timescale for the improvement, when it will be reviewed, and the consequences of failure to improve. These

could be a further warning, a final warning or dismissal.

When giving the warning the employer must inform the employee of any right of appeal and how long the warning will remain on their file. Any record of a disciplinary proceeding, apart from those relating to some serious offences, should be removed from an individual's file after the specified period.

The contract of employment may allow, in some circumstances, for the employee to be suspended on full pay, reduced pay or even no pay while the investigation is being carried out. An employee dismissed as the result of a disciplinary proceeding must be given the usual statutory or contractual notice period, whichever is longer (see page 105), or pay in lieu of notice.

An employee who is accused of gross misconduct is generally suspended on full pay while an investigation and disciplinary interview are carried out. However, in some cases the contract may allow suspension on reduced pay. If the gross misconduct case against the employee is proven, the contract may allow for dismissal without notice and/or pay in lieu of notice. If the contract does not provide for dismissal without notice, statutory or contractual notice or pay in lieu of notice must be given where permitted in the contract.

For further information about dealing with disciplinary problems see chapter 10 of *Just about managing?*

Grievance procedures

Employers should develop a formal procedure to allow employees to bring a grievance to the attention of management and an employee to appeal against a disciplinary penalty.

Procedures should be simple and in writing, should allow for grievances to be dealt with rapidly and should include mechanisms to ensure that proceedings and records are kept confidential. The procedure could be developed along the following lines:

- The employee raises the matter with their manager or, if the grievance is with the line manager, with that person's manager
- A meeting is held promptly after a grievance is received to allow the employee to explain their grievance and how they think it should be resolved.
- A decision is made on what action, if any, to take. Decisions should be communicated to the employee immediately, with an explanation of any action that will be taken to resolve the grievance.
- An appeal is available for an employee who feels that their grievance has not been satisfactorily dealt with. The appeal should be heard promptly and at an agreed time and, where possible, be dealt with by a more senior manager than the one who sat at the first hearing.

It can be helpful in some circumstances, subject to the agreement of all parties concerned, to seek external advice and assistance during the procedure. However, dealing with the matter speedily is very important.

Employers may want to consider developing separate procedures for dealing with complaints about harassment, discrimination and whistle-blowing (see page 102). If so, it is essential to be absolutely specific about the circumstances in which each procedure is used. It may be better to have one policy that is appropriate and flexible for a range of situations. It is good practice to keep written records during grievance cases and a written record should be kept of the outcome.

Representation

Under the **Employment Relations Act 1999** workers have the right to be accompanied by a colleague or trade union official when asked by an employer to attend a disciplinary hearing that could result in the following:

- the administration of a formal warning
- other action (including suspension without pay, demotion or dismissal)

- confirmation of a warning issued or some other action taken.

A worker is entitled to the same representation if asked to attend a hearing relating to a grievance that concerns the performance of a duty by an employer in relation to a worker – that is, a duty arising from a statutory or contractual duty.

Unions

Workers' rights

Workers have the following rights:

- to belong to a trade union and to take part in union activities outside working hours
- to take part in union activities during working hours if this is agreed by the employer, but this need not be paid
- not to be victimised or discriminated against because of trade union membership
- to take part in lawfully organised industrial action
- not to belong to a union, and not to be discriminated against because of non-membership.

Union recognition

A union is 'recognised' when an employer agrees to negotiate with it on pay and conditions for a particular group of workers known as the **bargaining unit**. There are two types of recognition. **Voluntary recognition** is where the union makes a request in writing to the employer specifying the bargaining unit for which recognition is claimed, and the employer agrees. **Statutory union recognition**, governed by the **Employment Relations Act 1999** and the **Employment Relations Act 2004**, covers organisations employing 21 or more people. If the employer does not agree to recognition, or fails to respond to the request within ten working days, the procedure is as follows:

- The union may apply in writing to the Central Arbitration Committee (CAC).
- The CAC has to be satisfied that there is sufficient potential support for the union. It

will require evidence of at least 10% membership in the relevant bargaining unit and that a majority of workers is likely to favour recognition.

- If the union can show that the bargaining unit has more than 50% membership, the CAC may declare that the union should be recognised, otherwise it will authorise a ballot among all those in the relevant bargaining unit.
- A declaration will be made for recognition if a majority of the workers voting **and** at least 40% of those eligible to vote support the union in the ballot.

Employers must:

- cooperate with the CAC in organising any ballot
- share the costs of a ballot with the union
- allow the union reasonable access to workers
- allow workers to go to union meetings.

Employers cannot campaign unfairly (for example, by offering inducements or imposing sanctions) against a workforce's decision to set up a union, nor can they terminate a statutory agreement for recognition within three years.

Acas can help with the setting up of voluntary recognition and offers a conciliation service for organisations before they involve the statutory process. For further details on Acas's role see *Ask Acas – trade union recognition*, available at www.acas.org.uk. For further details on the statutory process see *Statutory recognition – guide for parties*, available at www.cac.gov.uk.

Union agreements

Collective agreements

When an employer voluntarily recognises a union it is usual for the parties to agree the scope of collective agreements. This may include negotiation on:

- terms and conditions of employment, such as pay, holidays and pensions
- procedural arrangements such as discipline, redundancy and grievance

- union arrangements such as facilities for officials and procedures for negotiation and consultation.

If the union required statutory recognition through CAC, negotiations are limited to pay, hours and holidays, although the parties may voluntarily agree to widen the scope.

When an employer recognises a trade union for collective bargaining, the relevant contracts of employment should expressly incorporate all collective agreements, so that individuals benefit from the negotiated terms.

If employees belong to more than one union, the employer may decide to recognise the union with the greatest number of members in a collective agreement and recognise the others for discussing individual rights only. An alternative is to ask the representatives of the various unions to form a joint committee, with whom the employer will negotiate.

Contact Acas for further information about union recognition and agreements.

The rights of recognised trade unions

Once an employer has given a union official recognition, that union acquires the rights to:

- receive information for collective bargaining purposes. Acas lists the following as possibly relevant to collective bargaining: pay and benefits; conditions of service; staffing; performance; finance (see Acas's *Code 2: Disclosure of information to trade union officials for collective bargaining purposes*, available from www.acas.org.uk)
- be consulted on a range of matters (see *Consultation with employees*, page 99)
- reasonable paid time off for union officials to perform union duties and undertake relevant training
- paid time off for trade union learning representatives (see page 99).

Union officials

The union should notify management of the names of the elected representatives or officials, who will have been given credentials (papers authorising them to act for their union). Officials have a right to some facilities, and it is good practice to provide others, including: a desk and a lockable filing cabinet, a union notice board, use of a telephone, computer and email facilities, and meeting space.

Officials have the right to reasonable paid time off to perform union duties such as:

■ negotiating terms and conditions of employment and helping with disciplinary or grievance procedures on behalf of union members, including accompanying employees at disciplinary or grievance hearings

■ discussing matters that affect members, such as redundancies

■ training for union work.

An employer can encourage people to join the union by:

■ negotiating with the union rather than with individuals

■ enabling union representatives to talk to new employees

■ arranging for union contributions to be deducted directly from pay ('check off') if members agree.

The main unions in the voluntary sector are Unite and Unison.

Time off for union learning representatives

Under the **Employment Act 2002** union learning representatives (ULRs) are allowed reasonable paid time off work to ensure that they are adequately trained to carry out their duties, including to:

■ analyse learning or training needs

■ provide information and arrange or promote learning or training

■ discuss learning or training with the employer

■ to train as a learning representative.

Members of a recognised union are allowed reasonable unpaid time off work to access their ULRs.

For further information see *Time off for trade union duties and activities*, from www.acas.org.uk.

Employee representatives

Employers may wish to set up a structure for informing and consulting their workers. The most common arrangement is the **works council**, also known as joint consultative committees or staff councils. Employee representatives are elected to sit on the council and have the same rights to reasonable time off with pay to carry out their duties as union officials.

Works councils can operate alongside the unions: for example, a union official could sit on the council as of right or, alternatively, a separate election could be held with officials standing for those positions. Acas advises that works councils need good will from both sides and a commitment from senior managers, who must be prepared to attend meetings and provide the money and time to enable representatives to perform their roles effectively. Acas also provides a checklist of other factors which help to make works councils effective.

For further details see the Acas booklet *Representation at work*, available from www.acas.org.uk

Consultation with employees

Employers must consult with appropriate representatives, who can be either officials of recognised unions or elected representatives, on the following:

■ when 20 or more staff are to be made redundant in a 90-day period

■ a transfer of undertakings to another employer (see page 100)

■ health and safety

- occupational pension schemes
- working time.

Where there is no recognised trade union, employees can also elect safety representatives (see chapter 5).

The Information and Consultation of Employees Regulations 2004

The Regulations apply to organisations with 50 or more employees. If 10% of employees make a valid request, employers must negotiate an agreement to provide information on and consult about the following:

- recent and probable developments in the organisation's activities and economic situation, which could include profit and loss, sales performance, productivity, market developments and strategic plans
- the situation, structure and probable development of employment, and any anticipated measures, especially where there is a threat to employment
- decisions likely to lead to substantial changes in work organisation or contractual relations. These could include working time and practices, training and development, health and safety, equal opportunities, pensions, and redundancies.

If you have already formally approved information and consultation agreements that cover all employees, you need only consider making changes if you receive a request, supported by 40% of employees, to negotiate new arrangements.

For further details see the BERR publication *Informing and consulting employees – a brief guide to the legislation*, from www.berr.gov.uk.

Taking on other organisations' staff

The **Transfer of Undertakings (Protection of Employment) Regulations 2006 (TUPE)** protects the continuity of employment and terms and conditions (except for certain occupational pension rights) when an organisation (the **transferor**), or part of one, is transferred to a new employer (the **transferee**).

There are two broad categories of transfer:

- an undertaking (or part of one) is transferred from one employer to another as a going concern. This is known as a 'business transfer'. In other words one organisation sells, or passes over, its business to another. Voluntary organisations undergoing a merger may fall into this category
- where a contract to provide goods or services is transferred to a new employer (outsourcing) or where that contract is reassigned, including bringing the work back in-house. This is known as a 'service provision change'. To meet the Regulations the service provision must involve an identifiable group or team of employees providing a particular service. Voluntary organisations delivering contracts for public authorities may fall into this category if, for example, an identifiable unit within the authority is currently providing the service.

TUPE can apply regardless of the size of the transferred undertakings, and could involve just one person if that person performs a specific contracted out service.

Employees have certain rights under TUPE:

- to transfer to the new employer on their existing terms and conditions of employment and with all their existing employment rights (other than pension rights, see page 101) and liabilities (for example, for past breaches of contract such as arrears of wages and statutory liabilities such as redundancy pay). The new employer cannot make any changes to the terms and conditions of employment of the transferred employees if the only or main reason for the change is connected to the transfer – unless there is an economical, technical or organisational reason (**ETO**) (see page 101)
- protection from unfair dismissal if the only or main reason for dismissal is the transfer, unless it is an ETO reason requiring a

change in the workforce. However, this will not normally apply to employees with less than one year's service, as they have not accrued this protection right

- to be informed and in some cases consulted through appropriate representatives about the transfer and any measures proposed (see *Consultation*, below).
- to have trade union recognition agreements recognised by the new employer, as long as the transferring group of employees maintains a distinct identity from the rest of the new organisation.

Information

TUPE places obligations on both parties to share information about the transfer, including:

- transferors must provide written information about employees that will enable the transferee to understand the rights, duties and liabilities in relation to the transferring employees. This includes:
  - their identity and age
  - information contained in their statements of employment
  - information on applicable collective agreements
  - disciplinary and grievance actions involving statutory procedures within the previous two years
  - any legal actions taken by the employees against the organisation within the previous two years.

The transferee must supply information on any proposed 'measures' in relation to the transferring employees. If there are such measures, the transferee consults with the appropriate employee representatives.

Consultation

Both the transferor and transferee must inform and, if they as employer are taking any 'measures', must consult the union or elected representatives of their respective employees who may be affected by the transfer. Sometimes this is done jointly. The following

information must be provided in writing long enough (a period has not been defined) before the proposed transfer:

- that the transfer is to take place
- its approximate timing
- the reasons for it
- the legal, economic and social implications for any affected employees
- the measures the employer envisages it will take in relation to the employees as a result of the transfer (or a confirmation that no such measures are envisaged).

An economic, technical or organisational justification (ETO)

An ETO may provide grounds for the prospective transferee to fairly dismiss transferring employees following a transfer. There is no statutory definition of an ETO, but guidance suggests it is likely to include a reason relating to:

- the profitability or market performance of the transferee's business (an economic reason)
- the nature of the equipment or production processes used (a technical reason)
- the management or organisational structure of the transferee's business (an organisational reason).

It must entail changes in the workforce which mean changes in numbers (for example, redundancies) or a change in the type of work. It will rarely be safe to rely on an ETO justification for changing terms of employment or for dismissal except where you are restructuring and making redundancies.

Pensions

Certain aspects of employees' occupational pension schemes do not transfer under TUPE. However, the **Pensions Act 2004** does apply to transfers taking place after 6 April 2005, which means in effect that provisions broadly equivalent to the TUPE regulations apply to pension rights from that date. So if the transferor provides a pension scheme then the transferee has to provide some form of pension arrangement for employees who are eligible for, or members of, the previous scheme. It does not have to be the same as the arrangement provided by the transferor but must meet a certain minimum standard specified under the Pensions Act.

The law in this area is complex, and subject to ever-changing interpretation by both the UK and European courts. Before committing yourself to taking over work previously done by another organisation, you should obtain legal advice on whether TUPE applies and the effect it may have. It is also essential to consider the financial implications. For example, under TUPE you will be taking on employees who have accrued rights dependent on length of service, such as redundancy pay, and will have to be able to meet these commitments. This may significantly increase the amount of reserves you must hold to meet potential redundancy liabilities.

For further information see *Employment rights on the transfers of an undertaking*, available from www.berr.gov.uk, and the *Code of practice on workforce matters in public sector service contracts*, available from http://archive.cabinetoffice.gov.uk/opsr/workforce_reform/code_of_practice/index.asp

Public interest disclosure – 'whistle-blowing'

The **Public Interest Disclosure Act 1998** protects employees and workers from being dismissed or victimised as a result of 'blowing the whistle' on any breaches of the law or dangerous activities carried out by their employer. To qualify for protection the worker must have a reasonable belief that the employer is guilty or is likely to be guilty of at least one of the following:

- a criminal offence
- a failure to comply with any legal obligation
- a miscarriage of justice
- threats to anyone's health and safety

- damage to the environment
- deliberately concealing information showing responsibility for any of the above.

The Act defines two categories of people to whom protected disclosures can take place: the 'first level' is the employer in question; 'second level' disclosure includes an 'appropriate person' such as a professional body or regulator. Disclosures to the media are not protected.

Protection is provided for the first level if a worker makes a disclosure in good faith:

- to their employer or through procedures which their employer has authorised
- to the person responsible for the concern (for example, the health and safety representative for concerns about health and safety).

Protection is provided for the second level disclosure if a worker makes the allegation in good faith and believes:

- that the allegation is substantially true
- that they are making the disclosure to the appropriate 'prescribed person'.

In certain circumstances a worker can make a disclosure to their legal adviser or to a professional standards body.

It is good practice for all employers to introduce their own whistle-blowing procedures. For more information on policy development see *Whistle-blowing* at www.cipd.co.uk; for further information on the legal aspects see *Disclosures in the public interest: protections for workers who 'blow the whistle'*, available from www.berr.gov.uk.

Redundancy

Under the **Employment Rights Act 1996**, redundancy arises when employees are dismissed for any of the following reasons:

- the employer has ceased or intends to cease carrying on the activities for which the employee was employed

- the employer has ceased or intends to cease carrying on the activities in the place where the employee was employed
- the need for the employee to carry out particular work has ceased or diminished or is expected to do so
- the need to carry out particular work in the place where the employee was employed has ceased or diminished or is expected to do so.

Change of place of work: Whether a new workplace involves redundancy will depend on the circumstances, including the contract of employment. If the contract specifies where someone is employed (for example, at a particular address), then any shutdown of the workplace and a move to a new address will be a redundancy situation. Even if the contract has a mobility clause, a redundancy situation will still arise if the relocation causes significant inconvenience and, for example, employees have to move house.

Change in the work required: There will be a redundancy situation only if the work the employee performed under their contract of employment has ceased or diminished. If, for example, someone else is going to be employed to do that work there is no redundancy.

Suitable alternative employment: An employee who is offered 'suitable alternative employment' on new terms and conditions, at a new place of work, or with a slightly different job, will not receive a redundancy payment if they unreasonably refuse the offer. It may be necessary to get legal advice about whether the alternative employment is 'suitable', see *Offers of alternative work*, page 105.

Notifying those involved

Consultation with those people affected by redundancy provides an opportunity to discuss the problem and identify possible solutions as well as to meet legal obligations.

The unions and employee representatives

Under the **Trade Union and Labour Relations (Consolidation) Act 1992** and the **Collective Redundancies and Transfer of Undertaking (Protection of Employment) (Amendment) Regulations 1999**, if 20 or more employees are to be made redundant at one establishment within a 90-day period or are to be transferred to another employer:

- employers must inform and consult recognised union or appropriate employee representatives. If necessary, representatives may be elected specifically for the purpose; the regulations detail how
- representatives of all employees who may be affected by redundancies or transfer must be consulted, not just those under threat of redundancy
- representatives have the right to paid time off for training and to be provided with facilities to fulfil their role (for example, a room, a phone and copying facilities)
- where no representatives are elected, the employer must pass on information to all affected employees.

Case law has established that in most redundancies employers have a duty to consult the individuals who are or might be affected as well as their representatives. It is therefore advisable, and best practice, to consult with individuals who are to be made redundant, regardless of the size of the organisation or the length of service of the employee.

For further information see the Acas booklet *Redundancy handling*, available from www.acas.org.uk, or *Redundancy consultation and notification*, from www.berr.gov.uk.

Minimum periods for consultation

The employer must begin the process of consultation in good time and in any event at least:

- 90 days before the first dismissal takes effect if there are 100 or more proposed redundancies in one workplace within a 90-day period

- 30 days before the first dismissal takes effect if there are between 20 and 99 proposed redundancies within a 90-day period.

Where there are fewer than 20 proposed redundancies there are no minimum periods of consultation, but consultation should be carried out within a fair and reasonable time frame and the employer must follow a fair procedure (until April 2009 the employer must follow the statutory dismissal procedure).

The union or employee representatives must be told in writing:

- the reasons for the proposed redundancies
- the numbers and categories of employees affected
- the total number of employees in these categories at the workplace
- how employees will be selected for redundancy
- how the redundancies will be carried out, taking account of any agreed procedure, and the period over which they are to take effect
- the proposed method of calculating redundancy payments.

The consultation must consider ways of avoiding or reducing the number of dismissals and minimising their consequences, and must aim to reach agreement with the union or representatives. It is good practice to address some or all of the following:

- the effect on earnings if alternative work or downgrading is accepted in preference to redundancy
- arrangements for travel, removal and related expenses, where work is accepted in a different location
- whether a redundant employee may leave during the notice period, or postpone the date of expiry of notice, without losing entitlement to statutory redundancy payment
- any extension of the length of the statutory trial period in a new job
- help with job seeking including arrangements for reasonable paid time off

to look for alternative work or make arrangements for training.

Ways of reducing the need for redundancies include:

- natural wastage
- restricting the recruitment of permanent staff
- reducing the use of temporary staff
- retiring all employees at the normal or default retirement age
- seeking applicants for voluntary redundancy and/or early retirement
- filling vacancies from among existing employees
- introducing short-time working or temporary layoff (if this is provided for in the contract of employment or by an agreed variation of its terms)
- retraining employers so that they can work elsewhere in the organisation.

Department for Business, Enterprise and Regulatory Reform (BERR)

The employer must notify BERR in writing of any proposal to make 20 or more people redundant within a 90-day period. This is to help government departments develop measures to help or retrain the employees affected. The notice requirements are the same as those for consultation with the unions or other representatives (see page 103). A copy of the notice must be given to the union or other representatives.

Employers may notify the BERR by letter or by using form **HR1**, available from any Redundancy Payments Office or Jobcentre Plus Office. For further information, see the *Redundancy consultation and notification*, available from www.berr.gov.uk.

The employees

Under the **Employment Rights Act 1996** each employee being made redundant must be given an individual written notice of a redundancy dismissal. Workers on fixed-term contracts must be given notice in the same way as employees on permanent contracts.

The amount of notice given should be either the statutory minimum or the period agreed in the contract of employment, whichever is the longer. Employers who do not give advance notice must pay wages for the period of notice. This is separate from any obligation to award redundancy pay (page 106). The statutory minimum notice required is:

- one month to two years' service – one week's notice
- two to twelve years' service – one week's notice for each complete year
- 12 or more years' service – 12 weeks' notice.

Selection for redundancy

The employer has a legal duty to select people for redundancy in a fair, reasonable and consistent manner. It is best to define precise and objective criteria when determining who is to be selected for redundancy. The criteria should meet the needs of the organisation and could include:

- skills and experience needed to maintain its activities
- work performance, which should be assessed through appraisal systems
- attendance records (but make sure they are accurate, exclude maternity, parental and adoption leave, and leave for family responsibilities. Exclude absences related to an employee's disability and avoid those relating to one long bout of illness.)

Someone selected for redundancy for any of the following reasons could automatically claim unfair dismissal:

- because of trade union membership or non-membership, or taking part in union activities
- carrying out duties as an employee representative
- taking part in the election of an employee representative for collective redundancy purposes or transfers of undertakings (TUPE, see page 100)
- exercising the right to be accompanied at a disciplinary or grievance hearing
- requesting flexible working arrangements

- taking action on health and safety grounds as a recognised health and safety representative
- performing or proposing to perform the duties of a occupational pension scheme trustee
- reasons relating to the national minimum wage or Working Time Regulations
- making a 'protected disclosure' (whistle-blowing) within the meaning of the Public Interest Disclosure Act 1998, or in breach of a previously agreed procedure
- taking lawfully organised industrial action lasting eight weeks or less (or more than eight weeks in certain circumstances)
- on grounds related to maternity or to other rights for working parents (for example, adoption leave and paternity leave)
- reasons relating to the **Part-time Workers (Prevention of Less Favourable Treatment) Regulations**
- reasons relating to the **Fixed-term Workers (Prevention of Less Favourable Treatment) Regulations**.

An employer must not discriminate on the grounds of race, sex or pregnancy, marital status, religion or belief, sexual orientation, age or disability. Make sure the criteria do not indirectly discriminate. For example, arrangements whereby part-time workers should be laid off first could affect women disproportionately, and 'last in first out' arrangements could be potentially discriminatory on the basis of age. Employees should be consulted on the proposed criteria.

Offers of alternative work

Under the **Employment Rights Act 1996** employers must offer an employee threatened with redundancy suitable alternative employment, if a suitable post exists. Factors such as pay, status, hours and location are relevant when deciding if a job is a suitable alternative. Any offer should be put in writing and show how the new employment differs from the old. Any new job must start within four weeks after the end of the old employment contract. A redundant employee who unreasonably refuses a suitable offer of alternative work may lose their entitlement to redundancy payment.

If the terms and conditions of the new job are different or the work itself is different, the employee is entitled to a four-week trial period before accepting the arrangement. This period can be extended by agreement if retraining is necessary. The right to redundancy pay is preserved during the trial period, but once the new job is accepted redundancy rights are lost.

Time off to look for work

Employees under redundancy notice who have a minimum of two years' service are entitled to reasonable time off work during working hours to look for another job or make arrangements for training for future employment. The employer must pay at least two-fifths of a week's pay, regardless of the amount of time off allowed. Where possible, all time off to look for work should be paid and such assistance should be offered to all employees, regardless of length of service.

Redundancy pay

The **Employment Rights Act 1996** governs statutory redundancy pay. To be eligible under the Act an employee must have been:
- continuously employed for more than two years
- dismissed for reasons of redundancy (people who have opted for early retirement will not be eligible).

The level of statutory redundancy pay depends on the employee's age, length of service and weekly pay. For each complete year of service up to a maximum of 20 employees are entitled to:
- for each year of service if aged under 22 – half a week's pay
- for each year of service at age 22 but under 41 – one week's pay

- for each year of service at age 41 or over – one and a half weeks' pay.

The government sets an upper limit each year on the amount of weekly pay that can be counted (£350 from February 2009). The employer is responsible for paying this lump sum. There is a redundancy calculator on the BERR website www.berr.gov.uk.

You must give an employee a written statement of how the redundancy payment is calculated.

Good practice

The law provides a safety net for employees who are made redundant. However, the provisions outlined above are far from generous. Employers should look at ways of introducing better terms into employees' contracts.

Improvements on the legal minimum include:
- helping people to find alternative work
- allowing all employees facing redundancy, including those who have worked for less than two years, time off to look for work or for training
- arranging for redundancy counselling
- extending the period of redundancy notice given to employees
- providing contractual redundancy pay entitlement above the statutory minimum – for example, by extending the number of weeks' redundancy pay, increasing the maximum figure for 'weekly' pay, or reducing the qualifying period.

You should consider the organisation's financial position carefully before agreeing to better financial provisions. The decision to make staff redundant will often be made when an organisation's assets and income do not cover its costs. The contractual liability to employees is a debt. If these liabilities are increased, an organisation may have to close earlier, which is against the interests of service users. Also remember that the management committee of an unincorporated organisation (unincorporated association or trust) may become personally liable if the organisation cannot pay its employees the amount stated in their contracts.

Claiming money owed

If the organisation's cash flow problems are so serious that making the redundancy payment would damage its business, BERR can arrange to pay the employee direct from the National Insurance Fund. The organisation will be expected to repay these funds as soon as possible. If the organisation is insolvent, again payment is made by BERR, and the organisation's share is recovered from its assets.

If the organisation becomes insolvent, employees may claim payment from the Insolvency Service's Redundancy Payments Offices for the following claims:

- redundancy pay
- arrears of wages (for at least one week but no more than eight weeks)
- outstanding holiday pay for up to six weeks
- notice pay
- basic award for unfair dismissal.

There are also some safeguards for occupational pension rights: trustees of occupational pension schemes may apply to the employer's representative for payment from the National Insurance Fund, within certain limits, in respect of relevant contributions which remain unpaid at the date of the employer's insolvency.

HMRC is responsible for the following claims (for entitlement continuing after the insolvency date):

- statutory sick pay
- maternity, paternity and adoption pay.

An employee of an incorporated organisation who is still owed money after receiving these awards (for example, for any additional arrears of wages) would have a claim for some priority debts against the employer. The employee would therefore become a preferential creditor. An employee of an unincorporated organisation may be able to bring a claim against some or all members of the management committee. Employees are always advised to seek help (for example, from their union or a law centre).

Providing references

An employee who leaves or applies for another job will often request a reference. It is good practice to provide one wherever possible. Failure to give a reference may be discriminatory or in breach of contract. To ensure that future managers or management committee members can provide such references, it is good practice to preserve enough information in the employee's file to enable an accurate reference to be written.

All references provided must be fair and accurate. If unfairly critical, an employee could make a financial claim against your organisation. Ensure that you stick to the facts. You can, for example, say that 'Disciplinary proceedings are pending and matters are under investigation'. That is a pure statement of fact and does not say that the employee is guilty. If you are proposing to write a critical reference for a former employee, send them a draft and ask them to agree the reference before it is provided. Also beware of writing artificially good references; there is a danger of being sued by the new employer for misrepresentation.

The Information Commissioner's *Employment practices code*, available from www.ico.gov.uk, includes a section on references, which provides the following benchmarks:

- Set out a clear policy stating who can give references on behalf of the organisation, in what circumstances, and how references are accessed. Make sure that anyone who is likely to become a referee is aware of this policy.
- Do not provide confidential references about someone unless you are sure this is their wish.

- When someone's employment ends, establish whether the person wishes references to be provided to future employers or to others.

In relation to receiving references:

- When responding to a request from a worker to see their own reference which would enable a third party to be identified, make a judgement as to what information it is reasonable to withhold.

Employment tribunals

Employees who consider their employment rights to have been infringed usually have the right to apply to an employment tribunal. These are part of the UK tribunals system, are administered by the Tribunals Service, and are regulated and supervised by the Administrative Justice and Tribunals Council.

Matters dealt with include unfair dismissal, breach of contract, discrimination and a range of claims relating to wages and other payments. You can get a full list, called a **jurisdiction list**, from any local tribunal office, the Employment Tribunals public enquiry line on 0845 795 9775, or from www.employmenttribunals.gov.uk.

Most complaints to an employment tribunal must be made within three months, although those related to redundancy pay and equal pay must be made within six months and extensions are permitted in certain other circumstances for other types of complaint. Redundancy and equal pay complaints can sometimes be extended (if the employer deliberately concealed relevant facts or if the individual concerned was under the age of 18 or mentally incapable).

An employment tribunal has the power to award compensation for unfair dismissal up to a statutory limit (£66,200 in 2009). There is no financial limit to compensation that can be awarded in cases involving discrimination.

In most cases, once the employment tribunal has accepted a case, Acas will invite you to take part in a conciliation process. For straightforward cases such as redundancy payments and breach of contract seven weeks are allocated to reach a settlement. For most other cases, the limit is 13 weeks, but discrimination cases have no time limit.

For more information about the Acas scheme see *Heading for a tribunal? Choose the Acas arbitration scheme*, available from www.acas.org.uk. For alternative ways of resolving disputes see *Managing conflict at work*, available from www.cipd.org.uk. For information about the employment tribunals see the Tribunal Service website www.employmenttribunals.gov.uk or ring the helpline on 0845 795 9775.

Chapter 4

Recruiting and paying people

This chapter starts by describing the law and good practice relating to making an appointment, then looks at how to recruit and manage freelance and self-employed workers and take on volunteers. The following sections look at possible restrictions on recruitment, firstly through the Criminal Records Bureau and Independent Safeguarding Authority, and then relating to taking on workers from abroad. The rules on paying wages and statutory sick pay are then explained, together with a discussion of pension schemes and regulations. The next section presents employers' rights on monitoring emails and internet access along with an email internet policy. The final section looks at the implications when reorganising an organisation's structure and activities.

Making an appointment

The legal requirements

During recruitment and selection it is illegal to discriminate against anyone on the grounds of their:

- race (colour, ethnic origin or nationality), age, gender, transgender status, religion or other belief or sexuality, or because they have a disability (unless one or more of these factors is a genuine occupational requirement for the post – see *Discrimination*, in chapter 3)
- membership or non-membership of a union.

It is illegal to employ someone who is not entitled to work in the UK (see *Taking on workers from abroad*, page 122)

Voluntary organisations working in partnership with, or providing services on behalf of, a public authority may have a duty to promote racial, sexual and disability equality in employment. This includes examining procedures for staff recruitment (see *Equality schemes*, in chapter 3)

As recruitment may involve collecting 'sensitive' information about candidates, employers should also be aware of the requirements of the **Data Protection Act 1998**.

See the Information Commissioner's *Employment practices code,* available from www.ico.gov.uk.

Reviewing posts

As soon as there is a vacant post, prepare the job description and specification (see page 110). Examine how the post can meet equal opportunities objectives by considering, for example, whether:

- it is suitable for a flexible working arrangement (see *Flexible working arrangements*, in chapter 3)
- it is particularly appropriate for a disabled worker and what adjustments or adaptations could be made to ensure that disabled people are not disadvantaged. It is not unlawful to say that a particular position is open only to disabled people (as there is no law making it illegal to discriminate against able-bodied people). However it would be unlawful to say that a post was only open to people with a particular disability
- it is possible to apply the genuine occupational requirement criteria to limit recruitment to people of a specific racial group, sex, religion or other belief, or sexuality (see *Genuine occupational requirement*, in chapter 3)
- it is appropriate to encourage any groups of people currently under-represented in your workforce to apply. Under the law certain groups can be encouraged to apply but their race, sex, age, religion and sexuality cannot be taken into account when shortlisting or appointing (see *Positive action*, in chapter 3).

Selection panels

The composition of the selection panel will depend on the nature of the job and the organisation. It could include the line manager, committee member(s) and someone authorised to give information about terms and conditions. Some organisations invite external people with specialist human resource knowledge to participate. Where possible panels should have a racial and gender balance and, if a disabled person applies, include someone with experience or knowledge of that disability. Panel members should have been trained in interviewing techniques and equal opportunities law and good practice. Generally, panels have between three and five members.

The recruitment process

Making an appointment is a lengthy process. Allow enough time to:

- finalise the job description and person specification
- establish the assessment criteria: application form, interview and/or tests, examples of work, references
- identify how the post is to be advertised and design the advertisement, produce an application form and background information for enquirers
- advertise
- shortlist
- make arrangements for any tests or other assessments
- draw up the interview procedure and questions
- prepare for the interview
- interview the candidates (generally allow one day per five or six candidates)
- take up references (if not done before interview)
- if necessary, carry out medical, criminal records and other pre-employment checks.

From advertisement to starting date could therefore take at least ten weeks:

week 1	advertisement appears
week 4	closing date
week 4/5	shortlisting
week 6	interviews
	offer of appointment made verbally, and accepted
	offer made in writing
	candidate hands in notice to current employer
week 10	employee starts (if four weeks' notice given)

The process could take much longer if the job offer is conditional on satisfactory references, medical checks and/or criminal records checks. An employer must be satisfied that employees are entitled to work in the UK: to ensure everyone is treated equally, ask for evidence from all applicants before making an offer of work. See *Taking on workers from abroad*, page 122.

Job descriptions

A job description is not a legal requirement but it is good practice for employees to have a written statement of their tasks and responsibilities. If it forms part of the contract of employment, any change will have to be made through a variation of contract procedure, which usually means obtaining the employee's agreement. It is preferable to keep the job description separate from the contract of employment.

The job description should include:

- the job title
- the person(s) to whom the employee will report and those for whom the employee is responsible
- the location(s) of the job
- a summary of the main purpose of the job
- a list of the main duties.

Job sharers

You must include information about how responsibilities will be shared in job descriptions for job sharers (see *Flexible working*, in chapter 3). If relevant, separate the tasks specific to one post from shared work.

Person specifications

A person specification describes the knowledge, abilities, skills, attributes and experience needed for the post, based on the tasks outlined in the job description. Many specifications distinguish between essential attributes (for example, the knowledge that someone must have) and desirable (the knowledge someone ideally has).

Assess all criteria to ensure that they are necessary and not discriminatory.

Specifications should state the minimum qualifications and experience needed. For example, is an academic qualification or previous experience in similar employment essential? Other qualities may be just as important: for example, personal knowledge of a community, or personal experience of a disability. A requirement to have GCSE maths may indirectly discriminate against people who have not been educated in Britain, but a requirement to have 'maths to GCSE standard' is not discriminatory. If specifying knowledge of named software packages, such as Microsoft Word, say that equivalent packages will be acceptable, as disabled candidates may use adapted technology with their own software.

You should also consider how each candidate will be measured against the criteria. For example, 'A commitment to equal opportunities' cannot be easily assessed. A better phrase may be 'Demonstrable evidence of promoting equal opportunities'.

Application forms

An application form makes it easier to compare applications without bias than using curricula vitae (CVs) and letters of application. Forms should be clear and well structured, and ask only for information relevant to the particular post being recruited. Always offer disabled candidates alternative approaches to an application form, perhaps in a different format, such as typewritten, by telephone, on tape or by email.

Application forms should ask for:

- name (ask for 'first name' rather than 'Christian name', or even just initials, to reduce the possibility of race or sex discrimination)
- address and contact details
- details of current or most recent employment, duties involved, date of joining and leaving, if appropriate
- details of past employment
- relevant education and qualifications
- relevant experience (paid and voluntary, and general life experience)

- the earliest date the applicant would be able to take up the post
- names and addresses of two referees, one of whom should generally be the current or most recent employer, or a college or school (ask whether the current employer may be contacted before interview and whether the applicant wishes to be informed before referees are contacted)
- evidence to show that the person can work in the UK
- whether the person is disabled and would require any adaptations to attend for interview or to carry out the work as described in the job
- if the post is exempt under the Rehabilitation of Offenders Act (see *Ex-offenders*, in chapter 3), the form should include the statement: 'This post is exempt under the Rehabilitation of Offenders Act 1974 and you are required to reveal all convictions, even those which are spent.' Because the application may be seen by people who do not have a right to see this information, tell the applicant to provide details of all convictions separately, in a sealed envelope addressed to the person in charge of the recruitment process
- if the post is not exempt but you need to know about convictions, the form should ask whether the person has any criminal convictions and include the statement: 'You should not reveal any convictions which are spent under the Rehabilitation of Offenders Act 1974.' Again, tell the applicant to provide the information in a sealed envelope
- where relevant, the form should state that a Criminal Records Bureau disclosure will be sought for the successful applicant (see *Criminal Record Checks,* page 120).

Advise applicants to address their answers to the person specification; an effective method is to include the specification headings on the application form.

Avoid potentially discriminating questions about matters such as age, marital status and caring responsibilities.

Monitoring applications

A form to monitor applicants by race, gender, age and disability should be included in application forms (see *Monitoring effectiveness*, in chapter 3). Some organisations include questions on religion and sexuality. The questions should be on a separate sheet, used only for monitoring purposes. Explain why the information is needed and state that it will remain confidential; emphasise that completing the form is voluntary and failure to do so will not affect the success of an application.

Unless the monitoring form is separate from the application form and is anonymous (that is, there is no possibility that an individual could be identified), there are likely to be implications under the Data Protection Act 1998. Employers need the individual's explicit consent to handle 'sensitive' information. For further information see *Data protection*, in chapter 9.

Job advertisements

In addition to the local or national press, consider advertising in papers targeted at specific readerships: for example, *The Voice, Caribbean Times, New Nation, Asian Times, The Pink Paper, Disability Now* and *Disability Times.*

Also consider local organisations – including the council for voluntary service or equivalent – places of worship, radio stations and local publications such as a talking newspaper or the local disability organisation's newsletter. It is good practice to inform the Disability Employment Adviser at the local Jobcentre Plus of all vacancies.

There are also a number of web-based recruitment sites for voluntary organisations such as www.charityjob.co.uk, jobs.thirdsector.co.uk, www.jobsincharity.co.uk, www.charitypeople.co.uk and www.charitycareers.co.uk. There is also a dedicated site for disabled jobseekers, www.Jobability.com.

Adverts should be available in a range of formats, including large print, tape, disk and email.

Think carefully about the wording. It is important not only to attract good applicants, but also to deter unsuitable enquirers and avoid wasting their time and yours.

Advertisements should include:
- the organisation's name
- job title (and department, if appropriate)
- brief description of the job
- brief summary of skills, knowledge, experience and qualifications needed
- salary (and salary scale if appropriate)
- hours, stating whether full or part-time and any flexible working arrangements
- whether the post is open for job sharing
- whether the post is intended to be permanent or fixed term
- name, address, telephone number and/or email address of the contact for further information and application forms
- closing date for applications
- date(s) when interviews will be held, if this is known
- a statement that you have an equal opportunities and diversity policy
- any further information – for example, whether applications are particularly welcome from certain sections of the community (see *Positive action*, in chapter 3)
- if the organisation is a registered charity, a statement to this effect.

If the post is limited to specific applicants under a genuine occupational requirement this should be stated, together with the section of the relevant legislation under which the post is advertised (see *Genuine occupational requirement*, in chapter 3). Get legal advice before advertising such a post, as people who are wrongly excluded can claim for discrimination.

Some funders specify that recipients must acknowledge their support in all publicity material, including job advertisements. Check your conditions of grant aid to see if this applies.

Information for enquirers

Enquirers should be sent copies of the job description and person specification, together with a statement of your equal opportunities and diversity policy and details of the main conditions of service (see *Statement of employment particulars*, in chapter 3) including:

- salary and salary scale, including any cut-off point for starting salary
- method and frequency of pay
- hours of work including any flexible working arrangements
- place of work, and whether this can be varied
- whether overtime is paid or time off given in lieu of pay for extra hours worked
- annual leave and whether this includes bank holidays
- pension scheme, if any, and whether it is contributory or non-contributory
- the name of any recognised union(s)
- maternity/parental/adoption/paternity leave arrangements if these are more favourable than statutory entitlements
- any other points – for example, travel allowance or removal expenses.

Let candidates know the interview date. Be sensitive when arranging dates to avoid clashes with religious observance (for example, Friday afternoons).

Enquirers should also receive details of the organisation, ideally including a copy of the latest annual report and details of funding sources.

Shortlisting

Before shortlisting, separate the monitoring forms from the application forms, analyse them and store the results for future reference.

Shortlist soon after the closing date. The selection panel should have copies of the job description and person specification. The decision to shortlist a candidate must be based on whether that person fulfils the requirements in the person specification.

The panel should record why each applicant has or has not been shortlisted. An applicant who feels discriminated against on grounds of race, age, sex, sexuality, religion or belief or disability, or who has been refused employment on the grounds of membership or non-membership of a union has up to three months to complain to an employment tribunal. Shortlisting forms should therefore be kept for a minimum of three months. The tribunal can grant an extension, so it is advisable, as well as good practice, to keep the forms for 12 months.

Invite the shortlisted people to an interview, and let others know they have not been successful. Ask for the candidates' consent if references are to be taken up before interview, then write to the referees, enclosing a stamped addressed envelope and a copy of the job description and person specification. Even if references are taken up at this stage they should not be read until after a decision has been made, unless essential to the selection process.

Letters to interviewees should state:

- the date, time and length of the interview
- its location, how to get there (provide a map if necessary) and whether travel expenses will be paid
- who the candidate should ask for on arrival
- information about members of the interview panel
- any documents a candidate should bring, such as examples of reports
- whether there will be any tests and if so, their nature and length
- whether there is more than one interview stage
- whether referees have been contacted (if appropriate)
- that disabled applicants should contact you to discuss any adjustments or other help they require to attend the interview or take part in testing.

Ask candidates to confirm the time as soon as possible.

Interviews

Preparing for the interview

It is essential to plan interviews well. Identify any support a candidate may need and the best way to provide it. For example, if a candidate needs a signer ask them if there is someone they would prefer.

The panel should agree a list of questions relating to the skills and qualities appropriate to each key task and allocate to each member a set of linked questions. Look at the individual forms to see if there are specific questions that should be asked. Nominate someone to chair the interviews and decide who will answer candidates' questions on specific topics.

Never ask questions on the following topics in an interview: future family plans, marital status, sexuality, partner's occupation, caring responsibilities and domestic arrangements. Questions about union activities should only be asked if explicitly mentioned in the job description. If the job involves evening or weekend work, ask all candidates about their availability.

Make sure someone is available to welcome applicants, and that there is a suitable waiting area with access to a toilet. Have material prepared for any skills being tested (for example, bookkeeping, writing or word processing). This should be the same for each candidate, unless the material needs to be adapted for a disabled candidate. Organise arrangements for paying expenses, if appropriate.

Tests

A presentation or a test may assess some aspects of the person specification, but should never be used as the only method of selection and should only be included if relevant to the job. Make sure applicants are aware of the nature of the presentation or test, how long they will have and what is being tested. If a test involves use of a computer, wherever possible make sure the applicant is able to use a program they know. Remember a disabled person may need extra time and other adjustments when making a presentation or performing a test. People with dyslexia may need, for example, speech to text software or a computer screen with a coloured background to documents. For further details visit www.beingdyslexic.co.uk/information/workplace/adjustments_in_the_workplace.

Conducting the interview

The aim of the interview is to assess the applicant's suitability for the job in relation to the person specification.

Ask each candidate the same core questions, give them the same tests and allocate each an equal amount of time for their interview. However, disabled candidates may need more time if, for example, they use an interpreter or signer to communicate with the panel. The chair should inform each candidate of the time allocated and keep track of time during the interview.

Allow at least ten minutes between each interview for the panel to make notes, but wait until all the interviews have been completed before discussing the candidates.

Whoever is chairing the interviews should welcome each candidate, introduce panel members, outline the interview structure and explain when the decision will be made and how the candidate will be notified. Once the interview starts, encourage the candidates to do most of the talking and avoid questions that can produce one-word answers. If a candidate seems particularly shy, or unclear about what is being asked, try rephrasing the question or encouraging them to provide more information. Always allow time for candidates to ask questions and do not let the interviews overrun.

Selection

Panel members should make notes on each candidate during and after the interview. One method is to have a list of the skills, qualities and type of experience needed and record whether each has been fully, partly or not met. Candidates must always be assessed on the selection criteria, and not against each other. Panel members must be able to justify individual decisions with evidence. Under the **Data Protection Act 1998** applicants are entitled to view any interview notes which contain personal data about them. Make sure the panel is aware of this and that any defamatory or discriminatory comments could lead to claims of unfair treatment.

Once all the interviews are over, the panel should discuss the applicants and take the decision on whom to appoint; options for action if a decision cannot be made are given at the end of this section. If references have already been taken up this is the time to read them.

Contact the successful candidate as soon as possible. A telephone call should be immediately followed up by a formal written offer. If the offer is subject to any conditions, make this clear in the telephone call and subsequent letter (see *Letter of appointment*, below). Let unsuccessful candidates know as soon as possible and ask them if they want you to keep their application for future vacancies (if appropriate) or have their details removed from file. If they want you to keep their information, tell them how long it will be kept for.

It is important to record why people were not selected, for equal opportunities monitoring. However, you must be able to justify keeping any personal data following the interviews as being relevant to and necessary for the recruitment process itself, or for dealing with any challenges to the decision by an unsuccessful candidate. Make sure that any personal data is securely stored.

As with shortlisting, a candidate who feels discriminated against on grounds of age, race, sex, sexuality, religion or belief or disability has up to three months to apply to an employment tribunal (see *Discrimination*, in chapter 3). Interview records should therefore be kept for a minimum of three months. The tribunal can grant an extension, so it is advisable, as well as good practice, to keep the records for 12 months.

If the panel cannot reach a decision because there are two or more suitable candidates, it may be useful to re-interview just these people. If the panel cannot gather adequate evidence because of the questions asked, some or all of the candidates could be re-interviewed about those matters, perhaps through phone conversations. If none of the applicants were suitable, re-advertising is the only option. If this is the case, review the job description, person specification and advertising process to see whether they can attract the suitable candidates.

Letter of appointment

The letter of appointment may form part of the contract of employment (see chapter 3) and should include the following:

- starting date, subject to any conditions being met
- starting salary
- job title
- any conditions of appointment – for example, whether it is subject to a satisfactory medical check, references or criminal records check (see page 120), and the fact that the offer of employment is conditional on these being satisfactory
- the obligation to provide documents required to comply with the **Asylum and Immigration Act 1996** (see *Taking on workers from abroad*, page 122) and the fact that the offer of employment is conditional on the person providing these and having no restrictions on their right to work in the UK
- a request for any further information or necessary documentation – for example, a P45 (see *Paying staff*, page 124)
- details of any probationary period (see page 116)
- a request for confirmation in writing that the person accepts the offer (and any conditions included in it) and the date they expect to start provided that all conditions have been met.

Employees must receive a statement of terms and conditions within two months of commencing employment. The statement must contain certain particulars (see chapter 3).

Probationary periods

Some contracts allow for probationary periods – often of three or six months – to enable the employer and employee to assess how they are getting along in their new employment. An employee has all statutory rights during the probationary period and all contractual rights unless the contract explicitly states otherwise. For example, the contract might specify a reduced notice period and/or a simplified disciplinary procedure during the probationary period.

If employment is subject to a probationary period it is usual to make this clear in the letter of appointment, and it must be made clear in the contract. At the end of the probationary period either the employment will be confirmed, the probationary period extended (normally for a further four weeks) or the employment terminated. The probationary period can be extended only if the contract allows for this. If employment is terminated at the end of the probationary period, notice must be given as required by law or by the contract, whichever is longer.

For details of managing a probationary period see 'Managing staff recruitment and selection' in *Just about managing?*

Taking on freelance and self-employed workers and consultants

You may decide that it is appropriate to outsource a piece of work to an external worker or consultancy agency if, for example, specialised skills are needed or current staff do not have the time to do that work. If so, it is good practice to set up policies and procedures to ensure that the work is effectively managed and allocated fairly and that the parties involved understand their responsibilities.

Those who are not genuinely self-employed people are likely to be included within the definition of 'workers' (see *The definitions*, in chapter 3), and be entitled to some rights, including those relating to equal pay, the minimum wage and paid holidays. They are also protected by the equality legislation – an organisation must be able to show that it did not use race, age, sex, sexuality, disability or religious belief as a factor when making an appointment.

When to advertise

As small pieces of work may not justify advertising and staff costs it is useful to specify the size and type of contracts that do not have to be openly advertised. You should monitor any informal recruitment processes to safeguard against possible discrimination. Always ask those appointed for examples of previous work and for references.

Contracts

A contract for services is essential to spell out the responsibilities of both the organisation and the worker. It could simply be in the form of an exchange of letters, but should include the following:

Names of the organisation and the worker.

Work to be done: this information may be in a separate brief to which you can refer. It needs to be specific, and for long pieces of work it should include provision for reviews to ensure the brief remains appropriate and work is being done to the required quality and timescales. It is also useful to give the name of the key contact within the organisation.

Start and completion dates.

The agreed fee, and, if applicable, whether the fee is inclusive or exclusive of VAT.

Expenses. Whether any expenses (for example, travel, telephone) are payable; if so, you may want to give a maximum budget, state how expenses will be agreed and ask for proof of how they have been incurred.

Invoicing and payment. Payments can be made monthly or weekly in arrears, at the end of the piece of work, or at specified stages during a longer contract. Sometimes work is paid partly in advance. Ensure that you continue to owe the worker money until the work has been completed to your satisfaction.

Payment terms. Generally that payment is due within 14, 21 or 30 days of invoice date.

Copyright or patent. Unless explicitly assigned to your organisation, the copyright or patent of written material or a new product will belong to the person who produced the work and not to the organisation that paid for it. It is possible to have joint copyright. If a worker is contracted to produce a publication that may run to a second edition or be translated, the parties' rights and responsibilities in relation to that edition must be clear. Copyright on the design of databases, computer programs, websites etc. are particularly complex and it is advisable to take legal advice. (For further information on copyright and patents see www.ipo.gov.uk.)

Self-employment, tax and national insurance. Make it clear that the agreement does not create a contract of employment, that the worker is self-employed and remains so, and is responsible for their own tax and national insurance. **Note:** in general, organisations are responsible for deducting tax and national insurance from all payments made to individuals. Merely including the above statement does not exempt you from this obligation. Only HM Revenue & Customs (HMRC) can confirm someone's self-employed status and you should take advice from your PAYE office before paying anyone gross rather than deducting tax and national insurance, especially if the contract is relatively long-term, is based in your office, or is otherwise more like an employment relationship than a relationship with an outside person. Include an indemnity from the worker for respect of liability for taxation suffered by the organisation if that worker is deemed to be an employee.

Illness or accident. The contract should say who the worker needs to inform if they become ill and cannot perform the duties in

the contract. It should also state that no fee shall be payable if services are not provided.

Insurance. Depending on the kind of work, it may be necessary for the worker to have public liability insurance and/or professional indemnity insurance (see chapter 7). If so, the contract should ask for a copy of the policy or schedule to be submitted as proof of cover. In some situations the policy should also indemnify the organisation for any claims brought against it arising from the worker's negligence.

Organisational policies. The contract should state that the worker is expected to comply with your policies on, for example, equal opportunities and diversity, health and safety and environmental matters.

Confidentiality. Include a clause restricting disclosure of information. This should make clear the worker's duty to comply with data protection law and your data protection policy, and should detail the type of information considered to be confidential. The clause should cover confidentiality both during and after the engagement.

Variation. The contract should state that it can be varied by agreement with both parties, and should indicate who is authorised to agree variation on behalf of the organisation (and on behalf of the consultant, if it is a consultancy company).

Controlling quality of work. The contract should include provision for regular review of the work, and for the steps to be taken by the worker to rectify the position if you are dissatisfied with any aspect of the work.

Termination. Either party should be allowed to terminate the contract with an agreed notice period, usually one month, and in writing. Clarify the circumstances in which the agreement could be terminated immediately: for example, if the worker:

- fails to comply with any aspect of the contract
- cannot complete the work within the agreed timescale or any agreed extension, or
- has brought the organisation into disrepute.

Similarly, the worker should be able to terminate the contract if the organisation fails to supply information or anything else necessary for the work (in such cases the worker must be paid any fees owing).

The agreement. There should be a simple phrase stating that the worker (or a suitable substitute) agrees to carry out the work within the timescale (or any agreed variation) and on the terms and conditions included in the contract in exchange for the fee. It should be signed by or on behalf of both parties. The person signing on behalf of the organisation should be explicitly authorised to do so.

The following may be included:

Increased time required. It is sometimes difficult to assess accurately the time required for a piece of work. It may therefore be helpful to set out what will happen if the job overruns. You should state the circumstances under which the worker is expected to complete the work without additional fees if more time is required, and those that allow the option for renegotiation or additional payment.

Other responsibilities on the worker. For longer pieces of work the contract should require regular progress reports on specified dates with details of the time worked and expenses incurred.

Return of property. You may also wish to specify that you have access to or the right to keep any documents paid for by the organisation in connection with the work.

Obligations on the organisation. Always agree to supply any information needed to carry out the work. If you are providing any form of administrative or other support this should be specified.

Arbitration. If included, this clause should contain a procedure for an arbitrator, agreed by both parties, to be appointed in the event of a dispute.

Taking on volunteers

Volunteers do not have employment rights. However, it is good practice to spell out your responsibilities towards volunteers through a volunteer policy in an accessible format. These can describe:

- recruitment, including references and other screening arrangements and, if necessary, criminal record checks
- the tasks volunteers will or could be asked to do, and possibly those they will not be asked or expected to do
- details of any induction, training, supervision and support offered and whether the volunteer is obliged to undertake training before carrying out certain tasks
- any arrangements for reviewing the volunteer's work and role
- any arrangements for accrediting the volunteer's achievements
- arrangements for reimbursing expenses. Be clear that only actual expenses can be recovered and that evidence of expenditure will be needed. If volunteers are given cash in advance for expenses, they should be asked to return any unspent money
- copyright. Volunteers will own the copyright or intellectual property rights to any work they create unless they explicitly assign the copyright to the organisation
- a requirement to comply with your organisational policies
- insurance arrangements
- what the volunteer can do if dissatisfied with any aspect of their volunteering
- the procedure you will follow if dissatisfied with the volunteer's work
- how you can end the arrangement with the volunteer
- any minimum time commitment you hope the volunteer will make
- your rules on confidentiality (see chapter 9)
- the obligation of volunteers to abide by health and safety and equal opportunity policies (make sure you provide access to these policies).

For further information see *Get it right from the start. Volunteer policies – the key to diverse volunteer involvement*, published by Volunteering England and available from www.volunteering.org.uk. The UK Workforce Hub has published a new set of standards for the management of volunteers: *The National Standards for the Management of Volunteers*, which can be downloaded from www.ukworkforcehub.org.uk.

Expenses

It is important that volunteers are aware of their position under tax, benefits and employment legislation. A person who is a volunteer need not declare expenses received provided they are direct reimbursement for sums incurred. Any fixed allowances or other payments of any kind may cause difficulties because they could be treated as remuneration and be subject to tax and possibly national insurance. If the volunteer is on state benefits such payments could affect entitlement. They could also potentially create a contractual relationship, entitling the volunteer to workers' rights such as the national minimum wage, or even full employment rights.

People on some state benefits have to notify the relevant office of the mere fact that they are volunteering, even if they are not receiving payment of any type.

Even where a volunteer is not paid, a contractual relationship can be created if they receive training or other benefits or perks which are not necessary for the work. A contractual relationship can also be created even where training or benefits necessary to do the work are provided, if the volunteer is required to make a specified time commitment or is similarly obligated to the organisation.

Volunteering England advises that the following expenses would not classify as taxable earnings and can be claimed without creating a contractual relationship or affecting a volunteer's entitlement to benefit:

- travel to and from the place of volunteering
- travel while volunteering

- meals taken while volunteering
- postage and phone costs, and other costs incurred for the volunteering
- care of children or other dependants while volunteering
- the cost of any necessary protective clothing/specialist equipment.

Volunteering should not have an effect on someone's right to benefit or their ability to be available for work in order to claim Jobseeker's Allowance, as long as volunteers declare expenses claimed, keep receipts, and inform the benefits agency or personal adviser at Jobcentre Plus. Volunteering England warns that volunteers in receipt of benefits can receive out of pocket expenses only. Claimants receiving more than their actual expenses may lose part of their means tested benefit, and the nature of their volunteering may also be called into question. Money over and above out of pocket expenses is regarded as income by HMRC, and is therefore taxable. The entire sum a volunteer received would be taxed, not just the portion above the actual expenses. It is also likely that the organisation would have to put such volunteers through PAYE, as HMRC would treat them as they would employees. For further details see *A guide to volunteering while on benefits*, available at www.dwp.gov.uk/publications.

Since April 2000, asylum seekers (people in the process of applying for refugee status) have been allowed to volunteer. Volunteering England guidance states that organisations must ensure that activity undertaken by an asylum seeker does not amount to either employment or job substitution, and that asylum seekers are entitled to receive out of pocket expenses just like other volunteers.

Volunteering England (0800 028 3304, www.volunteering.org.uk) publishes a number of books and information sheets on all aspects of taking on and managing volunteers.

Restrictions on employing people

Criminal record checks

Offering paid or voluntary employment involving access to vulnerable adults and children is controlled by a number of acts, including the **Protection of Children Act 1999, Care Standards Act 2000, Criminal Justice and Court Services Act 2000** and the **Safeguarding Vulnerable Groups Act 2006**. Management committee members working closely with vulnerable people may also fall within the scope of the legislation.

The **Police Act 1997** established the **Criminal Records Bureau (CRB)** to carry out checks on people working with vulnerable people, who are defined under the Act as children and young people aged under 18 and adults with a:

- learning or physical disability
- physical or mental illness, chronic or otherwise, including an addiction to alcohol or drugs, or
- reduction in physical or mental capacity.

The CRB has two levels of check depending on the nature of the post.

Standard disclosures are primarily for posts (both paid and voluntary) that involve working with vulnerable adults and children, and some posts involving money or administration of the law. They contain details of convictions, cautions, reprimands and warnings held in England and Wales on the Police National Computer; most of the relevant convictions in Scotland and Northern Ireland may also be included. If the position involves working with vulnerable people, the disclosure will include details from:

- the **Protection of Children Act List (PoCA)**
- the **Protection of Vulnerable Adults List (PoVA)**
- information that is held under **section 142 of the Education Act 2002** (formerly known as List 99).

An **enhanced disclosure** is for posts involving a far greater degree of contact with children or vulnerable adults: for example, jobs involving caring for, supervising, training or being in sole charge of such people. It contains the same information as the Standard Disclosure, along with non-conviction information held on local police records if that is seen as relevant to the position sought.

Application to the CRB

Only a registered organisation can apply for a CRB check. As one requirement for registration is to meet the threshold of submitting at least 100 applications a year, most voluntary organisations will need to use an umbrella body to obtain a check on their behalf. The CRB website (www.crb.gov.uk) has a database of umbrella bodies from which you can find a local one or one which specialises in your type of work.

CRB checks are only available where an organisation is entitled to ask exempted questions under the Exceptions Order to the **Rehabilitation of Offenders Act (ROA) 1974** (see *Ex-offenders*, in chapter 3). Someone applying for a post that involves regular contact with children or vulnerable adults must reveal both spent and unspent convictions. Other past convictions should not automatically prevent someone from volunteering or employment.

The CRB has produced a Code of Practice that organisations seeking disclosure information must adopt, which states that an organisation must:

- have a written policy on the recruitment of ex-offenders that can be given to applicants
- ensure that application forms for positions where disclosures will be requested contain a statement to that effect
- where relevant, discuss with an applicant information revealed in a disclosure before withdrawing an offer of appointment
- ensure its confidentiality policy states who has access to sensitive information
- have guidelines on how information from CRB checks will be stored, and when it will be destroyed (in general no later than six months after the recruitment date).

Sample policies are available on the CRB website (www.crb.gov.uk).

It is a criminal offence to disclose information obtained under these procedures except for specified purposes.

For further information see www.crb.gov.uk or ring the CRB Information Line (0870 90 90 811).

See chapter 2 for Charity Commission requirements for trustees of organisations that work with vulnerable adults and children.

Independent Safeguarding Authority (ISA)

From October 2009, when you recruit **a new paid worker or volunteer** to work with children or vulnerable adults you will need to check their ISA status. This will determine whether you can employ them (or take them on as volunteers), and may affect what activities they can undertake. The **Safeguarding Vulnerable Groups Act 2006** defines two types of activity with vulnerable groups: **regulated** and **controlled**. The definition of vulnerable adult is much wider under ISA than under the present PoVA scheme. It includes anyone aged over 18 who:

- is in residential accommodation owing to a need for care or nursing
- is in sheltered housing
- receives domiciliary care in their own home
- receives any form of healthcare
- is in prison
- is under a supervision order
- receives welfare services and/or
- requires assistance in the conduct of their own affairs.

Regulated activity is any paid or voluntary activity which involves contact with children or vulnerable adults, such as:

- any activity of a specified nature that involves frequent, intensive and/or overnight contact with children or vulnerable adults. Such activities include teaching, training, care, supervision, advice, treatment and transportation

- any activity allowing contact with children or vulnerable adults in a specified place frequently or intensively. Such places include schools and care homes
- fostering and childcare
- activities that involve people in certain defined positions of responsibility (such as trustees of certain childcare charities).

Organisations providing a regulated activity must be registered with the ISA. It is a criminal offence to employ an unregistered person, that is, someone who has either not applied to register or is on an ISA **Barred List** – a list of people barred from working with children or vulnerable adults.

Controlled activity is:

- frequent or intensive support work in general health settings, the NHS and further education (including cleaners, caretakers, shop workers and catering staff)
- individuals working for specified organisations who have frequent access to sensitive records about children and vulnerable adults
- support work in adult social care settings (for example, day centre cleaners and those with access to social care records).

It will be a criminal offence to take on someone in a controlled activity without checking that person's status. A barred individual can work in a controlled activity, but only if sufficient safeguards are place.

Employers and service providers of regulated and controlled activities have a duty to inform the ISA of their concerns about any individual causing harm to children and/or vulnerable adults.

Existing employees

From 2010, you must also ensure that **existing employees** are ISA-registered. First ask those who have not been previously checked by the CRB to apply for ISA registration. Then ask those who have been CRB checked to apply, beginning with staff whose CRB checks are the oldest.

It is the applicant's responsibility to apply to register with the ISA. If they have not applied for registration you cannot employ them. Employees, but not volunteers, will be charged a small fee.

Relationship with the CRB

An ISA check does not replace the need for a CRB check. An ISA check will reveal if someone is registered and able to work with children and/or vulnerable adults. A CRB check will show if someone has a criminal record or any relevant non-conviction information.

The ISA will not check for malpractice or for all criminal convictions, so registration does not guarantee that a person has no criminal history. Further enhanced CRB checks will be at the employer's discretion and you may still wish to apply for CRB enhanced disclosure to obtain an applicant's full criminal record. At the time of writing it is envisaged that the existing statutory requirements for CRB enhanced disclosures will still apply.

The CRB will provide a 'one stop shop' to enable access to both of these checks, and employers will be able to apply for ISA registration and a CRB check (including an ISA check) on the same form.

For further details, contact ISA on 0300 123 1111 or see www.isa-gov.org.uk.

Taking on workers from abroad

Under the **Asylum and Immigration Act 1996** employers have a duty to prevent illegal working in the UK and to carry out checks on workers employed from 1997. The **Immigration, Asylum and Nationality Act 2006** introduced:

- civil penalties for employers who employ illegal migrant workers – the maximum civil penalty per illegal worker is £10,000
- a new criminal offence for employers who knowingly employ illegal migrant workers

- a continuing responsibility for employers of migrant workers with a time-limited immigration status to check their entitlement to work in the UK.

The main groups that can be employed without any restrictions are:
- British citizens
- members of the Common Travel Area – citizens of the UK, Ireland, Channel Islands and Isle of Man
- Some Commonwealth citizens
- European Economic Area (EEA) nationals and Swiss nationals. EEA members are: Austria, Belgium, Cyprus, Czech Republic*, Denmark, Estonia*, Finland, France, Germany, Greece, Hungary*, Iceland, Irish Republic, Italy, Latvia*, Liechtenstein, Lithuania*, Luxembourg, Malta, Netherlands, Norway, Poland*, Portugal, Slovakia*, Slovenia*, Spain, Sweden and the United Kingdom. (Most employees from countries marked * must register with the Workers Registration Scheme – see below. Bulgaria and Romania are also members of the EEA, but nationals from these countries cannot work in the UK without permission from the UK Border Agency.)
- family members of EEA and Swiss nationals living in the UK.

For further details see the UK Border Agency (BIA) website www.bia.homeoffice.gov.uk.

The Workers Registration Scheme

Most nationals from the following eight countries that joined the EU in 2006, referred to as **A8** workers, must register with the UK Border Agency within one month of starting work: Czech Republic, Estonia, Hungary, Latvia, Lithuania, Poland, Slovakia and Slovenia. It is the worker's responsibility to apply, but employers must provide them with evidence of their employment. For more information, including exemptions from registration, go to www.bia.homeoffice.gov.uk.

Bulgarian and Romanian nationals (A2 workers): Most nationals will need an accession worker card which is available to those with a work permit, or a Tier 1 general permission (see *Other workers*, below). For further information see www.bia.homeoffice.gov.uk.

Checking eligibility

To establish a defence against a civil penalty and/or a conviction for employing an illegal migrant worker, employers must show they carried out the required checks on a prospective worker's documents. Documents checks have to be repeated at least annually for those employees hired on or after 29 February 2008 and who have limited leave to enter or remain in the UK. The BIA has produced a list of documents that a candidate may produce to establish their eligibility to work in the UK and the check required to establish that these documents are genuine. These include:

- a passport
- a national identity card
- a residence permit, registration certificate issued by the Home Office or UK Border Agency
- a biometric immigration document
- other travel documents endorsed to show that the holder is exempt from immigration control
- evidence of a permanent national insurance number.

Employers must copy the relevant page or pages of the document, in a format which cannot be subsequently altered: for example, a photocopy or scan. These copies must be kept securely for the duration of the person's employment and for a further two years after their employment has ceased. See *Prevention of illegal working: Immigration, Asylum and Nationality Act 2006* available at www.bia.homeoffice.gov.uk.

You should carry out checks on all new workers to demonstrate consistent, transparent and non-discriminatory recruitment practices, and to avoid claims of

discrimination: for example, to check workers who are not British citizens solely on the basis of race or ethnicity could be construed as racial discrimination. The BIA has produced an anti-discrimination code of practice: see *Guidance for employers on the avoidance of unlawful discrimination in employment practice while seeking to prevent illegal working* available at www.bia.homeoffice.gov.uk.

Other workers

Under the **Immigration, Asylum and Nationality Act 2006** a points-based system (PBS) is being phased in to become the sole means of accessing work, training and studying opportunities in the UK. Underpinning the system will be a five-tier framework:

Tier 1: Highly skilled individuals (already introduced)

Tier 2: Skilled workers with a job offer from an approved sponsor (already introduced)

Tier 3: Limited numbers of low-skilled workers needed to fill specific temporary labour shortages (at the time of writing the introduction date was still to be confirmed)

Tier 4: Students (already introduced)

Tier 5: Youth mobility and temporary workers, such as musicians, actors (already introduced)

For each tier, applicants will need enough points to obtain the right to enter or remain in the UK. Points will be awarded on workers' skills to reflect aptitude, experience, age and also the demand for those skills in any given sector.

Employers wishing to recruit someone through the PBS must apply to become licensed as a sponsor. For further details contact the BIA at www.bia.homeoffice.gov.uk or its employers' helpline on 0845 010 6677.

For further information on employing people from abroad contact the Joint Council for the Welfare of Immigrants (www.jcwi.org.uk).

Paying people

Employers are responsible for paying everyone employed under a contract of service, including full-time, part-time and casual workers. They must make the necessary PAYE deductions from their wages, and provide them with an itemised pay statement.

To operate a payroll system for the first time you must register as an employer with HM Revenue and Customs (HMRC) by contacting the New Employer Helpline on 0845 60 70 143. You will receive:

- a PAYE reference number
- the option of receiving a *New employer starter pack* which contains the employer's CD-ROM and PAYE calculators, and the forms and information needed to operate PAYE.

For each employee you will need a tax code and NI number (normally on form **P45,** filled in by their previous employer). If an employee does not have a tax code, you should use the emergency tax code to work out their PAYE, and you and the employee should complete a **P46**. If the employee does not know their NI number complete form **CA6855** so that HMRC can trace it.

For advice on any aspect of paying people contact HMRC's Employer Helpline (08457 143 143) or New Employer Helpline (0845 60 70 143).

Payslips

All employees must be given an itemised pay statement, often known as a **payslip**, at or before the time they are paid. It must contain the following:

- the gross pay before deductions and the take-home pay
- the amounts of any fixed deductions (for example, union subscriptions), their frequency and why they are made. Alternatively, fixed deductions can be given as a total sum, provided the employee is given a written statement in advance or at the time of the fixed payment, and then at least annually afterwards

- the amounts of any variable deductions and why they are made
- the breakdown and method of any part-payment of wages – for example, the separate figures for a cash payment and a balance credited to a bank account.

An employee must be notified of any changes to fixed deductions either in writing or as an amended standing statement of fixed deductions, which is then valid for up to 12 months before reissue.

For further details see *Pay statements: what they must itemise*, from www.berr.gov.uk.

You can buy pre-printed payslips from office stationery suppliers, and compatible versions are available for use with various types of payroll software.

Deductions

You must also make the following deductions:

- **PAYE** if the person's tax situation or tax code requires this
- **national insurance** (NI), if the person earns more than the weekly NI employee's earnings threshold (see page 125)
- where relevant, repayments of **student loans** (see page 126)
- **pension contributions**, where relevant (see page 126).

The **Employment Rights Act 1996** prohibits any deduction from wages unless:

- the deductions are required by statute (for example, tax and NI)
- it is a term of the contract of employment that the deduction will be made
- the employee consented before the action which led to the deduction, or
- the deductions are ordered by a court.

There are other exceptions, which include:

- reimbursing an employer's previous overpayment
- deductions made under agreed arrangements for payment to a third party to which the employee has agreed (for example, union dues, payroll giving)

- deductions where an employee is on strike or engaging in industrial action
- sums due to the employer under an employment tribunal settlement or court settlement.

You must complete a **deductions working sheet (P11)** for each employee. These should be kept for at least three years after the end of the tax year to which they apply.

Income tax (PAYE)

Employers must operate PAYE on the payments made to employees if their earnings reach the NI lower earnings limit (LEL) (in 2009/10 this is £95 a week, £412 a month or £4,940 a year). You must send the amounts owed to HMRC by the 19th of each month, or by the 22nd if payments are made electronically. You can opt to send the amounts due every quarter if average monthly payments are likely to be less than £1,500. Tax quarters end on 5 July, 5 October, 5 January and 5 April.

PAYE is applied to all the payments an employee receives as a result of working for you, including:

- salary and wages and any bonuses
- certain expenses allowances paid in cash
- statutory sick pay
- statutory maternity, paternity or adoption pay.

Employees are also taxed through PAYE on benefits in kind, such as a company car, medical insurance and other benefits.

The PAYE deduction depends on the amount employees are paid and on current rates, allowances and limits, which are generally reviewed each year. To make the calculations use the following tables from the HMRC website:

- pay adjustment tables (www.hmrc.gov.uk/taxtables/pay-adjustment-tables)
- taxable pay tables (www.hmrc.gov.uk/taxtables/srbd).

National insurance contributions (NICs)

Employees aged between 16 and state pension age, currently 60 for a woman (gradually increasing to 65 for women from 2010–2020) and 65 for a man, may have a liability to pay NICs. Employers have a duty to manage their employees' NICs and must also pay NICs:

- for each person they employ who is aged 16 or over and whose earnings are above the defined thresholds
- on benefits in kind such as a company car.

There are six classes of NI, depending on the employment status of the person. Employers usually operate the Class 1 NICs, which are calculated by using three levels of earnings set by the government: the **primary earnings threshold (PET)**, the **lower earnings limit (LEL)** and the **upper earnings limit (UEL)**. The types in Class 1 are:

- **Class 1 primary contributions**. Paid by employees earning over the PET – 11% on their earnings over the PET and below the UEL and 1% of earnings over the UEL. They are deducted at source from wages
- **Class 1 secondary contributions**. Paid by employers on gross earnings above the PET at 12.8%. Paid with the employees' primary contributions
- **Class 1A contributions**. Paid annually, on benefits in kind.

For further details of NIC rates and thresholds see www.hmrc.gov.uk/helpsheets/e12_2.

Employers can calculate NICs themselves by using either HMRC NI tables or by the exact percentage method (see below). The tables are included in the Employers Pack, or are available from www.hmrc.gov.uk, or from New Employers Helpline (0845 60 70 143). There are different tables according to whether employees are:

- in a pension scheme which is contracted in, or out of, the state pension scheme
- aged over state retirement age
- classified as a special case (for example, women claiming the former married women's allowance).

If you use the exact percentage method, you must base calculations on your employee's gross pay. You then multiply their earnings over the PET level by the appropriate percentage rates. This method is explained in full in *Employer's further guide to PAYE and NICs*, available at www.hmrc.gov.uk/guidance/cwg2.

For further information see *Employer's further guide to PAYE and NICs*, available at www.hmrc.gov.uk/guidance/cwg2.

Student loan deductions

Employers are responsible for collecting repayments of student loans on behalf of HMRC by making deductions from wages where total pay exceeds a certain threshold, currently (2008/09) £15,000. You must make deductions:

- when HMRC sends you a **Start Notice (form SL1)** for a current employee
- if a new employee has a Y for Yes in the 'Continue student loans deduction' box of their P45, which means that a start notice was issued to their previous employer.
- when as a new employer who does not have a P45 for the employee you have completed a P46 and ticked Box D 'Student loans'.

Payments must be made until you receive a **Stop Notice (form SL2)** from HMRC, or if an employee leaves. In the latter case you should issue a form P45 in the normal way and enter a Y in the 'Continue student loan deductions' box.

Keep a record of all wages sheets and other documents relating to the calculation and deduction of student loan repayments, including forms SL1 and SL2, for at least three years after the end of the tax year to which they relate. Enter the amount of student loan deductions in the appropriate box on the employee's form **P14 end of year summary**, and **P60** and the total student loan deductions made in the tax year on form **P35 employer annual return**.

For further information use the Employer's CD-ROM or *Collection of student loans: employer's guide*, available from the Employer's Orderline on 0845 7 646 646 or www.hmrc.gov.uk/employers/emp-form.htm.

Pension deductions

Employers are not obliged to run a pension scheme, but those employing five or more people must offer their employees access to a stakeholder pension scheme if they don't already offer an occupational scheme, or access to a personal pension scheme into which they contribute at least 3% of salary (see *Pensions*, page 134).

If employees have access to a pension scheme, whether this is run in-house or administered by a third party, you must deduct your employees' pension contributions from their pay:

- Contributions to a registered pension scheme attract tax relief and are deducted from an employee's gross pay.
- Contributions to an occupational pension scheme that uses the 'net pay' arrangement (a system under which people get tax relief on contributions paid to occupational pension schemes) are deducted from employees' gross pay.
- Contributions to a personal pension scheme must be deducted from employees' net pay after deduction of tax and NI.

Deductions for pension contributions should be shown separately on the employee's payslip.

You must pay employees' pension contributions into the pension scheme within 19 days of the end of the month in which you made the deductions.

Organisations that administer an in-house pension scheme must register with and use HMRC's Pension Schemes Online. For further details see www.hmrc.gov.uk/pensionschemes/pensionschemes-online.

Employees leaving

When someone leaves:

- work out their final salary, tax and NI and enter them on form **P11** in the usual way
- enter the date of leaving on form **P11**
- make out a **P45** for the employee

- send part 1 of the P45 to the tax office (make a photocopy first for your records)
- give the employee parts 1A, 2 and 3 of the P45.

At the end of the tax year

At the end of each tax year (5 April) you must complete a form **P14** for each employee by transferring information recorded on P11 throughout the year. The first two pages must be sent to the tax office (see below). Page 3 is the **P60** certificate, which gives totals of earnings, PAYE and NICs for the whole tax year. Form P60 must be given, by 31 May, to all employees who were employed on 5 April.

Send to the tax office:

- form **P14 – end of year summary** (a summary of the P11) for each employee for whom a P11 has been used at any time in the year, and
- a **P35 – employer annual return**, listing all employees for whom you have completed a P14, with details of their PAYE and NICs.

Form **P14** can be obtained from your PAYE tax office; P35 is sent to the organisation by the tax office.

These make up the **end of year return** and must be filed by 19 May following the end of the tax year concerned.

Expenses that have been reimbursed and/or any taxable benefits or perks must be declared to HMRC on form **P11D** for each employee who has earned over £8,500 in the year and on form **P9D** for those who have earned £8,500 or less (2008/09 figures). Where employees receive only properly documented reimbursements it is possible to apply to the tax office for exemption from having to file these forms. Complete form **PD11(b)** stating that the information given on the PD11 forms is accurate and say which tax office they were sent to and when.

Copies of these forms are available from www.hmrc.gov.uk or the Employer's Orderline (0845 7 646 646).

Filing accounts

Employers with 50 or more employees must file their P35 and P14 (see *At the end of the tax year*, above) online. Under government proposals, from 2009/10 this will apply to all employers. Currently, employers with fewer than 50 employees can receive tax-free payments for using online filing. For more information about online filing and the tax-free payment offered see www.hmrc.gov.uk/payeonline.

From 6 April 2009 employers with 50 or more employees must send forms P45, P46 and similar pension information online. All employers will have to send this information online from April 2011. See www.hmrc.gov.uk for more information.

Temporary and casual staff

For PAYE purposes a casual worker is one who:

- does not produce a current P45
- is engaged to work for a single occasion of no more than one week in the current tax year.

If you are sure that the worker is a 'casual', and that they earn less than the PAYE threshold, you just need to keep a record of their name and address, the amount paid, dates of their employment and NI number.

Otherwise casual and temporary staff must go through your payroll systems in the same way as permanent staff.

Students

Full-time students in the UK, working only during holiday periods and planning to return to study after the period, must complete a **P38**. This exempts them from paying tax until earnings exceed individual tax allowances; thereafter the basic rate will be deducted. They must still pay NI if they earn more than the weekly threshold. Students working during term time should be treated like any other employee.

Volunteers

Provided volunteers only receive reimbursement for documented expenses, and do not receive anything of monetary value in return for their work, they do not count as employees, temporary or casual staff for tax purposes. However, employers must keep records of all reimbursements to them.

For further details on defining volunteering activity see *Volunteers*, in chapter 3.

Employers' childcare contributions

Employers can claim tax relief for the day-to-day costs of providing or subsidising the following types of childcare:

- workplace nurseries
- directly contracted childcare (for example, places bought direct from a local childminder or nursery)
- childcare vouchers.

The following conditions must be met:

- facilities have to be available to all staff
- a child qualifies up to 1 September following their 15th birthday, or 1 September following their 16th birthday if they are disabled
- the child must be the child/stepchild of the employee or a child for whom the employee has parental responsibility
- childcare provided has to be registered or approved by the local authority.

For further details see *How to help your employees with childcare* (E17) available from www.hmrc.gov.uk or the Employer's Helpline (0845 7 143 143).

The Daycare Trust can advise employers about helping parents with childcare. Information is available from www.daycaretrust.org.uk or 020 7840 3350.

Maternity, paternity and adoption pay and benefits

To qualify for **statutory maternity pay (SMP), statutory paternity pay (SPP)** or **statutory adoption pay (SAP)** or **statutory paternity pay (SPP) (adoption)** an employee must:

- have been in continuous employment with the employer for at least 26 weeks up to and including the 15th week before the expected week of childbirth, or by the week they are notified they have been matched with a child for adoption, and
- have average weekly earnings at least equal to the national insurance lower earnings limit in the eight weeks up to and including that week (in 2009/10 this is £95 a week, £412 a month or £4,940 a year)
- in the case of SMP, have stopped work because of the pregnancy.

The employer pays SMP, SPP and SAP in the same way, and usually on the same day as normal pay.

Statutory maternity pay

An employee must give at least 28 days' notice (in writing if requested) of the date she wishes to start receiving statutory maternity pay (SMP) along with form **MAT B1**. In practice most women choose to give notice for SMP when they give notice for leave. She does not have to intend to return to work to receive SMP, but must give her employee the correct advance notice of her intention to take leave (see *Starting maternity leave*, in chapter 3).

The earliest date that SMP can start is the 11th week before EWC and the latest the day following the birth. Women who continue to work after the 11th week before EWC can choose when they want SMP to start. This means that their SMP should start on the first day of maternity leave.

SMP is paid for a maximum of 39 weeks. The first six weeks are payable at the higher rate (90% of the woman's average weekly earnings in the eight weeks up to and including the 15th week before the EWC) and the remaining 33 weeks at the standard rate of £123.06 (2009/10) or 90% of her average weekly earnings, whichever is the lower.

The government intends to extend paid maternity leave to 12 months by 2010.

Maternity allowance

Women who do not qualify for SMP will be entitled to maternity allowance (MA) for up to 39 weeks if:

- they have been employed/self-employed for at least 26 weeks in the 66 weeks (the test period) before the baby is due, and
- their average weekly wage is at least £30 in the test period averaged over 13 weeks.

MA awards a standard weekly rate of £117.18 (in 2008/09) or 90% of the average gross weekly earnings (before tax), whichever is the lower, and is payable through the local Jobcentre Plus, from where further information is available.

Statutory paternity pay

Parents must give their employer at least 28 days' notice of the date they expect any SPP payments to start and must provide a self-certificate as proof of their entitlement. Leave must be taken in periods of either one week or two continuous weeks. The rate of pay is £123.06 (2009/10) or 90% of the average weekly earnings, whichever is the lower.

Statutory adoption pay

The rates of both **statutory adoption pay (SAP)** and **statutory paternity pay (SPP) (adoption)** are (in 2009/10) £123.06 per week or 90% of weekly earnings, whichever is the lower. SAP is payable for 39 weeks and SPP (adoption) for a maximum of two weeks.

Adopters must provide documentary evidence from their adoption agency to prove their entitlement to SAP.

Recovering payments

Small employers (those paying £45,000 or less annually in NICs) can deduct 100% of SMP, SPP or SAP from their next payment(s) of PAYE to HMRC plus an additional 4.5% (in tax year 2009/10) in compensation for the employer's NICs.

Larger employers can deduct 92% of SMP from their next payment.

Outsourcing payroll services

Some banks and accountants offer a low cost salary-paying service to small businesses, including voluntary organisations. Community accountancy projects and some local councils for voluntary service and similar organisations provide payroll services for a small charge. Many employers use commercial payroll agents, accountants or internet based services to run their payroll systems. Remember that you remain responsible for your payroll even if you don't prepare the records yourself.

An outside organisation used for payroll management becomes a 'data processor' under the Data Protection Act (see chapter 9). The Information Commissioner's code of practice includes a section on outsourcing data. Before asking another organisation to manage the payroll system, the Commissioner advises the following:

- ensure that it has appropriate security measures both in terms of the technology used and how data is managed
- have a written contract that requires the organisation to process personal information only on your instructions, and to maintain appropriate security
- check whether the arrangement would involve a transfer of information about a worker to a country outside the European Economic Area.

For further information see *The employment practices code*, available from www.ico.gov.uk.

Sick pay and leave

Statutory sick pay

Employees must receive rules on sick leave and pay in a written statement of employment particulars or accompanying document within two months of their starting work.

The aim of **statutory sick pay (SSP)** is to provide a level of earnings replacement for employees unable to work because of short-term sickness. It is paid to employees who are sick for four or more days in a row – known as **Period of Incapacity for Work (PIW)** – for a maximum of 28 weeks. SSP is subject to income tax and national insurance contributions (NICs). Part-time, temporary and casual workers may all be eligible for SSP if they meet the conditions described below. Agency workers whose contracts last for 13 or more weeks are also eligible.

·The procedures for managing SSP are complex, and you should refer to the HMRC guide *What to do if your employee is sick*, available from www.hmrc.gov.uk/helpsheets/e14 or the Employer's Helpline on 0845 7 143 143. The basic rules are described below.

An employee must meet **all** the following conditions to get SSP:

- they must have done some work under their employment contract before going off sick. Liability for SSP can arise if a new employee becomes sick on their first day of employment
- they must have been sick for four or more consecutive days
- the days they receive SSP must be qualifying days (see *Operating the scheme*, page 131)
- their earnings must be at least as much as the lower earnings limit (LEL) for NICs

- they must have earnings for which employers are liable for class 1 NICs, or would be but for the employee's age (see *National insurance,* page 125)
- they can't have already received the maximum amount of SSP for the PIW, or for a series of linked PIWs (28 weeks)
- they must have notified you about their sickness, either within your own time limit or within seven days, and they must give evidence of their incapacity.

Some people are ineligible for SSP. They include those who, if on the first day of their PIW:

- had average weekly earnings in the 'set period' (over the eight weeks before the sickness began) below the LEL for NI purposes
- are within the disqualifying period due to pregnancy or recently having had a baby. SSP will stop for those women who are entitled to Maternity Pay (MP) or Statutory Maternity Allowance (SMA) within the four weeks before their baby is due and their entitlement to MP or SMP will start automatically and will continue for 39 weeks
- have already received 28 weeks' worth of SSP and this new spell of sickness links to their last one
- are sick within eight weeks of receiving a social security benefit
- are a new employee and have not yet done any work for you.

If an employee has been sick for at least four consecutive days but is not entitled to SSP, or if you know the employee will still be sick when their entitlement to SSP is exhausted, you must issue form **SSP1** and advise them to contact Jobcentre Plus to claim **Employment and Support Allowance (ESA)**.

Rates of SSP

There is one flat rate. Up-to-date figures can be obtained from the HMRC website at www.hmrc.gov.uk/employers/employee_sick.htm. SSP is paid at a daily rate and only for qualifying days, usually an employee's normal working days. The daily rate is calculated by dividing the weekly rate by the number of days someone is unable to work (excluding the first three 'waiting days').

If someone has been sick for two spells or more of at least four days in a row with eight weeks or less between them, this is counted as one PIW. This means that waiting days will not be served for the second period of sickness.

Operating the scheme

Before operating the scheme, the employer needs to:

- agree qualifying days (days for which SSP is paid) with employees. These are usually regular working days. If an employee's working pattern varies, the employer must agree a qualifying day. If none is agreed regulations provide for this to be a Wednesday
- decide rules for employees notifying absence through sickness
- tell employees what evidence of incapacity is needed. It is normal practice to phone in on the first day of sickness or as soon as possible. Many employers require the employee to send in a completed self-certification form (**SC2**) for absences of between four and seven days and a doctor's statement for longer periods.

Record keeping

Employers must keep:

- records of dates of sickness lasting at least four calendar days in a row – that is, the PIW – reported by your employees
- records of all SSP payments made during PIW
- dates on which SSP was not paid and the reason
- copies of medical evidence.

You can use form **SSP2** to record this information or your own equivalent form.

Other forms you will need are:

- **SC2**, the employee's statement of sickness used to record absences of between four and seven days
- **SSP1(L)** if an employee leaves while they are receiving SSP.

These forms are available on the Employer CD-ROM (included in the *New employer starter pack*) or from the HMRC website. You can also order them from the Employer's Orderline (08457 646 646; textphone 0800 959 598). Keep copies of these completed forms for at least three years.

SSP1 (available from www.dwp.gov.uk/lifeevent/benefits/statutory_sick_pay) is issued to employees who have received their full SSP entitlement (28 weeks) and are still sick and therefore need to be transferred to ESA, or who have been sick for four or more consecutive days but are not entitled to SSP.

Employers should also record SSP payments on:

- form **P11** – the **deductions working sheet** – for each week or month that SSP is paid
- form **P14** – the **end of year summary** – all SSP paid to each employee for all tax months where you recovered some, or all, of that SSP
- form **P35** – the **employer annual return** – any SSP recovered under the percentage threshold scheme (see below).

It is good practice to give each employee a copy of the leaflet *Statutory Sick Pay,* available from www.dwp.gov.uk/lifeevent/benefits/statutory_sick_pay.

Percentage threshold scheme (PTS)

It may be possible to recover some or all of the SSP paid through the PTS, which is designed to help employers who have a high proportion of their workforce sick at any one time. If SSP paid in a tax month exceeds 13% of an employer's and employees' gross Class 1 NICs for that month, you can claim for the excess.

Contractual sick pay

Employers can opt out of SSP by providing their own contractual sick pay scheme, usually known as an **occupational sick pay scheme**. Under any employer scheme, the wages paid or sick pay must be of at least the same value as SSP and for the same qualifying days.

Details of contractual sick pay must be included in the statement of particulars or an accompanying document.

When designing your own sick pay scheme you will need to consider:

- whether to offer payment on sick days for which SSP is not payable, that is, the first three days of sickness
- the maximum rate of contractual sick pay available and for what period (for example, a specified number of weeks or months at full pay, and a specified number at half pay in each leave year or in any rolling 12-month period)
- whether to offer payment for more than the 28 weeks for which SSP is payable.

Always examine the financial implications before agreeing more generous provisions. Small organisations can be hit particularly hard by costs arising from staff illness. If large sums are needed to cover employees' sick pay, there may be none available to buy in temporary workers to ensure that their work continues.

An employer that operates a contractual scheme will still need to keep basic records of sickness absence of at least four days or more and amounts paid, plus sufficient records to complete:

- form **SSP1**, to enable employees to transfer to ESA if, for example, they have:
  - received their maximum 28 weeks' SSP, or
  - run out of their entitlement to contractual sick pay and were not entitled to SSP
- form **SSP1(L)**, if an employee moves to another job.

Sickness/ill health policies and procedures

All employers can help to reduce absence levels by promoting a healthy working environment, paying special attention to:

- **working conditions**, providing special equipment if necessary

- **job design**, including flexible working arrangements and working practices, and jobs that enable workers to exercise greater control over the way they do their day-to-day work
- **support**, having line managers who are confident and trained in people skills
- **training**, ensuring line managers know how to manage common health problems such as mental health, lower back pain and repetitive strain injuries
- **induction**, for example, training workers in using equipment safely
- **employment relations**, so that employees feel valued and involved in the organisation
- **health and safety measures**, including attention to stress (see *Stress*, in chapter 5)
- giving workers opportunities to discuss problems relating to attendance in performance appraisals
- **promoting well being**, for example, by encouraging exercise and by providing information and advice on diet and the risks of smoking and alcohol abuse.

For further details see the Acas publication *Health, work and well-being*, available from www.acas.org.uk.

It is good practice to develop absence policies that spell out employees' rights and obligations when taking time off from work due to sickness. The policy should cover:

- who to notify if an employee cannot come to work, when they need to submit a self-certificate form and when a medical certificate is required
- details of any contractual sick pay and its relationship with statutory sick pay
- when time off may be permitted – for example, to perform public duties or for emergencies when looking after dependents
- a commitment to improving health at work
- procedures for monitoring absence
- procedures for managing sickness including, for example, return-to-work interviews and whether the organisation reserves the right to request a report from a doctor

- references to other policies and terms and conditions – for example, health and safety, discipline and grievance, holiday entitlement, maternity/paternity/adoption and parental leave.

Monitoring absence

To identify potential problems and provide evidence for any action you may wish to take, keep accurate attendance records to measure:

- how much time is lost across the organisation through absence as a whole and through different types of absence: long-term sickness, short-term certified or uncertified sickness, unauthorised absence and lateness
- when absence occurs most
- whether particular departments are especially affected
- whether some people are absent more often than others.

You must get employees' consent to keep details of individual records of sick absence, which are 'sensitive personal data' under the **Data Protection Act 1998** (see chapter 9). They should be assured that this data will be kept only for as long as necessary and accessed only by named individuals.

Managing sickness

Return-to-work interviews help to ensure that employees know their absence has been noted and their attendance is valued. They also help managers to identify and resolve any deep-seated problems that are causing the absence.

When absence becomes a problem, you will need to adopt different approaches to address long-term and frequent short-term absences.

In the case of long-term absence you need to consider:

- how to communicate with the sick person so that they are kept in touch with developments (including whether anyone is providing cover) and consulted over actions taken under the sickness procedure. The aim of the communication should be to provide information and show concern, rather than to ask for help on work matters

- access to medical reports. An employer can ask for a medical report from an employee's GP, an independent specialist or an occupational health provider but must first obtain written consent from the employee, and if obtaining the report from the GP or employee's consultant must give certain prescribed information to the employee. Under the **Access to Medical Reports Act 1988** employees have a right to see their medical reports, and it is good practice to ensure that any practitioner is acceptable to all parties involved. The employer should cover the cost of any medical report and discuss its findings and recommendations with the employee
- whether the employee has a disability as defined under the **Disability Discrimination Act** (see *Discrimination*, in chapter 3), and if you must consider making adjustments to their working environment to help their return to work.

If an employee is taking frequent short-term absences you should have an informal discussion to explain your concerns and to discover why. If there are stress or other health-related problems at work, these must be addressed, and if there is an underlying health problem a medical report may be needed. Otherwise you should offer the employee the opportunity to improve their attendance within a specified timescale. If there is no such improvement then you may need to take further action under your procedure (see *Disciplinary and grievance policy and procedures*, in chapter 3). Throughout the process the employee should be kept fully informed, and an appeal against any decision should be allowed. Employees have the right to be accompanied to disciplinary hearings.

A number of resources are available to help organisations manage absence problems. These include the Acas publications *Tackling absence problems* and *Attendance management*, available from www.acas.org.uk, and the Business Link publication *Managing absence and sickness*, available from www.businesslink.gov.uk. The Chartered

Institute of Personnel and Development (CIPD), the Health and Safety Executive and Acas have produced a free online toolkit to help managers with absence management, available from www.cipd.co.uk/subjects/hrpract/absence/absmantool.

Pensions

State pensions

Basic state pension

Everyone who has paid enough national insurance contributions (NICs) will receive the **basic state retirement pension** when they reach state pension age. This is a flat rate benefit: that is, it is not directly linked to the amount of NICs paid, only to the number of years during which the employee has contributed. It is not possible to opt out of the basic state pension; any additional pensions are paid on top.

To qualify for the full basic state pension, men currently need 44 qualifying years and women need 39. A qualifying year is one in which someone has paid, or been deemed to have paid, sufficient NICs. Those who reach state pension age on or after 6 April 2010 (which will then be 65 for both men and women) will need 30 qualifying years for a full basic state pension. Credits are awarded in certain circumstances where NICs have not been paid, such as during periods of unemployment or where a person has caring responsibilities, such as looking after children or caring for a relative.

Additional state pension

The additional state pension acts as a top-up to the basic state pension and is based on the amount earned between the lower and upper earnings limits (£4,940 to £43,888 for 2009/10) during an employee's working life. Broadly, the amount awarded increases in line with the amount contributed, although currently low earners and those non-earners with certain caring responsibilities build up their entitlement at a higher rate than those on higher earnings.

Since April 2002 the additional state pension has been known as the **State Second Pension (S2P)**. Before this date it was calculated by a different method and was known as the State Earnings Related Pension Scheme (SERPS). It is financed by a percentage of employees' and employers' NICs and is run by the government.

Contracting out

Depending on the type of pension scheme offered by the employer, or the type of personal or stakeholder scheme chosen (see pages 136–7), employees may be **contracted out** of S2P. Where this applies, employees (and the employer, where applicable) pay lower NICs but do not accrue the full amount of S2P during the time they are contracted out.

Employees who join an employer's contracted-out scheme are contracted out by default. In all other cases, an employee can choose whether to contract out of S2P. If they do so they can set up a personal pension scheme (a rebate-only personal or stakeholder plan) specifically to accept rebated NICs. The employee would not be able to pay any contributions other than the NI rebates into the plan and this scheme would be independent of any other arrangements. Employees can contract out when they first take out their personal or stakeholder pension, or at a later date.

Those who choose to contract out will still be entitled to any SERPS or S2P built up beforehand and will also continue to accrue a reduced entitlement to S2P whilst they are contracted out.

From 2012, contracting out on a money purchase basis will be abolished and members of affected schemes automatically contracted back in. Therefore, from 2012 it will no longer be possible for an employee to contract out on an individual basis.

Additional provision

The state schemes do not give a pension on earnings above the NI upper earnings limit, nor do they provide a lump sum on retirement or a benefit on death other than a widow's or widower's pension in certain circumstances. Many people therefore choose to make additional provision for their pension, and employers with five or more employees must provide access to some form of pension arrangement.

Employers cannot advise employees on their pension options. For example, they cannot insist that employees join a particular pension scheme or the organisation's designated scheme. However, an employer may choose to enrol all new employees into its pension scheme automatically provided employees are given the right to opt out. Every employee must make up their own mind about which option suits them best, but they must have access to information about any scheme(s) offered by the employer, usually in the form of a booklet. See also *Further information*, page 138.

Occupational pension schemes

Types of schemes

There are two main types of occupational pension scheme.

Defined benefit (salary-related) schemes. The pension received depends on the number of years the employee has belonged to the scheme, and how much they earn. In a **final salary** scheme, the earnings used to calculate the pension are, as the name suggests, those at or close to retirement. There is an increasing shift to **career-average (CARE)** schemes, where the final pension is based on an employee's average earnings over their working life.

Many employers are no longer offering defined benefit schemes to new employees and some have closed them to any future accrual of benefits. This is because of difficulties in ensuring there will be adequate funds to meet the pension entitlements and because costs can fluctuate significantly for employers funding defined benefit schemes.

Defined contribution (money purchase) schemes. The money (or fund) built up in this type of scheme is used to buy an **annuity** (often from an insurance company), which is an agreement to pay a pension for life when the employee retires. The employer's and employees' contributions are invested, and the pension received is dependent on the level of payments into the fund, how well these investments have performed and the cost of purchasing an annuity at retirement.

Tax implications for employees

Under either defined benefit or defined contribution schemes it is usual for both employer and employee to contribute, although an employer can choose to pay the full cost of providing a scheme (by making it non-contributory for employees). Pension contributions attract full tax relief for both employer and employee.

Since 6 April 2006 (**A-day**) there has no longer been any limit on the amount that employees or employers can contribute. Tax charges are applied to those who see very large growth in the value of their pension benefits in the course of a year (more than £235,000 for 2008/09), or those with total benefits that exceed the 'lifetime allowance' (currently £1.65 million). These charges will generally only affect very high earners; for further information see the *Registered pension schemes manual* which is held on the HMRC website at www.hmrc.gov.uk/manuals/rpsmmanual/index.htm.

Contracted-out schemes

Some occupational pension schemes choose to contract out of S2P (see *Additional state pension*, page 134). In such cases both employer and employee pay NICs at a reduced rate. When the employee retires, they should still receive a basic state retirement pension, but will only be entitled to a reduced amount of S2P (although they would receive their full entitlement of S2P for any previously contracted-in period).

Any contracted-out scheme must meet certain standards laid down by HMRC. This can greatly increase the amount of administration, which may be a problem particularly for small schemes.

From 2012, contracting out on a money purchase scheme will be abolished.

Not contracted-out schemes

If an employee is in an employer's pension scheme which is not contracted out, both employer and employee pay full rate NICs. An employee who wants to contract out of S2P can set up a personal pension scheme (a rebate-only personal or stakeholder plan) into which HMRC will pay some of these NICs (see *Contracting out,* page 134).

Membership

Membership of an occupational pension scheme cannot be restricted to full-time employees; any rights granted to full-time workers must also be granted to comparable part-time workers (see *Part-time workers*, in chapter 3). Employees on short-term or fixed-term contracts of less than two years, whether full or part-time, do not have to be given the same pension rights as comparable permanent employees. However, if they are not, they must receive higher pay or other benefits to compensate for lack of access to the pension scheme.

Occupational pension schemes can be very complex and, dependent upon the type of scheme chosen, may require an organisation to make a long-term commitment which it may not be able to sustain. So although it is good practice to give some form of pension provision, an occupational pension scheme requires careful thought beforehand.

Organisations funded by local authorities may be able to become 'admitted bodies' to the Local Government Superannuation Scheme. This enables them to provide their employees with occupational pensions without having to set up their own scheme.

Many organisations belong to the Pensions Trust, which is the leading multi-employer occupational pension fund for employees involved in the charitable, social, educational, voluntary and not for profit sectors. Multi-employer schemes give employers in a similar sector the opportunity to group together to offer an occupational pension scheme which is more cost efficient as a result of being able to pool investments and ancillary expenses such as administration and legal costs. The Pensions Trust is a not for profit organisation, accountable to its members; its aim is to provide a low-cost comprehensive pensions service to employers and employees in this sector. For further information contact the New Business Team on 0113 394 2697 or email contact@thepensionstrust.org.uk.

The Pensions Trust's website provides helpful information on current issues affecting the voluntary sector. These can be found in the 'General' section of the 'Document Library' at www.thepensionstrust.org.uk.

Stakeholder pensions

Currently organisations meeting the following criteria must generally offer employees membership of a stakeholder scheme:

- five or more people have been employed by the organisation for at least three months and earn above the NI lower earnings limit (£4,940 for 2009/10)
- no other type of pension scheme is available to employees.

There is no requirement for an employer to contribute to a stakeholder pension.

The Pensions Regulator registers and regulates stakeholder pension schemes. It is also responsible for ensuring that, where necessary, employers offer access to such schemes.

The Pensions Regulator's website contains detailed information on stakeholder pensions including a 'decision tree', which guides employers through the process of determining whether they need to make a stakeholder plan available. See www.thepensionsregulator. gov.uk/stakeholderpensions or ring 0870 6063636.

The limited take-up of stakeholder pensions has resulted in the government's introduction of **personal accounts** (see below), which is expected in 2012.

Personal pension plans

An employee can take out a personal pension plan as an alternative or supplement to an occupational pension scheme. An employer may or may not choose to contribute to a personal pension plan.

Group personal pensions

Some employers organise group personal pensions (GPPs) for their employees, to which the employer may or may not contribute. The advantage of this for the employee is that charges may be lower than for individual personal pensions.

Employers that offer a GPP scheme will be able to continue with the GPP without having to provide access to stakeholder pensions as long as all employees are eligible to join the GPP and:

- the employer agrees to contribute at least 3% of the employee's basic pay into a personal pension on the employee's behalf
- the employer offers a payroll deduction facility to scheme members
- employees who transfer out of the scheme or stop making contributions do not incur any penalties.

Recent and forthcoming changes

Civil partners

Pension schemes must treat a civil partner in the same way as a legal spouse in relation to any pension benefits built up from 5 December 2005, although some schemes already had this type of provision before it became a statutory requirement.

A-day (6 April 2006)

A-day brought in many changes to the laws governing pension schemes. One of the most beneficial is that which gives employees the option to start receiving their pension whilst remaining in employment. This is particularly helpful to those employees who wish to reduce their working hours gradually over a number of months or years. Some schemes will also permit such members to build up further pension benefits at the same time as drawing some of their pension.

Prior to A-Day it was not possible to contribute to more than one pension arrangement at the same time. Since A-Day concurrent membership of more than one scheme has been permitted.

Age discrimination regulations

These regulations came into effect (in relation to pension schemes) in 2006. One of the key changes is that employees can continue contributing to their occupational pension scheme beyond the scheme's normal retirement age, and up to age 75, provided they continue in employment. However, an employer may still set lower and upper age limits for admission to a pension scheme.

Personal accounts

Personal accounts are the government's response to the fact that millions of people do not save towards their retirement; the intention is to introduce them in 2012. In general, all employees between the ages of 22 and state pension age who do not contribute to a pension scheme will be automatically enrolled into a personal account by their employer. Employees will be able to opt out by giving written notice to their employer.

Personal accounts will be funded jointly by the employee, who will pay 4% of earnings that fall within the £5,200 to £35,000 (in today's terms) range, the employer (3%) and the government (1% as tax relief). The employer contribution is likely to be phased in over three years, increasing by 1% each year.

Further information

The Financial Services Authority (FSA) has published a useful guide, *Promoting pensions to employees*, which can be downloaded from the FSA website www.fsa.gov.uk. The Pensions Service publishes a range of guides for employers and employees, available free by phone on 0845 7313233, or online at www.thepensionservice.gov.uk/resourcecentre. Employees can also get free advice and information from the Pension Advisory Service (TPAS) online at www.pensionsadvisoryservice.org.uk or by phone on 0845 6012923.

Keeping records

Employers have a legal duty to keep records of:

- gross pay
- tax and NI deductions or refunds
- any student loan deductions
- statutory sick pay
- statutory maternity leave and statutory maternity pay
- statutory paternity leave and statutory paternity pay
- absence due to adoption and statutory adoption pay
- accidents
- immigration status.

It is also useful to keep other information about employees, such as:

- personal details, including address, NI number, next of kin
- employment details – application form, references received, job description, signed copy of the employment contract
- employment particulars
- details of annual leave and any parental and/or dependants' leave taken
- contractual maternity, paternity and adoption leave taken
- sickness and other authorised absence
- any unauthorised absence including lateness and sickness

- any disciplinary action, unless it has been agreed that this will be removed from the employee's file
- training and development courses
- copies of references written (see *Providing references*, in chapter 3)
- pension records
- termination of employment and redundancy details/records.

Personnel records should be kept in a locked cabinet. Under the **Data Protection Act 1998** employees are entitled in most circumstances to access their personal details whether held on computer or manually. The **Access to Medical Reports Act 1988** gives employees the right to see medical reports supplied by their medical practitioner for employment purposes.

The Data Protection Act lays down eight principles relating to the collection, storage and management of personal data. Make sure that you understand and follow these principles, including those relating to personnel records. See chapter 9.

Part 2 of *The employment practices code*, published by the Information Commissioner and available from www.ico.gov.uk, covers employee records. *Data protection for voluntary organisations*, by Paul Ticher, published by the Directory of Social Change, is another useful resource.

Monitoring emails and internet access

Under the **Telecommunications (Lawful Business Practice) (Interception of Communications) Regulations 2000** an employer can monitor employees' use of email and the internet for a variety of purposes, as long as the employees are given reasonable notice that such activities will be monitored or where the employer is in notice of an abuse taking place. Examples of circumstances where monitoring is justified include:

- establishing whether communications are for business or private purposes
- preventing misuse of systems

– emails distributed do not contain information that would damage the organisation's reputation. For example, emails distributed through work should not be used to advertise a product or for political campaigning
– the system is not used to distribute chain mail or junk material.

You may wish to state that personal use of email facilities will be kept under review.

■ The appropriate use of email in relation to other forms of communication. For example, it is better to use email than posted letters if people need to be reached quickly, and in order to reduce paper use. Telephones should be used for urgent messages (but in some cases backed up with an email or letter). Email should not be seen as a secure medium, and other forms of communication should be used for sensitive or confidential information.

■ Distribution of emails. Only send an email to those who need it; unnecessary distribution wastes time and computer space.

■ Disclosure of status. Emails sent outside the organisation are likely to be 'business letters' and must include the same information about charitable and company status as any other business letter (see *Documentation*, in chapter 2). If the organisation is registered for VAT, some emails may need to include its VAT registration number (see chapter 8).

■ Legal status. Users must be made aware that emails have the same legal status as any other form of communication and that it is possible to make a legally binding contract via email. The policy should forbid anyone communicating via emails in a way that could lead to a contractual agreement without authorisation from their manager. Alternatively, all emails should contain a statement stating that no contract can be made via email.

■ Procedure to cover wrong delivery. For example, the policy could state that a wrongly delivered email should be redirected to the correct person and that if the message contains confidential

information, use must not be made of that information, nor must it be disclosed.

■ The penalties for sending offensive, abusive or defamatory messages or making any improper or discriminatory reference to someone. Any of these activities could be classified as harassment and could amount to gross misconduct. Users should also be aware that libel laws apply to emails.

■ Warnings to managers not to use bullying or stressful tactics (for example, sending a request with unreasonable deadlines that is copied to the management committee). Emails should not be used to rebuke or criticise staff.

■ Maintaining the security of the systems, especially the dangers of importing viruses. Users should be told, for example, what to do if an email has a suspect attachment or they are sent a chain email, and how to deal with spam messages.

■ Ensuring users are aware of the laws governing data protection when recording or obtaining information about individuals.

■ Email etiquette. Make sure users are aware of how easy it is to misinterpret the words or tone of an email and how abrupt, inappropriate or insensitive language can be construed as bullying and possibly offensive. For example, capital letters are sometimes interpreted as shouting. Users should always check the contents of an email before sending it (including spellchecking), just as they would a letter.

Good housekeeping practices

These could include clauses on the following:

■ All emails should include a disclaimer. You may want to add a note saying that under certain circumstances monitoring may take place.

■ Managing passwords (for example, they must not be shared and may need to be regularly changed) and security (for example, users leaving their screen unattended for any reason must either lock access to their workstation or log off).

- Procedures for dealing with emails when away from the office for extended periods. These could include forwarding emails, or granting colleagues access to your inbox.
- Procedures for deleting or archiving email information. This must be based on the data protection principles that the information recorded is adequate, relevant, not excessive and kept for no longer than necessary.

Reorganisation

Voluntary organisations, like other employers, sometimes have to reorganise. This may involve changes to conditions of employment: for example, a change in the workplace, different jobs and, in some cases, different terms and conditions of employment.

Some contracts of employment contain clauses that allow employers to make reasonable changes without consent:
- a variation clause to change a particular term or condition
- a flexibility to change duties performed
- a mobility clause to change of place of work.

You must obtain the employee's consent if there are no such clauses, or other changes are proposed; major changes imposed without agreement will be a breach of contract. If the breach is significant (for example, through having different working hours imposed), an employee with at least one year's service could argue that the change has forced them to resign and then make a claim for constructive dismissal. You should always discuss any proposed changes in good time, explaining why they are necessary, seek alternative ideas and take into account the impact of changes on each employee.

Employees who oppose changes should be asked to put their objections in writing.

A recognised union must be consulted about changes made to terms and conditions of a collective agreement; any changes made are binding on all employees, regardless of union membership.

You must give employees written notice of any changes to employment particulars within one month of the change taking effect.

If you cannot reach agreement about changes to the contract of employment there are two options. The first is to offer reasonable alternative employment. If this is a possibility, employers must consider the effects on each employee of any revised terms and conditions, pay, job description or place of work and, where necessary, make suitable adjustments (see *Offers of alternative work*, in chapter 3).

If there is no alternative work available, the only option is to terminate the contract and re-employ the people concerned on a new contract containing the new terms and conditions. Employees must be given the required notice to bring the old contract to an end. It is essential to seek legal advice before proceeding with this option.

Unfair dismissal

The **Employment Rights Act 1996** states that employees are dismissed fairly if they are dismissed 'for some substantial reason which justifies dismissal'. The courts have ruled that a necessary reorganisation by the employer may count as a 'substantial reason'. Provided there are good reasons for a reorganisation, an employee who has been dismissed, or who has been offered reasonable alternative terms and conditions and refused them, is unlikely to be able to claim unfair dismissal. But an employment tribunal will assess whether the offer of alternative employment was suitable and whether the refusal of the offer was reasonable.

Procedures for reorganisation

To protect themselves from claims for redundancy payments or unfair dismissal, employers should ensure that:

- the need for reorganisation has been seriously considered so that it can be objectively justified
- all possible alternatives to reorganisation have been examined
- the proposals have been discussed with recognised union and/or employee representatives
- employees affected by any reorganisation have been consulted and reasons for the proposed changes have been explained
- concerns expressed by those employees and their representatives have been considered, and suggested alternative strategies examined
- the final decision is not made until employees' views have been taken into account
- each employee's needs are considered when amending their contracts of employment.

Chapter 5

Health and safety

Legislation

The **Health and Safety at Work Act 1974 (HSW Act)** forms the basis of health and safety law. The Act sets out employers' general duties to employees (including anyone working remotely – for example, homeworkers) and others using an organisation's premises and equipment, including the public, trainees, volunteers, committee members, self-employed workers and contractors. It also covers duties employees have to themselves and to each other. The Act has been supplemented by regulations, approved codes of practice and guidance.

The **Health and Safety Executive (HSE)** is responsible for promoting health and safety at work. The HSE website www.hse.gov.uk/legislation provides information on existing and forthcoming legislation.

Regulations

Details of how employers must comply with their responsibilities under the HSW Act are given in regulations. They include:

- the management of health and safety
- health, safety and welfare in the workplace
- personal protective equipment
- provision and use of work equipment
- manual handling (for example, lifting)
- control of asbestos at work
- display screens
- fire precautions.

Guidance

The HSE publishes guidance on the regulations, most of which can be downloaded from www.hse.gov.uk.

Approved codes of practice

Approved codes of practice (ACoPs), which have a special legal status, advise on how to comply with the law. A court may, for example, take into account whether an employer followed an ACoP when assessing a breach of health and safety law.

Enforcement

Inspectors from the HSE or the local authority enforce health and safety legislation. They have the right to enter any workplace without notice and inspect the premises, test equipment, take photographs and samples and, if necessary, remove equipment for testing or preserving. They can also question staff, committee members and safety representatives (see *Safety representatives*, page 147) about health and safety matters.

If necessary, an inspector may specify measures to be implemented to comply with the law. If the breach is more serious, the inspector may issue an **improvement notice**, setting out measures to be taken, with a timescale. Where an activity involves, or will involve, risk of serious personal injury (including any disease or physical or mental impairment), the inspector may serve a **prohibition notice,** requiring an organisation to stop the activity until remedial action has been taken. Failure to comply with either type of notice is a criminal offence.

The inspector can also **prosecute** an organisation for failing to carry out its responsibilities. This is only likely to happen if an accident occurs in which someone is seriously injured or killed, or if an organisation:

- has failed to address health and safety issues
- is considered to be unwilling to implement health and safety measures or is believed to be deliberately delaying them
- has ignored obvious and imminent risks.

Anyone injured because of an organisation's failure to comply with health and safety law can claim compensation. Those employing staff must take out employers' liability insurance to cover claims by employees, and must display the certificate. They should also take out public liability insurance to cover other claims (see chapter 7 for further information on insurance).

Responsibilities of committee members and staff

The HSW Act imposes both collective and individual responsibility for health and safety. So if an organisation has committed an offence under the Act, anyone who has failed in their individual responsibilities could also be liable. This will always include committee members, and may also cover senior staff with health and safety responsibilities. HSE guidance recommends that every committee should appoint a member to take on particular responsibility for health and safety.

For further details see *Leading health and safety at work* (INDG417), available from www.hse.gov.uk. This explains how committee members can ensure their organisation has an effective approach to managing health and safety risks, and includes a health and safety leadership checklist.

Registering

Under the **Offices Shops and Railway Premises Act 1963** organisations that employ staff in shop or office premises may need to register with the HSE or the local authority. For further information contact your local authority or telephone the HSE InfoLine on 0845 345 0055.

General duties under the HSW Act

The HSW Act imposes general health and safety duties on employers, employees, self-employed workers and manufacturers and suppliers.

Duties to employees

Employers owe a duty 'so far as reasonably practicable' to ensure their employees' health, safety and welfare at work.

This duty includes:

- providing and maintaining machinery, equipment, appliances and work systems that are safe and free from health risks

- having arrangements for ensuring articles and substances are safely used, handled, stored and transported, without risk to health
- providing appropriate information, instruction, training and supervision to ensure the health and safety of staff
- maintaining any workplace in a safe condition and without risk to health
- maintaining workplace access and exit so that it is safe and without risk to health
- providing and maintaining a safe, risk-free working environment with adequate arrangements for staff welfare.

An employer cannot charge staff for any measures required for health and safety.

Reasonably practicable

Employers are not expected to guarantee total protection against accidents or ill health, as this would be impossible. Essentially, you have to balance the activities needed to achieve the organisation's objectives and the cost of safety measures against the risks staff face and the measures that can be taken to reduce or avoid those risks.

Home-based workers

Most of the regulations under the HSW Act also apply to home-based workers. For further details see *Homeworking: Guidance for employers and employees on health and safety* (INDG226), available from www.hse.gov.uk, and Telework guidance, available from www.berr.gov.uk/employment.

Duties to non-employees

You also have a duty to ensure 'so far as reasonably practicable' that people who are not employees but who might be affected by your activities are not exposed to health or safety risks.

Such people would include trainees, volunteers, committee members, self-employed workers, users, the general public and people temporarily working on an

145

organisation's premises. Any contractors appointed will also have a duty of care, so it is important to discuss with them how they will limit risks (for example, minimising noise or fumes resulting from their work).

It is good practice to take all reasonable steps to comply with the requirements of the Act, even if your organisation has no employees.

Duties to users of premises

Anyone responsible for non-domestic premises has a duty to non-employees who work there or who use equipment or substances provided on the premises. They must ensure 'so far as reasonably practicable' that the premises, access and exit routes, equipment and materials are free from health and safety risks. People considered responsible include owners, tenants, anyone with responsibility for repairs and those who, under a licence or tenancy, have responsibility for the health and safety of people using the premises.

This duty is owed to trainees, volunteers, committee members and self-employed workers, contractors, visitors, anyone sharing the premises and, in some cases, people hiring the premises.

Duties of employees

Each staff member must take reasonable care for their own health and safety and that of anyone who may be affected by anything they do or fail to do. Staff must cooperate with employers to fulfil their responsibilities.

You may wish to include a clause about employees' responsibilities in the statement of terms and conditions of service (see chapter 4). However, remember that the strength of duty is greater for the employer than the employee.

Other general requirements of the HSW Act

Health and safety policy statement

An organisation with five or more employees (including temporary, sessional and part-time employees) must have a written health and safety policy. This must:

- state the general policy on health and safety
- describe responsibilities for health and safety management
- outline systems and procedures for ensuring health and safety
- be brought to the attention of all employees
- be revised whenever appropriate, and every revision must be brought to the employees' attention
- be signed and dated by the employer.

It is good practice for *all* employers (and organisations that use only volunteers) to produce a written health and safety policy.

The policy should cover:

- managers' and supervisors' responsibilities
- employees' and volunteers' duties (both statutory and organisational)
- consultation arrangements (for example, safety committees), including name(s) of any employee representative(s)
- training arrangements (including induction and job specific training)
- hazard identification
- findings of general risk assessments
- findings of specific risk assessments for employees aged under 18 (see *Young workers*, page 151) and fire risks (see *Fire safety*, page 160)
- fire evacuation arrangements
- location of health and safety poster or leaflets
- accidents, first aid and work-related ill health
- monitoring arrangements
- emergency procedures.

An introduction to health and safety: Health and safety in small businesses (INDG259(rev1)), available from www.hse.gov.uk, and *The health and safety handbook for voluntary and community organisations*, published by the Directory of Social Change (DSC), both include a sample health and safety policy statement. The DSC policy covers volunteers as well as staff.

Health and safety poster

You must display the statutory poster *Health and safety law – what you should know* or distribute copies of the HSE leaflet *Your health and safety – a guide for workers* to all employees. Both are available from www.hse.gov.uk.

Safety representatives

Any recognised trade union (see *Unions*, in chapter 3) may appoint safety representatives. Wherever possible, they should have worked for the organisation for at least two years or have at least two years' experience in similar work.

Employers must consult safety representatives when drawing up their health and safety policies.

Safety representatives have the right to:

- investigate potential hazards and dangers and examine the causes of any accidents
- investigate complaints by staff relating to health, safety and welfare
- submit proposals on any health and safety matters at work and, in particular, suggestions relating to complaints, hazards and accidents
- carry out workplace inspections and inspect relevant documents
- represent employees in discussions on health, safety and welfare and with health and safety inspectors
- receive information from inspectors about matters identified during inspections
- attend meetings of safety committees where these have been set up (see *Safety committees*, page 148).

Safety representatives have the right to inspect the workplace or any part of it:

- at least once every three months, or
- where there has been any substantial change in the conditions of work – for example, when new machinery has been introduced or the HSE has issued new guidance relating to that type of work or workplace, or
- where there has been a serious accident, a dangerous incident or a notifiable disease.

Representatives must give the employer reasonable notice before carrying out the inspection. In turn, the employer must give safety representatives reasonable assistance, including facilities for independent investigation and private discussion with employees, and must let them inspect and take copies of any health and safety documentation.

There are exceptions to information provision, which include:

- an employee's health records where the individual can be identified
- information which cannot be disclosed by law (for example, under the **Data Protection Act 1998**, see chapter 9)
- information relating to any individual without their consent
- information that would substantially injure the employer's business.

You must allow safety representatives reasonable paid time off to carry out their responsibilities and for health and safety training. *Safety representatives and safety committees* (L87), available from HSE Books, sets out the relevant rules.

Consultation with employees who are not represented by a recognised trade union

Under the **Health and Safety (Consultation with Employees) Regulations 1996 (HSCER 1996)** employers must consult employees who are not represented by trade union safety representatives about health and safety.

Employees must be consulted on the following:

- any change that may substantially affect their health and safety, such as introducing new equipment or ways of working
- arrangements for appointing competent people (see *Getting advice*, page 150)
- the content of health and safety information to be provided to employees
- planning and organisation of health and safety training
- health and safety consequences of introducing new technology.

The employer can choose to consult employees directly or through the staff elected to represent them on health and safety matters (**representatives of employees' safety – ROES**).

The regulations do not specify the election procedure for ROES.

Elected ROES have the right to:

- receive the information they need to carry out their functions
- specifically receive information included in any records of accidents, injuries and diseases kept by the employer, with the same exceptions as apply to trade union representatives (see *Safety representatives*, page 147)
- make representations on potential hazards and dangerous incidents at the workplace that affect their colleagues
- make representations on general matters affecting health and safety at work and, in particular, the matters on which employers are obliged to consult (see above)
- represent their colleagues in consultations with inspectors at the workplace
- receive a reasonable amount of training, with costs, including travel and subsistence, paid for by the employer
- use any other facilities or receive reasonable assistance needed to carry out their functions
- take paid time off during working hours as necessary to perform their functions and to stand as candidates in an election for ROES.

Although ROES have many of the same rights as trade union representatives, they do not have the right to inspect or investigate, and will not have access to trade union resources such as legal help and advice.

Safety committees

Any two safety representatives can require an employer to set up a safety committee to review health and safety measures, within three months of the request. The employer must consult the safety representatives and recognised trade unions when setting up the committee and publicise members' names to staff. Membership could include volunteers and users, as well as paid staff and management committee members, and should be balanced between management and others.

Regulations under the HSW Act

The management of health and safety at work

The **Management of Health and Safety at Work Regulations 1999** cover the matters listed below. Full details can be found in *The management of health and safety at work. Approved code of practice and guidance* (L21), from HSE Books. The HSE InfoLine (0845 345 0055 or hse.infoline@natbrit.com) can help with many queries. See also *Health and safety regulation – a short guide* (HSC13(rev1)), available from www.hse.gov.uk.

Risk assessment

Every employer must:

- assess the health and safety risks employees are exposed to at work
- assess risks to the health and safety of others (for example, users, volunteers, committee members, self-employed workers and the public) arising from the organisation's activities

■ take action to eliminate any hazard or, if impracticable, reduce the risk as far as possible

■ review and revise the assessment whenever necessary

■ carry out a specific assessment of the health and safety risks affecting young people before employing anyone aged under 18 (see *Young workers*, page 151)

■ carry out a separate fire risk assessment (see *Fire safety*, page 160).

The regulations require a systematic examination of your activities. This must involve:

■ identifying hazards arising from activities (whether from the type of work, fire hazards or other factors – for example, the condition of the premises)

■ deciding who might be harmed, and how

■ evaluating the extent of the risks, taking into account any existing precautions, including fire safety arrangements

■ identifying what is already being done to minimise the risk, or to minimise the negative effects of any harm, and what else you could be doing to reduce exposure to the hazard to an acceptable level of risk

■ producing a health and safety policy for reducing risks, with named responsibilities and deadlines (see *Health and safety policies*, page 167)

■ putting the plan into action.

Employers must also carry out a risk assessment of work activities carried out by homeworkers, and workers and volunteers who visit other people's homes. This may involve visiting their homes, although people working from home can also help in identifying hazards. They must also assess the risks to personal safety of such workers and volunteers by conducting a lone worker risk assessment. For more information see *Homeworking: Guidance for employers and employees on health and safety* (INDG226) and *Working alone in safety* (INDG73), available from www.hse.gov.uk, and *Telework guidance*, available from www.berr.gov.uk/employment.

Reviews

You should regularly review your risk assessments as well as continually monitoring health and safety. If you develop a new area of work, move into new premises or buy new equipment, you must carry out further assessments.

Carrying out the assessment

In a small organisation with few hazards non-specialist staff or a committee member can carry out the assessment, as long as they have had appropriate training. In larger organisations or where there are special hazards, a non-specialist can carry out an overall assessment, followed by a specialist assessment of particularly hazardous activities. In organisations with several workplaces, some risks will be common and can be included within an overall assessment, but each site and its equipment must be assessed separately.

The risk assessment must take account of what *actually* happens in the workplace rather than what is supposed to happen. It should, for example, examine existing precautionary measures, the extent to which they are actually being used, and their effectiveness. So if, for example, staff ignore safety instructions on the use of equipment or keep fire doors closed, note this in the risk assessment and decide what action to take.

You should pay particular attention to those who may be especially at risk: for example, inexperienced or new staff, volunteers, disabled people, people who work unusual hours or who work alone, such as cleaners and security staff, and those who have difficulty understanding written or spoken English.

Organisations with five or more employees must produce a written record of the significant findings of the assessment. It is good practice for all organisations to do so. The record should include:

■ significant hazards identified

■ who might be harmed and how

- existing control measures and the extent to which they control, minimise or eliminate the risks
- risks that are not adequately controlled and the action taken.

Management and safety representatives should sign the form.

Getting advice

Employers must appoint at least one competent person, where possible a staff member, to help them carry out the risk assessment and take necessary preventative and protective measures. The assessor must have appropriate training, experience and knowledge, including knowledge of fire safety, and must be given all the necessary information, including details of anyone working on short-term contracts. Assessors must also be given enough time and the means to fulfil their functions.

Guidance on risk assessments is included in the *Management of health and safety at work. Approved code of practice* (L21), available from HSE Books. *An introduction to health and safety: Health and safety in small business* (INDG259(rev)) and *Five steps to risk assessment* (INDG163(rev2)), from www.hse.gov.uk, include a sample recording form. *Five steps* is particularly useful for small organisations.

Publications and other information

Employers and employees should read health and safety publications. Publications mentioned in this chapter (many of which are free) and many others are available from HSE Books on 01787 881165 or www.hsebooks.co.uk. Other information is available from www.hse.gov.uk and the HSE InfoLine 0845 345 0055, minicom 0845 408 9577 (8am-6pm) or hse.infoline@natbrit.com. Guidance is available in the following translations: Bengali, Chinese, Gujarati, Hindi, Polish, Urdu and Welsh.

Preventative and protective measures

Every employer must have arrangements for effective planning, organisation, control, monitoring and review of preventative and protective measures and, where there are five or more employees, must record these arrangements in writing. It is good practice for all organisations, regardless of size, to put such arrangements in writing.

An employer must use the following hierarchy of preventative measures:
- Avoid risk altogether if possible.
- Address risks at source rather than mitigating them (for example, it is better to design out a risk than to put up a warning notice).
- Wherever possible, adapt work to the individual – for example, in workplace design, choice of equipment and work methods.
- Take advantage of any technological progress that enables work to be done more safely.
- Ensure risk prevention measures are part of a coherent policy and approach, and aim progressively to minimise risks that cannot be prevented or avoided altogether.
- Give priority to those measures that affect the whole workplace and so yield the greatest benefit.
- Ensure that all workers, including trainees and volunteers, understand their responsibilities in relation to health and safety.
- Aim to make the need to avoid, prevent and reduce health and safety risks an accepted part of the organisational culture.

Health surveillance

This regulation requires all employers to introduce health surveillance where needed. The HSE recommends that this should be done where the risk assessment shows that:
- there is an identifiable disease or health condition relating to the work carried out
- techniques are available to detect indications of the disease or condition

- there is a reasonable likelihood that the disease or condition may arise in the work environment
- health surveillance will improve protection for staff against the disease or condition.

For further information see *Understanding health surveillance at work – an introduction for employers* (INDG 304), available from www.hse.gov.uk.

Emergency procedures

All employers must have appropriate procedures to follow in the event of serious and imminent danger to people at work, and nominate enough competent staff to evacuate premises in an emergency.

The procedures must ensure that all staff exposed to serious and imminent danger are informed of the hazard and know about the steps to be taken to protect them. The procedures must also enable people to stop work, leave the danger area if exposed, and not return until it is safe to do so.

The risk assessment should identify events that will lead to the implementation of emergency procedures: for example, a fire, bomb alert or building collapse.

The procedures should set out what is required of employees in an emergency: for example, when to fight a fire and when to evacuate, whether to notify emergency services, shut down machinery or secure essential documents, and how the emergency procedures will be activated.

Information to employees

You must give all employees clear and relevant information on the risks identified, the preventative and protective measures and the emergency procedures, together with the names of those responsible for evacuation. They must also be told about risks, including fire risks, identified by any other employers using the same workplace or premises.

It is important to recognise the needs of staff who have difficulties with communicating in written or spoken English: for example, by producing information in different languages, on tape, or in a simplified or pictorial format for workers with learning disabilities.

Visiting employees and contractors

You have a responsibility to visiting employees (for example, someone coming in to fix the photocopier or attend a meeting) and self-employed people working on site. You must notify self-employed people and the employer of anyone working on your premises (for example, cleaning and service contractors or recruitment agencies) of any health and safety risks and the precautionary measures taken. They must also be given instructions and information about any hazards or risks identified.

Staff capabilities and training

Staff capabilities in health and safety must be taken into account when allocating work. You should provide adequate health and safety training to new staff and to all staff if exposed to any new or increased risks. Training should take place during working hours and be repeated periodically. Employers have a specific responsibility to consider the health and safety training needs of people aged under 18 before their employment. Health, safety and emergency procedures must be covered as part of induction training for all staff and volunteers.

Temporary workers

Agency staff and anyone employed on a temporary or fixed-term contract must be given accessible information about any special qualifications or skills required to carry out work safely and any necessary health surveillance before they begin work.

Young workers

Before you employ anyone aged under 18, your risk assessment (see page 148) must take specific factors into account:

- young people's inexperience, immaturity and lack of awareness of risk
- the fitting out and layout of the workplace and workstation

- the nature, degree and duration of exposure to physical, biological and chemical agents
- the form, range and use of work equipment and the way it is handled
- the organisation of processes and activities
- the extent of the health and safety training to be provided for the young person and the special risks set out in health and safety guidance.

People aged under 18 must not be employed for work:

- which is beyond their physical or psychological capacity
- involving harmful exposure to radiation or agents which are toxic, carcinogenic, cause genetic damage or harm to unborn children or chronically affect human health
- involving the risk of accidents which would not be recognised or avoided by young people because of a lack of experience, training or attention to safety
- in which there is a risk to health from extreme cold, heat, noise or vibration.

This does not prevent 16 or 17 year-olds being employed for work that is part of their training if they are supervised by a competent person and where any risk will be reduced to the lowest level reasonably practicable.

Before employing someone under the school-leaving age, their parent or guardian must receive accessible information on:

- the health and safety risks identified by the risk assessment (see *Risk assessment*, page 148)
- the preventative and protective measures (see *Preventative and protective measures*, page 150)
- any risks notified by other employers using the same premises.

Work experience trainees

Work experience trainees have the same status as employees under the HSW Act.

For further information see www.hse.gov.uk/youngpeople/.

New and expectant mothers

If you employ women of childbearing age you must consider any risks to a new or expectant mother or her child when carrying out the risk assessment (see *Risk assessment*, page 148). A new mother is defined as one who has given birth within the previous six months, or who is breastfeeding.

If a risk to a new or expectant mother or her child(ren) cannot be avoided by other measures, you must alter her working conditions or hours of work if it is reasonable to do so and would avoid the risk. If this is not reasonable, you should offer her suitable alternative work at the same rate of pay, and if that is not feasible, suspend her from work for as long as is necessary to protect her health and safety. The **Employment Rights Act 1996** requires that this suspension be on full pay.

If a new or expectant mother who normally works at night presents a medical certificate stating that she should not continue to do so, you must offer her suitable alternative daytime work, on the same terms and conditions. If this is not feasible, you must suspend her on full pay for the period specified in the certificate as long as this remains necessary for health and safety reasons.

You need take no action until the employee has provided written confirmation that she is pregnant, has given birth within the previous six months or is breastfeeding. It is good practice not to require this information in writing, but you should record the date you were told.

Further guidance is contained in *New and expectant mothers at work: A guide for employers* (HSG122), from HSE Books. The leaflet *A guide for new and expectant mothers who work* (INDG373) can be downloaded from www.hse.gov.uk/mothers.

Cooperation between employers

Employers who share a workplace must cooperate on health and safety matters and wherever possible coordinate their health and safety measures, including those relating to fire safety in the workplace. Cooperation may involve carrying out a joint risk assessment for the whole premises as well as a more limited assessment for each employer's activities. In any event, each employer must provide information about any risks arising from their activities to other employers' staff. The HSE recommends that either one employer (for example, the owner or tenant) takes responsibility for the premises, that a health and safety coordinator is jointly appointed or a dedicated premises health and safety committee is formed.

Workplace health, safety and welfare

The **Workplace (Health, Safety and Welfare) Regulations 1992** apply to all workplaces. Full details can be found in *Workplace health, safety and welfare. Approved code of practice* (L24) and are summarised in *Workplace health safety and welfare: A short guide for managers* (INDG244(rev2)). *Welfare at work: Guidance for employers on welfare provisions* (INDG293(rev1)) includes suggestions for good practice. All are available from HSE Books (www.hsebooks.com).

Premises and equipment

Premises and equipment must be kept in a good state of repair, in proper working order and should be properly maintained. Defects should be rectified immediately or steps taken to protect anyone who might be at risk (for example, by preventing access). You should have suitable servicing and maintenance procedures that identify potentially dangerous defects and ensure they are remedied. Keep a record of any defects and of any maintenance carried out.

Ventilation

There must be effective and suitable ventilation. This may simply involve windows that open. Any air conditioning or mechanical ventilation must be cleaned, tested, maintained and serviced, and must operate effectively. Recycled air must be filtered.

Temperature

The workplace must be neither too hot nor too cold, with enough thermometers to enable people to establish the inside temperature. Unless there are special reasons for lower temperatures, in most cases the minimum acceptable temperature is 16°C. As a guide, 19–20°C is the recommended temperature in offices, as internal heat gains from equipment and lighting will raise the temperature to a comfortable level. (See *The green office*, in chapter 6.)

Lighting

Every workplace must have suitable and sufficient lighting. As far as practicable, this should be natural light. There must also be emergency lighting if there is no natural light source in escape routes or if anyone working in any part of the premises would be in danger if normal lighting became defective. The light should be sufficient for people to work and move around safely without eye strain. Stairs should be well lit and without shadows on treads. Individual workstations and places of particular danger should be lit separately. Windows and skylights should be cleaned regularly.

Cleanliness and rubbish disposal

Workplaces, furniture and fittings must be kept clean and there should be additional cleaning if there is a spillage or soiling. Rubbish should not be allowed to accumulate except in rubbish receptacles. The standard of cleanliness should be adapted according to how the workplace or area is used.

Room dimensions and space

There must be enough space in workrooms to enable staff to move easily and safely. This will depend on the layout and the space needed for furniture and fittings. A worker should normally have an absolute minimum of 11 cubic metres of space (approximately two metres square, including workstation and chair, but excluding filing cabinets), discounting any height above three metres. This minimum may be insufficient if a high percentage of the space is taken up by furniture.

Workstations and seating

A workstation is the place where someone works, including for example a desk, chair, computer, immediate shelving and drawers. It must be suitable for the individual(s) concerned as well as for their work, and must take account of the specific needs of disabled staff members. It should be:

- protected from the weather
- designed so that someone can leave it quickly in an emergency
- designed to ensure that no one will slip or fall
- provided with a suitable seat and foot rest where necessary
- designed so that work equipment and materials are within easy reach without undue bending or stretching.

There are specific workstation requirements for computer use (see *Display screen equipment*, page 158).

Floors and internal traffic routes

Floors must be suitable for their purpose without any dangerous holes, slopes or slippery or uneven surfaces and with drainage where necessary. Handrails should be provided on all staircases except where they would obstruct a traffic route.

Preventing people and objects from falling

You should take suitable and effective measures to prevent anyone from being injured through falling or being hit by a falling object. Any area where there is a risk of this happening should be clearly indicated. Wherever possible, fence off any place where someone could fall and injure themselves.

Storage units should be strong and stable enough for their task and should not be overfilled. The height of stacking should be limited and checks made on the safety of stored objects.

Windows

All windows should be made from material that does not cause danger: for example, by making them robust enough not to break, or by using shatter-proof glass. Transparent surfaces should be marked so that they are visible.

It should be possible to reach windows, skylights and ventilators so that they can be safely opened and closed. There should be controls to prevent people falling out of any window.

It should be possible to clean windows and skylights safely: for example, by having pivoting windows or using ladders.

Vehicles

There should be measures to protect pedestrians from vehicles. Traffic routes for pedestrians and vehicles should be clearly marked, and if possible separated. Pay particular attention to the safety of wheelchair users and people with visual and hearing disabilities.

Doors and gates

Doors and gates should be suitably constructed. Sliding doors should be fitted with a device to prevent them from being derailed, and upward opening doors with a device to prevent them from falling back. Powered doors must have features preventing them from trapping anyone and enabling them to be overridden if power fails. It should be possible to see through doors that open both ways.

WCs

WCs must be suitable, adequately ventilated and lit, kept clean and tidy, and be sufficient for the number of staff. Exact requirements are shown below.

Number of employees	Minimum number of toilets/washrooms
1–5	1
6–25	2
26–50	3
51–75	4
76–100	5

There must one additional WC and one additional washing station for every 25 people (or fraction of 25) above 100.

Men and women must have separate facilities unless each WC is in a separate room with a door that can be locked from the inside. There must be at least one women-only WC for every 25 women and one men-only WC for every 25 men.

Washing facilities

There must be suitable and sufficient washing facilities if required by the nature of the work or for health reasons. The facilities must be sited by each WC and changing area, with hot and cold running water, soap or other washing agent and a means of drying hands (for example, towels or a hot air dryer). The rooms must be ventilated and properly lit and be kept clean and tidy. Men and women must have separate facilities unless they are provided in a room with a lockable door and one person at a time uses the facilities in each room.

Acas guidance points out that some religions and beliefs do not allow individuals to undress or shower in the company of others. If staff need to change their clothing or shower in the interests of health and safety, it is good practice to discuss with them how such needs can be met. Insisting on communal shower and changing facilities could constitute indirect discrimination or harassment. For further details see *Religion or belief and the workplace*, available from www.acas.org.uk.

Drinking water

Drinking water must be easily accessible from marked places. Taps and containers must be clearly and correctly labelled as drinking water, and cups provided unless the water comes in a jet.

Storage and changing facilities

Staff needing separate clothes for work must have secure storage facilities for home and work clothes – two areas if the two types of clothes need to be kept separate for hygiene or health reasons. There should also be facilities for drying clothing.

If changing requires privacy, there should be separate facilities for men and women.

Rest and eating facilities

Workplaces should have suitable rest facilities at convenient places. There must be enough tables and seating with backs for the number of people likely to use them at any one time and enough suitable seating for the number of disabled people at work. If food eaten in the workplace is likely to become contaminated, there should be separate eating facilities. There must also be suitable facilities to enable pregnant women and breastfeeding mothers to rest, and it is good practice to provide somewhere private and safe to express milk. Toilets are not suitable for this purpose.

Remember that some religions or beliefs have special dietary requirements. If staff bring food to work they may need to store and heat it separately.

Personal protective equipment (PPE)

Full details of the **Personal Protective Equipment at Work Regulations 1992** can be found in the HSE's *Personal protective equipment at work. Guidance on regulations* (L25(2nd edn)). The regulations do not apply if there are more specific regulations relating to the use of cutting machinery.

Personal equipment and clothing must be provided to protect staff against the weather and risks to their health and safety, unless risks are controlled by other, equally effective means. This includes, for example, providing helmets, gloves, rainwear, high visibility jackets, aprons, eye protectors, lifejackets and safety harnesses.

Protective equipment and clothing must be readily available and:

- be appropriate for the risks involved, the conditions where the risks may occur and the period for which it is worn
- take account of the practicality of its use and the state of health of the person wearing it, and of the characteristics of each person's workstation

- be capable of fitting the worker correctly
- be effective in preventing or controlling the risks involved.

You must carry out an assessment of the general suitability of PPE before supplying it. You must also assess the needs of individual workers and whether the equipment meets those needs. If more than one piece of PPE is required, ensure the equipment is compatible.

Unless there is a suitable cleaning process, only one person may use equipment that needs to be hygienic and otherwise free of risk to health.

Equipment must be well maintained, in good working order and replaced when necessary, and there must be adequate storage facilities for equipment not in use.

Staff must receive clear information, instruction and training to enable them to know:

- the risks avoided or limited by the equipment
- what the equipment is for and how to use it
- steps they should take to maintain the equipment.

Employers must take reasonable steps to ensure that protective equipment is used. In turn, employees must use the protective equipment and report any defects or loss.

Work equipment

Details of the **Provision and Use of Work Equipment Regulations 1998 (PUWER)** can be found in the HSE's *Safe use of work equipment. Approved code of practice and guidance* (L22) and in the *Simple guide to the Provision and Use of Work Equipment Regulations 1998* (INDG 291).

The regulations impose a duty on employers and on any organisation controlling premises where people work and where machinery is used. If an organisation shares its premises and equipment, it will owe a duty to the employees of those organisations sharing the premises as well as to its own staff.

Mobile work equipment

Under Part III of PUWER, mobile work equipment used for carrying people must be suitable for this purpose. You should take measures to reduce the risks (for example, from the equipment rolling over) to the safety of the people being carried, the operator and anyone else.

Suitability and maintenance of equipment

Ensure that work equipment is suitable for the purpose for which it is used and for those who use it. This includes taking into account any special needs. When selecting equipment, consider working conditions, existing risks and any additional risk posed by the equipment. There are separate requirements relating to the maintenance of equipment to meet fire safety regulations (see *Fire safety*, page 160).

You must ensure that equipment is in good repair, and its maintenance should be recorded in a log book.

Ladders and access equipment

The **Work at Height Regulations 2005** cover the use of ladders and access equipment at work, including stepladders, working platforms and cherry pickers. Employers must avoid the need for working at height where possible, and where this is unavoidable use work equipment and other measures to prevent falls. Where risks cannot be eliminated, use work or other equipment to minimise the distance and consequences of any fall.

Employers must assess the need for working at height. Any ladders or equipment must be fit for purpose and well maintained, and staff or volunteers must receive appropriate training before working with such equipment.

For further information and guidance see *The Work at Height Regulations – a brief guide* (HSE INDG401) and the CD-ROM *Height aware*. Both are available from www.hsebooks.com.

Specific risks

If any equipment is likely to involve a specific risk to health or safety, only specifically authorised and suitably trained staff can use it.

Information and instruction

Everyone who uses work equipment, and their managers, must have adequate, clear health and safety information and, where appropriate, written instructions on its use. Instructions should include details of:

■ how the equipment should be used

■ possible problems (for example, likely faults) and the action to be taken if they occur

■ comments from those with experience of using the equipment.

Training

You must ensure that everyone using equipment, and their managers, has received adequate health and safety training which includes:

■ ways to use the equipment

■ possible risks from its use

■ precautions to be taken.

Other requirements

More specific requirements apply to machinery, covering:

■ dangerous parts of machinery

■ protection against specific hazards

■ high or very low temperatures

■ stop controls

■ isolation from sources of energy

■ stability

■ lighting

■ maintenance operations

■ markings

■ warnings.

For further information on reducing risks from work equipment see *Using work equipment safely* (INDG229(rev1)), available from www.hse.gov.uk.

Manual handling

General duties on employers

Manual handling covers physically lifting, lowering, holding, pushing, pulling, carrying or moving an object or load (which includes a person). This would include helping people in and out of vehicles, lifting wheelchairs, moving furniture and other equipment, pushing trolleys, clearing rubbish and gardening. Employers should, wherever possible, avoid the need for manual handling which involves a risk of injury. If a task cannot be avoided, assess the risks involved against a series of factors set out in the regulations, including those listed below. If your manual handling activities include moving and handling people (such as assisting people in wheelchairs to transfer to a car), you must conduct a separate risk assessment, and staff must receive appropriate (people handling) training.

Tasks involved in the handling

Do they involve:

■ working with loads at a distance from the body

■ awkward body movements

■ excessive lifting or lowering distances

■ excessive carrying distances

■ excessive pushing or pulling

■ risks of loads moving suddenly

■ frequent or prolonged physical effort?

Type of load

Is it:

■ heavy

■ bulky or unwieldy

■ difficult to grasp

■ unstable?

Working environment

Are there:

■ space constraints, preventing good posture

■ uneven, slippery or unstable floors

■ variations in floor levels or work surfaces

■ extremes of temperature or humidity

- poor lighting conditions
- conditions causing ventilation problems or gusts of wind?

An individual's capability

Consider the following:

- strength
- height
- physical suitability
- clothing, footwear or other personal effects the person is wearing
- whether the activity requires a certain level of stamina or fitness
- experience, knowledge and training
- whether a risk assessment has identified the employee as being especially at risk
- whether the activity creates a hazard for pregnant women
- age
- information or training needed.

Other factors

These could include, for example, whether movement or posture could be hindered by personal protective equipment or by clothing.

Full details of the **Manual Handling Operations Regulations 1992** can be found in *Manual handling. Guidance on regulations* (L23). The guidance provides a model checklist that can be used for making the assessment. *Getting to grips with manual handling: a short guide* (INDG143(rev2)) explains the problems associated with manual handling and sets out best practice in dealing with them. Both are available from HSE Books.

The HSE has developed the online *Manual handling assessment chart* to help identify high risk workplace manual handling activities – see www.hse.gov.uk/msd/mac.

Managing asbestos

Under Regulation 4 of the **Control of Asbestos Regulations 2006**, building owners, tenants and anyone else with legal responsibilities for non-domestic premises must:

- take reasonable steps to find asbestos-containing materials in the premises and check their condition
- presume materials contain asbestos unless there is strong evidence to suppose they do not
- keep an up-to-date written record of the location and condition of asbestos-containing materials
- assess the risk of exposure to asbestos-containing materials
- prepare and put into effect a plan to manage the risk
- give adequate training, including information and instruction, to anyone who is, or may be, exposed to asbestos.

Work with most asbestos-containing materials requires a licence from the HSE.

Anyone who controls or has information about the building must cooperate with the duty holder. For example, landlords must pass on relevant information to new tenants and leaseholders must allow access for inspection by managing agents.

For further details see *The management of asbestos in non-domestic premises*, available from www.hse.gov.uk/asbestos.

Display screen equipment

Full details of the **Health and Safety (Display Screen Equipment) Regulations 1992** can be found in *Display screen equipment. Guidance on regulations* (L26). This provides useful guidance on safe methods of using display screens (VDUs), including diagrams of seating arrangements. *Working with VDUs* (INDG36(rev3)) includes a summary of the regulations, suggestions for simple adjustments users can make to workstations and screens and a list of sources of further advice. It also draws attention to the role of employees and safety representatives in risk assessments. Both publications are available from www.hsebooks.com.

The regulations impose duties only in relation to **users** – employees who use display screen equipment as a significant part of their normal work. The code of practice gives examples of staff who are likely to be included and excluded by the regulations.

Analysis of workstations

You must carry out thorough analysis of workstations to assess the health and safety risks and update the assessment as often as necessary. Identified risks must be reduced to the lowest reasonably practicable extent. All display screens, not just those used by 'users' (see previous paragraph), must comply with the regulations.

Requirements for workstations

Workstations should be set up to ensure:

- the display screen is adequate for the type of work, with legible characters and adjustable brightness and contrast
- the screen is detachable and adjustable, in height and swivel, to allow for the operator's individual preferences
- the screen is properly and regularly cleaned to ensure dirt and grime do not affect legibility; there should be wipes at each workstation
- the keyboard is adjustable
- each workstation has a wrist rest and a foot rest
- each workstation has an anti-static mat, a lamp and a document holder
- direct light does not fall on the screen and, where possible, the screen is at a right angle to the window
- the work desk is non-reflective
- there is adequate space on work surfaces surrounding computer equipment
- the work chair is adjustable for both height and back support, and stable
- there is sufficient space at each workstation for each user to vary their position comfortably.

Daily work routine for users

It is important to consider the organisation of VDU work:

- Jobs should be designed to allow for changes in activity.

- Staff should take regular breaks (at least ten minutes away for every hour at the screen). Short, frequent breaks are better than occasional longer breaks. Individuals should have some discretion over when to take breaks; some people prefer to take frequent micro-breaks.

Portable computers

The design features necessary to make portables easy to carry, such as small keyboards, can make prolonged use uncomfortable.

The HSE advises that it is better to use full-sized equipment if possible. People who must use portable computers should be trained in how to minimise risks. This includes sitting comfortably, angling the screen so it can be seen clearly with minimal reflections, and taking frequent breaks. Wherever possible, portables should be used on a firm surface at the right height for keying.

Eye and eyesight tests

The employer must pay for all staff defined as users (see *Display screen equipment*, page 158) to have eyesight tests. These should take place at regular intervals, including before someone starts using the equipment, if requested, and at any time they may be experiencing difficulties attributable to their work with VDUs. You may wish to pay for eye tests for all regular VDU operators.

If a test shows that, as a result of work with VDUs, a staff member needs to purchase special corrective appliances (usually glasses) the employer should pay for these. The employer would not be expected to pay for glasses used for purposes other than work with VDUs.

Upper limb disorders

Work-related upper limb disorders (**ULDs**) are often associated with keyboard work and mouse use. The term repetitive strain injury (**RSI**) is often used to refer to pain resulting from working with computers (although ULDs cover more than 20 medical conditions). The employer should provide VDU, keyboard and mouse equipment and furniture which help prevent the development of these musculoskeletal disorders. Staff, however, can contribute to their own safety and welfare by:

- avoiding sitting in the same position for long periods
- adjusting equipment and furniture to appropriate/comfortable positions
- taking short pauses from mouse work to relax their arm
- taking rests from VDU work (at least ten minutes away every hour or frequent micro-breaks).

Using a mouse

Because use of a mouse, trackball or similar pointing device concentrates activity on one hand and one or two fingers, users may experience more problems with their fingers, hands, wrists, arms and shoulders than with keyboard work. They can reduce risks by adopting a good posture and technique, and taking their hand away from the mouse when they are not using it.

The HSE booklets *Aching arms (or RSI) in small businesses* (INDG171(rev1)) and *Working with VDUs* (INDG36(rev3)), available from www.hsebooks.com, give advice on reducing disorders such as RSI.

Pregnant women

The level of electromagnetic radiation emitted from VDUs is well within the safe levels set out in international recommendations, and employers are not obliged to check radiation levels or provide any special devices, such as screens or aprons. It is now generally accepted that there is no link between miscarriages or birth defects and working with VDUs. However, a pregnant woman who believes she is at risk, however much she is reassured, should not be forced to work with VDUs, and wherever possible employers should arrange alternative ways of working.

Training

All users of display screen equipment must receive health and safety training before they start using the equipment. Further training must be provided if a workstation is modified.

Information

Staff must be given information on all aspects of health and safety relating to their workstations, together with the measures taken to analyse risks and comply with the regulations. Employers must also provide information about the steps they are taking to ensure breaks in equipment use and the training they are providing.

Fire safety

The **Regulatory Reform (Fire Safety) Order 2005 (RRO)** governs fire safety in England and Wales. The order came into force in October 2006 and replaced over 70 pieces of fire safety legislation. It applies to all non-domestic buildings, including offices, shops, community halls, premises that provide care, and tents and marquees. Fire authorities no longer issue fire certificates and certificates previously in force have no legal status.

In most cases enforcement will be the responsibility of the local fire and rescue service.

Responsible person

Legal responsibility for implementing the order lies with the 'responsible person' (or people) – whoever has control of the premises or certain areas or systems. In a workplace this is likely to be the employer and anyone else who has control over any part of the premises, such as the owner or occupier.

The responsible person must, as far as is reasonably practical, make sure that everyone on the premises or nearby can escape safely if there is a fire. This applies to visitors, volunteers and the public as well as employees.

Risk assessment

The responsible person must carry out, or nominate someone to carry out, a fire risk assessment that involves five steps:

1. **Identify fire hazards.** How could a fire start? What could burn?
2. **Consider people at risk.** People in and around the premises and people who may be especially at risk (for example, people working near to fire dangers, people working in isolated areas, children or parents with babies, disabled people or people with special needs).
3. **Evaluate, remove or reduce, and protect from risk.** Think about what you have found in steps 1 and 2 and reduce any risks in order to protect people and premises.
4. **Record, plan, inform, instruct and train.** Keep a record of the risks identified and action taken to reduce or remove them. Make a clear plan of how to prevent fires and how you will keep people safe if a fire starts. Make sure staff are trained so that they know what to do in the event of a fire.
5. **Review.** Regularly review the risk assessment and make changes if necessary.

Employees must cooperate with the employer to make a workplace safe from fire and not do anything that would place themselves or others at risk.

If you share a building you should coordinate your risk management plan with the other occupants.

Emergency plan

You must ensure that there are emergency exit routes from a workplace, which are kept clear at all times.

Taking account of the extent of the risk, you must ensure that:

- people can evacuate the premises quickly and safely
- emergency routes and exits lead as directly as possible to a place of safety
- emergency routes and exits are clearly signed
- the number, distribution and dimensions of emergency routes and exits are adequate

- emergency doors open in the direction of escape and can be immediately opened: that is, they should not be locked or fastened
- sliding or revolving doors are not used as emergency exits
- routes and exits have emergency lighting if normal lighting fails (in smaller workplaces this could take the form of battery-operated torches placed in suitable positions – for example, along the emergency exit routes).

All equipment and devices must be regularly and efficiently maintained to avoid risk of fire.

When designing evacuation procedures remember to take into account the needs of people who may be especially at risk: for example, physically disabled people and those who have difficulty understanding written or spoken English.

Fire detection and warning systems

All non-domestic premises must have a suitable fire detection and warning system. The type of system needed depends on the size of the building and how easy it would be to hear an alarm: for example, in premises with only a few rooms, a handbell would be enough so long as everyone could hear it. You should also consider installing alarms with flashing lights to alert people with hearing impairment. The Disabled Living Foundation (www.dlf.org.uk) has details.

Fire alarms must be tested weekly, and the system tested and inspected quarterly.

Fire fighting equipment

Premises must have adequate means of fighting fires, including fire extinguishers and possibly fire blankets (these are particularly important if there is a kitchen), and sprinklers or foam inlets. Only people who have been trained should use fire extinguishers, which must be inspected annually and be recharged as soon as they have been let off. Any non-automatic fire fighting equipment must be easily accessible, simple to use and indicated by signs.

You must ensure all fire precautions are maintained in efficient working order and keep a fire log book.

Further information

For further details see *A short guide to making your premises safe from fire*, available from www.communities.gov.uk/fire. The Fire Gateway website (www.fire.gov.uk/Workplace+safety) includes a range of useful information, and your local fire and rescue service may provide advice and training.

Other health and safety laws and regulations

Smoking

Premises

Under the **Smoke-free (Premises and Enforcement) Regulations 2006** (in England) and similar regulations in Wales, Scotland and Northern Ireland, smoking is not allowed in any 'enclosed' or 'substantially enclosed' public place or workplace in the UK. This includes both permanent structures and temporary ones such as tents and marquees.

Premises are considered enclosed if they have a ceiling or roof and (except for doors, windows or passageways) are wholly enclosed on either a permanent or temporary basis.

Premises are considered substantially enclosed if they have a ceiling or roof, but have an opening in the walls that is less than half the total area of the walls.

Vehicles

Vehicles must be smoke-free at all times if they are used:

- to transport members of the public
- by more than one person in the course of paid or voluntary work, regardless of whether they are in the vehicle at the same time.

It is the legal responsibility of anyone who drives, manages or is responsible for order and safety on a vehicle to stop people smoking.

Signage

Premises

You must display no-smoking signs in a prominent position at every entrance to smoke-free premises. They must:

- be at least A5*
- display the international no-smoking sign (a single burning cigarette enclosed in a red circle with a red bar across it) at least 70mm in diameter*
- carry the following words in characters that can be easily read: 'No smoking. It is against the law to smoke in these premises' (in Wales this must also appear in Welsh).

You can display a smaller sign showing just the no-smoking symbol at entrances to premises that:

- are only used by members of staff (but there must be at least one A5 sign* in the premises)
- are located within larger smoke-free premises.

Vehicles

Smoke-free vehicles must display a no-smoking sign showing the international no-smoking symbol at least 70mm* in diameter in each compartment of the vehicle in which people can be carried.

For further information and downloadable signs see www.smokefreeengland.co.uk, www.clearingtheairscotland.com, www.smokingbanwales.co.uk or www.spacetobreathe.org.uk (for Northern Ireland). The signs are available in a number of community languages.

These sizes differ slightly in Scotland and Wales

Enforcement

Local councils are responsible for enforcing the law. Employers are responsible for ensuring all staff, service users/customers and visitors are aware of the regulations, and must display the proper signage. Employers who do not display the required signs in premises or vehicles face a £200 fixed penalty or a fine of up to £1,000; those who fail to prevent smoking can face fines of up to £2,500. People who smoke in no-smoking premises or vehicles face a fixed penalty of £50 or a fine of up to £200.

Smoke-free policy

Having a smoke-free policy will help ensure that everyone who uses your premises and vehicles is aware of the law and knows how to comply. You should develop a policy in consultation with employees and their representatives. The policy could cover:

- purpose
- policy statement
- who is responsible for implementation
- non-compliance
- help to stop smoking.

A sample policy can be downloaded from www.smokefreeengland.co.uk.

Help for smokers who want to quit

If staff, volunteers or users want to stop smoking they can contact:

- their local NHS Stop Smoking Service (call 0800 169 0 169 or visit www.gosmokefree.co.uk)
- the NHS Smoking Helpline (0800 169 0 169)
- www.gosmokefree.co.uk
- the support programme 'Together' (details from the NHS Smoking Helpline (0800 169 0 169) or www.gosmokefree.co.uk).

Electrical apparatus

The **Electricity at Work Regulations 1989** set out requirements for the construction, use and testing of electrical systems in all workplaces. For further information see the HSE's *Memorandum of guidance on the Electricity at Work Regulations* (HSR25(2nd edn)).

The regulations impose a general duty on employers to ensure that, so far as is reasonably practicable:

- systems are constructed to prevent danger
- systems are maintained to prevent danger
- systems are used in a manner to prevent danger arising.

The regulations also have specific requirements about earthing and types of connectors, and state that users must be properly trained and supervised to avoid injury.

Maintaining portable electrical equipment in offices and other low risk environments (INDG236), available from www.hsebooks.com, sets out precautions that can be taken in premises where risks are generally low and includes suggestions for good practice. The HSE microsite www.hse.gov.uk/electricity includes further information about electricity safety at work.

Hazardous substances

The **Control of Substances Hazardous to Health Regulations 2002** (**COSHH**) require employers to identify hazardous substances and assess risks to those who may be affected. Hazardous substances could include, for example, photocopier toner and cleaning fluids. The assessment must be reviewed whenever necessary. Exposure to substances identified must then be prevented or controlled, or protective equipment issued. Employers must prepare plans and procedures to deal with accidents, incidents and emergencies involving hazardous substances, and must ensure employees are properly informed, trained and supervised. Any protective equipment or control methods must be regularly monitored and reviewed.

You must record both the assessment and the maintenance tests, keep these records safely and make them available for inspection.

For further guidance see *A step by step guide to COSHH assessment* (HSG97), available from HSE Books, and *COSHH: a brief guide to the regulations* (INDH136(rev3)), available from www.hse.gov.uk/coshh.

Registration, Evaluation, Authorisation and Restriction of Chemicals (REACH)

REACH requires chemical manufacturers and importers to improve the quality of advice and information about the product to end users. It can apply to everyday workplace items such as cleaning materials, glues, paints, solvents and plastics. Where end users are provided with additional information about the safe use of certain chemicals, this may require an amendment to their COSHH assessments. However, most organisations using products routinely as specified by the supplier are unlikely to be significantly affected by these regulations.

For further information see www.hse.gov.uk/reach/index.htm.

First aid

Under the **Health and Safety (First Aid) Regulations 1981** all workplaces, regardless of size, must have adequate and appropriate equipment, facilities and personnel to give first aid to employees if they are injured or become ill at work.* The level of provision will depend on the circumstances at the workplace, identified through the risk assessment (see *Risk assessment*, page 148).

* *Revised regulations, particularly relating to first aid training, are likely to come into force during 2009.*

The minimum requirements are:
■ a suitably stocked first aid box
■ an appointed person to take charge of first aid arrangements.

The regulations do not apply to non-employees, but the HSE strongly recommends including provision for them.

The HSE booklet *First aid at work: The Health and Safety (First Aid) Regulations 1981* (L74), available from www.hse.gov.uk/firstaid, contains an approved code of practice and guidance.

First-aiders

Organisations with fewer than 50 employees in a 'very low risk' environment (such as an office) have no legal obligation to have a trained first-aider on the premises, but it is good practice for all organisations to have at least two people with first aid training.

Training

First-aiders must have undertaken training and obtained qualifications approved by the HSE. First aid certificates are valid for three years, and refresher courses must be started before they expire, otherwise the first-aider will have to take a full course again.

Appointed person

Organisations with no trained first-aiders must have an appointed person authorised to take charge if there is a serious injury or illness (for example, by calling an ambulance). Consider providing emergency first aid training for all appointed persons.

First aid boxes

First aid boxes and kits should contain only the items that a first-aider has been trained to use; they should not contain any medication.

Information

Employees and volunteers should be told about first aid arrangements, given the names of the first-aider(s)/appointed person and the location of the first aid box. Remember to take into account the needs of people with reading or language difficulties.

For further information about first aid, including contents of first aid boxes and good practice suggestions, see *First aid at work: your questions answered* (INDG214), available from www.hse.gov.uk/firstaid.

Occupational road risk

The HSW Act places a duty on employers to adopt a proactive approach to **managing occupational road risk (MORR)** and to do all that is reasonably practicable to protect any staff (including volunteers) who may be on the road as part of their job. This applies regardless of who owns the vehicles.

When assessing risks associated with any transport services the organisation provides, remember that older or disabled service users may have particular difficulties escaping from a vehicle in the case of an accident.

RoSPA (the Royal Society for the Prevention of Accidents) publishes a number of free guides on road safety for employers, including *Managing occupational road risk in voluntary organisations: a pilot study*, which are available from www.rospa.org.uk. *Driving at work*, available from www.hse.gov.uk/ workplacetransport, covers managing risk to drivers' health and safety.

Using mobile phones in vehicles

It is illegal to use a hand-held mobile phone while driving. It is also an offence to 'cause or permit' a driver to use a hand-held mobile phone while driving, therefore employers, as well as the individual driver, can be liable if they expect employees to use a hand-held phone while driving. It can also be illegal to use a hands-free phone if this can be shown to have caused dangerous driving. RoSPA recommends not using mobile phones while driving. The leaflet *Driving for work: Mobile phones*, available from www.rospa.org.uk, includes a sample policy on mobile phones and driving.

Working hours

The **Working Time Regulations 1998** include requirements for leave, rest breaks and maximum working weeks to protect workers' health and safety The regulations contain specific provisions for night workers. For further details see chapter 3.

Noise

The **Control of Noise at Work Regulations 2005** aim to protect employees' hearing from being damaged by excessive noise at their workplace.

Employers must:
- assess the risk to employees from noise at work
- take action to reduce the noise exposure that produces those risks
- provide employees with hearing protection if it is not possible to reduce exposure by other methods
- make sure the legal limits on noise are not exceeded
- provide employees with relevant information, instruction and training
- carry out health surveillance where there is a risk to health.

Judging noise

You will probably have to do something about noise if any of the following apply:
- the noise is intrusive – like a busy street or a vacuum cleaner – for most of the working day
- employees have to raise their voices to carry out a normal conversation when about two metres apart for at least part of the day
- employees use noisy powered tools or machinery for more than half an hour each day.

For further information see *Noise at work: Guide for employers on the Control of Noise at Work Regulations 2005,* available from www.hse.gov.uk/noise.

Corporate manslaughter

The **Corporate Manslaughter and Corporate Homicide Act 2007** applies to all companies and other corporate bodies, including within the voluntary sector. Under the Act an organisation can be found guilty of corporate manslaughter if the way in which its activities are managed or organised causes a death and amounts to a gross breach of a duty of care to the deceased. A substantial responsibility for the failure within the organisation must have been at a senior level (people who make significant decisions about the organisation or substantial parts of it). When reviewing your health and safety management systems it is important to consider how activities are managed and organised by senior management.

For further information see www.justice.gov.uk/publications/ corporatemanslaughter2007.htm.

Duties relating to premises

The **Occupier's Liability Act 1957** states that reasonable care must be taken to ensure that anyone using the premises with permission will be reasonably safe. This includes service users, staff, committee members, volunteers, guests and people delivering goods or mending appliances.

The **Occupier's Liability Act 1984** also applies to trespassers (for example, children who come onto a site when it is closed). There is in all circumstances a duty to take reasonable care to avoid the risk of people being injured or killed: for example, a site that is dangerous to unsupervised children may have to be securely fenced.

Public health laws

Public health legislation is very detailed and broad in scope, and includes many local by-laws. It is therefore important to meet the local authority's environmental health officer, preferably on site, to discuss your obligations. The main scope of public health legislation is outlined below.

The quality of the air

Any building in which people work or meet must have proper ventilation. The property must be free from pollution (for example, from a badly maintained boiler or the burning of rubbish).

The quality of housing

For organisations running hostel accommodation or with resident workers, further public health laws, concerned with housing, come into force. Environmental health officers have powers to insist on standards of cleanliness, fire precautions, the provision of WCs, hot and cold water supplies, heating, rubbish disposal and proper repairs. Their exact powers will depend on whether the building is classified as having a single tenant or as being a 'house in multiple occupation'.

Drainage and refuse disposal

Any faults in drainage and refuse disposal systems can create serious health risks, and the environmental health officer will look carefully at the systems provided.

Organisations that burn rubbish or allow it to accumulate can be prosecuted. You may need to pay for trade refuse to be removed.

Pests and vermin

If pests such as rats, mice or cockroaches are found on the premises, contact the local authority's environmental health department immediately. After an outbreak, review the arrangements for cooking, cleaning and storing food. Regularly inspect the premises, especially behind boilers and pipe runs and under floors. Call in a specialist firm to carry out a complete spring clean if necessary.

If there are young children on the premises look out for head lice. If any are found contact the health visitor or nurse from the health authority.

The quality of food

The **General Food Regulations 2004** cover the provision of any food served on the premises: for example, pensioners' lunches and refreshments at socials. Many local authority environmental health departments publish guides to the regulations. For further information on issues relating to food see the Food Standards Agency website (www.food.gov.uk) and *Selling, preparing and storing food*, in chapter 9.

Public entertainment

Premises used for public entertainment have to meet particular conditions, especially on fire precautions, ventilation and sound insulation. A group will usually need a licence (see *Licensing premises*, in chapter 9); the licensing authority will provide details.

Accidents and diseases

All employers (regardless of the number of employees) must keep a record of all accidents. Records must be kept for at least three years. An **official accident book (B1 510)** is available from HSE Books. Safety representatives are entitled to inspect the book.

Under the **Reporting of Injuries, Disease and Dangerous Occurrences Regulations 1995 (RIDDOR)**, employers must report the accidents and incidents at work described below to the enforcing authority (usually the local authority). Alternatively, you can report incidents via the HSE Incident Contact Centre (ICC) on 0845 300 9923 or online at www.hse.gov.uk/riddor/index.htm. The ICC will send you a copy of the completed form for checking and then pass it on to the relevant enforcing authority.

If there is an accident connected with work and an employee or a self-employed person working on the premises is killed or suffers a major injury (including as a result of physical violence) or a member of the public is killed or taken to hospital you must make the report immediately.

Any accident connected with work (including an act of physical violence) that results in an employee or a self-employed person working on the premises being unable to work for more than three consecutive days must be reported within ten calendar days.

The enforcing authority must be informed if a doctor tells the organisation that an employee suffers from a reportable work-related disease.

If an incident happens that does not result in a reportable injury, but which clearly could have done, then it may be a dangerous occurrence, which must be reported immediately.

For further information see *Incident at work?*, available from www.hse.gov.uk, and www.hse.gov.uk/riddor/. The accident book (see above) includes information about employers' duties under RIDDOR.

Health and safety policies

Good practice

The highest duty under health and safety legislation is to protect employees. Voluntary organisations must develop health and safety policies to protect volunteers, trainees and users (who could be invited to join the safety committee).

Implementation

Implementing a health and safety policy may appear daunting and, certainly in larger organisations, involves substantial work. One way of producing information in a manageable form is to use a series of headings, following the format used in the risk assessment (see *Risk assessment,* page 148). These could be:

- hazard identified – for example, shelves overloaded, floor slippery
- risk – for example, items may fall, a person may slip
- priority – for example, high, medium or low
- preventative or protective steps required – for example, new shelving in neighbouring room, new floor covering
- committee or staff member responsible for implementing preventative or protective steps
- costs involved
- timescale for completion of steps identified
- information and training required for staff
- timescale for completion of training and information.

You can use a similar format to identify the steps required to comply with the workplace, personal protective and work equipment, manual handling, display screen equipment and fire safety regulations. Details of new hazards (for example, from new equipment) can be added as necessary.

Information presented in this way helps you to carry out monitoring and reviews easily: you can see whether the steps and training required have been delivered within the agreed timescale. If a particular hazard has become more urgent (for example, if it proves to be more dangerous than envisaged), you can change the priority and revise the timescale.

Also see the implementation checklist at the end of the chapter.

Stress

Work-related stress is a serious problem: workers can suffer serious medical problems, which may result in severe under-performance at work and cause major disruptions to an organisation. The HSE defines stress as 'the adverse reaction people have to excessive pressure or other types of demand placed upon them'.

According to HSE-commissioned research, work-related stress accounts for over a third of all incidents of ill health; in 2006/07 13.8 million working days were lost as a result of stress and related conditions.

Stress is a workplace hazard that must be dealt with like any other. Thus the responsibility for reducing stress at work lies with both employer and employee.

The primary causes of stress at work, as identified by the Health and Safety Executive, are shown on page 172.

Employers and employees should not make unrealistic demands on other workers by imposing impossible deadlines and/or increasing others' workloads to a level they cannot cope with.

An organisation as a whole should develop an atmosphere of mutual respect amongst staff and ensure that interpersonal conflicts are avoided or dealt with sensibly.

In order to deal with stress if it does occur, there must be appropriate procedures and support for affected staff. Managers should investigate the cause(s) of any stress and take appropriate action to remove them. Organisations should neither discriminate nor tolerate discrimination against employees suffering from stress.

The HSE has compiled a set of management standards for work-related stress to help employers, employees and staff representatives manage the issue and minimise its impact on the organisation. The standards cover six areas:

1. **Demands.** Workload, work patterns, work environment.
2. **Control.** How much say someone has in the way they do their work.
3. **Support.** Encouragement and resources provided by the organisation, line management and colleagues.
4. **Relationships.** Promoting positive working to avoid conflict and dealing with unacceptable behaviour.
5. **Role.** Whether people understand their role within the organisation and whether the organisation ensures the person does not have conflicting roles.
6. **Change.** How organisational change is managed and communicated.

For full details of the standards, and a five-step programme for tackling stress, see www.hse.gov.uk/stress/standards/index.htm.

Working together to reduce stress at work: A guide for employees discusses the management standards from an employee's viewpoint, suggests how employees can support their employer and advises what an employee can do if they are feeling stressed. This, and other free leaflets, can be downloaded from the HSE stress microsite www.hse.gov.uk/stress/index.htm.

Checklist:

Health and safety policy

Organisation

☐ Ensure the management committee decides who is responsible and, if necessary, delegates decision-making powers. Even if powers are delegated, the management committee as a whole is ultimately responsible and potentially liable, and must be aware of this.

☐ Appoint staff members to be given overall responsibility for health and safety and for implementing the policy on a day-to-day basis – for example, the director may take overall responsibility and an administrator could be given day-to-day responsibility.

☐ Set up a safety committee including those management committee members and staff members with responsibility for health and safety, together with trade union representatives and/or employee representatives and other staff and volunteers.

☐ If premises are shared, cooperate with other employers in all health and safety matters, but especially in carrying out a fire safety risk assessment and appointing a coordinator.

Ensure the costs of health and safety requirements are included in the annual budget.

Information and training

☐ Obtain the necessary advice and publications (for example, from the HSE, your local authority and trade unions), and guidance on fire safety from Communities and Local Government (www.communities.gov.uk/fire/).

☐ Identify the training needs of committee members and staff with health and safety responsibilities and design a training programme.

Risk assessment

☐ Carry out a preliminary risk assessment of the workplaces and activities in consultation with staff and trade unions. Before starting, list the headings covered by the health and safety regulations. Assess the risks to users and members of the public as well as to staff. Include homeworkers if appropriate.

☐ Carry out a thorough inspection of workplaces to identify the steps required to comply with the workplace and fire safety regulations.

☐ Carry out a thorough inspection of work and display screen equipment to identify any steps required to comply with regulations.

☐ Assess any manual handling operations using the checklist in *Manual handling. Guidance on regulations* (see page 158).

☐ Carry out a fire safety risk assessment.

☐ Before employing anyone aged under 18, ensure a risk assessment is carried out specific to that person and the work they will be doing (see *Young workers*, page 151).

☐ Arrange to bring in external expertise if needed to complete the assessment.

☐ Make a written record of the assessment and discuss the findings with the members of the safety committee and other staff.

☐ Decide on a review date for the assessment.

For further details see *Five steps to risk assessment*, available from www.hse.gov.uk.

Preventative and protective measures

☐ Identify preventative and protective measures to reduce or avoid any risks. These may include providing personal protective equipment, health surveillance, eye tests and regular servicing of equipment.

☐ Identify any necessary changes to new or expectant mothers' working hours or conditions to reduce risks to them and their child(ren).

☐ Identify the modifications to display screen and work equipment and the workplace necessary to comply with the regulations.

☐ Establish the costs of preventative and protective measures and any necessary modifications and draw up a timescale for their implementation in consultation with the safety committee.

New premises and equipment

Ensure a risk assessment is made before acquiring new premises or equipment and that the costs of removing any risks are identified.

Emergency procedures

Draw up emergency procedures to deal with risks identified during the assessment and identify those responsible for evacuation and other tasks in the event of an emergency. These must include what to do in the event of fire.

Training, instructions and information for staff

☐ Inform staff of the risks identified, the steps they should take to reduce the risks and the steps you (as employer) will be taking.

☐ Ensure that all staff are properly trained and instructed in the use of all protective equipment, work and display screen equipment and on safe manual handling techniques.

☐ Ensure that staff who work outside normal working hours, at home or in isolation are given necessary health and safety information.

☐ Ensure that new and temporary staff are given necessary health and safety information.

☐ Pay particular attention to staff who may be more vulnerable to accidents (for example, inexperienced or young staff and disabled people).

☐ Ensure information is available in alternative formats – for example, accessible for people with learning disabilities or visual impairment.

☐ Include the cost of staff induction, training and instruction in the annual budget.

Accidents

☐ Establish a policy requiring all accidents and near-accidents and their causes to be reported and recorded, and reported to the safety committee.

☐ Establish procedures for dealing with accidents and ensure that there are sufficient staff with first aid training.

☐ Ensure that all reportable accidents under RIDDOR (see *Accidents and diseases*, page 167) are reported to the relevant authorities.

Monitoring and review

☐ Ensure that those responsible for health and safety regularly receive updated information and training.

☐ Regularly monitor the implementation of the policy in consultation with the safety committee, and revise the assessment and targets as necessary.

☐ Consult with employees and safety representatives in good time.

☐ Revise the assessments and the steps required whenever circumstances change, including new kinds of work, new premises, new equipment or changes in good practice.

Work-related stressors

Culture

Lack of communication and consultation

A culture of blame

Denial of potential problems

Expectation of excessively long working hours or taking work home

Job demands

Too much to do, too little time

Too little or too much training for the job

Boring or repetitive work

Too little to do

Poor working environment

Control

Lack of control of work activities

Relationships

Poor relationships with others

Bullying, racial or sexual harassment

Change

Uncertainty about what is happening

Fears about job security

Role

Conflicting demands

Confusion about how everyone fits in

Support and the individual

Lack of support from managers and colleagues

Conflicting demands of home and work

Chapter 6

Premises and environmental concerns

Buying or renting property is a major step and involves considerable responsibilities for both staff and management committees. Always get legal and surveyor's advice before taking on property.

The way in which the property is held will depend on whether the organisation is unincorporated or incorporated (see chapter 1).

Unincorporated organisations

An unincorporated organisation cannot hold property in its own name. To enable such an organisation to buy property or hold a lease, the property is often put into the names of two or more individuals as trustees (**holding trustees**). Although legally only two holding trustees are needed, you should consider having three or four. It is also advisable to draw up a separate trust deed setting out holding trustees' and management committee members' respective rights and obligations and the position of holding trustees in relation to the committee.

Another option is to put the property in the name of a **custodian trustee** or the **Official Custodian for Charities** (a Charity Commission staff member appointed to hold land on behalf of charities).

These options are discussed later in the chapter.

Incorporated organisations

Incorporated organisations can own property in their own right, so the deed or lease will be in the name of the organisation itself, rather than in the name of holding trustees or a custodian trustee.

The Ethical Property Foundation's website (www.ethicalproperty.org.uk) includes a wide range of useful information about many aspects of finding, renting, buying and managing properties.

Types of property interests

Generally, the following types of property interests are available: freehold, long leasehold, leasehold and licence. The management committee must understand the implications of whichever form of tenure it is considering.

Freehold land with **title absolute** gives the owner the greatest freedom to deal with the land as they see fit, subject to other constraints such as planning and building regulations, restrictive covenants and easements (rights over the land). Your solicitor will identify such constraints and explain these to you.

A **long leasehold** interest in a property normally involves paying a capital sum to acquire the lease (for example, 99 years), together with an annual, and usually small, rent. Such a lease provides long-term security of tenure.

Mortgages for freehold and long leasehold properties

It is crucial to obtain advice from a solicitor and surveyor before signing a mortgage agreement. Remember that one or more named individuals may have to stand as a guarantor for any mortgage (but it is strongly recommended that any request for such guarantors is resisted). Guarantors, and their estate after they die, remain liable until the lease ends or the mortgage is paid in full. No one should ever stand as a guarantor without taking independent legal advice.

Under **Section 38** of the **Charities Act 1993** a charity considering taking out a mortgage must get 'appropriate' advice from people with necessary experience and practical ability.

A company that takes out a mortgage must notify Companies House on form **395** and enter specified details in a **register of charges** (a list of mortgages and other loans secured on its assets). There is no such requirement for industrial and provident societies.

Advantages and disadvantages

The advantages of buying a freehold or long leasehold are long-term security, independence and the potential for income generation from subletting spare space, although leaseholders are subject to some controls and have to pay a small rent. However, these options are available only if you can raise a substantial capital sum or obtain a mortgage. Arguably, the main disadvantages are the legal costs of buying and selling the property and the lack of flexibility, so that it will be a much longer process if the organisation decides to move. Buying property is best considered as a long-term commitment.

Further information

The Ethical Property Foundation's online guidance *Through the maze: A guide to buying property for charities and social enterprises* provides a step by step guide to buying a building.

Leasing premises

Leasing premises usually involves paying a market (or near-market) rent and always grants the tenant an exclusive right to occupy a property. A lease (or tenancy) imposes obligations on both the landlord and tenant.

Exclusive possession means the tenant has the right to exclude everyone else from the premises, including the landlord (although leases often include exceptions, such as allowing access for emergency works or to do work on adjoining properties).

Before signing a lease, make sure everyone involved fully understands the meaning and implications of all the clauses, the costs of complying with the obligations and the risks if the obligations are not met. It is essential to get independent legal advice and, where necessary, advice from a surveyor when negotiating the terms of a lease (see *Points to check in a lease or licence*, page 178). All leases of seven or more years must be registered with the Land Registry. This will usually be done by a solicitor, although you can do it yourself. For details see *Land Registry practice guide 25*, available from www.landregistry.gov.uk.

Advantages and disadvantages

Leasing premises offers a number of advantages, including flexibility (a shorter term commitment), no substantial capital outlay and tax advantages (for example, rent paid can be offset against taxable income).

The main disadvantages are that the tenant does not own the property outright, money is paid as rent which does not result in the acquisition of a capital asset and occupation is subject to numerous obligations and restrictions imposed by the landlord.

The Landlord and Tenant Act 1954

The **Landlord and Tenant Act 1954** gives security to tenants (including voluntary organisations) in business premises in England and Wales. Where a lease is protected by the Act's security of tenure provisions a landlord can seek repossession only if a business tenant breaches a term of the lease. Otherwise, they can serve notice only under the terms of the Act and even then, tenants may be able to ask a court to grant a new tenancy if they are unable to agree terms (but see next paragraph). Landlords can oppose such applications on certain specified grounds: for example, because they need the premises for themselves. If the landlord does not oppose the application, the court will grant a new tenancy.

Some business tenancies do not have renewal rights. These include:

- those granted for less than six months, where either the tenant has been in occupation for less than 12 months or there is no provision for extension or renewal
- those where both parties have agreed, before entering into the lease, that renewal rights should not apply. Under the **Regulatory Reform (Business Tenancies) (England and Wales) Order 2003** the landlord must serve a warning notice of the proposal for a lease to be excluded from **Sections 24 to 28** of the **Landlord and Tenant Act 1954**. Where a tenant receives at least 14 days' notice they will need to sign and date a simple declaration. If a tenant receives less than 14 days' notice they need to swear a statutory declaration before a solicitor. Both types of declaration state that the tenant has received the warning notice and accepts the exclusion. Many landlords will only lease premises to organisations willing to agree to exclude security of tenure. Think carefully before agreeing to an exclusion, as some funders will grant-aid refurbishment or redecoration only if you have adequate security of tenure.

Voluntary code of conduct for business leases

The property industry has a voluntary code of practice for business leases, which includes recommendations for landlords and tenants when they negotiate new business leases. The code covers such matters as rent reviews, break options, service charges and repairs, and can be viewed at www.leasingbusinesspremises.co.uk.

Holding a licence

Unlike a lease, which gives an exclusive legal interest in a property, a licence grants only a permission to occupy the premises; it is generally a temporary agreement, and the Landlord and Tenant Act does not apply.

A licence details the obligations of both **licensor** (the person or body granting the licence) and **licensee** (the person or body taking the licence) more simply than a lease. Before signing a licence always obtain legal advice and ensure you have the financial resources to meet the obligations under the terms of the licence.

If you have exclusive use of the property, an agreement is likely to be legally considered a lease even if described as a licence.

Advantages and disadvantages

The main advantages are that the licensee generally has no obligation for repairs, maintenance or buildings insurance, and it may be easier to terminate the agreement by **surrendering** (returning) the licence to the landlord. Also, because many local authorities do not consider licensees to be occupiers for the purposes of non-domestic rates (see *Paying rates*, page 187), a licence may be cheaper than a lease. However, the landlord may charge the licensee all or part of the rates, so check this before signing. Licensees may still be responsible for water charges.

As properties held under licence are not protected by the Landlord and Tenant Act, the licensee has very little security of tenure. A licence will usually be either for a fixed period (for example, one year) or will continue indefinitely but have a fixed notice period. Once notice has been given and expired the occupant must leave. If the licence continues on a weekly or monthly basis and no notice period is mentioned, the law would imply that the licensee is entitled to 'reasonable notice'.

The main disadvantage of a licence is the lack of security of tenure. The ultimate decision may depend on the organisation's finances.

Finding premises

One place to start looking is your local authority. The property department or the department responsible for economic and business development keeps a record of vacant council premises available under a lease or a licence.

The local authority may charge a commercial rent but include an equivalent amount in an organisation's grant, or it could charge a

peppercorn (nominal) rent. It may state as a condition of tenure that an organisation must use the premises only to carry out the activities for which it is being funded. If the organisation changes its activities without permission, it could be evicted; it is therefore advisable to discuss such changes in activities with the local authority.

The outcome of a 2007 government review into transferring assets from local authority to community ownership, with the subsequent establishment of the community assets fund, has brought, and will bring, more local authority buildings into community ownership. This, in turn, is likely to result in greater availability of office space to let and properties suitable for sharing (see *Sharing premises*, page 182). For further information about the transfer of community assets contact the Development Trusts Association (www.dta.org.uk).

Local estate agents have lists of property belonging to commercial and private landlords, which will charge market rents. Landlords may be willing to negotiate the terms of a lease. For example, it may be possible to persuade them to reduce the rent, agree to a rent-free period, redecorate the premises or pay for repairs. Any concessions need to be balanced against the possibility of future rent increases.

The local council for voluntary service or rural community council, churches, community centres and housing associations may also know of vacant premises. There are also some office providers that specialise in providing space to voluntary organisations, in particular social enterprises. These include the Ethical Property Company (www.ethicalproperty.co.uk), Community Action Network (www.can-online.org.uk) and Workspace (www.workspacegroup.co.uk).

When looking for premises, consider:

- proximity to public transport and access on foot and bicycle
- access for disabled people and those with children, including car parking (see *Access for disabled people* below)
- local facilities for staff – for example, basic lunchtime shopping and banking

- the immediate locality and whether members would be happy attending activities in the premises and how people would feel if they had to work late or attend evening meetings
- time restrictions on access
- the neighbours – for example, noisy activities may not be popular next door to residential accommodation
- whether goods can easily be delivered. This is particularly important if an organisation receives regular deliveries of heavy items
- any planning permission granted on a property.

Access for disabled people

Employers

Under **Part II** of the **Disability Discrimination Act 1995** (**DDA**) employers must make reasonable changes to any physical features of their premises which may put a disabled employee or prospective employee at a disadvantage. Physical features include a building's design and construction, approach and exit, fixtures, fittings, furnishings, equipment and materials. 'Reasonable' will be defined by a number of factors, including the practicality and cost of making the change, the resources available to the employer and the ability to raise finance.

Service providers

Under **Part III** of the **DDA** all providers of goods, services or facilities must make reasonable adjustments to their premises' physical features (see previous paragraph) for disabled people. If a physical feature makes it unreasonably difficult or impossible for a disabled person to use a service, the organisation will have to take measures, where reasonable, to:

- remove the feature, or
- alter it so that it no longer has that effect, or
- provide a reasonable means of avoiding the feature, or
- provide a reasonable alternative method of making the service available to disabled people.

Wherever possible, consider removing or altering physical features, so that disabled people can receive services in the same way as other users.

The duty to comply with the DDA (and pay for reasonable adjustments to be made) is on the employer or service provider. This will generally be the tenant, but could be the landlord where, for example, the lease says the landlord is responsible for common parts of a building. So the landlord of a multi-tenanted building may need to assess the accessibility of its common parts such as walkways, stairs and toilets.

Where a tenant needs to make alterations to the property to comply with the DDA he will usually need the consent of the landlord. A landlord cannot unreasonably withhold consent, but may impose 'reasonable' conditions.

The DDA does not override planning or historic buildings legislation. Organisations making adaptations to buildings should therefore ensure they get all necessary planning permissions, and occupiers of listed buildings or buildings in conservation areas should take specialist advice.

Signage

The legislation also applies to signage; both employers and service providers must consider how disabled people, particularly those with visual impairments or learning disabilities, would be able to find their way around the premises. Signs that work best are:

- simple and short
- easily read and understood with clear typefaces in a mixture of upper and lower case
- well contrasted with the background
- supplemented by visual/pictorial symbols.

Signs covered with glass can be hard to read because of light reflection, as can lettering applied directly onto glass.

RNIB's publication *See it right*, available from www.rnib.org.uk, includes guidance on producing accessible signage for visually impaired people. For information about signage for people with learning disabilities contact the Makaton Charity (01276 61390; www.makaton.org). The *Sign design guide*, available from www.signdesignsociety.co.uk, provides guidance on accessible signage.

Policies and procedures

You should take DDA requirements into account in your equal opportunities and diversity policy and procedures.

Access audit

Both employers and service providers should carry out an access audit, looking at the following:

- approach and parking areas
- routes and external level change, including ramps and steps
- entrances, including reception, and exits
- corridors, internal doors and internal ramps
- lifts, stairlifts and internal level changes
- toilets and washing facilities
- facilities for cooking or refreshments
- fixtures and fittings
- lighting and ventilation
- emergency exits and evacuation procedures
- public facilities, such as telephones and service desks
- signage
- acoustic environment.

The RNIB (www.rnib.org.uk) and the Centre for Accessible Environments (www.cae.org.uk) can carry out accessibility audits. The Ethical Property Foundation's website www.ethicalproperty.org.uk includes an accessibility checklist.

The access audit handbook, published by the Centre for Accessible Environments (www.cae.org.uk), offers guidance on undertaking access audits.

Further information

More details about the DDA are available from the businesses and organisations section of the Equality and Human Rights Commission's website www.equalityhumanrights.com. The website also has links to downloadable publications including *Top tips for small employers. A guide to employing disabled people* and *Making access to goods and services easier for disabled customers: A practical guide for small businesses and other small service providers.*

Deciding about premises

In an unincorporated organisation individual committee members or trustees may be personally liable for complying with the terms of any lease or licence. The full committee should therefore participate in the final decision (although a subcommittee could make recommendations, if your constitution permits this). Always allow enough time for getting appropriate advice and making informed decisions. Although you may want to move into premises quickly, it is important to consider the risks of taking on an inappropriate lease and to ensure committee members understand their responsibilities and potential liabilities.

Points to check in a lease or licence

Below are some of the main points to consider when negotiating a lease or licence. Where a landlord is eager to rent out premises, you may be in a strong negotiating position. Always get a lease checked by a solicitor before signing it.

Note: For the sake of brevity 'lease' is used to refer to both leases and licences throughout this section. Any differences between leases and licences are noted.

The duration

Leases are usually for a fixed period, although they can be weekly, monthly or annual. There may be an option to renew a fixed-term lease at the end of a specific time. The duration is important because an organisation must meet its obligations for the whole period of a fixed-term lease, even if it no longer uses the building. Committee members of an unincorporated organisation will be personally liable for the rent for the full term of a lease even if it has run out of funds and no longer operates.

Committee members can avoid or reduce their personal liability by making sure the organisation can **assign** the lease (transfer to a third party who will become the new tenant) or **sublet** (grant a sublease to a third party but remain liable to the head landlord under the obligations in the lease). They can also seek to avoid liability completely if they persuade the landlord to include a clause that excludes any personal liability for the rent and any other payments due under the lease. However, few commercial landlords are prepared to accept such a clause.

A **break clause** (see *Break clauses* below) allows the organisation to end the lease before the end of the contractual term, normally subject to complying with certain conditions. A lease may also be **surrendered** (brought to an end) but only if the landlord agrees.

Under the **Landlord and Tenant (Covenants) Act 1995** a tenant is normally released from future liabilities for a lease once it is assigned. However, in many cases the landlord may only agree to the assignment on the condition that the original tenant remains liable for the rent. This has the effect of overriding the provisions of the Act. If this is the case, you must ensure that the new tenants are financially viable, otherwise you could be responsible for their debts. Take legal advice on this point when assigning a lease. Charities have to go through certain formalities before surrendering or assigning a lease (see *Disposing of premises*, page 188).

Finally, you should be aware that some funders specify the minimum duration of a lease they will accept when considering applications for building or refurbishment.

Break clauses

A break clause is an agreed term incorporated into the lease that allows either the landlord or tenant, or both, to end the lease before the expiry date. The date on which the lease may end and who may exercise that right will depend on what has been agreed and the wording incorporated into the lease. Be cautious about accepting any break option in favour of the landlord. If the landlord exercised the break option you would have to find new premises, with all the staff and financial resources this implies. In practice, a right to a break clause for the landlord can rarely be justified.

Rent levels and payment periods

Always check whether the rent includes VAT. Most leases give landlords the option to introduce VAT at any stage unless it has been agreed that such right shall be specifically excluded. Also, note the payment period; leases often require rent to be paid quarterly in advance.

Rent review

Longer leases often include a clause allowing the landlord to review the rent periodically. In such cases, it would be wise to negotiate a break clause so that you could surrender the lease (see page 178) if you could not afford a higher rent.

Service charges

Many leases of shared premises include a clause requiring the tenant to pay a service charge in addition to the rent. Check the lease carefully to see how this is calculated, what it will cover and when it will be reviewed. If, for example, a building needs a new roof, a tenant could end up having to pay a proportion of the cost even if the lease is short term.

Although it is appropriate for tenants on a short-term lease to pay a contribution towards, for example, heating and lighting of communal parts, make sure you are not responsible for paying service charges towards long-term maintenance and repairs.

There are two ways in which a lease may be amended to protect a tenant from excessive service charges:

- ensure the service charge provision makes clear that it cannot include maintenance and repair costs or major structural repairs and maintenance costs

- specify a fixed amount for service charges or impose a top financial limit (known as a service charge cap) on repair and maintenance costs during any financial year. A fixed sum could be written in as the contribution for repairs and maintenance, or added to the rent (known as an inclusive rent).

Responsibility for repairs

The landlord and tenant will each agree in the lease the extent of their respective repairing responsibilities.

Where a lease is for part of a building, the most common arrangement is for the tenant to be required to repair the interior of the leased area (including the landlords' fixtures and fittings) and the landlord to have responsibility for repairing the building's exterior.

If the lease is for the whole building, the tenant normally takes responsibility for repairing both the interior and exterior.

The extent of the repairing liability varies. Examples include the following:
- A full repairing lease requires a tenant to put, keep and return the property to the landlord in 'good and substantial' repair and condition. This is the highest standard of repairing liability that can be imposed on a tenant.
- A tenant may be required to keep the property in 'good condition'. This requires the tenant to monitor the condition of the property and put, keep and return the property to the landlord in good condition.
- Alternatively, a tenant could simply be required to keep the property in no worse a state and condition than that listed by a **schedule of condition**, prepared by a surveyor, which will describe the state of the property before the tenant moves in. The landlord and tenant should agree in advance who will pay for the schedule, which must be approved by both parties and annexed to the lease.

Before signing a lease it is always advisable to instruct a surveyor to inspect the premises to give an idea of the cost of complying with whatever repairing obligation has been agreed.

If the premises are not in very good condition it is advisable to ask for the repairing obligation to be qualified so that you will not have to place the premises in any better condition than that shown by a schedule of condition. Make sure at least one person in the organisation takes responsibility for monitoring the condition of the property.

When a tenant moves out, the landlord will inspect the premises and may commission a **schedule of dilapidations** (a list of items of disrepair where the tenant has failed to comply with the repairing clauses) and the tenant may have to pay for any repairs needed to put the property back into the original state or pay the costs of the landlord doing so.

It is worth noting that, just as the organisation, or its committee members in an unincorporated organisation, is responsible for the rent throughout the duration of the lease, it will also be responsible for complying with the repairing obligation, which could involve paying the costs of putting the property in the state of repair required by the lease.

Insurance

Most leases require either that the tenant insures the premises or, more usually, pays the premium to the landlord, who will arrange insurance (in which case the lessee has to be able to inspect the policy). A lease will require the tenant to have public liability insurance and, where relevant, insurance for fixed glass – for example, shop fronts. Insurance is discussed further in chapter 7.

Rates and water charges

Tenants are usually responsible for non-domestic (or business) rates (see *Paying rates,* page 187) and water charges.

The costs of drawing up the lease

It is normal for both parties to pay their own legal costs arising from drafting and agreement of lease documentation. If the landlord's solicitor insists on their costs being paid make sure this is capped at an agreed level.

Permitted activities

Check whether any activities are restricted under the terms of the lease – for example, music or alcohol consumption. Most leases specify permitted uses; make sure these cover your intended activities. Try to ensure that the lease allows a sufficiently wide range of uses to make it easier to assign if necessary, but remember that a wider range of uses may also mean a higher rent. Also check whether the property has planning permission for any intended use.

Subletting and use by others

Most leases permit subletting. Some leases also allow the hiring out of rooms or the sharing of the premises with other organisations, which would not normally amount to a subletting. If you plan to hire out rooms or anticipate sharing your premises (see *Sharing premises*, page 182), make sure the lease allows this and, if necessary, negotiate an amendment.

Alterations to the structure of the building

Most leases do not permit structural alterations, but most do permit non-structural alterations with the landlord's consent (such consent not to be unreasonably withheld or delayed). If alterations are necessary, try to get the landlord's permission before signing the lease; do not assume that you are free to make improvements if you take on a property in poor condition. If possible, try to negotiate a provision allowing the tenant to install and remove internal demountable partitioning without the landlord's consent.

Under the Disability Discrimination Act, the requirement for service providers to adapt premises (see *Access*, page 176) automatically implies the inclusion of provisions in leases to enable tenants to make necessary alterations with the landlord's consent. Landlords cannot withhold their consent unreasonably.

The **Equality Bill 2008** (at the time of writing due to be debated in the 2008/09 parliamentary session) proposes creating a duty on landlords and managers of premises to make disability-related alterations to the common parts of residential premises where reasonable and when requested by a disabled tenant or occupier.

Is the lease or licence right for you?

Always get independent advice (from a solicitor and/or surveyor) about your obligations and likely expenditure before making a decision to take on a lease or licence. You should also:

- understand all the provisions of the agreement and its obligations, particularly those that will incur expense and/or involve long-term obligations
- have funds to meet the likely expenditure, including rent, VAT, insurance, service charges, non-domestic rates, water charges, repairs, decorations and structural alterations, and to cover health and safety requirements (see chapter 5) and any alterations necessary to comply with the Disability Discrimination Act (see *Access*, page 176)
- make sure there are no **covenants** (restrictions) in the lease which prevent you using the property in the way that you want
- obtain planning permission for use of the premises, where relevant (see *Obtaining planning permission*, page 186)
- have building regulation approval for any intended alterations (see *Planning and building regulations*, page 185)
- have the landlord's consent for any proposed adaptations
- ensure there is a way of terminating the lease if you want to move, or run out of money; this is particularly important for unincorporated organisations
- consider the implications if individuals are being asked to guarantee the lease (see page 178) and encourage potential guarantors to seek independent legal advice.

Signing deeds, including leases and mortgage agreements

Check your constitution for any powers relating to signing leases or other documents.

Unincorporated associations and trusts

There are a number of ways in which unincorporated associations and trusts can enter into legal arrangements relating to premises.

- **Appoint holding trustees**. The constitution of an unincorporated association may either require or allow the committee to appoint holding trustees (see page 173). If this option is used, the committee should agree a trust deed with the holding trustees clearly setting out their responsibilities and obligations and their position in relation to the committee. A model trust deed (deed of appointment) is given at the end of this chapter.

  If the premises are owned or held on a long lease, you may need to change the holding trustees and enter into new legal agreements if holding trustees die or wish to withdraw from the arrangement. The landlord's consent may be required for any changes made under a lease.

  In a trust, property can be held in the name of the trustees and a separate trust deed is not necessary. All the trustees can sign or, unless prohibited by the trust deed, under **Section 82** of the **Charities Act 1993** (see page 182) they can pass a resolution that authorises at least two trustees to enter into legal agreements on behalf of the trust. However, when the trustees change, the property will need to be transferred to (**vested in**) the new trustees.

- **Apply to the Charity Commission** to appoint the **Official Custodian for Charities** as a trustee. The advantage is that there will be no need to change trustees. For further details see the Charity

Commission booklet *The Official Custodian for Charities' land holding service* (CC 13).

■ **Appoint an incorporated body as a custodian trustee** to hold the property on behalf of the organisation. The custodian trustee will provide a trust deed setting out its relationship with the organisation. There is likely to be a charge for this. As with the Official Custodian (see previous bullet point), there will be no need to change trustees. **This option may be appropriate for non-charities, which cannot use the Official Custodian.**

■ **Pass a resolution that authorises at least two members of the committee to sign legal documents** on behalf of the committee under **Section 82** of the **Charities Act 1993**. Any such document must then contain a specific clause stating that it has been executed in pursuance of Section 82 of the Charities Act 1993 by people signing on behalf of the charity, who are then deemed to have signed on behalf of the whole committee. This method has two advantages. There is no need to draw up a deed of trust between the committee and the holding trustees, and it does not place two or three individuals in a more risky position than the whole committee. Check the constitution to see if it includes any restrictions on passing such a resolution.

■ Apply to the Charity Commission for incorporation of a charity's trustee body (management committee) under **Section 72** of the **Charities Act 1993**. This will enable the committee to hold the property in the same way as an incorporated organisation, and avoids the need to appoint separate holding trustees or a custodian trustee, or have the property held by trustees in a charitable trust. Remember, this type of incorporation does not provide limited liability for management committee members. They still remain personally responsible for any liabilities under the lease that cannot be met by the organisation. For further information see *Incorporation of charity trustees* (CC43). Applications must be made on the form in the application pack *How to apply to the Charity Commission for a Certificate of Incorporation* (CHY 1093), available from Charity Commission Direct (0845 3000 218; textphone 0845 3000 219).

Incorporated organisations

The organisation itself (as opposed to individuals) can be a named party to a lease. For companies, a lease can be executed by using the company seal (if it has one) in the presence of two directors (committee members), or the company secretary and one director. If the company does not have a seal it must be signed by:

■ two directors, or

■ one director plus the company secretary, or

■ one director in the presence of a witness.

The last option is a change brought about by the **Companies Act 2006**; you will need to check whether your constitution requires two signatures and if so, you may wish to change it.

An industrial and provident society must attach its seal in the presence of the secretary and one committee member, or two committee members. If it does not have a seal, the lease can be signed by one committee member and the secretary or two committee members.

Sharing premises

Those belonging to another organisation

One way of obtaining premises is to share property belonging to or rented by another organisation, as either a subtenant or (more likely) a licensee. The arrangements between the two organisations must be clear from the start. The following points therefore need to be clarified in writing:

■ the areas that will be for exclusive use (for example, an office) and those to be shared (for example, kitchen, WCs and meeting rooms)

■ how the use of shared facilities (for example, reception services) will be organised

- that insurance companies are notified of plans to share premises
- whether furniture or equipment will be provided
- use of resources such as a photocopier and fax, and charging policies
- whether adaptations to the premises are permitted (this is unlikely in a licence) (also see *Alterations to the structure of the building*, page 180)
- responsibilities for safety and security arrangements
- responsibilities for cleaning
- payment for utilities' bills
- confidentiality agreements
- any restrictions on activities
- requirement to adhere to any policies – for example, environmental, equal opportunities and diversity, health and safety (including fire drills)
- other rules and regulations – for example, relating to noise.

Those belonging to your organisation

Renting out or licensing parts of your premises can be a useful way of raising funds. As well as the points made later in this section about security and safety when hiring out premises, you need to consider the following.

Subletting: Always check the terms of the lease to ensure that subletting is allowed before entering into any arrangement, and always check the conditions attached to sublettings: for example, it may be a condition that subleases must be excluded from the protection of sections 24–28 of the Landlord and Tenant Act 1954 (see page 174).

If you sublet any part of the premises you may create a business tenancy and be unable to regain the right to use the whole premises. Just because a document is called a licence rather than a tenancy or lease does not prevent it creating a subtenancy. A tenancy or lease is created only if an occupant has exclusive use of some part of the premises. You can avoid this situation by, for example,

retaining the right of access for regular cleaning or to use equipment held in that part of the building.

Restrictions in the lease: Check whether other restrictions in the lease might prohibit sharing the premises. For example, some leases contain a provision allowing only the tenant to use the premises. A landlord may be prepared to waive that requirement provided it is clear that no subtenancy is being created.

Avoiding disputes: It is advisable to draw up a formal agreement that clarifies the relationship between the two organisations. The points made under *Sharing premises – Those belonging to another organisation* (page 182) could form the basis of such an agreement.

Legal advice: Always take legal advice before making any arrangement for the continuous use of any part of the premises by another organisation.

Co-locating

In recent years it has become more common for voluntary organisations to share a building, or 'co-locate'. There are two main models:

- One organisation (the landlord) acquires premises, establishes a shared building and lets out space to a range of tenants under a licence agreement.
- A group of organisations come together to acquire a property jointly for their own occupation, sometimes with additional space to let to other tenants.

Such arrangements have a variety of titles, including 'hubs', 'charity centres' and 'resource centres'.

There are a number of benefits, for both landlords and tenants. Co-location can enable a landlord to reduce costs through sharing office overheads, to generate unrestricted income from rent, or to contribute to their charitable objectives by housing small organisations. For a tenant, co-location opens up opportunities to share information, resources and facilities, some of which would not be available or affordable if they had premises on their own. It can also help organisations to work more strategically together.

A co-location scheme requires careful planning to ensure that it has an appropriate structure and governance, that it is financially viable, and that the most suitable property interest is acquired. Major schemes can take several years to set up, and it is essential to consider exit arrangements for any party that wants or needs to leave.

For further information on sharing property see the property advice section of the Ethical Property Foundation (EPF)'s website (www.ethicalproperty.org.uk).

Hiring out parts of premises

Hiring out rooms for meetings and functions can raise funds as well as provide a community facility.

The key points to consider when other organisations are using your premises are:
- complying with the law
- security
- safety
- retaining control.

Legal requirements

The legal requirements to consider include:
- restrictions imposed by the lease or licence – for example, some leases state that the premises cannot be used by other organisations, or that music must not be played
- licensing laws if alcohol is to be sold, or if the premises are to be used for public entertainment or music (see chapter 9)
- planning laws – for example, a condition may be that the building cannot be used after 11pm
- noise limits under the **Environmental Protection Act 1990**
- whether corporation tax is payable: even charities may be required to pay corporation tax on rents and licence fees. If in doubt, check with HM Revenue & Customs or an accountant.

Security

Consider the following security precautions when the building is in use by the hirer:
- checking the identity of those entering (in large buildings this may involve identity passes)
- locking internal doors to private areas (but fire doors must remain unlocked)
- warning staff to take special care of their belongings when other people will be in the building
- providing secure storage for personal belongings
- locking away cash, cheques and other valuables
- securing expensive office equipment.

Remember that security includes protecting staff from possible intruders who may gain access to offices or other parts of the premises. This is especially important if staff work in the evening or if several activities are taking place.

You need to be clear about who is responsible for the following procedures to secure the building at the end of an event:
- ensuring that everyone has left the building before it is locked up
- locking up – this could involve appointing a caretaker, worker or management committee member to lock up after use and set the burglar alarm, or to ensure the hirer has done so.

Insurance

You must inform your insurance company that the premises will be hired out. It may impose additional conditions on the policy.

Safety

An organisation letting out a building is likely to be responsible for any injury or damage sustained by visitors caused by the state of the premises. It may also be responsible if someone is injured because the fire fighting apparatus is not functioning or a fire escape is blocked. Consider adding specific clauses to the conditions of hire to require the hirer to take certain precautions. The agreement should certainly require the hirer to ensure that fire escapes are not blocked and to take all reasonable steps to ensure the safety of people taking part in their activities.

You must take out public liability insurance to cover injury or loss sustained by visitors and others (see chapter 7). The cost can be passed on to the hirer(s) through the hiring charges. Again, make sure you tell your insurance company that the building will be hired out. The hirer may also need to take out public liability insurance, as your insurance will not cover claims brought against the hirer.

For an example of a hiring agreement see Community Matters' information sheet 61 *Rules and hiring agreement for a community centre*, available from www.communitymatters.org.uk.

Planning and building regulations

Planning laws govern many aspects of a building and its surroundings and can restrict activities, regardless of tenure. The primary legislation is found in the **Town and Country Planning Act 1990**. The local planning authority, by granting or refusing planning permission, enforces its detailed planning regulations, often called **development control**.

The planning system can be extremely complicated. Check with the local planning authority if in doubt. Planning Aid (www.planningaid.rtpi.org.uk) can provide free advice on planning matters to voluntary organisations.

Development

Some minor developments are given automatic permission by the **Town and Country Planning (General Permitted Development) Order 1995**, which also allows certain changes of use (see *Use of buildings and land*, below). Some temporary developments are possible without planning permission: for example, land used for certain activities for 28 or fewer days in any calendar year.

Planning permission is needed for:
- certain changes in the use of buildings and land
- major changes to the external appearance of a building
- changes to the internal or external appearance of listed buildings (listed building consent)
- erection of new buildings.

Use of buildings and land

The **Town and Country Planning (Use Classes) Order 1987** as amended by the **Town and Country (Use Classes) (Amendment) Order 2005** sets out 16 classes of use for land and buildings, collected into four groups. To change from one use to another within the same group does not require planning permission.

The four basic uses are:
- **class A**: retail shops, financial and professional services and food and drink shops
- **class B**: offices, industrial and commercial uses
- **class C**: residential, including houses, hotels, hostels, hospitals and residential institutions
- **class D**: public places, including churches, schools, libraries, art galleries, cinemas, nurseries and arts centres.

The subclasses particularly relevant to voluntary organisations include:
- **class A1**: shops, including charity shops
- **class A2**: financial and professional services – this could apply to advice centres
- **class A3**: food and drink – relates to the sale of food or drink to be consumed on the premises or hot food to be taken away
- **class B1**: business – includes office premises used by charities; could cover small manufacturing processes such as making poppies or Christmas cards
- **class B8**: storage and distribution – includes warehousing and storing the products of small manufacturing processes (see class B1, above)

- **class C1**: hotels and hostels – hostel accommodation would be included where there is no significant element of care provided
- **class C2**: residential institutions – residential accommodation with care
- **class C3**: dwelling houses – includes houses providing accommodation for not more than six residents living together as a single household, including those with care provided for residents
- **class D1**: non-residential institutions – for example, day centres, crèches, halls, arts centres and educational uses
- **class D2**: leisure use.

The appearance of a building

Planning permission for painting or repairs is not necessary in most cases (apart from buildings in some conservation areas or where a building is listed). However, permission is needed for a major change to a building's appearance, for example:

- installing a shop front
- building an extension (although certain extensions to a house may, subject to certain restrictions, be classed as permitted development)
- erecting a garage.

The **Town and Country Planning (Control of Advertisements) Regulations 1992** govern planning permission for advertisements. Illuminated and hanging signs usually need planning permission, but non-illuminated signs do not. Check with the local authority's planning department if in doubt.

Listed property and buildings in conservation areas

There are extra restrictions imposed on buildings in conservation areas or listed as being of special architectural importance. These apply to both external and internal alterations to listed buildings and to certain works to buildings in conservation areas. Conservation area consent is required to demolish any building in a conservation area.

Again, if in doubt, check with the local authority.

Tree preservation orders

Local authorities have the power to make a tree preservation order, applicable to individual or groups of trees and woodlands. Such an order can prohibit cutting down, topping or lopping trees without the consent of the local planning authority. The local authority will confirm whether a tree is covered by such an order.

New buildings

Most new non-domestic buildings need planning permission, which is a two-stage process. You must first submit an outline application, and the local planning authority will decide whether the development is acceptable 'in principle'. If so, permission will be subject to the approval of the details (**reserved matters**), which include siting, design, external appearance, access and landscape. Building work cannot begin until the local planning authority has approved all these details.

Obtaining planning permission

If you are buying or moving into a building, your solicitor will check the need to apply for planning permission as part of the searches. If you wish to make alterations to a building you already occupy you should contact the local authority's planning department. The staff there will need to know:

- the address of the premises
- the floors being occupied, if applicable
- what the premises are (or have been) used for
- what new activity is intended
- any alterations being considered.

Making an application

All planning applications must be submitted on a form provided by the planning department, together with plans showing the location of the premises and the details of the proposed development, such as external appearance, siting, car parking and layout and a certificate of ownership. The fee payable depends on the nature of the application. If you do not own the land or buildings in question you must serve notice on the owner and any other parties with an interest in the land, informing them that an application has been made.

The local authority has to notify neighbours of an application, through an advertisement in the local press, a site notice and/or a letter. If an application might be seen as controversial, explain to the neighbours what is involved.

When considering alterations to the building you must take into account the needs of disabled people. This applies to current and potential members of staff and to anyone else who uses the building.

The British Standards Institution's *Design of buildings and their approaches to meet the needs of disabled people* (**BS 8300**), available from www.standardsuk.com, explains how the built environment can be designed to anticipate and overcome restrictions that prevent disabled people from making full use of premises and their surroundings. It includes recommendations for the design of new buildings and their approaches to meet disabled people's needs.

If permission is refused

Permission could be refused altogether, or conditions imposed, such as restricting the hours of certain activities. There is a right of appeal to the Secretary of State against refusal or the imposition of conditions. An appeal must be made within six months of a local authority's decision, and decisions can take a long time. It is however possible to agree to lease or buy subject to obtaining planning permission.

For further information see www.planningportal.gov.uk.

Building regulations

Building regulations apply to new buildings and extensions or major structural changes to existing property, whether domestic, commercial or industrial. In general the regulations control:

- structure
- fire safety
- site preparation
- toxic substances
- sound insulation
- ventilation
- hygiene
- drainage and waste disposal
- fuel storage systems
- protection from falling, collision and impact
- conservation of fuel and power
- access and facilities for disabled people
- glazing.

The regulations are enforced by the local authority's building control service, which must check the work as it progresses. It is usually the builder's responsibility to make the arrangements, but it is important to confirm this before work starts. Also remember that the building's owner, not the builder, will be served with an enforcement notice if work does not comply with the regulations. It may also be necessary to consult the environmental health department and fire brigade.

For further information see *Building regulations: Explanatory booklet*, available from www.planningportal.gov.uk.

Paying rates

The occupiers of premises must pay **non-domestic rates** and **water charges**. Although non-domestic rates are usually referred to as **business rates** or the **uniform business rate**, they are payable on any premises not used as a dwelling, which includes most premises occupied by voluntary organisations. Organisations that occupy premises under a lease will normally be the occupiers and will therefore be liable for both non-domestic rates and water charges. However, a licence to occupy premises may state that the landlord is still in occupation and is therefore responsible for non-domestic rates.

In unincorporated organisations the management committee will be the occupier, and members will be personally responsible for paying rates and water charges if the organisation fails to do so.

Mandatory rate relief

Property used wholly or mainly for charitable purposes is entitled to 80% relief on non-domestic rates. The same rate relief applies to registered community amateur sports clubs, under the **Relief for Community Amateur Sports Clubs (Designation) Order 2002**.

There is no statutory requirement for charities to submit applications for rate relief but it is advisable to inform the rating authority as soon as you occupy the premises. Also, as charity law requires trustees to safeguard the organisation's assets, spending them unnecessarily on rates could be seen as a breach of trust.

Discretionary rate relief

Under **Section 47** of the **Local Government Finance Act 1988** local authorities have the discretion to grant additional relief to charities on all or some of the remaining 20% of non-domestic rates. They also have the discretion to grant additional relief to registered community amateur sports clubs and relief of up to 100% where properties are occupied wholly or partly by non-profit making bodies which are not charities. All voluntary organisations should therefore consider applying for relief from non-domestic rates.

Discretionary relief can only be backdated to the beginning of the rating year in which the local authority agrees to grant relief (1 April to 31 March). Once relief is given it can continue automatically each year, but this decision is up to the local authority.

If the end of the rating year is close it may be necessary to ask for relief in advance.

Empty rate relief

Charitable relief will be available if a charity owns empty non-domestic property where the intention is to reoccupy it for wholly or mainly charitable purposes. However, rates may be payable if a charity is marketing empty property for non-charitable use. In all cases the full business rate is payable on empty non-domestic property after three months (office and shop space) or six months (warehouses).

Disposing of premises

Organisations can dispose of their premises in a number of ways including:

- selling
- leasing or granting subleases
- assigning a lease
- returning the lease to the landlord (surrendering the lease or giving notice to quit).

Always take legal advice before disposing of premises and, if appropriate, consult the Charity Commission.

Requirements of Section 36 of the Charities Act 1993

Section 36 of the **Charities Act 1993** places obligations on non-exempt charities (see chapter 1) when disposing of property.

The provisions of Section 36 aim to ensure that charities obtain the best value for any property disposed of. There are two ways of complying: by obtaining a Charity Commission Order (authorisation) or by the committee taking the advice of a property expert, usually a surveyor.

Disposals covered by Section 36

Section 36 applies to disposals of land held by, or on trust for, a non-exempt charity, including freehold sales, grants of leases, surrenders of leases and grants of easements (rights over the land). A grant of a genuine licence to occupy (see page 175) is not a disposal for the purposes of the Act.

Not all disposals require compliance with Section 36. The main exceptions include:

- disposals authorised by statute or a Charity Commission Scheme
- disposals made to other charities other than for best value, authorised by the disposing charity's constitution
- the grant of a lease to another charity for other than the best rent that can reasonably be obtained, to allow the premises to be occupied for the purposes of the charity
- disposals by exempt charities
- disposals by way of mortgage or other security (in such cases section 38 applies, see page 173).

You will need to obtain a Charity Commission Order or third party advice for disposals that require compliance. You must take legal advice on when and how to deal with such compliance.

A charity must obtain a Charity Commission Order before disposing of land to a **connected party:** for example, a committee member or employee. There are other occasions when it may be useful to obtain an Order: for example, where the time and costs involved in obtaining third party advice (see below) would be disproportionate.

Third party advice

If a charity plans to let or sublet premises for seven years or less without charging a **premium** (a non-returnable lump sum), before entering into the lease the committee must get advice about property values from someone they believe has the necessary ability and practical experience. The committee then has to be satisfied that, having considered the advice, the proposed terms are the best that can be reasonably obtained in the circumstances. This also means that a charity must charge a market rent if it leases any premises to a trading subsidiary (see *Trading*, in chapter 1).

The committee must obtain written advice from a qualified surveyor (that is, a member of the Royal Institute of Chartered Surveyors – see www.rics.org) if it proposes to do any of the following:

- sell its property
- enter into a lease for more than seven years, or a shorter lease where a premium is charged
- transfer its property or lease to another organisation
- surrender its lease to the landlord.

Again, the committee must be satisfied that the proposed terms are the best that can reasonably be obtained. The charity must advertise the property for sale or lease publicly unless the surveyor has advised that this would not be in its best interests. The Charity Commission has the authority to waive the requirements.

Premises held on trust

If premises were given or sold to a charity to fulfil a specific purpose, certain restrictions apply on their disposal. The committee must give at least one month's public notice of its intention to dispose of the premises, so that people who may be affected can give their views.

These rules do not apply if:

- the property disposed of will be replaced with other property, or
- the premises are being let for two years or less, or
- the Charity Commission has said that the rules should not apply to the charity generally, or to the particular disposal in question.

Documentation

The **Charities Act 1993** sets out requirements for specific clauses that must be included in any document disposing of a charity's property. You should take legal advice when such a document is drawn up.

Equipment leases

Many organisations enter into leasing contracts, for example for office equipment. There are advantages and disadvantages to leasing as opposed to outright purchase. Leasing equipment means that you can spread the cost and plan ahead because of regular fixed payments. The downside is that you will not own the equipment, and the long-term cost will almost always be higher. However, the additional cost may be worth it if the owner (**lessor**) pays for maintaining the equipment and for its insurance.

Types of agreement

There are two main types of leasing agreement:

- **Operating leases** are often used for less valuable items of equipment – the lease will run for the agreed term and the lessor will take the equipment back. Generally the lessor will maintain the equipment and make sure it is insured.
- **Finance leases** run for the estimated valuable lifetime of the equipment. At the end of the term the lessor will often allow you to dispose of the equipment or continue paying reduced rent. You will generally be responsible for maintenance and insurance.

Leases are often for a fixed term and then continue automatically unless the lessee gives the required notice to terminate them. A lessee who wants to dispose of equipment before the term has finished must either pay off all the charges until the end of the contract or acquire other equipment from the owner.

Before signing any leasing agreement make sure that you understand the full terms and conditions and, in particular, note:

- any routine charges made and whether VAT is charged in addition
- whether the lessor can increase any charges and, if so, whether there is a maximum limit on any increases

- whether any servicing or maintenance is provided and, if so, whether it is for the full period of the lease (this is often not the case, and it can cost a substantial amount to take out a maintenance contract when the service period has finished, as lessors wish to encourage the purchase or hire of a new machine)
- whether the maintenance contract is limited – for example, does it exclude breakdown if the lessee is at fault, or are certain expensive parts of the machine excluded?
- whether the lessee is responsible for insuring the equipment against loss, theft or damage.

Hire purchase

Hire purchase agreements are similar to leasing arrangements, but at the end of the term you will be able to buy the asset from the lessor, usually for a nominal sum. The main advantage is that the payments will not be 'wasted money', although it will usually cost more than paying for the equipment outright. Check any hire purchase agreement to ensure that the terms relating to the final payment are satisfactory and that there are no hidden charges.

Other points to consider are:

- If you default on any lease or hire purchase agreement, the lessor will be able to seize the goods.
- There may be tax implications in choosing one route over another. If the lease is particularly long-term, or if the payments are high, you should consult a specialist.
- The lease may contain a change of control clause. This enables the lessor to terminate the arrangement if a 'new entity' takes control of the organisation – for example, if it merges with another organisation, or changes its legal structure. This does not happen very often, but it is advisable to consult the lessor if you know a change is likely.

All equipment and hire purchase agreements should be discussed and agreed by the management committee.

For further information see the finance and grants section of the Business Links website (www.businesslinks.gov.uk).

The green office

Voluntary organisations were amongst the first to expose the damage inflicted on the environment by human activity and the impact this has on people, especially the poorest. The sector now has a key role in developing environmental policies and procedures.

- As a significant employer of paid staff and volunteers, the sector is a major consumer of resources.
- Climate change disproportionately affects the poorest people both in the UK and globally, and will increase the number of people in need of assistance. Without taking steps to minimise their environmental impact, organisations risk exacerbating the problems they aim to tackle and undermining their own objectives.
- Organisations have a responsibility to promote good practice and deliver change by, for example, increasing awareness, engagement and action amongst their members and local people, and by encouraging other voluntary organisations and agencies to develop policies and services to support sustainable development.
- Environmental policies make economic sense: reducing energy and cutting down on waste saves money, as does avoiding green taxes such as those on energy consumption and congestion charging.
- Many funding bodies now require grant or service contract recipients to have an environmental policy in place or to be working towards one. In some cases they expect recipients to be using, or working towards, an environmental management system such as **BS 8555** or **ISO 14001** (see the environment and efficiency section of the Business Link website www.businesslink.gov.uk).
- Saving energy demonstrates good overall management; again an attraction to funders.

The Department for Environment, Food and Rural Affairs (Defra) funds Every Action Counts (EAC) to support voluntary sector involvement in environmental action. The EAC website (www.everyactioncounts.org.uk) contains much useful information, including advice on how to develop an action plan to improve environmental performance. EAC has also published two free guides, *Changing the way we work – a guide to greening your office* and *Your community building counts*, which show how to improve and develop offices, village halls and community centres. They can be downloaded from the website; printed copies are also available.

This section starts by looking at the law in relation to the environment, and then discusses how organisations can develop environmental policies.

Legislation

Much environmental legislation is focused on industrial, extractive and agricultural processes, details of which can be found on www.netregs.gov.uk.

The legislation most likely to affect voluntary organisations concerns waste management. The regulations change frequently but the core principles are set out in the **Environmental Protection Act 1990**, which puts a 'duty of care' on all waste producers, including households, businesses (including voluntary organisations) and the public sector. The Act covers how waste from business premises is handled, collected and disposed of, with special arrangements – which may attract charges – for the safe disposal of hazardous items such as batteries, paint, waste oil, pesticides and asbestos.

All such items are referred to as **controlled wastes** and have specific regulations. Most voluntary organisations commission a waste contractor to take their waste away (in a multi-occupancy building this may be managed by the landlord). The contractor should be your first port of call for any queries about specific wastes. The Netregs site (www.netregs.gov.uk)

also has detailed information on waste management.

There is some specific legislation that may affect offices, including:

- the **Hazardous Waste Regulations 2005**
- the **Waste Electrical and Electronic Equipment (WEEE) Regulations 2006**
- **End of Life Vehicles Directive 2000** and **End of Life Vehicles Regulations 2003**.

Hazardous Waste Regulations 2005

If you produce, move, receive or dispose of hazardous waste, there are certain procedures you must follow. Like other regulations, these change over time. The Environment Agency, which has responsibility for waste, has produced some useful guidance. If you are unsure whether waste is hazardous, see the Agency's guidance at www.environment-agency.gov.uk/subjects/waste, which includes a link to a 16-page guide.

Electrical and electronic equipment (EEE)

Disposal of electrical and electronic equipment must now follow legislation as set out in the **Waste Electrical and Electronic Equipment (WEEE) Directive**.

The **Waste Electrical and Electronic Equipment (WEEE) Regulations 2006** set out how the Directive is implemented, and affect most voluntary organisations. They set criteria for the collection, treatment, recycling and recovery of waste electrical equipment, including household appliances, IT and telecommunications equipment, audiovisual equipment (TV, video, hi-fi), lighting, electrical and electronic tools with a voltage of up to 1000 volts for alternating current or 1500 volts for direct current. For all non-household electrical or electronic equipment either the producer or the end user is responsible for disposing of the products. See the Environment Agency website for more information (www.environment-agency.gov.uk/business).

The regulations state that users:

- must store, collect, treat, recycle and dispose of WEEE separately from other waste

- keep proof that their WEEE was given to a waste management company, and was treated and disposed of in an environmentally sound way.

Disposal options

You can dispose of WEEE by:

- returning it to the manufacturer (if you bought it on or after 13 August 2005)
- taking it to a professional waste disposal facility
- donating it to a non-profit organisation.

Returning the product to the manufacturer. The responsibility for WEEE depends on when it was placed onto the UK market. Products placed before 13 August 2005 are called historic WEEE; those placed on or after that date are called future WEEE. You can return future WEEE free if you are replacing it with new equivalent EEE, or if you rent or lease EEE.

If disposing of historic WEEE and not buying an equivalent replacement, you are responsible for collection, treatment, recovery and environmentally sound disposal.

When buying new EEE make sure you keep the producer registration number so that you can contact the producer when you need to dispose of the products.

Using a professional waste disposal facility. You must arrange and pay for the transfer of WEEE to an appropriately licensed facility if you:

- are discarding historic WEEE and are not replacing it with equivalent EEE, or
- cannot trace the producer or its compliance scheme.

You must keep proof that your WEEE was given to a waste management business, and was treated and disposed of in an environmentally sound way. If your equipment contains information covered by the Data Protection Act (see chapter 9), ensure that the waste disposal business you used holds a relevant certificate in information security management.

For a list of approved schemes see the business and industry section of www.environment-agency.gov.uk.

Donating the goods to a non-profit organisation. A number of non-profit organisations collect EEE either for reuse or recycling. If donating computers, ensure that the organisation has an appropriate data destruction process (some will issue data erase certificates) and a strategy for waste management once the equipment becomes obsolete. For information on UK computer recyclers and refurbishers visit www.wasteonline.org.uk.

For more information about WEEE see www.netregs.gov.uk.

End-of-life vehicles (ELVs)

The **End of Life Vehicles Directive 2000** and **End of Life Vehicles Regulations 2003** aim to prevent waste from vehicles that can no longer be used, and promote the collection, reuse and recycling of their components. Included are requirements that:

- ELVs can only be scrapped by authorised treatment facilities (ATFs)
- owners are given a certificate of destruction when the vehicle is scrapped. The ATF should notify the DVLA. However, keep the certificate as proof that, as the last registered keeper, you are no longer responsible for the vehicle
- cars or vans can be taken to an ATF free of charge providing they have the essential components of a vehicle – such as the engine, transmission, coachwork and wheels – and the ATF is part of the appropriate manufacturer's network.

Make sure the site you use has a waste management licence and is listed as an ATF. For more information about ELVs and a list of ATFs visit www.netregs.gov.uk.

Energy performance

Energy performance certificates

Under **Article 7** of the **EU Energy Performance in Buildings Directive**, all commercial buildings over 50m^2 require an energy performance certificate (EPC), giving information on the energy efficiency and carbon emissions of the building, on sale or rental, or upon construction.

Certificates grade performance on a scale from A to G, similar to the system used for grading white goods. Each certificate is accompanied by a **recommendation report** that lists cost effective improvements to the building to make it more energy efficient.

If your organisation is a landlord you must commission an EPC when renting or selling a property; if a tenant, you should ask for an EPC from your prospective landlord; you also need an EPC if you are subletting, but as they are transferable you can use the one provided by your landlord.

Display energy certificates

Buildings over 1000m^2 occupied by a public authority or an institution that is providing a public service to, and visited by, a large number of people, need a **display energy certificate** (DEC). Its purposes are to raise public awareness of, and inform visitors about, the building's energy use. Depending on how they are funded and the extent to which they are open to the public, some community buildings may require DECs. If you are unsure about whether your building requires a DEC, phone the Communities and Local Government helpdesk on 0845 365 2468.

DECs provide an energy rating of the building from A to G, based on the **actual** energy usage – measured by gas, electricity and other meters over 12 months. The DEC should be clearly visible to the public at all times. A DEC is always accompanied by an advisory report that lists cost effective measures to improve the building's energy rating.

EPCs and DECs can only be produced by an accredited energy assessor who is part of an accreditation scheme. A list of approved accredited schemes is available on the Communities and Local Government website http://tinyurl.com/5mln6l.

Voluntary sector environmental organisations

Organisations involved in activities such as waste recycling and reuse, wildlife and landscape conservation, allotments and food growing, city farms, cycling, walking and community transport may be subject to more specialist environmental law.

For example, handling, storing, processing and distributing waste materials and products for recycling or reuse is subject to detailed regulation. There may be assessment, planning and site management obligations for environmental conservation projects. There are stringent regulations governing composting or treatment of organic waste, particularly kitchen waste. The management of animals and animal waste is strictly regulated, and the management of transport is subject to regulations relating to emissions, waste oil and fluids and, as noted on page 193, vehicle disposal.

The Community Recycling Network (0117 942 0142; www.crn.org.uk), the national umbrella organisation for community-based, not for profit and cooperative waste management organisations, can help with developing a reuse or recycling initiative.

The best sources of advice on legal and planning matters are organisations already active in the same field, most of which offer advice freely to new entrants. Planning Aid (www.planningaid.rtpi.org.uk), which works regionally, can provide free, independent and professional help, advice and support on planning issues to voluntary organisations.

Environmental policy and practice

An environmental policy sets out your aims and your commitment to improving your environmental performance and the priorities for your action plan. The action plan describes how and when (with both long-term and short-term goals) you will make changes, particularly in relation to:

- reducing waste
- reusing material
- recycling
- energy use and efficiency
- water conservation
- purchasing
- travel.

Implementing the policy

The policy must have the commitment of all staff, volunteers and the management committee, and should include the following:

- named individuals, ideally a staff member and management committee member, who will take responsibility for day-to-day management of the policy, possibly with the support of an action group
- training and awareness raising initiatives for staff and volunteers
- a strategy for communicating the policy throughout the organisation
- measurable targets with timescales
- procedures for regular reporting on progress
- a commitment to review the policy at regular intervals
- procedures for working with funders, suppliers, service users and other organisations (and especially those that share your premises) to develop good practice.

Information

There is a lot of help available. *Green Officiency,* which can be downloaded from www.envirowise.gov.uk, is a useful starting point for office-based voluntary organisations. It includes benchmarking information and tools on waste, paper use, energy and water. Organisations such as Global Action Plan (www.globalactionplan.org.uk) and Groundwork (www.groundwork.org.uk) can help you identify opportunities to reduce waste at source, improve energy efficiency and reduce water consumption, and will provide guidance on procurement and environmental management systems. Also see EAC's website www.everyactioncounts.org.uk. The Carbon Trust provides technical guidance on energy efficiency and has produced a number of useful guides that can be downloaded free of charge from www.carbontrust.co.uk. Friends of the Earth Scotland (www.green-office.org.uk) has developed an online audit to help organisations gather basic information about current green office practices, take further action and track progress.

The action plan

Changing how we use energy

Cutting energy use is an essential first step in addressing climate change.

The forthcoming Climate Change Act will set national targets to reduce CO_2 emissions by 60–80% by 2050. Voluntary organisations can play an important role in promoting local awareness and engagement in meeting this new target, especially as it will impact on workplaces and homes. For more information see the EAC's 'Third Sector Declaration on Climate Change' (available at www.everyactioncounts.org.uk/declaration/).

Using energy efficiently is a matter of common sense and prudent budgeting. Begin by looking at your bills or your meter to see how much energy you use; this can act as a baseline against which to measure future use. Make sure you keep everyone informed of progress in cutting down on use.

Try to create a culture in which everyone uses simple checklist measures, particularly in relation to office equipment, lighting, heating and air conditioning. How far you can act depends on how much control you have over the workspace. If you share a building, consider talking to the other occupants and the landlord about investing in energy efficiency.

Office equipment

- Only switch on computers, copiers, printers and other powered equipment when necessary. Switch off monitors (VDUs) if they are not in use. This will not only save energy but will also extend the equipment's life span and reduce maintenance costs.
- Where possible share printers through a network. Set computers to go on stand-by after ten minutes of inactivity or, better still, put the monitor to sleep. Avoid using energy consuming screen savers.
- When buying new equipment remember that laptops are more energy efficient than desktop computers, and that flat screen (LCD) monitors are more energy efficient than bulky monitors.
- Locate desks and workstations to derive maximum benefit from natural light.

Lighting

- Switch off lights when rooms are not in use (making sure that neither security nor health and safety are compromised).
- Use low energy light bulbs.
- Ensure that any lighting control systems work properly.
- If daylight is not sufficient, use individual desk lamps rather than lighting an entire office.

Heating

- Ensure that any thermostats or other heating control systems work, are maintained and used. Turn radiators down rather than open windows.
- Do not block radiators with furniture, and put reflective panels behind those on outside walls.
- Maintain the heating at the appropriate level: as a guide, 19–20°C is the recommended temperature in offices, and internal heat gains from equipment and lighting will raise the temperature to a comfortable level.
- Ensure that only occupied areas are heated and that heating is switched off or reduced during non-working hours.
- In buildings with several rooms, consider creating zones where separate time and temperature controls are installed to suit different uses.
- Check that the office is well insulated and draughtproofed.

Air conditioning

- If possible open doors and windows for natural rather than mechanical ventilation, but always consider security and noise implications.

- Avoid simultaneously cooling and heating your office by setting the air conditioning to come on only when the temperature reaches 24°C, and adjusting your heating system to switch off when it gets above 19°C.
- Make sure that the system is not running when people are out of the building, keep doors and windows closed in air conditioned areas, and switch off lighting and office equipment where possible to reduce heat gains.
- Regularly maintain the system.

Conserving water

- Install a water meter to monitor consumption.
- Fix dripping taps, use spray taps for hand washing and put up signs to remind people not to leave taps running.
- Keep any water-saving devices such as automatic taps and urinal flushers in good working order.
- Install waste-saving devices in the cistern and if upgrading toilets go for dual flush ones.
- Adopt obvious but often overlooked good housekeeping measures such as not overfilling kettles, and using a plug or bowl when washing dishes.
- Install water butts to water any garden or lawn areas.

Other measures will depend on the control or influence you can exercise over your premises or landlord, and on your budget. They include:

- installing draught proofing, lightweight secondary double glazing, roof space insulation and hot water system lagging
- specifying a green tariff from an electricity supplier, under which the supplier buys energy from renewable sources such as wind, solar and hydro (although this may cost more). For information about different tariffs see the Green Electricity Marketplace website at www.greenelectricity.org. To find out more about how to buy electricity from a green supplier see www.uswitch.com/Energy/Green-Energy.html
- when planning to replace heating or lighting systems, getting advice from the Energy Saving Trust (0800 512 012 or www.energysavingtrust.org.uk) on energy saving installations such as energy efficient light fittings with reflectors and motion sensors that automatically switch off lights in empty rooms
- if moving into a new building or redeveloping an existing one, exploring the possibilities of using renewable energy systems, such as heat pumps, solar panels or a wind turbine. For further information contact the Low Carbon Buildings Programme (08704 23 23 13 or www.lowcarbonbuildings.org.uk). Renewable energy specialist www.windandsun.co.uk has an online reference guide to help you assess the appropriate systems for your building.

The Carbon Trust provides energy efficiency loans for replacing or upgrading existing equipment with a more energy efficient version (see www.carbontrust.co.uk/loans). Organisations can borrow from £5,000 to £100,000 on an unsecured, interest-free loan, payable over up to four years. First check your constitution to make sure you have the power to take out a loan.

Reducing waste

Measures to reduce waste include:

- use washable crockery and cutlery rather than disposable kitchenware
- buy bottled milk and avoid disposable containers
- disciplined reuse of file hangers, lever arch files and other office stationery items
- introduce simple but effective paper saving policies, for example:
  - reusing single sided or discarded paper for scrap, internal memos, drafts, file, fax and email copies (but be aware of the data protection and confidentiality implications of reusing paper that contains personal or sensitive information – see chapter 9); email rather than print documents
  - print only the necessary pages from documents
  - run a spell check before printing

– put up memos in communal areas rather than distributing them to all staff
– develop e-filing systems rather than printing file copies
– ensure everyone knows how to use a photocopier's double sided function
– put public information on your website.

For other ideas see *Changing the way we work*, available from www.everyactioncounts.org.uk.

Reusing materials

A number of voluntary organisations resell or, in some cases, give away the following used items:

- IT equipment
- office furniture
- white and other electrical goods
- leftover paint.

For details of organisations that refurbish and redistribute IT, furniture and electrical goods see Waste Watch WasteOnline (www.wasteonline.org.uk).

Surplus paint can be offered to a Community RePaint scheme. For information on the nearest scheme visit www.communityrepaint.org.uk or phone 0113 200 3959.

Unused, surplus building or decorating materials as well as unused stationery items, cloth, card and plastic sheeting might be of interest to a scrapstore for reuse by a school or children's project. Details of scrapstores can be found in the National UK Scrapstore Directory (www.childrensscrapstore.co.uk).

Recycling

Waste paper recycling is the simplest way of participating in practical environmental improvement (but shred any documents with information about individuals, the organisation's internal business or other sensitive information). For details of local office waste paper recycling schemes see www.wasteonline.org.uk.

Some waste paper recycling initiatives are themselves non-profit or small community enterprises. Some schemes charge for collections to help cover costs, but the fee is usually small, and may be reduced for voluntary organisations. Most waste paper collectors specify a minimum quantity they will collect and prefer to take unshredded paper for space reasons. They usually provide an accredited security shredding service to meet confidentiality requirements. Your arrangements for recycling waste paper must be compatible with your confidentiality policy (see chapter 9).

Other office items that should be recycled include toner cartridges (many of which can be returned to the supplier), mobile phones, glass and plastic bottles (check local collection systems) and vending cups.

For details contact Waste Watch WasteOnline (www.wasteonline.org.uk).

Green procurement

Organisations can minimise the environmental and social impacts of the goods and services they buy through examining the following.

Whether the purchase is necessary

Do you need this product or service? If an appliance has stopped working, before discarding it see if it can be repaired. Can the need be met in another way – for example, can the product be leased, borrowed or shared with another organisation? Are you buying the right amount? Does the product meet the needs of all potential users, including people with specialist needs?

What each product is made of

Is it made of recycled or reused materials? For example, choose recycled stationery and remanufactured or refilled toner cartridges for printers and copiers (but check that the use of such products does not invalidate any warranty on the equipment). WasteOnline (www.wasteonline.org.uk) has details of computer recyclers and refurbishers. The non-profit social enterprise Green-Works (0845 230 2 231; www.green-works.co.uk)

supplies recycled office furniture to community organisations at low cost. The Green Stationery Company (www.greenstat.co.uk) specialises in recycled paper and green office products, and all good stationery suppliers should have a range of recycled stationery.

If not, is it made of renewable or biodegradable materials? For example, choose biodegradable, non-toxic cleaning materials; Forest Stewardship Council certified furniture; organic paints for decorating; rechargeable or mercury-/cadmium-free batteries.

Where it comes from

Buying locally reduces the resources used in transporting goods and means that your local traders enjoy the benefits.

Who has made it

Does the product meet recognised fair trade standards? This guarantees that the producers are getting decent wages at a fair price, and goods are likely to have been produced with less impact on the environment. The Ethical Consumer Research Association (0161 226 2929 or www.ethicalconsumer.org) provides information on the social and environmental impacts of companies and their products.

Is the product energy efficient?

The following labelling schemes identify energy efficient products:

- The Energy Saving Recommended logo, managed by the Energy Saving Trust, endorses products that are amongst the most energy efficient available. The Trust also has a database of energy saving products. see www.energysavingtrust.org.uk.
- The European Union Energy label rates products for energy efficiency from A (best) to G (worst).
- The Energy Star logo means that the energy consumption of an appliance is below an agreed level in stand-by mode. The logo appears on some types of office equipment, such as computers, monitors, printers and fax machines.

How they will be disposed of: end of life management

Can the product serve a useful purpose after its initial use? If not, how will it be disposed of? Is it biodegradable? Is it designed for disassembly – can it be easily taken apart so that materials can be recycled?

Services

Consider the environmental and ethical implications when buying services. There are, for example, some 'ethical' cleaning companies that pay a better wage to their employees and use environmentally friendly products; see the Ethical Products Organisation's website (www.ethicalproducts.org.uk).

Minimising the environmental impacts of travel

You can help reduce the environmental impact of travel by encouraging staff, volunteers and visitors to use public transport, cycle or walk, and by minimising the use of cars for journeys connected with your work. You can do this by developing a simple green transport plan or policy, which might include the following points:

- Take account of the quality of public transport if considering locating to new premises.
- Advertise for staff and volunteers locally.
- Encourage use of public transport by:
  - giving staff, volunteers, committee members and visitors up-to-date information on public transport. Publicise how to get to your office and events by public transport on your literature and website. Traveline's website (www.traveline.info) includes links to sources of information on planning journeys using public transport
  - offering interest free or low interest loans to buy season tickets. Staff do not have to pay tax or national insurance contributions (NICs) if they repay the cost of the loan in full and the total outstanding amount of all individual loans is less than £5,000.

- Encourage staff and volunteers to cycle, by:
  - providing secure facilities for bicycles at the office (including a changing room and if possible a shower) and at project locations
  - instituting a mileage allowance for bicycle use on work-related journeys. HM Revenue & Customs allows a tax-free mileage allowance of up to 20p per mile (2008/09) for work-related bicycle journeys
  - use a Cycle to Work scheme (see www.cyclescheme.co.uk) to operate a 'salary sacrifice' arrangement to provide a bicycle and equipment free of VAT, tax and NICs. Under the scheme the organisation buys the bike and equipment and then recovers the cost by leasing it to the employee, reducing their gross salary by the necessary amount each month over 12 or 18 months. By the time the scheme has expired, the fair market value of the bike has generally depreciated to such an extent that it can be offered for sale to the employee at the cost of one or two months' lease
  - holding designated cycle to work days and providing refreshments for participating staff. Up to six 'cyclist breakfasts' a year, per employee, are exempt from tax
  - providing information on local cycle routes and cycle training schemes; see www.cyclenetwork.org.uk for details of your local cycle campaign group and www.cycletraining.co.uk for information on cycle training.
- Where car use is necessary (for example, travel by people for whom public transport is inaccessible, travelling to multiple or remote locations, transporting equipment or materials, late night travel or where personal security might be compromised), reduce its impact by:
  - encouraging staff and volunteer car sharing
  - selecting fuel efficient, low emission models when buying, leasing or renting vehicles

  - investigating whether there is a local car share scheme. Participants are charged only for the costs of what can be very short hire times. For further information contact Carplus on 0113 234 9299 or visit www.carshareclubs.org.uk.
- Reduce the need to travel by:
  - encouraging flexible working arrangements and allowing staff to work from home when practicable (see *Flexible working arrangements*, in chapter 3)
  - making use of telephone, electronic or virtual conferencing (see *Virtual meetings*, in chapter 2).

For further details on travel plans see *The essential guide to travel planning* available from www.dft.gov.uk. For further details on tax and NIC concessions see *A fact sheet for employers setting up green travel plans*, available from www.hmrc.gov.uk.

When encouraging bicycle or alternative transport you must be sensitive to the needs of disabled people and others who for various reasons may need to use cars.

Further information

The EAC guides to green offices and workplaces *Changing the way we work – a guide to greening your office* and *Your community building counts* (available from www.everyactioncounts.org.uk) include a lot of relevant information. *Better places, better planet*, published by the Community Development Foundation (www.cdf.org.uk), provides a plain English guide to community action on climate change and the environment, which includes relevant advice for smaller groups.

Model deed of appointment

This model is reproduced from the second edition of *The Voluntary Sector Legal Handbook*, with permission from Russell-Cooke Solicitors (www.russell-cooke.co.uk).

This Deed of Trust is made on the . . . . day of *[month] [year]* between:

[Name of organisation] ('the Organisation'),

acting by its Management Committee *[or insert what the governing body is called]* ('the Governing Body');

and *[Names and addresses of holding trustees]* ('the Trustees').

Background

The Organisation is an unincorporated association // an unincorporated association registered as a charity // a charitable trust.

The Organisation wishes property that it owns which includes items in the attached schedule and other property acquired from time to time ('the Property') to be vested in the Trustees.

At a duly convened meeting of the Governing Body // a general meeting of the Organisation held on *[date]* at *[place]* it was resolved that the Trustees named above should be appointed to hold the title to the Property for the purposes of the Organisation.

Note that if the organisation is a charitable association or charitable trust, the property should be held 'for the purposes of the Organisation'. If the organisation is not charitable, the property should be held 'for the benefit of the members for the time being of the Organisation'.

At the same meeting it was resolved that *[names of two persons authorised to sign]* were authorised to sign this Deed on behalf of the Governing Body // the members of the Organisation.

Agreement

It is agreed that:

1. The Organisation hereby appoints the Trustees to act as trustees of the Organisation for the purpose of holding the Property.
2. The Trustees agree jointly and severally to hold the Property for the Purposes of the Organisation // for the benefit of the members for the time being of the Organisation.
3. The Trustees undertake that they will promptly follow all lawful and reasonable directions given by the Organisation, and that they will act only in accordance with such directions.
4. The Organisation agrees that it will indemnify the Trustees against all costs, claims and liabilities properly incurred or arising out of their trusteeship of the Property.

5. The Trustees have the following rights during the period of their trusteeship and during any further period in which they may be liable to any claim arising out of their trusteeship:
   a. the right to receive notice of all meetings of the Governing Body and all general meetings of the Organisation
   b. the right to attend and speak at any meeting of the Governing Body or general meeting on any matter relevant to the Property
   c. the right of access to information reasonably required to discharge their duties as trustees
   d. the right to immediate payment of any outstanding liability arising from trusteeship of the Property.
6. The Trustees agree to provide the Organisation with copies of all correspondence and to notify them of all communications in respect of the Property.
7. The Trustees agree to notify the Organisation of any change of their name or address.
8. New trustees may be appointed only by a resolution of the Governing Body or general meeting of the Organisation.
9. Trustees may be removed only by a resolution of the Governing Body or a general meeting of the Organisation.
   Unless it is made explicit that the power to appoint and remove trustees rests solely with the governing body of the organisation, trust law will place the power to appoint and remove in the hands of the holding trustees.
10. If a Trustee wishes to resign from his or her trusteeship the Organisation will use its best endeavours to obtain the Trustee's release from any obligation connected with the Property.

Signed and delivered as a Deed

by *[signature of authorised person]*

on behalf of the Governing Body *[name of organisation]*

acting on their authority by resolution on *[date]*

in the presence of *[witness's signature, name, address and occupation]*

Signed as a Deed

by *[signature of Trustee no 1]*

in the presence of *[witness's signature, name, address and occupation]*

[and the same for the remaining trustees]

Chapter 7

Insurance

This chapter describes general rules about insurance contracts and looks at compulsory and discretionary insurance.

The organisation's governing body is responsible for ensuring that all insurances are taken out, paid and kept up to date. You can buy cover directly from an insurance company or through a broker; get several quotes before taking out any policy. The British Insurance Brokers' Association has a list of registered brokers for each area (available online at www.biba.org.uk) and can identify members with a particular interest. It is also worth asking other local voluntary organisations, particularly the council for voluntary service or rural community council, which company they use.

A number of voluntary organisations have negotiated specialist insurance packages, including Community Matters, the London Voluntary Service Council, the National Association for Voluntary and Community Action, the National Council for Voluntary Organisations, Wales Council for Voluntary Action and the Scottish Council for Voluntary Organisations.

General rules

In insurance contracts, an application for insurance is a **proposal** and the person or organisation taking out the insurance the **proposer**.

When taking out insurance the proposer owes a duty of the **utmost good faith** to the insurance company. This means that the company can refuse to pay out on any insurance claim if, when making the proposal (usually by completing an application form or giving details over the phone or internet), the proposer has failed to disclose or has misrepresented a **material fact** (see page 203).

The extent of the duty

The proposer must disclose all material facts until the proposal is accepted, and must inform the insurance company if additional material facts arise or existing facts change during the course of the policy.

The obligation to disclose material facts includes providing information that could be discovered by making reasonably prudent enquiries.

Who should be covered?

Any action, or the failure to perform any action, by an organisation is, in practice, the responsibility of one or more individuals within that organisation or the organisation itself. Who is liable depends on what has or has not been done, and by whom. It is therefore advisable to cover employees, committee members and volunteers as well as the organisation for any liability they may incur in carrying out the organisation's work. This would include cover by professional indemnity insurance, trustee indemnity insurance, employer's liability insurance, public liability insurance and road traffic insurance (if they are driving the organisation's vehicles).

Most insurance companies design their policies for individuals or businesses. Their standard policies may cover staff (in terms of both staff protection and third party liability) but do not usually cover volunteers or unpaid management committee members, so it may be necessary to get specific extensions to standard policies. A specialist policy designed for the voluntary sector may therefore be preferable and cheaper (see above), as it will probably give volunteers protection under the employer's liability section, and include their third party liability under the public liability section.

Incorporated organisations

Incorporated organisations (companies, industrial and provident societies and charitable incorporated organisations – see chapter 1) can take out insurance in the name of the organisation.

Unincorporated organisations

One named individual will be required to take out the policy on behalf of the other committee members and should sign the proposal form. If that person leaves, the insurance must be transferred to someone else's name.

Material facts

A material fact affects the degree of risk the insurance company is accepting. Examples are given below.

All insurance

- Previous refusals of similar insurance
- Special conditions imposed on previous insurance
- Unspent criminal convictions of staff or management committee members. The type of conviction and time limits vary between insurance companies and between types of policies
- Previous claims on similar insurance

Theft insurance

- Use of the premises by other organisations or the public

Fire insurance

- Defective fire fighting equipment
- Internal blocking of fire exits
- Regular blocking of fire access (for example, by cars)
- Use of the premises by other organisations or the public

Motor insurance

- Drivers' ages
- Drivers' road traffic convictions
- In the case of minibus drivers, lack of specialist training (some policies offer discounts if drivers have had specific minibus driving training)
- The use of vehicle(s)

Public liability insurance

- Use of the premises by other organisations or the public

- The organisation's activities and the extent of any associated risks

Professional indemnity insurance

- Professional services provided (for example, giving information or advice about legal, financial, health or similar matters or providing medical treatment)

Renewals

You must disclose all material facts each time you renew insurance (even if not specifically asked to do so). These include changes and additional material facts that have arisen since the last renewal.

Exclusions

All insurance policies include a list of circumstances excluded from cover (the **small print**). Make sure you understand them before taking out a policy.

Amount of cover

It is essential to be covered for the right amount.

- **Contents** would normally be insured for the cost of replacing the lost or damaged goods.
- **Buildings** would normally be insured for the reinstatement cost, including VAT, all professional fees and site clearance.

Other insurance

For other types of insurance, you will need to work out the likely maximum claim that might be made against the organisation. Take advice from a reputable insurance broker who understands your organisation and its work.

Under-insurance

A policy usually states that the organisation must insure for a sufficiently large sum to cover any claim. If it is under-insured, some policies allow the insurance company to reduce the claim payment or refuse to pay out at all.

Other policies operate an **average clause**. This means that the insurance company pays out only a proportion of any loss. For example, if a building valued at £400,000 is insured for £100,000, the insurance company would pay only one quarter of any claim made, however small. So if you claimed for £4,000 worth of damage to a roof during a storm, the insurance company would only pay £1,000.

Completing the proposal

When completing a proposal on behalf of an organisation you must be aware of the consequences of making a mistake. Leaving a blank space on a proposal form, for example, is taken to mean that no material fact exists in reply to that question; if in doubt give the insurance company too much rather than too little information.

If an insurance broker completes the proposal form, make sure all the necessary information has been recorded accurately, and that you receive a copy. As a matter of good practice, a committee member should read and sign all insurance proposals.

Some insurers now issue a **statement of facts** in place of a proposal form when insurance is arranged over the phone or on the internet. The insurer will send you a copy of the statement with the insurance policy. It is essential to check this carefully – some can be very detailed – and send the insurer an amended statement of facts if necessary.

Make at least two copies of all information supplied: keep one copy away from the premises so that it can be referred to if other papers are lost through fire or theft.

Liability

If a material fact is not disclosed or the application form is inaccurate, the insurance company may refuse payment of a claim. If the insurance company refused to pay a claim against an unincorporated association (see chapter 1), the committee members could be personally liable to pay compensation to the person making the claim out of their own assets.

Making a claim

As soon as there is a possible insurance claim make sure the organisation complies with any conditions. These may include, for example, reporting the matter to the police or submitting a claim within a specific period.

Contact the insurance company as soon as possible, giving full details and quoting the policy number. If a claim involves a question of legal liability and the organisation is insured for this type of claim, the insurer will liaise with the other party.

Never admit responsibility for an accident, however obvious it is that the organisation is at fault, because this could prejudice an insurer's position.

Types of insurance

You should consider obtaining cover above the legal minimum for all types of insurance (but see *Risk management*, page 210).

Compulsory insurance

Two types of insurance are required by law.

Employer's liability insurance

Under the **Employer's Liability (Compulsory Insurance) Act 1969** all employers must insure against claims by workers for injury or illness caused by the employer's negligence or failure to comply with a statutory duty such as health and safety. The insurance must be for at least £5 million to cover any one claim, and the current insurance certificate must be displayed in all workplaces (this can be done electronically, as long as it is reasonably accessible to the relevant employees) and be retained by the employer for 40 years.

This insurance does not usually cover:

- injury or illness caused to committee members, trainees, consultants, self-employed people working for the organisation, volunteers or service users – although some specialist policies (see page 202) automatically cover volunteers. You need public liability insurance to cover these categories (see page 206)
- injury through an accident rather than employer's negligence (for this, see *Insurance for accidents, medical care and assault*, page 209)
- claims brought by an employee for breach of employment or equality legislation (for this, see *Legal expenses insurance*, page 210).

Motor insurance

Under the **Road Traffic Acts** all organisations that use vehicles on the road must insure drivers against **third party risks** – injury or death caused to other people (including passengers) and damage caused to other people's property. The certificate of insurance must be readily available.

Third party insurance does not cover theft of, or damage to, a vehicle. It is therefore worth extending the insurance either to **third party, fire and theft** (which covers theft and fire damage to the vehicle) or **comprehensive** (which covers all damage). Some comprehensive policies may cover death or injury of the driver, but cover will be very limited. Such circumstances need to be covered by personal accident insurance (see page 209).

You must tell the insurance company about how the vehicle is used and who is likely to be driving it. Insurance may be cheaper if the number of named drivers is limited.

If employees and/or volunteers use their own vehicles to carry out your work you must ensure that their insurance policies cover such journeys. Using a vehicle for work purposes is called 'business use' even in voluntary organisations using volunteer drivers.

An organisation may be liable for personal injury or damage to property as a result of a traffic accident in the course of work, so it is essential to ensure adequate cover. Check the following:

- the insurance is current
- it covers the employee and/or volunteer for use in connection with their work (including voluntary work)
- the nature of the work has been accurately disclosed to the insurance company
- the insurance company has been notified of any particular risks associated with how the vehicle will be used – for example, to carry service users or for unusual activities such as off-road driving.

The above apply equally if the employee or volunteer uses a car owned by someone else (for example, their partner).

Some specialist policies will cover the costs incurred by an employee or volunteer through loss of a no claims discount and/or having to pay the excess on a claim.

Insurance that may be required

There are a number of other types of insurance which, although not required by law, may be required by, for example, a landlord, funder or a service contract, or may be in your best interest.

Buildings insurance

Generally the landlord takes out insurance for a leased building (including rebuilding costs, rent if the building is vacated during refurbishment and possibly plate glass) and adds reimbursement of the insurance costs to the terms of the lease. If so, the tenant should have the right to inspect the policy.

In the few cases where the landlord does not organise the buildings insurance, the tenant would insure the building, normally as a condition of the lease, thus protecting the landlord.

Organisations are under no statutory obligation to insure premises they own. However, as there is a duty under charity law to protect a charity's assets, charities have a duty to take out buildings insurance. A committee that left a building uninsured would be negligent in its duty to the charity, and therefore in breach of trust. If a loan or mortgage is secured on a building the lender will normally insist the building is insured.

It is usual to insure for the cost of rebuilding the premises (including VAT) if completely destroyed, and to include all professional and site clearance fees.

It is also worth considering cover for the cost of alternative accommodation while the rebuilding takes place. You may also want to consider 'business interruption insurance' (see *Discretionary insurance*, page 208).

Insurance for plate glass windows

Leases of properties with shop fronts often require tenants to insure any plate glass windows against breakage, either accidentally or through criminal damage. Check the lease to see whether the insurance is the landlord's or the tenant's responsibility.

Public liability insurance

This covers claims made against the organisation (or committee members of an unincorporated body) for injury, loss or damage caused to anyone other than an employee (who will be covered under employer's liability insurance) as a result of an organisation's negligence. It would include injury suffered by someone using the organisation's premises as a result of a breach of the duties under the **Health and Safety at Work Act 1974** or **Occupier's Liability Act 1957** (see chapter 5). It does not cover:

- injury, damage or loss caused by the provision of professional services (see *Professional indemnity insurance*, below)
- the supply of goods (see *Product liability insurance*, page 207).

When taking out public liability insurance, make sure the insurance policy or schedule includes liability for damage, injury or loss caused by anyone who carries out work on behalf of the organisation. In other words, it should cover not only the organisation itself but also staff, trainees, committee members and volunteers. Most policies will automatically cover paid staff, but you may need a specialist policy for voluntary organisations (see page 202) to cover volunteers and committee members.

Always inform the insurance company of the nature of your work and if you use volunteers, trainees, outside workers and/or secondees.

Examples of situations covered by public liability insurance include injury to a person (other than an employee) who trips on loose flooring or is injured by faulty equipment, damage to clothing caused by failure to put up 'wet paint' signs, or food poisoning suffered by people attending a lunch club.

Although not compulsory, it would be extremely unwise not to have some form of public liability insurance if you run premises and/or provide activities or services. It may be a condition of a lease or grant aid, and organisations providing services under contract will usually be required to have public liability insurance. Check the value of insurance required: make sure you have least £5 million worth of cover.

Professional indemnity insurance

Public liability insurance does not cover injury or damages arising from negligence in the course of providing a professional service, even if the service is free. You will therefore need to take out professional indemnity insurance to cover any claims resulting from incorrect advice or negligent services which cause damage, injury or loss to a service user. It is sometimes included in trustee indemnity insurance (see page 207).

Examples include a person injured by a massage therapist, someone losing out on housing or welfare benefits because they are given incorrect or misleading information, or an organisation facing an employment tribunal claim because it was given incorrect advice about employment law. If your organisation uses volunteers make sure they are covered by the policy.

Professional indemnity policies can be expensive, as some insurers have high minimum premiums, but this cover can be included in specialist policies for voluntary organisations (see page 202).

Some national umbrella and support organisations have negotiated lower-rate policies for members. For example, adviceUK, the umbrella body for independent advice-giving organisations, arranges insurance for members on a block policy.

Self-employed people

Public liability and professional indemnity insurance only cover employees. You must therefore ensure that self-employed people who carry out work on behalf of the organisation have their own public liability and/or professional indemnity insurance where there is any element of risk, and make this a condition of appointment. Check that their insurance is in force, that it covers the work they are doing for the organisation, and that it indemnifies (repays) the organisation if it faces any claims because of their negligence. At the same time check that your public liability and/or professional indemnity insurance covers any liabilities incurred as a result of the worker's activities.

Defamation and unintentional breach of copyright

Insurance against defamation (slander or libel, see chapter 9) or unintentional breach of copyright can either be included with another type of cover – for example, public liability insurance, professional indemnity or trustee liability insurance – or be available separately.

There is always a risk of either of these occurring if an organisation represents people, writes letters on their behalf or publishes any kind of material, including in emails or on the internet.

Product liability insurance

If your organisation manufactures, sells or supplies any goods, it is advisable to take out product liability insurance to cover any illness, injury, death or damage that may arise from faulty goods. This is normally available as an extension to public liability insurance.

Trustee and directors' indemnity insurance

This insurance protects trustees or directors against personal liability when their organisation or a third party makes a legal claim against them or, in the case of an incorporated organisation, for liability for wrongful trading in some situations. However, it will not protect against deliberate wrongful trading (see *Liability for debts* in chapter 10).

Some insurers include other types of insurance with trustee/directors' indemnity: for example, professional indemnity, defamation, fidelity (theft by staff or committee members) and/or loss of documents. If this is the case, make sure you do not duplicate cover already held.

People may not be prepared to serve as committee members unless they are protected by this type of insurance, and some local authorities require it before making nominations to management committees. It is important to understand the extent of this cover. Many people wrongly assume, for example, that it covers committee members for personal liability for the organisation's debts, or negligence to third parties.

Before buying trustee/directors' indemnity insurance, committee members should focus on putting procedures and policies in place to help reduce any potential risk.

There are restrictions on the circumstances in which an organisation can take out this form of insurance, and because it covers committee members rather than the organisation, there is a potential conflict of interest between the individuals and the organisation they are managing.

Charities

Charities no longer need explicit constitutional power to take out and pay for trustee indemnity insurance. The 2006 Charities Act inserted a provision into the 1993 Act that gives trustees legal authority to buy this insurance as long as:

- the governing document does not expressly forbid its purchase
- it is in the best interests of the charity
- trustees observe a 'duty of care'.

So a charity only needs to obtain approval from the Charity Commission if there appears to be an express prohibition against the purchase of trustee indemnity insurance set out in its governing document. If this is the case it is possible to apply to the Commission to overturn it.

The insurance must include a clause to ensure that it does not cover:

- criminal fines or penalties arising from regulatory action
- costs of unsuccessfully defending criminal prosecutions for offences arising out of a committee member's fraud, dishonesty or reckless misconduct
- liability resulting from conduct which the trustee knew, or should have known, was not in the charity's interests.

Given these exclusions, the only circumstances likely to be covered by trustee indemnity insurance are where committee members entered into an arrangement that turned out to be in breach of trust, having made an honest but reasonable mistake. But as explained in chapter 1 (see *Breach of trust*), charity committee members who have acted reasonably in good faith and made an innocent mistake can be excused personal liability and so are unlikely to be held liable for such inadvertent breach of trust.

Where the charity is a company or charitable incorporated organisation, or carries out a part of its business through a separate company, trustees' personal liability for 'wrongful trading' (see *Incorporated organisations*, in chapter 10)

is similarly covered, provided it does not cover deliberate insolvent or reckless trading. It would cover committee members only if they made an honest and reasonable mistake.

For further details see the Charity Commission's information sheet *Trustee indemnity insurance* (CSD-1279), available from www.charity-commission.gov.uk.

Trustee or directors' liability insurance does not cover committee members for losses or debts arising from contracts, negligence or other obligations to third parties: for example, the inability to pay bills or meet redundancy costs.

Discretionary insurance

Organisations should also consider the following types of insurance, depending on their activities and the extent of their property.

Contents insurance

This normally covers the contents of a building for theft or damage (for example, by fire), but usually excludes theft by employees or volunteers (for this, you would need theft by employee insurance, see *Fidelity or theft by employee insurance*, page 209). Check whether the policy includes:

- **accidental damage**. Damage caused directly by individuals – for example, by spilling coffee over a keyboard. If not, it may be worth extending the cover
- **property** while it is out of the organisation's building, or during a move to other permanent premises (see *All risks insurance*, page 209).

Note: A charity's duty to protect its assets may require it to insure contents, and take out all risks insurance if it hires, leases or borrows equipment.

You must tell the insurance company about the building's likely users. The insurer may impose conditions on the policy: for example, installing additional locks or an alarm. If the policy is to cover theft of cash, the company may require cash to be stored in a safe, may set a limit on how much cash can be kept on the premises and/or may place conditions on its transit.

It is especially important to inform the insurance company if you have volunteers or other organisations using your premises.

All risks insurance

This is usually an extension of contents insurance, to cover property when it is outside the building (for example, laptops and presentation equipment). It is especially useful for organisations that shift around expensive equipment to different venues (for example, theatre or music groups), or where staff take the organisation's laptops home.

Business interruption insurance

It is possible to get cover for the cost of interruption to business if you need to move premises because of damage. Examples include losing income through being unable to provide a fee-paying service, or incurring extra costs through additional rent, installing phone lines and advising service users of a change of address.

Equipment failure insurance

You can insure major equipment, such as boilers and lifts, against damage and breakdown. Most policies require regular maintenance checks and servicing.

Engineering inspection insurance

This provides an inspection and reporting service for major equipment such as passenger lifts, stairlifts and tailboard lifts that have to be inspected to comply with relevant legislation (for example, the **Factories Act 1961** and the **Offices, Shops and Railway Premises (Hoists and Lifts) Regulations 1968**). Such insurance could cover all major equipment failure.

Fidelity or theft by employee insurance

Organisations dealing with large amounts of cash or holding high value stock or equipment should consider insuring against employees'

dishonesty. The ease of electronic transfer for salaries and other payments makes this particularly relevant nowadays. The insurance company would want details of any convictions against employees.

You may wish to consider insuring against dishonesty by members of the management committee and/or other volunteers. This is not a standard type of insurance, but an insurance company might supply it as an extension to a policy covering employees' dishonesty, and a specialist insurance policy (see page 202) may also cover volunteers. Again, members and volunteers would have to disclose any previous convictions.

Computer insurance

Specially tailored insurance for computers can be arranged which, as well as covering loss of, or damage to, the computer and/or its peripherals (such as a printer or scanner), also covers reinstatement of data and the increased costs of working as a result of the damage (for example, running a manual system at the same time as a computerised system).

Insurance for accidents, medical care and assault

It is possible to insure against the cost of sick pay. There are other policies that pay out standard sums to staff for specific injuries at work: for example, loss of a limb, or injuries through being assaulted. You may want to extend this to cover volunteers and committee members.

Insurance for outdoor events

It is possible to take out cover against losses arising from cancellation of outdoor events due to bad weather. This is commonly known as **pluvius** (rain) insurance. It usually involves strict time limits and arrangements for measuring rainfall.

Events of all sizes require public liability insurance (see page 206). If this is not provided under an annual policy it can be arranged on a stand-alone basis. You must give your insurers full details of the event.

Legal expenses insurance

This could cover legal expenses incurred in:

- employment and equality legislation disputes
- defending prosecutions against the organisation under legislation such as the Health and Safety at Work Act and Trade Descriptions Act
- property damage and claims from third parties
- in-depth investigation by HM Revenue & Customs into the organisation's tax affairs
- disputes with HM Revenue & Customs regarding VAT
- contract disputes.

In case of a claim or potential claim, the insurer usually requires the organisation to comply with its advice, and failure to do so may invalidate the insurance. This can reduce the scope for dealing with a claim in other ways (for example, the insurer may recommend making an out-of-court settlement in a situation where you might prefer to go to court to clear your name).

Legal advice helplines

Some legal expenses and other insurance policies include free access to legal advice, usually via a telephone helpline. This can be a useful service if you require immediate advice about a problem that might develop into a loss or claim.

Risk management

Insurance premiums are likely to continue to rise. Also, some insurers no longer offer insurance in what they consider to be high-risk areas, because of their experience of increased claims.

These factors are significant for voluntary organisations. Before taking out insurance, committee members need to consider a number of questions, including the following:

- Do the type of activities and services present risk of a particular form of loss or liability?
- How much would it cost to insure against such risks?
- Is there any way to reduce this cost, for example:
  - by taking steps to reduce the likelihood of a claim
  - by asking an insurance broker to seek competitive quotes
  - by collaborating with other organisations when buying insurance?
- How can the organisation ensure it can afford to meet the insurance costs?
- Should the organisation reduce or abandon the activity that gives rise to the risk?
- Should the organisation stop (or not take out) that type of insurance? What are the potential implications if something goes wrong and the organisation is not insured for it?

For further information see *Charities and risk management*, available from www.charity-commission.gov.uk/investigations/charrisk.asp.

Further information

For further information see the Charity Commission's booklet *Charities and insurance* (CC 49), available from www.charity-commission.gov.uk, which includes information that would be useful for any voluntary organisation. For further information about insurance relating to volunteers, see Volunteering England's information sheet *Insurance and volunteers*, available from the 'Resources' section of the website www.volunteeringengland.org.uk.

Chapter 8

Financial management

All voluntary organisations should keep accounts and most are legally obliged to. Properly kept accounts will help to show funders, members and the public that an organisation is operating effectively. Keeping well-organised records will also help an organisation manage its activities by showing how actual income and expenditure compare with budgeted figures.

This chapter covers the legal requirements and the committee and treasurer's duties relating to accounts, annual reports and other financial records. Throughout the chapter a charity's committee members are referred to as trustees, and a company's as directors.

The charity treasurer's handbook by Gareth Morgan, referred to in the chapter, is published by the Directory of Social Change.

Legal requirements – accounts

Regulations governing accounting records, statements of account and auditing requirements vary according to an organisation's legal status, whether it is charitable (see chapter 1), and its annual income and expenditure.

At the time of writing, the Office of the Third Sector had agreed some increased financial thresholds recommended by the Charity Commission, which are shown in brackets throughout this section. These are likely to apply to accounting periods starting from 1 April 2009, but as the changes require secondary legislation, you should check with your accountant or the Charity Commission whether they have come into force.

Charities

Charities Act 1993

Part VI of the **Charities Act 1993** (as amended by the **Charities Act 2006**) governs accounting, reporting and auditing rules for unincorporated charities and charitable incorporated

organisations (CIOs). All charitable associations, charitable trusts and CIOs are required to:

- prepare and maintain proper financial records
- prepare annual accounts and, in most cases, a trustees' annual report
- except for the very smallest, to have the accounts independently scrutinised (see *Audit or examination of accounts*, page 216), and
- make their most recent annual accounts and report available to a member of the public on request.

Many of the detailed requirements are included in regulations made under the Act – the latest version is the **Charities (Accounts and Reports) Regulations 2008** – and in the **Charities SORP** (see page 214) or guidance and directions from the Charity Commission.

The obligations for charitable companies (under company law) and charitable industrial and provident societies (IPSs) (under IPS law) are very similar – and for accounting years following April 2008 the scrutiny rules for charitable companies are largely identical to those for other charities. However, the accounts and reports of charitable companies must include some additional information to comply with company law, and similarly with IPS charities.

The accounting rules for charitable incorporated organisations (CIOs) are expected to be the same as for charitable trusts and associations.

Charitable incorporated organisations

At the time of writing, the final regulations for CIOs had not been published. The draft regulations did not include any additional requirements, but in the consultation document the Office of the Third Sector and the Charity Commission were seeking views on this. Any additional requirements will be contained in the **Charitable Incorporated Organisations (General) Regulations 2009**.

Charities whose annual income is £10,000 (£25,000) or less are subject to less onerous accounting requirements than larger charities, sometimes referred to as the 'light touch regime'. There are also concessions for charities with up to £100,000 and up to £250,000 income: only those with over £500,000 income (or over £2.8 (£3.26) million assets) have to follow the full requirements. It is important to be clear on these thresholds and know what is required at each level.

All registered charities with an annual income or expenditure of more than £10,000 (£25,000) have to submit annual accounts and reports to the Charity Commission; those (apart from CIOs) whose annual income is below this threshold need only submit annual accounts and reports on request (all CIOs must file accounts and reports with the Commission, whatever their income). Excepted charities (see chapter 1) must still comply with the accounting rules set out here, but only need submit accounts and reports to the Commission if explicitly requested.

Some charities are affiliated to national bodies that have their own accounting rules; such rules may add to the legal requirements set out here but cannot replace them.

Charities registered in Scotland

As explained in chapter 1, English and Welsh charities which work wholly or partly in Scotland often need to register with OSCR as well as with the Charity Commission; they are then known as 'dual-registered charities'. In such cases, their accounts will have to comply with the Scottish rules, as set out in the **Charities Accounts (Scotland) Regulations 2006**, as well as the rules under the Charities Act.

In general, the Scottish rules are stricter than those for England and Wales, for example:

- There are precise rules on what must be included even when the accounts are on a receipts and payments basis.

- A professionally qualified independent examiner is needed whenever the accounts are on an accruals basis (not just for charities with over £250,000 income).
- Charities with £10,000 (£25,000) or less income are not exempted from independent examination.

If financial thresholds are increased under the Charities Acts this will not affect the Scottish rules. So, in general, a dual-registered charity should follow the Scottish rules, even if only a small part of its work is in Scotland. For further details, see chapters 1 and 8 of *The charity treasurer's handbook*. Guidance on Scottish charity accounting is also available from the OSCR website www.oscr.org.uk.

Accounting records

All charities must keep accounting records that record the financial transactions – money spent and received – on a day-to-day basis, and show the nature and purpose of each transaction. The records must also show all **assets** (what the charity owns and is owed) and **liabilities** (what it owes).

Although records do not have to be updated each day, accounts must be able to show the charity's financial position on any particular date in the past.

Unincorporated charities must keep accounting records for at least six years from the end of the financial year to which they relate. This applies even if the charity folds before the end of six years.

All companies, whether charitable or non-charitable, must maintain records to the same standard, under the **Companies Act 2006**. Although companies need only keep records for three years, funders may require that records be kept for longer periods and it is good practice to keep them for at least six years from the end of the financial year; moreover, any tax-related records (such as Gift Aid, see page 224) must be kept for six years from the end of the year concerned.

Charity funds

One of the main issues that makes charity accounting different from commercial accounting is the need to manage separate funds, and this can apply to even the smallest organisation. A charity may typically have:

- **unrestricted funds** which can be spent on whatever purposes the trustees feel is most important – this includes a *general fund* (and sometimes also *designated funds* where trustees have set unrestricted funds aside for the future)
- various **restricted funds** holding grants or donations for specific projects.

Some charities may also have **endowment funds** which cannot be spent at all, but which are held just for investment purposes.

You do not need separate bank accounts for each fund – in fact, this can cause a lot of extra work (for example, if a payment is split between more than one fund) – but the books must be kept in a way that allows income and expenditure for each fund to be separately identified. For example, if a charity employs staff working on different projects, it cannot just have a single expenditure column for 'salaries'; a separate salaries expenditure account is needed for each fund that includes staff costs. This applies to all categories of income and expenditure. Also, if the charity has several restricted funds, it cannot just split the income and expenditure into two columns for 'unrestricted' and 'restricted'; it must be possible to track each fund separately through the books. For more details on accounting for multiple funds, see chapter 5 of *The charity treasurer's handbook*.

A charity with several funds must ensure that costs are properly shared between funds. Most charities, like other voluntary organisations, now try to use the principles of **full cost recovery** so that the full costs of each project (including organisational overheads) are properly allocated to the funds concerned. However, all expenses charged to a fund must meet any restrictions made by the funder or donor.

Fund accounting in non-charitable organisations

The principle of fund accounting relates to the notion of trust law, where funds are given 'on trust' to an organisation for specific purposes. It is only in charities that strict regulations apply. However, sometimes a non-charitable organisation will receive a grant where the funder imposes restrictions, which effectively creates a trust relationship, and so some voluntarily choose to follow the same principles of fund accounting as used by charities (even, in some cases, producing accounts in the Charities SORP format, see page 214) as a means of demonstrating accountability to funders.

Annual accounts

The **Companies Act 2006** governs the requirements for preparing charitable and non-charitable companies' annual accounts and the committee's report on the accounts; IPSs are governed by the **Friendly and Industrial and Provident Societies Act 1968**, and non-company charities (including CIOs) by the **Charities Act 1993**. For further Charity Commission guidance on charity accounting see *Charity reporting and accounting: The essentials April 2008* (CC 15a).

For more on the specific requirements, and examples of accounts in each format, see chapter 7 of *The charity treasurer's handbook*.

Receipts and payments accounts

Unincorporated charities whose income does not exceed £100,000 (£250,000) may produce their final accounts on a **receipts and payments (R&P)** basis. In England and Wales there are no specific rules on what is required, except that there must always be two financial reports:

- a **receipts and payments account** showing monies received and paid out during the year under suitable headings (and broken down by funds if the charity has more than one fund); and
- a **statement of assets and liabilities (SOAL)**.

R&P accounts are simpler to produce, because they only show money received and paid out during the year; they do not include income due but not yet received or expenditure committed but not paid out. For this reason, care is always needed in interpreting such accounts. However, even smaller charities using the R&P basis must still keep records of income due or payments not yet made, so these can be shown as debtors and creditors on the SOAL.

The Charity Commission publication *Receipts and payments accounts pack* (CC16) gives more details and, if desired, a charity can produce R&P accounts simply by completing the forms in this pack.

Note that R&P accounts are not permitted for charitable companies or for IPS charities.

Charities SORP and accruals accounts

For **charities with annual income over £100,000 (£250,000), non-company charities that use accruals accounting** (whatever their income), **charitable companies** and **IPS charities,** the requirements for accounts and annual reports are laid down in *Accounting and reporting by charities: Statement of recommended practice* (usually referred to as the **Charities SORP** or **SORP 2005** for the latest version). Although using SORP is not a legal requirement, it is backed by the **Charities (Accounts and Reports) Regulations 2008,** which refer to the SORP on many occasions, and the Charity Commission expects charities to comply.

Any significant divergence from SORP's recommendations must be explained in the accounts, although a few simplifications are allowed for charities below the audit threshold (that is, with income not over £500,000 and assets not over £2.8 (£3.26) million).

SORP 2005 is available from www.charitycommission.gov.uk (though it runs to 138 pages); printed copies can be purchased from CCH Publications (020 8547 3333). SORP 2005 was reissued in 2008 with notes on the latest legal changes, but the SORP itself has not changed, so notes to a charity's accounts should still refer to SORP 2005.

Accounts prepared to comply with SORP comprise:

- a **statement of financial activities (SOFA)** – this is similar to an income and expenditure account, but divided into columns for the different types of funds, and there are rules about the various headings which must be used
- a **balance sheet** – showing amounts for all the assets and liabilities as at the last day of the year, balanced to the total of all the funds
- extensive **notes to the accounts** – such as accounting policies, explanation of the different funds and any transactions with trustees or their relatives (including expenses). The notes also give a breakdown for many of the figures on the SOFA and balance sheet.

However, the SORP framework is not just about presentation: all the figures must be calculated on the **accruals basis** – the R&P basis is not permitted. This means that figures will show **accrued income** for the year – that is, the total income the charity has earned (including amounts promised but not received) – and the total **accrued expenses** for the year (including relevant expenditure which may not have been paid for by year end). Amounts paid or received which relate to a different year are excluded, such as paying a bill included as a creditor in the previous year's accounts. In accruals accounts, the balance of a fund shows the total resources belonging to that fund, which could comprise fixed assets, debtors and creditors, not just cash.

The layout of the SOFA and balance sheet and the content of the notes are covered in the regulations and the SORP.

Companies

All companies, whether charitable or non-charitable, must under company law prepare a set of accounts. Companies set up on a not for profit basis must prepare an **income and expenditure (I&E)** account, a **balance sheet** and **notes to the accounts**. But in most cases the SOFA required under the Charities SORP covers more than is needed for an I&E account, so a separate I&E account is not usually needed. A company's report and accounts must be submitted to Companies House within nine months of the end of the financial year (note that this is a month less than the time limit under charity law).

Small and medium companies (see below) can submit abbreviated accounts, although this is rarely helpful for charities, since full accounts complying with the Charities SORP must be produced for the Charity Commission, and funders are rarely satisfied with abbreviated accounts. However, some of the other concessions for smaller companies can be useful.

Small companies

To be a small company, at least two of the following conditions must be met:

- annual turnover (that is, income or expenditure) must be £6.5 million or less
- the balance sheet total must be £3.26 million or less
- the average number of employees must be 50 or fewer.

These tests must be satisfied for both the current year and the two preceding years. The figure for employees is determined by taking the average monthly number of employees (including full-time, part-time and casual employees).

Small companies are exempt from complying with the full range of accounting standards approved by the Accounting Standards Board, such as Financial Reporting Standards (FRSs), which normally apply to all companies. Instead they can choose to follow an all-in-one *Financial Reporting Standard for Smaller*

Entities (FRSSE). So, for small charitable companies, there are only two standards to consider – the FRSSE and the Charities SORP.

Small companies are exempt from audit under company law, but if they are charities they will need an audit or independent examination under charity law (see *Audit or examination*, page 216) if their income is more than £10,000 (£25,000).

Medium companies

To be a medium company, at least two of the following conditions must be met:

- annual turnover must be £25.9 million or less
- the balance sheet total must be £12.9 million or less
- the average number of employees must be 250 or fewer.

Medium companies are also allowed some exceptions from the full requirements of the Companies Act 2006 in terms of the preparation of their accounts and reports. However, their accounts will always require an audit (whether or not they are charities).

Filing of accounts by charitable companies

Charitable companies whose income is over £10,000 (£25,000) must submit accounts to the Charity Commission as well as to Companies House. Those whose income is £10,000 (£25,000) or under must submit accounts to Companies House, but to the Charity Commission only if requested.

Industrial and provident societies (IPSs)

IPSs must prepare an annual **revenue account** and **balance sheet**. The revenue account can cover the whole society, or there can be two or more revenue accounts dealing with specific aspects of the society's work. The balance sheet must cover the whole society. The accounts and balance sheet must be submitted to the Financial Services Authority (FSA), which charges a fee when accounts are filed.

At present, IPS charities are exempt charities (see chapter 1), and so not registered with the Charity Commission, but this will change under the Charities Act 2006 (starting with those over £100,000 income – probably some time in 2009). Once they become registered charities, IPSs will need to file accounts with both the FSA and the Charity Commission. However, many IPS charities may find it easier to take advantage of the provisions in the Charities Act 2006 and convert to a CIO, which will remove the need to report to the FSA.

Non-company charities (including CIOs*)

Income £100,000 or less (£250,000)

Non-company charities with a gross annual income of £100,000 (£250,000) or less may prepare accounts on an R&P basis (see *Receipts and payments accounts*, page 213). Unless the income is £10,000 (£25,000) or less, the accounts must be **independently examined** (see page 217) and they must still prepare a trustees' annual report to accompany the accounts (see page 218).

However, if a charity of this size chooses to prepare accruals accounts, they must follow the requirements of the Charities SORP (apart from the provisions which only apply to charities over the audit threshold) (see below).

It is possible that the final regulations could impose additional accounting requirements on CIOs beyond those mentioned here.

Income over £100,000 (£250,000)

Non-company charities with a gross annual income over £100,000 (£250,000) must prepare a full statement of accounts for each financial year on the accruals basis, in accordance with the **Charities (Accounts and Reports) Regulations 2008** and complying with the Charities SORP (see *Charities SORP and accruals accounts*, page 214).

Some simplifications to the SORP 2005 requirements are allowed provided the charity is not subject to a statutory audit (that is, its income does not exceed £500,000 and the total assets on the balance sheet do not exceed £2.8 (£3.26) million). These include:

- the breakdown of income and expenditure on the SOFA does not have to follow the functional breakdown prescribed in the SORP – charities below the audit threshold can use those headings they feel are most appropriate
- the notes to the accounts do not have to disclose departures from the SORP.

Audit or examination of accounts

All charities are holding funds on trust, given (or raised through trading) to support charitable purposes. This means that their accounts must normally be subject to independent scrutiny, either an audit or (for small/medium charities) an independent examination. The auditor's or independent examiner's report must be attached to and circulated with all copies of the accounts. Only the smallest charities – those with income not over £10,000 (£25,000) – are exempt from this requirement. However, much higher audit thresholds apply to non-charitable organisations (including CICs) as the special trust relationship which applies to charities is not applicable.

Legal requirements are given on pages 217–218; the process of working with an auditor or independent examiner is described in *Working with auditors and examiners*, page 220. The details given are the minimum scrutiny requirements by law; some charities may need to do more – for example, their constitution or funder may require an audit. However, if a charity is below the audit threshold (£500,000 income in most cases) it is always worth asking funders whether they would be willing to accept independently examined accounts, as this is still a thorough form of scrutiny required by law. Also, the Charity Commission has indicated that trustees may interpret 'audit' sensibly (that is, treat it as including an independent examination) if constitutions were prepared before 1992 and not subsequently amended, as long as the term does not specifically imply a professional audit.

Non-charitable companies (including CICs)

Non-charitable companies that fall outside the definition of a 'small company' (see page 215) must have a full audit by a registered auditor. 'Registered auditor' means a firm eligible to act as auditors under the Companies Act 2006. Such firms will always be regulated by the Institute of Chartered Accountants in England and Wales, the Chartered Association of Certified Accountants or the Institutes of Chartered Accountants in Scotland or in Ireland. However, note that not all accountants who are members of these Institutes will be registered auditors.

Many non-charitable companies will fall within the small company threshold and will not need an audit. However, the accounts must comply with company law and be signed by the directors. But an audit is necessary if, for example, it is required in the constitution or by its members or funders. In these circumstances, it must be an audit under company law by a registered auditor.

Charities – unincorporated, CIOs, companies

For accounting years following 1 April 2008, the scrutiny requirements are virtually the same for company and non-company charities. There are essentially four possible levels of scrutiny, and the rules are slightly different according to the total value of assets on the balance sheet.

Not more than £2.8 (£3.26) million assets

■ For charities with up to (and including) £10,000 (£25,000) income, no independent scrutiny is required. However, trustees must still approve the accounts (and it is always good practice for a trustee other than the treasurer to conduct independent checks before the trustees as a whole agree to sign).
■ For charities whose income is between £10,000 (£25,000) and £250,000 the

accounts must have an independent scrutiny report, but this can be an **independent examiner's report** rather than a full audit (see *Independent examination* below). At this level, the independent examiner does not have to hold any specified qualifications, but must have a good understanding of charity accounting.
■ For charities from £250,000 up to £500,000 income, an independent examination is still permitted, but the independent examiner must be professionally qualified (see *Independent examination* below).
■ For charities with over £500,000 income, a full audit by a registered auditor is needed. If the charity is a company, this will still be an audit under the Charities Act unless the company is outside the 'small' definition (see page 215), in which case a Companies Act audit is needed.

More than £2.8 (£3.26) million assets

■ The rules are the same as above, except that a full audit by a registered auditor is needed if the income exceeds £100,000 (£250,000) (rather than £500,000).

All these financial limits under charity law now apply purely to the total income (or total assets) for the current year – there is no need to consider previous years, nor to consider expenditure if it is larger than income. Also note that until the thresholds are amended, the asset limit remains £2.8 million under charity law (even though it is now increased to £3.26 million under company law in the definition of a 'small company').

For the definition of total income, and for Charity Commission guidance on the selection of independent examiners and their duties, see the Commission's publication *Independent examination of charity accounts* (CC31).

Independent examination

An independent examination covers slightly less than a full audit, but it is still a demanding process laid down in the **Charities (Accounts and Reports) Regulations 2008** and the Directions of the Charity Commission, which appear in CC31.

Where a professionally qualified independent examiner is needed – that is, for charities with over £250,000 and up to £500,000 income and with not more than £2.8 (£3.26) million assets – the examiner must be a member of one of the professional bodies listed in CC31.

The Association of Charity Independent Examiners (ACIE) was established specifically to provide advice, training and qualifications for independent examiners (see www.acie.org.uk). ACIE can help charities find an independent examiner, and offers courses for those wishing to train to become independent examiners.

Industrial and provident societies

For IPSs a slightly older scrutiny regime still exists. This is quite complex and may well be subject to further amendment – IPSs should always use accountants who are familiar with the specific requirements of IPS law.

For a non-charitable IPS, an audit is generally only compulsory if it has more than £2.8 million assets or £5.6 million turnover (unlike under company law, an audit is triggered if *either* of these is exceeded, and there is no test based on numbers of employees). However, this exemption does not apply to credit unions, which must always have an audit.

An audit is required for a charitable IPS if the turnover exceeds £250,000 (or, as above, if the assets exceed £2.8 (£3.26) million).

In either case, where the IPS is below the relevant audit threshold, a **reporting accountant's report** is needed if the turnover is above £90,000. The reporting accountant must be eligible to be an auditor under IPS law – although the duties are much less onerous than those of a charity independent examiner.

Where an IPS is not required by law to have an audit, members must vote each year in a general meeting to agree that an audit is not needed (otherwise, an audit must still take place).

All the financial thresholds mentioned apply to the current *or* previous year – so a charitable IPS must have turnover not exceeding £250,000 in the year concerned *and* in the previous year if it is to escape an audit.

Where an audit is needed, it is an audit under the **Industrial and Provident Societies Act 1968** (as amended). Normally the auditor must be qualified to act under the provisions of the Companies Act. It is possible, in principle, to appoint two individuals to act as auditors provided they are properly independent, though the Financial Services Authority as the regulator of IPSs can require a society to use a qualified auditor.

Excepted and exempt charities

Charities excepted from registration (see chapter 1) are subject to the same scrutiny rules (independent examination or audit) as registered charities.

Under the **Charities Act 2006**, from autumn 2009 most exempt charities (see chapter 1) will lose their exempt status unless they are subject to a 'principal regulator' (such as universities, registered social landlords), in which case audit requirements will be as determined by their own regulators. Other exempt charities (such as IPSs) will initially become excepted charities and will thus follow the normal scrutiny rules for charities of the size concerned.

Trustees' annual reports

In general, any set of charity accounts should be accompanied by a **trustees' annual report (TAR)**, which gives certain legal information about the charity, and explains its work during the year. The Charities SORP places great emphasis on the links between the accounts and the TAR. Registered charities must send the TAR to the Charity Commission, with the annual accounts (and the report of the auditor or independent examiner where applicable) within ten months of the end of the financial year (although the Commission encourages charities to file well before the deadline).

The TAR is not a legal requirement for excepted charities, but it is strongly recommended in order to give a clear picture of the organisation's work.

Charities (other than CIOs) whose income is £10,000 (£25,000) or below do not have to send the TAR and accounts to the Commission, but they must still prepare these documents and make them available to anyone on request. All CIOs, whatever their income, must send the TAR and accounts to the Commission.

A TAR is not necessarily a glossy publicity document; it is a straightforward report that must include certain information. If a charity wishes to produce a publicity document that may not contain all the information required in a TAR, it is better to call it an 'annual review'. However, a publicity document *can* serve as the legally required report if it includes all necessary information; in many cases it requires less work to produce one document that, in addition to meeting the legal requirements for the TAR, provides other information such as photos, comments from service users or reports on particular projects.

The legal requirements for the contents of the TAR are set out in the **Charities (Accounts and Reports) Regulations 2008**, and some are further explained in the Charities SORP. Different requirements apply to charities above and below the statutory audit threshold (see definitions on page 216).

A TAR is usually clearest if it has three sections:

- **factual information** – such as official names, registration numbers and trustees
- **narrative information** – about the work of the charity in relation to its objects
- **policies section** – stating the trustees' policy on key issues.

The following is a checklist of the minimum requirements under the 2008 Regulations. Bear in mind that a report that only meets the minimum legal requirements may do little to impress funders or others who ask to see the annual report and accounts. So always consider the prospective audience – it is always possible to include more than the legal minimum.

Factual section

- Official name of the charity (and any working names)
- Registered charity number (if registered) and company number (if applicable)
- Official address of the charity*
- Particulars of the constitution (including date of last amendment)
- Description of the charity's objects (usually this is easily obtained from the constitution)
- Names* of the charity trustees as at the date of approving the report
- Names* of all other trustees who served for any part of the financial year
- Any external persons* or bodies entitled to appoint trustees to the charity
- Names* of holding trustees at date of approval
- Any other holding trustees* during year.

If disclosing trustees' names or an official address would put anyone in personal danger, the charity can apply to the Charity Commission for permission to omit them.

Narrative section (public benefit report)

- Statement that the trustees have considered Charity Commission guidance on public benefit
- Charities below the audit threshold: a brief review of the main activities undertaken during the year in terms of public benefit achieved
- Charities over the audit threshold: review of significant activities undertaken during the year in terms of public benefit achieved, including the trustees' aims for the year, progress against the aims, contribution of volunteers and principal funding sources.

Policies section

- Policy on level of reserves
- Action being taken on any funds in deficit.

Extras needed for charities over the audit threshold

- Organisational structure
- Risk assessment
- Policy on trustee induction and training
- Investment policy and review of investment performance
- Grant making policy.

Other information is often included, such as a note of the charity's bankers and professional advisers, a statement of trustees' responsibilities and details of the appointment (or reappointment) of the auditor or independent examiner.

The trustees as a whole must approve the TAR before it is circulated; typically the following is added at the end: 'This report was approved by the trustees on [date] and is signed on their behalf by . . .'. In principle a single trustee could sign, but if two trustees are normally required to sign cheques and financial documents, it is clearer if the TAR is signed by at least two trustees. In a charitable company, a director (trustee) or the company secretary (if appointed) must sign the directors' report (which is often combined with the TAR).

Companies

A TAR prepared as above will also cover most of the requirements of a **directors' report** under company law. However, if the company is small (see definition on page 215) and has not had an audit under company law, the directors' report must include a clear statement above the signature that it is prepared in accordance with the provisions for small companies.

If a company (whether charitable or not) is subject to an audit under the **Companies Act 2006**, statements must be made confirming that the directors have made available all relevant information to the auditors.

CICs must also provide a **community interest report** to the CIC Regulator, although the information is often included within the directors' report.

Working with auditors and examiners

In most cases, the TAR and the accounts are prepared as a single document. Auditors and independent examiners can advise on the legal requirements for TARs and directors' reports, and may be willing to help in their preparation. However, people who have working knowledge of the charity must write the body of the TAR.

Risk management

Under the **Charities (Accounts and Reports) Regulations 2008**, the TAR for charities over the audit threshold must include a risk management statement, confirming that the trustees have identified and reviewed the major risks to which the charity may be exposed, and have set up systems to mitigate those risks. The Charity Commission encourages smaller charities to do the same.

Possible financial risks include accuracy of financial information, adequacy of reserves and cash flow, diversity of income sources and investment management. There are also a number of other areas of risk, often classified into governance, operational, external and compliance with law and regulation. For more details on identifying, reporting and managing risk see *Charities and risk management*, published by the Charity Commission, available from www.charitycommission.gov.uk.

Public access to accounts

Anyone can ask any charity for a copy of its most recent accounts and report. These must be provided within two months of a written request. The charity can charge a reasonable fee. However, the Charity Commission now publishes all accounts and reports for registered charities over £25,000 income online, so nowadays it is more common for people to access the accounts this way.

Anyone can obtain the latest report and accounts of any company electronically from Companies House for a fee of just £1. IPSs must display the latest accounts (or at least the balance sheet and audit report where applicable) conspicuously on their premises (at the registered office).

Unincorporated non-charitable voluntary organisations are not generally required to publish accounts, so their financial affairs can be kept confidential to members. However, if they have trading activities, they must prepare accounts, as they will need to make a corporation tax return to HM Revenue & Customs (HMRC).

Legal requirements – PAYE

Organisations employing staff must keep extensive records to comply with employment law (see chapter 4), and the basic information in a contract of employment or statement of employment particulars, such as rates of remuneration and hours worked, forms part of the financial records.

Most organisations must also register with HMRC and operate a Pay as You Earn (PAYE) scheme to deduct income tax and employee's national insurance (NI) contributions from staff wages or salaries, and to pay employer's NI. Any organisation operating PAYE must also be able to handle statutory sick pay and statutory maternity, paternity and adoption pay payments, and student loan repayments. All PAYE records form part of an organisation's financial records, so they need to be available at year end to the auditor or independent examiner, and HMRC also has a right to inspect them.

See chapter 4 for more on PAYE. It is advisable (and, for charities, essential) to keep PAYE records for at least six years.

Legal requirements – value added tax

Contrary to popular belief, the law on value added tax (VAT) applies to charities in much the same way as to any other organisation. However, there are a few specific concessions applicable to charities, as outlined in the following paragraphs (note that in general these do not extend to non-charitable voluntary organisations).

There are two quite separate issues to consider:

- how an organisation is affected by the VAT on goods and services purchased (known as **input VAT**)
- whether an organisation needs to charge VAT on goods and services it provides (**output VAT**).

Output VAT only arises if an organisation has to be registered for VAT (see below), but *all* organisations are affected by input VAT.

An organisation whose turnover from sources other than grants, donations, investments and other proceeds defined as 'non-business' under VAT law exceeds the compulsory registration threshold (£67,000 in 2008/09) must register for VAT. Services classed as 'VAT exempt' do not count towards the threshold; this includes much work undertaken by charities that falls within the VAT definitions of education or welfare services.

When considering VAT implications, it is vital to distinguish between grant income and contract income. A genuine grant (even if subject to detailed restrictions on how the money can be used) is a gift, and is not subject to VAT. But a contract is an agreement for the supply of services (even if the services are charitable) and the relevant contract income counts towards the VAT threshold. Proceeds from selling goods or services for fundraising purposes (such as in charity shops or coffee shops) are treated as trading income and thus count towards the VAT threshold. (However, sales at clearly identified fundraising events, such as sponsored swims, are VAT exempt.)

Once registered, you must charge VAT at the appropriate rate on goods and services, and keep detailed records complying with VAT law. However, you will then be able to recover the input VAT paid when purchasing related VAT-taxable goods and services.

There are currently three rates of VAT: the **standard rate** of 17.5% (reduced to 15% until 31 December 2009), the **lower rate** of 5% (applicable, for example, to home and charity energy bills, and to contraceptive and sanitary products) and the **zero rate** of 0%, which applies, for example, to sales of books, publications, children's clothes, donated goods (such as in charity shops) and cold food not consumed on the premises. (See VAT publications, available from www.hmrc.gov.uk, for detailed definitions.) Even the zero rate counts as a rate of VAT, and items sold at 0% VAT still count towards the VAT turnover.

The impact of this depends very much on who is paying for an organisation's services. If it is mainly working under contract for a local authority, the local authority will generally be able to reclaim the VAT amounts added on the organisation's invoices, and by becoming VAT registered, the organisation will be able to reclaim its input VAT costs. So in this case the organisation will be better off. But an organisation which is mainly selling services to individuals or to purchasers who cannot reclaim the VAT will find it hard to increase prices by 15% (17.5% from 1 January 2010) and may therefore have to absorb some of the output VAT by lowering the price before VAT.

If services are **VAT exempt,** you don't have to charge VAT on goods and services sold (output VAT), but cannot reclaim VAT on the corresponding inputs. So VAT exempt supplies are very different from zero-rated supplies. For example, an organisation whose main income is selling publications will be able to reclaim most or all of its input VAT, because the publications will be sold at 0% VAT, but a charity whose main income is through welfare services (which are VAT exempt) will not be able to recover any input VAT.

Overall, you need to distinguish five kinds of income: VATable trading income (at 15% (17.5% from 1 January 2010), 5% or 0%), trading income which is VAT exempt, and non-trading income (such as grants, donations and interest).

An organisation must register for VAT if:

- at the end of any month, the value of taxable supplies (VATable income) in the past 12 months has exceeded the annual threshold, or

- at any time, there are reasonable grounds for believing that the value of taxable supplies in the next 30 days will exceed the annual threshold (this will only apply to a large organisation launching a major new service).

If either of these applies, you have one month in which to register, by completing registration form **VAT1** (available from the National Advice Service or www.hmrc.gov.uk). HMRC will stipulate a date from which an organisation is registered and provide a VAT number. It is unlawful to charge VAT before being registered. Once registered, you must charge VAT on all relevant sales or other VATable income sources (remember that any kind of contract income will count as trading income, even if the funder does not require invoices). Invoices, order forms or similar documents showing VAT separately on prices must include the VAT registration number (in addition to the company number and registered charity number if applicable).

For further details see *Should I be registered for VAT?* (**VAT700/1**), available from HMRC's National Advice Service (0845 010 9000) or www.hmrc.gov.uk.

You need to make a quarterly VAT return to HMRC with details of the sales and purchases for the relevant quarter, and the corresponding amounts of output and input VAT. The output VAT charged over the quarter less the input VAT reclaimed is paid over to HMRC. Unless an organisation applies to operate the VAT cash accounting system (where VAT amounts are calculated at date of payment, rather than date of invoice) these calculations are based on the invoice dates (accruals accounting, see page 214) rather than on the actual payment dates.

Unfortunately, most charities that need to register for VAT find they have some VATable income, combined with other income sources which are VAT exempt or non-trading (outside the scope of VAT). This will also apply to non-charitable organisations if they have significant grant income (unrelated to their business activities) as well as trading income. In such cases, they are described as **partially exempt** for VAT purposes and can only reclaim a proportion of their input VAT. It is vital to be aware of this, as many VAT-registered charities can only reclaim a small proportion of their input VAT, so in these cases budgets must continue to allow for the input VAT costs when making purchases. The partial exemption calculations in such cases can be quite complex and considerable effort may be needed to agree a reasonable method with HMRC.

There are substantial penalties for failing to register for VAT or registering late. It is therefore essential to be fully aware of which of your supplies are subject to VAT and to keep a regular check on the level of turnover for those supplies to see whether you will reach the annual threshold. This must be monitored monthly (taking total sales for the last 12 months, which may span two accounting years). But remember that income from grants, donations, legacies and VAT-exempt services does not count towards the threshold.

An organisation that has at least some VATable trading income can register for VAT voluntarily, even if the VATable income is below the threshold. Although you would have to charge VAT on some goods or services provided, you can recover VAT on some goods or services purchased, and this may result in an overall saving. It is essential to take professional advice before considering voluntary registration.

VAT is a complicated subject, particularly for charities, and cannot be covered in full in this book. Particularly complex issues can arise with building projects. A broader discussion is available in chapter 11 of *The charity treasurer's handbook* and a more in-depth explanation appears in *A practical guide to VAT for charities and voluntary organisations* by Kate Sayer and Alastair Hardman (Directory of Social Change). For further details contact your accountant or auditor, or an adviser experienced in charity VAT issues. Assistance with straightforward queries is also available from the HMRC Charities helpline (0845 302 0203).

Legal requirements – income tax and corporation tax

Corporation tax is a tax on the profit of associations and incorporated bodies (including CIOs); income tax (in this context) is a tax on the income of trusts. Grants and donations are not subject to income or corporation tax.

Charities

Charities are frequently exempt from corporation tax or income tax on their trading activities, but a clear distinction must be made between:

- **primary purpose trading income** – where the goods or services are sold directly as part of the charity's work in carrying out its objects (such as an educational charity charging fees for training courses), and
- **trading for fundraising purposes** – where, although the proceeds will support the charity, the actual provision of goods or services is not part of the charitable work (such as sales of mugs, T-shirts or tickets for fundraising events, or consultancy income for work not linked to the charity's beneficiaries).

Primary purpose trading income is always exempt from corporation tax (or income tax) and there is no need to set up a subsidiary company to handle such trading activities.

Trading for fundraising purposes is, however, potentially taxable if a charity makes a profit. However, there are a number of exemptions including:

- **trading by the beneficiaries** (so, for example, if a charity's objects are to provide therapeutic work for people with particular needs, no tax is payable on profits from the sales of the goods made by the beneficiaries)
- **fundraising events** (if clearly advertised as such, and not in competition with commercial traders)

223

- **small-scale trades** of any kind, provided the total annual turnover from such activities does not exceed £5,000 or 25% of the charity's total income if larger (subject to a maximum of £50,000 of non-charitable trading where the charity's income is over £200,000).

Where a charity plans to undertake substantial trading for fundraising purposes that falls outside these limits – for example, a commercial café or restaurant – it is possible to establish a separate non-charitable trading subsidiary company which undertakes the activity and then donates its profit back to the charity under Gift Aid. This means the trade can be undertaken in a legal and tax efficient manner.

However, there are many complications in running a trading subsidiary company alongside a charity, and it is easy to end up with the charity subsidising a non-charitable body, which is in breach of charity law. With the exemptions above, trading subsidiaries are nowadays only needed where charities wish to undertake very substantial forms of non-charitable trading. For further details about trading subsidiaries see *Using a separate trading company*, in chapter 1.

Non-charitable organisations

It is vital to remember than the concessions above only apply to charities; non-charitable organisations that have trading activities and/or investment income will, in general, pay tax in the same way as businesses. There are no special concessions for CICs.

In 2009/10 the rate of corporation tax is 21% on annual profits up to £300,000 (rising to 28% on the largest businesses), so a non-charitable organisation that makes a profit on its activities must set aside funds to pay this. It is the responsibility of the committee to make a corporation tax return to HMRC.

However, grants and donations do not count as trading income. Also, there is an important exemption for the profits of 'mutual trading',

where members of an organisation are trading with one another. So an organisation that organises events for members will not generally have to pay taxes on any profits from such events if only the organisation's members participate.

Gift Aid

Charities that reclaim tax on Gift Aid donations (see chapter 9) must keep sufficient records to show that their tax reclaims are accurate. This includes keeping individual Gift Aid **declarations** for as long as the donor is supporting the charity, and an audit trail for the last six years, allowing gifts to be traced back to the donor concerned. HMRC has the power to waive small numbers of errors, and charities should be given the opportunity to correct errors before penalties are raised; however, where there are problems with Gift Aid records that fall outside these concessions a charity can be required to repay tax which has been reclaimed for up to six years.

It is important that Gift Aid claims are made promptly to HMRC. From 2008/09 to 2010/11 a Gift Aid supplement is paid in addition to tax reclaimed (to compensate charities for the reduction in the basic rate of income tax from 22% to 20%) but the supplement is only paid for claims made within two years of the end of the tax year concerned.

Further information is available from HMRC Charities (0845 302 0203 or www.hmrc.gov.uk/charities).

Duties of the committee – financial procedures and responsibilities

All committee members of any type of organisation have a duty to see that the organisation is properly managed and that funds are spent correctly. Under charity law trustees must ensure that funds are being spent appropriately for charitable purposes within the charity's objects and powers. Although the treasurer oversees the finances on behalf of the committee, the trustees have overall responsibility for the charity's money and property and cannot delegate their responsibility. Trustees who fail to carry out their duty properly may be in breach of trust (see chapter 1) and personally liable for any losses caused.

In a company, committee members will be directors and have extensive legal responsibilities under the **Companies Act 2006**. In a charitable company, it is best to refer to the committee members as 'directors/ trustees' so everyone is aware of the dual responsibilities under company law and charity law. IPS committee members have responsibilities under the **Friendly and Industrial and Provident Societies Act 1968** (as amended).

The committee's main financial responsibilities are to:

- comply with legal requirements – these will vary according to the organisation's legal structure and whether it is charitable, but the basic principles are the same for all
- approve and monitor budgets
- ensure proper financial records are kept
- ensure proper control is exercised over income and expenditure
- oversee fundraising policy and activities, and trading activities
- ensure tax affairs, including VAT if applicable, are managed properly
- ensure the organisation's funds are used in accordance with its constitution, committee decisions and funders' conditions
- ensure proper financial reports are provided to the committee, funders and others who have a right to see them
- ensure annual accounts and reports, audited or independently examined if required, are produced.

The committee members of any organisation must ensure that the treasurer and finance staff carry out their jobs properly. This means being satisfied that the treasurer and all staff who handle money, whether paid or voluntary, are honest and competent.

There are several ways in which the committee can minimise risks. For example, it can:

- make sure that anyone who stands for election as treasurer has experience of handling money and accounts
- arrange additional training for the treasurer if necessary
- appoint a finance subcommittee to oversee day-to-day management of finances and regularly examine the accounts
- require the treasurer to make regular financial reports to the committee
- have careful procedures for handling cash, involving at least two people
- require two signatures on cheques and ensure that blank cheques are never signed, for any reason (no cheque should ever be signed without documentation, for example an invoice, explaining the expense)
- ensure that the treasurer, manager or other authorised person authorises all expenses, that no one can authorise expenses paid to themselves, and that all expenses are paid by cheque rather than in cash
- ensure that no one can sign a cheque to themselves or to a close relative
- employ a bookkeeper to carry out day-to-day transactions.

Charities and risk management, available from www.charitycommission.gov.uk, includes a list of potential financial risks, with their potential impact and steps to mitigate the risk.

Specific duties of the treasurer

In a small organisation, the treasurer may deal with all aspects of financial management, including keeping records. Larger organisations with paid staff may delegate day-to-day financial management to a finance worker who would report to the treasurer or senior staff member.

However, final responsibility for financial matters always rests with the committee as a whole.

The treasurer's responsibilities may include the following:

- general financial oversight
- managing income, including funding, contracts, fundraising and sales, in particular ensuring that all income due to the organisation is invoiced where applicable or reminders are sent to donors, and that Gift Aid tax claims on donations are made
- ensuring payments are made (subject to proper authorisation)
- payment of wages or salaries (including operation of PAYE if needed; see *PAYE*, page 221 and in chapter 4)
- budgeting and associated monitoring of income and expenditure
- banking, bookkeeping and record keeping
- control of fixed assets and stock
- investments
- insurances (see chapter 7)
- premises, if there is no premises subcommittee (see chapter 6).
- managing the organisation's different funds (see *Charity funds*, page 213), transfers and recharges between funds, advising when new funds need to be established, and making arrangements when funds are closed (including any negotiations with funders on balances remaining in restricted funds)
- VAT and other tax issues (see pages 221 and 223)
- preparing annual accounts at year end (or liaising with external accountants to undertake this) and arranging for audit or independent examination (see *Annual accounts*, page 213).

Although it is usually appropriate for the treasurer to take the lead on these tasks, only in the very smallest organisations will the treasurer personally do all the work; in larger organisations much will be delegated to staff members. Even if there are no paid staff it is good practice to share the financial responsibilities between several committee members: for example, one person may take the lead on fundraising records (including Gift Aid if applicable) and another on premises, leaving the treasurer to manage the organisation's books and the financial policies as a whole.

Never rely on one person alone to understand the organisation's finances. This could expose it to risks of fraud, or create terrible difficulties if a treasurer is suddenly incapacitated. Any relationships with auditors or independent examiners should involve the committee as a whole (sometimes a dishonest treasurer has found a 'friend' to examine the accounts, and has thus kept the committee unaware of funds going astray). It is also very dangerous, in organisations with paid staff, if the committee relies entirely on, for example, a finance officer, and does not really understand the finances itself; there is no way it can exercise proper control and oversight or take effective financial decisions.

Financial systems and procedures

For any organisation to operate effectively, proper financial procedures are needed, linked to appropriate systems such as the bookkeeping system. All procedures (or at least the high-level procedures in a large organisation) need to be approved by the management committee. But there is no point in preparing procedures which are ignored: the committee members need to establish ways of monitoring them so they will know if key procedures are not being followed. However, few organisations will be able to devise procedures for every eventuality, so flexibility is needed, otherwise the organisation may end up stagnating and be unable to respond to new opportunities. An arrangement where two committee members can agree urgent variations to procedures may be helpful.

Some common areas where procedures are needed are outlined below.

Banking, bookkeeping and record keeping

- Deciding which banks or other financial institutions the organisation should use, the type of bank accounts it should have and the appointment of signatories (see *Bank accounts*, page 230).

- Arrangements for approval of different kinds of expenditure (different approaches are needed for straightforward project expenses which fall within a previously agreed budget and the approval of unplanned expenditure on a speculative fundraising event).
- Systems for counting, banking and recording the cash when an organisation needs to take cash payments (such as at fundraising events or cash donations). The procedures should require that all cash remains in sight of at least two people until it is recorded.
- Where cash payments are made, procedures for a petty cash system (however, the risks of error, fraud and burglary are considerable and a prompt system for reimbursing staff and volunteer expenses may make it unnecessary to hold petty cash). An insurance company may require certain precautions for cash insured (for example, keeping it in a safe), or you may wish to take out insurance against theft by employees (see *Fidelity or theft by employee insurance,* in chapter 7). Never keep more cash than is necessary on the premises; pay any surplus into the bank as soon as possible. Only authorised people should have keys to the safe, with a duplicate copy kept at the bank. Remember that staff may be more vulnerable to attack if there is cash on the premises.
- Procedures should specify how often bookkeeping systems (whether manual or computerised) are to be updated, what checks are to be done (such as bank reconciliation) and, with a computer system, what reports are to be printed (see *Record keeping*, page 231).
- Ensuring membership records are kept and subscriptions collected.
- Ensuring other money due is collected and that there are procedures for non-payment which are carried out if necessary.
- Payment of bills, including confirmation that the expenditure is agreed, and ensuring that proper documentation is retained.
- PAYE procedures.

- Ensuring that everyone handling money for the organisation keeps appropriate records and documentation.

Control of fixed assets and stock

- Ensuring that a fixed asset register is maintained for all items of furniture, equipment and vehicles which are to be kept on a long-term basis (the register should include date of purchase, supplier, value, model and serial number, date of disposal, and the depreciation policy if the organisation uses accruals accounting – see *Charities SORP and accruals accounts*, page 214).
- Establishing systems for stock control and reorders.
- Ensuring the organisation has all necessary insurances and keeps them up to date (see chapter 7).

Investments

- Setting investment policy: deciding on issues such as whether to aim for capital growth or income and the level of risk – this must always be a matter for the committee. In a charity, funds can only be invested in 'qualifying investments': that is, investments regarded as reasonably safe for holding other people's funds, such as with recognised banks on a listed stock exchange (for details see HMRC's guidance notes at www.hmrc.gov.uk/charities). Moreover, the trustees must take proper financial advice on any investments unless they have suitable expertise themselves
- arrangements are needed to ensure that no new investments can be made without the committee's formal approval. Any delegation to an investment manager must be clearly agreed, with proper arrangements for the committee to review investment decisions periodically
- it may be useful to have procedures that allow the treasurer or another individual to switch funds when needed without other authorisation: for example, to move funds between current and deposit accounts according to cash flow requirements

- arrangements for monitoring investments and reporting regularly to the committee. Normally this will include 'benchmarking': that is, comparing the interest received on bank accounts against published rates, or comparing the returns on equities against indexes such as the FTSE 250.

Budgets and cash flow

Budgets are important, but are not an end in themselves; their only value is if they help the committee and staff manage the organisation more effectively.

There is no legal requirement for any organisation to prepare budgets, but they are an important part of effective governance. Very few organisations can work effectively with no budgets at all.

The budget process

Clear procedures are needed when preparing budgets. In particular, it is vital to know the implications of agreeing a budget: is the document simply a list of targets the committee will monitor? Does it mean that all the expenditure limits are 'approved' and no further authorisation is needed for expenditure up to these limits? Or is the budget a proposal for a new project, which will form the basis of a submission to a funder?

Also, there is not much point in preparing a single budget for the whole organisation if there are significant restricted funds (see *Charity funds,* page 213). In such cases, separate budgets must be prepared for each fund, which becomes a considerable task. At this stage policy decisions must be made, such as how overheads are to be apportioned between funds, otherwise the budget decisions are meaningless.

Where a budget is agreed in advance (whether for a project, a fund or a whole organisation) it needs to cover both the anticipated income and the anticipated expenditure. Care is needed, particularly on the expenditure side, to ensure that all costs are included, including inflation if the budget covers more than a year.

Such a budget must be presented to the full committee for approval, although an initial discussion by a finance subcommittee can be helpful. Members must ensure they understand what is being presented and ask the right questions:

- do I understand where the income comes from?
- do I understand the headings used for expenditure?
- do the figures balance?
- are estimates and assumptions reasonably justified?

A balanced budget is one in which anticipated income equals anticipated expenditure. If anticipated income is greater than anticipated expenditure the excess may be shown as 'surplus transferred to reserves' to balance the budget. If the reverse is true, the difference will be shown as a deficit. If this is the case, the committee needs to know how the organisation will cover it. It is not appropriate to 'balance' a budget by saying the money will come from fundraising (or whatever) unless it is likely that the money really will be raised.

Using budgets for decision making

Normally the committee will receive regular reports of income and expenditure against budget; this is the most common form of **management accounts**. An important part of the role of a treasurer or finance officer is to provide such information.

However, when reviewing reports of actual figures against budget it is vital to consider both sides together: for example, if the income is 20% up on the anticipated budget this is not good news if there has been a 30% increase in anticipated expenditure. Also, there can be many problems with differences in timing, where income comes in either before or after the corresponding expenditure, and often budget reports only make sense if these are understood.

Also, where separate budgets are needed for each fund, a full report of actual income and expenditure against budgets for a whole organisation can be a huge document, and providing this kind of information can overwhelm the committee with figures rather than help them. However, reports of actual figures against budgets are not the only form of management accounts; often a summary of movements of all funds can be helpful (with one line for each fund), perhaps supported by a detailed budget statement for one or two key funds.

Budget and cash flow forecasts

In cases where cash flow is tight, the most important report for the committee is a cash flow projection for the next few months. Cash flow means just that – the flow of money (cash and cheques) into and out of the organisation. A cash flow forecast shows, usually on a monthly basis, when in the year payments are made and income is received. It is therefore a useful method for forewarning of a cash shortage.

Forecasts can also be prepared on an income and expenditure (accruals) basis rather than a cash flow basis. Often a budget forecast is produced which revises the organisation's anticipated income and expenditure by considering developments since the budget was drawn up and which helps the committee to make financial decisions. Ideally forecasts should be produced every quarter, and at the least every six months. They can also be built into the financial reports/management accounts (see page 213).

When examining forecasts, committee members should consider the following:
- does the budget for income or expenditure need to be adjusted, either upwards or downwards?
- what are the implications of any adjustments?
- do they take account of inflation or interest rate changes?

- does the organisation need to take steps to ensure that future budgets are more accurate?

Overdrafts and loans

If an organisation has a short-term cash flow problem, an arranged overdraft will ease the crisis, but constant overdrafts are not a good form of financial control. They are expensive, which can make the financial situation even worse, and the bank will probably want security, in the form of collateral (the organisation's assets) or personal guarantees from committee members. Overdrafts can also be called in at any time. An organisation which does not have a constitutional power to borrow may not be able to take out an overdraft.

For major long-term projects, organisations may sometimes take out significant loans. Charities may borrow money as long as the trustees are satisfied that it is in the interests of the charity to do so, and provided there is a constitutional power to permit this. For example, loans are often used to enable a charity to proceed with a major building project sooner than would otherwise be the case, or to invest in new skills and resources in order to launch new services. There are now several loan schemes designed for the voluntary sector including, at the time of writing, the government-backed Futurebuilders programme, which provides loan finance to assist third sector organisations to deliver public services (see www.futurebuilders-england.org.uk) and bodies such as CharityBank (see www.charitybank.org).

However, there must always be an income source from which the loan could be repaid: for example, contract income from services or long-term committed giving from donors. It would be irresponsible of the committee members of any organisation (and possibly even fraudulent) to take on a loan unless they were reasonably confident that it could be repaid within the timescale agreed with the lender. Moreover, lenders will normally charge interest so (apart from interest-free loans) any borrowing will always mean repaying more than the amount borrowed. The committee members must therefore be clear that the interest cost is justified and that funds will be available to cover the interest as well as repaying the capital.

Committee members who give personal guarantees become personally liable for loans or overdrafts if the organisation cannot repay what it has borrowed. In unincorporated organisations the committee members will always be responsible whether or not they provide personal guarantees – although some lenders may make a policy decision not to pursue individual committee members unless there is evidence of dishonesty.

If the organisation does not have a reasonable prospect of being able to meet its financial obligations, it needs to get advice urgently from a qualified accountant or insolvency practitioner.

In a company it may be unlawful under the **Insolvency Act 1986** to carry on operating in such cases. The directors should contact the company's accountant or auditor immediately. If it carries on despite being in such financial difficulty, individual directors could lose their limited liability and be held personally liable for the organisation's debts (see chapter 10).

Charitable incorporated organisations

At the time of writing the final regulations for CIOs had not been published. The draft regulations proposed that the provisions of the Insolvency Act 1986 should also apply to CIOs, and that a CIO's trustees would therefore have similar responsibilities and liabilities to those of company directors. The full rules will be in the **Charitable Incorporated Organisations (Insolvency and Dissolution) Regulations 2009**.

Bank accounts

To open an account in the name of an organisation the committee needs to pass a resolution – the wording of which is set out on a form supplied by the bank (the **Form of Mandate**) – which must be completed by officers of the organisation. A copy of the organisation's constitution should be attached and, if incorporated, a copy of the certificate of incorporation. Individuals authorised to draw cheques on behalf of the organisation must be named on the form.

Banks will often require detailed information about the individual signatories and, under regulations to combat money laundering, must take steps to confirm their identity for new accounts. This will also include confirming the identity of the organisation itself (through its constitution, and charity and/or company registration if applicable) and the identities of the main office holders. Check the bank's procedures on signatories before opening the account, especially if the signatories cannot easily get to the bank in person; some banks have much simpler procedures than others.

In a charity, confirmation of charitable status should also be supplied to the bank to enable it to pay interest gross (without deduction of tax). Also, cheques must make clear if they are issued on behalf of a registered charity: the simplest approach is to ask the bank to add the words 'registered charity' after the account name.

The constitution may include rules on cheque signatories. Many organisations choose to have three or four and state that cheques must be signed by at least two; however, this protection only has value if both signatories check the supporting documentation carefully before signing. If there are paid staff, it may be convenient for one or more of them to be a signatory up to a certain amount. As most organisations need to withdraw small amounts for cash, it is possible to arrange that cheques below a certain figure require only one signature, but above that two signatures would be necessary.

Blank cheques must never be signed; this could amount to a breach of trust and any individual who signs a blank cheque might have to repay the organisation for any loss that resulted. Even a cheque which shows the name of the payee but not the amount (or vice versa) could easily be used fraudulently, so cheques should never be signed until all other information is provided. The same applies to documents authorising salary transfers or any type of BACS payment.

It is important to have proper controls over how and by whom expenditure is authorised (see *Financial systems and procedures*, page 226). Although a control at the cheque signing stage is necessary, it may be too late to do anything about the payment if the goods or services have already been ordered.

Organisations with extra cash should consider opening a deposit account. When choosing banking arrangements it is worth establishing what deposit accounts are available and the interest rates (it is usually much simpler administratively if the current and deposit accounts are held at the same bank).

Two accounts (current and deposit) should be adequate for short-term banking by almost all organisations. There is no need to open new accounts for new funds or projects within one organisation; it is perfectly possible to keep track of different funds within the charity's own books (see *Accounting records*, page 212).

Many banks now provide internet banking facilities, but they are generally unsuitable for organisations governed by a reasonably sized committee. For example, two signatories may be needed to establish the online banking facility, but if one person can then authorise payments of any amount, all the security of two signatures is lost. However, some banks have schemes whereby, when one signatory requests a payment, an email is sent to the second signatory for authorisation, and payment is only made once both signatories have separately logged on, entered their passwords and authorised the transaction. This can be effective, but even so, great care is needed with security of passwords.

Bank charges vary and can add a significant amount to an organisation's expenditure. It is worth spending some time talking to a number of banks in order to get the best deal. If the organisation may need overdraft facilities, it is worth discussing this at the outset (see *Overdrafts and loans,* page 229).

Some less well-known banks specialise in accounts for charities and voluntary organisations. Many offer free banking to smaller charities for normal short-term transactions (but there could still be significant charges for matters such as replacing lost statements). Always get written details of how charges are calculated.

Record keeping

Financial responsibility involves keeping records (**accounts** or **books**) of how much money has come into the organisation, where it has come from, and how it has been spent. This process is called **bookkeeping**. Along with the books you must keep documentation, such as invoices and receipts, to prove the money was spent in the way shown; the books and supporting documents constitute the accounting records required by law (see *Accounting records*, page 212).

There are many forms of bookkeeping, depending on the complexity of the organisation. It is tempting to keep records on a personal computer, especially using spreadsheets, but this is not always appropriate for bookkeeping as figures can be easily changed and few spreadsheets are maintained on a double entry basis (where each transaction is posted to two accounts, in one case as a credit, in the other case as a debit).

For the smallest organisations, manual books may be the most reliable method. Larger organisations could consider buying a computerised accounting system where transactions are allocated to accounts, with an audit trail that makes it possible to trace figures back to the original entries. Such systems allow the use of many more accounts than could easily be handled in the columns of manual books, and almost always work on a double-entry basis. There are accounting packages designed specifically for charities and other non-profit organisations, with support for fund accounting; the most sophisticated can even handle data such as partially exempt VAT calculations. However, changes in hardware and software mean that it is often hard to go back six years, so if you use a computerised accounting system you should print all the relevant reports at year end and treat the printed reports as the long-term accounting records.

Any accounting system, whether manual or computerised, must enable the relevant information to be extracted in order to prepare the accounts at year end (see *Annual accounts*, page 213). The treasurer or bookkeeper must therefore have a thorough understanding of the organisation's legal accounting requirements. For example, an organisation that will produce its year end accounts on an R&P basis (see page 213) can manage with books which are a good deal simpler than one that needs to use accruals accounts in SORP format (see page 214). However, even R&P accounts will often require accounting for more than one fund.

For more details on different bookkeeping approaches, including ways of drawing up books for organisations of different levels of complexity, see chapter 5 of *The charity treasurer's handbook*.

Checking the records

Any bookkeeping system is only of value if the information is reliable and up to date. Of course, any treasurer or bookkeeper will make occasional errors, and it is important to have some means of identifying these, so they can be corrected. Bank reconciliation (see below) is probably the most important regular check. Also, if books are being kept manually on a double entry basis (see page 231), a regular **trial balance** (checking that all the debits and credits balance) is very important (though few

bookkeepers nowadays maintain full double entry accounts on a manual basis).

Checks can also be made on specific accounts in the books: for example, an organisation using petty cash should count the physical amount of cash in the box and check that it agrees with the petty cash figure in the books. Also debtor and creditor accounts are worth checking to make sure that balances outstanding agree with records of unpaid invoices.

Other checks include the normal management accounting processes of reviewing actual figures against budgets (see page 228) and looking for obviously incorrect figures.

A person other than the treasurer/bookkeeper should be involved in checking the records from time to time (including looking at bank reconciliations).

Bank statements and bank reconciliation

A bank statement is the bank's record of the organisation's finances. This record may not agree exactly with what is in the organisation's own books, because of uncleared items: for example, cheques that have been written but not yet paid in by the recipient. There is also usually a few days' delay before deposits appear on the bank statement.

Checking whether the books agree with the bank statement is called **bank reconciliation**. In the books it is vital to identify all bank transactions as 'cleared' (that is, they have appeared on a bank statement) or 'uncleared'. When you receive a bank statement, mark all items in the books which are now cleared (most computerised accounting systems have a bank reconciliation facility built in; in manual books just use a tick, preferably in a different colour). Then add up the items in the books which are still uncleared and the following formula should balance:

Balance at bank – uncleared cheques + uncleared receipts = Balance in books

If the calculation does not balance, you need to go through the books looking for discrepancies, missing items or duplicated entries; see chapter 6 of *The charity treasurer's handbook* for more specific guidance.

Charities' reserves

A charity's committee has a legal duty to use charity funds within a reasonable time of receiving them unless they are being held for a specific future purpose. However, charities need to be able to secure their future, absorb setbacks and take advantage of change and opportunities. Many provide for this by putting aside, when they can afford to, some of their current income as a reserve for future plans or against future uncertainties.

To overcome the possible perception that a charity is hoarding its money, and asking the public for funds that are not immediately needed, it is essential to be able to justify and explain the position on reserves. Responsibility for this lies with the trustees. Usually a reserves policy is stated in terms of the number of months of reserves felt to be needed: for example, 'The trustees' policy is to maintain sufficient reserves to cover six months' expenditure.'

The Charity Commission's publication *Charities' reserves* (CC19) provides guidance on developing a reserves policy and justifying reserves. A statement of the reserves policy must be included in the trustees' annual report (see page 218); this is a legal requirement even for the smallest charities.

When applying for funds you should establish funders' policies on reserves. Most funders will accept reasonable reserves provided they are clearly justified. (Note that amounts held in restricted funds do not count towards reserves as they cannot be spent at will. The trustees' report should make this clear, indicating how the reserves figure is calculated.)

Working with auditors or independent examiners

Each year the annual accounts may have to be audited or examined (see *Audit or examination of accounts*, page 216). There are many practical issues to consider when working with an auditor or independent examiner.

Responsibilities of the auditor or examiner

The legal duties of auditors and independent examiners are to prepare an independent report on the accounts of the organisation. For an auditor, the key task is to ensure there is reasonable certainty that the accounts are free from material misstatement: that is, to confirm that they give a 'true and fair view'. An independent examiner aims to provide a 'negative assurance' that no material problems were identified (but only after following the Charity Commission Directions).

As explained under *Audit or examination of accounts* (page 216), these requirements mainly apply to charities. Independent examination is specific to charities, and non-charitable organisations will rarely be subject to a statutory audit unless they have over £6.5 million income (see page 215 for specific rules). However, where a non-charitable organisation opts for a non-statutory audit, similar principles will apply.

However, in both cases, the legal duties are framed in terms of the auditor or independent examiner reporting on a set of accounts the organisation has prepared and which the committee members have approved. In practice, most organisations find it helpful to use their auditor or examiner to assist in preparing the accounts as well as auditing or examining them. This is permitted, so long as the auditor or examiner is independent of the underlying decisions and record keeping. But in such cases, it is important to distinguish between the auditor's or examiner's role in preparing the accounts (which is simply assisting the trustees to fulfil their duties) and the independent review of the accounts – even though both may be taking place at the same time.

If the auditor or examiner is asked to help prepare the accounts they will, of course, need to have the books and records and all supporting information, such as an explanation of the organisation's different funds, details of transactions with committee members and, for charities, all other issues which require disclosure under the Charities SORP (see *Annual accounts*, page 213).

To undertake the actual audit work, an auditor may:

- check that the organisation has spent money within the terms of its constitution or aims and objectives, committee decisions, agreed accounting policies and funders' requirements (normally this will include reviewing the committee's minutes and other documents such as grant letters)
- check that all money received and spent has been entered in the books
- verify that vouchers (such as receipts, used cheques or cheque stubs) and subsidiary records exist to back up the entries in the cash book
- verify that the treasurer, staff and others with financial authority have followed instructions from the committee and officers
- review the trustees' annual report to identify any major discrepancies with the accounts
- verify that the final accounts give a 'true and fair' view of the organisation's financial position and transactions (or, in the case of R&P accounts, that they are 'properly presented').

With an independent examiner, similar steps are involved. The examiner will first need to understand the organisation, and then will check that its income falls within the band where independent examination is permitted, will carry out various checks to see if the accounting records are complete and will review the range of transactions (focusing on larger or more unusual items, seeking explanations as needed).

Much of this work usually takes place while the accounts are in draft format. This applies whether the drafting is being done by the auditor/examiner or by the organisation itself. This approach means that minor concerns can usually be addressed by amending the draft accounts, for example to revise a figure or add an explanatory note, and thus avoid a 'qualified report' (see page 235).

Once all amendments to the draft accounts have been made, the accounts must be submitted for formal approval by the committee. To avoid calling a special meeting, the timescales are normally planned around the relevant meeting. Even if one trustee, such as the treasurer, has been largely responsible for preparing the draft, the whole committee must approve the accounts, which must then be signed (normally two trustees are appointed to sign the balance sheet). Usually the trustees' annual report is approved at the same time as the accounts.

For this process to be meaningful, committee members who were not involved in the preparation of the accounts must be given the chance to suggest amendments: for example, they may feel notes or explanations are unclear, or (occasionally) they may even identify incorrect figures, such as where something has been missed out. To reduce the risk of changes being raised at the last minute, the draft accounts should be circulated in good time before the meeting. Alternatively, many organisations find it helpful to have a finance subcommittee meeting a week or two before the full committee meeting to review the draft accounts in detail and identify any changes needed.

Once the accounts are approved by the full committee, the auditor or independent examiner now has a final set of accounts to report on, and the committee will then be given the auditor's or independent examiner's signed report: a public document that must be circulated with all copies of the accounts. These reports are quite detailed, and normally require at least a page to cover all the legal background.

The aim is always to obtain an 'unqualified report': a report where the auditor or examiner is essentially satisfied with the accounts and does not express any qualifications or reservations. Sometimes a minor qualification in the report is unavoidable (for example, if certain overseas expenditure could not be verified) but a serious qualification, where the auditor or examiner expresses major concerns, is likely to have a serious impact on the charity's reputation. In the most serious cases, auditors and examiners are required by law to report matters directly to the Charity Commission (and to the Serious Organised Crime Agency if they find possible indications of fraud, theft, tax evasion, money laundering or use of funds for terrorism).

As well as the formal report on the accounts, many auditors and examiners will provide feedback on the organisation's accounting procedures and suggest ways of improving controls and accounting records – this is called a **management letter**. Unlike the formal audit or independent examination report, the management letter is not public but is issued in confidence to the committee. Any comments should be taken seriously: an issue raised in a management letter could, if not resolved, lead to a qualified report the following year.

Appointing an auditor or examiner

Many constitutions include a clause stating that the auditor must be appointed by the AGM. Some also state that the AGM must set the fee or delegate responsibility for this task.

In the case of a charity, if a full audit is needed, it is necessary to appoint a firm of registered auditors (not all firms of accountants have this status). However, if the constitution specifies an audit but the organisation's income only requires an independent examination, it is often worth amending the constitution so that the form of scrutiny is simply as required by the Charities Act 1993 (see *Changing the structure*, in chapter 1). For

an independent examination the choice is much wider: examiners can be drawn from firms of accountants, specialist freelancers or community accountancy services, or (for smaller charities) you may find someone who has some relevant experience who is willing to be trained to be an independent examiner.

For a non-charitable organisation, any audit or scrutiny requirements will be purely as laid down in the constitution, unless the organisation is a company falling outside the 'small company' definition (see page 215), or is an IPS large enough to require a compulsory audit (see *Audit or examination of accounts*, page 216). Sometimes, for example, a small unincorporated voluntary organisation may have a constitution which requires the appointment of an 'honorary auditor' but (unless otherwise stated) this could just be an independent person who is not connected to the committee members.

For charities, however, the auditor or independent examiner must have relevant charity accounting experience. Where a professionally qualified independent examiner is needed, the examiner must be a member of one of the bodies listed in *Independent examination of charity accounts* (CC31).

Before engaging an auditor or independent examiner, get quotations and check the expertise of the person or firm concerned. It may be useful to seek advice or recommendations from your local council for voluntary service or rural community council, community accountancy project or other voluntary organisation. Larger charities may undertake a tender process where they invite firms to bid for the work (but selections should never be made on fees alone – expertise is critical).

Once you have made a decision, the auditor or independent examiner should ask you to sign an 'engagement letter' which confirms exactly what they are being engaged to do. This will require approval by the committee, and should be carefully checked before signing; any services not covered by the engagement letter normally mean additional fees.

It is also essential to agree timescales well ahead. First consider your year end, and how long after that you will need to get the books up to date, complete your bank reconciliations and have everything ready. Even if you are highly organised, the audit of an organisation with a 31 March year end cannot normally begin before late April; mid May is perhaps more realistic (bear in mind that some information may be held by others). (If you commit to a start date for the audit but do not have everything ready, you may incur extra fees.) Then consider deadlines: for example, if you need final accounts for an AGM in October, work back to a date before this when the accounts will be approved by the trustees (perhaps in mid September). You will then need to make sure the auditor or examiner can schedule the work between the relevant dates (mid May and mid September in this case) and at a time when you are not on holiday.

Records the auditor needs

The main items the auditor or independent examiner will require to carry out an end of year audit are:

- a copy of the constitution
- committee minutes (including any supporting documents)
- the books (manual or computerised; for computer systems, check whether the information should be supplied electronically or as printouts)
- any subsidiary records kept (for example, records from subgroups)
- PAYE records if applicable (including details of wages and salaries, and written evidence of salary changes)
- VAT returns if applicable (and supporting VAT records if not included in the main books)
- any fundraising records kept separately from the accounts, such as a donor register (including Gift Aid records if applicable)
- bank statements and bank reconciliations
- bank paying-in book and cheque-book stubs

- sales invoices if the organisation is doing work under contract
- daily cash register totals if the organisation runs a shop
- all vouchers, including bills/receipts obtained for money paid out
- funding agreements, including conditions of grants from funders
- the previous year's annual accounts (final signed version)
- the draft accounts for the current year if being prepared
- all legal documents signed during the year
- a copy of the organisation's written financial procedures, if any
- a list of debtors (people who owe money to the organisation) and creditors (people to whom the organisation owes money)
- a list of liabilities, including loans or overdrafts and items contracted but not yet paid for.

In many cases, auditors and examiners will have a checklist of information they want at the start and will request further evidence as the process proceeds. For example, rather than wanting all bills and receipts, they may do a selection and ask for certain items only.

Chapter 9
Services and activities

This chapter looks at the law and good practice governing a range of services and activities carried out by voluntary organisations. It starts by describing how organisations should review their activities in the light of equal opportunities legislation. Subsequent sections outline the law and good practice relating to contracting with public authorities to provide services, handling information and confidentiality policies, meetings, marches and protests, fundraising, human rights and freedom of information.

Reference is made to the content of the **Equality Bill 2008**, which, at the time of writing, was due to be debated in the 2008/09 parliamentary session.

Equal opportunities in service delivery

The voluntary sector is a major provider of services and activities. It is essential that current and potential users know what is available, feel confident about seeking help or asking to participate, and believe the services are appropriate and sensitive to their needs. You should examine how services are delivered, and take positive measures to make sure they comply with the law and are accessible and relevant to anyone entitled to use them.

The Equality Bill proposes the adoption of a more harmonised approach to how the law treats delivery of public functions and the provision of goods, facilities and services.

Legal requirements

It is unlawful to discriminate when providing goods, facilities or services (whether free or paid for) to the public on the grounds of sex, race, disability, sexual orientation, and religion or belief. Discrimination in providing services means:

- refusing to provide a service
- providing a lower standard of service, or
- offering a service on different terms than you would to other people.

Sex discrimination

The **Sex Discrimination Act 1975** generally prohibits discrimination against men or women in the supply of goods or services. There are two major exceptions for voluntary organisations:

- where an organisation's main object is the provision of services to one sex – but only if it is a proportionate means of achieving a legitimate aim or for the purpose of preventing or compensating for a disadvantage linked to a person's sex
- where a non-charitable organisation restricts membership to one sex and provides services only to its members; again, only if this is a proportionate means of achieving a legitimate aim or for the purpose of preventing or compensating for a disadvantage linked to a person's sex.

The **Sex Discrimination (Amendment of Legislation) Regulations 2008** make the following unlawful when providing services (apart from those not normally provided on a commercial basis in premises used for organised religions):

- indirect discrimination and harassment on grounds of sex
- direct discrimination and harassment on grounds of gender reassignment unless, in relation to communal accommodation or services limited to one sex for propriety or privacy, such discrimination is a proportionate (appropriate) means of achieving a legitimate aim or, in relation to participation in sport or other competitive activities, such discrimination is necessary to ensure fair competition or the safety of competitors
- direct and indirect discrimination on the basis of pregnancy or because a woman has given birth within the previous 26 weeks, unless the service provider reasonably believes the service would pose a risk to her health or safety and has an equivalent policy for people with other physical conditions.

The Equality Bill proposes further protection against discrimination in the exercise of public functions to cover pregnancy and maternity. It will make clear that breastfeeding mothers are protected against discrimination in the provision of goods, facilities and services.

Race discrimination

The **Race Relations Act 1976** generally prohibits discrimination in the provision of goods and services on the basis of race. There are the following exceptions:

- Organisations with fewer than 25 members may use racial group as a factor in selecting members.
- Organisations of any size can limit their membership and services to people of a specific racial group (not defined by reference to colour) if the main object of the organisation is to enable the benefits of membership to be enjoyed by people from that group.
- Charities can limit their services to a particular racial group if their constitution explicitly allows this, provided the group is not defined by reference to colour.
- A charity may restrict access to some services or allocate services first to members of a specific racial group if:
  - it can be shown that members of the group have a need that is different in kind from, or is the same as but proportionately greater than, the other population of the area covered by the charity
  - the need is attributable to and distinguished by a characteristic specific to the racial group, and
  - the special need relates to education, training, welfare or ancillary benefits.

Disability discrimination

The **Disability Discrimination Act (DDA) 1995** and the **Disability Discrimination Act 2005** prohibit discrimination in the provision of goods, facilities and services by:

- refusing to serve a disabled person for a reason relating to their disability

- offering a substandard service to disabled people
- providing a service on different terms
- failing to comply with the duty to make reasonable adjustments (see below), in circumstances in which the failure makes it impossible or unreasonably difficult for a disabled person to use a service.

The government is considering whether to introduce powers in the Equality Bill 2008 to protect disabled people against harassment in the provision of goods, facilities and services and public functions.

Reasonable adjustments

The duty to make reasonable adjustments to ensure disabled people can use the services more easily involves:

- **changing policies, practice and procedures** that make it impossible or unreasonably difficult for disabled people to access goods, services or facilities
- **providing auxiliary aids and services** to enable disabled people to use a service or to use it more. Examples include:
  - producing information on audio tape, in Braille and in large print
  - providing induction loops, textphones and sign language interpreters
  - using simplified text
  - designing accessible websites
  - having well designed signage, portable ramps and designated car parking
- **overcoming physical features** that make it impossible or unreasonably difficult for disabled people to use a service by:
  - providing services by an alternative means, for example at a location other than an office, at home, by telephone or by video link
  - removing or altering any physical features in their premises that make it impossible or unreasonably difficult for a disabled person to use a service, or provide a reasonable means of avoiding the feature.

Private clubs with 25 or more members are covered by the DDA 2005 in respect of their members, associates and guests, and prospective members and guests.

Service providers must not think they can ignore this legislation because disabled people do not use their services. Larger organisations, in particular, are expected to take positive steps to identify any barriers which prevent disabled people from knowing about, or attempting to use, services which they might otherwise use.

Exceptions

The following reasons might justify less favourable treatment, but cannot be used as an excuse to exclude all disabled people:

- The health or safety of the disabled person or someone else may be endangered if the same service or facility is provided.
- The disabled person is not capable of understanding the terms of a contract: that is, the nature of the agreement or their obligations. However, without clear evidence to the contrary, you should assume that the disabled person is able to enter into a contract. This exemption does not apply if someone is legally acting on behalf of the disabled person.
- Providing the service to the disabled person would stop the service being provided at all. You would have to show that other users would be prevented from using the service, and not just inconvenienced.
- You can charge a disabled person more for a service if that charge reflects the additional cost of meeting their specification – that is, the service is individually tailored to the disabled person's requirements.
- You do not have to make any adjustments that would fundamentally alter the nature of the service, profession or business.

For further details of these requirements see the *Code of Practice: Rights of access: services to the public, public authority functions, private clubs and premises*, available from www.equalityhumanrights.com, *Making access to goods and services easier for disabled customers: A practical guide for small businesses and other service providers* from www.dwp.gov.uk/employers, and the Business

Link publication *Access and facilities for disabled people*, available from www.businesslink.org.uk.

In the Equality Bill, the government aims to replace different justification defences with a single 'objective justification' test, which would require that the conduct in question is 'a proportionate means of achieving a legitimate aim', and to introduce a single threshold for making reasonable adjustments: that is, whenever a disabled person would be at a 'substantial disadvantage' compared with a non-disabled person if no adjustment were made. It is also considering whether to introduce protection against harassment in the provision of goods, facilities and services and public functions because of a person's disability.

Religion and belief

The **Equality Act 2006** makes discrimination unlawful in the area of goods, facilities and services on the grounds of religion or belief.

There are exceptions:
- faith-based schools can select pupils on the basis of faith
- faith-based charities and other organisations can discriminate in favour of one faith in the provision of services.

Sexual Orientation Regulations 2007

The **Equality Act (Sexual Orientation) Regulations 2007** (the Regulations) outlaw discrimination on the grounds of sexual orientation in the provision of goods and services. There are exceptions where it is lawful to discriminate:
- Charities can be set up for people of a specific sexual orientation to provide services only to that group.
- Any provider can offer people of a particular sexual orientation access to goods, facilities or services to meet their specific educational or welfare needs.
- in private clubs and associations, if the main object of the organisation is to enable the benefits of membership to be enjoyed by people of a particular sexual orientation.

Religious organisations carrying out purely faith-based activities are exempted from this requirement.

Age discrimination

The Equality Bill contains powers to outlaw unjustifiable age discrimination against adults aged 18 or over in the provision of goods, facilities and services. To allow organisations to prepare, and to make sure the law does not prevent justified differences in treatment for different age groups, there will be further consultation on the design of the legislation and a transition period before any new legal protections from age discrimination are implemented.

The government also intends to introduce protection against harassment in the provision of goods, facilities and services and public functions because of a person's age.

Working for public authorities

Public authorities have a duty to tackle discrimination and promote equality in relation to race, gender and disability, either individually or under the umbrella of a **single equality scheme.** Organisations working in partnership with, or providing services on behalf of, a public authority (either through grant aid or contracts) may need to comply. In any event it is good practice to adopt the measures listed below.

Generally duties include:

- preparing a publicly stated policy on equality
- setting out arrangements for assessing and consulting on proposed policies with employees and users
- monitoring the policies' impact
- publishing the results of assessments, consultations and monitoring
- giving staff relevant training.

The Equality Bill proposes a new equality duty on public authorities which will bring together the three existing duties and include gender reassignment, age, sexual orientation and religion or belief. Public authorities will be required to report on gender pay, minority ethnic employment and disability employment.

Good practice

Organisations should draw up an equal opportunities and diversity policy relating to service provision that extends beyond the legal requirements. The policy should state your commitment to ensuring equal access to your services, and identify ways in which they can be monitored and adapted so that they meet the needs of everyone in the community. Measures to consider are given below.

Think about the image of the organisation. If it is seen as predominantly made up of or controlled by people from one sex, racial group or social class, many people may be deterred from using its services. One way of changing this image is to ensure that your management committee, staff composition (at all levels of the hierarchy) and volunteers reflect the make up of the community (see *Equal opportunities in employment*, in chapter 3). Make sure any information about your services uses language and images that are inclusive and welcoming.

Identifying needs

Ensure that equality of access is designed into current and new projects and, where appropriate, set targets. Ask your users and potential users about their needs and how your services could be adapted to meet these needs by, for example, arranging conferences, group discussions, workshops, interviews, open days and visits. Make recommendations from this consultation process publicly available so that you can demonstrate progress in making changes. The management committee should regularly discuss and record progress.

Remember to budget for producing information in accessible formats at the beginning of the financial year, or at the outset of each project.

Monitoring

Set up systems to monitor the extent to which your services are meeting everyone's needs. Ideally, monitoring should be based on a system of records covering race, gender, age and disability. You may wish to discuss with users (see *Identifying needs*, page 240) whether to monitor other characteristics, such as religion, sexuality, marital status and caring responsibilities. For more information about monitoring see *Monitoring effectiveness*, in chapter 3.

When collecting data about service users, follow these principles:

- Participation in monitoring is voluntary – if users don't want to provide the information themselves you should never complete the forms on their behalf. You can only explain why it matters to you and encourage them to respond.
- It is preferable to ensure the information is anonymous, with no way of identifying the user from the information provided.
- If collecting monitoring information which is not anonymous,* you must:
  - tell people that you will be using the information for monitoring
  - make it clear they do not have to provide it
  - explain how you will handle the data (for example, that you will release it only as statistics and you will not keep the individual forms after the statistics have been compiled)
  - tell respondents that they do not have to provide personal details in order to receive the service being used for monitoring purposes.

The purpose must be genuine monitoring; the information must not be used to make decisions about the individual.

These principles apply in particular to monitoring on the basis of race or ethnicity, disability or religion. They are good practice when monitoring on the basis of age, gender or less contentious criteria (such as postcode or ward). Monitoring on the basis of other 'sensitive' data, including sexuality, criminal record or political views, can only be done with consent (again, unless it is anonymous). In other words, even if you already have the data

for other reasons, you must still check that it is acceptable to use it for monitoring.

The rules also apply to monitoring information collected over the phone. You must use a standard script that explains everything thoroughly before asking any questions.

For further information see *Equal opportunities in enployment*, in chapter 3.

Information

When producing your information, consider the needs of people with different types of disability and those whose first language is not English.

Translation

Consider translating information into other languages; your local council for voluntary service or rural community council may be able to signpost you to a local group that can help. Most local authorities will have a list of translation and interpreting agencies.

Disabled people

The government's Office for Disability Issues has developed five core principles for providing services and information:

- ensure that disabled people are involved from the start
- provide information through a range of channels and formats
- ensure your information meets users' needs
- clearly signpost other services
- always define responsibility for information provision.

For further details see *Five principles for producing better information for disabled people*, available from www.officefordisability.gov.uk/docs/ODI_FivePrinciples_2007.pdf.

Written material. All written material should be easy to read and understand, and use plain, jargon free language. Avoid long sentences, hyphenation and abbreviations. Pay particular attention to the layout: use unjustified text, a sans serif font (one without short lines at the end of characters) such as

Arial, Helvetica or Verdana, in at least 12 point. Avoid excessive use of capital letters, bold, italic and underlining. Black type on white or yellow paper is easiest to read; remember people with colour blindness may have problems distinguishing reds or greens. Choose uncoated or matt rather than glossy paper; the glare makes it difficult to read.

Two checklists on producing accessible information are available from www.rnib.org.uk: *See it right checklist* (for printed information) and *See right Microsoft Word checklist* (for electronic information).

Other formats – for blind and partially sighted people. Wherever possible consider producing information in different formats including Braille, audio tapes, CDs, computer disk and large print. The Royal National Institute of Blind People (RNIB) can help with transcription; for details of your local Regional Transcription Centre contact RNIB on 0845 766 9999.

Other formats – for deaf and hard of hearing people. To book a **British Sign Language** interpreter, contact the Royal National Institute for Deaf People (RNID) Communication Services on 0845 685 8000, textphone 0845 685 8001, or email communication.services@rnid.org.uk. RNID has produced a fact sheet on using sign language interpreters, *Working with a British Sign Language/English interpreter*, available from www.rnid.org.uk.

Type-Talk is a national telephone relay service run by RNID for deaf, deafened, hard of hearing, deafblind and speech-impaired people. It allows people to use a textphone to access services available on standard telephone systems. Calls are charged at your telephone communication provider's standard rate. For further details contact the Customer Support Helpdesk on 0800 7311 888, textphone 18001 0800 7311 888, or see www.typetalk.org.

For more information on these services and other forms of communication, including lipspeakers, speech-to-text reporters, deafblind interpreters, communication support workers and video interpreting, see the RNID's publication *Types of communication support*, available from www.rnid.org.uk.

For people with learning disabilities. The **Easy Read** format and the signing and symbols system **Makaton** are widely used by people with learning disabilities. Easy Read uses clear, short sentences and avoids difficult words and acronyms. Pictures are often used to illustrate points. A tape or CD-ROM is often provided alongside the text, with the words spoken slowly and guidance given on when to turn the page. For more information see *How to use easy words and pictures*, available from www.equalityhumanrights.com, and the Mencap guides *Communicating with people with a learning disability* and *Make it clear: a guide to making information clear and easy to read for people with a learning disability*, available from www.mencap.org.uk/guides. For further information about using Makaton see www.makaton.org.

Signalong is a sign-supporting system based on British Sign Language, designed to help children and adults with communication difficulties, mostly associated with learning disabilities; for further information see www.signalong.org.uk.

For more information about making services accessible for people with learning disabilities, contact Mencap's accessibility unit on 020 7454 0454.

Accessible web design. Under the **Disability Discrimination Act 1995** organisations must make 'reasonable adjustments' to ensure their websites accommodate all users, regardless of ability or disability. There are a number of resources available for improving accessibility. These include:

- Web Accessibility Initiative (WAI) guidelines for developing accessible websites, available from www.w3.org/wai
- RNID guidance on designing a website, including *Producing information for deaf and hard of hearing people*, available from www.rnid.org.uk

- AbilityNet offers a range of support on web access, including training courses and audits of websites, together with a number of useful fact sheets such as *Free web accessibility resources*. Contact them on 01926 312847 or visit www.abilitynet.co.uk
- RNIB's Web Access Centre (www.rnib.org.uk; follow links from 'Good Design') includes frequently asked questions about web accessibility and a blog on accessibility debates. The web access team offers a range of consultancy services
- The Dyslexia Online Magazine for Parents outlines the principles of good web page design for a dyslexic audience in *Designing web pages for dyslexic readers*, available from www.dyslexia-parent.com/mag35.html
- The BBC has developed a site in partnership with AbilityNet, 'My web, my way' (www.bbc.co.uk/accessibility), which explains how you can change your browser, computer, keyboard and mouse settings to make the web more accessible.

Public events

Planning for access should be an integral part of planning for all public events. Always use the broadest definition of access – to include not only physical access for people with mobility impairments but also, for example, how someone with learning disabilities can access information about the event – and ask potential participants about their access requirements.

Give plenty of notice of an event to allow people enough time to make travel and caring arrangements. Provide information on available access facilities.

Visit any external venue before making a booking to assess the accessibility of the premises and facilities. This will include looking at transport facilities, including car parks with clearly signed disabled parking bays near to the main entrance, toilets, corridors, lifts, catering areas, workshop rooms and entrance lobbies. Check that:

- there is space near the main entrance for minicabs and taxis to park

- access facilities such as induction loops are maintained
- there is level access to and from all rooms, including toilets and refreshment areas
- the signage is clear and consistent; if necessary arrange to install temporary signage
- there are enough tables and chairs, and the furniture is suitable for a variety of needs
- rooms are well lit with no glare or shadows
- there is enough space for a sign language interpreter to sit or stand, positioned away from windows or busy backgrounds
- evacuation procedures take account of disabled people, including those with sensory impairments and mobility impairments, and information about evacuation and emergency procedures is available in different formats.

Some disabled people may need help from a support worker or personal assistant, so remember to ask beforehand whether any participants need an extra place.

Carry out a risk assessment to help you identify and remove or reduce any health and safety risks, such as slippery surfaces, and risks from vehicles (see *Risk assessment*, in chapter 5).

Provide information on how people with limited mobility can access your events. Your local dial-a-ride group may be able to provide transport; all Computer Cabs' taxis are wheelchair accessible and all drivers have undergone disability awareness training. For details see www.computercab.co.uk or ring 020 7763 5001.

Consider providing crèche or childminding facilities at public events, conferences and training courses. Crèche providers should be able to offer an accessible service for disabled children. People with school-aged children may prefer events between 10am and 3pm, and if possible avoid dates that coincide with school holidays. Remember that people with children or other dependants may find it difficult to attend evening meetings.

Take into account the dates of festivals for all faiths when arranging events (see *The Shap calendar of religious festivals*, published by the Shap Working Party, available from www.shap.org). Ensure venues have a quiet room available for prayer, reflection and meditation.

Ask participants about any special catering needs and be prepared to offer vegetarian, vegan, gluten-free and nut-free, halal and kosher food, and herbal and caffeine-free hot drinks. Vegetarian, vegan, meat and fish dishes must be served on separate plates, with meat products containing ham, bacon or pork plated separately. Label food where necessary.

For more information see *Organising accessible events*, available from www.equalityhumanrights.com.

Feedback

Develop monitoring and evaluation systems to assess service delivery and user satisfaction. Aim to identify trends according to users' gender, age, ethnicity, religion or belief, disability and sexual orientation.

Complaints

Introduce a complaints procedure for people who feel they have been discriminated against and ensure it is well advertised on your premises. Direct and indirect discrimination, victimisation and harassment by a member of staff against any user should be a disciplinary offence (see chapter 3).

Relationships with other organisations

Voluntary organisations can help to promote equality amongst other agencies. Make sure your commitment to equalities is made clear to all your partner agencies. Before deciding to affiliate with or become a member of another organisation, examine its commitment to equal opportunities. Where appropriate and possible, offer to help other organisations develop an equal opportunities strategy, and if necessary challenge discriminatory practices.

Contracting to provide services

Types of funding agreements

The Charity Commission has produced the following useful summary of funding arrangements:

A grant is a gift or donation. The donor has no right to receive anything in return, but may attach terms and conditions specifying how the grant is to be spent, which could make it a restricted fund within the charity's accounts (see chapter 8). Spending the grant on anything else would be a breach of trust. Any surplus funds will be subject to the same restrictions unless the terms of the grant stipulate otherwise.

A contract is a legally enforceable agreement between two (or more) parties where one party agrees to provide goods or services in return for payment. A payment under a contract is a fee, not a grant, and is subject to the application of the VAT rules (see chapter 8). Any surplus under a contract is not a restricted fund, but might be subject to contractual terms and conditions.

Service level agreement (SLA) is not a legal term. An SLA is usually a document setting out the understandings of the contractor and the charity about the service to be provided. It would only be a contract if it fulfilled all the legal criteria for a valid contract, including that both parties intended it to be legally binding.

Until recently the relationship between the statutory and voluntary sectors has centred on grant aid, with statutory agencies using their discretionary powers to support voluntary organisations by awarding grants, usually on an annual basis. This relationship has changed, as voluntary organisations are bidding for or negotiating contracts to provide services.

The contracting process

A range of law and procedures governs how statutory agencies commission or procure services:

■ European Union directives (which increasingly are adopted as UK law) require public agencies to advertise contracts over a certain value and ensure that all bidders are treated equally.

■ UK law requires statutory agencies to work in a fair and transparent manner.

■ Most statutory agencies have standing orders or financial regulations that describe their procedures for working with external providers.

Although not legally enforceable, the Compact between the government and the community and voluntary sector, and the adoption of the Compact principles by local authorities, has established a code of practice setting out key principles in building relationships between the sectors. The Compact and its codes can help to create a positive relationship between parties. See, in particular, the *Funding and procurement code*, available from www.thecompact.org.uk.

In practice, statutory agencies commission services in four main ways:

■ **Competition**. A statutory agency may advertise its intention to contract a defined service and invite potential providers to bid to a specification that sets out what it wants to purchase. Organisations need to produce a bid or tender setting out how they would deliver the service, their relevant experience and the cost.

■ **An approved list**. Many statutory agencies maintain a list of organisations that have successfully demonstrated, generally through an application process, that they have the required level of experience and systems to deliver a contract. When a need for a provider is identified, only those organisations on the approved list are invited to bid.

■ **Preferred supplier**. In some cases a statutory agency might decide to appoint directly an organisation as a preferred supplier, usually for a specialist service where there are few or no alternatives.

■ **Converting a grant to a contract**. Some statutory agencies have formalised grant aid terms by adding clear expectations, responsibilities and conditions. The grant may not be called a contract but all the elements that make up a binding agreement are in place.

Information about researching tendering opportunities is available on the Finance Hub website at www.financehub.org.uk.

Should an organisation take on a service?

The decision to take on a contract raises a range of legal, organisational and policy issues for voluntary organisations. The following questions will help you to assess whether to bid for or take on a contract.

Is it in line with the organisation's aims and objectives?

An organisation's constitution will set out what it can and cannot do. In particular, the objects clause defines the scope of the organisation's activities and may, or may not, specify a limited area of benefit (see chapter 2). Committee members are responsible for ensuring that the organisation keeps within these limits. Taking on a service that would involve operating outside the organisation's constitutionally defined objects is beyond its legal authority and would place its trustees in breach of duty (see *Liability of committee members*, in chapter 1).

Is it something we want to do?

Taking on a service at the request or encouragement of a statutory agency may not always be in the best interests of a voluntary organisation. The type of work might not fit with other activities, or the organisation's ethos or style of work. You also need to consider whether you have the capacity to take on the service, its possible impact on current work and relationships with users and how it may affect volunteers. A good strategic or business plan should set out a clear organisational direction into which all new activities should fit.

Is it what our users (current and potential) want and need?

To what extent have users been consulted about and influenced the service specification? Has the statutory agency researched the level and nature of need?

Does the contract fee cover the full cost of the service?

The true cost of a service is made up three elements:

- the **direct costs** of delivering the service – expenditure involved in operating the service and employing the staff to deliver it
- **support costs** – the costs of supporting, organising and supervising the service
- a share of **indirect costs** – the costs or overheads involved in governing and developing the organisation. Each specific service or project should pay a share towards these costs. The price should include a 'reasonable surplus', to cover development cost and reasonable reserves.

It is essential to ensure that the service has been properly costed and includes both the full direct costs of delivering and operating the service and a fair share of the organisation's overall management costs.

Charities

A charity's decision must be based on the interests of the organisation and the needs of its beneficiaries. The Charity Commission advises that if a charity is considering taking up or renewing a funding agreement for public service delivery where the funding on offer will not cover the full cost of the service, it can:

- negotiate for more funding
- offer a lower level of service, commensurate with the funding on offer
- decide to use other funds to make up the shortfall, or
- reject the funding agreement and not deliver the service.

Trustees must only agree to use the charity's funds if they are satisfied that this is in the interests of the charity and its beneficiaries and fully in line with its objects. Any decision to subsidise or supplement a service must be made by the charity and should not be imposed on it as a condition of funding.

For guidance on full cost recovery see *Full cost recovery – a guide and toolkit on cost allocation*, available from www.fullcostrecovery.org.uk.

Do we have the relevant skills and expertise to submit a bid?

Putting together a tender requires skills in identifying needs, developing service plans, costing activities and writing and making bids.

Do we have the relevant skills and expertise to deliver the service?

It is essential to check whether the organisation has the necessary skills and expertise to deliver the activities to be carried out under the contract. Will additional training be required or new staff employed? The contract specification might set out specific requirements relating to the use of qualified staff and the application of particular standards.

Are we able to manage and support the service?

Taking on a new activity will place requirements on the organisation's management and organisational systems. Often statutory agencies require service providers to produce a range of contract monitoring information, carry out evaluation exercises and take part in contract reviews and other events. Adding on new activities could test and strain the organisation's management processes.

Do we need to review policies and procedures?

As part of the contracting process statutory bodies often require that organisations have up-to-date and robust policies and procedures covering, for example, health and safety, data protection and confidentiality, complaints procedures and the protection of children or vulnerable adults. At an early stage in the contracting process check that you have such policies, that they are up to date, legally compliant, reflect best practice and are used.

Might the contract involve taking over an existing service?

The **Transfer of Undertakings (Protection of Employment) Regulations (TUPE)** protects employees' terms and conditions of employment when a business or service is transferred from one organisation to another. At its simplest, employees of the organisation that owns or operates the service when the business changes hands automatically become employees of the new employer on the same terms and conditions. Their continuity of service and other rights are preserved (see *Taking on other organisations' staff*, in chapter 3). It is therefore essential to check if a contract could involve a service transfer. If so, the costs of taking on the existing employees need to be included in the contract bid.

Are there any tax implications?

A contract is usually formed to create or further a business relationship, whereas a grant is funding that is freely given by one party to another. A contract between a voluntary organisation and a commissioner will be a business supply or trading relationship and, as such, VAT rules will need due consideration (see *VAT*, in chapter 8). It is important to establish the VAT status of a proposed activity, taking advice as appropriate. It is important to state in the contract that the price is exclusive of chargeable VAT, otherwise there is a risk of the price being deemed to be inclusive of VAT and so, effectively, reducing the actual intended price.

Is the structure appropriate for trading?

There are important restrictions on a charity's trading activities, and it may be worth considering setting up a trading subsidiary to manage the contractual income-generating activity. (For further information on charities and trading see *Trading,* in chapter 1). It is important to set up and manage the relationship between a charity and its trading company properly, as a charity must not subsidise non-charitable activity. A trading subsidiary is not needed where non-charitable trading activity will generate less than £50,000 gross annual trading income, provided the non-charitable trading activity amounts to less than 25% of the charity's total income. Otherwise the threshold is £5,000.

Could the time-limited nature of the contract have a negative effect on our users?

Contracts are often fixed term. Before taking on such agreements, think carefully about what might happen at the end of the contract, particularly in relation to how users' needs will continue to be met, and whether the organisation can continue without contract funds. You should develop an exit strategy for fixed-term activities.

What happens if there are problems or under-performance?

The contract should set out a process for dealing with failure to perform or deliver any aspect of the agreement. It is worth remembering that failure to perform can happen on either side: for example, a statutory agency could fail to pay on time. It is also important that not all the risks involved in a service should be loaded onto one party to the agreement. The process for resolving problems and dealing with failure should be clear and reasonable.

Have we analysed the risks of taking on a contract?

The Charity Commission has identified four areas of risk associated with taking on a contract:

- **financial**, including use of reserves and sustainability
- **governance**, including constitution and independence

- **service**, including contractual risks and quality of service
- **reputational**, including public perception and relationship with public authorities.

For further information see *Charities and public service delivery* (CC37), available from www.charity-commission.gov.uk.

Liability

In unincorporated organisations any contractual liabilities beyond the value of the organisation's assets would fall on the trustees personally. Any organisation that is contemplating public service delivery should first consider establishing an incorporated structure, or set up a separate company specifically to deliver a service or services under contract. In incorporated organisations the organisation itself rather than individual committee members would generally be liable for breach of contract or contractually limiting liability to the value of the assets of the organisation. For further details see *Liability of committee members*, in chapter 1.

Main headings of a contract

Contracts vary in shape and size, but any agreement should contain the following.

- **Who it is between:** Setting out the parties to the contract.
- **Definitions:** Explaining the key terms and language used in the agreement.
- **Purpose:** The overall purpose of the agreement, possibly including a statement of values to which both parties adhere.
- **Duration of the contract and termination arrangements:** If fixed term, can it be renewed or extended?
- **The user:** Who is the service for? How will people become users? What is the anticipated number of users?
- **Services to be provided:** A statement of the services to be provided in order to deliver under the contract. This will usually have been set out in the specification, which may be attached to the contract and form part of it.

- **Quality assurance:** A list of any specific standards, performance indicators, best practice requirements (for example, user involvement, equality and diversity policies) and procedures for dealing with complaints, and confidentiality.
- **Monitoring and management:** The information the provider will collate and produce (including frequency of reports) to monitor and evaluate the performance of the contract.
- **Finances:** The fees for the contract – the payment schedule, VAT if relevant, any costs that might vary during the contract, including provision for inflation, late payment interest (reliance could be placed on the statutory right to claim interest, or specific contractual provision could be made), and requirements for financial monitoring, including annual accounts. Procedures and timetables for negotiating budgets for future years.
- **Disputes and non-compliance:** How any disagreements between the parties will be resolved.
- **Changes to the agreement:** A description of how to change, vary or extend the agreement. This may include allowing the provider to subcontract some or any element.
- **Insurance:** Requirements for any specific insurance.
- **Agreement:** The signatures of responsible officers.

Futurebuilders England can offer investment and support to develop the capacity of third sector organisations to deliver public services. It offers loans, often with additional grant and professional support, to help organisations that need investment to help them bid for, win and deliver public service contracts. It also provides sustained, flexible and individual support to ensure organisations have the right financial, managerial and governance structures to take on a loan and compete successfully for contracts in the public sector. For further details visit www.futurebuilders-england.org.uk or ring 0191 269 5200.

For further information see *Charities and public service delivery* (CC37), available from www.charity-commission.gov.uk, *Surviving contracts* by Alan Lawrie and Jan Mellor (Directory of Social Change) and *Hearts and minds: Commissioning from the voluntary sector* (The Audit Commission), available from www.audit-commission.gov.uk. NCVO's website (www.ncvo-vol.org.uk) has two useful publications, *Before signing on the dotted line: all you need to know about procuring public sector contracts* and *Introductory pack on funding and finance: Guide to procurement and contracting*. Also see the guide produced by Social Economy Scotland, *Tendering for public sector contracts*, available from www.socialeconomyscotland.info.

Handling data and information

Data protection

Organisations that record and use personal information about recognisable, living individuals will almost certainly be **data controllers** and must comply with the **Data Protection Act 1998**. Personal data includes both facts and opinions about an individual. People to whom information relates are **data subjects**.

The following is likely to be covered by the Act:

- information held on computer (including in email systems) about an individual who can be identified from the data (even if the person's name is not used) or from the data plus any other information in, or likely to be in, the data controller's possession (for example, a list of codes that includes the person's name)
- information held in manual (paper) filing systems where it is possible to access information about particular people very easily – for example, in an alphabetically organised filing cabinet or card index files
- information collected with the intention of storing it on a computer or in a manual (paper) filing system as above.

Data protection principles

Anyone responsible for processing personal data must follow the eight data protection principles. **Processing** covers everything that could be done to data, including collecting, recording, storing, organising, consulting, using, disclosing and destroying it.

The principles ensure that data is:

- processed fairly and lawfully
- collected only for specified and lawful purposes; any further processing must be compatible with these purposes
- adequate, relevant and not excessive
- accurate and up to date
- not kept longer than necessary
- processed in line with the data subject's rights under the Act
- secure (against loss, destruction or unauthorised use)
- not transferred to countries outside the European Economic Area without adequate protection (publication on the internet is potentially regarded as an overseas transfer).

When data is obtained from data subjects, the data controller must ensure that the data subject is sufficiently aware of the situation and, in particular, knows:

- who is obtaining their data
- what purposes they are going to use it for
- to whom (in general) they might disclose it
- how to exercise his or her rights – for example, how to contact the data controller.

In addition, at least one of the following circumstances must apply:

- the data subject has given informed consent to the processing. Explicit consent is needed for 'sensitive' personal data (see page 250)
- the data is needed in connection with a contract involving the data subject
- the information is necessary to protect the data subject's 'vital interests' (that is, life or death) or to carry out public functions

- there is a legal obligation to process the information (for example, for sick pay records)
- it is in the legitimate interests of the data controller or third parties to whom it is disclosed to process the data except where such processing is unwarranted because of the prejudice to the data subject's rights. This requires a balancing exercise to decide if processing is appropriate.

Sensitive personal data

Special rules apply to sensitive personal data, which includes information about someone's racial or ethnic origin, their political opinions, trade union membership, religious beliefs, health, sex life and any criminal proceedings and convictions. In many cases, the data controller should get consent in writing to hold or use such data.

There are special rules permitting certain activities without consent, including the processing of sensitive personal data needed for monitoring racial or ethnic origin, disability or religion to ensure equality of opportunity. This information can be collected and used for monitoring purposes provided there are adequate safeguards for the data subject's rights and freedoms. The Information Commissioner's *Employment practices data protection code* includes a chapter on record keeping for equal opportunities purposes.

You are also permitted to process sensitive data without consent in a number of other limited circumstances, including where you are providing a confidential service and it is either impossible to get consent or reasonable to go ahead without it.

Data subjects' rights

Under the Act, data subjects have the right to see information about themselves held on computer and in some manual records (see page 249). In response to a **subject access request** the data subject must receive:

- a copy of the information held about them and any available information about its source

- a description of why the data is being processed
- details of anyone who may see the data or to whom it may be passed or disclosed.

Subject access requests must be made in writing and data controllers can charge a fee of up to £10. They must deal with requests within 40 days. If additional information is needed to confirm the identity of the data subject or locate the data, the data controller does not have to deal with the request until this has been received. The 40-day period begins when all the necessary information and the fee, if charged, has been received. However, data controllers need to be aware that the Information Commissioner's advice is that a data controller should act promptly in requesting the fee or any further information necessary to fulfil a subject access request.

If data is inaccurate the court may order the data controller to correct or destroy the data. However, if the data accurately records the information given, and the data controller has done the best to ensure the information was accurate, the court may require the data to be supplemented with a statement of the true facts.

Individuals also have the right to prevent their data being used for direct marketing by post, fax, telephone, email, text message or other electronic means. This includes for fundraising purposes and could include volunteer recruitment or similar communications.

Registering

All data controllers must comply with the Act. In addition, many have to **notify** (register with) the Information Commissioner. Data controllers do not need to notify if they keep only the following data:

- manual systems (that is, no personal data on computer, microfilm or other electronic media except as specified in the following bullet points)
- computerised accounts and payroll activities, and limited amounts of marketing

■ computerised membership records, where members have consented to the records being kept and those records are used only for sending information to all members. Organisations that record preferences to enable certain categories of members to receive different mailings must register.

There are a number of additional exemptions from the requirement to notify for certain activities, including advertising and public relations as well as for certain non-profit making organisations. Further information is available from the notification helpline 01625 545740 and in *Notification exemptions: a self assessment guide*, available from www.ico.gov.uk.

Developing a data protection policy

The following action points could form the basis of an organisational policy on data protection, perhaps linked to the confidentiality policy (see chapter 4). They are taken from the *Guide to the 1998 Data Protection Act* by Paul Ticher, produced by Lasa (revised version *Data protection* available to download from www.lasa.org.uk).

■ **Ensure that everyone about whom the organisation holds information knows it is held**, what it is used for, and to whom it might be passed. Often a short statement on forms and leaflets, or a notice in the waiting room, will be sufficient.

■ Wherever possible get **consent** for holding a significant amount of someone's information, and get explicit consent, in writing if possible, for any sensitive information the organisation wants to hold (see *Sensitive personal data*, page 250).

■ Make sure people have the chance to **opt out** of any direct marketing.

■ **Modify the organisation's systems** to record, where necessary, consent, direct marketing opt-outs and opt-ins.

■ **Design or modify the systems** so that the organisation can easily comply with any request by data subjects (see *Data subjects' rights*, page 250) to see the records held on them.

■ **Make appropriate security arrangements**, for both manual and computer systems,

depending on the sensitivity of the information.

■ **Train or brief staff** in what they are and are not allowed to do with people's information, and whom they have to ask if they are unsure.

■ **Notify the Information Commissioner** about any non-exempt data processing activities.

■ Appoint a member of staff as **data protection compliance officer**, so that part of their job is to find out about data protection in more detail and keep the organisation within the law.

■ **Appoint a member of the management committee to oversee data protection** on behalf of the committee, and to liaise with the staff data protection compliance officer.

Further information

The Information Commissioner has published a data protection code, *The Employment Practices Code*, which consists of four parts: recruitment and selection, employment records, monitoring at work and workers' health. It can be downloaded from www.ico.gov.uk/what_we_cover/data_protection/guidance/codes_of_practice.aspx

If you handle any kind of personal data you should obtain further information about the effect of the 1998 Act. For further information and guidance contact the Information Commissioner's enquiry/information line (01625 545 745), visit www.ico.gov.uk or see *Data protection for voluntary organisations* (3rd edn), by Paul Ticher, published by the Directory of Social Change.

Electronic marketing

Under the **Privacy and Electronic Communications (EC Directive) Regulations 2003**, it is an offence to send individuals and unincorporated organisations unsolicited marketing emails (spam), text messages or faxes unless they have given prior consent. Email and text message marketing to existing customers is permitted if the marketing relates to similar goods or services, being offered by the same organisation.

Organisations should therefore use an opt-in statement on any publicity, fundraising and membership materials, along the lines of 'We may want to send you information about our work and products by email, text, fax or other electronic means. Please tick here to give your consent', rather than the currently widely used 'tick here if you don't want to hear from us' opt-out. If you send direct marketing emails, you must make clear in the subject line what they are and explain how people can opt out.

The regulations also prohibit phone marketing if the subscriber's line is on the Telephone Preference Service register, unless an individual gives specific consent to the contact. For further details see www.tpsonline.org.uk.

Freedom of information

Under the **Freedom of Information Act 2000** any person can ask to see information held by a public authority. All public authorities, and those providing services for them, must have schemes for publishing information which specify the classes of information to be published, the manner of publication and whether they make a charge.

It is extremely unlikely that any voluntary organisation will be covered by the Act because it applies to organisations that meet both of two conditions:

- The organisation must be set up by the Crown, statute, a government department, the National Assembly for Wales or a minister.
- At least one appointment to the organisation must be made by the Crown, a government department, the National Assembly for Wales or a minister.

The Ministry of Justice maintains a definitive list of the organisations to which the Freedom of Information Act applies at www.foi.gov.uk/yourRights/coverageguide.htm.

The legislation applies to any organisation holding information on behalf of a statutory body. It is therefore advisable to clarify the Freedom of Information situation if you accept any contracts with a statutory organisation.

For further information see www.justice.gov.uk/whatwedo/freedomofinformation.htm.

Copyright

Copyright protects original literary, dramatic, musical and artistic works, sound recordings, films (including videos and DVDs) and broadcasts. These works can include databases, computer programs, designs and logos.

The copyright on any material belongs to the person who originally created it, unless:

- they have assigned (transferred) that copyright, or
- it has been produced by an employee as part of their work, in which case the copyright will normally belong to the employer.

You should ensure that any contracts of employment make clear who owns the copyright if employees may produce material or documents for the organisation outside their normal work. Normally the employer would own the copyright of anything produced by an employee as part of their job, but the employee would own the copyright of anything produced outside the normal course of work.

It is also essential to clarify who will own the copyright of material or documents produced in contracts with self-employed workers, designers and consultants, and in volunteer agreements. Unless agreed otherwise, copyright will belong to the person who created the work. It is possible to have joint copyright between two or more parties, but you should take legal advice to ensure the provisions are fair to all parties and are workable. They should state, for example, what happens if one party dies (if an individual) or is wound up (if an organisation).

If the organisation is planning to publish material written, designed or created by anyone other than an employee who did the work as part of their employment, check that the copyright holder has given permission, or that the material is in the public domain or copyright has expired. This applies to illustrations, photographs, logos and material on the internet as well as to written material. There are some exceptions, such as incidental use or 'fair dealing', which can cover use for the purposes of criticism or news reporting. The fair dealing exception generally applies only if the source of the material is acknowledged. It is possible to insure against unintentional breach of copyright (see chapter 7).

Electronic copyright

Material published in electronic format (such as software or online databases) has the same protection as its printed equivalents.

Copyright material sent over the internet or stored on a website is protected in the same way as material in other media. It is advisable to mark each page of a website with the copyright symbol (©) – this is most useful in the context of enforcing copyright outside the UK – and to include a statement explaining the extent to which content may be used without permission.

If in doubt take legal advice.

For further information on handling data and information see chapter 43 of *The voluntary sector legal handbook*.

Reproduction of copyright material for visually impaired people

Under the **Copyright (Visually Impaired Persons) Act 2002** voluntary organisations can make multiple accessible copies of publications and literary, dramatic, musical or artistic work for use by visually impaired people, where the material exists only in an inaccessible form. This exception does not apply where making the accessible copies would involve recording a music performance or would infringe copyright in a database. For further information see the RNIB website, www.rnib.org.uk.

Music

If you wish to play a music recording in public you must obtain a licence from the copyright owner. Phonographic Performance Limited (PPL) enforces performance rights in sound recordings and performances; the Performing Right Society (PRS) manages performance rights in composition (that is, music and lyrics). So to play recorded music in public involves getting permission from both bodies, unless the use is exempt (see *Exemptions* below). Public performance and public playing covers virtually everything outside home use, including background music in a café and a TV in a staff room.

Exemptions

There are currently two exemptions to the rights managed by PPL. These apply to charitable bodies that:

- play CDs or other recorded music if certain conditions are met
- play radios or TVs if the broadcasts include recorded music and the audience has not been charged entry.

At the time of writing the Intellectual Property Office was conducting a consultation on copyright exemptions relating to sound recordings.

Further information

For further details see *Copyright basic facts*, available from www.ipo.gov.uk.

Defamation

Defamation covers both **libel** (involving the written word or any other permanent record such as a photograph, tape recording or video) and **slander** (involving speech in a non-permanent form, including a conversation between two or more people). For example, a verbal statement made in a speech at a meeting could be slander, and if recorded in the minutes or on tape, reported in a newsletter or on a website or repeated in a letter or email could be libellous.

Anyone suing for defamation has to prove that their reputation has been damaged. This means that an untrue statement has been made to a third party which tends to:

- lower the victim in the estimation of society, or
- make people view them with feelings of hatred, fear, ridicule, dislike or contempt.

Simply making one of the following accusations is likely to be defamatory:

- saying that someone has committed a criminal offence serious enough to be punished by imprisonment
- alleging something calculated to disparage the person as to their office, trade or profession.

A general comment could be defamatory if:

- someone's name is mentioned in conjunction with damaging circumstances: for example, 'Only criminals go to the XYZ club. Pat was seen there last week.'
- someone could deduce a meaning by implication or innuendo: for example, 'A person not a million miles away from Pat was seen handing money over to a police officer'.

Anyone defaming an unnamed member of a small identifiable group could be sued by each person in that group. So if, for example, six members of a management committee are accused of being dishonest, one or all of them could take action.

The five means of defence against an accusation of defamation are:

- proving that the **statement was true**
- showing that the words were **fair comment** – correctly stated facts giving an opinion, not malicious, about a matter of public concern. This defence cannot be used against defamation of a person's moral character
- **privilege** – this would include statements made by MPs in parliament or judges in court
- **qualified privilege**, which covers people fairly and accurately reporting court cases, parliamentary proceedings and, in some

cases, public meetings. It also includes reporting an allegation, when under a legal or moral duty, to an enforcement authority – for example, social services or the police

- **innocent defamation**, which claims that the statement was unintentional and reasonable care was taken to avoid making the mistake. An offer of amends, such as publishing a correction and an apology in a newsletter, should be made as soon as possible.

It is possible to insure against unintentional defamation (see chapter 7).

Activities

Meetings

Private meetings

Organisers of a private meeting (that is, one not open to members of the public) can refuse entry or ask someone to leave, regardless of whether the meeting is held on private or public premises or whether an entry fee is charged, without giving a reason. The police can attend private meetings only if invited by the organisers or if they believe there is likely to be a breach of the peace.

Hiring out rooms

Anyone hiring a room must comply with any terms and conditions laid down by the owners. For further details see *Hiring out parts of premises,* in chapter 6.

Public meetings

A public meeting is one that is open to the public to attend, with or without payment, and is held in a public place. It can involve any number of people.

People who force their way into a meeting are trespassing and can be evicted using reasonable force. If there is no admission charge, you can ask someone to leave at any time without warning. However, people who have paid an entrance fee can only legally be asked to leave if they are acting in such a disorderly way that the meeting cannot continue. Under the **Public Meeting Act 1908** it is illegal to try to break up a public meeting by acting in a disorderly manner or incite someone to do so, although anyone has the right to heckle within reasonable limits. Stewards, who should be easily identifiable (but should not wear a uniform to promote a political objective or signify membership of a political organisation), can help to control disorder or remove members of the public who go too far in their heckling. However, they must not try to take over the functions of the police or use force to promote a political objective – these actions would be illegal.

In addition, several local by-laws and Acts of Parliament control public meetings in parks and open spaces and in some streets. Details are available from your local authority. Under local laws you may need to give notice to the council's chief executive or local police.

Public assemblies

Under the **Public Order Act 1986 (POA)**, amended by the **Anti-Social Behaviour Act 2003**, a senior police officer has the power to impose conditions on 'public assemblies' – meetings of two or more people held partly or wholly in the open air. The officer must believe that:

- conditions are necessary to prevent serious public disorder, serious damage to property or serious disruption to the life of the community, or
- the purpose of the person organising the assembly is to intimidate others.

Conditions can relate to:

- the location of the assembly
- its duration
- the maximum number of people who may attend.

The police do not have the power to ban a public assembly altogether.

There is normally no need to give prior notice of an assembly. However, those within the vicinity of Parliament do require notice (see *Parliament*, page 256).

Processions

The POA also governs processions (which includes marches). There is no legal minimum number of people who constitute a procession. You must give the police notice of any procession that is intended to:

- demonstrate support for, or opposition to, any views or actions of any group
- publicise a cause or campaign, or
- mark or commemorate an event.

Under section 11 of the POA you must give the police at least six clear days' written notice (delivered by recorded delivery or by hand) of the date, time, route and organiser's name and address. If the procession is planned at short notice, you must hand-deliver a written notice as soon as is practicable. You must also inform the police of any change in the planned route.

There is no need to give notice if it is not reasonably practicable (for example, if a procession is spontaneous) or if the procession is held regularly in the same area. However, it is advisable to let the police know.

The police may impose conditions on a procession (including directing the route or prohibiting it from entering a specific public place) and can, in limited circumstances, have it banned. Failure to comply with the conditions is a criminal offence.

Marches and processions may also be governed by local by-laws or Acts of Parliament. Ask your local authority for details.

Protest and private land

The police have powers under the **Criminal Justice and Public Order Act 1994** as amended by the **Anti-Social Behaviour Act 2003** to control organised protests. It is a criminal offence to trespass on land (which includes buildings) with the intent of intimidating other people engaged in lawful activity, or to obstruct or disrupt them. This would include, for example, disrupting the building of a new road or entering and intimidating people conducting medical research on animals.

A senior police officer who reasonably believes that an offence has been committed or is planned and that at least two people are trespassing with the intent to intimidate people or disrupt their activity, can require them to leave the land. It is then a criminal offence to stay on the land or to return within three months.

The police can also apply to the local authority for an advance ban on any organised protest that is likely to involve trespass on private property if they believe protest would result in serious disruption to community life or would damage any historic monument or building.

Protests in London

In London the police have additional powers under the **Metropolitan Police Act 1839** to prevent traffic congestion caused by demonstrations or meetings.

Parliament

A 'demonstration' near the Houses of Parliament that falls within the 'designated area' (which includes Whitehall, some parts of the South Bank, Westminster and Parliament Square, but excludes Trafalgar Square) will be regulated by the **Serious Organised Crime and Police Act 2005**. The organiser must give written notice to the Metropolitan Police Commissioner stating the date and time of the demonstration, how it is to be carried out, and whether it is to be carried out by the organiser. If reasonably practicable, the notice must be given not less than six clear days before the day the demonstration will start, or if not reasonably practicable, as soon as possible and not less than 24 hours before the start of the demonstration.

There is no definition of a demonstration, but it could involve just one person. Processions that require notice under the POA (see *Processions*, page 255) are not covered by SOCPA.

The Commissioner must give authorisation if the required notice is given. However, he may impose conditions if these are necessary to prevent:

- serious disorder
- serious damage to property
- disruption to the life of the community
- risk to security or to health and safety
- hindrance to the proper operation of Parliament or to any person wishing to leave or enter Parliament.

For further details, including a map of the designated area, see www.met.police.uk/ events/protest_march.htm or ring the Public Order Branch of the Metropolitan Police on 020 7230 9801/9805.

Public squares and parks

For information about meetings held in Trafalgar Square and Parliament Square, contact the Squares' Management Team in the Greater London Authority (www.london.gov.uk/ squares/index.jsp); for meetings in royal parks contact the Royal Parks Agency (www.royalparks.org.uk); and for other parks, the relevant local authority. For other information and guidance contact the Public Order Branch of the Metropolitan Police Service on 020 7230 9801/9805.

Further information

For further details about meetings, processions and demonstrations see the 'The right of peaceful protest' section of http://yourrights.org.uk/.

Loudspeakers

Local by-laws govern the use of loudspeakers; for details contact your local authority. It is usually necessary to give 48 hours' written notice to the police before using a loudspeaker for non-commercial purposes. Under the **Control of Pollution Act 1974** as amended by the **Noise and Statutory Nuisance Act 1993** loudspeakers cannot be used in public places between 9pm and 8am.

Street parties

If you are planning to hold an event on publicly owned space or in the street you should contact the police, as well as the local authority engineer's and housing departments, to make sure there are no objections. The police can advise on certain aspects of organising an event, such as safety, access and traffic problems. You will need to apply to the traffic or highways department six to twelve weeks in advance for permission to close a road: there may be a charge. The engineer's department can advise on services such as gas, electricity and toilets. You have to arrange any temporary water supplies through the water company, which will ask you to sign an indemnity form absolving it of any responsibility. Make sure your organisation is adequately insured; some local authorities require public liability insurance (see chapter 7). For further information about organising street parties see www.streetparty.org.uk.

Selling, preparing and storing food

Rules of food hygiene are contained in the **Food Hygiene (England) Regulations 2006 (as amended)** (and equivalent regulations in Scotland, Wales and Northern Ireland). Most of the regulations cover movable or temporary premises (for example, stalls at a fete, mobile vans or vending machines), as well as fixed premises, and apply whether food and drink is sold at a profit, at cost or less, or is given away.

You must also put in place food safety management procedures (that is, you must be able to show what you do to make or sell food that is safe to eat, and have this written down) and review them as necessary.

Under the temperature control requirements of the regulations hot foods must be kept at or above 63°C and cold foods at or below 8°C. This applies to all types of food premises (including those out of doors).

For further information contact your local environmental health department or the Food Standards Agency helpline (020 7276 8829) or see Community Matters' information sheet 11 *Food safety and food hygiene*, available from www.communitymatters.org.uk, or *Food hygiene, a guide for businesses*, available from www.food.gov.uk.

Licensing premises

Much of this section has been adapted, with permission, from Community Matters' information sheet 20 *The Licensing Act 2003*, available from www.communitymatters.org.uk.

The **Licensing Act 2003** established an integrated scheme for licensing premises. A single **premises licence** can now cover the retail sale of alcohol, the supply of alcohol by clubs, the provision of regulated entertainment and the provision of late night refreshment, and is not time limited. Each licensed premises must appoint a **designated premises supervisor (DPS)**. If the licence covers the sale of alcohol, the DPS must also hold a personal licence (see below).

Anyone supervising or authorising the sale of alcohol must hold a **personal licence**, which enables the holder to work in any licensed premises. A personal licence is initially issued for ten years, and may be renewed. Licensed premises may have more than one personal licence holder.

Premises and personal licences can only be issued to people aged 18 or over.

Local authorities issue both types of licence. A fee is usually payable, related to the rateable value of the premises.

Temporary event notices (TENs) can be used to authorise relatively small-scale and ad hoc events, and events on premises with a premises licence that does not cover any or all of the activities planned (for example, supply of alcohol). The event must last no longer than 96 hours and involve no more than 499 people.

The system requires an event organiser to give a TEN to the licensing authority (with a fee – £21 in 2008/09) and a copy to the police no less than ten working days before the start of the event.

Anyone aged 18 or over can give up to five TENs in a calendar year. Personal licence holders (see page 257) can give a maximum of 50 TENs per calendar year. Each property can have up to 12 TENs a calendar year, for a maximum total of 15 days. There must be a minimum of 24 hours between events.

Registered social clubs

Clubs that meet certain criteria may be granted a **clubs premises certificate**. This entitles the club to certain benefits, including the authority to supply alcohol to its members and sell it to guests without anyone needing to hold a personal licence or having to specify a designated premises supervisor. The application process is similar to that for a premises licence. Criteria include:

- no one can become a member until at least two days after applying
- members must wait at least two days before enjoying the privileges of membership
- the club must have at least 25 members and be established and conducted in good faith as a club.

A club, if it prefers, can apply for a premises licence instead of, or as well as, a club premises certificate.

Regulated entertainment

The Act describes regulated entertainment as:
- the performance of a play
- an exhibition of a film
- an indoor sporting event
- boxing or wrestling
- live music
- playing of recorded music
- a dance performance
- entertainment of a similar description to live music, recorded music or dance.

To be regulated, the entertainment must take place in the presence of an audience with the aim of entertaining that audience. So, for example, a play performed to students for educational purposes would probably not be covered, and a choir's rehearsal would certainly not be covered. If in doubt, check with your local authority.

Exemptions

Some public entertainment does not require a premises licence if neither alcohol nor late night refreshment (see below) is provided. The main exemptions include:

- entertainment incidental to religious services or meetings or at places of public religious worship
- Morris dancing or similar dancing
- incidental music
- garden fetes and similar functions (if not held for private gain).

Late night refreshment

Late night refreshment means the supply of hot food or drink to the public, for consumption on or off the premises, between 11pm and 5am. Registered charities are exempt from the requirement to obtain a licence for this purpose.

Fee exemptions

The following require a premises licence but are exempt from the associated fees if only entertainment is provided (that is, there is no alcohol or late night refreshment):

- church or chapel halls or other similar places of public religious worship, and village, parish or community halls and other similar buildings
- schools and sixth form colleges (where the school provides the entertainment).

For further information see www.culture.gov.uk/ what_we_do/alcohol_and_entertainment.

Campaigning and political activity

In 2008 the Charity Commission updated its guidance on political activity. The law has not changed, but the revised guidance is much clearer. In particular it clarifies the distinction between **non-political campaigning** (raising awareness of issues, mobilising support and ensuring the law is observed) and **political campaigning** (trying to change the law or to change policies of local, national or international governments). This section outlines some of the main areas covered by the guidance; for further details see *Campaigning and political activities by charities* (CC9), available from www.charitycommission.gov.uk.

Some charities have a parallel non-charitable organisation to carry out their political activity. For example, Liberty is not a charity, and so is free to carry out political campaigning. The linked but separate Civil Liberties Trust is registered as a charity. If you adopt this strategy you must ensure that the charitable and non-charitable bodies have completely separate accounts, committees and decision-making procedures. If the charity's premises, equipment and staff time are used by the non-charity, the charity must charge an appropriate amount. Take advice from an accountant or solicitor if considering this approach.

Trustees' duties

Trustees (a charity's committee members) must be satisfied that any campaigning activities will support or further the charity's purposes, to an extent justified by the resources used.

The main factors to consider are:
- whether the campaigning activities are prohibited by the charity's constitution (the constitution does not need to contain an express power to campaign)
- where the charity has educational purposes, it is particularly important to ensure that any campaigning activity is balanced and presents both sides of the argument

- the balance between the benefits to the charity and its beneficiaries and the risk to the charity, particularly its independence and reputation
- compliance with the general law and other regulatory requirements (see *Legislation*, page 260).

Trustees must identify and review any major risks and put systems in place to reduce that risk.

Permitted activities

Examples of the types of activities a charity is allowed to carry out are:
- supporting or opposing the passage of a parliamentary bill (or Welsh Assembly Proposed Measure)
- publishing comments on proposed or possible changes in the law or government policy
- supplying relevant information to politicians
- promoting the need for a particular piece of legislation
- providing politicians' voting patterns to supporters and the public in order to influence them to change their position
- seeking to influence central or local government or other public bodies such as NHS trusts on public opinion issues relating to the charity's purposes or to the wider well-being of the charitable sector. It can also support a government policy
- supporting a policy advocated by a political party or candidate, although it cannot support a political party or individual politician.

A charity may:
- affiliate to a campaigning alliance where the alliance will help to further or support the charity's purposes, but it must carefully consider the risks involved
- focus most or all of its resources on political activity for a period. In such a case the trustees must have considered all the options open to them and have decided that, for the time being, the charity's purposes are most effectively pursued through political activity.

Remember that any activity must support or further the charity's purposes.

Campaigning methods

A charity can use any reasonable method to campaign. Seek specialist advice if you are unsure about the legality or propriety of any campaigning method.

A charity can:

- give its supporters or members of the public material to send to politicians, as long as it can demonstrate that a considered decision was made to engage in the activity and there was a rationale for using the chosen material
- use emotive or controversial material based on well-founded evidence in a campaign, where this can be justified. But trustees must consider the possible consequences of using such materials, as they may change public perception of the charity
- use its resources to carry out or commission research to back up a campaign, or endorse existing research, as long as the trustees are sure that it is robust
- organise and present a petition in support of a campaign. The petition and supporting material should make clear the purpose of the petition and the charity should be able to demonstrate, on request, that the petition's authenticity can be verified
- organise, promote or participate in demonstrations or direct action by providing information. This can extend to taking part in marches, rallies, or peaceful picketing, but again the trustees must consider the risk to public perception.

Elections

Once a local, regional or national election has been called, charities that are campaigning will need to take special care to ensure their political neutrality. A charity must never indicate which candidate to support. For details about acceptable activities in the run up to elections see the Charity Commission guidance *Charities and elections*, available at www.charitycommission.gov.uk/supportingcharities/elect.asp.

At the time of writing the Commission was developing further guidance outlining the implications and provisions of electoral law for charities, which will be available on its website.

Use of premises

A charity whose purpose includes providing premises to community groups can allow local political or campaigning groups to use its premises, but only on the same terms as other non-commercial organisations. A charity may refuse to allow a particular organisation or individual to use its premises if:

- their activities would conflict with the charity's purposes
- there is a risk of public disorder
- there is a risk of alienating the charity's users or supporters (for example, if the organisation in question is associated with racist beliefs).

Under the **Representation of the People Act 1983** certain charities may be required to allow election candidates to use their premises free of charge. For further details see *Charities and elections*, available at www.charitycommission.gov.uk/supportingcharities/elect.asp.

Legislation

Trustees must be aware of the following legal and regulatory requirements, as well as charity law:

- The Advertising Standards Authority (ASA) and Broadcast Committee of Advertising Practice (BCAP): charities should take all reasonable steps to comply with the ASA and BCAP Codes (see www.asa.org.uk). Serious or persistent breaches of these Codes may result in the Charity Commission taking regulatory action.
- The **Communications Act 2003** prohibits political advertising in the broadcast media.
- The **Serious Organised Crime and Police Act 2005** places restrictions on campaigning, including demonstrations (see *Protests*, page 255).

Other legal requirements include the civil law on defamation (see page 253) and the criminal law on incitement.

Charities that overstep the mark on campaigning may receive a demand for income tax or corporation tax on at least part of their income. Trustees may, in rare cases, be liable for breach of trust. If non-charitable activities continue, the Charity Commission may be prompted to take investigative action, but the Commission has stated that serious problems are rare.

Further information

To clarify whether a proposed campaigning activity (including the content of publications or advertisements) would be acceptable, see CC9 or telephone Charity Commission Direct on 0845 3000 218.

The National Council for Voluntary Organisations' Campaigning Effectiveness Programme (campaigning@ncvo-vol.org.uk or www.ncvo-vol.org.uk/ce) supports organisations that want to increase the impact of their campaigns. It publishes *Campaigning in collaboration*, by Sarah Shimmin and Gareth Coles, available from www.dsc.org.uk.

Fundraising

This section looks at some of the forms of fundraising available to voluntary organisations. The Directory of Social Change publishes a range of books on many other ways of raising funds; for details see www.dsc.org.uk. The website www.how2fundraise.org is another useful resource for volunteer fundraisers.

Regulation

The Fundraising Standards Board (www.frsb.org.uk) was set up to oversee a self-regulatory scheme for fundraising in the UK. Both charities and fundraisers can subscribe. Members are expected to comply with the Institute of Fundraising Practice's codes of practice, which provide a guide to the law and best practice in relation to fundraising activity.

The codes, and a code of practice, can be downloaded from www.institute-of-fundraising.org.uk. The **Charities Act 2006** gives the government the power to introduce statutory regulation of fundraisers should self-regulation fail.

Fundraising statements

Under the **Charities Act 1992** professional fundraisers appealing for money on behalf of a charity must have a written contract with the charity that satisfies legal regulations. Any request for funds must be accompanied by a statement indicating who will benefit, the way in which the proceeds will be distributed, the method of calculating the fundraiser's remuneration and the actual amount, or a reasonable estimate, of their total remuneration.

Paid employees and committee members of a charity or company connected with the charity who are acting as collectors in a public collection must also make a statement to potential donors. The content will vary, according to whether the collection is for a named charity or for particular charitable purposes, but should include the person's position within the organisation, that they are paid to be in that position, and the name of the organisation(s) for which they are collecting.

Both cases only apply to those earning at least £5 a day, £500 a year or, if paid in a lump sum, at least £500.

At the time of writing the Charity Commission had recommended increasing these thresholds to £10 and £1,000 and the government had supported that recommendation.

For further information see *Draft guidance on professional fundraising and commercial participation*, available from www.cabinetoffice.gov.uk/third_sector/law_and_regulation.aspx, and *Guidance for employees and paid officers or trustees of a charity required to make a solicitation statement*, available from www.cabinetoffice.gov.uk/third_sector/law_and_regulation.aspx.

Right to a refund

Anyone who gives £50 or more in response to a radio or television appeal made by a professional fundraiser using a debit or credit card is entitled to a full refund, less reasonable administration expenses, if they decide to cancel their donation within seven days. The right to a refund must be made explicit in the appeal; failure to do so is a criminal offence.

At the time of writing the Charity Commission had recommended increasing the minimum amount to £100 and the government had supported that recommendation.

If a donor has bought goods following representations made on the radio or on television to the effect that a percentage of the purchase price will be given to a charity, there is a similar right to a refund, but this is dependent on the return of the goods.

Trading

Charities are not in general allowed to trade regularly. However, there are exceptions; for details see *Trading,* in chapter 1.

Car boot sales

Under the **Local Government (Miscellaneous Provision) Act 1982**, more than five cars or stalls constitute a market and therefore an application must be submitted to the local council at least a month before such an event. However, if all the proceeds of a car boot sale are for charitable purposes, or sales are carried out on private property with the owner's permission, the Act does not apply.

Regular events may require planning permission. If in doubt check with the local authority's planning department.

Exempt fundraising events

Charities, and some other non-profit making bodies, are exempt from charging VAT on up to 15 fundraising events of any kind held in any one location, within a financial year. An exempt event is defined as one organised and promoted primarily for the purpose of raising money, and includes those accessible through electronic communication.

There is no restriction on the number of small-scale events of any one kind, such as coffee mornings, as long as weekly gross takings for such events do not exceed £1,000.

A fundraising event that meets these criteria for VAT exemption will automatically be exempt from tax on the profits (income tax if the organisation is a charitable trust, or corporation tax if it is an association or company). Profits from events that do not meet these criteria may be subject to VAT and/or to tax.

For further information see CWL4 *Fundraising events: exemptions for charities and other fundraising bodies*, available from www.hmrc.gov.uk/charities.

Gift Aid

The Gift Aid scheme enables UK taxpayers (both individuals and companies) to make tax effective donations to charities. Donations can be regular or one-off and of any amount. Where an individual makes a donation, a charity can reclaim the basic rate of tax paid from HM Revenue & Customs (HMRC). Until 5 April 2011 the government will pay a supplement of 3p in the pound for all donations, to compensate for the reduction in the basic tax rate from 22% to 20% (claims must be made within two years from the end of the tax year concerned). This means that until that date a £10 donation is worth £12.80, instead of £12.50.

Individual donors must give the charity a Gift Aid **declaration**. The declaration can be made in writing, electronically or orally, cover one or more donations, be backdated up to six years, and also cover future donations. Charities must send the donor a written record of an oral declaration. Declarations must include certain information, but you can design your own form: a model is available from www.hmrc.gov.uk/charities/giftaid-charities/how.htm.

To recover tax on individuals' donations you must write to HMRC Charities, with proof of the organisation's charitable status. You must keep sufficient records to show that tax reclaims are accurate, otherwise you may have to pay back the tax reclaimed, with interest (see *Gift Aid*, in chapter 8).

Companies wanting to make Gift Aid donations get corporation tax relief on the value of their gift. They can increase its value by giving an amount that includes the corporation tax they would otherwise have to pay on that figure and then claim tax relief on the gift when calculating their profits for corporation tax.

For further details see www.hmrc.gov.uk/charities/giftaid-charities/how.htm or phone 0845 302 0203.

Payroll giving

Under the payroll giving scheme employees can authorise their employer to deduct charitable donations from their pay before calculating PAYE. Employees will get tax relief on their donations at their highest rate of tax (but still must pay the usual rate of national insurance) and benefiting charities receive a regular donation. There is no limit on the amount that can be given under the scheme.

The employer pays the donations to a payroll giving agency, which must pass on the donations to nominated charities within 60 days of receipt. Agencies generally deduct an administrative charge (unless the employer pays this on the donor's behalf). The fee is normally a maximum of 4% or 25p (whichever is greater), so a charity would receive £9.60 of a £10 donation.

For further details contact HMRC Charities (www.hmrc.gov.uk/payrollgiving/charities or 08453 020203) or the Payroll Giving Centre (www.payrollgivingcentre.org.uk or 0845 602 6786).

Gifts of shares and securities

Individuals and companies can get tax relief for gifts of certain shares and securities to a charity when calculating their income or profits for tax purposes. The tax relief applies when the shares or securities are donated without conditions.

For further information, including clarification of which shares and securities qualify, contact HMRC Charities on 0845 302 0203 or see www.hmrc.gov.uk/incometax/relief-charity-assets.htm.

Collections

To collect money on **private premises** you just need the owner's permission. This includes a single collection or a static collection box in a pub or shop, but you will need a street collection permit if a collection is to be held 'in a street or public place'. A 'public place' is a 'place where the public has access'. It is advisable to check with your licensing authority if you are in any doubt about whether an area constitutes 'private premises'. Collections from shop to shop or from pub to pub need a house-to-house collection permit. For further details see below.

For details of collecting from underground stations contact the Charities Team at Transport for London (0845 330 9874; email charities@tube.tfl.gov.uk). For collections at railway stations contact the station manager.

The **Charities Act 2006** introduces a new system regulating public charitable collections in England and Wales. For details see *Public charitable collections,* page 264. This is unlikely to come into force until 2010. Until then, the following applies.

The **House-to-House Collections Act 1939** and the **Police, Factories, etc. (Miscellaneous Provisions) Act 1916** as amended by the Local Government Act 1972 currently govern **house-to-house** and **street collections** and collections on private premises where the public has right of access. For such collections you must apply in writing to the licensing authority no later than the first day of the month preceding the month in which the collection takes place. It is likely the licensing authority will have an application form for you to complete, providing information such as the purpose of the collection, where you propose to collect, the number of collectors and what they will be paid.

In London the licensing authority is the Metropolitan Police Service's Charities Office (020 7321 7129, www.met.police.uk/charities) or, for collections in the City, the Corporation of London (020 7332 3226). Elsewhere it is the local authority. The regulations apply to collecting goods as well as cash.

If a licence is refused or revoked, you can appeal to the Minister for the Cabinet Office within 14 days of when notice is given.

There is currently no law controlling face-to-face fundraising (direct debit solicitation) but this will be covered in the new legislation (see *Public charitable collections, below*). *The Public Fundraising Regulatory Association has a code of practice for this type of fundraising (see www.pfra.org.uk).*

Some national charities have been granted an **Order of Exemption**, enabling them to make house-to-house collections anywhere in England and Wales at any time. However, under best practice guidelines issued by the Cabinet Office to exemption order holders, a charity with such an exemption order should inform the local authority (or in London, the police) of its plans and try to avoid overlapping with other collections by notifying other exemption holders of future collections.

Regulations

Under the **House to House Collection Regulations 1947** the promoter of a **house-to-house collection** must comply with a number of rules, including the following:

- collectors are aged 16 or over
- each collector carries a certificate of authority and a prescribed badge (available from the Stationery Office) which conforms to Home Office regulations and is signed by the promoter

- collectors produce their badges on request and give their names to the police if asked
- collectors do not annoy passers-by or householders
- any collecting boxes are numbered and sealed
- any envelopes used have a gummed flap
- if neither boxes nor envelopes are used, receipts are given from a receipt book with consecutively numbered pages
- a record is kept of each box, authorisation badge and permit issued.

After the collection, the boxes or envelopes must be opened in the presence of the promoter and a witness, unless the sealed box is taken to the bank. The contents should be recorded.

A statement of accounts must be sent to the licensing authority, showing the amount collected and the expenses incurred, the number of boxes distributed and confirmation that all have been returned.

The licensing authority can make rules covering **street collections** in its area. Contact your local licensing authority for details of local regulations. In most cases these rules are virtually the same as for house-to-house collections.

Collection boxes can be purchased from Angal Limited (0845 130 9963/01903 787 978).

Public charitable collections

The **Charities Act 2006** introduces a new regime, which covers house-to-house and street collections, including face-to-face fundraising (direct debit solicitation). This is unlikely to come into force before 2010. An outline is given in the following paragraphs; details will be included in regulations to be produced by the Office of the Third Sector and the Charity Commission.

Promoters of such collections will need to hold a **public collections certificate (PCC)**, issued by the Charity Commission for up to five years (although there are exceptions – see page 265). Once a PCC is issued, the Commission will be able to suspend, withdraw or vary the certificate. No further permit will be needed for house-to-house collections, although the promoter must notify the local authority in advance.

For collections in public places (which will include some privately owned land to which the public has unrestricted access, such as station ticket halls and supermarket forecourts), the promoter will also require a permit from the local authority. The local authority's decision whether to issue a permit must be based solely on whether the collection would cause a public nuisance. It will be possible to appeal against the refusal or withdrawal of a permit.

Local short-term charitable collections will not need a PCC or a permit. The types of collection covered will be set out in regulations, but are likely to be events such as carol singing and collecting for a school jumble sale. The organiser will still need to let the local authority know about the collection beforehand.

The national exemption scheme will be abolished.

Regulations are likely to deal with requirements to keep and publish accounts, the form of badges to be worn and the minimum age for collectors.

Sponsored activities

Events such as sponsored walks, swims or bicycle rides can be financially rewarding, although they can take a lot of organisation. Keep a record of the names and addresses of everyone who is being sponsored. Include the following on sponsorship forms:

- a description of the event
- its purpose and date
- a statement that all money raised will go to the charity: 'All money raised will go direct to . . . No expenses will be deducted'
- the name, address and (if under 18) age of the sponsored person
- each sponsor's name, address and amount pledged

- if the funds raised will be donated to a charity, a Gift Aid statement suitable for a sponsorship form and space for sponsors to tick if they want their donations to be treated as Gift Aid donations (for the correct wording, see HMRC's *Gift Aid guidance*, available from www.hmrc.gov.uk/charities)
- the statement 'I certify that . . . has walked . . . miles/swum . . . lengths/danced for . . . hours', followed by the signature of the organiser and the date
- registered charity status if appropriate
- a statement clarifying whether any money raised before the event will be retained or returned if the person doesn't participate or doesn't complete the event.

Keep a record of the value of the sponsorship on each form and whether the money has been handed in. You may find it helpful to look at other organisations' sponsorship forms for ideas.

Note that if sponsorship is collected door to door, you will need a house-to-house collection permit (see *Collections*, page 263).

It is very important to discuss the insurance implications of any sponsored event with an insurance broker, and where events involve children, to consider potential Children Act requirements. Where sponsored activities are held overseas or are intrinsically dangerous (such as parachuting) it is especially important to ensure that all insurances are in order (see chapter 7).

Sustrans's guide to sponsored events (available from the 'rides and events' section of www.sustrans.org.uk) includes useful information about what to consider when organising such an event.

Lotteries, raffles and bingo

The following sections are largely drawn from Community Matters' information sheets 24 *The Gambling Act* 2005 and 26 *Bingo*, available from www.communitymatters.org.uk.

The law relating to most forms of gambling, including lotteries (apart from the National

Lottery), raffles and bingo, is now contained in the **Gambling Act 2005**. The regulatory body is the **Gambling Commission.**

Licences

Under the Act, there are three types of licence:

- **operating licences** (issued to businesses and other organisations promoting gambling)
- **premises licences** (issued to premises where gambling activities take place)
- **personal licences** (issued to individuals who have an ability to affect the outcome of gambling).

Premises licences

Local authorities issue premises licences for various forms of gambling including bingo and betting, and permits for gaming machines in alcohol-licensed premises and members' clubs, other gaming activities in members' clubs and Category D machines, which can be used by children and have the lowest level of stakes and prizes. However, many smaller voluntary organisations will be classed as small-scale operators and will be exempt from needing a licence. If in doubt contact your local authority's licensing department.

Personal management licences

Certain individuals working in the gambling industry will need to hold a personal management licence. However, there is an exemption for small-scale operators, which will apply to most smaller voluntary organisations. Further information is available on the Gambling Commission's website www.gamblingcommission.gov.uk and in the Commission's publication *Lotteries and the law*.

Lotteries

The Act defines a lottery as any arrangement whereby:

- people have to pay to enter
- one or more prizes are allocated
- prizes are allocated by a process which relies wholly on chance (a **simple** lottery), or

- prizes are allocated by a series of processes, the first of which relies wholly on chance (a **complex** lottery).

Exempt lotteries

Exempt lotteries do not require a licence from the Gambling Commission. They include the following.

Incidental non-commercial lotteries (or raffles). Lotteries that are incidental to a non-commercial event (that is, all the money raised, including entrance fees, goes entirely to purposes that are not for private gain). Tickets must be sold at the event location during the event, and the result must be made public during the event. The promoters can deduct a maximum of £100 from the proceeds for expenses (such as printing tickets) and no more than £500 for the cost of prizes.

Private lotteries. These are of four types:

- private society lotteries – only open to members of the society and those on society premises
- work lotteries – limited to people who work together on the same premises
- residents' lotteries – for people who live at the same premises
- customer lotteries – for customers at the business premises.

Private lotteries can only be advertised and promoted, and tickets sold, at the premises of the relevant society, work, residence or business. Tickets must show the people to whom the promoter can sell or supply tickets, and the fact that they are not transferable.

Society lotteries. Lotteries promoted on behalf of an organisation wholly or mainly for charitable purposes, participation in, or support of, athletic sports, games or cultural activities, or other purposes not for private gain or commercial undertaking. There are two types:

- **Small society lottery:** this applies where annual ticket sales do not exceed £20,000 for a single lottery and £250,000 for all lotteries. Small society lotteries are exempt lotteries (see above) but they must be registered with the local authority.

- **Large society lottery:** lotteries that exceed the above limits must be registered with the Gambling Commission and require an operating licence.

Tickets, prizes and expenses. Lottery tickets must not be sold to or by anyone aged under 16. There is no maximum price, but all tickets must cost the same (so, for example, five tickets cannot be sold for the price of four). Every ticket must specify:

- its price
- the name of the society promoting the lottery
- the promoter's name and address
- the date of the draw
- where appropriate, the fact that the society is licensed by the Gambling Commission.

Tickets can be sold from door to door but not on the street.

No prize may exceed £25,000 or 10% of the total value of the tickets sold, whichever is the greater. Proceeds must not exceed £4 million for a single lottery or £10 million within one calendar year. A minimum of 20% of the gross proceeds must go directly to the purposes of the society; the promoters can choose how to divide the remainder between prizes, expenses and any further contribution to the charity.

Records – Gambling Commission. Societies licensed by the Gambling Commission must submit a return to the Commission within three months of the draw or, in the case of a scratch card lottery, within three months of the last date on which tickets were on sale. The return must show the total proceeds and how they were distributed between prizes and expenses and the amount applied directly to the society's purpose.

Accounting records, including details of the total proceeds and expenses of each lottery and the number of sold and unsold tickets, must be kept for a minimum of three years, and must be available for inspection by the Commission on request. Where the cumulative proceeds exceed £1 million in a calendar year,

the society must send the Commission written confirmation from a qualifying auditor that the proceeds have been fully accounted for in audited accounts, within ten months of the end of the period to which the accounts relate.

Records – local authority. Societies registered with the local authority must submit a statement showing:

- the date on which tickets were available for sale and the date of the draw
- the total proceeds
- the amount deducted for prizes and costs
- the amount applied directly to the purpose for which the society is conducted
- details of expenses not covered by deduction from proceeds.

For further details of all aspects of holding lotteries see *Lotteries and the law*, published by the Gambling Commission, available from www.gamblingcommission.gov.uk.

Gaming machines

Gaming machines can be a useful source of revenue for clubs but as some people object to them it is important to consult members before acquiring one. Premises licensed for the on-premises supply of alcohol (see *Licensing premises,* page 257) have an automatic entitlement to two gaming machines.

Other members' clubs (see *Members' clubs* overleaf) will need a **club machine permit** from the local authority. They can have up to three machines, from four categories: B3A (maximum £1 stake and £500 prizes); B4 (maximum £1 stake and £250 prize); C (maximum 50p stake and £35 prize); and D (maximum stake 10p and £5 prize; these can also give non-cash prizes up to a value of £8, with a maximum stake of 30p). There is no statutory minimum payout. Machines can be used only by club members or signed-in guests. People aged under 18 can only play type D machines.

Only authorised people can remove money from the machine; these would usually be committee members or club employees.

Contact your local authority about the use of a gaming machine at a one-off event such as a bazaar, fete or social.

For further details contact the Gambling Commission on 0121 230 6666.

Bingo

Members' clubs

Under the Gambling Act 2005 a members' club must have at least 25 members and be established and conducted wholly or mainly for purposes other than gaming, for the benefit of their members and with the intention of operating on an ongoing basis.

Such clubs can provide facilities for bingo under the 'exempt gaming' provisions in **Part 12** of the Act (**section 269**). The following rules apply:

- no amounts may be deducted from sums staked or won (that is, expenses and other costs must be covered from the admission fee)
- the admission fee can be no higher than £1 per person per day
- people can only participate if they have been a member for at least 48 hours, or are genuine guests of a member.

There are no limits on individual stakes or prizes, but clubs that wish to offer stakes or prizes exceeding £2,000 a week will need a bingo operating licence from the Gambling Commission.

Bingo for 'good causes'

Organisations that wish to provide bingo for charitable or other non-commercial purposes may do so under **Part 14** of the Act. Non-commercial gaming may only take place at events where none of the proceeds are used for private gain, and participants must be told that the purpose of the game is to raise money for a specified purpose. There are two types:

- **Prize gaming**: where the prizes are put up in advance and are not dependent on the number of players or the amount staked. There are no limits on stakes, prizes, participation fees or other charges.
- **Equal chance gaming**: where the amount or value of the prizes varies according to the number of players who participate and/or the amount of money they stake. A single daily charge of £8 can be made, to cover admission, stakes and any other charges for playing. The total value of prizes must not exceed £600 a day (apart from the final event in a series, in which case the prize fund can be up to £900).

Under-18s may participate in such games.

Premises licensed for the sale of alcohol

Premises holding a premises licence that includes the sale of alcohol (see *Licensing premises*, page 257) may provide facilities for bingo under **section 279** of the Act. The following conditions apply:

- players may be charged a fee for participating
- the maximum stake is £5
- no amounts may be deducted from money staked or won (that is, expenses must be taken from the participation fee)
- under-18s may not participate.

If stakes or prizes exceed £2,000 a week the premises will need a bingo operating licence from the Gambling Commission.

For further information see the fact sheets *Bingo under the Gambling Act 2005* and *Gaming and gaming machines in clubs and miners' welfare institutes under the Gambling Act 2005*, available from www.culture.gov.uk, or contact the Gambling Commission on 0121 230 6666.

Minibuses and coaches

Organisations that own a minibus or coach with nine or more passenger seats require a **Section 19 permit** (9–16 passenger seats) or a **large bus permit** (17 or more seats) if they use the vehicle for 'hire or reward'. This includes any arrangement where there is payment for the trip, even if the charge includes other items such as a meal, or the payment is treated as a donation. Organisations running a service for profit need a **Public Service Vehicle (PSV) Operators' Licence.**

Section 19 permits can cover five types of passenger: class A – members of the organisation holding the permit; class B – the organisation's beneficiaries and people who help them; class C – disabled people and people with learning disabilities, people who are seriously ill, and their carers; class D – pupils or students and staff or other helpers; class E – other classes of people specified in the permit.

You do not need a permit or licence if passengers are not charged in any way.

Application forms for Section 19 permits are available from the local authority, a designated body (a national voluntary organisation that can issue permits), Traffic Area Offices or www.vosa.org.uk. All drivers must be aged 21 or over. Drivers who passed their test before 1 January 1997 are automatically entitled to drive minibuses with 9–16 passenger seats not used for hire or reward. Drivers who passed their test on or after 1 January 1997 and have held a licence for at least two years may be entitled to drive minibuses of gross weight not exceeding 3.5 tonnes (4.25 tonnes including any specialised equipment for carrying disabled passengers).

Permits for large buses are issued to umbrella organisations by the local Traffic Commissioner. Drivers of such vehicles need a full PCV (Passenger Carrying Vehicle) Category D on their licence.

For further information see *Passenger transport provided by voluntary groups under the Section 19 or 22 permit*, from www.vosa.org.uk (this includes a list of designated bodies and Traffic Area Offices), or contact the Community Transport Association Advice Line on 0845 130 6195.

Hiring to other organisations

An organisation that hires your minibus and intends to charge passengers may need its own permit. This can be avoided if you (as the permit holder) also appoint the driver. Passengers must then pay you, the permit holder, and not the hiring organisation, although that organisation could collect the money.

If you are hiring out your vehicle, make sure the passengers of the hiring group are covered by your permit, drivers are licensed to drive a vehicle of that type and the vehicle meets all safety requirements. Remember to inform your insurance company. A standard vehicle insurance policy excludes use for 'hire or reward' so the policy will need to be extended to cover this, which may greatly increase the premium.

At the time of writing the Local Transport Bill was going through parliament, which will result in further opportunities being available to the voluntary sector in 2009. For further information contact the Community Transport Association Advice Line on 0845 130 6195.

Confidentiality and information sharing

Organisations should consider developing a confidentiality policy to ensure workers and volunteers understand how to manage information and users know how their confidential information will be treated.

Those managing information must also know the implications of any breach of confidentiality. It is a criminal offence for anyone to obtain unauthorised access to personal data 'knowingly or recklessly', and in response to persistent high profile security breaches there is a likelihood that eventually the law will be changed to make managers personally liable for serious breaches of confidentiality.

There is no single piece of legislation regulating the collection, use and sharing of personal information; these activities are governed by a range of statutory provisions, common-law rules and a duty of care to service users. The main legislation governing information management includes:

- the **Data Protection Act 1998**, which covers the storage and use of personal data in written and electronic formats (see page 249)
- **Article 8** of the **Human Rights Act 1998** (see page 272), which stresses the respect for private and family life. Although this only applies to public authorities it is good practice for voluntary organisations to comply
- the **Freedom of Information Act 2000** (see page 252), which governs the right of access to information held by public authorities.

Common law rather than statute governs the law of confidence. Where express obligations of confidence are lacking, implied duties of confidentiality will need to be considered. An implied duty of confidence may arise where confidential information is given to a worker or volunteer in circumstances which make it clear that it is being communicated subject to restrictions of confidentiality.

For information to be regarded as confidential it must have the necessary 'quality of confidence' about it. This means that it must be of limited availability to the public and limited in nature: that is, referring to specific people, ideas or documents. Furthermore, the information must have been communicated to, obtained by or become known to the worker or volunteer in circumstances imposing a duty of confidence (for example, marked 'Confidential') or where someone has been made aware of, or is aware, that the information is confidential. If the information is already independently and widely available to the worker or volunteer no obligation arises.

The duty of confidentiality is likely to be breached where there has been an unauthorised use of the information. This will include situations where a worker or volunteer knew or ought to have known that the information should not be disclosed. If

someone has shared the confidential information with the express permission of the person who provided it or to whom it relates, there will be no breach of confidence. Similarly, if the information was given on the basis that it would be shared with a limited number of people or for limited purposes, then sharing it in that way will not be a breach of confidence.

Common law can be overridden if there is a public interest in disclosure of the information.

Contractual agreements can also provide the basis for collecting, using and sharing personal information, and organisations and individual practitioners should also take into account any relevant professional guidance or industry code.

There are exceptions where organisations may have a duty to disclose information. These include:

- the **Money Laundering Regulations 2003**, where suspicions of money laundering have to be reported to the police
- the **Prevention of Terrorism Act 2000**, where it is an offence to withhold information which may prevent acts of terrorism
- the **Criminal Justice Act 1993**, where it is an offence to withhold information on drug trafficking
- to ensure that an organisation provides a duty of care in a life threatening situation (for example, suicide or self-harming behaviour)
- under a contractual obligation – for example, an organisation may be obliged to share information if it is providing services to a local authority
- where disclosure is required by a court order.

Voluntary organisations should develop their own policies on circumstances in which disclosure is necessary. For example, there is no specific legal duty for an individual to report child abuse, but organisations working with children should develop a child protection policy within their workplace which requires their employees and volunteers to safeguard and promote the welfare of children and which would include reporting abuse to the relevant authorities.

Employees' contracts should contain an explicit requirement to adhere to the organisation's confidentiality policy.

Confidentiality policies

A confidentiality policy should set out the rules for managing information, which could include:

- the information the organisation will hold, why it is being held and for how long
- who has access to each type of information, for what purpose(s) and whether access to certain categories of information needs to be authorised.

Handling and storing information

The security measures that each organisation takes should be proportional to the risks it identifies. Typical provisions of a security policy for confidential information might include:

- Users' records must be labelled 'confidential' and kept in a locked cabinet.
- Computerised records must be password protected.
- Confidential information must not be left on desks, in filing trays or on public view such as on computer screens.
- Information in electronic form should only be removed from the office if strictly necessary.
- If confidential information has to be sent by email (which is probably more secure than fax), the address to which it is sent must be carefully verified beforehand, and it may be advisable to password-protect the information in attached documents.
- If any files, disks, memory sticks or laptop computers are taken away from the office they must be fully encrypted, password-protected, carried securely and never left unattended.
- Records that need to be destroyed must be shredded.

- If a computer is being disposed of, the data must be wiped off beforehand (see *The green office*, in chapter 6).
- Staff should also be warned against breaching confidentiality through gossip, or through disclosing information without checking the bona fides of the person they are disclosing it to.

Informing users of their rights

When information is being treated as confidential, it is often worth spelling out what this means. For example, your approach could be that:

- users will be told from the outset how information about them will be used. They will also be told:
  - under what circumstances it could be shared with other agencies
  - why the information will be shared
  - the implications of sharing the information
  - that their written consent will be sought beforehand
- users will also be told of any circumstances where disclosure to a third party without their consent will be necessary under the law or under the organisation's policy
- workers must ascertain users' preferences about how they should be contacted – for example, by letter to their home, by telephone, email or text
- users' names and/or photos will not appear in any reports of the organisation without their permission
- users have the right to access any information held about them.

Sharing information with other agencies

This should state that:

- any information shared must be accurate and up to date, necessary for the purpose for which it is being shared, shared only with those who need to see it, and shared securely
- individuals must be informed before their data is shared, either as part of a general policy statement or on a case by case basis

- workers must seek advice from their line manager before sharing users' information against their wishes.

There should also be procedures for training new staff and volunteers in the policy and informing them of the consequences of any breach in the rules. The policy should be made available to everyone and posted on your website.

For further information see the Home Office publication *Information sharing – the legal framework*, available from www.crimereduction.homeoffice.gov.uk, and the Information Commissioner's guidance *Sharing personal information: our approach*, available from www.ico.gov.uk. Another useful publication is *Information sharing: practitioners' guide*, available from www.everychildmatters.gov.uk. Although the guidance is designed for organisations working with children and young people, it is applicable more widely.

Human Rights Act

The **Human Rights Act 1998** incorporates the **European Convention on Human Rights (ECHR)** into domestic law. It includes the following key provisions:

- the right to life
- the right to respect for private and family life, home and correspondence
- the right not to be subjected to torture or inhuman treatment
- the right to a fair trial
- freedom of thought, conscience and religion
- freedom of expression
- freedom of assembly and of association
- the right to marry and found a family
- prohibition of discrimination in the enjoyment of Convention rights
- the right to peaceful enjoyment of possessions
- the right to education.

The Act makes it unlawful for public authorities, including private bodies that carry out public functions, to act in a way that is incompatible with the rights and freedoms guaranteed by the ECHR.

Organisations with public functions

Many voluntary organisations have a contract or service agreement with local or health authorities, and so may be considered to be carrying out public functions for the purposes of the Human Rights Act.

Although the functions determine whether the organisation is a 'public authority', it is the relationship with the individual that will come under scrutiny when the Act is applied.

Implications

An organisation that breaches the Human Rights Act would be liable to remedies available in the courts. The level of damages awarded by UK courts must be commensurate with those awarded by the European Court of Human Rights.

Even if most voluntary organisations are relatively unlikely to be defined as carrying out public functions, they should build the principles of human rights into their policies and procedures to help develop and implement good practice and improve attitudes and behaviour towards people they work with and help.

For further information see the Ministry of Justice's website at www.justice.gov.uk/whatwedo/humanrights.htm and *The promotion of human rights* (RR12), available from www.charitycommission.gov.uk.

Chapter 10

Closing down

There are many reasons why a voluntary organisation might close down. For example, it may have achieved its goals and decide to stop operating, or it may be forced into closure through lack of funds. Whatever the organisation's legal status, closure is extremely serious if it cannot meet its financial obligations.

When closing down, there are certain legal procedures to follow when an organisation employs staff, rents or owns property, leases equipment, is incorporated (see chapter 1) and/or is a registered charity.

There is a range of information available on the subject. *Managing financial difficulties and insolvency in charities* (CC12) from the Charity Commission (www.charitycommission.gov.uk or 0845 3000 218) provides guidance for charities that are in financial trouble, and describes how to recognise when a charity may be in danger of becoming insolvent. Companies House has produced the booklet *Liquidation and insolvency* (GBW1) which covers the winding up of a company limited by guarantee; available from www.companieshouse.gov.uk. The government's Insolvency Service website www.insolvency.gov.uk also provides information about insolvency matters in general, including redundancy payments.

A note of caution: this chapter is not intended to be a substitute for expert legal and financial advice. When your organisation is facing closure, professional expertise is essential and should ideally be sought at the earliest opportunity.

Below is a glossary of terms used in this chapter.

Glossary of terms used

An organisation becomes **insolvent** if:

- it cannot pay its debts when they are due, or
- its total assets are worth less than its total liabilities, including possible, contingent and prospective liabilities.

An organisation is often described as **technically insolvent** if:

- the balance sheet shows its assets are worth less than its liabilities, but there is other cash to pay debts as they fall due, or
- its assets are worth more than its liabilities and it has no ready cash to pay debts but:
  - assets can be sold to pay the debts, or
  - enough funds can be borrowed, or
  - creditors are prepared to postpone the time for payment of their debts until cash is available.

Administration. Where an Administrator is appointed to run a company, usually to enable it to continue to operate whilst protected from action by creditors, and with the purpose of the organisation surviving or a sale taking place on better terms than would be achieved by a liquidation of the organisation. The alternative is usually that a liquidator will be appointed who will gather in and sell the assets of the organisation, with the net proceeds, after the costs of the liquidation have been deducted, being used to pay a dividend to creditors.

Assets. All the property an organisation owns that has some value: for example, stock and equipment, land and buildings, machinery and intellectual property rights.

Balance sheet. A statement that lists the total assets and total liabilities of an organisation and reveals its net worth at a given date.

Cash flow. The flow of cash into and out of an organisation. This is one measure of an organisation's financial health.

Company voluntary arrangement (**CVA**). A means by which a company may reach a legally effective agreement with its creditors for payment of all or part of its debts, over a period, to give directors time to focus on the recovery of the business.

Creditors' voluntary liquidation (**CVL**). When a company stops trading due to insolvency, and a liquidator is appointed who sells its assets and makes a payment to creditors, if funds are available. Company members and creditors start the process, which is managed by a licensed insolvency practitioner.

Creditors. Those to whom money is owed.

Debtors. Those who owe money for services provided. These are classed as a **current asset**.

Dissolution. A company that no longer wishes to trade can be dissolved. To start the process it must have stopped trading for at least three months. This is also known as **voluntary striking off**.

Fraudulent preference. Preferring one creditor to another at a time when a company is known to be insolvent.

Fraudulent trading. When directors continue trading in a company or industrial and provident society (IPS) knowing that it has no reasonable prospect of repaying debts and avoiding an insolvent liquidation. This is a criminal offence. Directors can also be held personally liable and required to make a contribution to the company's assets as the court thinks proper.

Insolvency practitioner (**IP**). Usually an accountant or solicitor who is licensed under the Insolvency Act to hold office in insolvency proceedings and who closes a company in a way that protects the legal interests of all parties involved.

Liabilities. Money an organisation owes, including, for example, debts, tax, wages, loans and rent.

Liquidation. Usually occurs when a company reaches the end of its life. Once a decision to liquidate has been made, the liquidation of the company is administered by a liquidator (who must be an IP), who gathers in and sells the assets and distributes the proceeds to creditors in accordance with the provisions of the Insolvency Act.

Liquidity. The ease with which an asset can be turned into cash.

Wrongful trading. When the directors allow a company to continue trading once they know, or ought to know, that there is no reasonable prospect of the company avoiding an insolvent liquidation.

Is closure necessary?

It is essential for the management committee to understand and control an organisation's finances. (Chapter 8 describes the systems for financial management of accounts.) The committee must consistently monitor its current financial position to spot potential problems as early as possible. If the answer to any of the following questions is 'yes', then your organisation is running into financial difficulties, and you should either start thinking of closure or Implementing a rescue plan.

- Is there an unanticipated overdraft? Are you regularly reaching your overdraft limit? Has your bank refused to increase your overdraft?
- Are there large debts you have difficulty in paying on time?
- Do you regularly have to dip into reserves without being able to top them up?
- Is anticipated future income at considerable risk?
- Is expenditure greater than income, with inadequate reserves available to cover the shortfall?
- Are current assets (including any investments) worth less than current liabilities? (See *Cash flow forecast*, below.)
- Are total assets and reasonably foreseeable income worth less than total liabilities and reasonably foreseeable expenditure? (See *Balance sheet*, below.)

There are two key indicators of insolvency. The first is the **cash flow forecast**, which will highlight whether you can pay debts when they are due for payment. The second is the **balance sheet**, which will determine whether the organisation has enough assets (fixed and current) to meet its actual and anticipated liabilities.

Cash flow forecast

The cash flow forecast will reveal **current expenses**. These could include:

- wages and employer's national insurance and pension contributions
- rent and rates for premises and rent on leased equipment

- the direct costs of providing your activities and services
- overheads, such as electricity, water, insurances, telephone and building repairs
- administrative costs, such as stationery, post and travel
- bank charges and auditor's fees
- HM Customs & Revenue (HMRC) payments including VAT payments, if registered for VAT.

It will also reveal current **income**. This could include:

- grant payments
- fees
- income from sales
- income from any investments.

Balance sheet

The balance sheet will determine the **value of your assets**. These could include:

- money in the bank and cash in hand
- money owed to the organisation
- the realistic resale value of stock: for example, unsold publications
- the realistic resale value of fixed assets such as land, buildings, furniture, equipment and vehicles.

When preparing the balance sheet examine any restrictions attached to the assets. Many funders do not allow organisations to sell premises or equipment bought with their grants. Check whether your constitution has restrictions on selling assets. Some sales of land and buildings by charities are regulated by the Charities Act 1993 (see chapter 6).

When assessing liabilities you must also consider potential liabilities, including those that would be incurred through closure. These include:

- legal and financial advice
- the legal fees for disposing of a lease or freehold property
- any outstanding rent for the remaining period of leases on equipment and premises

- the legal and accountancy fees for winding up a limited company or an industrial and provident society (see *Winding up*, page 281)
- redundancy payments (see chapter 3)
- any outstanding holiday, maternity, paternity and adoption payments (see chapters 3 and 4).

You must identify any financial difficulties as early as possible, as it may be possible to prevent insolvency and/or reduce committee members' risk of personal liability. If there are any concerns whatsoever about your organisation's financial position you should seek advice from an accountant or solicitor immediately. Such advice should be confirmed in writing, and any remedial action suggested should be considered, implemented so far as possible and monitored, along with the regular monitoring of budgets and cash flows. The management committee should be prepared to meet more often, and should minute the basis of all decisions as well as the decisions themselves.

An organisation heading for insolvency has two choices. It can either implement a rescue plan with a view to ensuring that it remains solvent, or it has to wind up. The next section examines ways of rescuing an organisation in financial difficulties.

Planning for survival

This section looks at ways of reducing costs, increasing income and raising capital to provide more financial security for your organisation, and describes how to prioritise in order to make decisions. It then looks at more radical ways of ensuring your activities survive through merging with other organisations.

Reducing staff costs

As staff costs often form the largest proportion of expenditure, it is likely that the greatest savings can be made through redundancies or by changing terms and conditions. Reducing costs in this way will involve difficult choices. The committee is responsible for these

decisions, but should obtain the cooperation of staff by consulting with them throughout; even if redundancy and redeployment can be avoided, restrictions on expenditure will affect working conditions. Consultation with staff or their representatives is a legal requirement if redundancies are proposed (see *Notifying those involved*, in chapter 3). Before making any decisions, consider how any reduction in staff or staff hours would affect your services, specifically those performed under a contract or a service level agreement (see *Contracting to provide services*, in chapter 9). Your organisation could be held liable for any failure to meet its contractual obligations.

Although redundancy is an obvious way of reducing costs, there may be other options. These include:

- restricting recruitment
- redeploying staff (but providing retraining if necessary) with their consent
- seeking applicants for voluntary redundancy
- introducing short-time working (reducing hours), if this is allowed under the contract of employment or with the agreement of staff
- ending the use of contract or temporary staff
- laying off staff temporarily in the hope of obtaining new funding. If liability is to be avoided this must be allowed for under the contract of employment, which may also specify whether the laid-off employee will be paid and, if so, how much. People who are either laid off (that is, receive no wages) for four consecutive weeks or put on short time (that is, receive less than half a week's pay) for six or more weeks (of which not more than three were consecutive) in any 13 week period, may claim redundancy payment. The claim must be in writing and employers may refuse payment if they believe that within four weeks they can offer at least 13 weeks' work
- outsourcing a specific piece of work (for example, producing a newsletter) to a self-employed worker. This may be a cheaper option as the employer no longer pays costs such as employer's national insurance

and pension contributions and, in the longer term, there will also be savings on overheads such as training, holidays and sick pay. However, a self-employed worker's daily rate is invariably higher than that of people on an organisation's payroll, so consider the financial implications carefully. For further details see *Self-employed people*, in chapter 3. You should not make an employee redundant and then outsource to that person the same work they were doing as an employee.

Chapter 3 looks at the legal rights of staff where reorganisation is necessary and results in redeployment, and describes the law and good practice governing redundancy procedures.

Reducing costs of premises

Premises can form another large element of expenditure. Moving to cheaper accommodation or sharing or subletting existing premises may reduce expenditure, although there may be substantial upfront costs. Chapter 6 looks at the implications of these options in more detail. It also describes the process to be followed when disposing of property.

Reducing other costs

Equipment

It may be possible to sell equipment both to save on running costs and to raise capital. Before doing so, establish who owns each item and if there are restrictions on selling: for example, some funders attach conditions to grant aid which prevent organisations from selling off equipment purchased with a grant.

Once a company or IPS enters into a form of insolvency, whether liquidation or administration, the power to sell equipment (or other assets) lies with the IP appointed. As an insolvent organisation has a general responsibility to try to do its best for its creditors, any equipment sold before liquidation or administration should be sold at the best obtainable price. If it is unlikely that all the creditors are to be paid off in full, there is a risk that accusations of fraudulent preference could be made, resulting in possible personal liability of the management committee members.

Another possibility is to give equipment away to save on running costs. A charity must give equipment to another charity with similar objects. Check your constitution and funders' restrictions to see whether this option is permitted. Such a decision would need to be justifiable by reference to the value of the equipment to be given away and the savings to be made. If insolvency is imminent it is advisable to seek professional advice before disposing of equipment, especially if it is valuable.

Check the terms of the agreement of any equipment bought on credit or hire purchase. Under some credit agreements the purchaser merely rents the equipment until the payments are completed; with others it owns the purchases immediately. Also check warranties; they may be invalidated when the equipment is sold or transferred.

If equipment is rented, check the terms of the lease (see chapter 6). It may be for a fixed term, in which case the organisation could be liable for the rent of the whole period. As with premises it is possible – although unlikely – that the owner will be prepared to accept an early termination of the lease or allow it to be transferred.

Reducing administrative costs

Ways of cutting administrative costs include using email instead of post, reducing staff travel, limiting the use of external printing facilities and restricting the use of external consultants. It may be tempting to reduce costs associated with professionals such as auditors, accountants and solicitors, but remember that an organisation facing insolvency is likely to need more, rather than less, professional advice.

You can also make savings by using the telephone, including conference calls, or through email or faxes, rather than getting people together in one place for a meeting. This approach also has environmental benefits (see chapter 6). The constitution must allow decisions to be made in this way, but if not, they could be made provisionally and ratified at the next face-to-face meeting (see *Running the organisation*, in chapter 2).

Increasing income

As well as reducing running costs, there are ways of increasing income. The Directory of Social Change publishes a range of books on fundraising (see www.dsc.org.uk/publications) and runs a subscription-based website, www.trustfunding.org.uk. Visit www.governmentfunding.org.uk for information on central government funding. Local development agencies throughout the country can advise on funding sources and making applications. FunderFinder has produced a computerised database of grant-making trusts and other funding sources. It also runs a very helpful website providing advice and contact points at www.funderfinder.org.uk. A number of organisations, including councils for voluntary service and the Directory of Social Change, have copies of the database available for use, usually on an appointment basis. The *Introductory pack on funding and finance – guide to fundraising* available at www.financehub.org.uk covers fundraising from the public, business and the local community.

Ways of increasing income

- **Introduce or increase charges for membership or services**. Although increased costs may discourage those most in need of services, it may be possible to introduce a tiered charging structure.
- **Improve cash flow** by invoicing regularly and promptly, and chasing up any debts owed to your organisation.
- **Improve marketing**. Some organisations may be able to raise substantial sums by marketing their services more effectively. As well as increasing income, an expanded market means an organisation is reaching many more people and improving its service delivery. But remember that any marketing will almost certainly incur extra costs. It is also important to be realistic about how much extra demand an organisation can cope with, especially at a time when it may have to wind down.
- **Put funding on a more secure basis**. It may be possible to get a two or three-year commitment from funders, or to change from grant funding to contractual funding (which is legally more secure, provided the organisation complies with its side of the contract; see chapter 9).
- **Launch an emergency appeal**. Make sure any funds raised are unrestricted and can be used to pay existing creditors and that donors are informed that their funds raised may be used to pay off debts.
- **Borrow money** from your supporters, possibly on an interest free basis, or from a bank on commercial terms. Remember you will have to demonstrate that you have robust financial management systems in place and produce a sound business case for a loan. First check that your constitution gives you the power to raise loans and if necessary pledge assets as security. When taking on a commercial loan, committee members are legally binding the organisation to an agreed repayment schedule, terms and conditions and possibly security in the form of a charge on the organisation's assets. They will not be personally liable for any loan as long as they can show they have:
  - acted prudently and lawfully
  - avoided any losses by acting outside the terms of the constitution
  - not committed the organisation to debts worth more than its assets.

NCVO has useful advice on borrowing and bank loans, including sources of loans suitable for voluntary organisations, on its website www.ncvo-vol.org.uk/askncvo. The publications *A brief guide to loan finance for trustees* and *The guide to loans and other forms of finance*, produced by the Sustainable Funding Project for the Finance Hub, are available at www.ncvo-vol.org.uk/sfp/loanfinance.

Mergers

A further option is to amalgamate with, or be taken over by, another organisation. The most common forms of merger are when:

- one (or more) organisation dissolves and transfers its/their assets to another existing organisation
- two (or more) organisations dissolve and combine their assets to create a new organisation.

Charities

Any charity wishing to merge must have appropriate powers in its constitution to proceed. Some constitutions include an explicit clause giving power to merge with another charity. It may also be possible to rely on other powers, such as a clause which states that once the charity is wound up its assets will be passed over to a charity with similar purposes. You should seek legal advice on whether your constitution contains the necessary powers.

Charity Commission consent is not generally needed before carrying out a merger. Note however that a charity must usually gain the Commission's consent before making any changes to its objects clause (see *Drafting and agreeing the constitution,* in chapter 2).

The objects of the merging charities must be compatible, so that current users will continue to benefit after the merger. It is important to check for any restrictions on how assets (for example, restricted funds) can be used, as this will have an effect on how the merger takes place.

The Charity Commission has identified the following main issues to consider when exploring a merger proposal:

- whether the merger will be in the best interests of the charity's beneficiaries

- ensuring that all legal issues have been addressed and the process complies with the constitution
- how to maintain confidentiality
- employment implications, such as TUPE requirements and pension liabilities (see *Taking on other organisations' staff*, in chapter 3, and *Pensions*, in chapter 4)
- handling of staff issues, such as managing redundancies, and addressing staff morale in a period of change.

Note: The Commission warns that a merger should not be pursued primarily to keep one charity going, and that users' best interests should be of central concern. It advises that if a merger is initiated to rescue one of the parties, trustees of the solvent organisation must ensure that this does not present an unjustifiable risk.

Due diligence

Trustees considering a merger should ensure that the proposed partners carry out an appropriate disclosure or due diligence exercise, proportionate to the size and nature of the merger. The main elements of due diligence are:

- **financial** – including accounting systems
- **legal** – for example, constitutions, employment contracts, leased equipment, service contracts
- **strategic and operational** – for example, organisational structure, culture and policies or IT systems.

Due diligence can be carried out in house, by an organisation's auditors or by other professional advisers.

Register of mergers

The Charity Commission has established a public register of charity mergers. The main advantage of the register is that if a merger is registered, any gifts made to a charity that has merged and subsequently ceased to exist but which do not take effect until after the merger – such as legacies – will generally transfer automatically to the successor charity after the merger. This removes the need to maintain a 'shell' charity that exists only to receive such legacies.

Registration also allows the merging charities to transfer property from one charity to another using a special document called a **vesting declaration**.

Note that not all mergers can be registered. Registration is not possible, for example, where some but not all activities of one charity are transferred to another, or when one charity becomes a subsidiary of another.

More information about registering a merger is available via the 'Apply for it' link at www.charitycommission.gov.uk.

Further information

For further details on charity mergers see the Charity Commission booklets *Collaborative working and mergers* (RS4) and *Collaborative working and mergers – an introduction* (CC34), available from www.charitycommission.gov.uk.

The Institute of Chartered Secretaries and Administrators has produced a series of guidance sheets on charity mergers, available from www.icsa.org.uk. The Collaborative Working Unit at NCVO has developed a range of good practice tools and guidance material including *Due diligence demystified: What it is and how you can manage it*, available from www.ncvo-vol.org.uk/collaborativeworkingunit or call the help desk on 0800 2 798 798.

Notification of a merger

Organisations planning a merger must inform the following where relevant:

- the Charity Commission if a new charity is being created or an existing one is dissolved, and in order to register the merger (see *Register of mergers,* page 279)
- the Registrar of Companies if a new company is being created or an existing one is dissolved or changes are made to a constitution
- HMRC if the merger will affect tax or trading arrangements
- the Land Registry if land or property is being transferred

- local authorities for change of details for obtaining charitable rate relief (see *Paying rates*, in chapter 6)
- the Information Commissioner in relation to data protection (see *Data protection*, in chapter 9).

Also see *Notification of closure*, page 286.

The rescue plan

Prioritising objectives and services should be an integral aspect of managing an organisation; however, it is particularly important when services may have to be reduced.

There is no single method of prioritising services to cut costs, but gathering the following information will help in making decisions:

- services that must be provided under the terms of a contract where failure to do so could lead to breach of contract claims against the organisation
- the services, in order of priority, that must be provided to meet the organisation's objectives
- the best estimate of the cost of each service
- possible additional income that could be generated from or for each service
- the additional cost of, and possible income from, any new service
- other methods of generating income, the amount that might be raised and the expenditure, including staff time, involved
- ways of reducing the costs of premises, equipment and administration, possible savings and the effect of any changes on services
- savings that could be made by freezing recruitment, redeployment, short-time working and redundancy.

Staff will almost certainly be affected by any decision to cut costs. It is therefore essential to consult them throughout the process of drawing up a rescue plan.

Winding up

The process of winding up an organisation will depend upon whether it is:

- solvent or insolvent
- unincorporated or incorporated
- registered as a charity.

It is therefore imperative to get professional advice about the appropriate procedures for your organisation.

Solvent organisations

A solvent organisation may decide to close down, for example, because it has achieved its goals, or to avoid a potential future insolvency. If it can pay all its debts, including redundancy payments, the cost of disposing of premises and equipment, and pay the costs and fees associated with the winding up, there are no restrictions on who can be paid during the closing down process. If, by ceasing activities, an organisation can pay off all its debts, it could consider maintaining a legal existence, albeit dormant. For example, a company can remain an inactive shell, and an unincorporated organisation can retain a steering committee, ready to start again if new funding becomes available. The Charity Commission will want to be assured that any registered charity is still fulfilling its objectives.

Planning for closure is essential and it is good practice to prepare a formal written plan with realistic timescales (which may require professional advice) and the appointment of key people to be responsible for each task.

You should still take advice to ensure that all necessary procedures have been carried out thoroughly and correctly, and that all required notifications have been made (see *Notification of closure*, page 286).

Unincorporated organisations

The procedure for winding up an unincorporated organisation is often set down in its constitution. It usually requires members at a general meeting to pass a resolution agreeing to the dissolution.

A solvent organisation will also need to consider how to transfer any assets remaining after it has paid its debts, before it is dissolved. This decision should be made at the meeting that formally winds it up. The constitution may also state how any balance or remaining assets should be distributed, usually by allowing the committee or a general meeting to select another organisation to which the assets can be transferred.

If a charity's constitution does not have a specific power for it to be dissolved but all its funds are unrestricted, the committee may generally close the charity by spending all assets in line with its objectives or transferring them to a charity with similar objectives. In the latter case the committee can and should specify how the receiving charity may use the assets.

The committee will also need to ensure that any grants or donations received for a specific purpose are used for that purpose or used for a different purpose only with the funder/donor's agreement, or returned to the funder or donor, although this can give rise to complications and legal advice may be necessary.

Before the organisation is wound up, it will need to prepare final accounts and submit them to the final meeting for approval. Once the organisation has been wound up, it should follow the advice outlined in *Notification of closure* (page 286) and *Record retention* (page 287).

The Charity Commission has published guidance for winding up charities. See *Small charities: dissolutions and removals from the register* (CDS 1344A) and *Dissolution, winding up and removal from the register for medium sized charities* (CDS 1077A), both available from www.charitycommission.gov.uk.

Incorporated organisations

A solvent company can be dissolved in two ways.

Voluntary striking off

A company that is not trading may apply to be struck off the Register of Companies if it is no longer needed (for example, it has fulfilled its objectives), if it:

- has not operated in the previous three months (apart from settling its affairs, including disposing of assets)
- has not changed its name
- is not the subject of insolvency proceedings (see *Insolvent organisations,* page 283).

Companies applying for voluntary striking off are advised to warn all potential creditors and interested parties beforehand, as any of them may object to the company being struck off. Any loose ends, such as closing the bank account, should be dealt with before applying. It is important that directors (management committee members) are satisfied that all debts have been met and there are no contingent liabilities.

The advantages of this approach are that it is inexpensive and it may still be possible to restore the company to the Register in the future for certain purposes. Complete and send Form **652a**, signed by the majority of directors, to the Registrar of Companies. Within the next seven days, copies of the form should be sent to all other directors, all company members, creditors and prospective creditors (including HMRC, employees and managers and trustees of any employee pension fund). VAT registered companies must notify the relevant VAT office. The Registrar advertises the proposed striking off, and if no one objects the company is struck off three months later.

Members' voluntary winding-up

The directors (or if more than two, the majority of directors) must make a formal declaration of solvency, no more than five weeks before a resolution to wind up a company is passed, that they have fully examined the company's affairs and believe it can pay all its debts within 12 months of the start of the winding-up. The declaration must include an up-to-date statement of the company's assets and liabilities.

The liquidation starts when members, in a general meeting, pass a special resolution for the company to be wound up voluntarily and then appoint a liquidator (who must be an authorised IP). Notice of the special resolution for voluntary winding-up of the company must be published in the *London Gazette* (or the *Edinburgh Gazette* for companies in Scotland and the *Belfast Gazette* for companies in Northern Ireland) within 14 days of the general meeting. The company must also send a copy of the declaration and the special resolution to the Registrar of Companies within 15 days of the general meeting. As soon as the resolution is passed, the company ceases to operate apart from engaging in activities required to wind up.

The process of winding up is managed by a **liquidator**, as follows:

- Following consultation with members, the liquidator will decide on the disposal of assets and the payment of debts. In practice, most constitutions will require the surplus assets to be given to another organisation with similar objects.
- The liquidator will present a report and accounts to a general meeting, and then submit these to the Registrar of Companies and the company's creditors.
- The company is dissolved three months later.

A **solvent IPS** is wound up using an **instrument of dissolution**.

An application to terminate a solvent society's registration by instrument of dissolution may be made if:

- it is signed by at least 75% of its members
- the intended distribution of remaining assets is in line with the registered rules, and
- the society has submitted up-to-date accounts to the Mutual Societies Registration (MSR) at the Financial Services Authority (FSA).

Societies must submit two copies of Form **AA** (the instrument of dissolution) and one copy of Form **AB** (the statutory declaration) to the MSR. The MSR will then publish notice of the dissolution in the appropriate Gazette (see *Members voluntary winding up*, page 282), and send you Form **AG**. As long as there have been no objections to the dissolution within three months after the notice appears, you may distribute remaining assets, and then submit Form AG to state you have done so.

Alternatively, many IPSs choose to amalgamate with another IPS or company; see *Mergers*, page 279.

Charitable incorporated organisations

At the time of writing the final regulations for CIOs had not been published. The draft regulations published for consultation in September 2008 proposed that the provisions of the Insolvency Act 1986 should also apply to CIOs, and that a CIO's trustees would therefore have similar responsibilities and liabilities to those of company directors. The full rules will be in **The Charitable Incorporated Organisations (Insolvency and Dissolution) Regulations,** which will probably be published in 2009.

Insolvent organisations

Once a decision has been taken to wind up an insolvent organisation, you must not interfere with remaining assets, including money in the bank, cash in hand, stocks, equipment and possibly the premises. You must not pay any sums to creditors, include the utility companies, phone companies and the landlord, unless and until authorised by the IP to do so, as this could result in a **fraudulent preference** claim.

In practice, this means you cannot pay any money into an overdrawn bank account, allow any equipment to be moved from the premises, or even pay staff wages. You should, however, continue to collect any

money owed, but must deposit it into a bank account that is in credit.

You must keep records of all relevant decisions made and actions taken, including documenting the reason for them, to protect committee members against any possible later claims of wrongful trading or fraudulent preference.

Unincorporated organisations

Legal advice is essential if an unincorporated organisation becomes insolvent. Any liabilities incurred can be treated as personal liabilities for its management committee members (see *Liability for debts*, page 286). There is no legal procedure for winding up unincorporated associations, but they are generally advised to pay debts in the same order of preference as companies (as set out in the Insolvency Act).

The management committee should nominate an individual or individuals to take responsibility for closing down the organisation: for example, the chair, finance officer or treasurer or a combination of these.

If the organisation is in debt, consider calling a creditors' meeting to see whether creditors will accept a percentage of what is owed based on what assets remain. This should be done only with specialist legal advice from accountants and lawyers.

Incorporated organisations

It is important to realise that a company or IPS becomes insolvent when the directors know, or should have realised, that it has no reasonable prospect of avoiding an insolvent liquidation.

Under the **Insolvency Act 1986** an insolvent company or IPS must appoint an insolvency practitioner (IP). The Insolvency Service website (www.insolvency-service.co.uk) includes a database of all IPs, and your professional advisers will be able to make recommendations. The IP will decide whether the organisation should cease operating, and will notify the appropriate people and organisations (see *Notification of closure*, page

286). Once the liquidator is appointed, committee members lose their powers completely. The organisation must cease operating from the date of the resolution to wind up, and carry out only those activities deemed necessary by the liquidator to the winding up.

Alternatives for an insolvent incorporated organisation are to apply for a **moratorium** to give it breathing space to review future options through:

- corporate voluntary arrangements
- administration

or winding up by going into **liquidation** through:

- creditors' voluntary liquidation
- using the courts to appoint the Official Receiver (**compulsory liquidation**).

Moratorium

Company voluntary arrangement (CVA). A CVA allows a company owing money to make a proposal to its creditors asking them to agree to accept a reduction in their debt or a delay in payment. It can be used as a way of moving the organisation out of its current crisis into recovery or to wind down its affairs in an orderly fashion.

Directors of small companies can also apply to the courts for a moratorium, normally lasting for a minimum of 28 days, to protect the organisation against any creditor wishing to take action. A small company is defined as meeting any two of the following criteria:

- a turnover of no more than £5.6 million
- a balance sheet of no more than £2.8 million
- no more than 50 employees.

The directors produce a proposal, which includes details of the organisation's financial position and the offer being made to pay creditors. They then appoint an IP (**the nominee**), who will report to a court within 28 days on whether they believe it is necessary to call a creditors' meeting to discuss the proposal. A creditors' meeting must be held within 28 days of any moratorium.

To be approved, the proposal must be supported by 75% of creditors present or represented at the meeting. Once approved, it binds all creditors who were entitled to vote at the meeting or would have been if they had had notice of it whether or not present or represented. The nominee becomes responsible for implementing the arrangement.

Administration. This is a procedure that, like a CVA, gives a company some breathing space by means of a moratorium from any action by creditors. The administration must aim to achieve one of a number of purposes, most commonly:

- the survival of the company, or part of it, as a going concern

or, if that is not possible:

- a more advantageous realisation of its assets than would be possible if the company went into liquidation.

The company itself, its directors or one or more of its current, contingent or prospective creditors can present a petition for an administration order. If the court agrees the application it appoints an administrator (an IP), who becomes responsible for managing the company's property and affairs with the approval of the company's creditors. Generally, the administration must be concluded within a year.

Note that it is not always necessary for an application to be made to the court.

If the company itself wishes to appoint an administrator, it must pass a resolution in a general meeting or gain the consent of all shareholders before the appointment can be made. In the case of the directors, a resolution of the board of directors or the assent of all the directors will be required.

If the board of directors makes such a resolution it becomes the duty of all the directors, even those who may have voted against such an appointment, to take all necessary steps to put the resolution into effect. Any director has the authority to make the appointment on behalf of the board, though a properly drafted resolution will give the power to one or more directors to sign the necessary documents to effect the appointment.

There are some restrictions on the power of the company or the directors to appoint an administrator: for example, if the company is already in liquidation or administration or, within the previous 12 months, has been subject to certain types of appointment (including a previous administration) or a moratorium. It is therefore essential to take legal advice before either the company or its directors start the process of appointing an administrator.

Five business days' written notice must be given to any person who is, or may be, entitled to appoint an administrative receiver of the company or an administrator (under the **Insolvency Act 1986**). During the period of five business days, a qualifying floating charge holder (a lender who has security over a company's assets and who has the power to appoint an administrator) may either agree with the appointment or appoint their own administrator – the floating charge holder has an effective right of veto in this regard.

Where a company or its directors appoint an administrator, a **Notice of Appointment** must be filed with the court on the prescribed form and contain a statutory declaration by or on behalf of the person who makes the appointment that:

- the person appointing is entitled to appoint
- the appointment is in accordance with Schedule 16 of the Act, and
- the statements made and information given are accurate.

The Notice must identify the administrator and state that in his or her opinion the purpose of the administration will be achieved.

The administration procedure in general is full of potential traps for the unwary, so obtaining professional assistance is essential.

Liquidation

Creditors' voluntary liquidation. Where the directors become aware that a company is, or is likely soon to be, insolvent, they may take the initiative and call an extraordinary general meeting for the purpose of the members resolving that the company should voluntarily enter liquidation. If the members agree, the meeting passes an extraordinary resolution to wind up the company and an ordinary resolution to nominate a liquidator.

A copy of the resolution to wind up must be published in the appropriate *Gazette* (see *Members' voluntary winding up*, page 282) within 14 days of it being passed and be filed with the Registrar of Companies within 15 days.

A creditors' meeting must then be called. At least seven days' notice must be given to creditors and the creditors' meeting must be held within 14 days of the company meeting at which it resolved to enter into liquidation. The directors must prepare a statement of affairs for the meeting.

The creditors then usually resolve to appoint the nominated liquidator at the meeting of creditors or petition the court to appoint the Official Receiver as the liquidator. The liquidator manages the gathering in and sales of assets and creditors' claims and makes payments to creditors in the statutory order of priority (the order of preference when distributing the assets of an organisation to its creditors). Once any dividends have been paid to creditors, the liquidator will call a general meeting of the creditors and members to provide a final report on the liquidation.

Compulsory liquidation. This is when a court orders a company to be wound up.

The following can petition the court to make an order for the compulsory liquidation of the company (though it is the court that will decide whether the company should be wound up):

- any creditor who is owed at least £750
- any shareholder or member

- the company itself
- the company's directors.

The Secretary of State for Business Enterprise and Regulatory Reform, the FSA and the Official Receiver also have powers to petition the court to wind up a company.

The Official Receiver will investigate the company's affairs and the causes of its failure, and will then manage the winding up or, as is usual if funds are available and if the creditors prefer, this can be done by an IP appointed as liquidator.

Liability for debts

The final responsibility for debts depends on the organisation's legal structure (see chapter 1).

Unincorporated organisations

An unincorporated organisation does not have a separate legal existence independent of its members. This means it cannot enter into any financial or legal commitments in its own right; instead the members themselves – or more commonly the committee members – do so on behalf of the organisation. If the organisation cannot pay its debts, a creditor is entitled to bring a court case against those responsible for authorising transactions to recover any money owed unless the terms of the agreement under which the liability arises state otherwise.

A committee member cannot avoid liability by resigning before the organisation runs into debt, as former committee members can also be liable if the debt was incurred while they were on the committee. The exception is when the liability stems from an employment contract, where any claims would be against current committee members.

In practice it is sometimes possible to negotiate with creditors to waive or reduce debts, or to raise funds to cover them. But committee members should not depend on this being possible.

An unincorporated organisation facing insolvency should take financial advice immediately. Individual committee members may consider taking their own independent legal or accounting advice.

Incorporated organisations

In an incorporated organisation, the organisation, rather than committee members, is responsible for the debts. In companies limited by guarantee, members are liable only up to the value of the guarantee set out in the memorandum of association (usually £1 or £5); in IPSs they will have to pay only the amount due on any shares (usually £1). Committee members may lose their normal protection against personal liability and be held personally responsible for the organisation's debts if they carry out wrongful trading, that is:

- they continue to trade against the advice of the IP, or
- they fail to call in an IP as soon as the committee members are, or should have been, aware of the pending insolvency.

Committee members could also be found guilty of fraudulent preference if they allow an insolvent company or IPS to pay debts without following the very strict order of preference set out in the Insolvency Acts.

Individuals who back a loan with a personal guarantee remain responsible for its repayment, even if the organisation is incorporated. Likewise, individuals who have guaranteed payment of rent or equipment under a lease will remain personally responsible for payments.

If an organisation has no reasonable prospect of being able to pay debts when they are due or cannot negotiate realistic repayment dates, the committee members must immediately seek advice from an IP. The practitioner will advise whether the organisation should stop trading immediately, start running down its activities, or implement a rescue plan.

Notification of closure

Once a formal decision has been made to close an organisation down you should inform, as relevant, the following:

- the employees, employee representatives and unions (see *Redundancy*, in chapter 3)
- your accountant, auditor and solicitor
- your bank manager
- managers or trustees of any pension fund
- the Charity Commission (see below)
- the registration body (Companies House or the FSA)
- your funder(s)
- past and current committee members
- anyone with a fixed charge or mortgage over the organisation's property
- HMRC
- Department for Work and Pensions
- Information Commissioner
- all creditors
- service users
- your website host
- your internet service provider.

In some cases notification will be the task of the appointed (or to be appointed) IP.

Notifying the Charity Commission

Trustees of registered charities must inform the Charity Commission if the charity ceases to exist.

Trustees of a charitable company must notify the Charity Commission of its dissolution and removal from the Companies House Register. You will need to send the Commission:

- a declaration using form **CSD 1077** (if you choose this option you must ensure you have complied, or are able to comply, with all the statements in part 2 of the form), or a copy of the charity's final accounts showing where the assets have gone and a nil balance, along with either:
  - a certified copy of the minutes of the meeting at which the decision to dissolve the charity was taken, or
  - certified copies of the relevant resolutions.

The Commission will remove the charity from the Charity Register after it has checked that the charity has been removed from the Companies House Register and that it has all

the directors' reports, annual accounts and annual returns it should have received.

Unincorporated registered charities whose gross income was not more than £20,000 and whose gross assets were valued at no more than £200,000 in the last accounting period should send to the Charity Commission:

- a declaration form, **CSD 1344B** (available from the Charity Commission), or
- where there is a dissolution clause in the constitution, a certified copy of the resolution or minutes of the meeting at which the decision to dissolve the charity was taken, certified and dated by a trustee, the secretary or clerk to the trustees. The minutes or resolutions should indicate how the assets of the charity have been used after settling any outstanding liabilities, or
- where there is no dissolution clause, a copy of the charity's final accounts showing a nil balance and the destination of the assets, or
- a letter, signed on behalf of the trustees, which details how and why the charity was dissolved and where remaining money was passed.

Unincorporated charities with income between £20,000 and £10 million and whose assets are worth less than £100 million should submit to the Charity Commission:

- a declaration form, **CSD 1077** (available from the Charity Commission), or
- a copy of the charity's final accounts showing the destination of assets and a nil balance together with either:
  - a certified copy of the minutes of the meeting at which the decision to dissolve the charity or spend all its assets was taken, or
  - certified copies of the relevant resolutions.

Record retention

After a charity has been wound up, the trustees have to ensure its accounts and records are preserved for at least three years (for a charitable company) or six years (for an unincorporated charity). If property has been transferred to another charity, the Commission recommends asking the recipient charity to hold the records. Otherwise trustees may be able to arrange for records to be held by a former trustee, a solicitor or accountant, another local charity or an umbrella body.

Retention periods for key records are as follows:

Record	Statutory retention period
Accounts	
Company accounts	At least three years by law, but six years is recommended
VAT records	Six years
PAYE	Six years from the year end for companies
	Five years after 31 January of the following year of assessment for unincorporated organisations
Employment records	
Accident reports	Three years after date of last entry
Income tax and NI returns/records	At least three years after the end of latest tax year
Statutory sick/ maternity pay	Three years after end of relevant tax year
Health and safety records	Three years

For a more comprehensive list of records that must be kept, see *Document retention periods* on the AskNCVO section of www.ncvo-vol.org.uk.

Copies of key documents can be stored on a computer, CD-ROM or microfilm. It may be worth thinking about scanning important documents to save space; electronic copies are fully admissible as long as you produce the copy of the record upon request.

Finally, destroy any information that is no longer needed:

- paper records that do not have to be kept should be shredded
- headed notepaper, compliment slips etc. should be destroyed
- computer hard drives should be cleaned to delete permanently documentation relating to the organisation.

Glossary

ACIE	Association of Charity Independent Examiners		**EEE**	electrical and electronic equipment
AcoP	approved code of practice		**EHRC**	Equality and Human Rights Commission
AGM	annual general meeting		**ELV**	end-of-life vehicle
APL&P	additional paternity leave and pay		**EPC**	energy performance certificate
ATF	authorised treatment facility		**ESA**	Employment and Support Allowance
AtW	Access to Work		**ETO**	economic, technical or organisational justification
BERR	Department for Business, Enterprise and Regulatory Reform		**EWC**	expected week of childbirth
BIA	UK Border Agency		**FRS**	Financial Reporting Standard
CAC	Central Arbitration Committee		**FRSSE**	Financial Reporting Standard for Smaller Entities
CCNI	Charity Commission for Northern Ireland		**FSA**	Financial Services Authority
CIC	community interest company		**GOR**	genuine occupational requirement
CIO	charitable incorporated organisation		**GPP**	group personal pension
CIPD	Chartered Institute of Personnel and Development		**HMRC**	Her Majesty's Revenue and Customs
COSHH	Control of Substances Hazardous to Health Regulations 2002		**HSCER**	Health and Safety Consultation with Employees Regulations
CRB	Criminal Records Bureau		**HSE**	Health and Safety Executive
CV	curriculum vitae		**ICSA**	Institute of Chartered Secretaries and Administrators
CVA	company voluntary arrangement		**I&E**	income and expenditure
CVL	creditors' voluntary liquidation		**IP**	insolvency practitioner
DDA	Disability Discrimination Act		**IPS**	industrial and provident societies
DEC	display energy certificate		**IRD**	intended retirement date
Defra	Department for Environment, Food and Rural Affairs		**ISA**	Independent Safeguarding Authority
DPS	designated premises supervisor		**LEL**	lower earnings limit
EAC	Every Action Counts		**MA**	Maternity Allowance
ECHR	European Convention on Human Rights		**MORR**	managing occupational road risk
EEA	European Economic Area		**MP**	Maternity Pay

Glossary

MSR	Mutual Societies Registration
NCVO	National Council for Voluntary Organisations
NI	national insurance
NIC	national insurance contribution
OSCR	Office of the Scottish Charity Regulator
PAYE	pay as you earn
PBS	points-based system
PCC	public collections certificate
PCV	passenger carrying vehicle
PET	primary earnings threshold
PIW	period of incapacity for work
POA	Public Order Act 1986
PoCA	Protection of Children Act List
PoVA	Protection of Vulnerable Adults List
PPE	personal protective equipment
PPL	Phonographic Performance Limited
PRS	Performing Right Society
PSV	Public Service Vehicle
PTS	percentage threshold scheme
PUWER	Provision and Use of Work Equipment Regulations 1998
R&P	receipts and payments
REACH	Registration, Evaluation, Authorisation and Restriction of Chemicals
RIDDOR	Reporting of Injuries, Disease and Dangerous Occurrences Regulations 1995
RNIB	Royal National Institute of Blind People
RNID	Royal National Institute for Deaf People

ROA	Rehabilitation of Offenders Act 1974
ROES	representatives of employees' safety
RRO	Regulatory Reform Fire Safety Order 2005
RSI	repetitive strain injury
S2P	State Second Pension
SAP	Statutory Adoption Pay
SLA	service level agreement
SMA	Statutory Maternity Allowance
SMP	Statutory Maternity Pay
SOAL	statement of assets and liabilities
SOFA	Statement of financial activities
SORP	Statement of Recommended Practice, Accounting and Reporting by Charities
SPP	Statutory Paternity Pay
SSP	Statutory Sick Pay
TAR	trustees' annual report
TEN	temporary event notice
TPAS	the Pension Advisory Service
TUPE	Transfer of Undertakings Protection of Employment Regulations 2006
UEL	upper earnings limit
ULD	upper limb disorders
ULR	union learning representative
VAT	value added tax
WAI	Web Accessibility Initiative
WEEE	waste electrical and electronic equipment

Contacts

Sandy Adirondack
39 Gabriel House
Odessa Street
London SE16 7HQ
www.sandy-a.co.uk

Acas
08457 47 47 47 (helpline)
08456 06 1600 (textphone)
08702 42 90 90 (publications orders)
www.acas.org.uk

Age Positive Team
Department for Work and Pensions
Room N10
Moorfoot
Sheffield S1 4PQ
0113 232 4444
agepositive@dwp.gsi.gov.uk
www.agepositive.gov.uk

Angal Limited
K2 Brookside Avenue
Rustington BN16 3LF
0845 130 9963/01903 787 978
sales@angal.co.uk
www.angal.co.uk

Association of Charity Independent Examiners
Bentley Resource Centre
High Street
Bentley
Doncaster DN5 0AA
01302 828338
info@acie.org.uk
www.acie.org.uk

British Insurance Brokers' Association
14 Bevis Marks
London EC3A 7NT
0870 950 1790
enquiries@biba.org.uk
www.biba.org.uk

Business Link
0845 600 9 006
0845 606 2666 (textphone)
www.businesslink.gov.uk

CarPlus
SII
Hanover Walk
Leeds LS3 1AB
0113 234 929
www.carplus.org.uk

Centre for Accessible Environments
70 South Lambeth Road
London SW8 1RL
020 7840 0125
info@cae.org.uk
www.cae.org.uk

Chartered Institute of Personnel and Development
151 The Broadway
London SW19 1JQ
020 8612 6200
www.cipd.co.uk

Charity Bank
194 High Street
Tonbridge
Kent TN9 1BE
00 44 (0) 1732 774040
enquiries@charitybank.org
www.charitybank.org

Charity Commission Direct
PO Box 1227
Liverpool L69 3UG
0845 3000 218
0845 3000 219 (textphone)
www.charity-commission.gov.uk

Charity Law Association
admin@charitylawassociation.org.uk
www.charitylawassociation.org.uk

Communities and Local Government
Eland House
Bressenden Place
London SW1E 5DU
020 7944 4400
contactus@communities.gov.uk
www.communities.gov.uk

Contacts

Community Development Foundation
Unit 5, Angel Gate
320–326 City Road
London EC1V 2PT
020 7833 1772
admin@cdf.org.uk
www.cdf.org.uk

The Community Interest Regulator
CIC Team
Room 3.68
Companies House
Crown Way
Maindy
Cardiff CF14 3UZ
029 20346228
cicregulator@companieshouse.gov.uk
www.cicregulator.gov.uk

Community Matters
12–20 Baron Street
London N1 9LL
020 7837 7887
communitymatters@communitymatters.org.uk
www.communitymatters.org.uk

Community Recycling Network
57 Prince Street
Bristol BS1 4QH
0117 942 0142
info@crn.org.uk
www.crn.org.uk

Community Repaint
Resource Futures
3rd Floor, Munro House
Duke Street
Leeds LS9 8AG
0113 200 3959
www.communityrepaint.org.uk

Community Transport Association
Highbank
Halton Street
Hyde SK14 2NY
0845 130 6185
info@ctauk.org
www.ctauk.org

Companies House
Crown Way
Maindy
Cardiff CF4 3UZ
0870 33 33 636
02920 381245 (textphone)
enquiries@companies-house.gov.uk
www.companies-house.gov.uk

Criminal Records Bureau
PO Box 110
Liverpool L3 6ZZ
0870 90 90 822 (registration/application enquiries)
0870 90 90 844 (disclosure application line)
0870 90 90 223 (Welsh line)
0870 90 90 344 (textphone)
www.crb.gov.uk

Daycare Trust
21 St George's Road
London SE1 6ES
020 7840 3350 (helpline)
info@daycaretrust.org.uk
www.daycaretrust.org.uk

Department for Business, Enterprise and Regulatory Reform
1 Victoria Street
London SW1H 0ET
020 7215 5000
020 7215 6740 (textphone)
enquiries@berr.gsi.gov.uk
www.berr.gov.uk

Department for Children, Schools and Families
Sanctuary Buildings
Great Smith Street
London SW1P 3BT
0870 000 2288
01928 794274 (textphone)
info@dcsf.gsi.gov.uk
www.dcsf.gov.uk

Department for Culture, Media and Sport
2–4 Cockspur Street
London SW1Y 5DH
020 7211 6200
enquiries@culture.gov.uk
www.culture.gov.uk

Department for Transport
Great Minster House
76 Marsham Street
London SW1P 4DR
FAX9643@dft.gsi.gov.uk
www.dft.gov.uk/

Department for Work and Pensions
www.dwp.gov.uk

Department of Health
Customer Service Centre
Richmond House
79 Whitehall
London SW1A 2NL
020 7210 4850
020 7210 5025 (textphone)
dhmail@dh.gsi.gov.uk
www.dh.gov.uk

Directory of Social Change
24 Stephenson Way
London NW1 2DP
08450 77 77 77
enquiries@dsc.org.uk
publications@dsc.org.uk
www.dsc.org.uk

Disabled Living Foundation
380–384 Harrow Road
London W9 2HU
0845 130 9177 (helpline)
020 7432 8009 (textphone)
advice@dlf.org.uk
www.dlf.org.uk

Energy Saving Trust
21 Dartmouth Street
London SW1H 9BP
0800 512 012
www.energysavingtrust.org.uk

envirowise
0800 585 794
www.envirowise.gov.uk

Environment Agency
National Customer Contact Centre
PO Box 544
Rotherham S60 1BY
08708 506 506 enquiries@environment-agency.gov.uk
www.environment-agency.gov.uk

Ethical Consumer Research Association
Unit 21, 41 Old Birley Street
Manchester M15 5RF
0161 226 2929
www.ethicalconsumer.org

Ethical Property Foundation
Development House
56–64 Leonard Street
London EC2A 4JX
020 7065 0760
mail@ethicalproperty.org.uk
www.ethicalproperty.org.uk

Equality Direct
Helpline on equality in the workplace
0870 242 90 90

Every Action Counts
33 Corsham Street
London N1 6DR
0845 241 0957
www.everyactioncounts.org.uk

Financial Services Authority
25 The North Colonnade
Canary Wharf
London E14 5HS
0845 606 1234/020 7066 1000)
0845 730 0104 (textphone)
www.fsa.gov.uk

Food Standards Agency
Aviation House
125 Kingsway
London WC2B 6NH
020 7276 8000
www.food.gov.uk

Funder Finder
65 Raglan Road
Leeds LS2 9DZ
0113 2433008
www.funderfinder.org.uk

Futurebuilders England
Level 14, Cale Cross House
156 Pilgrim Street
Newcastle-upon-Tyne NE1 6SU
0191 269 2850
info@futurebuilders-england.org.uk
www.futurebuilders-england.org.uk

Contacts

Gambling Commission
Victoria Square House
Victoria Square
Birmingham B2 4BP
0121 230 6666
info@gamblingcommission.gov.uk
www.gamblingcommission.gov.uk

Global Action Plan
8 Fulwood Place
London WC1V 6HG
020 7405 5633
all@globalactionplan.org.uk
www.globalactionplan.org.uk

Groundwork
Lockside
5 Scotland Street
Birmingham B1 2RR
0121 236 8565 info@groundwork.org.uk
www.groundwork.org.uk

Greenworks
94–96 Queensbury Road
Wembley HAO 1QG
0845 230 2 231
info@green-works.co.uk
www.green-works.co.uk

Health@Work
Orleans House
Edmund Street
Liverpool L3 9NG
0151 236 6608
info@healthatworkcentre.org.uk
www.healthatworkcentre.org.uk

Home Office
2 Marsham Street
London SW1P 4DF
020 7035 4848
020 7035 4742 (textphone)
public.enquiries@homeoffice.gsi.gov.uk
www.homeoffice.gov.uk

HMRC Charities
0845 302 0203
www.hmrc.gov.uk/charities

HMRC National Advice Service
0845 010 9000

HMRC Employer Orderline
0845 7 646 646
0800 95 95 98 (textphone)

HMRC New Employer Helpline
0845 60 70 143
0845 602 1380 (textphone)

HSE Books
01787 881165
www.hsebooks.com

HSE Infoline
0845 345 0055
hseinfoline@natbrit.com

Independent Safeguarding Agency
0300 123 1111
scheme.info@homeoffice.gsi.gov.uk
www.isa-gov.org.uk

Information Commissioner
Wycliffe House
Water Lane
Wilmslow SK9 5AF
01625 54 57 45/0845 30 60 60
www.informationcommissioner.gov.uk

The Insolvency Service
0845 602 9848 (insolvency)
0845 145 0004 (redundancy)
insolvency.enquiryline@insolvency.gsi.gov.uk
www.insolvency.gov.uk

The Institute of Chartered Secretaries and Administrators
16 Park Crescent
London W1B 1AH
020 7580 4741
info@icsa.co.uk
www.icsa.org.uk

International Cooperative Alliance
www.ica.coop

Joint Council for the Welfare of Immigrants
115 Old Street
London EC1V 9RT
020 7251 8708
info@jcwi.org.uk
www.jcwi.org.uk

Liberty
21 Tabard Street
London SE1 4LA
020 7403 3888
www.liberty-human-rights.org.uk

London Voluntary Service Council
356 Holloway Road
London N7 6PA
020 7700 8107
www.lvsc.org.uk

Low Carbon Buildings Programme
0800 915 0990
info@lowcarbonbuildings.org.uk
www.lowcarbonbuildings.org.uk

Makaton Charity
Manor House
46 London Road
Camberley GU17 0AA
tel 01276 606760
info@makaton.org
www.makaton.org

Mencap
123 Golden Lane
London EC1Y 0RT
020 7454 0454
help@mencap.org.uk
www.mencap.org.uk

Metropolitan Police Public Order Branch
www.met.police.uk/publicorder

Ministry of Justice
102 Petty France
London SW1H 9AJ
020 3334 3555
general.queries@justice.gsi.gov.uk
www.justice.gov.uk

National Association for Voluntary and Community Action
177 Arundel Street
Sheffield S1 2NU
0114 278 6636
0114 278 7025 (textphone)
navca@navca.org.uk
www.navca.org.uk

National Council for Voluntary Organisations
Regent's Wharf
8 All Saints Street
London N1 9RL
020 7713 6161
0800 2 798 798 (helpline)
0800 01 88 111 (textphone)
www.ncvo-vol.org.uk

National Scrapstore Directory
www.childrensscrapstore.co.uk

Office of the Scottish Charity Regulator (OSCR)
2nd Floor, Quadrant House
9 Riverside Drive
Dundee DD1 4NY
01382 220446
info@oscr.org.uk
www.oscr.org.uk

Office of the Third Sector
35 Great Smith Street
London SW1P 3BQ
020 7276 6400
OTS.info@cabinet-office.x.gsi.gov.uk
www.cabinetoffice.gov.uk/third_sector

The Pensions Advisory Service
11 Belgrave Road
London SW1V 1RB
0845 601 2923
enquiries@pensionsadvisoryservice.org.uk
www.pensionsadvisoryservice.org.uk

Pensions Regulator
The Pensions Regulator
Napier House
Trafalgar Place
Brighton BN1 4DW
customersupport@thepensionsregulator.gov.uk
0870 6063636
www.thepensionsregulator.gov.uk

The Pensions Trust
6 Canal Street
Leeds LS11 5BQ
0113 234 5500
enquiries@thepensionstrust.org.uk
www.thepensionstrust.org.uk

Planning Aid
Unit 419, The Custard Factory
Gibb Street
Birmingham B9 4AA
0121 693 1201
info@planningaid.rtpi.org.uk
www.planningaid.rtpi.org.uk

Registrar of Companies
see Companies House

Royal Parks Agency
www.royalparks.org.uk

Contacts

Scottish Council of Voluntary Organisations
15 Mansfield Plane
Edinburgh EH3 6BB
0131 556 3882
enquiries@scvo.org.uk
www.scvo.org.uk

Shap Working Party
PO Box 38580
London SW1P 3XF
020 7898 1494
info@shapworkingparty.org.uk
www.shapworkingparty.org.uk

Squares Management Team
www.london.gov.uk/squares/management.jsp

Stamp Taxes Helpline
0845 603 0135

The Stationery Office
0870 600 5522
www.tso.co.uk

Streets Alive
86 Colston Street
Bristol BS1 5BB
0117 922 5708
events@streetsalive.net
www.streetparty.org.uk

Transport for London Charities Team
Customer Service Centre
55 Broadway
London SW1H 0BD
0845 330 9874 charities@tube.tfl.gov.uk

TUC
Congress House
Great Russell Street
London WC1B 3LS
020 7636 4030
www.tuc.org.uk

UK Border Agency
Customer Contact Centre
PO Box 3468
Sheffield S3 8WA
0114 207 4074 (work permit enquiries)
wpcustomers@ind.homeoffice.gsi.gov.uk
www.bia.homeoffice.gov.uk

UK Intellectual Property Office
Concept House
Cardiff Road
Newport NP10 8QQ
0845 9 500 505
0845 9 222 250 (textphone)
enquiries@ipo.gov.uk
www.ipo.gov.uk

Unison
1 Mabledon Place
London WC1H 9AJ
0845 355 0845
www.unison.org.uk

Unite
Hayes Court, West Common Road
Hayes
Bromley BR2 7AU
0845 850 4242
www.unitetheunion.org.uk

Volunteering England
Regent's Wharf
8 All Saints Street
London N1 9RL
020 7520 8900
volunteering@volunteeringengland.org
www.volunteeringengland.org

Wales Council for Voluntary Action
Baltic House
Mount Stuart Square
Cardiff CF10 5FH
029 20431700
029 2043 1702 (textphone)
enquiries@wcva.org.uk
www.wcva.org.uk

Waste Watch
56–64 Leonard Street
London EC2A 4LT
020 7549 0300
info@wastewatch.org.uk
www.wastewatch.org.uk

WasteOnline
www.wasteonline.org.uk

Working Families
1–3 Berry Street
London EC1V 0AA
0800 013 0313 (advice line)
office@workingfamilies.org.uk
www.workingfamilies.org.uk

Index

Abroad, workers from 122
Absence, monitoring 133
Acas code of practice on discipline and
  grievance 95
Access
  audit 177
  disabled people 176
  public events 243
Access to Medical Reports Act 1988 . . . 138
Access to Work 76
Accidents 167
  accident book 167
  insurance 209
Accidental damage insurance 208
Accounting records 212
Accounts, clauses in constitution 33
Accounts 46, 211, 213
  companies 215
  filing 43
  industrial and provident societies 215
  non-company charities 216
  public access 220
Accruals accounts 214
Activities 254
Acts
  Access to Medical Reports Act 1988 . . 138
  Anti-Social Behaviour Act 2003 255
  Asylum and Immigration Act 1996 . 115, 122
  Care Standards Act 2000 120
  Charities Act 1992 261
  Charities Act 1993 . . . . 12, 213
  Charities Act 1993, Part VI (amended) . . 211
  Charities Act 1993 9, 29, 173, 182, 188, 189
  Charities Act 2006 . . 6, 11, 12, 18, 38, 218,
    263, 264
  Charities Act (Northern Ireland) 2008 . . 11
  Charities and Trustee Investment (Scotland)
    Act 2005 11
  Civil Partnerships Act 2004 73
  Communications Act 2003 260
  Companies Act 1985 . . . . 5, 33
  Companies Act 2006 . 5, 27, 30, 41, 43, 44,
    212, 213
  Companies (Audit, Investigations and
    Community Enterprise) Act 2004 5
  Control of Pollution Act 1974 256
  Cooperatives and Community Benefit
    Societies Act 2003 . . . . 7, 38
  Corporate Manslaughter and Corporate
    Homicide Act 2007 165

Acts—*continued*
  Criminal Justice Act 1993 270
  Criminal Justice and Court Services Act
    2000 120
  Criminal Justice and Public Order Act
    1994 . . . . 93, 255
  Data Protection Act 1998 . . . . . . 115, 249
  Disability Discrimination Acts 1995 and
    2005 . . . . 72, 176, 238
  Employment Act 2002 . . . . 80, 86, 99
  Employment Rights Act 1996 . . 65, 66, 102,
    104, 105, 124, 142
  Environmental Protection Act 1990 184, 191
  Equal Pay Act 1970 79
  Equality Act 2006 239
  Freedom of Information Act 2000 252
  Friendly and Industrial Provident Societies
    Act 1968 213
  Gambling Act 2005 266
  Health and Safety at Work Act 1974 . 61, 65,
    93, 144, 148
  Human Rights Act 1998 272
  Industrial and Provident Societies Acts 1965,
    1968 . . . . 7, 11, 218
  Insolvency Act 1986 . . . . 33, 283, 284, 285
  Landlord and Tenant Act 1954 175
  Landlord and Tenant (Covenants) Act
    1995 178
  Local Government Finance Act 1988,
    Section 47 188
  Local Government (Miscellaneous Provision)
    Act 1982 262
  Metropolitan Police Act 1839 256
  National Minimum Wage Act 1998 68
  Noise and Statutory Nuisance Act 1993 . 256
  Occupier's Liability Act 1957, 1984 . . . 166
  Offices Shops and Railway Premises Act
    1963 145
  Pensions Acts 1995, 2004 . . . . 9, 80, 101
  Police, Factories etc (Miscellaneous
    Provisions) Act 1916 263
  Prevention of Terrorism Act 2000 270
  Protection from Harassment Act 1997 . . 93
  Protection of Children Act 1999 120
  Public Interest Disclosure Act 1998 . . . 102
  Public Meeting Act 1908 255
  Public Order Act 1986 255
  Race Relations Act 1976 . . . . . . 72, 238
  Rehabilitation of Offenders Act 1974 80, 120

297

Index

Acts—*continued*

Representation of the People Act 1983 . 16, 260

Safeguarding Vulnerable Groups Act 2006 120

Serious Organised Crime and Police Act 2005 260

Sex Discrimination Act 1975 72

Town and Country Planning Act 1990 . . 185

Trade Union and Labour Relations (Consolidation) Act 1992 103

Work and Families Act 2006 . . . 84, 87, 90

Additional paternity leave and pay 87

Additional state pension 134

Address for administrative purposes 38

Administration, insolvency 284

Administrative office, moving 46

Adopting the constitution 34-36

Adoption

leave 87

pay 128

Advertisements, job 112

Age discrimination 73, 240

pensions 137

Agency staff 62

AGM, see *Annual general meetings*

Agreements, unions 98

Air quality 166

Alcohol 257

All risks insurance 209

Altering the constitution 33

Alternative work

new or expectant mothers 85

redundancy 105

Annual accounts, see *Accounts*

Annual general meetings 44, 27

checklist 55

Annual reports 46, 218

Annual return

charity 47

employer 127

Annual turnover limit, charity trading 16

Antenatal care 85

Anti-Social Behaviour Act 2003 255

Appealing, decision on flexible working . . 91

Appearance, building 186

Application forms 111

Appointed person, first aid 164

Appointing auditor or examiner 235

Appointing staff, see *Recruitment*

Appointment, letter 115

Approved codes of practice 144

Articles of association 6

Asbestos 158

Assault, insurance 209

Assigning a lease 178

Asylum and Immigration Act 1996 . . 115, 122

Audit 216

Auditors

appointing 235

records for 236

responsibilities 233

working with 220, 233

Average clause 204

Balance sheet 214, 215, 275

Bank accounts 38, 230

Bank mandates 38

Bank reconciliation 232

Bank statements 232

Bargaining unit 97

Basic state pension 134

Belief, discrimination 239

Beneficiaries 24

BERR, see *Department for Business, Enterprise and Regulatory Reform*

Bingo 268

Blindness 72

Board, see *Committee, management*

Bookkeeping 231

Breach of copyright, insurance 207

Breach of statutory duties

Breach of trust 20

Break clause 178

Budgets 228, 229

Building regulations 185, 187

Buildings

altering the structure 180

appearance 186

classes of use 185

insurance 205

new 186

Business interruption insurance 209

Business leases, voluntary code of conduct 175

Business rates 187

Campaigning 16, 259, 260

Capital gains tax 15

Car boot sales 262

Care Standards Act 2000 120

Career breaks 93

Career-average pension schemes 135

Carers 90

Cash flow 228, 229

forecast 275

Casual staff, paying 127
Changes
   constitution 47
   recording 45
Changing facilities 155
Changing structure 8
Charges' register 42
Charitable companies, accounts 215
Charitable incorporated organisation 6
   converting to 10
   accounts 216
   financial regulations 211
   insolvency 34, 230
   membership 24, 25
   registers 42
   trustees 29
   winding up 283
Charitable Incorporated Organisations
   (General) Regulations 6
Charitable Incorporated Organisations
   (Insolvency and Dissolution) Regulations 283,
   230
Charitable purposes 12
Charitable status 11
Charitable trusts 3
Charities (Account and Reports) Regulations
   2008 . . 211, 214, 216, 217, 218, 219, 220
Charities Accounts (Scotland) Regulations
   2006 212
Charities Act 1992 261
Charities Act 1993 . . . . 12, 189, 213
   Part VI (amended) 211
   property disposal 189
   Section 26 188
   Section 38 173
   Section 72 182
   Section 72(4) 29
   Section 74 (as amended) 9
   Section 82 182
Charities Act 2006   6, 11, 12, 18, 38, 218, 263,
   264
Charities Act (Northern Ireland) 2008 . . . 11
Charities and Trustee Investment (Scotland)
   Act 2005 11
Charities SORP 211, 214
Charities
   accounts scrutiny 217
   campaigning 16, 259
   collections 264
   dual registration 14
   financial management 211
   funds 213

Charities—*continued*
   mergers 279
   registration 36
   reserves 233
   Scottish 212
   small 15
   tax 223
   tax relief 15
   trading 223
   trustee indemnity insurance 208
Charity Commission, notifying of closure . 287
Checklist
   annual general meeting 55
   committee members' roles and
     responsibilities 57
   electing committee members 56
   health and safety policy 169
Childcare contributions 128
CIC, see *Community interest companies*
CIO, see *Charitable incorporated organisations*
Civil partners, pensions 137
Civil Partnerships Act 2004 73
Claiming money owed, redundancy 107
Claims, insurance 204
Classes of use, buildings and land 185
Clauses, constitution 22-34
Cleanliness 153
Closing down 273
Club machine permit 267
Clubs premises certificate 258
Coaches 268
Collections 263
Collective agreements 98
Collective Redundancies and Transfer of
   Undertaking (Protection of Employment)
   (Amendment) Regulations 1999 103
Co-locating 183
Committee, management 4, 37
   financial procedures 224
   first members 37
   meetings 28, 32
   meetings, first 38
   meetings, observers 33
   members, elections 29
   members, liability 20
   members, misconduct 48
   members, payments 18
   members, removing 31
   members, selecting 29
   members' register 41
   members' roles 37

Index

Committee, management—*continued*
members' roles and responsibilities,
    checklist 57
    membership 28, 45
    officers 28
    titles 1
Communications Act 2003 260
Community amateur sports clubs, rate
    relief 188
Community benefit society 7
Community interest companies 5
    annual report 220
    accounts, see *Companies, accounts*
Community interest report 43, 220
Community interest test 5
Companies (Audit, Investigations and
    Community Enterprise) Act 2004 5
Companies (Particulars of Usual Residential
    Address) (Confidentiality Orders) Regulations
    2002 41
Companies Act 1985 . . . . 5, 33
Companies Act 2006 5, 27, 30, 41, 43, 44, 212,
    213
Companies, also see *Community interest
    companies* 4
    accounts 215
    adopting constitution 34
Company voluntary arrangement 284
Compressed hours 93
Compulsory insurance 204
Compulsory liquidation 285
Compulsory maternity leave 86
Computer insurance 209
Computers, health and safety 159
Confidentiality 269
    self-employed/freelance workers 117
Conflicts of interest 32
Conservation areas 186
Constitution, also see *Trust deed, Rules* . . 1
    adopting 34
    altering 33
    changing 47
    charitable incorporated organisation 6
    charitable trust 3
    community interest company 6
    drafting 22
    models 34
    unincorporated association 3
Consultants 116
Consultation
    employees 99
    health and safety 147

Consultation—*continued*
    redundancy 103
    TUPE 101
Contents insurance 208
Contracting out, state pension 134, 135
Contracting to provide services 244
Contractors, health and safety 151
Contracts
    converting grant to 245
    employment 66
    freelance/self-employed workers 116
    personal liability 21
    service 244, 248
Contractual rights 63
Contractual sick pay 131
Control of Noise at Work Regulations . . . 165
Control of Pollution Act 1974 256
Control of Substances Hazardous to Health
    Regulations 2002 163
Controlled activity 121
Controlled wastes 191
Cooperation between employers, health and
    safety 152
Cooperative society 7
Cooperatives and Community Benefit Societies
    Act 2003 . . . . 7, 38
Co-option 30, 38
Copyright 252
    electronic 253
    material, visually impaired people 253
    freelance/self-employed workers 117
    music 253
    volunteers 118
Copyright (Visually Impaired Persons) Act
    2002 253
Corporate Manslaughter and Corporate
    Homicide Act 2007 165
Corporation tax 15, 223
Covenants, premises 181
Cover, insurance 202, 203
CRB, see *Criminal Records Bureau*
Creditors' voluntary liquidation 285
Criminal Justice Act 1993 270
Criminal Justice and Court Services Act
    2000 120
Criminal Justice and Public Order Act 1994 93,
    255
Criminal record checks, employees 120
Criminal Records Bureau 120
Crises, dealing with 48
Custodian trustee 173, 182
Data handling 249

Data protection 249
  policy 251
  principles 249
Data Protection Act 1998 . . . . . . 115, 249
Data subjects 249, 250
Dates, noting important 42
DDA, see *Disability Discrimination Act*
Declaration of trust 3
Deductions
  pay 124
  pensions 126
  student loans 126
Deductions working sheet 125
Deed of appointment, model 200
Deed of trust 3
Deeds, signing 181
Defamation 253
  insurance 207
Defined benefit pension schemes 135
Delegating powers 39
Department for Business, Enterprise and
  Regulatory Reform, notifying 104
Dependants' leave 89
Designated premises supervisor 257
Development control 185
Dignity at work 93, 94
Direct discrimination 74, 80
Directors 4
  report 220
Disability discrimination 72, 238
  Equality Bill 2008 73
  Disability Symbol 77
Disability Discrimination Act 1995 and 2005 72,
238
Disability Discrimination Act 1995, Part II . 176
Disability Discrimination Act 1995, Part III . 176
Disability Discrimination Act 1995
  (Amendment) Regulations 2003 . . . 72, 74
Disability Discrimination (Blind and Partially
  Sighted Persons) Regulations 2003 . . . 72
Disabled people
  access 176
  employment schemes 76
  providing information 241
  rights 75
Disciplinary policy and procedures 95
Disclosures, standard 120
Discretionary insurance 208
Discretionary rate relief 188
Discrimination 64
  by association 74
  age 240

Discrimination—*continued*
  context 71
  disability 72, 238
  gender reassignment 72
  liability 78
  post-employment 75
  protection from 64
  race 238
  religion and belief 239
  sex 237
  sexual orientation 239
Dismissal, protection from 64
Dispensing with members' meetings . . . 27
Display energy certificates 193
Display screen equipment, see *VDUs*
Disposals, land 188
Disposing of premises 188
Dissolution, constitution 33
Diversity policy, see *equality and diversity
  policy*
Documentation 40
Donations 15
Doors, health and safety 154
Drainage 166
Drinking water 155
Dual registration 14, 36, 37
Due diligence 279
Duration, lease/licence 178
Eating facilities 155
Economical, technical or organisational
  justification 101
Electing
  committee members 29
  committee members, checklist 56
  officers 38
Election meetings, charities 16
Elections, charities and campaigning . . . 260
Electrical apparatus 163
Electrical and electronic equipment,
  disposal 192
Electricity at Work Regulations 1989 . . . 163
Electronic communication 40, 43
Electronic copyright 253
Electronic marketing 251
Electronic meetings 44
ELV, see *End-of-life vehicles*
Email
  policy 139
  monitoring 138
Emergency decisions 48
Emergency plan, fire safety 161
Emergency procedures 151

Index

Employee representatives 99
  redundancy 103
Employee
  definition 61
  health and safety 145, 146
  leaving 126
  notifying re redundancy 104
  on the committee 19
  rights 64
Employers, also see *Employment*
  annual return 127
  childcare contributions 128
  disabled people 176
  liability insurance 204
Employing people, restrictions 120
Employment tribunals 108
Employment Act 2002 . . . . 80, 86, 99
Employment and Support Allowance . . . 130
Employment Equality (Age) Regulations
  2006 . . . . 73, 77
Employment Equality (Religion or Belief
  Regulations) 2003 . . . . 73, 74
Employment Equality (Sexual Orientation)
  Regulations 2003 . . . . 73, 74
Employment Relations Act 1999 . . 65, 89, 97
Employment Relations Act 2004 97
Employment Rights Act 1996 65, 66, 102, 104,
  105, 124, 142
Employment, also see *Employers*
  contracts 66
  equal opportunities, good practice 83
  rights, summary 63
  schemes, disabled people 76
Empty rate relief 188
End of year return 127
End of year summary 127
End-of-life Vehicles Directive 2000 193
End-of-life Vehicles Regulations 2003 . . . 193
Endowment funds 213
Energy efficiency 195
Energy performance 193
Enforcement
  health and safety 144
  smoking 162
Engineering inspection insurance 209
Environment, also see *Green office*
  legislation 191
  policy and practice 194
  voluntary sector organisations 194
Environmental Protection Act 1990 . 184, 191
Equal opportunities
  employment 83

Equal opportunities—*continued*
  service delivery 237
Equal pay 79
Equal Pay Act 1970 79
Equal Treatment Amendment Directive 2002 74
Equality Act 2006 239
Equality Bill 2008 . . . . 24, 49, 73
  discrimination 79
  harassment 75
  pay 80
  positive action 79
  premises 181
  public bodies 81
Equality Act (Sexual Orientation) Regulations
  2007 239
Equality and diversity policy 49
Equality and Human Rights Commission . 79
Equality legislation, scope 74
Equality schemes 81
Equality standard 81
Equipment
  failure insurance 209
  fire fighting 161
  health and safety 153, 156
  leases 190
  suitability and maintenance 156
EU Agency Workers Directive 62
EU Energy Performance in Buildings
  Directive 193
European Convention on Human Rights . . 272
Excepted charities 12
  account scrutiny 218
Exceptions, DDA 239
Exclusions, insurance 203
Exempt charities 12
  account scrutiny 218
Exempt fundraising events 262
Ex-offenders 80
Expected week of childbirth 85
Expenses, volunteers 119
Express terms 66
Extent of duty, insurance 202
Eyesight tests 159
Face-to-face fundraising 264
Fallback scheme, parental leave 88
Falling, preventing 154
Family legislation 84
Family responsibilities, time off 65
Fee exemptions, premises licence 258
Fidelity insurance 209
Filing accounts 43
Final salary pension schemes 135

Finance leases 190
Financial management 211
Financial responsibilities, committee 224
Financial systems and procedures 226
Financial year 39
Finding premises 175
Fire detection and warning systems 161
Fire fighting equipment 161
Fire safety 160
First aid 164
Fixed asset register 227
Fixed-term employees 81
  rcdundancy 104
Fixed-term Employees (Prevention of Less
  Favourable Treatment) Regulations 2002 81,
  105
Flexible working 90
  good practice 91
  ways 92
Flexitime 92
Floors 154
Food Hygiene (England) Regulations 2006 257
Food 166
  selling, preparing and storing 257
Form of Mandate 230
Fraudulent preference 282
Freedom of information 252
Freedom of Information Act 2000 252
Freehold land 173
Freelance workers, also see *Self-employed
  people* 116
Friendly and Industrial Provident Societies Act
  1968 213
Full cost recovery 213
Fund accounting, non-charitable
  organisations 213
Funding agreements 244
Fundraising 261
  exempt events 262
  face-to-face 264
  statements 261
Funds, charity 213
Gambling Act 2005 266
Gaming machines 267
Gender reassignment, discrimination . . . 72
General Food Regulations 2004 166
Genuine occupational requirement 78
Gift Aid 224, 262
Gifts, shares and securities 263
Glossary of terms, closing down 273
Good practice
  disabled people 76

Good practice—*continued*
  equal opportunities in employment . . . 83
  flexible working 91
  health and safety 167
  redundancy 106
  service provision 240
Governing document, see *Constitution*
Grants 244
  converting to contract 245
Green office 191
Green procurement 197
Grievance policy and procedures . . . 95, 96
Gross misconduct 95
Group personal pensions 137
Harassment 74, 75
  intentional 93
  third party 75
Hazardous substances 163, 164
Hazardous Waste Regulations 2005 192
Health and safety 144
  duties 145
  information to employees 151
  policies 167
  policy statement 146
  poster 147
  pregnant women and new mothers 85, 152
  temporary workers 151
  training 151
  work experience trainees 152
  young workers 151
Health and Safety (Consultation with
  Employees) Regulations 1996 147
Health and Safety (Display Screen Equipment)
  Regulations 1992 158
Health and Safety (First Aid) Regulations
  1981 164
Health and Safety at Work Act 1974 61, 65, 93,
  144, 148
Health surveillance 150
Helplines, legal advice 210
Hire purchase 190
Hiring out
  premises 184
  vehicles 269
Holding trustees 30, 173, 181
Holidays 70
Home-based workers, health and safety . 145
House to house collections 263, 264
House-to-House Collections Act 1939 . . . 263
House-to-House Collections Regulations
  1947 264
Housing quality 166

Index

Human Rights Act 1998 272
Ill health policies 132
Immigration, Asylum and Nationality Act
   2006 . . . . 122, 123
Implied terms 66
Income and expenditure account 215
Income tax 15, 125, 223
Income, increasing 278
Incorporated organisations 4, 6
   insolvency 283
   insurance 202
   liability for debts 286
   premises 173
   signing deeds 182
   winding up 282
Incorporation, trustees 2, 182
Increasing income 278
Indemnity insurance 207
Independent examination 216, 217
Independent examiners
   appointing 235
   responsibilities 233
   working with 220, 233
Independent Safeguarding Authority 121
Indirect discrimination 74, 80, 92
Industrial and provident societies 7
   accounts 215, 218
   rules 7
   converting to company 11
Industrial and Provident Societies Act 1965 . 7,
   11
Industrial and Provident Societies
   Act 1968 (as amended) 218
Information and Consultation of Employees
   Regulations 2004 100
Information
   accessible 241
   data protection 251
   handling and storing 271
   health and safety 151
   insurance 210
   job enquirers 113
   sharing 269, 271
Insolvency Act 1986 . . . . . 33, 283, 284, 285
Insolvency, charitable incorporated
   organisations 34
Insolvent organisations, winding up 282
Instrument of dissolution 282
Insurance 202
   accidental damage 208
   accidents, medical care and assault . . . 209
   all risks 209

Insurance—*continued*
   business interruption 209
   compulsory 204
   computer 209
   contents 208
   defamation and unintentional breach of
     copyright 207
   discretionary 208
   employee theft 209
   engineering inspection 209
   equipment failure 209
   fidelity 209
   hiring out premises 184
   legal expenses 210
   outdoor events 209
   premises 180
   product liability 207
   self-employed people 207
   that may be required 205
   trustee and directors' indemnity 207
Intentional harassment 93
Internet
   monitoring 138
   policy 139
Interviews 114
Investments 227
IPS, see *Industrial and provident societies*
ISA, see *Independent Safeguarding Authority*
Job advertisements 112
Job descriptions 110
Job Introduction Scheme 76
Job sharing 92
Keeping in touch days, maternity leave . . 86
Keeping records 138
Ladders, health and safety 156
Land, classes of use 185
Landlord and Tenant Act 1954 175
Landlord and Tenant (Covenants) Act 1995 178
Large bus permit 268
Late night refreshment 258
Learning disability, information 242
Leases, equipment 190
Leases, property
   points to check 178
   signing 181
   surrendering 175
Leasehold property 173
Leasing premises 175
Leave
   adoption 87
   annual 70
   dependants 89

Leave—*continued*
  maternity 85
  parental 88
  paternity 86
Legal expenses insurance 210
Legal structures 1
Letter heads 40
Letter of appointment 115
Liability
  contracts 248
  for debts 286
  committee members 20
  insurance 204
Libel 253
Licence, property 175, 178
Licences, gambling 266
Licensing Act 2003 257
Licensing premises 257
Light touch, Charity Commission 15
Lighting 153
Limited companies, see *Companies*
Liquidation 285
Liquidator 282
Listed property 186
Loans 229
Local authority influence 11
Local Government (Miscellaneous Provision)
  Act 1982 262
Local Government Finance Act
  1988, Section 47 188
Lotteries 266
Loudspeakers 256
Machinery, health and safety 156
Maintenance, equipment 156
Management accounts 228
Management committee, see *Committee,*
  management
Management of Health and Safety Regulations
  1999 148
Managing sickness 133
Mandatory rate relief 188
Manual handling 157
Manual Handling Operations Regulations
  1992 158
Marches 255
Marketing, electronic 251
Material fact, insurance 202, 203
Maternity 84
  allowance 129
  leave 85
  pay 85, 128

Maternity and Parental Leave Regulations
  1999 . . . . 84, 88
Medical care, insurance 209
Medium companies, accounts 215
Meetings 27, 254
  committee 28, 32
  members' 27
  notice 43
  virtual 44
Members' register 41
Members' voluntary winding-up 282
Membership 24, 38
  changes, organisational 44
  charitable incorporated organisations . . 24
  terminating 26
Memorandum of association 6
Mergers 279
Metropolitan Police Act 1839 256
Minibuses 268
Minimum wage 68
Minutes 32
Misconduct, officers/committee members   48
Mobile phones, in vehicles 165
Mobile work equipment 156
Model constitutions 34
Model deed of appointment 200
Money Laundering Regulations 2003 . . . 270
Monitoring
  absence 133
  effectiveness, equal opportunities 83
  applications 112
  email and internet 138
  service provision 240
Moratorium 284
Mortgages 173
  agreements, signing 181
Motor insurance 205
Mouse, using 160
Moving administrative office 46
Music, copyright 253
National insurance 125
  self-employed/freelance workers 117
National Minimum Wage Act 1998 68
Negligence 20
New buildings 186
New mothers, health and safety . . . 85, 152
Noise and Statutory Nuisance Act 1993 . . 256
Noise 165, 256
Non-charitable companies
  accounts scrutiny 216
  fund accounting 213
  tax 224

Non-company charities, accounts 216
Non-domestic rates 187
Non-employees, health and safety 145
Non-primary purpose trading 16
Notes to the accounts 214, 215
Notice of Appointment 285
Notification of closure 286
Notification, redundancy 103
Notifying, data protection 250
Noting important dates 42
Observers, committee meetings 33
Occupational pension schemes 135
Occupational road risk 164
Occupier's Liability Act 1957, 1984 166
Officers, committee 28, 30
  electing 38
  misconduct 48
  removing 31
  register 41
  roles 37
Offices Shops and Railway Premises Act
  1963 145
Official Custodian for Charities 173, 181
Officials, union 99
Older people 77
Operating leases 190
Operating licences 266
Order of Exemption 264
Ordinary resolution 28
Organisation, running 43
Organisational membership, changes . . . 44
Organisations with public functions 272
Outdoor events, insurance 209
Outsourcing 116
  payroll 129
Overdrafts 229
Parental leave 88
Parks, meetings in 256
Parliaments, protests near 256
Part VI, Charities Act 1993 (amended) . . . 211
Part-time workers 82
Part-time Workers (Prevention of Less
  Favourable Treatment) Regulations 2000 82,
  92, 105
Paternity 86
  leave 86
  pay 128
Paying people 63, 68, 124
  redundancy 106
  deductions from pay 124
PAYE 125, 221
Payments, committee members 18

Payroll giving 263
Payroll, outsourcing 129
Payslips 124
Pensions 80, 134
  changes 137
  TUPE 101
Pensions Act 1995 80
Pensions Act 2004 . . . . 9, 101
Peppercorn rent 176
Percentage threshold scheme 131
Period of Incapacity for Work 130
Permitted activities, campaigning 259
Person specifications 110
Personal accounts, pensions 137
Personal liability 20
Personal licence, alcohol 257, 266
Personal pension plans 137
Personal Protective Equipment at Work
  Regulations 1992 155
Pests 166
Planning for survival 276
Planning permission 186
Planning regulations 185
Plate glass windows insurance 206
PoCA, see *Protection of Children List*
Police, Factories etc (Miscellaneous
  Provisions) Act 1916 263
Policies, developing organisational 39
  confidentiality 269, 371
  data protection 251
  dignity at work 94
  disciplinary and grievance 95
  environmental 194
  equality and diversity 49-52
  health and safety 167, 169
  internet/email 139
  sickness/ill health 132
  smoke-free 163
Policy statement, health and safety 146
Political activity 259
Portable computers 159
Positive action 78, 79
Post-employment discrimination 75
Posts, reviewing 109
PoVA, see *Protection of Vulnerable Adults List*
Powers, delegating 39
Pregnant women, health and safety . 85, 152,
  160
Pregnant Workers Directive 1992 72
Premises licence 257, 266
Premises 173
  access 176

Premises—*continued*

deciding 178

disposal 188

health and safety duties 153, 166

held on trust 189

hiring out 184

in campaigning 260

licensing 257

reducing costs 277

sharing 182

smoking 162

Preparing food 257

Preventative and protective measures . . . 150

Prevention of Terrorism Act 2000 270

Primary purpose trading 16

Principles, data protection 249

Privacy and Electronic Communications (EC
Directive) Regulations 2003 251

Private lotteries 266

Private premises, collections 263

Probationary periods 116

Processing data 249

Processions 255

Procurement, green 197

Product liability insurance 207

Professional indemnity insurance 206

Proposal, insurance 204

Protection from Harassment Act 1997 . . . 93

Protection of Children Act 1999 120

Protection of Children List 120

Protection of Vulnerable Adults List 120

Protests 255

in London 256

Providing references 107

Provision and Use of Work Equipment
Regulations 1998 156

Proxy voting 43

Public access, accounts 220

Public assemblies 255

Public authorities, equality schemes 240

Public benefit 14

Public charitable collections 264

Public collections certificate 264

Public events, access 243

Public functions, organisations with 272

Public health laws 166

Public interest disclosure, see *Whistle-blowing*

Public Interest Disclosure Act 1998 102

Public liability insurance 206

Public Meeting Act 1908 255

Public Order Act 1986 255

Public Service Vehicle Operators' Licence 269

Public squares, meetings in 256

PUWER, see *Provision and Use of Worker
Equipment Regulations 1998*

Quorum 28, 48

Race discrimination 238

Race Relations Act 1976 . . . . 72, 238

Race Relations Act 1976 (Amendment)
Regulations 2003 74

Raffles 266

Rate relief 188

Rates, paying 187

Reasonable adjustments, disabled people 238

Receipts and payments accounts 213

Recognition, union 97

Recommendation report, energy
performance 193

Record keeping

finance 231

statutory sick pay 131

record retention 287

Records

auditor 236

lotteries 267

Recruitment 40, 109

freelance, self-employed workers,
consultants 116

Recycling 197

Reducing costs 276, 277

Reducing waste 196

Redundancy 102

pay 106

claiming money owed 107

good practice 106

References, providing 107

Refreshment, late night 258

Refund, fundraising appeals 262

Refuse disposal 166

Registered social clubs 258

Registering

charity 36

data protection 250

health and safety 145

Registers

charges 174

charitable incorporated organisations . . 42

setting up 40

mergers 279

Registration, Evaluation, Authorisation and
Restriction of Chemicals 164

Regulated activity 121

Regulated entertainment 258

Index

Regulatory Reform (Business Tenancies)
  (England and Wales) Order 2003 175
Regulatory Reform (Fire Safety) Order 2005 160
Rehabilitation of Offenders Act 1974   80, 120
Religion, discrimination 239
Rent 179
Reorganisation 142
Repairs, responsibility 179
Reporting accountant's report 218
Reporting of Injuries, Disease and Dangerous
  Occurrences Regulations 1995 167
Representation of the People Act 1983 16, 260
Representation, disciplinary hearing 97
Representatives of employees' safety . . . 148
Rescue plan 280
Reserves, charities 233
Resolutions 28, 32
Responsible person, fire safety 160
Rest facilities 155
Restricted funds 213
Restrictions, employing people 120
Retirement 77
Reusing materials 197
Revenue account 215
Reviewing posts 109
Rights
  contractual 63
  employees' and workers' 61
  members' 26
  recognised trade unions 98
  statutory 63
Risk assessment 148
  fire safety 161
Risk management 210
  trustees' annual report 220
Risks, taking on contracts 247
ROA, see *Rehabilitation of Offenders Act*
Road Traffic Acts 205
Roles
  committee members 37
  officers 37
Room dimensions 153
RSI, see *Upper limb disorders*
Rubbish disposal 153
Rules, industrial and provident societies . . 7
Running the organisation 43
Safeguarding Vulnerable Groups Act 2006 120
Safety, also see *Health and safety*
  committees 148
  representatives 147
  hiring out premises 184
SAP, see *Statutory adoption pay*

Schedule of condition 179
Schedule of dilapidations 180
School-hours working 93
Scottish charities 11, 212
Seating 154
Seconded staff 62
Section 142, Education Act 2002 120
Section 19 permit 268
Section 36, Charities Act 1993 188
Section 38, Charities Act 1993 173
Section 47, Local Government Finance Act
  1988 188
Section 72, Charities Act 1993 . . . . 173, 182
Section 72(4), Charities Act 1993 29
Section 74, Charities Act 1993 (as amended) 8,
  9
Section 82, Charities Act 1993 . . . . 181, 182
Securities, gifts 263
Security, hiring out premises 184
Selection for redundancy 104
Selection panels 109
Self-employed workers 62
  contracts 116
  insurance 207
  recruiting 116
Selling and storing food 257
Sensitive personal data 250
Serious Organised Crime and Police Act
  2005 260
Service charges 179
Service contracts 244
Service, deciding whether to take on . . . 245
Service level agreement 244
Service providers, disabled people 176
Services and activities 237
Setting up an organisation 22
Sex discrimination 237
Sex Discrimination Act 1975 72
Sex Discrimination Act 1975 (Amendment)
  Regulations 2003, 2008 . . . . 75, 84
Sex Discrimination (Amendment of Legislation)
  Regulations 2008 237
Sex Discrimination (Gender Reassignment)
  Regulations 1999 72
Sexual orientation, discrimination 239
Shares, gifts 263
Sharing premises 182
Shortlisting 113
Sick pay 130
Sickness
  policies 132
  managing 133

Signage
   disabled people 177
   smoking 162
Signing deeds 181
Single equality scheme 81, 240
Slander 253
Small charities 15
Small companies, accounts 215
Smoke-free (Premises and Enforcement)
   Regulations 2006 162
Smokers, help for 163
Smoking 162-163
SMP, see *Statutory maternity pay* . . . .
SOAL, see *Statement of assets and liabilities*
Society lotteries 266
SOFA, see *Statement of financial activities*
Solvent organisations, winding up 281
SORP, see *Charities SORP*
Special resolution 28
Sponsored activities 265
SPP, see *Statutory paternity pay*
SSP, see *Statutory sick pay*
Staff, also see *Employees* and *Workers*
   costs, reducing 276
   agency 62
   appointing 40
   seconded 62
Stakeholder pensions 136
Stamp duty land tax 15
Standard disclosures 120
Standing orders 31
State pensions 134
Statement of assets and liabilities 213
Statement of employment particulars . . . 66
Statement of financial activities 214
Statements, fundraising 261
Statutory adoption pay 128, 129
Statutory duties, breach of 21
Statutory maternity pay 128
Statutory paternity pay 128, 129
Statutory rights 63
Statutory sick pay 130
Statutory union recognition 97
Storage 155
Street collections 263, 264
Street parties 257
Strengthening enforcement, discrimination 79
Stress 168, 172
Structural alterations, leases 180
Structure, changing 8
Student loan deductions 126
Students, working 127

Subcommittees 30
Subletting 178, 183
Subscriptions 26
Subsidiary trading company 17
Surrendering a lease 175, 178
Survival, planning for 276
Tax relief, charities 15
Tax, pension schemes 135
Tax, self-employed/freelance workers . . . 117
Telecommunications (Lawful Business
   Practice) (Interception of Communications)
   Regulations 2000 138
Temperature 153
Temporary event notices 257
Temporary staff
   paying 127
   health and safety 151
Terminating membership 26
Terms and conditions 68
Term-time working 93
Theft by employee insurance 209
Third party advice, premises 189
Third party harassment 75
Time off, also see *Holidays*
   public duties 71
   to look for work 106
   union learning representatives 99
Town and Country Planning Act 1990 . . . 185
Town and Country Planning Orders and
   Regulations 185, 186
Trade Union and Labour Relations
   (Consolidation) Act 1992 103
Trade unions 64, 97, 98
   redundancy 103
   union learning representatives 99
Trading 262
   charities 16, 233
   trading company 17
Trainees 63
Training
   equipment 157
   first aid 164
   health and safety 151
   VDUs 160
Transfer of Undertakings (Protection of
   Employment) Regulations 2006, see *TUPE*
Translation 241
Travel, minimising environmental impact . 198
Treasurer, duties 225
Tree preservation orders 186
Trial balance 232
Trust deed 3

Trust, breach of 20
Trustee and directors' indemnity insurance 207
Trustees
  annual report 218
  annual report, companies 220
  charitable incorporated organisations . . 29
  duties, campaigning 259
  holding 30
  incorporated body 2
Trusts, charitable 3
  signing deeds 181
TUPE 66, 100, 247
  consultation 101
Under-insurance 203
Unfair dismissal 108, 142
Uniform business rate 187
Unincorporated associations 2
  constitution 3
  signing deeds 181
  insolvency 283
  insurance 203
  liability for debts 286
  premises 173
  winding up 281
Unions, see Trade unions
Unrestricted funds 213
Upper limb disorders 159
Use of buildings and land 185
Users on the committee 18
Users
  health and safety 146
  rights 271
  VDUs 158, 159
Utmost good faith, insurance 202
Vacancies, filling 30
Value added tax, see VAT
VAT 15
  legal requirements 220
  rates 221
VDUs 158
  training 160
  users 158, 159
Vehicles
  hiring out 269
  health and safety 154
  smoking 162
Ventilation 153
Vermin 166
Vicarious liability 78
Victimisation 64, 74
Virtual meetings 44, 32
Visiting employees, health and safety . . . 151

Visual display units, see VDUs
Visual impairment 72
  copying material for visually impaired
    people, ... 253
Voluntary code of conduct for business
  leases 175
Voluntary recognition, unions 97
Voluntary sector environmental
  organisations 194
Voluntary striking off 282
Volunteers 61, 118
  records 128
Voting procedures 28
Washing facilities 155
Waste disposal 191
Waste Electrical and Electronic Equipment,
  Regulations 2005 192
Waste, reducing 196
Water, drinking 155
WCs 154
Web-design, accessible 242
WEEE see Waste Electrical and Electronic
  Equipment 192
Whistle-blowing 102
Winding up 281
Windows 154
  insurance 206
Work and Families Act 2006 . . . . 84, 87, 90
Work at Height Regulations 2005 156
Work experience trainees, health and
  safety 152
Worker
  definition 61
  from abroad 122
  rights 63, 97
Workers Registration Scheme 122
Workforce agreement, parental leave . . . 89
Working at home 92
Working hours 165
Working Time Regulations, 1998 . 69, 70, 165
Workplace (Health, Safety and Welfare)
  Regulations 1992 153
Work-related stressors 172
Works council 99
Workstations 154, 159, 160
Young workers
  employment rights 70
  health and safety 151